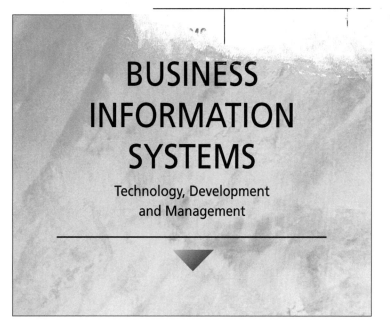

BUSINESS INFORMATION SYSTEMS

Technology, Development
and Management

BUSINESS INFORMATION SYSTEMS

Technology, Development and Management

PAUL BOCIJ

DAVE CHAFFEY

ANDREW GREASLEY

SIMON HICKIE

Edited by Dave Chaffey

FINANCIAL TIMES

Prentice Hall

An imprint of **Pearson Education**

Harlow, England · London · New York · Reading, Massachusetts · San Francisco
Toronto · Don Mills, Ontario · Sydney · Tokyo · Singapore · Hong Kong · Seoul
Taipei · Cape Town · Madrid · Mexico City · Amsterdam · Munich · Paris · Milan

Pearson Education Limited
Edinburgh Gate
Harlow
Essex CM20 2JE
England

and Associated Companies around the world

Visit us on the World Wide Web at:
http://www.pearsoneduc.com

First published in Great Britain in 1999

© Pearson Education Limited 1999

The rights of Paul Bocij, Dave Chaffey, Andrew Greasley and Simon Hickie
to be identified as Authors of this Work have been asserted by them in
accordance with the Copyright, Designs and Patents Act 1988.

ISBN 0 273 63849 1

British Library Cataloguing in Publication Data
A CIP catalogue record for this book can be obtained
from the British Library

10 9 8 7 6 5 4 3
04 03 02 01 00

Typeset by Pantek Arts, Maidstone, Kent.
Printed and bound in Great Britain by Ashford Colour Press Ltd, Gosport, Hampshire

Contents

Contents

Contents

A Companion Web Site accompanies Business Information Systems
by Paul Bocij, Dave Chaffey, Andrew Greasley and Simon Hickie.

Visit the Business Information Systems Companion Web Site at www.booksites.net/chaffey
to find valuable teaching and learning material including:

For Students:
- Study material designed to help you improve your understanding
- Multiple choice questions for every chapter, to help reinforce learning
- A host of links to useful websites, including:
  - professional computing magazines
  - perspectives from industry analysts and management consultants
  - academic and practitioner-oriented articles
  - case study materials
  - sites linked to particular activities in the book
- Glossary of key terms in BIS

For Lecturers:
- A secure, password protected site with teaching material
- Downloadable Overhead Masters to assist in lecturing
- A bank of further multiple choice questions for use in student assessment
- Complete, downloadable Lecturer's Guide and teaching Handbook, incorporating:
  - teaching hints for specific materials
  - suggested answers for all assignments in the book
  - further exercises and case studies for tutorial sessions
  - suggested extended assignments
  - notes on mapping the book for courses in a variety of disciplines and levels

This regularly maintained and updated site will also have a syllabus manager, search functions, and e-mail results functions.

Preface

▶ INTRODUCTION

Writing in *The Economist* of 16 June 1990, John Browning stated that:

> Information Technology is no longer a business resource; it has become the business environment.

Through the 1990s, and into the millennium, the truth of this statement has been supported by the ever increasing expenditure on the information technology (IT) which is used to build information systems (IS): in 1998, the *Financial Times* reported that annual expenditure would soon top $2000 billion worldwide.

With the growth in use of business information systems (BIS) within organisations, the need for all working professionals to have a good knowledge of IT and IS has also increased. With the vast, rapidly changing choice of IS available, important business skills are understanding and assessing the range of options available, and then choosing the solution best suited to the business problem or opportunity. This is, essentially, our aim in writing this book; to provide a source of knowledge which will explain how the right systems can be chosen by a business, then developed appropriately and managed effectively.

Despite the rising expenditure on IS, surveys also show that the potential of IS are often not delivered, often due to problems in the management, analysis, design or implementation of the system. The intention in this book is to acknowledge that there are great difficulties with developing and using IS and explain the measures that can be taken to try and minimise these difficulties in order to make the systems successful.

▶ WHY STUDY BUSINESS INFORMATION SYSTEMS?

Information systems form an integral part of modern organisations and businesses. Computer-based IS are now used to support all aspects of an organisation's normal functions and activities.

New technology creates new opportunities for forward-thinking companies. Higher levels of automation, high speed communications and improved access to information can all provide significant benefits to a modern business organisation. However, the benefits of new and emerging technologies can only be realised once they have been harnessed and directed towards an organisation's goals.

▶ The hybrid manager

The traditional view of managers is as functional specialists having specialised knowledge and expertise in a particular area, such as finance. The modern business environment requires a new kind of manager, often called a *hybrid manager*. The hybrid manager combines management and business skills with expertise in the areas of IT and IS. This type of manager is able to undertake a wide variety of roles and can operate across functional areas. The study of IS plays an important part in the development of an individual so that they may become a competent and effective manager as well as providing prospective managers with important problem solving skills that can be applied to a range of situations and problems. Specifically, the hybrid manager will need to:

- define the IS strategy for their workgroup, department or company;
- identify potential uses of IS to improve company performance;
- select and then acquire new IS from appropriate suppliers;
- oversee the development and implementation of these new systems;
- manage the IS to ensure they are effective in delivering information of the appropriate quality to users.

▶ AIMS

This book is intended to provide a comprehensive, yet accessible, guide to choosing the right systems for an organisation, developing them appropriately and managing them effectively. The book was conceived as a single source book that undergraduate business students would refer to throughout their course, without the need to purchase a separate book for different topics such as IT; information management; systems analysis and design; and strategy development. It covers, in detail, the software and hardware technologies which form IS; the activities involved in acquiring and building new IS and the elements of strategy required to manage IS effectively.

Key skills necessary to participate in the implementation of IT in businesses are developed and these skills, which form the main themes of the book are:

- understanding of the terms used to describe the components of IS to assist in selection of systems and suppliers;
- managing IS development projects;
- systems analysis and design;
- developing an IT strategy and managing its implementation.

The book assumes no prior knowledge of IS or IT. New concepts and terms are defined as simply as possible, with clear definitions given in the margins of the book. It explains the importance of information in developing a company business strategy and assisting decision making. The use of relevant hardware and software components of computer systems are defined and explained in the context of a range of business applications. The book also explains the benefit of specialised innovative applications such as the Internet and intranets; office automation using groupware and workflow products such as Lotus Notes, and marketing analysis using tools such as data warehouses and geographical information systems. The application of IS to business process reengineering and initiatives is also described.

After using the book, in conjunction with IS modules on their course, students will be able to:

- evaluate and select IT solutions for deployment within different functional parts of a business to achieve benefits for a business;
- actively participate in IT projects, applying skills such as selection of suppliers, procurement of hardware and software, systems analysis and design, and project management;
- communicate effectively with IT specialists when collaborating on a task or project;
- use IT to access a wide range of information sources for research and acquisition of knowledge.

▶ THE STRUCTURE OF THIS BOOK

The book is divided into three parts, each covering a different aspect of how BIS are used within organisations to help achieve competitive advantage:

- *Part 1* focuses on the hardware and software technologies, known collectively as IT, which comprise IS. It is intended for introductory courses in IT and BIS;
- *Part 2* explains how IS are acquired and developed by considering the activities involved with each of the stages of developing an IS. This part is intended for more advanced courses in systems analysis and design;
- *Part 3* describes how IS need to be managed, and a strategy developed, to ensure they effectively support the mission of the business. This part is appropriate for courses which consider the strategic management of IS.

Each part is self-contained and is the equivalent of what might be covered in a single module, or course, in a programme of study.

▶ Part 1 Introduction to information systems

Part 1 introduces the basic concepts of IS. Its main focus is the technology which forms IS, but it starts by reviewing the importance of information and what makes good quality information. Many people who work in the IT industry tend to believe it is the technology part of IT which is important, whereas most business people will tell you it is the information part of IT which is crucial to business performance. As Evans and Wurster, writing in the *Harvard Business Review* of September 1997 put it:

> ... every business is an information business ... information is the glue that holds together the structure of all businesses.

To enable a business user to communicate effectively with their suppliers of IT, a knowledge of the often, bewildering terminology, used to describe the components of IS, and a basic idea of how these components interact is important. To aid understanding, basic concepts and characteristics of IS are reviewed in Chapter 2. Hardware, software, communications and networking technologies are then described in subsequent chapters.

The different aspects of IT are introduced as follows:

◆ *Chapter 1: Basic concepts – understanding information* provides an introduction to how information is used within a business;

◆ *Chapter 2: Basic concepts – an introduction to information systems* introduces the different types of IS and how they can be used to gain strategic advantage;

◆ *Chapter 3: Hardware* describes the different hardware components of IS which are used to capture, process, store and output information;

◆ *Chapter 4: Software* reviews the use of general purpose applications software, such as word-processors, spreadsheets and databases, which are often referred to as productivity software;

◆ *Chapter 5: Networks and telecommunications* explains how IS are linked using telecommunications links which form networks, within and between, businesses;

◆ *Chapter 6: Business applications of information systems* reviews how these technologies are applied in different types of business. The business applications are considered from several perspectives: how IS can support decision making at different levels of the organisation such as at senior management level and an operational level; how IS are used in different functional areas of an organisation to support different processes such as sales order processing, manufacturing or recruitment.

▶ Part 2 Information systems development

Part 2 focuses on how IS are acquired and built. A basic understanding of this is necessary to every business user of IS so that they can appreciate the context of their use of the system and this can be of particular importance when they are involved in testing or using a new system since they will need to understand the reason for introducing new systems as well as their limitations. A more detailed understanding of building IS is important to users and managers who are responsible for, or are involved in a systems development project. In this case they will need to know the different stages of systems development to help plan the project or work with the developers of the system. They will also need to be aware of the different alternatives for sourcing IS, such as buying pre-written 'off-the-shelf' systems or specially written 'bespoke' systems, to decide which is best for their company or department.

This book provides a reference framework known as the systems development lifecycle which puts all the activities involved with building a system into a business context. Chapters give guidelines on how best to approach system development giving examples of activities that need to occur in order to avoid any pitfalls and enabling a quality system to be produced which meets the needs of the users and the business. The chapters in Part 2 are sequenced in the order in which activities occur in the systems development lifecycle:

◆ *Chapter 7: An introduction to acquiring and developing information systems* gives an introduction to alternatives for acquiring new systems. It also introduces the software development lifecycle which acts as a framework for the next chapters;

◆ *Chapter 8: Initiating systems development* covers the initiation phase of system development when the need for the new system and the feasibility of different development methods are assessed;

◆ *Chapter 9: Systems project management* describes how project management can be used to ensure the new system is built within the time and budget constraints, while also providing the features and quality required by the business and end-users;

◆ *Chapter 10: Systems theory* provides a theoretical foundation for chapters on systems analysis and design;

◆ *Chapter 11: Systems analysis* details system analysis techniques including methods of capturing the requirements for the system, and then summarising them using different diagramming techniques;

◆ *Chapter 12: Systems design* reviews different aspects of the design of IS from overall architectural or system design to aspects of detailed design, such as database and user interface design;

◆ *Chapter 13: System build, implementation and maintenance* describes the final stages of a systems development project when the system is released to end-users, following programming, testing and installation, and is then maintained.

▶ Part 3 Information systems management

Part 3 considers issues involved with the management of IS within an organisation. Of these, probably the most important is ensuring that the strategy defined is consistent with the mission and objectives of the business. Techniques for achieving this are reviewed, together with trends in IS strategy, such as location of IS within a large company and outsourcing IS management to third-party companies. Key issues in implementing the strategy are detailed in the areas of ensuring IS are secure; managing end-user facilities such as desktop-PCs, development tools and the help desk; managing a company intranet and its Internet

presence and ensuring the company is acting within moral, ethical and legal guidelines.

The chapters are structured as follows:

◆ *Chapter 14: Information systems strategy* stresses the importance of basing the IS strategy on the business strategy and looks at alternative techniques for achieving this. Setting investment levels and locating the IS function are also considered;

◆ *Chapter 15: Protecting information systems against security breaches* describes how information and systems can be protected through controls from threats such as destruction, failure or loss as part of business continuity planning;

◆ *Chapter 16: End-user computing – providing end-user services* explains why managing use of systems and, in particular, development by end-users is a significant trend in IS;

◆ *Chapter 17: Managing internet- and intranet-based information systems* details how Internet technologies can be used to support business activity and how they should be managed effectively;

◆ *Chapter 18: Ethical, legal and moral constraints on information systems* discusses the importance of protecting personal data and other ethical, moral and legal requirements which must be met by the IS manager;

◆ *Chapter 19: Information systems in the future* summarises best IS practices. This is achieved by reviewing future technologies and trends in the way that businesses operate, such as virtual organisations, teleworking and organisational learning. This chapter reviews the difficulties of managing the pace of technological change and questions whether the rate of change represents an opportunity or threat to a business.

▶ WHO SHOULD USE THIS BOOK?

The book discusses key aspects of IS development and management for students who need to understand the application of IT to assist businesses. It is designed for college students, undergraduate degree and postgraduate students taking courses with modules giving a grounding in the practical IT skills of selection, implementation, management and use of business information systems (BIS). The main type of reader will be:

◆ *undergraduates taking general business courses* such as Business Administration and Business Studies or *specialised business courses* such as Accounting, Marketing, Tourism and Human Resources Management;

◆ *undergraduates on computer science courses* which involve the study of business applications of information technology and the management of the development of IS;

◆ *students at college aiming for vocational qualifications* such as the HNC/HND in Business Management or Computer Studies;

◆ *postgraduates students on MBA, Certificate in Management, Diploma in Management Studies or specialist masters degrees* which involve courses on information management or IS strategy.

Managers in industry involved in the development and use of IS who will also find the practical sections in this book of use are:

◆ *business analysts* working with customers to identify business problems and propose solutions;

◆ *systems analysts and software designers* specifying how the solution will be implemented;

◆ *'hands-on' managers* responsible for implementing IT solutions either as a supplier or client.

▶ WHAT DOES IT OFFER TO LECTURERS TEACHING THESE COURSES?

The book is intended to be a comprehensive guide to the business applications, development and management of IS. As such, it can be used across several modules to help integrate different modules. Lecturers will find the book has a good range of excellent case studies to support their teaching. These include industry case studies of the applications of IS together with problems encountered and simplified practical exercises for systems analysis and design. Web references are given in the text to important information sources for particular topics.

▶ STUDENT LEARNING FEATURES

A range of features have been incorporated into this book to help the reader get the most out of it. They have been designed to assist understanding, reinforce learning and help readers find information easily. The features are described in the order you will encounter them.

At the start of each chapter:

◆ *chapter introductions*: succinct summaries of why the topic is relevant to the management of IS and its content and structure;

◆ *learning objectives*: lists describing what readers should learn through reading the chapters and completing the exercises;

◆ *links to other chapters*: a summary of related information in other chapters.

In each chapter:

◆ *definitions*: when significant terms are first introduced the main text contains explanations and succinct definitions in the margin for easy reference;

◆ *web references*: where appropriate, web addresses are given as reference sources, which provide further information on a particular topic. They are provided in the main text where they are directly relevant as well as at the end of the chapter;

◆ *case studies*: real-world examples of how technologies are used to support businesses. Case studies are taken from around the world but there is a particular emphasis on the UK and Europe. They are referred to from related material within the text they support. Questions at the end of the case study are intended to highlight the main learning points from each case study;

◆ *mini case studies:* short examples which give a more detailed example, or explanation, than is practical in the main text. They do not contain supplementary questions;

◆ *activities*: exercises in the main text which give the opportunity to practice and apply the techniques described in the text. They are not relevant to all chapters, but are used to support the chapters on systems analysis and design;

◆ *focus on sections*: used to consider topical issues of IS in more detail. Such sections may be used to support the essay or discussion-style questions, or may provide areas for further student research, perhaps giving ideas for student dissertations and projects;

◆ *chapter summaries*: intended as revision aids which summarise the main learning points from the chapters.

At the end of each chapter:

◆ *self-assessment exercises*: short questions which will test understanding of terms and concepts described in the chapters;

◆ *discussion questions*: require longer essay-style answers discussing themes from the chapters, and can be used for essays or as debate questions in seminars;

◆ *essay questions*: conventional essay questions;

◆ *examination questions*: typical short answer questions which would be encountered in an exam and can also be used for revision;

◆ *references*: these are references to books, articles or papers referred to within the chapter;

◆ *further reading*: supplementary text or papers on the main themes of the chapter. Where appropriate a brief commentary is provided on recommended supplementary reading on the main themes of the chapters.

At the end of the book:

◆ *glossary*: a list of all definitions of key terms and phrases used within the main text;

◆ *index*: all key words, abbreviations and authors referred to in the main text.

▶ SUPPORT MATERIAL

A range of free supplimentary materials are available on a Companion Web Site @ see page x for more details.

About the authors

Dave Chaffey, BSc, PhD has extensive experience of working in industry on corporate information systems projects for British companies such as Ford Europe, WH Smith, North West Water and the Halifax Bank in roles varying from business/ systems analyst, programmer and trainer to project manager. He is currently senior lecturer in Business Information Systems in the Derbyshire Business School at the University of Derby. He is involved in teaching at all undergraduate and post graduate levels including a first year undergraduate module in Information Technology for Business, HND module in Managing Business Computing, CM/MBA modules in Information Management and Managing IS, MSc in Strategic Management and more specialist modules in Systems Analysis and Design and IS strategy. His main research interests are the application of workflow and groupware to computer supported co-operative work in service-oriented business and software project management techniques. He is author of *Groupware, Workflow and Intranets*, published by Digital Press in 1998 and the forthcoming *Internet Marketing: Strategy, Implementation and Practice*, to be published by Financial Times Management. He directs regular seminars for the Chartered Institute of Marketing on strategic Internet marketing. He is a member of the UK Academy for Information Systems and an associate member of the British Computer Society.

Paul Bocij is a graduate of the University of Nottingham and the University of Derby. He is an experienced lecturer, having worked for a wide variety of institutions, including universities, colleges and numerous commercial organisations. He is an active researcher and his research interests are largely concerned with the use of educational technology in higher education, with a particular emphasis on computer-based assessment. His commercial experience includes time spent in the fields of programming, management, training and consultancy. In addition, he has also worked as a professional writer and is the author of numerous books, articles and papers related to Information Systems and Information Technology. At present, he is the managing director of an independent IT training and consultancy company.

Andrew Greasley, MBA is a lecturer in the Derbyshire Business School. He lectures on modules in systems analysis and design, information management and operations management. His research interest is in the use of discrete-event simulation modelling and its role in process improvement. He has directed a number of projects in both the public and private sector in the area including work for Adtranz Ltd, Stanton Plc and Derbyshire Constabulary. He is author of several publications including papers in *SIMULATION* and the *International Journal of Operations and Production Management*. He is also author of the forthcoming text *Operations Management in Business* to be published by Stanley Thornes Ltd. He is a member of the Society for Computer Simulation International.

Simon Hickie is a senior lecturer in Business Information Systems in the Derbyshire Business School. He studied Economics and Politics at Keele University, and took his PGCE at Leicester University. After teaching Economics for two years, he retrained in 1980 as a commercial computer programmer. During a ten year career working for a variety of organisations including the NAAFI, Hogg Robinson and Kenner Parker he undertook a variety of roles including analyst programmer, systems programmer, project manager and training consultant, before returning to education in 1990 as a senior lecturer in Information Systems in the department of Mathematics and Computing at the University of Sunderland. He moved to the University of Derby in 1992. He is module leader of the systems analysis and design and information systems management modules and MSc Strategic Management strategic information management module. In addition to his teaching role, he is also a Senior Academic Counsellor, Head of Operations for the second stage of the University's Combined Subject Programme and Head Of Programme for combined business subjects within the Derbyshire Business School.

Acknowledgements

The authors would like to thank the assistance of the team at Financial Times Management in the compilation of this book. In particular, Pat Bond, Julianne Mulholland, Michelle Graham and Penelope Woolf. Thanks also go to the team of reviewers for their constructive comments which have helped develop the book. The book has also been shaped by discussion with colleagues in the Derbyshire Business School and the School of Mathematics and Computing. Valuable feedback has also been obtained from students completing exercises and case studies. We thank everyone who has contributed in this way. Dave Chaffey would like to thank Sal for copy-editing drafts and her patience in sharing her husband with the book. John Chaffey provided inspiration for the quality of text we wanted to achieve. Simon Hickie wishes to thank Fr. Ken Nugent SJ, Ian Soden, Mike Elliot, Viv Oliver, Bob Bell, John Clifford, Kate Murray and Professor David Gowland who have all had roles to play in making the book possible. Simon would also like to thank his children, Charlotte, Jonathan and Dominic who kindly gave him permission to use his computer when they were not doing homework or zapping aliens, and his wife Clare for putting up with the chaos in the study. Andrew Greasley would like to thank his wife Kay for her support.

List of reviewers

The following people contributed to this book by commenting on the initial plan, or by providing detailed feedback on the entire manuscript:

Linda Charnley	Robert Gordon University
Neil Doherty	Loughborough University
Glenn Hardaker	University of Huddersfield
Alan Hunt	Robert Gordon University
Chris Percy	Oxford Brookes University
David Rowe	Kingston University
Daune West	University of Paisley

Plan of the book

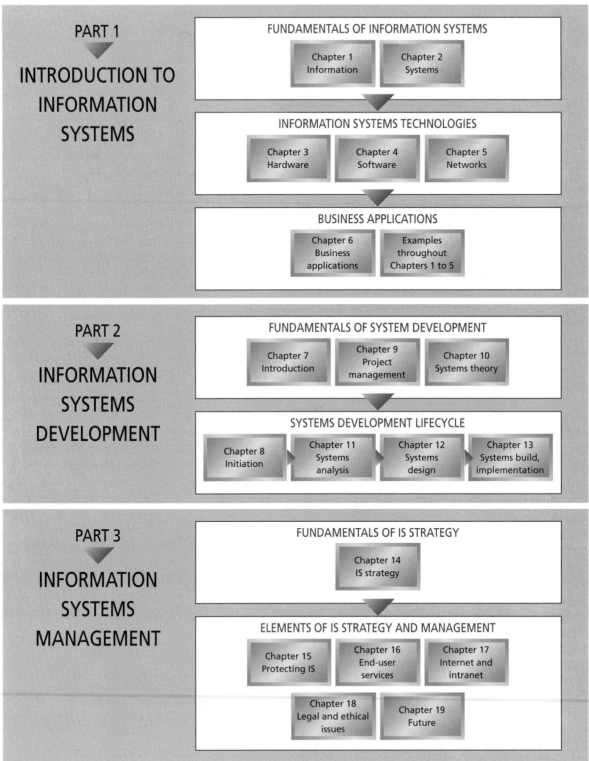

PART 1

INTRODUCTION TO INFORMATION SYSTEMS

FUNDAMENTALS OF INFORMATION SYSTEMS

Chapter 1 Information | Chapter 2 Systems

INFORMATION SYSTEMS TECHNOLOGIES

Chapter 3 Hardware | Chapter 4 Software | Chapter 5 Networks

BUSINESS APPLICATIONS

Chapter 6 Business applications | Examples throughout Chapters 1 to 5

PART 2

INFORMATION SYSTEMS DEVELOPMENT

FUNDAMENTALS OF SYSTEM DEVELOPMENT

Chapter 7 Introduction | Chapter 9 Project management | Chapter 10 Systems theory

SYSTEMS DEVELOPMENT LIFECYCLE

Chapter 8 Initiation | Chapter 11 Systems analysis | Chapter 12 Systems design | Chapter 13 Systems build, implementation

PART 3

INFORMATION SYSTEMS MANAGEMENT

FUNDAMENTALS OF IS STRATEGY

Chapter 14 IS strategy

ELEMENTS OF IS STRATEGY AND MANAGEMENT

Chapter 15 Protecting IS | Chapter 16 End-user services | Chapter 17 Internet and intranet

Chapter 18 Legal and ethical issues | Chapter 19 Future

PART

1

INTRODUCTION TO INFORMATION SYSTEMS

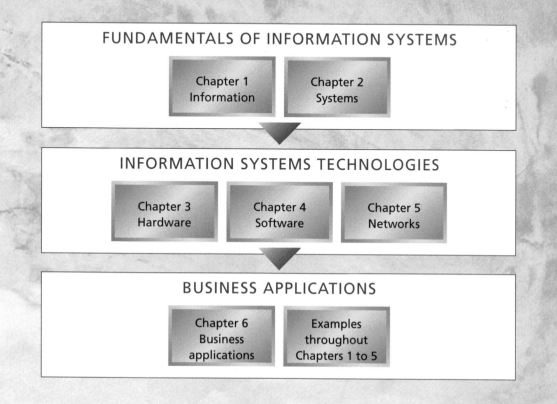

FUNDAMENTALS OF INFORMATION SYSTEMS

Chapter 1
Information

Chapter 2
Systems

INFORMATION SYSTEMS TECHNOLOGIES

Chapter 3
Hardware

Chapter 4
Software

Chapter 5
Networks

BUSINESS APPLICATIONS

Chapter 6
Business
applications

Examples
throughout
Chapters 1 to 5

When beginning the study of the use of information systems (IS) in business, it is important to understand a number of concepts drawn from a variety of different fields. In order to create, improve and manage business information systems (BIS), one must combine an understanding of information, systems concepts, business organisations and information technology (IT). Part 1 is intended as an introductory section to IS which provides a background supporting further study in Parts 2 and 3. In addition to explaining basic terms and concepts, Part 1 shows, through examples in Chapters 3, 4, 5 and 6, why IS are vital to business today.

Understanding the terms and components that define IS is necessary in order that business users can communicate with the IT suppliers building and maintaining their systems. All systems involve transforming inputs such as data into outputs such as information by a transformation process. The UK Academy for Information Systems defines information systems as follows:

> Information systems are the means by which organisations and people, using information technologies, gather, process, store, use and disseminate information.

In simpler terms, a business information system can be described as a system that provides the information needed by managers to support their activities in achieving the objectives of a business. A computer-based information system can be described as an IS which uses information technology in the form of hardware, software and communications links. The term information and communication technology (ICT) is sometimes used to emphasise the growing importance of communications technology such as the Internet. Note that an IS can be paper-based or computer-based. For simplicity, computer-based information systems and business information systems are referred to as IS throughout this book.

1

Basic concepts – understanding information

INTRODUCTION

The general aim of this chapter is to introduce readers to the basic concepts needed to gain a thorough understanding of information systems. However, before looking at information systems themselves, it is important to understand something of the nature of information. For an information system to be effective, the quality of the information it provides is vital. In this chapter we look at how we can assess and improve the quality of data and information. The topics covered are intended to give readers an understanding of:

◆ the nature of data and information;

◆ the value of information;

◆ the characteristics that can be used to describe information quality;

◆ managerial decision making, including the characteristics of decisions at different organisational levels;

◆ the information needed to support decision making.

> ▶ Learning objectives
>
> After reading this chapter, readers will be able to:
>
> ◆ describe and evaluate information quality in terms of its characteristics;
>
> ◆ classify decisions by type and organisational level;
>
> ◆ identify the information needed to support decisions made at different organisational levels.

> ▶ Links to other chapters
>
> Chapter 2   builds on the concepts described in this chapter and introduces new ideas, such as information systems and computer-based information systems.
>
> Chapter 6   describes in more detail how decision support systems assist decision making.
>
> Chapter 10   describes some of the techniques used in analysing information systems. Diagramming techniques that can be used to show information flows within an organisation are described in detail.
>
> Chapter 14   looks at strategic decision making and the ways in which information systems can support an organisation's business strategy.
>
> Chapter 15   considers how the quality and security of information can be maintained.

▶ DATA AND INFORMATION

As will be shown in later sections, much of a manager's work involves making use of information in order to make decisions. The material that follows provides an insight into the natures of data and information, providing a foundation for greater understanding.

▶ What is data?

Data

A collection of non-random facts recorded by observation or research.

Data consists of raw facts or observations that are considered to have little or no value until they have been processed and transformed into information. Unrelated items of data are considered to be essentially without meaning and are often described as 'noise'. It is only when data has been placed in some form of context that it becomes meaningful.

> Although 'data' is commonly used to refer to both the singular and plural forms, it should be noted that the singular form is *datum*.
>
> However, despite having made this distinction, the popular use of this term has been adopted in this text.

There are several definitions for data in common use:

(a) *A series of non-random symbols, numbers, values or words.*

(b) *A series of facts obtained by observation or research.*

(c) *A collection of non-random facts.*

(d) *The record of an event or fact.*

Data can exist naturally or be created artificially. Artificial data is often produced as a by-product of another business process. Processing an organisation's accounts, for example, might produce the number of sales made in a particular month.

> Examples of data include:
>
> ◆ today's date;
> ◆ measurements taken on a production line;
> ◆ records of business transactions.

Naturally occurring data needs only to be recorded in some way. The person recording the data tends to have little influence or control over the data itself, since it already exists in one form or another.

▶ What is information?

As with the concept of data, there are several definitions of **information** in common use:

Information

Data that has been processed so that they are meaningful.

(a) *Data that has been processed so that they are meaningful.*

(b) *Data that has been processed for a purpose.*

(c) *Data that has been interpreted and understood by the recipient.*

Three important points can be drawn from this definition. First, there is a clear and logical process that is used to produce information. This process involves collecting data and then subjecting it to a **transformation process** in order to create information. The concept of a transformation process will be discussed in more detail in the next section. Second, information involves placing data in some form of meaningful context, so that it can be understood and acted on. Third, information is produced for a purpose, to serve an **information need** of some kind.

Transformation process

A transformation process is used to convert inputs into outputs.

Information need

Information is produced to meet a specific purpose or requirement.

> Some examples of information include:
>
> ◆ a bank statement;
> ◆ a sales forecast;
> ◆ a telephone directory.

It is worth noting that information is subjective in nature: a piece of information found to be of value to one person may be meaningless to another. Similarly, what might be regarded as information by one person may be seen as data by another. It is for this reason that many definitions insist that information must be placed within a meaningful context.

A somewhat different view of information can be examined by introducing an additional definition:

(d) *Information acts to reduce uncertainty about a situation or event.*

It may help understanding to explain the meaning of 'uncertainty' in the context of this definition.

It is not possible to predict the outcome of a situation or the behaviour of a person with absolute certainty. Even the simplest of situations will be subject to a number of random factors. Consider the act of switching on an electric light. It is reasonable to predict that switching the light on will result in the bulb glowing. However, this is not necessarily a certain outcome. The bulb, switch or electrical wiring might suddenly develop a fault, or there might be a power outage, or some other unpredictable event might occur that prevents the light from working.

Although uncertainty can never be eliminated entirely, it can be *reduced* significantly. Information can help to eliminate some possibilities or make others seem more likely. Returning to the example of the electric light, the chances of making an accurate *prediction* can be increased by gathering additional information. One might, for example, find out whether or not the electricity supply is likely to be interrupted at the time when the light will be switched on. Holding such information would improve the likelihood of the prediction being accurate.

Decision making can also be improved by using information to reduce uncertainty. Information is said to influence **decision behaviour**, the way in which people make decisions. Managerial decision making is dealt with in more detail later on page 15.

Decision behaviour

Describes the way in which people make decisions.

It may be valuable to summarise some of the points made in the preceding sections. Information:

◆ involves transforming data using a defined process;

◆ involves placing data in some form of meaningful context;

◆ is produced in response to an information need and therefore serves a specific purpose;

◆ helps to reduce uncertainty, thereby improving decision behaviour.

▶ CREATING INFORMATION

It is necessary to process data to place it into a meaningful context so that it can be easily understood by the recipient. Figure 1.1 illustrates the conversion of data into information.

Data process

A process used to convert data into information. Examples include summarising, classifying and sorting.

A number of different **data processes** can be used to transform data into information. The next section describes a range of common data processes.

▶ Data processes

Some examples of data processes include the following.

◆ *Classification*. This involves placing data into categories, for example categorising an expense as either a fixed or a variable cost.

Fig 1.1 Transforming data into information using a data process

- *Rearranging/sorting*. This involves organising data so that items are grouped together or placed into a particular order. Employee data, for example, might be sorted according to last name or payroll number.
- *Aggregating*. This involves summarising data, for example by calculating averages, totals or subtotals.
- *Performing calculations*. An example might be calculating an employee's gross pay by multiplying the number of hours worked by the hourly rate of pay.
- *Selection*. This involves choosing or discarding items of data based on a set of selection criteria. A sales organisation, for example, might create a list of potential customers by selecting those with incomes above a certain level.

In the context of a student attending a university course, which of the following might be examples of information? Which might be examples of data?

(a) the date;

(b) a bank statement;

(c) the number 1355.76;

(d) a National Insurance number;

(e) a balance sheet;

(f) a bus timetable;

(g) a car registration plate.

ACTIVITY

▶ Value of information

It is often possible to measure the value of information directly. The **tangible value** of information is often measured in terms of financial value. An example might be the use of inventory information to improve stock control procedures. A simple calculation can be used to determine the value of a given item or collection of information:

value of information – cost of gathering information

However, in many cases it is not possible to calculate the value of information directly. Although it is certain that the information is of benefit to the owner, it is difficult – or even impossible – to quantify its value. In such cases, the information is said to have **intangible value**. A good example might involve attempting to measure the extent to which information can improve decision behaviour. Such a calculation might appear as shown below:

improvements in decision behaviour – cost of gathering information

There can be little doubt that the ability to make better decisions can be of great value to any organisation. However, one cannot easily quantify any improvements in decision making, since a large number of other factors must also be taken in account.

Tangible value

A value or benefit that can be measured directly, usually in monetary terms.

Intangible value

A value or benefit that is difficult or impossible to quantify.

ACTIVITY

When information is used effectively, it can bring about many of the improvements listed below. State whether each of the items listed illustrates a tangible or intangible value of information:

(a) improved inventory control;

(b) enhanced customer service;

(c) increased production;

(d) reduced administration costs;

(e) greater customer loyalty;

(f) enhanced public image.

▶ Sources of information

Formal communication

Formal communication involves presenting information in a structured and consistent manner.

Informal communication

This describes less well structured information that is transmitted by informal means, such as casual conversations between members of staff.

Information can be obtained via both formal and informal communication. **Formal communication** can include reports and accounting statements. **Informal communication** can include conversations and notes.

Each form of communication has characteristics that make it appropriate for certain applications. Some of these characteristics are explained in the material that follows.

Formal communication

Information transmitted by formal communication tends to be presented in a consistent manner. Company reports, for example, will often use the same basic format. This allows the recipient to locate items of interest quickly and easily. Since formal communication tends to be presented in a more structured manner, it is also more likely to present a more comprehensive view of the situations or circumstances it describes. In addition, the information transmitted in this way is likely to be accurate and relevant, since it is normally created for a specific purpose.

It is not uncommon for organisations to adopt a 'house style' for standard documents. Memos, reports and other documents are produced by making use of the templates that are found in most modern wordprocessing packages. These templates contain the basic structure of a given document and can be compared to completing a standard form.

In some cases, the template can also contain detailed instructions that specify what information should be included in the document and, more importantly, what information should be excluded.

However, formal communication also has several disadvantages. The structure imposed on information is often inflexible, sometimes limiting its type, form and content. In addition, formal communication often overlooks information obtained by informal means. This can lead to a number of negative effects, for example managers are less likely to be able to gain an in-depth understanding of a particular situation if they do not have access to all relevant information. In turn, this can affect the decision-making process, reducing the quality and accuracy of any decisions made.

Finally, formal communication often ignores group and social mechanisms. A formal report, for example, might marginalise or ignore staff opinions, causing offence and leading to reduced morale.

Informal communication

In general, very little of the information transmitted by word of mouth is retained by the recipient. A number of factors, for example 'noise', can reduce the amount of information retained to as little as 20 per cent. In the context of communication, noise refers to any factor that serves to hinder the transmission of information or distort its meaning.

Informal communication is always present in an organisation, regardless of its size or nature. Information of this kind can be considered a valuable resource and can be harnessed to work for the benefit of the organisation. Perhaps the most common means by which informal communication takes place is by word of mouth. In a sales organisation, for example, a casual conversation between a salesperson and a client might yield information that can be used to enhance a product or find new ways of making it more attractive to customers.

Consider the role of informal communication within an organisation such as a local government department or hospital.

ACTIVITY

1 In what ways can informal communication support the day-to-day activities of the organisation?

2 How important is the role of informal communication within the organisation? Could the organisation function effectively if informal communication were restricted?

3 How can informal communication be controlled or harnessed for the benefit of the organisation?

4 What negative results might occur if overly strict controls are imposed on informal communication?

Informal communication tends to offer a high degree of flexibility, since there is more freedom to choose how information is structured and presented. Information obtained in this way also tends to be highly detailed, although it may often contain inaccuracies and may not be entirely relevant.

The scope of information obtained in this way is often very narrow, relevant only to localised problems and situations. However, even at a local level, this can improve problem solving and decision making, since it allows managers to gain a more detailed and in-depth understanding of a given situation.

One of the main disadvantages of informal communication is that it cannot deal with large volumes of information. Furthermore, as a means of communication it is relatively slow and inefficient. Informal communication can also be highly selective, for example a person taking part in a conversation may be able to restrict what information is transmitted and who is able to receive it. Perhaps a more serious disadvantage is that informal communication is often ignored in favour of formal communication.

The case study on National Westminster Insurance Systems considers the types of information that one particular company needs to support its business. It also considers information quality and how the development of a new database system has improved information delivery.

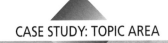

CASE STUDY: TOPIC AREA

FT

National Westminster Insurance Systems

Database management systems: A better understanding of clients

by Rod Newing

There was a time when executives complained that information was never timely 'and was never what they really wanted,' says Julie Pratten, who oversees a management information project at National Westminster Insurance Services.

'We were about to build a new operational system and we wanted to exploit the information it would capture for us.'

NatWest Insurance Services (NWIS) is one of the largest independent insurance intermediaries in the UK and is wholly owned by National Westminster Bank. The organisation has 30 different operational systems.

'We didn't just want statistics, but information about the key drivers of the business,' Ms Pratten explains. 'We needed a large database to hold all the data in a common format and make it available to a range of tools.'

At the end of 1996, the team built a prototype using data from the 'household claims' department to prove the concept of migrating data from one system to another and then interrogating it.

'The prototype proved this and actually solved some of our problems,' says Ms Pratten. 'It shifted our focus from moving data to the quality of data.'

The first phase of development was to complete the 'household' system and build routines so that the database could be updated daily and weekly. The team then moved on to the 'business insurance' department. Summarised financial data from the general ledger followed, using Microsoft Excel (spreadsheet) files created by finance.

Human resources data about people and their grades followed, also using Excel. Sales information was transferred from an RDB database. Twice-yearly customer satisfaction surveys giving feedback on sales and service levels were transferred from a Microsoft Access database.

Nobody works directly with the database. Most users access it through specialised software, which creates different view of business performance from the data.

Some power-users download data to Microsoft's Access desktop database for off-line planning models, margin management models and cross-selling. These will be replaced by a series of departmental databases fed from the central database.

'Building the database has been invaluable in improving the quality of data in the company because we have refined and cleaned it en route,' says Ms Pratten.

An important aspect of data quality is ensuring that users understand the data they are using. For instance, 'gross premium' in one business area may be different to that in another. The team has helped the business to agree a standard set of data definitions and terminology that everybody understands.

A cross-company 'information management group' was set up to focus on best-practice on information usage. It helps users to develop their analytical skills as they use the information in the database. The team is about to embark on a data mining prototype for the business insurance department.

'As a company, we need to train our staff and move beyond reporting into modelling and analysis,' says Ms Pratten. 'The main benefit of using the software we chose is being able to manage a database with a very small team,' she adds. 'It has proved very cost-effective and we've been able to build a database without investing millions of pounds.'

'We recognised that within NWIS we have been "data-rich", but "information-poor",' concludes Ms Pratten.

'If we are to achieve our strategic objectives, we need to understand more about our customers and more about our key business drivers and where we can make changes. The database has highlighted our awareness of data and how it is being used in the business. It has brought us more business focus.'

Source: *Financial Times*, 18 March 1998

Questions

1 Why was National Westminster Insurance Services considered 'data rich' but 'information poor'?

2 Outline some of the steps taken by National Westminster Insurance Services to make better use of the data it holds and improve its quality.

3 Having found new ways to make use of the data held by the organisation, what are some of the business benefits that might be realised by National Westminster Insurance Services?

QUALITIES OF INFORMATION

Information can be said to have a number of different characteristics that can be used to describe its quality. The differences between 'good' and 'bad' information can be identified by considering whether or not it has some or all of the **attributes of information quality**.

Lucey (1994) provides a list of characteristics likely to be present in information considered to be of good quality. However, others, such as O'Brien (1993), take a more organised approach and describe the attributes of information quality as being divided into three basic categories: time, content and form. Table 1.1 summarises information characteristics that can be used to assess quality.

Attributes of information quality

A group of characteristics by which the quality of information can be assessed, normally grouped into categories of time, content and form.

Table 1.1 Summary of attributes of information quality

Time	Content	Form	Additional characteristics
Timeliness	Accuracy	Clarity	Confidence in source
Currency	Relevance	Detail	Reliability
Frequency	Completeness	Order	Appropriate
Time period	Conciseness	Presentation	Received by correct person
	Scope	Media	Sent by correct channels

▶ Time dimension

The **time dimension** describes the time period with which the information deals and the frequency with which the information is received:

◆ *Timeliness*. The information should be available when needed. If information is provided too early, it may not be relevant. If the information is supplied too late, it will be of no use.

◆ *Currency*. The information should reflect current circumstances when provided. One can go further and suggest that in addition to being up to date, the information should also indicate those areas or circumstances liable to change by the time the information is used.

◆ *Frequency*. In addition to being available when needed, information should also be available as often as needed. This normally means that information should be

Time dimension

Characteristics of information quality such as timeliness, currency and frequency which are related to the time of collection and review.

supplied at regular intervals, for example some organisations may require weekly sales reports while others need only monthly reports.

◆ *Time period*. The information should cover the correct time period. A sales forecast, for example, might include information concerning past performance, current performance and predicted performance so that the recipient has a view of past, present and future circumstances.

▶ Content dimension

Content dimension

Characteristics of information quality such as accuracy, relevance and conciseness which are related to the scope and contents of the information.

The **content dimension** describes the scope and content of the information:

◆ *Accuracy*. Information that contains errors has only limited value to an organisation.

◆ *Relevance*. The information supplied should be relevant to a particular situation and should meet the information needs of the recipient. Extraneous detail can compromise other attributes of information quality, such as conciseness.

◆ *Completeness*. All of the information required to meet the information needs of the recipient should be provided. Incomplete information can compromise other attributes of information quality, such as scope and accuracy.

◆ *Conciseness*. Only information relevant to the information needs of the recipient should be supplied. In addition, the information should be provided in the most compact form possible. As an example, sales figures are normally provided in the form of a graph or table – it would be unusual for them to be supplied as a descriptive passage of text.

◆ *Scope*. The scope of the information supplied should be appropriate to the information needs of the recipient. The recipient's information needs will determine if the information should concern organisational or external situations and whether it should focus on a specific area or provide a more general overview.

▶ Form dimension

Form dimension

Characteristics of information quality related to how the information is presented to the recipient.

The **form dimension** describes how the information is presented to the recipient:

◆ *Clarity*. The information should be presented in a form that is appropriate to the intended recipient. The recipient should be able to locate specific items quickly and should be able to understand the information easily.

◆ *Detail*. The information should contain the correct level of detail in order to meet the recipient's information needs. For example, in some cases highly detailed information will be required, while in others only a summary will be necessary.

◆ *Order*. Information should be provided in the correct order. As an example, management reports normally contain a brief summary at the beginning. This allows a manager to locate and understand the most important aspects of the report before examining it at a high level of detail.

◆ *Presentation*. The information should be presented in a form that is appropriate to the intended recipient. Different methods can be used to make information clearer and more accessible to the recipient, for example it is common to present numerical information in the form of a graph or table.

◆ *Media*. Information should be presented using the correct media. Formal information, for example, is often presented in the form of a printed report, whereas a presentation might make use of a slide projector.

▶ Additional characteristics

In addition to the attributes described above, one might add several others.

Of particular importance is *confidence* in the source of the information received. Recipients are more likely to accept and trust the information they obtain if it is received from a source that has been accurate and reliable in the past. It can be argued that attempts should be made to obtain information from sources considered to be reliable and trustworthy.

This view can be extended to suggest a further attribute of information quality, that of *reliability*. Recipients should be confident that they can rely on information being available when required and that the information will be of a consistent quality in terms of other attributes of information quality, such as accuracy and conciseness.

The widespread use of computer-based information systems raises a number of issues related to the sheer quantity of information that is freely available via sources such as the Internet. In addition, it raises concerns in relation to security. In view of this, one might suggest that a further attribute of information quality is that the information provided should be *appropriate* to the recipient's activities. This might restrict information from being supplied if it is of a confidential nature or beyond the duties or responsibilities of a person's role.

It also seems natural to require some confirmation that the information has been *received by the correct person*. Unless the information has been received and acted on, it is of no value. Thus, it can be suggested that an additional attribute of information quality is that it can be verified that the information has been received and understood.

Finally, information should be capable of being transmitted via the *correct channels*. Most organisations have formal policies and procedures for dealing with particular situations. For example, a complaint against a member of staff is normally presented in a written form and travels upwards through the management hierarchy until it is received by the correct person. If the information were to be sent in any other way, for example by word of mouth, it might not reach its destination or might become garbled during the journey.

> Locate at least two different examples of information. For each example determine whether the information is of 'good' or 'poor' quality. Explain your reasoning with reference to the characteristics of information described in this chapter.

ACTIVITY

▶ THE BUSINESS ENVIRONMENT

All business organisations operate within an environment that influences the way in which they operate. Legislation, for example, will act to control some of the organisation's activities. However, the actions of an organisation may also influence parts

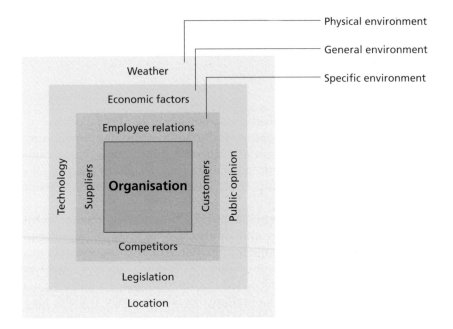

Fig 1.2 **The environment in which an organisation functions and some of the factors that influence the organisation**

of the environment. For example, companies may launch an advertising campaign designed to draw customers away from a competitor.

Figure 1.2 illustrates some of the elements that may influence the way in which an organisation operates.

Business resource base

The resources that a company has available to it which are made up of physical and conceptual resources known as tangible and intangible assets.

Physical resources

Tangible assets or resources owned by a company such as land, buildings and plant.

Conceptual resources

Non-physical resources or intangible assets owned by a company. Such as organisational knowledge.

▶ The business resource base

Organisations also have access to a **business resource base** that supports their activities. The resource base consists of physical resources and conceptual resources.

Making the best use of physical and conceptual resources can help an organisation to reduce costs, improve productivity and enhance overall efficiency.

Physical resource base

Physical resources are often known as tangible assets and are normally directed towards the production of a product or service. Examples of physical resources include money, land, plant and labour power.

Conceptual resource base

Conceptual resources are often known as intangible assets and are normally used to support an organisation's activities, for example by helping managers to make better decisions. Examples of intangible resources include data, information, experience, motivation, knowledge, ideas and judgement.

▶ MANAGERIAL DECISION MAKING

In order for an organisation to function effectively, all activities must be managed in an efficient and organised manner. Although a general review of management principles is well beyond the scope of this book, a brief look at two general management theories may help to illustrate their importance to the field of information systems.

▶ The role of managers

Henri Fayol (1841–1925) devised a classic definition of management that is still widely used today in both industry and academia:

To manage is to forecast and plan, to organise, to command, to co-ordinate and to control.

As will be seen in Chapter 2, elements of this statement can be found in many modern definitions of the term 'information system'.

Fayol's definition should make it clear that much of a manager's work involves making decisions about the best way to achieve the organisation's objectives and that there is a direct link between a manager's decision-making and planning activities. A forecast, for example, is created to help managers decide what actions are necessary to prepare the organisation for the future. The success of *all* of the activities described in Fayol's definition depend on access to high-quality information. It is here that information systems have a role, as a means of supporting the manager's work by providing the information he or she needs. The next sections discuss managerial decision making in more detail.

Max Weber's (1864–1920) view of a bureaucratic form of organisation suggests that as an organisation grows in size and complexity, it becomes more difficult to control. For Weber, an ideal organisation displays a number of characteristics, such as a well-defined hierarchy or legitimate authority, the division of labour based on functional specialism and the existence of rules and procedures to deal with all situations and decisions. Large organisations, such as public utilities, often adopt some or all of the characteristics of a bureaucracy.

Although seen as being superior to other forms of organisation, bureaucratic organisations have a number of disadvantages. The relatively inflexible structure of a bureaucracy means that it cannot adapt to change quickly or easily. Furthermore, there is a tendency to adhere to rules and procedures regardless of whether or not they help the organisation to reach its objectives.

As organisations grow in size or complexity, the importance of effective and efficient management increases. In turn, greater reliance is placed on the information systems used by the organisation. Put simply, as an organisation becomes larger, effective information systems become critical to continued survival.

▶ Decision behaviour

The way in which managers make decisions and the factors that influence those decisions are often described as **decision behaviour** (see page 6).

Decisions can be classed as structured or unstructured (sometimes referred to as programmable and unprogrammable decisions). In reality, however, many decisions fall somewhere between the two extremes and are known as semistructured decisions.

Decision behaviour

Describes the process and factors involved when people make decisions.

Structured decisions

Situations where the rules and constraints governing the decision are known.

Unstructured decisions

Complex situations, where the rules governing the decision are complicated or unknown.

Cognitive style

This describes the way in which a manager absorbs information and reaches decisions. A manager's cognitive style will fall between analytical and intuitive styles.

Structured decisions tend to involve situations where the rules and constraints governing the decision are known. They tend to involve routine or repetitive situations where the number of possible courses of action is relatively small. A good example involves stock control. The decision to reorder a given item will be governed by a fairly simple set of rules and constraints. When the amount of stock held falls below a certain point, a fixed quantity of new stock will be ordered.

Unstructured decisions tend to involve more complex situations, where the rules governing the decision are complicated or unknown. Such decisions tend to be made infrequently and rely heavily on the experience, judgement and knowledge of the decision maker. A good example of an unstructured decision might be whether or not an organisation should open a new branch in a particular area.

The behaviour of a manager will influence the way in which he or she absorbs information and reaches a decision. This is often referred to as a person's **cognitive style**. A manager's cognitive style will fall between analytical and intuitive styles.

The analytical manager typically displays a high level of analytical thought and is able to provide detailed justifications for any decisions made. He or she tends to prefer quantitative information as the basis for a decision and will often overlook any qualitative information received. This type of manager examines situations in fine detail and often overlooks the wider issues that might influence a decision.

Systems to assist in decision making are described in Chapter 6.

Data is often described as hard data or soft data

Hard data, also known as **quantitative data**, tends to make use of figures, such as statistics. Hard data is often collected in order to measure or *quantify* an object or situation.

  Soft data, often known as **qualitative data**, tends to focus on describing the *qualities* or characteristics of an object or situation. Interviews, for example, are often used to collect qualitative data related to a person's opinions or beliefs.

Hard data

See Quantative data.

Quantitative data

Includes use of figures, such as statistics. Also known as *hard data*, often collected in order to measure or quantify an object or situation.

Qualitative data

Describes without the use of figures, the qualities or characteristics of an object or situation. Also known as *soft data*.

The intuitive manager relies heavily on prior experience, judgement and intuition. He or she tends to examine situations as a whole, adopting a holistic view that takes into account the wide range of factors that might influence a decision. This kind of manager will also be more willing to accept qualitative information when making a decision.

It should be evident that a manager with an analytical cognitive style is likely to be most effective when making structured decisions. Intuitive managers are likely to be most effective when making unstructured decisions.

▶ A model of decision making

The work of H. Simon (1977) provides a framework from which to examine the way in which managerial decisions are made. Although presented in a modified form, this framework can be used to show how the act of making a decision involves moving through five stages. Each stage must be completed before it is possible to move on to the next. Table 1.2 provides an overview of the decision-making process.

Table 1.2 A model of decision making

Stage	Activities
Intelligence	◆ Awareness that a problem exists ◆ Awareness that a decision must be made
Design	◆ Identify all possible solutions ◆ Examine possible solutions ◆ Examine implications of all possible solutions
Choice	◆ Select best solution
Implementation	◆ Implement solution
Evaluation	◆ Evaluate effectiveness or success of decision

The *intelligence* stage involves gathering information concerning the decision to be made. It recognises that managers must be made aware that a problem exists before any action can be taken. Once a problem has been identified, information is collected in order to achieve a thorough understanding of the problem and the circumstances in which it arose. Unless this understanding is achieved, managers may take an inappropriate approach to the problem, resulting in a less efficient or ineffective solution.

In the *design* stage, as many as possible of the potential solutions to the problem are identified and evaluated. At this point, the decision maker will begin to discard unsatisfactory solutions in order to reduce the number of alternatives as far as possible. The solution that will be implemented is then chosen during the *selection* stage.

Having made a decision, the action required to achieve a resolution to the problem is taken in the *implementation* stage. Following implementation, the *evaluation* stage considers how successful the solution has been. If further action is required, the decision maker returns to the intelligence stage and examines the problem again.

This model can be used to highlight a number of important points. First, it is important to recognise that information plays a critical part in arriving at an effective and successful decision. In the design stage, for example, it is essential to examine the implications of each possible solution. Unless the decision maker has access to adequate information, he or she may reject or accept possible solutions for the wrong reasons.

Second, the information required to support the decision-making process is determined by the decision itself. In other words, *decision needs determine information needs*.

Third, although many models of decision making consider the implementation stage as the end of the process, this is not necessarily the case. If the chosen solution has been unsuccessful or only partially successful, then the problem effectively remains unsolved. In this event, the entire process must be repeated until a satisfactory solution is achieved.

The case study on enterprise resource planning considers how a company uses information from the perspective of enterprise resource planning systems (ERP). ERP systems are an important category of information systems that are intended to be integrated across an organisation.

ERP systems are described in more detail in Chapters 6 and 19.

CASE STUDY: TOPIC AREA

FT

Enterprise resource planning

Corporate intelligence: Distributed data and connectivity

by Geoffrey Wheelwright

Effective use of information is often the vital factor in determining whether a company will succeed, stagnate or die. Demand for new ways to strategically track, manage and manipulate corporate information – and maximise its use – has given birth to a whole new sector of the computer industry aimed squarely at providing such services to 'the enterprise'.

It goes by any number of names, with the hottest acronym at the moment being ERP (enterprise resource planning).

More important than what it is called, however, is what it actually *does*. An ERP system helps an organisation assess the data that it holds, looks at how that data can be better managed, what manipulation can be carried out on it to create better corporate intelligence – and perhaps what further data is needed to complete the picture. Perhaps most importantly, ERP deals with the issue of managing the data already within the organisation.

According to the London-based PA Consulting Group, the solution to properly implementing distributed data and connectivity solutions lies not only in choosing the right technology: it suggests that a strong set of a 'best practices' needs to be developed alongside the technology, which create a situation in which:

Information is treated as a shared business resource and, through appointed stewards, is actively and strategically directed.

Users understand what information is available within the company and what their own further data needs are likely to be.

The company works to continuously improve the quality of its information resources and formally audit its information resources.

Information storage, security, availability and accessibility are managed efficiently, effectively and economically.

All information is openly and easily accessible to those who need it.

Employees have the necessary capability to manage, use and exploit those resources in accordance with goals for improved business excellence and continued business success.

Innovation in using and enriching information is encouraged and rewarded.

There is strong evidence that these ideas apply more widely across more sectors of the economy than ever before. A global study released by Microsoft, in conjunction with McKinsey & Company, suggests that a growing percentage of the world's workforce is primarily knowledge workers. This, in turn, means that the way in which staff use and manage and access information is fundamental to their jobs.

According to Steve Ballmer, Microsoft executive vice president, the results of the survey show that in 'semi-developed' economies, about 47 per cent of people are knowledge workers.

'It's clear that those numbers are higher in advanced economies such as the US or Germany, while the figures are lower in developing economies,' he says. 'But certainly there's a shift in the workforce as economies develop, where for more and more of the people, their fundamental job is working with information.'

Bob Muglia, vice president of server applications at Microsoft, suggests that the challenge now lies in making this 'knowledge' as useful and relevant as possible.

'A key problem is that corporations have so much information, created by staff in so many different formats, that taking that information, and creating useful, easy-to-find documents and a valuable knowledge-base is a major challenge,' he says. 'And it's something in which the right technology can make a very great difference.'

It appears that corporations everywhere are taking this message to heart for both their employees and their cus-

tomers. The impact of this need to use and work with distributed information was recently demonstrated in a
decision by British Airways to develop and run a serviced
technology centre for its frequent flyers.

At the airline's new business centre in London Heathrow's
Terminal One, BA's Silver and Gold Club Members, as well as
Club Europe passengers, can access the World Wide Web and
check their e-mail.

Hewlett-Packard and Computacenter developed the
centre for BA.

The airline reports that, so far, accessing the internet has
been one of the most popular services used by travellers,
along with the sending of 'last minute' e-mails and faxes.

Source: Financial Times, 18 March 1998

Questions

1 Identify some of the factors that cause modern business
organisations to generate the large volumes of information described in the case study.

2 What are some of the problems faced by organisations
in dealing with large quantities of business information?

3 In addition to developing more effective computer-
based information systems, why is it also important to
develop new procedures and guidelines for dealing
with business information?

4 In what ways can enterprise resource planning systems
support an organisation's business activities?

▶ Levels of decision taking

The characteristics of the decisions taken in an organisation vary according to the
level at which they are taken. Figure 1.3 shows the distribution of managerial responsibility within a typical organisation. As can be seen, the largest proportion of
managers is located at the operational level of the organisation. The smallest proportion of managers, typically less than 10 per cent, is located at the strategic level.

◆ At the *strategic* level, managers are largely concerned with long-term organisational planning. Decisions tend to be unstructured and are made infrequently.
However, the decisions made at this level are likely to have a large impact on the
organisation as a whole and cannot be reversed easily. An example of a decision
taken at the strategic level might be a choice of new markets into which to move.

◆ At the *tactical*, level managers are largely concerned with medium-term planning.
They monitor the performance of the organisation, control budgets, allocate
resources and set policies. Decisions taken at this level are used to set medium-
term goals that form stages leading to the accomplishment of the organisation's
strategic objectives. An example of a decision taken at the tactical level might be
setting a departmental budget.

◆ At the *operational* level, managers deal with short-term planning and the day-to-
day control of the organisation's activities. The decisions taken at this level direct
the organisation's efforts towards meeting the medium-term goals, abiding by the
budgets, policies and procedures set at the tactical level. Operational decisions
tend to be highly structured and have little impact on the organisation as a whole.
An example of a decision taken at the organisational level might be setting a daily
or weekly production schedule.

A direct relationship exists between the management level at which a decision is
taken and the characteristics of the information required to support decision making.
Tables 1.3 and 1.4 illustrate how the characteristics of the information needed by
managers change according to the type of decision being made.

Fig 1.3 Levels of managerial decision taking

Table 1.3 Decision characteristics and management level

Management level	Decision			
	Type of decision	Timescale	Impact on organisation	Frequency of decisions
Strategic	Unstructured	Long	Large	Infrequent
Tactical	↔	Medium	Medium	↔
Operational	Structured	Short	Small	Frequent

Table 1.4 Information characteristics for decisions by management level

Management level	Information					
	Time period	Frequency	Source	Certainty	Scope	Detail
Strategic	Wide	Infrequent	External	Less certain	Wide	Summarised
Tactical	↔	↔	↔	↔	↔	↔
Operational	Narrow	Frequent	Internal	More certain	Narrow	Detailed

ACTIVITY

Classify the following decisions by type (structured, semistructured, unstructured) and organisational level (strategic, tactical, operational). In addition, determine whether or not the decision-making process could be automated.

(a) At what level should we set the budget for next year?

(b) Does this customer qualify for a discount on a large order?

(c) How should we deal with a takeover bid?

(d) Should we employ more staff to cope with an urgent order?

(e) Should we expand abroad?

(f) Should we launch an advertising campaign?

(g) Should we take a short-term loan to help our current cashflow position?

(h) What new markets should we move into?

(i) What should we do about a faulty machine?

▶ SUMMARY

1 Data can be described as a collection of non-random facts obtained by observation or research.

2 Information can be described as data that has been processed so that it is meaning-ful. An alternative view of information suggests that it acts to reduce uncertainty about a situation or event.

3 Information can have tangible or intangible value. One view suggests that the value of information can be measured in terms of the improvements it brings to managerial decision making.

4 The quality of information can be described by using the attributes of information quality.

5 The functions of management include forecasting, planning, organisation, co-ordination and control. One of the key management functions that information systems seek to support is managerial decision making.

6 Decisions can be structured, semistructured or unstructured. A simple model of decision making includes five stages: intelligence, design, choice, implementation and evaluation. Decisions can be taken at a strategic, tactical or operational level. The characteristics of a decision will vary according to the organisational level at which it is made.

▶ EXERCISES

▶ Self-assessment exercises

1 What are the three dimensions of information quality?

2 How can the value of information be measured?

3 What are the functions of management?

4 What are the stages involved in making a decision?

5 How will a manager's cognitive style affect the decisions that he or she makes?

▶ Discussion questions

1 Some people argue that employees should be restricted in terms of the information to which they have access in the course of their duties. Others argue that they are able to work more efficiently if they have access to *all* of an organisation's information resources. Using relevant examples, make a case for one side of this argument.

2 It has been said that decision needs should determine information needs. Is this always true or is there a case for an organisation gathering *all* available data and information?

▶ Essay questions

1 Select an organisation with which you are familiar. Identify at least one major decision that the organisation has taken recently. Describe the decision-making process that took place, paying particular attention to the following points:

   (a) Describe how managers became aware that a problem existed and that a decision was required.
   (b) Describe what information was gathered so that managers could achieve a good understanding of the problem.
   (c) Provide examples of any alternative solutions that were considered and explain why these were eventually rejected.
   (d) Explain why the final solution was selected and describe how it was implemented.
   (e) Discuss how the solution was evaluated and whether or not it was successful.

2 The survival of a large organisation depends on access to high-quality information. Discuss this statement, providing relevant examples where necessary.

3 The Microsoft Corporation is arguably the most successful company in the world. Conduct any research necessary to complete the following tasks:

   (a) Provide an overview of the company and its activities.
   (b) Selecting appropriate examples, describe the company's physical and conceptual resource bases.
   (c) Identify and describe some of the factors in the company's business environment. Provide examples of factors that act either to support or obstruct the company's activities.

▶ Examination questions

1 It is generally agreed that one of the key functions of management is decision making. Using specific examples, you are required to:

  (a) describe the types of decisions that managers are required to take;
  (b) explain the stages involved in making a decision;
  (c) describe the characteristics of decisions taken at different levels in an organisation.

2 An understanding of the nature of information is fundamental to the study of information systems. Using specific examples, you are required to:

  (a) define information;
  (b) describe the characteristics that will be present in information of high quality;
  (c) describe how the value of information can be determined.

3 Information can be transmitted via formal and informal means. Using specific examples, you are required to:

  (a) describe the advantages and disadvantages of each method;
  (b) discuss each method in terms of the attributes of information quality that are likely to be present.

▶ References

Lucey, T. (1994) *Management Information Systems*, 6th edn, DP Publications, London.

Newing, Rod (1998) 'Database management systems: a better understanding of clients', *Financial Times*, 18 March.

O'Brien, J. (1993) *Management Information Systems: A Managerial End User Perspective*, 2nd edn, Richard D. Irwin.

Simon, H. (1977) *The New Science of Management Decision*, Prentice-Hall, Englewood Cliffs, NJ.

Wheelwright, Geoffrey (1998) 'Distributed data and connectivity', *Financial Times*, 18 March.

▶ Further reading

Cashmore, C. and Lyall, R. (1991) *Business Information Systems and Strategies*, Prentice-Hall, New York.

Gordon, S. and Gordon, J. (1996) *Information Systems: A Management Approach*, The Dryden Press, London.

Laudon, K. and Laudon, J. (1995) *Management Information Systems: Organization and Technology*, 3rd edn, Macmillian, Upper Saddle River, NJ.
    Chapter 5 covers concepts related to data and information, the functions of management and managerial decision making. In addition, Chapter 16 deals with the use of computer-based information systems to improve managerial decision making.

Lucey, T. (1994) *Management Information Systems*, 6th edn, DP Publications, London.

O'Brien, J. (1993) *Management Information Systems: A Managerial End User Perspective*, 2nd edn, Richard D. Irwin, Boston, USA.
    Chapter 10 provides detailed coverage of managerial decision making.

O'Hicks, J. (1993) *Management Information Systems: A User Perspective*, 3rd edn, West Publishing, St Paul (Minneapolis), USA.

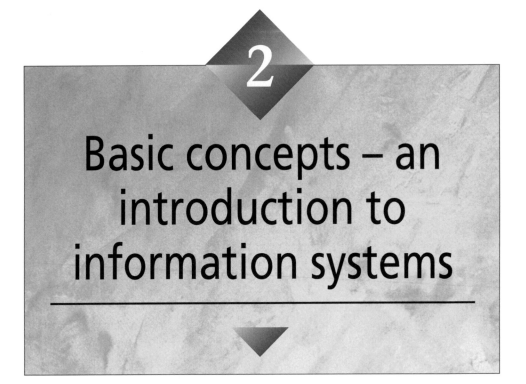

Basic concepts – an introduction to information systems

INTRODUCTION

This chapter builds on the concepts introduced in Chapter 1 and introduces the features of systems. The topics covered are intended to give readers an understanding of:

◆ the basic characteristics of systems;

◆ the behaviour of systems;

◆ types of information systems;

◆ applications for information systems;

◆ applying information systems for competitive advantage.

▶ Learning objectives

After reading this chapter, readers will be able to:

◆ identify systems and their components;

◆ identify the behaviour of systems;

◆ identify computer-based information systems, distinguishing them by category and the organisational level at which they are used;

◆ identify basic strategies and methods used to gain competitive advantage through the use of information systems.

▶ Links to other chapters

Chapter 1   provides an introduction to concepts related to data, information and managerial decision making.

Chapter 6   describes how information systems support the functional areas of business.

Chapter 10   reviews systems theory in more detail as background to systems analysis and design, which are covered in Chapters 11 and 12.

Chapter 14   looks in more detail at developing a company strategy for introducing and using information systems effectively.

Chapter 15   deals with maintaining the quality of the information provided by computer-based information systems and considers the security of information systems.

▶ INTRODUCTION TO SYSTEMS

Systems theory provides a powerful means of analysing and improving business processes. It can be applied to a wide variety of different areas and is one of the fundamental concepts required to gain a good understanding of the field of information systems.

▶ What is a system?

A **system** can be defined as a collection of interrelated components that work together towards a collective goal. The function of a system is to receive inputs and transform these into outputs. Figure 2.1 illustrates the organisation of the input, process, output model. Note that natural systems such as the solar system may not have an obvious goal, but that business systems usually have multiple goals such as profit or improving the quality of a product.

An example might help to illustrate this concept and aid understanding. On page 6, the concept of a transformation process was used to explain how data can be converted into information. Using the model shown in Fig 2.1, it can be said that data is used as the **input** for a **process** that creates information as an **output**.

However, this model illustrates a system that is essentially static. The performance of the system cannot be adjusted and there are no checks to ensure that it works correctly. In order to monitor the performance of the system, some kind of **feedback** mechanism is required. In addition, **control** must be exerted to correct any problems that occur and ensure that the system is fulfilling its purpose.

If these additional components are added to the basic model of the system, it can be illustrated as shown in Fig 2.2. The model shown in the diagram is sometimes referred to as an **adaptive system**, in order to signify that it has the ability to monitor and regulate its own performance.

Fig 2.1 A basic model of a transformation process

Systems theory

The study of the behaviour and interactions within and between systems.

System

A collection of interrelated components that work together towards a collective goal.

Output

A product that is created by a system.

Process

Inputs are turned into outputs by a transformation process.

Input

The raw materials for a *process* that will produce a particular *output*.

Feedback mechanism

Provides information on the performance of a system which can be used to adjust its behaviour.

Control

If alterations are needed to the system, adjustments are made by a control mechanism.

Adaptive system

A system with the ability to monitor and regulate its own performance.

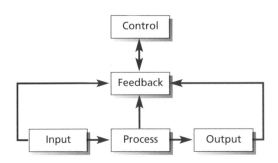

Fig 2.2 A generic model of a system

▶ System components

At this point, it can be argued that a generic system includes five components: input, process, output, feedback and control. Each of these components can now be described in more detail.

◆ The **input** to a system can be thought of as the raw materials for a process that will produce a particular output. Inputs can take many forms and are not necessarily purely physical in nature. Examples of inputs might include data, knowledge, raw materials, machinery and premises.

◆ Inputs are turned into outputs by subjecting them to a transformation **process**. The concept of a transformation process was described on page 6.

◆ The **output** is the finished product created by the system. Again, the outputs produced by a system can take many forms. Examples might include information, products and services.

◆ Information on the performance of the system is gathered by a **feedback** mechanism (sometimes known as a feedback loop). An example of feedback might include quality control measurements taken on a production line.

◆ If alterations are needed to the system, adjustments are made by some form of **control** mechanism. In general, control is exerted as the result of feedback information regarding the performance of the system. The function of the control component is to ensure that the system is working to fulfil its objective (which is normally the creation of a specific output). Control tends to be exerted by adjusting the process and input components of the system until the correct output is achieved.

System objective

All components of a system should be related to one another by a common objective.

Environment

The surroundings of a system, beyond its boundary.

Boundary

The interface between a system and its environment.

▶ Other characteristics

As mentioned earlier, the components of a system work towards a collective goal. This is known as the **system objective**. The objective of a system is normally very specific and can often be expressed in a single sentence. As an example, the objective of a car might be expressed as simply to transport people and goods to a specified location.

It should also be recognised that systems do not operate in complete isolation, they are contained within an **environment** that contains other systems and external agencies. The scope of a system is defined by its **boundary**. Everything outside of the boundary is part of the system's environment, everything within the boundary forms part of the system itself. The boundary also marks the **interface** between a system and its environment. The interface describes exchanges between a system and the environment or other systems.

Systems can be extremely complex and can be made up of other, smaller systems known as **subsystems**. Systems composed of one or more subsystems are often referred to as **suprasystems**. The objective of a subsystem is to support the larger objective of the suprasystem. Consider the example given earlier, that of a car. The car can be considered a suprasystem that is made up of numerous subsystems, including the engine, the steering mechanism, the brakes and so on. Each of the subsystems has an objective that supports the overall objective of the car, for example the objective of the engine might be to move the car in a specified direction at a specified speed. By fulfilling this objective, the engine supports the overall objective of the car, to transport people and goods from one location to another.

▶ INFORMATION SYSTEMS

In this section, we introduce the concept of an information system and consider the nature of computer-based information systems.

▶ What is an information system?

Having examined concepts related to information, general systems theory and decision making, it is possible to suggest a basic definition of an **information system**:

> An information system is a group of interrelated components that work collectively to carry out input, processing, output, storage and control actions in order to convert data into information products that can be used to support forecasting, planning, control, coordination, decision making and operational activities in an organisation.

Although quite long, it should be clear that the definition offered makes use of many of the concepts described in Chapters 1 and 2. These include data, information, managerial decision making and aspects of systems theory.

It should be noted that a number of alternative definitions exist and it is worth taking a brief look at some aspects of these definitions:

◆ Many definitions refer to 'data resources' that are converted into 'information products'. This underlines the notion that data forms part of an organisation's resource base and that the information derived from it is provided in a finished, useful form. The concept of a resource base was described on page 14.

◆ Many of the definitions in common use also specify that information systems involve the use of information technology. However, this can be disputed, since it is possible to provide many examples of information systems that do not involve information technology at all. A simple example of such a 'manual' information system is a set of accounting ledgers.

◆ Some definitions specify that information systems are used only to support decision making. Again, this can be disputed, since it is apparent that managers make use of information in a number of other ways, for example as feedback on various aspects of a company's performance.

Interface

Defines exchanges between a system and its environment, or other systems.

Subsystem

Large systems can be composed of one or more smaller systems known as subsystems.

Suprasystem

A larger system made up of one or more smaller systems (*subsystems*).

Information system

A system designed to produce information that can be used to support the activities of managers and other workers.

◆ Although some definitions refer to organisations in general, others specify that they are concerned only with business organisations. However, it can be argued that it is sometimes very difficult to distinguish between profit-making and non-profit-making organisations. In recent years, many non-profit-making organisations have started to operate more like businesses. In the UK, Oxfam, for example, operates a national chain of stores that enjoy a healthy share of the clothing market.

▶ RESOURCES THAT SUPPORT INFORMATION SYSTEMS

Although it has already been pointed out that information systems need not involve the use of information technology, some definitions suggest that information systems rely on four basic resources: people, hardware, software and data. It is worth considering this idea further, since it is certainly true that we can describe an information system in these terms.

▶ People resources

People resources include the users of an information system and those who develop, maintain and operate the system. Examples of people resources might include managers, data-entry clerks and technical support staff.

▶ Hardware resources

The term *hardware resources* refers to all types of machines, not just computer hardware. Telephones, fax machines and switchboards are all valid examples of hardware. The term also covers any media used by these machines, such as magnetic disks or paper. These resources are described in Chapter 3.

▶ Software resources

In the same way, the term *software resources* does not only refer to computer programs and the media on which they are stored. The term can also be used to describe the procedures used by people. Within this context, examples of software resources include instruction manuals and company policies. These resources are described in Chapter 4.

▶ Communication resources

Resources are also required to enable different systems to transfer data. These include networks and the hardware and software needed to support them. These resources are described in Chapter 5.

▶ Data resources

Data resources describe all of the data to which an organisation has access, regardless of its form. Computer databases, paper files and measurements taken by sensors on a production line are all examples of data resources.

> What information systems might be found in your newsagent? For each system identified, list the people, hardware, software and data resources involved.

ACTIVITY

▶ Information technology

The terms information systems (IS) and information technology (IT) are often used interchangeably. This is an error, because their scope is different. The stress in IT is on the technology, while IS not only refers to the technology, but also considers the application of the system to a business context, i.e. its objective.

▶ Computer-based information systems

In modern organisations, most information systems make extensive use of information technology, such as personal computers. Further understanding of **computer-based information systems** of this kind can be gained by considering some of the advantages and disadvantages of computers and computer-based information systems in general.

> The term **computer-based information system** is used in this chapter. This helps distinguish computer-based IS from other IS, such as paper-based information systems. In the remainder of the book the general term **information system** will be used for simplicity to refer to computer-based information systems and business information systems.

Computer-based information system

An information system that makes use of Information Technology in order to create management information.

Information system

A system designed to produce information that can be used to support the activities of managers and other workers.

▶ Some advantages of processing by computer

◆ *Speed*. Computers can process millions of instructions each second, allowing them to complete a given task in a very short time.

◆ *Accuracy*. The result of a calculation carried out by a computer is likely to be completely accurate. In addition, errors that a human might make, such as a typing error, can be reduced or eliminated entirely.

◆ *Reliability*. In many organisations, computer-based information systems operate for 24 hours a day and are only ever halted for repairs or routine maintenance.

> Although many people consider computers to be infallible, this is not always the case. As an example, following the launch of the Intel Pentium processor, it was found that carrying out certain calculations produced incorrect results. Although the fault was corrected quickly, the company's reputation suffered a great deal of harm.

◆ *Programmability*. Although most computer-based information systems are created to fulfil a particular function, the ability to modify the software that controls them provides a high degree of flexibility. Even the simplest personal computer, for example, can be used to create letters, produce cashflow forecasts or manipulate databases.

These advantages combine to give major benefits to a business, as described on page 34.

▶ Some disadvantages of processing by computer

◆ *Judgement/experience.* Despite advances in artificial intelligence techniques, computer-based information systems are incapable of solving problems using their own judgement and experience. Although one might argue that more specialised systems, such as expert systems, can use prior experience, these are not typically found in most organisations.

◆ *Improvisation/flexibility.* In general, computer-based information systems are unable to react to unexpected situations and events. Additionally, since most systems are created to fulfil a particular function, it can be difficult to modify them to meet new or changed requirements.

◆ *Innovation.* Computers lack the creativity of a human being. They are unable to think in the abstract and are therefore restricted in their ability to discover new ways of improving processes or solving problems.

◆ *Intuition.* Human intuition can play an important part in certain social situations. For example, one might use intuition to gauge the emotional state of a person before deciding whether or not to give them bad news. Computer-based information systems cannot use intuition in this way and are therefore unsuitable for certain kinds of situations.

◆ *Qualitative information.* Managers often make decisions based on the recommendations of others. Their confidence in the person they are dealing with often has a major influence on the decision itself. Once again, computers cannot act on qualitative information of this kind.

▶ Areas of application for computer-based information systems

Data processing

The transformation of the large volumes of data that arise from an organisation's daily activities into information for decision making.

On page 20, it was shown how the characteristics of the decisions taken by managers vary according to organisational level. By way of example, consider the kinds of problems that managers encounter at the strategic level of an organisation. Most decisions tend to be unstructured and require managers to make use of facilities such as experience and judgement. In such cases, computer-based information systems are of only limited value and are therefore less common at this organisational level.

On the other hand, the problems and decisions dealt with at the operational level of an organisation tend to have a high degree of structure. Frequent access to highly detailed information is often required to support the decision-making process. Since computer-based information systems are well suited to such situations, they are more common at this organisational level.

Transaction processing

Processing the sales and purchase transactions that an organisation carries out in the course of its normal activities.

Perhaps another way of looking at this topic is to consider the work undertaken at each level of an organisation. The bulk of an organisation's work normally involves **data processing**, that is, handling the large volumes of data that arise from an organisation's daily activities. Although data processing describes a wide range of activities, the most common are transaction processing and process control.

Process control systems

Systems which manage manufacturing and other production processes.

Transaction processing involves dealing with the sales and purchase transactions that an organisation carries out in the course of its normal activities. Banks, for example, handle millions of deposits and withdrawals each day. **Process control systems** deal with the large volume of data generated by production processes. As an example, a machine producing a precision component might take hundreds of measurements and use these to adjust the manufacturing process. These types of system are described in more detail in Chapter 6.

The speed, accuracy and reliability of computer-based information systems mean that they are able to handle repetitive tasks involving large volumes of data. Furthermore, they are best utilised in situations governed by clear, logical rules. This makes them ideally suited to transaction processing or process control applications. From this, it is reasonable to suggest that the widest use of computer-based information systems will be at the operational level of an organisation.

Figure 2.3 illustrates areas of applications for computer-based information systems in a typical organisation. Note that there will be fewer applications and therefore lower levels of usage at the strategic level. A need for higher levels of automation and the structure of the tasks carried out mean that the highest levels of usage will be at the operational level.

► CATEGORIES OF BUSINESS INFORMATION SYSTEMS

In this book all types of information system that can be used within businesses are referred to as **business information systems (BIS)**. BIS can be divided into two broad categories: systems that support an organisation's business activities, and systems that support managerial decision making:

◆ **Operations information systems** are generally concerned with process control, transaction processing, communication (internal and external) and productivity.

◆ **Management information systems** provide feedback on organisational activities and help to support managerial decision making.

As shown in Table 2.1, both of these broader categories can be subdivided into a number of additional categories. The following sections introduce these types of system. They are described in more detail in Chapter 6. Figure 2.3 also illustrates the typical use of each category of computer-based information system by management level.

Business information systems

IS is used to support business processes and functional areas.

Operations information systems

Systems required for the day-to-day activities of a business such as process control, transaction processing, communications (internal and external) and productivity.

Management information systems

Systems providing feedback on organisational activities and supporting managerial decision making.

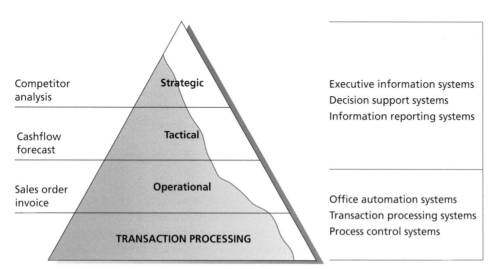

Fig 2.3 Usage and applications of business information systems by organisational level

Table 2.1 Categories of business information systems

Operations information systems	Management information systems
Transaction processing systems	Decision support systems
Process control systems	Information reporting systems
Office automation systems	Executive information systems

▶ Operations information systems

Transaction processing systems (TP)

As mentioned earlier, transaction processing involves recording and processing the data that results from an organisation's business transactions. Transaction processing can be carried out by batch processing or real-time processing. In **real-time processing** (sometimes known as online processing), transaction data is processed immediately. An excellent example of real-time processing is a cashpoint system, where balance enquiries and cash withdrawals are processed almost instantly. In **batch processing**, transaction data is collected and processed in bulk at regular intervals. A good example of batch processing is the production of bills for utilities and other services. Typically, customer data is collected and prepared for processing during the day. The processing itself takes place during the night, when the demands on an organisation's computer resources are lowest. Deciding whether to use a batch or real-time system is usually a design decision. This is described in more detail in Chapter 12.

Real-time processing

Data is processed immediately on collection. Such systems often involve user interaction.

Batch processing

Data is 'post-processed' following collection, often at times when the workload on the system is lower.

Process control systems

These systems are used to support and control manufacturing processes. A good example involves the modern computer numerically controlled (CNC) machines used in sophisticated engineering environments. Such machines use sensors to gather data concerning a variety of conditions that affect the manufacturing process, such as the level of wear and tear of a cutting tool. This data is processed in real time and used to adjust the operation of the machine. In the case of a worn cutting tool, corrective action might involve automatically changing the tool. Process control systems can also be used to automate routine decisions that influence the manufacturing process. An example is the ordering of raw materials automatically when the stocks held fall below a certain point.

Office automation systems (OAS)

Office automation systems

Systems intended to improve efficiency by applying information technology to common office tasks.

Office automation systems are concerned with improving efficiency by applying information technology to many of the common tasks carried out in a typical office. Technology is used to enhance communications and increase productivity. Examples include using a wordprocessor to produce business correspondence, setting up a video conference to hold a meeting or using a fax machine to send technical drawings to a supplier.

▶ Management information systems (MIS)

Management information systems are defined differently by different authors. For example, O'Brien (1993) refers to MIS as including operational systems and transaction processing systems that are only used indirectly by managers. It is believed that the term 'business information systems' to describe all types of IS used in business, including decision support systems and operational information systems is more appropriate than 'management information systems'. The term MIS implies that the use of these systems is limited to managers, which is clearly not the case. Management information systems are generally taken to include the following types of systems.

Information reporting systems (IRS)

Information reporting systems produce reports containing the information required to support a manager's day-to-day decision-making activities. The information provided can take a number of forms, ranging from a formal report to a display on a computer monitor. In addition, the information needed by a manager can be supplied at different times, depending on his or her information needs. Information can be supplied on demand, periodically or by exception. An *on demand* or *ad hoc* *report* fulfils an immediate information need, such as current stock levels for a particular item. *Periodic reports* (sometimes known as scheduled reports) are supplied at predetermined intervals, for example a sales summary might be provided weekly or monthly. *Exception reports* are created when an unexpected event occurs, for example if production falls below a specified level.

Information reporting systems

Systems used to generate reports containing information that can be used to support managerial decision making.

Decision support systems (DSS)

Decision support systems provide managers with the information needed to support semistructured or unstructured decisions. Unlike most information reporting systems, these provide information on an *ad hoc* (as needed) basis. Users work interactively with the system to identify and retrieve the information needed to support a decision or solve a business problem. Decision support systems come in a wide variety of forms, operating in different ways to achieve the same basic goal. Two suitable examples are as follows:

Decision support systems

Provide managers with information and tools to support semi-structured or unstructured decisions.

◆ Some systems allow users to evaluate their decisions by helping them define a problem or situation in a more structured way. For example, some systems help a user arrive at a list of criteria by which each potential solution to a problem can be judged.

◆ Some systems can be used to create a model of a situation so that *what if?* questioning can be carried out. This allows users to experiment with potential solutions and see what the results are likely to be. Spreadsheet models are an excellent example of this approach.

Executive information systems (EIS)

Executive information systems are used by senior management to select, retrieve and manage information that can be used to support the achievement of an organisation's business objectives. They need not be directly concerned with decision-making activities, but can help senior managers become more efficient and productive in a number of other ways. Personal information managers (PIM) can be considered an

Executive information systems

Systems used by senior management to select, retrieve and manage information that can be used to support the achievement of an organisation's business objectives.

example of an EIS. A PIM can be used to schedule meetings, make notes, store information on contacts and organise other items of information, such as personal expenses. In this way, a PIM can help a manager to manage time more effectively, improving his or her productivity.

It is shown in Chapter 6 that the categories of MIS are now supported by a new type of software known as business intelligence software, which includes data warehousing and data mining. These systems possess many of the characteristics of IRS, DSS and EIS and the terms business intelligence software or data warehousing are now used in their marketing.

▶ Other categories

In addition to operations information systems and management information systems, a number of other categories are often used to describe a more specialised range of applications.

Expert systems (ES)

Expert systems

These systems attempt to apply human knowledge and experience to a range of problems. In general, expert systems are used to support problem-solving activities by providing managers with advice and information.

Expert systems attempt to apply human knowledge and experience to a range of problems. A typical expert system is composed of a knowledge base and a series of rules. The knowledge base contains a representation of the knowledge and experience of one or more 'experts' in a given area. The rules contained in the system are used to organise the knowledge base and allow users to carry out questioning activities. Expert systems can be used for a variety of applications, from choosing the correct computer system for an organisation to performing a medical diagnosis. ES can be used to assist in both decision support and EIS applications. These applications and the structure of ES are described in Chapter 6.

End user computing systems

End-user computing systems

These systems are created and managed by end users in order to support their individual activities.

End user computing systems are created and managed by end users in order to support their individual activities. A simple example might involve a user creating a wordprocessing template to simplify the production of certain documents. End user computing is a rapid area of growth and is considered to have significant implications for the development of computer-based information systems over the next decade. Owing to its importance it is covered in a separate chapter (Chapter 16) which addresses the issues involved in its management.

Strategic information systems

Competitive advantage

In order to survive or expand, organisations must seek to gain competitive advantage by a variety of strategies to achieve control of a market or prevent others from achieving control.

Strategic information systems are concerned with creating and sustaining **competitive advantage**. The next section describes concepts related to competitive advantage and considers applications for strategic computer-based information systems.

▶ INFORMATION SYSTEMS AND STRATEGIC ADVANTAGE

In order to survive and grow in a competitive environment, organisations must seek to gain competitive advantage (or strategic advantage). Computer-based information systems play a crucial part in gaining and sustaining a competitive edge over the other organisations operating in the same industry.

This section introduces competitive or strategic advantage. Chapter 14 describes how IS strategy can be developed in more detail. Chapter 8 looks at how a company reviews the benefits of a new system when assessing its feasibility.

Michael Porter (1980) describes a business environment in which five competitive forces operate. These are:

(a) the threat of new entrants;

(b) the bargaining power of suppliers;

(c) the bargaining power of customers;

(d) the threat of substitute products or services;

(e) rivalry among existing competitors.

▶ Competitive strategies

In order to gain or maintain competitive advantage, organisations can adopt three basic strategies: cost leadership, differentiation or innovation.

Cost leadership

Cost leadership means simply providing goods or services at the lowest possible cost. In most cases this is achieved by reducing the organisation's costs in producing goods or providing services, for example by automating parts of the production process. However, cost leadership can also be achieved by helping suppliers and customers to reduce costs, usually by forming alliances and *linkages* that benefit all of the parties involved. In some cases, cost leadership is achieved by causing a competitor's costs to increase, for example by introducing new product features that will be expensive for a competitor to duplicate.

Product differentiation

Differentiation involves creating a distinction between the organisation's products and those of its competitors. In many cases, differentiation is used to concentrate on a specific niche in the market so that the company can focus on particular goods and services. A car manufacturer, such as Rolls-Royce, provides a good example of product differentiation. The cars produced by Rolls-Royce are perceived as luxury items that indicate status and importance in society. They are considered far superior to standard production models in terms of quality, reliability and comfort. By creating this image, Rolls-Royce has succeeded in differentiating its products from those of its competitors. Although the luxury market forms only a relatively small part of the market for cars as a whole, Rolls-Royce has succeeded in capturing a large share of this segment. This position in the market allows the company to concentrate organisational resources on maintaining and increasing market share.

Innovation

Innovation is concerned with finding new ways to approach an organisation's activities. Examples of innovation include improving existing products or creating new ones, forging strategic linkages, improving production processes and entering new markets. Intel is a company well known for frequent innovation. The case study on Intel: a Silicon Valley powerhouse shows how the company innovates and its methods for retaining competitive advantage. The case study also highlights how *responsiveness* to the market environment and the *flexibility* to be able to respond are important capabilities for a company to possess.

CASE STUDY: TOPIC AREA

FT

Intel: a Silicon Valley powerhouse

With the largest chipmakers in Japan and Korea now struggling with economic turmoil, there are few companies that could seriously challenge Intel's dominant role in the world's semiconductor industry, writes Louise Kehoe in San Francisco.

Intel is in a league of its own. The world's largest chipmaker with a market value of more than $134bn, the Silicon Valley powerhouse produces most of the microprocessors used by the global personal computer industry.

The huge scale of Intel's operations dwarf those of most semiconductor rivals. The company ended 1997 with annual sales of $25.1bn, up from $20.8bn in 1996. With gross profit margins of close to 60 per cent, the company generates cash at a rate far exceeding that of any of its competitors.

This enables Intel to spend heavily on research and development as well as on new plants and equipment. This year, for example, Intel has a research and development budget of $2.8bn and plans to spend an additional $5.3bn on new production lines, three times that of any other semiconductor maker.

Given the dominant market share of Intel's Pentium microprocessors and the rapid pace at which the company is pushing forward with new technology developments, it may appear that the company's leadership is unassailable.

Yet changes in the personal computer market are creating new challenges for Intel that might trim its future growth. In particular, the emergence of the 'basic PC', which sells in the US for under $1000, has forced Intel to rethink its strategy. Until now, despite the complexity of its products, Intel's strategy has been simple. The company relentlessly improves upon the performance of its microprocessors so that the PC bought a year ago, or even six months ago, is quickly overshadowed by new models with faster engines.

With the introduction of each new generation of microprocessors, Intel would drop the prices of older versions so that PC prices remained quite stable while performance increased rapidly.

Microsoft and other software companies have aided Intel by developing ever more complex programs that require the latest PC hardware. Then along came the 'basic PC' – typically based on a less powerful microprocessor from one of Intel's rivals. At first, Intel dismissed the significance of this new competition. 'Who would want a less capable PC?' Intel asked, rhetorically. But the price was right and millions of buyers flocked to purchase the bargain PCs. Last year an estimated 25 per cent of personal computers sold in the US were in the under-$1000 price category. The growth of this new market segment caught Intel by surprise, forcing the company to reassess the situation. Intel could offer its older microprocessors for use in these PCs, but that would put a dent in the company's vaunted profit margins. Instead, the company recently announced plans to develop microprocessors specifically designed for use in lower-priced PCs.

In November, Intel realigned its product groups to reflect the new strategy. Intel would 'embrace all segments' of the computer market, said Andrew Grove, chairman and chief executive. By mid-year it plans to offer a version of its latest Pentium II microprocessor for low end PCs. The company will shave the cost of its highest performance microprocessors by taking out costly memory chips that accompany the current version. This will put the Pentium II in the same price range as slower chips from competitors.

Intel is also developing new 'chip sets' – devices that work with the microprocessor – that further reduce costs by squeezing the functions of a PC into fewer chips.

Another cost-reducing trick up Intel's sleeve is to switch functions currently performed by chips into software that can be run on the microprocessor. While this increases the workload on the central processor, it means that even cheap PCs will need Intel's high performance microprocessors.

Even as Intel shifts gears to address the 'basic PC' market, the company is also aiming to ensure that its chips are used in a new generation of television set-top boxes. These units, which are expected to sell for about $200–$300, will enable cable TV viewers to receive digital television pictures and internet services and they represent a potentially huge new market.

While lower-cost PCs and set-top boxes may boost Intel's sales, analysts predict that the company's profit margins will decline as it moves into these very cost-sensitive markets.

However, Intel plans to compensate for this shift by expanding its sales of very high performance chips with much fatter profit margins.

Already, Intel's Pentium II chips are being used in computer workstations and in multi-processor servers. In the workstation market, computers based on Intel chips and running Microsoft's Windows NT operating system are displacing those with proprietary technologies and the Unix operating system.

Intel has also made significant inroads in the server market. Last year, the majority of servers selling for under $25 000 were powered by Intel microprocessors.

In 1999, Intel will launch a new generation of microprocessors, code-named Merced, that will be aimed at higher end servers. Hewlett-Packard, the second largest US computer company, is collaborating with Intel in the development of Merced and plans to base its future products on the Intel chips.

Several other computer manufacturers, including Digital Equipment, also see Merced playing an important role in their future products.

By 2001, Merced will enable Intel to achieve a 41 per cent share of the market for microprocessors used in high end computers, analysts at International Data Corporation, a market research group, predict.

This would establish Intel chips as the dominant standard for servers and make Intel the top 'engine builder' for the entire computer industry; a role that no other chipmaker can even aspire to.

With the largest chipmakers in Japan and Korea struggling with economic turmoil, there are few companies that could seriously challenge Intel's role. Even if another chipmaker came up with a better microprocessor design, none has the production capacity to match Intel.

However, Intel's growing dominance in the microprocessor market could make it more vulnerable to antitrust challenges, such as those currently facing Microsoft. Already, Intel is under investigation by the Federal Trade Commission, although it appears unlikely that the company will be charged with any wrongdoing.

Still, to achieve its 'Intel inside everything' goal, Intel must produce a flawless Merced, with none of the bugs that plagued its original Pentium chips. The company may also have to weather a year or so of slimmer profits as it addresses the immediate need for lower-priced chips to service the 'basic PC' and TV set-top box markets before Merced profits emerge.

Source: Financial Times, 4 February 1998

Questions

1 What entry barriers exist for Intel's competitors?

2 Describe Intel's competitive strategy in terms of the concepts described in this chapter.

3 As indicated by the case study, Intel has formed a number of strategic alliances with other organisations. What benefits might be gained by making such alliances?

▶ Value chain analysis

Michael Porter's work also describes the concept of a **value chain**, a series of connected activities that add value to an organisation's products or services. An analysis of an organisation's value chain can indicate which areas might provide an organisation with a competitive advantage.

Value chain analysis allows managers to separate an organisation's basic activities into primary and support activities. Primary activities include marketing, inbound and outbound logistics, operations and service. Support activities are those that make primary activities possible and include administration, management, personnel and procurement. Identifying the importance of activities makes it possible for an organisation to concentrate on the areas that add most value to products and services. Chapter 14 considers the elements of the value chain in more detail.

Value chain analysis
A series of connected activities that add value to an organisation's products or services.

▶ Using information systems for strategic advantage

Porter's work can be used to identify a number of ways in which computer-based information systems can be used to achieve competitive advantage. These include:

(a) improving operational efficiency;

(b) raising barriers to entry;

(c) locking in customers and suppliers;

(d) promoting business innovation;

(e) increasing switching costs;

(f) leverage.

Figure 2.4 summarises the main ways in which computer-based information systems can be used to achieve competitive advantage.

The case study on corporate strategy refers to some of these methods of achieving competitive advantage and is worth reading in conjunction with the following sections. It also considers who is the driving force for strategy within an organisation.

Fig 2.4 Applying computer-based information systems to achieve competitive advantage

CASE STUDY: TOPIC AREA

FT

Corporate strategy

Company strategy: the machines are taking over

by Tony Jackson

Based on an extract from Unleashing the Killer App, *by Larry Downes and Chunka Mui, 1998, Harvard Business School Press.*

There seems no end to the way technology is invading management thinking. The internet has already deeply affected whole areas such as marketing and procurement.

But technology now shows signs of taking over that most central of functions, corporate strategy.

Traditionally, strategy has come from the top of the company, with technology being one of the things used to implement it. But in more and more cases, technology *is* the strategy. What is more, it generally comes from below.

Most managers are uneasily aware of this. All kinds of business, from banking to travel agencies, are under threat from the internet. And if you find a new way of doing things – a killer app (application), in the jargon – it will probably come not from the top, but from your customers and those in the company closest to them.

But according to a US survey last year, senior executives have not quite grasped the implications. Most of those questioned confessed to anxiety and the feeling that they did not fully understand the issues. But they were agreed that 'in their organisation technology was only a tool to implement strategy'.

The forthcoming book, *Unleashing the Killer App*, from which this information is drawn does much to explain their difficulty. It also gives a remarkably clear picture of why technology is becoming so pervasive in the first place.

The authors begin with three forces, each powerful in itself and lethal when combined. The first is familiar: Moore's Law, which says the power of chips doubles every 18 months for the same cost.

The second is less well known: Metcalfe's Law, named after the founder of the US network company 3Com. This says that the utility of a network rises with the square of the numbers of people using it.

Suppose there are only two phones in the world, and the owners talk once a day. Result, one call. Add another phone and that becomes three calls. Make it 10 phones and – supposing everyone is still talking to everyone else – you have 45 calls. The use of the network, in other words, increases exponentially.

Third is an observation from 1937 by the Nobel prize-winning British economist Ronald Coase. The reason firms form in the first place, Mr Coase said, is to minimise their transaction costs. When they run out of things they can do more cheaply inside the firm than out, they stop growing.

Some surprising things follow from this. The combination of Moore's and Metcalfe's laws is driving down a number of transaction costs in the open market very fast indeed. It should follow from Mr Coase that as these costs approach zero, so does the size of the firm.

This seems rather at odds with the current wave of mega-mergers. As the authors point out, much of this – in financial services especially – is a defensive response to falling transaction costs. Whether that is the whole story seems doubtful.

And, of course, not all transaction costs are falling. The monstrous growth of computing consultants such as Andersen Consulting and EDS is a reminder that whereas computing may drive down transaction costs elsewhere, it has vast transaction costs of its own: choosing the system, installing it, and ensuring it does not bring the enterprise to its knees by going wrong.

That apart, the authors make one essential point: that customers are generally quicker to grasp the technology than established suppliers are. This is mainly because the suppliers have more to lose, in the form of sunk costs. Their assets, as the book remarks, are their liabilities.

If you are a conventional bookseller, the advent of a virtual internet rival such as Amazon poses a distinct dilemma. Of course, you can retaliate in kind; but then what happens to all your expensive stores?

Or suppose you are an established chemical distributor, complete with offices, trucks and warehouses. It must be thought-provoking to study the website of the virtual dealer ChemConnect, which tells you that 500 litres of isobutylnitrite are wanted in Germany, or that 400 tonnes of aluminium monostearate are on offer from South Africa at $3 a kilo.

What is needed in such cases, of course, is lateral thinking. The book is rather good at suggesting ways to go about this.

First, forget the conventional rules of strategy. For instance, Michael Porter of Harvard emphasises the importance of the value chain. Scrap it, say the authors, since it is hampering change. If you do not, someone else will destroy it anyway.

In the same heroic vein, you should not hesitate to cannibalise your product. And you should give as much of it away free as you can, since Metcalfe's Law says you will thereby increase its value.

That, after all, was exactly what Netscape did in releasing the browser that made internet commerce feasible in the first place; and in spite of its recent mishaps, Netscape still has a market value of some $2bn (£1.25bn) four years after being founded.

Perhaps most important, you should let your customers take the lead. Outsource as much of your business to them as possible. Holiday Inn has a website that allows customers to find the right hotel, check the availability of rooms and make a booking. There are no banks of phones or reservation agents. Customers do it on equipment – PCs, modems, phone lines – that they have paid for themselves.

Next, let the customer develop the product. What can be digitised can be customised, so customise everything. Or rather, let the customers do it for you. In the process, they will feed you priceless market data on who they are and what they like.

Finally, how can you be sure that you have avoided the trap of thinking, like those managers in the survey, that technology is merely a way of doing things? Simple, the authors say. You will know you have arrived when you can no longer tell where the business stops and the technology starts.

Source: Financial Times, 23 February 1998

Questions

1 'Traditionally, strategy has come from the top of the company, with technology being one of the things used to implement it. But in more and more cases, technology *is* the strategy.' Why might this be the case?

2 Why are changes in corporate strategy beginning to come from the bottom of the organisation?

3 The case study suggests moving away from Porter's concept of the value chain in order to encourage change. What arguments can be made in favour of this?

4 Can you think of other types of business that could adopt similar systems?

Improving operational efficiency

One of the most common ways of using computer-based information systems to achieve competitive advantage is by using them to improve *operational efficiency*. As an example, consider a typical manufacturing company wishing to adopt a cost leadership strategy. In a primary activity, such as production, an inventory control system might be used to manage stock levels, reducing storage and transportation costs. In addition, support activities, such as management and administration, might achieve higher levels of productivity through the introduction of office automation systems. The organisation might also realise additional benefits from this kind of approach, such as improved customer service.

Barriers to entry

In many industries, organisations have improved operational efficiency by investing heavily in computer-based information systems. Often, the systems employed are extremely complex and require ongoing maintenance and development. This means that newcomers to the industry must be prepared to make a large initial expenditure so that they can acquire the computer-based information systems they need to be able to compete effectively. The level of expenditure needed may be so high that an *entry barrier* is created that deters or prevents the new competitor from entering the industry. Investing heavily in computer-based information systems may also deter existing competitors, since they too must invest in their information systems in order to maintain or improve their position in the industry.

Lock in customers and suppliers

Linking an organisation's computer-based information systems to those of its customers and suppliers can help to strengthen business relationships. As an example, computer-based information systems can be used to provide higher levels of customer service, thereby encouraging clients to remain loyal to the company.

Close integration with a supplier's information systems can result in a number of business benefits, which include:

(a) the availability of raw materials or parts is more certain;

(b) cost savings can be realised through reduced administration overheads;

(c) suppliers are less likely to abandon the business relationship;

(d) the organisation can negotiate favourable terms and prices;

(e) competitors are excluded from the business relationship.

However, it should be noted that achieving high levels of integration can also have some significant disadvantages. Perhaps the single largest disadvantage is that the organisation may come to rely on a relatively small number of suppliers. This reliance might lead to some suppliers taking advantage of the relationship, for example by raising prices. Furthermore, it may be difficult to locate an alternative source of raw materials or parts if a problem arises with a particular supplier.

Promote business innovation

Investing in computer-based information systems often helps stimulate business innovation. Introducing a new process control system, for example, might ultimately result in the development of new product features or new product lines.

Organisations that have invested in building effective computer-based information systems are well placed to support business innovation. Such organisations are likely to have established a resource base that can be drawn on to develop new ideas.

On the other hand, an organisation that has failed to invest adequately in its information systems may lack essential resources, such as hardware, software and trained personnel, and be unable to explore new methods.

Increase switching costs

In general, an organisation that has invested time, money and effort in developing a computer-based information system will be reluctant to bear the *switching costs* of moving to a new system. In addition to the cost of new hardware and software, a range of other costs can be incurred. These might include costs connected with:

(a) converting data for use with the new system;

(b) training staff;

(c) interruptions to the company's operations;

(d) lost opportunities to gain new business.

When an organisation links its information systems to those of its suppliers or customers, it will often ensure that switching costs are as high as possible. In this way, the supplier or customer is discouraged from switching to a competitor's system and competitors are excluded from the business relationship.

Leverage

It was mentioned earlier that investment in computer-based information systems can help establish a resource base that can stimulate business innovation. However, access to a resource base of this kind can provide a number of other benefits to an organisation. First, the organisation is likely to be equipped to take advantage of any opportunities that arise in the business environment. Second, the organisation can begin to develop new products and services by maximising its use of existing resources. As an example, a travel agent might create a mailing list from its customer database so that it can offer customers new products or services, such as travel insurance or car rental.

Finally, the organisation may use its resources to gain competitive advantage through **information leadership**. Information leadership involves enhancing a product or service with an organisation's specialised information or expertise. In many cases, organisations achieve information leadership by selling information or

Information leadership

Enhancing a product or service using an organisation's specialised information or expertise.

41

expertise in the form of a separate product. A good example might be selling a mailing list created from an organisation's customer database.

MINI CASE

American Airlines

As early as 1953, American Airlines foresaw how important electronic reservation systems would become to the travel industry and began to develop a number of simple systems. In 1964, the company launched an electronic reservation system known as SABRE, although it was not until 1976 that the system gained significant popularity.

In 1976, the imminent launch of a rival system from a major airline caused American Airlines to take the unprecedented step of supplying SABRE to travel agencies free of charge. In addition to supplying all necessary hardware and software, the company also provided training and support services. Not surprisingly, travel agencies were keen to take up SABRE and it had been installed in 130 offices within a year.

An interesting feature of SABRE concerns the way in which information was displayed to travel agents. Although *all* flights to a given destination were displayed, those from American Airlines were always shown first. Since some 70 per cent of all bookings were for flights shown on the first screen of information, the company's income increased dramatically. In the first year alone, the company saw a return on its initial investment of more than 500 per cent. As SABRE became used more widely, American Airlines saw revenues from the system rising from approximately $20 million in the first year, to more than $77 million by 1981 and over $335 million by 1985.

▶SUMMARY

1 A system is composed of a group of interrelated components that work towards a common goal. These components include inputs, processes, outputs, feedback and control. A system also has a boundary that separates it from the environment. Systems can be made up of one or more smaller subsystems.

2 An information system converts data into information products. This information is used to support the activities of managers. Information systems make use of people resources, hardware resources, software resources and data resources.

3 Business information systems take advantage of the benefits of information technology and are often grouped into two broad categories. Operations information systems are concerned with process control, transaction processing and productivity. Management information systems provide feedback on organisational activities and support managerial decision making. For simplicity, business information systems are referred to as 'information systems' in the remainder of the book.

4 Operations information systems include transaction processing systems, process control systems and office automation systems.

5 Management information systems include information reporting systems, decision support systems and executive information systems.

6 Other categories of business information systems include expert systems, business information systems, end user computing systems and strategic information systems.

7 In order to gain strategic advantage, companies will often adopt one of three basic competitive strategies: cost leadership, product differentiation or business innovation. Strategic information systems can be used to support attempts to gain competitive advantage through a number of different approaches. These include improving operational efficiency, raising entry barriers, creating high switching costs and gaining information leadership.

► EXERCISES

► Self-assessment exercises

1 Answer the following questions in relation to your college or university:

(a) What are the institution's objectives?

(b) Identify a range of typical inputs, processes and outputs.

(c) What feedback mechanisms are in place and what kinds of information do they produce?

(d) What control mechanisms exist?

2 In what ways can information systems support a manager's activities?

3 How can computer-based information systems help an organisation achieve a strategic advantage over its competitors?

4 Match each term to the correct statement.

(a) input	1	provides information concerning the performance of a system
(b) process	2	describes exchanges between the system and its environment
(c) output	3	converts raw materials into a finished product
(d) feedback	4	contains everything outside of the system
(e) control	5	defines the scope of the system
(f) boundary	6	examples include raw materials, energy or labour power
(g) environment	7	examples include information, a product or service
(h) interface	8	adjusts the performance of the system

► Discussion questions

1 Can each of the following be described as a system? For each item, try to identify at least *two* inputs, processes and outputs. In addition, what feedback and control mechanisms exist?

◆ a human being;

◆ a plant;

◆ a house;

◆ a country;

◆ a computer.

2 A small company is considering the purchase of a computer and accounting software to help it keep track of its finances. In general, what are the benefits of processing by computer? What other benefits might the company gain by taking this step?

3 Locate an annual report or article that describes a large organisation, such as a supermarket chain. From the information contained in the annual report, identify and describe the information systems that the company might use.

▶ Essay questions

1 The classic American Airlines case study clearly demonstrates how computer-based information systems can be used to gain strategic advantage. Provide an analysis of the case study. Your response should include discussion of the following areas:

   (a) Describe how the overall approach adopted by American Airlines incorporated the basic competitive strategies of cost leadership, innovation and product differentiation.

   (b) In what ways did SABRE provide American Airlines with a competitive advantage? Your analysis should refer to concepts related to the strategic use of information systems, for example entry barriers.

   (c) Although SABRE was undoubtedly successful, American Airlines was not able to maintain its competitive advantage beyond the late 1980s. What factors played a part in the erosion of the company's lead over its competitors and how did it react?

2 Select an organisation with which you are familiar. You may choose a department within a large organisation, if you wish. Analyse the structure and behaviour of the organisation using systems concepts. Your response should include the following elements:

   (a) Identify and describe at least *two* examples of the following: inputs, processes, outputs, feedback and control.

   (b) Identify and describe *two* decisions that will be taken at the strategic, tactical and operational levels of the organisation.

   (c) For each of the decisions described, identify at least *two* items of information that may be required. Describe some of the characteristics that each item of information will have.

▶ Examination questions

1 Information systems play a critical part in supporting a company's activities. Using specific examples, you are required to:

   (a) define an information system;

   (b) describe the categories of computer-based information systems, providing relevant business examples for each category identified;

   (c) explain how computer-based information systems can support managers at each level of an organisation.

2 Computer-based information systems are critical to an organisation's survival in the modern competitive environment. Discuss this statement with reference to the following:

   (a) Porter's competitive forces model and the basic competitive strategies that can be used to gain advantage;

   (b) how computer-based information systems can support these strategies;

   (c) how an organisation's information resources can be used to create information leadership.

3 Large retail organisations employ a wide variety of computer-based information systems in order to support their activities. Considering a large supermarket chain, such as Sainsbury's, you are required to:

   (a) define the term 'computer-based information system';
   (b) identify the types of computer-based information systems that are likely to be found within a typical branch – your response should describe the function of each system identified and the category to which it belongs;
   (c) select one of the systems identified in (a) and describe the system in more detail, identifying the hardware, software, data and people resources it employs.

▶ References

Jackson, T. (1998) 'Company strategy: the machines are taking over', *Financial Times*, 23 February.

Kehoe, L. (1998) 'Intel: a Silicon Valley powerhouse', *Financial Times*, 4 February.

O'Brien, J. (1993) *Management Information Systems: A Managerial End User Perspective*, 2nd edn, Richard D. Irwin.

Porter, M. (1980) *Competitive Strategy*, Free Press, New York.

▶ Further reading

Cashmore, C. and Lyall, R. (1991) *Business Information Systems and Strategies*, Prentice-Hall, Englewood Cliffs, NJ.

Clifton, H. and Sutcliffe, A. (1994) *Business Information Systems*, 5th edn, Prentice Hall, Hemel Hempstead.
   Chapter 1 introduces a variety of basic concepts and includes topics such as business information systems.

Fuori, W. and Gioia, L. (1995) *Computers and Information Systems*, Prentice-Hall, Englewood Cliffs, NJ.
   Chapter 13 provides a slightly different – more pragmatic – view of computer-based information systems than other texts.

Gordon, S. and Gordon J. (1996) *Information Systems: A Management Approach*, The Dryden Press, London.

O'Brien, J. (1993) *Management Information Systems: A Managerial End User Perspective*, 2nd edn, Richard D. Irwin.
   Chapter 1 provides an overview of fundamental systems concepts and discusses the components of a computer-based information system. Chapter 2 provides a concise but thorough overview of competitive advantage.

O'Hicks, J. (1993) *Management Information Systems: A User Perspective*, 3rd edn, West Publishing.

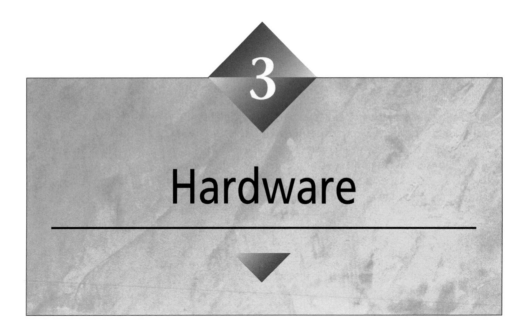

Hardware

INTRODUCTION

The aim of this chapter is to provide readers with a basic grasp of the often complex and technical language used to describe the computer hardware which is part of information systems. A knowledge of this language is necessary to help business users communicate with technical staff when discussing their requirements for new systems. An appreciation of how the different components of a computer interact is also useful when trying to understand problems that occur with hardware. For example, if your PC is running too slowly, what are the potential reasons for this? Finally, departmental managers (or home users) will need to specify the hardware requirements for their personal use or their staff. Specification of hardware 'kit' is not possible without a grasp of the terminology and an idea of what represents a basic specification, and an advanced specification.

The chapter is structured according to the different parts of a computer system, such as input devices, output devices, storage and processing. Different categories of computer system are defined at the start of the chapter.

> ▶ Learning objectives
>
> After reading this chapter, readers will be able to:
>
> ◆ categorise the type of computer system that a business uses;
> ◆ recognise the different components of a computer;
> ◆ specify the components needed for the purchase of a personal computer;
> ◆ make decisions based on a brief coverage of evaluation methods.

▶ Links to other chapters

Chapter 4	focuses on computer software and describes a number of common applications.
Chapter 5	provides a detailed view of networks and communications and describes the client/server architecture in more detail.
Chapter 12	gives details of client/server technology and the network computer.

▶ COMPONENTS OF A COMPUTER SYSTEM

Some of the concepts discussed in earlier chapters can be used to explain the notion of a computer system. Chapter 2 described a system as a collection of interrelated components that work together towards a collective goal. It was also said that an information system can be defined as a system whose purpose is to convert data into information. We can think of a **computer system** as consisting of a number of inter-related components that work together with the aim of converting data into information. In a computer system, processing is carried out electronically, usually with little or no intervention from a human user. The components of a computer system include **hardware** and software. This chapter considers hardware in depth, while Chapter 4 focuses on software.

▶ Computer hardware

Hardware describes the physical components of a computer system. The hardware of a computer system can be said to consist of different elements, whose relationship is shown in a simplified form in Fig 3.1. Data is input, then processed according to software instructions, then output, to the screen for example as information. Information that needs to be stored permanently will be placed in storage. This chapter is structured by describing the options available for each of these elements and assessing the criteria used for purchase decisions. The main elements of a computer system are:

◆ **Input devices**. Input devices are used to capture or enter data into the computer. Before data can be used within a computer system, it is usually necessary to convert it into a format that supports processing by computer. Most data is held in *human sensible form*, that is, in a format that makes it directly accessible to human beings. A bank statement, for example, contains text and numbers that are relatively easy for a human to understand. However, such data is almost meaningless to the electronic components of a computer system. Input devices convert data into a form that makes it *machine sensible*.

◆ **Central processing unit**. The central processing unit (CPU) performs processing by carrying out instructions given in the form of computer programs.

◆ Primary storage or **memory**. Memory is used as a temporary means of storing data and instructions. Memory is used to store:

Computer system

Interrelated components including hardware and software that work together with the aim of converting data into information.

Hardware

The physical components of a computer system: input devices, memory, central processing unit, output devices and storage devices.

Input devices

Hardware used to enter data, information or instructions into a computer-based information system.

Central processing unit (CPU)

The processor found in a computer system that controls all of the computer's main functions and enables users to execute programs or process data.

Memory

A temporary means of storing data awaiting processing, instructions used to process data or control the computer system, and data or information that has been processed.

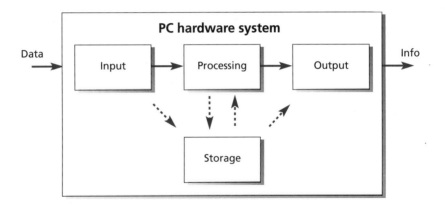

Fig 3.1 Basic hardware components of a computer system

(a) data awaiting processing;

(b) instructions loaded from software which are used to process data or control the computer system;

(c) data or information that has been processed.

◆ **Storage devices.** Storage devices provide a means of storing data and programs until they are required. As an example, a program can be stored on a hard disk drive until needed. When the program is activated, it is transferred from the storage device into the computer's memory. When the program has ended or is no longer needed, it can be removed from memory so that other programs or data can be used.

◆ **Output devices.** Output devices translate the results of processing – output – into a human readable form. The results of a calculation, for example, might be displayed on a screen or sent to a printer. An output device may also transfer data requiring further processing to a storage device.

Storage devices

A permanent means of storing data and programs until they are required.

Output devices

Translate the results of processing – output – into a human readable form.

▶ Computer software

Software describes the programs and procedures used by a business information system. Programs consist of detailed lists of instructions that control the operation of the computer system. Software is covered in more detail in Chapter 4.

▶ MAIN CATEGORIES OF COMPUTERS

We can begin to understand more of the technology of business information systems by looking at the ways in which computers themselves can be categorised. A traditional view of computer technology suggests three basic categories of computer: mainframe, minicomputer and microcomputer. By examining the characteristics of each category, it is possible to understand more of how industry makes use of computer technology.

Mainframe

Mainframes are powerful computers used for large-scale data processing.

▶ Mainframe

A traditional view of **mainframe** computers sees them as extremely powerful machines designed for large-scale data-processing activities. The use of mainframe computers in industry has declined steadily over the past two decades, but they are still responsible for the multibillion dollar revenues of companies such as IBM, Amdahl and Hitachi. The decline has been largely due to advances in technology that enable smaller, less expensive systems to compete squarely with mainframes in terms of speed and power. A modern personal computer, for example, could be considered many times more powerful than one of the very earliest mainframe systems.

Since the distinctions between the mainframe and the minicomputer have become blurred over time, it is not possible to provide a fixed, firm definition of each. However, we can understand something of the character of the mainframe by considering some of the main characteristics attributed to it. Taking the typical mainframe computer of the 1960s and 1970s, some of the main characteristics are as follows:

◆ Mainframes were considered extremely expensive to purchase and operate. Early systems were so expensive that only government departments, large multinational companies, public utilities and some universities could afford to purchase them.

◆ Early mainframe computers were extremely large and were often housed in their own specially designed buildings. Since systems were very susceptible to environmental conditions, it was often essential to maintain a dust-free, temperature-controlled environment.

◆ Users had little direct interaction with the mainframe itself. The system was connected to a number of simple terminals that consisted of little more than a visual display unit and a keyboard. The type of terminal is often referred to as a *dumb terminal*, meaning that it has little or no processing power of its own and is merely a means of communicating with the mainframe.

◆ Programming of mainframe computers was considered difficult and non-interactive. Programs were written in a low-level language and entered into the machine using punched cards or paper tape. Errors in programs were difficult to detect and were often only found when the program was actually executed. Mainframe programmers required a very high degree of technical expertise and frequently required extensive training. This meant that the costs associated with employing programmers, such as salaries and training costs, were extremely high.

In many organisations, mainframe computers are considered **legacy systems**, meaning that, while it is recognised that the existing system may not be entirely adequate to meet the company's needs, a changeover would be difficult – or even impossible – to implement. This can be for a number of different reasons:

Legacy systems
A system which has been superseded by new technologies or business practices.

◆ So much has been invested in developing and maintaining the mainframe system that a move towards more modern technology would be prohibited by the costs involved.

◆ The data and information produced by the mainframe system are critical to the company's operations. Since any changes might disrupt the company's activities, any new systems that are introduced are made compatible with the older mainframe system. In turn, this reinforces the need to retain the existing mainframe system.

◆ The links between the existing mainframe system and the company's main business activities are so strong that it is not possible to introduce new systems a little at a time. This can mean that the cost of introducing new systems across the entire organisation is too high. Furthermore, the risk of disruption to the company's activities may be so high that it is considered unacceptable.

ACTIVITY

> Although use of mainframe computers has declined quite sharply since the middle of the 1980s, many are still in use today. In many cases, retaining an existing mainframe system may be considered more cost effective than introducing a new system. As an example, consider a public utility that provides a service to a relatively stable base of customers. What are the arguments both for and against retaining the current mainframe system?

▶ Minicomputers

Minicomputer

Minicomputers offer an intermediate stage between the power of mainframe systems and the relatively low cost of microcomputer systems.

The **minicomputer** combines some of the characteristics of both the mainframe computer and microcomputer. Today, they are often referred to as *servers* by companies such as Sun and Hewlett-Packard. Different types of server may have different functions, such as managing a network or hosting a database. Further information on servers is given in Chapter 5. An understanding of minicomputers and servers can be helped by considering some of the characteristics of the minicomputer:

◆ Minicomputers can be programmed using tools that are more modern and sophisticated than those available for mainframes. Programming systems that are more interactive in nature are available, although programmers still require a relatively high level of technical knowledge.

◆ Since minicomputers are based on relatively modern technology, they are able to offer speed and power at levels similar to mainframe computers.

◆ The physical size of a minicomputer is far smaller than a mainframe. A typical minicomputer will consist of several large cabinets and will easily fit into a single room. Minicomputers are also more forgiving of environmental conditions, although an air-conditioned environment is still normally required.

◆ Many minicomputers are used to form the basis for a network system. Both local and centralised processing can be supported by the use of intelligent terminals. A typical terminal will have its own storage and processing facilities, enabling it to perform many tasks without drawing on the resources of the minicomputer. Access to large volumes of data and the ability to process more complex tasks are provided by the minicomputer.

◆ While still relatively expensive to purchase, minicomputers are available to a wider range of organisations. Even a modest university, for example, will normally own one or more minicomputers.

◆ Some organisations, such as IBM, have supported the development of minicomputers that can be expanded easily and at relatively low cost. This enables a computer-based information system based around a minicomputer to be developed further as an organisation's needs change.

Microcomputer

Microcomputers are considered less powerful than minicomputers and mainframes, but are more flexible and relatively inexpensive to purchase.

▶ Microcomputers

The **microcomputer** makes use of more modern technology to provide relatively powerful computing facilities at low cost. Microcomputers are now often referred to as the '*client*' machine which receives its data from a '*server*' machine. This client/server architecture is described in Chapter 5 as a common type of communications structure. Some of the main characteristics of the microcomputer are as follows:

◆ The physical size of a microcomputer is far smaller than a minicomputer. A typical microcomputer will easily fit on a desk; portable computers smaller than a brief-case are also available.

◆ Microcomputers are widely used with other computers and provide the best price/performance of the various types of computer.

◆ Since microcomputers can be very inexpensive, they are more accessible than mainframes or minicomputers. A typical microcomputer will be within the means of a small business or individual.

◆ Microcomputers are extremely flexible and are considered general-purpose machines capable of being used for a wide variety of applications. However, they are generally seen as being unsuitable for applications involving large volumes of data processing, such as transaction processing (Chapter 6).

◆ Microcomputers are considered easier to use than mainframes or minicomput-ers. Users require little technical knowledge and can be trained quickly and at low cost.

◆ Resources supporting the use of microcomputers are widely available and can gen-erally be obtained at relatively low cost. Resources such as blank media, training materials, replacement parts and off-the-shelf software are often available from high-street suppliers.

◆ Programming systems for microcomputers tend to be highly interactive. Non-technical users are able to develop applications quickly and easily. This area is described in more detail in the next chapter.

In industry, several types of microcomputer are in common use. The **IBM-compatible** or personal computer, commonly known as a PC, is considered the standard for gen-eral business use. The **Apple Macintosh** is often used for professional desktop publishing applications, such as the production of newspapers. **Workstations**, such as those produced by Sun, are typically used in the area of computer graphics. Typical applications include computer-aided design (CAD) and animation.

▶ TYPES OF MICROCOMPUTERS

▶ Desktop

As its name suggests, the **desktop computer** is intended for office use and supports the day-to-day activities of an organisation's employees. These machines tend to be placed in a fixed location and connected permanently to items such as printers, scan-ners and other devices. The desktop computer is the most common type of microcomputer and is found in the majority of organisations.

Desktop computers tend to have a modular design, that is, they are made up of components that can be removed or replaced individually. This means that repairs can be carried out quickly and easily. Since components are relatively inexpensive, it is possible to upgrade desktop machines at low cost. Many expansion devices can be fitted internally, protecting the device from accidental damage and helping to reduce its cost.

IBM-compatible

The modern personal computer found in most business organisations developed from a family of personal computers launched by IBM in the early 1980s.

Apple Macintosh

A family of personal computers produced by Apple Computers.

Workstation

A powerful terminal or personal computer system, usually applied to specialised applications, such as computer-aided design (CAD).

Desktop computer

Intended for office use to support the day-to-day activities of an organisation's employees.

▶ Portable

Portable computer

A self-contained computer with integrated power supply, keyboard, pointing device and visual display unit to facilitate carrying.

Notebook

A small portable computer, which is approximately the size of a sheet of A4 paper.

Subnotebook

A small portable computer which is usually significant smaller than a notebook due to a small screen and keyboard.

The **portable computer** is largely self-contained, featuring its own power supply, keyboard, pointing device and visual display unit. Early portable computers were relatively large and heavy, earning themselves the nickname of 'luggables'. However, modern portables tend to weigh very little and fit easily into a briefcase.

Portable computers are often described as notebooks or subnotebooks. A **notebook** or laptop is approximately the size of an A4 writing pad. The size of a **subnotebook** can vary considerably: some feature keyboards that can be used in the normal way, others have keyboards so small that a special pointing device is needed to press keys.

Some typical applications for portable computers include:

◆ Collecting data from a number of different locations. Salespeople, for example, might record order details and other information as they visit different clients.

◆ Remote working. Portable computers allow users to work in a variety of different locations and situations, for example an employee travelling to work might use a portable so that he or she can complete a task started in the office.

◆ Communication. Many portable computers contain telecommunications facilities that can be used to send and receive information in a variety of forms. A manager, for example, might compose and send a fax message while travelling.

Although they are undoubtedly useful, some common criticisms of portable computers include:

◆ Portable computers often have a limited battery life, sometimes offering only as little as an hour of continuous use before the battery needs to be recharged.

◆ The limited expansion capacity of a portable computer means that it is often not possible to install additional devices, such as CD-ROM drives. Expansion is often achieved by installing devices externally through the use of special cards.

◆ Many users find portable computers unsuitable for anything more than occasional use. Poor display units, small keyboards and clumsy pointing devices can sometimes make prolonged use of a portable computer very uncomfortable. They can be docked to a desktop computer to remove these limitations when in the office.

▶ Organiser/PDA

Personal digital assistant (PDA)

A hand-held device, often no larger than a pocket calculator with functions such as address book, appointment scheduler and calculator.

A **personal digital assistant** (PDA) can be thought of as a sophisticated personal organiser. A PDA is normally a hand-held device, often no larger than a pocket calculator. Its purpose is to help users manage their time more efficiently and effectively. The typical functions of a PDA can include: address book, appointment scheduler, calculator, expenses tracking, currency conversion, alarm clock, world time display and a variety of other features that allow users to store notes, such as to-do lists. More sophisticated models, such as the Psion Organiser or the PalmPilot, may include a more powerful range of tools, such as communications, spreadsheet and wordprocessing applications.

PDAs have several advantages over portable computers. First, they are relatively inexpensive to purchase. Second, they have a comparatively long battery life and there is often no need to purchase expensive rechargeable batteries. Third, since they have a rather limited range of functions, they tend to be easier to use than their larger counterparts. However, PDAs are considered to have only limited functionality and are therefore not appropriate to some applications.

▶ Network computer (NC)

A relatively recent development has been the introduction of inexpensive **network computers** (NC) by a number of leading manufacturers. Network computers are targeted at two distinct segments of the personal computer market: home users reluctant to purchase more expensive personal computers, and organisations seeking to reduce the costs associated with computer-based information systems. Since the concept of the NC was introduced, a further variant on this type of limited PC has been proposed. These are known as Net PCs that can be thought as a hybrid between a PC and a NC, with the aim, again being to reduce the cost ownership.

Network computer (NC)

A computer providing access to a network system, which to reduce cost, features limited disk storage, less powerful processor and less memory.

The philosophy behind the network computer is that it should be inexpensive to manufacture, purchase and maintain. For this reason, a typical network computer will feature limited disk storage, memory and expansion potential. In addition, the computer may also feature an older, less powerful processor than its desktop counterpart.

The purpose of the network computer is to provide access to a network system, such as the Internet, at minimal cost. Since the network computer is able to call on the resources of the network server, only limited processing power is required. Simple tasks can be carried out by the network computer itself. More complex tasks, such as those that make intensive use of a computer's processor, are dealt with by the network server and the results are passed back to the network computer. In a similar way, since software applications and data can be accessed via the network, only minimal storage capacity is required. This type of network architecture is often described as **thin client** and its design is described in more detail in Chapter 12.

Thin client

In a network system, this describes an architecture where the bulk of the processing is carried out by a central server.

Network computers are considered to reduce the *total cost of ownership* (TCO) associated with computer systems. The cost of ownership describes a range of different expenses incurred in purchasing and maintaining a computer system. Such costs include the original cost of the hardware and software, upgrades, maintenance, technical support and training. TCO is discussed further in Chapter 16 with regard to the cost of providing end-user services. Network computers act to reduce the cost of ownership in several ways:

◆ The initial purchase costs of hardware and software are low.

◆ Since network computers can be managed via a central network server, administration costs can be reduced. Network computers are often described as offering the potential to achieve **zero administration**, a point where the centralised management and control of the computers attached to a network server make administration costs almost negligible.

Zero administration

The point where centralised management and control of the computers attached to a network server makes administration costs almost negligible.

◆ Since the network computer contains fewer components than a conventional personal computer, it is less expensive to maintain, repair and replace.

◆ As network computers are often used for a relatively small number of applications, training and support costs can be reduced. As an example, a business organisation might purchase network computers for the sole purpose of data entry. Similarly, home users are likely to purchase network computers as a means of accessing the Internet.

The mini case study on Panalpina's use of network computers to reduce costs gives an example of an international company which has committed to NCs for the reduced costs that they promise.

MINI CASE

Panalpina uses network computers to reduce costs

Panalpina of Switzerland, a freight-forwarding company with a turnover of over £2 billion, is converting two-thirds of its 9500 users worldwide from PCs to network computers. Most users are located at ports and airports. The work is straightforward data entry, logging the arrival or departure of shipments. This does not require a state-of-the-art PC. Panalpina now uses Winframe software from Citrix which allows multiple user sessions on NC 'thin clients' to be run on a Microsoft Windows NT-based server. The Data General Aviion servers need about 8Mb per user. All the processing occurs on the server, with only screen updates and user events such as key presses and mouse clicks needing to be transmitted over the network. Cost reductions are anticipated on hardware purchase and reduced cost of support through the simplicity of the thin clients.

▶ INPUT DEVICES

Input devices are used to enter data or instructions. Device is used in this context to refer to an individual piece of hardware with a specific function. Mouse and keyboard are examples of input device. Before looking at some of the devices available, it is worth making some observations:

◆ It should be noted that modern computer-based information systems can make use of a wide variety of input devices. This should come as no surprise, since any

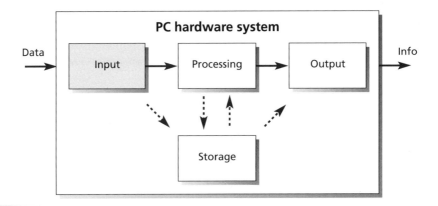

Fig 3.2 Input devices

large business organisation will deal with data originating from a wide variety of sources. In addition, the data flowing into the organisation may take a number of different forms.

◆ The choice of an input device will often depend on the quantity of data to be entered. Entering data on a small scale is normally carried out by human opera-tors, using a number of familiar input devices, such as the mouse or keyboard. However, large-scale data input may require the use of more specialised input devices. In many cases, a **direct capture** device will be used to acquire and store data automatically. Generally, the data is captured at source and stored with little or no human intervention. Data obtained from sensors on a production line, for example, might be stored and then processed automatically.

◆ A computer-based information system will seldom make use of only a single input device. Even a typical personal computer will often feature several different meth-ods for data entry, such as a keyboard, mouse, joystick and sound card.

◆ Many of the input devices traditionally associated with more expensive and spe-cialised computer systems can now be connected to a typical personal computer. Optical mark readers, touch screens and bar-code readers are all examples of devices that can now be connected to relatively inexpensive personal computers.

▶ Keyboard/keypad

The keyboard remains the most common input device and its basic design has remained largely unchanged for more than a century.

A common criticism of the keyboard is that inexperienced users find it difficult and uncomfortable to use. In answer to this, new keyboard designs have appeared that attempt to make them easier to use. **Natural keyboards** have the keys arranged so that users can locate them more quickly and easily. The keyboard itself is often shaped in a way that makes prolonged use more comfortable.

Keypads designed especially for data entry are also in common use. The electronic tills used in most supermarkets, for example, contain special keys for entering amounts of currency.

▶ Mouse

Computers featuring a **graphical user interface** often require the use of a **mouse** or other **pointing device**. Although there are many different kinds of mouse, all use the same basic method of operation: moving the mouse over a flat surface causes a corre-sponding movement in a small pointer on the screen (*see* Fig 3.3). Selections, such as menu items, are made by clicking one of the buttons on the mouse.

A mouse is especially suitable for controlling programs that make use of icons, menus or buttons. However, in most cases a keyboard is still required to enter other kinds of data, such as text. The mouse is also used in applications involving graphics, such as drawing packages. The case study on Douglas Engelbart gives a brief history of the mouse.

Direct capture

A method of acquiring and storing data automatically with little or no human intervention.

Natural keyboard

Keys are arranged so that users can locate them more quickly and easily in a way that makes prolonged use more comfortable.

Graphical user interface (GUI)

Allows the user to control the operation of a computer program or item of computer hardware using a pointing device, such as a mouse by selecting options from icons and menu options.

Mouse

A pointing device found on most modern personal computers.

Pointing device

An input device that allows the user to control the movement of a small pointer displayed on the screen that is used to select options.

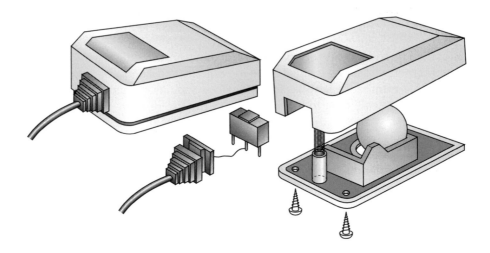

Fig 3.3 A mouse contains a small ball that rotates as the mouse is moved across a smooth surface. The direction and rate of movement is translated into the movement of the pointer on the screen

CASE STUDY: TOPIC AREA

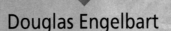

FT

Douglas Engelbart

The mouse: small but very useful rodent

It was far from an instant success, but who would be without the indomitable computer mouse, says Tom Foremski.

'People laughed at me,' says computer pioneer Douglas Engelbart, recalling the initial reaction to his development of the first computer mouse in the early 1960s. Yet where would we be without that ubiquitous computer pointing device?

In those days, Dr Engelbart says, the computer interface consisted of typing commands one line at a time into a mainframe. Working on a research project for the US Air Force, he was studying ways of improving computer interfaces. During the project he became convinced that all knowledge workers would some day have their own computer and needed a simpler way to interact with complex software.

'Remember, this was in the days when computers were very expensive, but I knew that eventually the technology would become less expensive over time,' he says.

Dr Engelbart's work led him to develop the concept of a graphical user interface with windows, graphics icons and text organised into hyperlinks, where highlighted words are linked to other computer documents. These are all con-cepts that form the bedrock of computer systems and internet software.

He quickly realised a graphical user interface required a simple pointing device, leading to the development of the computer mouse, which he called an 'X-Y Position Indicator for a Display System'. The mouse was far from an instant success, simply because there was no graphical user interface software, outside a handful of US research labs. Dr Engelbart faced laughter 'and much worse' in his efforts to promote the mouse as a serious device.

The first main commercial system to feature a mouse was Apple Computer's ground-breaking Lisa computer, introduced in 1983, the forerunner of the Macintosh and Microsoft Windows systems. Those first Apple computers were based on research carried out at the Xerox Palo Alto Research Center, where scientists who had worked with Dr Engelbart were based.

'I'm not surprised the mouse is the success it became, but I am a little surprised that nothing better has come along since,' he says. The first prototype mouse looked very similar to today's devices, although over the past few years there has been a move away from a mechanical mechanism towards optical-based mechanisms. For example, US-based Logitech, the biggest maker of computer mouse devices, offers a large range, with its high-end models using a tiny laser to read dots on marble, converting the information into data the computer understands.

Julie Goebel, global product manager for mouse products at Logitech, says: 'With an optical mechanism, the mouse is more accurate and you don't have to periodically clean the rollers as you would with a mechanical mouse.

'The computer mouse has become more useful than the keyboard,' she adds. 'This is especially true when you consider that millions of people are using the internet, which means they are mostly pointing and clicking on web page links.'

Today, consumers can buy a computer mouse designed for either the left or right hand. Some have a scrolling wheel that allows users to scroll up or down a computer screen without first having to click on a graphical user navigation bar. Logitech also offers a cordless mouse and even a 3D mouse with six degrees of movement, useful in specialist applications in computer aided design and in some computer games.

Other companies have developed a mouse with a 'force feedback system' so users can 'feel' texture or be pulled towards an icon on the computer screen through tiny magnets within the mouse. US-based Immersion last year introduced its Feelit Mouse using force feedback technology.

'Unfortunately there is not much software available that supports a force feedback mouse but that will change,' predicts Ms Goebel.

The mouse has been partly blamed for carpal tunnel syndrome, a painful condition caused by too much computer use. Logitech funds research into ergonomic issues and Ms Goebel says that, so far, there is no direct proof that too much use of the computer mouse causes carpal tunnel syndrome.

'It's really a personal issue, users have to find a mouse that they are comfortable with. There are also trackballs and touchpads available, which some users prefer,' she says.

Dr Engelbart's first mouse had one button, but his later models had three. 'I would have added more buttons if I'd have had the physical space,' he says. Apple Computer offers just one button on its mouse, Microsoft added an extra button for Windows systems. But for Dr Engelbart more buttons mean more efficiency.

'With one hand controlling the mouse, the left hand could be doing something. So I developed a device with five keys for the left hand, so that even before you click on something, you can communicate to the computer what it is that you want to do with it,' he says. With five keys, users can also input letters without resorting to a keyboard. He still uses his five key input device and hopes to find commercial interest in the design.

Source: Financial Times, 24 April 1998

Questions

1 For what applications is a mouse most suited?

2 List some of the advantages and disadvantages of the mouse.

▶ Lightpen

A **lightpen** is a pointing device that can be used to control applications by pointing to items on the screen. Lightpens are also used for applications involving graphics, such as drawing packages, since images can be drawn directly on to the screen. One of the disadvantages of the lightpen is that many users find them uncomfortable and awkward to work with. Since the graphics tablet and touch sensitive screens (*see* below) are simpler and more comfortable to use, the lightpen has declined in popularity over the past decade.

Lightpen

A pointing device used to control applications by pointing to items on the screen.

▶ Trackball

A **trackball** is a pointing device that is controlled by rotating a small ball with the fingertips or palm of the hand. Moving the ball causes corresponding movement to a small pointer on the screen. Buttons are used to select items in the same way as the mouse.

The trackball is especially suitable for controlling programs that make use of icons, menus or buttons. However, in most cases a keyboard is still required to enter other kinds of data, such as text. The trackball is also used in applications involving graphics, such as drawing packages. Since, unlike the mouse, the trackball does not need to be used on a flat surface, it is often used as the pointing device attached to a portable computer.

Trackball

A trackball is a pointing device that is controlled by rotating a small ball with the fingertips or palm of the hand.

▶ Joystick

The joystick is one of the most common input devices available and is primarily used for leisure activities, such as playing computer games. However, the joystick is also used for several other purposes. First, it can be used as a pointing device, much in the same way as the mouse or trackball. Second, it is particularly suited to certain graphics applications, including drawing packages and various simulators. Finally, the joystick is often used to control external devices, such as robotic arms.

▶ Optical scanner

Optical scanner

An input device used to capture graphics and text from printed documents.

The **optical scanner** can be used to capture graphics and text from printed documents. A photograph, for example, can be captured and converted into a form suitable for use with a number of different applications. Images captured in this way are normally incorporated into wordprocessing or desktop publishing documents.

Optical scanners can also be used to perform data entry by converting printed documents into text files that can be used by wordprocessing packages and other programs. **Optical character recognition** (OCR) involves using software that attempts to recognise individual characters. As a scanned image is processed, the program creates a text file containing all of the characters recognised. This file can then be edited further using a wordprocessor, text editor or other suitable program.

Optical character recognition (OCR)

Software that attempts to recognise individual characters.

Although a typical OCR package will be able to recognise a wide variety of different typefaces, more sophisticated programs are available that can deal with handwriting and documents containing complex formatting. Some packages, for example, are able to produce accurate translations of documents that contain tables, captions and even several columns of text. Some human intervention is usually necessary to correct documents. For example, the letter *i* is sometimes recognised as *l*.

Systems are also available that can process large volumes of documents very quickly. These document image processing applications are described in Chapter 6.

Optical mark recognition (OMR)

Detection and recognition of simple marks made on a document.

A variation on optical character recognition is **optical mark recognition** (OMR), which involves detecting and recognising simple marks made on a document.

MINI CASE

Optical mark recognition

Public examinations, such as the GCSE qualifications that most students take at school, often involve a multiple-choice paper. Students record their answers on a special sheet, usually by filling in small boxes corresponding to their choices.

The answer sheet used by students is a special document that has been prepared so that it can be read with an optical mark reader. The size and position of the boxes on the sheet, for example, have been designed so that the optical mark reader can process the sheet quickly and accurately.

The optical mark readers used by examination bodies are almost completely automatic and are able to deal with hundreds of answer sheets each hour. However, although this simplifies the process of marking the papers from the many thousands of examinations sat each year, problems can still arise. Common problems include equipment breakdowns, damaged answer sheets and answer sheets that have been completed incorrectly.

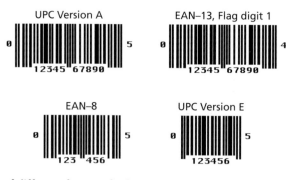

Fig 3.4 Example of different formats for bar codes

▶ Bar-code reader

A **bar code** is a means of displaying a unique identification number as a series of thick and thin lines. The sequence and width of the lines in the bar code can be translated into a sequence of digits. Bar-code numbers are normally produced according to a specific method. The **universal product code**, for example, is a standard method for creating and using bar codes.

A **bar-code reader** measures the intensity of a light beam reflected from the printed bar code to identify the digits making up the unique identification number. The digits making up the identification number are also printed at the foot of the bar code (*see* Fig 3.4). If a label containing a bar code becomes damaged or cannot be read for some other reason, it may still be possible to enter the identification number manually.

Perhaps the most common example of the use of the bar-code reader in industry is the supermarket checkout. However, bar codes are also used in a variety of other situations. Some examples include:

◆ In manufacturing organisations, supervisors often use handheld bar-code readers when making a manual inspection of stock levels. The bar-code reader is used to store information on the items scanned until the supervisor returns to the organisation. The information can then be transferred to an inventory control system for further analysis.

◆ Hospitals routinely use bar codes on the identity bracelets given to patients. Since each bar-code number is unique, this provides an effective means of storing and retrieving information on a given patient. As an example, a hospital's computer-based information system might store all information regarding a given patient against the bar-code number. When the patient receives further treatment, doctors can check to ensure that the patient is receiving the correct medication.

◆ Spare parts used for aircraft maintenance are often marked with bar codes. This helps to ensure that only the correct spare parts are used when replacing items.

◆ The bar codes carried on magazines and newspapers are used to record sales of particular titles. This helps vendors, distributors and publishers to monitor trends and plan possible promotions.

▶ Touch screen

The **touch screen** is a transparent, pressure-sensitive covering that is attached to the screen of the monitor. Users make selections and control programs by pressing on

---

Bar code

A means of displaying a unique identification number as a series of thick and thin lines.

Universal product code (UPC)

A standard for defining bar codes used frequently in retailing.

Bar-code reader

Measures the intensity of a light beam reflected from a printed bar code to identify the digits making up a unique identification number.

Touch screen

A transparent, pressure-sensitive covering that is attached to the screen of the monitor. Users make selections and control programs by pressing onto the screen.

the screen. Although touch screens are simple to use, they are comparatively expensive and require special software to operate.

Common applications for touch screens are interactive kiosks and booking systems. An **interactive kiosk** (*see* the section on multimedia in Chapter 4 for examples of kiosks) allows a user to purchase items or browse through a list of products by pressing buttons or other controls shown on the screen. Such kiosks are often found in banks, music stores and large catalogue stores. Many booking systems, such as those used by airlines, theatres and travel agents, also make use of touch screens.

▶ Graphics tablet

A **graphics tablet** is used in the same way as a writing pad. A stylus is used to draw images on a rigid pad located near to the computer. As the user draws with the stylus, the image is duplicated on the computer's display. Although graphics tablets can be used to control programs and select items shown on the screen, they are most often used for professional graphics applications.

▶ Video capture card

The **video capture card** records and stores video sequences (motion video) when connected to a digital video camera. A playback device, for example a video cassette recorder, is connected to the video capture card and special software is used to capture, edit and manipulate video sequences. Once a motion video sequence has been processed, it can then be output to a television, video cassette recorder or other device.

Video capture devices are used in a wide variety of applications. Some examples include:

◆ Television and film studios routinely use such devices to add special effects to their productions. The effects seen in many popular films and television programmes are created using this form of technology.

◆ In education and training, many organisations make use of computer-based learning (CBL) software. A large number of these packages feature video sequences, for example in order to demonstrate a particular procedure.

▶ Microphone/sound card

A **sound card** can be used to capture sound, music and speech from a variety of sources. Sound can be captured at a very high quality; even the most inexpensive sound cards are capable of producing results similar in quality to a compact disc recording. Examples of using the facilities of a sound card include:

◆ A microphone can be used to record speech, allowing users to create **voice annotations** that can be inserted into data files, such as wordprocessing documents. These annotations can be played back by the user or by any other person who receives the document.

◆ The use of **voice recognition** software allows a user to dictate text directly into a wordprocessing document. In many cases, a special microphone is required in order to ensure that the user's voice is not obscured by background noise. In addition, the software used normally requires 'training' so that it can adapt to a user's accent or the way in which he or she pronounces particular words. Even with this training, recognition rates are unlikely to exceed 95 per cent, so some modifica-

---

Interactive kiosk

A typical application for touch screen systems, an interactive kiosk allows a user to purchase items or browse through a list of products by pressing buttons or other controls shown on the screen.

Graphics tablet

Used in the same way as a writing pad; a stylus is used to draw images on a rigid pad located near to the computer.

Video capture card

The video capture card records and stores video sequences (motion video).

Sound card

A sound card allows a personal computer to play speech, music and other sounds. A sound card can also be used to capture sound, music and speech from a variety of sources.

Voice annotations

Spoken notes or reminders that can be inserted into data files, such as wordprocessing documents.

Voice recognition

The facility to control a computer program or carry out data entry through spoken commands via a microphone connected to a sound card.

tions are usually required after recognition. Some voice recognition packages also provide limited control over a graphical user interface.

The addition of a sound card and CD-ROM device provides a computer with **multimedia** facilities (*see* Chapter 4 for a description of this type of software). In order to ensure a degree of standardisation in terms of hardware and software requirements, most personal computers are designed to meet the MPC (Multimedia Personal Computer) standards set by organisations such as Microsoft.

▶ Digital camera

A **digital camera** captures and stores still images. Images are held in the camera's memory or stored on disk until they can be transferred to a personal computer.

> A digital camera is just one device that makes use of **non-volatile memory**. The memory found in a personal computer is considered volatile, that is, anything held in memory is lost once the power to the computer system is switched off. However, non-volatile memory retains its contents until altered or erased. Typically, non-volatile memory is housed in a small expansion card that can be inserted into a special slot on a digital camera, portable computer or other device.

Once an image has been transferred to a personal computer, it can be manipulated using specialised software. A picture that appears a little fuzzy, for example, could be enhanced using a special editing program.

Perhaps the greatest advantage of the digital camera is that it can be used in the same way as a conventional camera. This provides users with a portable method of capturing and storing images. The ability to store images in memory or on disk means that poor-quality pictures can be overwritten immediately. In addition, since there is no need to process film, images can be used at once. Digital cameras are increasingly used by estate agents to take photographs of properties. In the future, digital video of houses may be available over the Internet as an alternative to viewing.

However, digital cameras also have a number of disadvantages. First, current models are comparatively expensive and lack many of the features found in professional photography equipment. Second, memory limitations mean that cameras can store only a relatively small number of images – at present, few models are capable of storing more than 36 images at a time. Finally, current models capture images at relatively low resolution. This makes pictures produced in this way unsuitable for applications that require high-quality photographs.

▶ Specialised input devices

In addition to the items described in this section, a wide variety of specialised input devices are in common use. Some examples include the following:

◆ **Magnetic ink character recognition (MICR)** involves capturing data that has been printed using a special magnetic ink. This technology is normally associated with the banking industry, especially cheque processing. Some of the details on a cheque, such as the cheque number, are printed a special typeface using magnetic ink. The shape of each character means that it can be recognised by its magnetic field.

Multimedia

A combination of several media under the control of an interactive computer program including text, graphics, sound, video and animation.

Digital camera

A digital camera captures and stores still images in a camera's memory until they can be transferred to a personal computer. The image is recorded using a charge-coupled device which recognises the different colours and intensity of light in the image.

Non-volatile memory

Retains its contents until altered or erased, even if the device is not switched on.

Magnetic ink character recognition (MICR)

Capture and recognition of data that has been printed using a special magnetic ink.

Sensing devices

A variety of devices can be used to detect external variations in the environment: motion detectors, light sensors, infra-red sensors (that can detect heat), microphones and many others.

◆ Modern personal computers are capable of communicating with external devices via a number of different means. This allows them to be connected to a variety of **sensing devices**. Among these are motion detectors, light sensors, infra-red sensors (that can detect heat), microphones and many others.

◆ The joypad is similar to the joystick but uses a flat pad that is pressed with the fingertips. The pad tilts in the direction it is pressed and gives a wide range of movement.

◆ Specialised joysticks are available for a variety of purposes. The flight stick, for example, is specially designed for controlling flight simulation software. Other specialised controllers feature steering wheels and foot pedals.

Joypad

The joypad is similar to the joystick but uses a flat pad that is pressed with the fingertips. The pad tilts in the direction it is pressed and gives a wide range of movement.

SELECTING INPUT DEVICES

It is important to select an appropriate means of data entry in order to ensure that any computerised system works as efficiently as possible. The collection of data on a very large scale, for example, usually requires an approach that involves automating the process as far as possible. The selection of an input device is usually based on three basic criteria: volume, speed and accuracy.

▶ Volume

Some input devices are unsuitable for dealing with large volumes of data. An electricity company, for example, would be unlikely to use manual data-entry methods to record the details of payments made by customers. Instead, this data would be collected using more sophisticated methods, such as optical mark recognition (OMR) or optical character recognition (OCR) (*see* page 58). On the other hand, a small business dealing with far fewer transactions might prefer to enter data using the keyboard as an input device.

▶ Speed

If large volumes of data need to be entered, speed and accuracy may be an important consideration for many business applications. It would be unrealistic, for example, to enter text into a wordprocessor using only the mouse. Similarly, the electricity company mentioned earlier would be unlikely to employ data-entry clerks to record payment details – OCR and OMR can be many thousands of times faster than manual data-entry methods.

▶ Accuracy

In some business applications, it is essential to ensure that data entry is completely accurate. In engineering, for example, sensing devices are often required to measure components with an accuracy of plus or minus 0.01 cm. Obviously, if there are any errors in the data recorded, this may mean that components need to be scrapped.

In many cases, it may be acceptable if an input device generates a certain number of errors. This is often referred to as the **error rate**, and the acceptable level will vary according to the input device being used and the business application. Optical char-

Error rate

The frequency of errors which occur when using an input device to recognise patterns.

acter recognition, for example, is generally considered a comparatively unreliable means of entering data. At present, a typical OCR software package will have an error rate of between 5 and 10 per cent.

▶ Other criteria

Other considerations when selecting an input device might include:

- *Complexity of data*. Some methods are unsuitable for entering data of a complex nature. In many cases, data may need to be interpreted or altered before it is entered. In entering a letter into a wordprocessor, for example, a secretary may need to interpret shorthand notes or alter words and phrases as the document is typed.
- *Cost*. Although some methods offer high levels of speed and accuracy, an organisation may be unwilling or unable to purchase the hardware and software required. In such cases an alternative means of data entry may be required.
- *Frequency of data entry*. Some types of data entry may be carried out on an infrequent or *ad hoc* basis. In these cases, the acquisition of new or specialised input devices may not be justifiable.

▶ OUTPUT DEVICES

Output devices display the results of computer processing. Before looking at some of the devices available, it is worth making some observations:

- The output produced by some devices is temporary in nature. A display shown on a monitor, for example, is lost when a new image is shown or the computer system is switched off. On the other hand, a report produced on a printer is more permanent and may last for many years.
- Some forms of output may be used as the input for another process. Photographs, sounds and video sequences, for example, might be combined during the production of a training package or demonstration program.

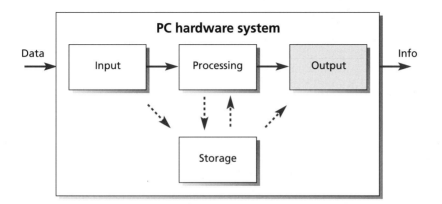

Fig 3.5 Output devices

◆ Business organisations have a wide range of requirements in terms of the *form* of the information they produce. These requirements mean that there are a large variety of specialised output devices available.

◆ A computer-based information system will seldom make use of only a single output device. Even a typical personal computer will often feature several different output devices, such as a monitor, sound card and printer.

▶ Display

Visual display unit (VDU)

A monitor connected to a computer system, traditionally used to describe character based terminals.

The most common output device is almost certainly the monitor, formerly referred to as a **visual display unit** (VDU), that is attached to all personal computer systems. The monitor has several advantages over other forms of output device:

◆ Information can be shown instantly, with only a negligible delay between the information becoming available and its being displayed. In addition, the monitor is one of only a small number of devices that allows users to view the progress of an activity as it occurs.

◆ As a standard component of a computer system, monitors are relatively inexpensive to purchase, repair or replace.

◆ The monitor is particularly suited to displaying certain kinds of information, for example charts and graphics.

◆ The cost of using the monitor as an output device is very low. Unlike printers, for example, a monitor does not require consumables, such as paper. In turn, this means that wastage does not occur.

However, the monitor also has several disadvantages:

◆ The output provided by a monitor is only temporary in nature.

◆ In the event of the monitor breaking down, users are unlikely to be able to continue using the computer system.

◆ A monitor is inappropriate for displaying some kinds of information, for example many users find reading lengthy sections of text uncomfortable.

Monitors are available in a range of shapes and sizes. Smaller computer systems may feature units with a 9" (23 cm) screen, while a graphics workstation may have a screen measuring 20" (51 cm) or more. Systems used for desktop publishing may have monitors shaped to provide an accurate representation of an A4 page, while multimedia systems may feature internal speakers or other hardware. Portable computers tend to make use of liquid crystal displays (LCD), similar to the much smaller displays found on pocket calculators.

Resolution

The 'fineness' of the image that can be displayed expressed as number of pixels (picture elements) – the individual dots that make up an image on the screen.

The quality of a monitor's display can be described in several ways. The **resolution** of the monitor describes the fineness of the image that can be displayed. Resolution is often expressed in terms of pixels (picture elements) – the individual dots that make up an image on the screen. Various standards exist that describe the resolutions that a monitor should be capable of displaying. A VGA monitor, for example, should be able to display an image that is 640 by 480 pixels in size. As screen sizes become larger, it becomes possible to display much higher resolutions. A typical 15" (38 cm) monitor can display images up to 1600 by 1200 pixels in size. The number of colours that can be displayed on the screen is also related to resolution. The number of colours that can be shown ranges from two (monochrome) to several million.

The number of colours that can be displayed on the screen becomes almost meaningless beyond a certain point. Since the human eye can only distinguish between a few hundred shades of the same colour, the ability to display several thousand shades is of little practical importance.

Another method of gauging the quality of a monitor's display involves measuring the distance – known as the **dot pitch** – between the pixels on the screen. The smaller the distance between pixels, the finer the image will appear. The image shown on a monitor with a dot pitch of 0.35 mm, for example, will often appear grainy. On the other hand, an image shown on a monitor with a dot pitch of 0.28 mm will normally appear sharp and clear.

A third indicator of image quality relates to the way in which an image is displayed on the monitor. The number of times the image is drawn on the screen each second is known as the **refresh rate** and is measured in Hz. A refresh rate of 60Hz, for example, means that the image will be drawn on the screen 60 times each second. However, as screen size and the complexity of the display increase, it becomes difficult for some monitors to refresh the image at a high enough rate. Some monitors attempt to refresh the screen in two stages, alternatively updating half of the screen at a time. This often results in a flickering effect that can cause difficulties, such as eye strain, for some users.

An **interlaced** display is one where each complete image is drawn in two steps. A **non-interlaced** monitor refreshes the display in a single pass. A good-quality monitor is normally capable of supporting a non-interlaced display at a refresh rate of 70Hz or more.

Another way of producing a large display is by making use of a **video projector**. A computer system can be connected directly to a projector so that output is directed to a projection screen. Some projectors convert the computer's output into a television picture before displaying it.

▶ Printers

The printer is one of the most common output devices and is considered an essential part of a computer-based information system.

Printers are described in more detail on page 68.

▶ Plotter

A **plotter** uses a number of different coloured pens to draw lines on the paper as it moves through the machine. Although they are capable of producing characters, the quality of the text created is often very poor. Plotters are primarily used to create technical drawings, such as engineering diagrams. They can also be used to record the results of the continuous monitoring of various events by creating charts. Some cardiac monitors, for example, use a simple plotter device to produce charts showing a patient's heart activity over time.

Dot pitch

A method of gauging the quality of a monitor's display that involves measuring the distance between the pixels on the screen.

Refresh rate

A method of gauging the quality of a monitor's display that involves measuring the number of times the image is drawn upon the screen each second.

Interlaced display

Each complete image shown on a monitor's display is drawn in two steps.

Non-interlaced display

The monitor refreshes the display in a single pass.

Video projector

A computer system can be connected directly to a projector so that output is directed to a projection screen.

Plotter

A plotter uses a number of different coloured pens to draw lines upon the paper as it moves through the machine.

▶ MIDI devices

The ability to link devices to a personal computer via MIDI (**musical instrument digital interface**) connections allows users to send information directly to one or more musical instruments. Specialised software is used to create a musical score that includes a range of different instruments. Once finalised, the score can be sent directly to one or more MIDI instruments for playback. The instruments synthesise any sounds or effects required in order to play the music. MIDI devices are used by a wide variety of individuals and organisations, including television and film companies, musicians and software developers.

▶ Microfilm

Computer output to microfilm (COM), also known as computer output microform, is often used to archive large quantities of information for future reference. Information is processed via a personal computer and sent directly to a device that produces microfilm negatives.

A related technology is known as **document image processing** (DIP). Documents are treated as pictures or images and stored directly to compact disc or tape.

▶ Sound

In addition to music and sound, a sound card can be used to output information in a variety of other forms. Two common examples include:

◆ **Voice annotations** consist of spoken comments that can be recorded and embedded within a document or other data file. A user working on the document can play back a voice annotation whenever required.

◆ **Speech synthesis** software allows text to be converted into speech. The contents of spreadsheet files, e-mail messages, wordprocessing documents and other files can be converted into speech and played back via a sound card or other device. Although primarily used to assist people with sight impairments, these techniques are also becoming more popular within business organisations. One example involves senior managers using these methods so that they can listen to e-mail and other messages while driving.

▶ Other output devices

In addition to the items described above, a wide variety of other output devices are also available. Some examples include the following:

◆ *Computer aided design* (CAD) and *computer aided manufacturing* (CAM) systems allow users to design and manufacture products via a computer system. The design of the product, including all technical details such as dimensions, is produced using CAD software. Once finalised, the design can be transferred to a CAM package for further processing. The CAM software produces a program that describes how to produce the finished item to a *computer numerically controlled* (CNC) machine. Many systems integrate the design and manufacturing process so that the direct output from the CAD/CAM system is a finished product.

◆ *Computer output to laser disk* (COLD). This is used to store management reports which would previously have been output as computer printout.

◆ **Visualisation** involves looking at graphical representations of data. Although still in its infancy, this technology makes use of various devices so that users can examine information from new and different perspectives. An important development concerns **virtual reality**, where users can explore an immersive computer-generated environment that is perceived as being three-dimensional. Using virtual reality goggles, for example, can allow a user to view and interact with a body of data that appears as a three-dimensional model.

◆ The computer leisure market has seen a rapid growth in sales of devices that simulate tactile responses from programs. Such devices attempt to simulate motion or physical contact when using programs such as flight simulators or racing games. Again, although this is still a relatively young area of technology, there remains a tremendous potential in terms of business applications. The most common example of such devices in the business environment is message pagers which can be set to vibrate when a message is received.

Visualisation

This describes a variety of methods used to produce graphical representations of data so that it can be examined from a number of different perspectives.

Virtual reality (VR)

An interactive, artificial reality created by the computer. Users perceive the environment in three dimensions and are able to interact with objects and people.

▶ SELECTING OUTPUT DEVICES

The selection of an inappropriate output device can incur unnecessary costs and lead to a variety of other problems. Some of the factors that should be considered when selecting an output device include appropriateness, permanence, speed, response time and cost. The following sections describe these factors in more detail.

▶ Appropriateness

An output device should be appropriate to the type of information produced as the result of a business process. A plotter, for example, provides an efficient means of producing large technical diagrams. However, it would not be an appropriate means of printing a business letter.

▶ Permanence

It is often necessary to make a permanent record of the results of a given activity, for example an organisation will normally retain a copy of a business letter sent to a client. However, in many other cases, for example when replying to an e-mail message, a permanent record is often unnecessary.

▶ Response time

Many activities require constant and immediate feedback. The user of a wordprocessor, for example, needs to see the results of his/her actions at all times – in other words, the **response time** between action and feedback must be very small.

Response time

The time it takes for a maintenance provider to fix a problem.

▶ Speed

In many applications, the speed of the output device can be of critical importance. As an example, consider a mailmerge operation, where personalised letters are produced by inserting the names and addresses of customers into a standard document.

Although generating each letter may take only a matter of seconds, printing each copy can take considerably longer. The time required to complete the process will depend heavily on the speed of the output device; the slower the device (in this case, the printer), the longer the overall time necessary to complete the task.

▶ Cost

The operating costs of certain output devices can be extremely low. A monitor, for example, costs relatively little to purchase, maintain and operate. However other output devices, for example printers, incur costs each time they are used.

▶ PRINTERS

The four basic types of printer are: laser, inkjet, dot-matrix and daisywheel. Note that variations exist for each type of printer.

▶ Laser printer

Laser printer

A laser is used to charge sections of a rotating drum which is then used to print using toner powder achieving a combination of speed with high print quality.

Page printer

A document is processed one page at a time.

Line printer

A document is processed one line at a time.

In a **laser printer**'s operation, a laser is used to charge sections of a rotating drum. The pattern of charged and uncharged areas on the drum corresponds to the image that will be printed. As the drum rotates, particles of dry toner powder are picked up. Heat is used to transfer the toner powder to the paper.

It is worth noting that laser printers are usually described as **page printers**, that is, an entire page is printed at a time. Other types of printers, such as dot-matrix printers, are known as **line printers**, since a document is printed line by line.

Some advantages of the laser printer are as follows:

◆ *Print quality*. Laser printers are capable of producing documents at a quality appropriate for business correspondence. Page 71 provides more information concerning print quality.

◆ *Speed*. A typical laser printer will be able to print at a rate of between four and twelve pages per minute. This compares well against other printing methods, for example a typical inkjet printer may only be capable of printing one or two pages per minute (ppm).

◆ *Volume*. Laser printers are normally capable of dealing with large volumes of work. Manufacturers often provide ratings for their printers that describe the typical workload appropriate for a given model. Whereas a dot-matrix printer may be suitable for a workload of 500 pages per month, it is not unusual to find laser printers capable of a workload of 5000 pages per month.

◆ *Noise*. Laser printers are almost completely silent in operation.

However, laser printers also suffer from a number of disadvantages:

◆ *Cost of printing*. The cost of printing via a laser printer is considered high. One reason for this is that all documents – including drafts – are printed at a high quality.

◆ *Colour printing*. A typical laser printer is not capable of printing in colour. Although special colour laser printers are available, these can cost thousands of pounds and are expensive to use and maintain.

◆ *Cost*. Laser printers are considered expensive to purchase in comparison with other types of printer.

▶ Dot-matrix printer

A **dot-matrix printer** arranges a series of pins (usually from 8 to 24) to form the shape of a required character. The character is transferred to the paper by striking the pins against an ink ribbon. The greater the number of pins used, the more detailed the character that can be produced, but this is still crude compared to other methods and these printers are not usually purchased today for this reason.

Dot-matrix printer

A character is transferred to the paper by striking pins against an ink ribbon.

▶ Inkjet printer

Although they were initially considered expensive and unreliable, **inkjet printers** have rapidly gained acceptance and are now found in many organisations. Changes in technology have resulted in models that are inexpensive to purchase, reliable in operation and capable of excellent results.

An inkjet printer uses a print-head containing 50 or more small nozzles. Each nozzle can be controlled individually by electrostatic charges produced by the printer. Characters are formed by squirting small droplets of ink directly on to the paper. **Bubble jet printers** work in a similar manner but transfer the character by melting the ink droplets on to the paper.

Some advantages of inkjet printers include:

Inkjet printer

An inkjet printer uses a print-head containing 50 or more small nozzles that squirt ink on to paper by varying electrostatic charges produced by the printer.

Bubble jet printer

Operates in a similar manner to an inkjet printer, but transfers the character by melting the ink droplets onto the paper.

- ◆ *Cost.* Inkjet printers can be purchased at a low cost and are relatively inexpensive to operate.
- ◆ *Reliability.* Since inkjet printers have very few moving parts, they are considered reliable and robust.
- ◆ *Colour printing.* Inkjet printers provide a relatively inexpensive means of printing in colour at an acceptable quality.
- ◆ *Versatility.* Inkjet printers are able to produce a variety of different documents, including overhead transparencies, card, labels and envelopes.
- ◆ *Noise.* Inkjet printers are almost completely silent in operation.

Some of the disadvantages of inkjet printers include the following:

- ◆ *Permanence.* The ink used by some printers is not waterproof, meaning that documents can easily become smudged or blurred.
- ◆ *Print quality.* Printing at the highest possible quality requires the use of special paper. This increases the cost of printing significantly.
- ◆ *Economy.* Most inkjet printers offer a variety of printing modes. This can provide economy by allowing internal documents to be printed in draft quality.
- ◆ *Speed.* Although considerably faster than dot-matrix and daisywheel printers, inkjet printers are still unable to compete with laser printers in terms of speed. Colour printing can be particularly slow, with some models taking six to eight minutes to produce a single page.

Daisywheel printer

Similar to a conventional typewriter. Characters are mounted on hammers arranged in the shape of a wheel. The wheel is rotated until the correct character is in position for printing.

▶ Daisywheel printer

A **daisywheel printer** functions in much the same way as a conventional typewriter. Characters are mounted on hammers arranged in the shape of a wheel. The wheel is rotated until the correct character is in the correct position for printing. The hammer then strikes a fabric ribbon against the paper to transfer the character. Different typefaces can be produced by changing the daisywheel for another for the new typeface.

It should be noted that daisywheel printers are seldom found in modern business organisations, having been superseded by laser and inkjet printers. They may be of value for impact printing on to duplicate or triplicate paper such as that used for invoices, so are often found in the accounting department.

▶ Other types of printer

Specialised printers exist for a number of different applications. Some of the types available include:

Thermal printer

A matrix of heated pins to melt ink from a ribbon directly on to the paper.

◆ **Thermal printers**. Thermal printers operate by using a matrix of heated pins to melt ink from a ribbon directly on to the paper. Although popular during the late 1980s, thermal printers have declined in popularity over recent years. Many thermal printers required the use of special paper which was relatively expensive and sometimes faded or yellowed when exposed to sunlight.

Wax printers

Printers which employ a ribbon with a coloured wax coating to form images by heating sections of the ribbon and pressing it against the paper (dye sublimation).

◆ **Wax printers**. The need to reproduce photographs and other graphic images at high quality has stimulated interest in a variety of printing technologies. Some printers employ a special ribbon with a coloured wax coating. Images are formed by heating sections of the ribbon and pressing it against the paper. This process, known as dye sublimation, is used to produce more natural tones and shades by merging together different colours. Although this method of printing is considered expensive, print quality is extremely high.

Label printers

These are small units specifically designed to print on rolls of self-adhesive labels.

◆ **Label printers.** These are small units specifically designed to print on rolls of self-adhesive labels. Although various kinds of label printer exist, one of the most common types is used for printing bar codes.

▶ SELECTING A PRINTER

A number of factors should be considered when selecting a printer for business use. The aim should be to acquire equipment that meets the business needs of the organisation and ensures high print quality at minimum cost. Some of the factors that should be taken into account include printing costs, print quality, speed, volume, any requirement to print in colour and paper handling. Each of these factors is described below.

▶ Printing costs

Cost per page

Figures refer to the costs of consumables such as ink and replacement components (toner cartridges, drums and so on).

The cost of printing is normally described in terms of **cost per page**. Two separate figures are usually given for the cost per page: the typical cost of a page containing only text and the typical cost of a page containing a large graphic image.

The cost per page provides a simple means of determining the overall running costs of a given printer. The figures given usually refer to the costs of consumables such as ink and replacement components (toner cartridges, drums and so on).

In general, laser printers and inkjet printers have slightly higher costs per page than other types. However, this is largely due to the fact these printers print at very high qualities. The cost per page tends to rise dramatically when printing in colour is carried out. In some cases, the cost per page can increase by a factor of more than ten.

▶ Print quality

Print quality is normally measured in **dots per inch (DPI)**. This describes the number of individual dots that can be printed within a space of one square inch. Quality is normally compared against professional typesetting, such as the equipment used to produce a book or magazine. A typeset document is normally produced at a quality of between 1200 and 1500 dpi. However, since business documents seldom need to be produced to this standard, the quality provided by a laser printer is considered acceptable for business correspondence, reports and other documents.

A simpler way of describing print quality is by comparing it to the quality normally used for business documents. A *draft quality* document can be printed quickly but quality will be comparatively low. Draft printing is normally used for internal documents, such as program listings or database reports. A slightly higher quality can be achieved by printing documents at *near letter quality* (NLQ). NLQ is often the highest quality possible with certain kinds of printers, particularly dot-matrix models. Documents to be sent outside the organisation need to reflect a professional approach and support the organisation's image. Such documents will be printed at *letter quality* (LQ).

Table 3.1 provides a basic guide to the print quality produced by using different methods.

Dots per inch (DPI)

This describes the number of individual dots that can be printed within a space of one square inch.

Table 3.1 Print quality

Method	DPI	Quality
Dot-matrix	90–360	Draft–NLQ
Inkjet	300–720	NLQ–LQ
Laser	300–1200	LQ
Daisywheel	–	LQ

▶ Paper handling

Many organisations require the capability to print on envelopes, overhead transparencies and card. In general, only inkjet and laser printers offer this facility. In addition, some laser and inkjet printers have special paper feeders that allow batches of envelopes or labels to be printed at a time.

The quantity of paper that a printer can hold is often an important factor when selecting a business printer. Laser printers feature one or more 'bins' that can contain hundreds of sheets at a time. Other types of printer may only be able to hold 30, 50 or 100 sheets at a time. Where a printer will be expected to deal with high volumes of work, a large paper capacity will reduce the need to refill the printer continually.

▶ Colour printing

At present, inkjet printers offer the best compromise between print quality and cost when producing documents in colour. Although other printers, such as colour laser printers, are capable of producing better results, the associated costs can be prohibitive. Few organisations use colour dot-matrix printing as quality tends to be poor in comparison with other methods.

▶ Volume

The volume of printing that will be carried out using a particular printer has implications for running costs, maintenance costs and reliability.

Manufacturers often provide ratings for their printers that describe the typical workload appropriate for a given model. This value is often described in terms of **pages per month**. An inkjet printer, for example, might be described as appropriate for home use where the average monthly workload is likely to be less than 1000 pages per month. A laserjet might achieve 8000 pages per month.

Pages per month

Manufacturers often provide ratings for their printers that describe the typical workload appropriate for a given model.

> A common problem experienced by organisations using inkjet printers concerns increased printing costs. Many organisations acquire inkjet printers so that they have the facility to print documents in colour. In many cases this is seen as a facility that will be used infrequently, for specific documents on specific occasions. However, employees often overuse this facility, even printing internal and draft documents in colour. There are two results: printing costs increase dramatically (sometimes by a factor of up to 20) and the working life of the printer is reduced significantly.

Characters per second (cps)

This describes a simple means of measuring the speed of a printer. Line printers, such as dot-matrix, daisywheel and some inject printers, are measured in terms of characters per second.

▶ Speed

The speed of a printer can have a significant impact on the work carried out within an organisation. Delays in printing documents can promote bottlenecks within administrative processes and are wasteful in terms of labour power. As an example, consider a household or motor insurance company. Such companies often print documents on demand, for example a motor insurance quotation may be printed while the customer waits at the service counter. Clearly, printing the document quickly and efficiently has implications for customer service and company image.

Printing speeds are usually measured in terms of **characters per second** (cps) or **pages per minute** (ppm). Line printers, such as dot-matrix, daisywheel and some inkjet printers, are measured in terms of characters per second. Page printers, such as laser printers and modern inkjet models, are measured in terms of pages per minute (ppm).

Some typical examples of printing speeds are given in Table 3.2.

Pages per minute (ppm)

A simple means of measuring the speed of a printer.

Table 3.2 Typical print speeds

Printer type	Draft speed	LQ speed
Dot-matrix	120 cps	45 cps
Daisywheel	–	30 cps
Inkjet	240 cps	150 cps
Laser	–	6 ppm

▶ STORAGE DEVICES

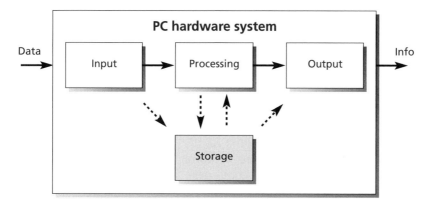

Fig 3.6 Storage devices

Storage devices are used to store programs, data awaiting processing and the information resulting from computer processing. Storage devices are categorised as **primary storage** when the data is loaded into computer memory, or **secondary storage** when the data is stored on a separate device, where the information will be retained even if the machine is switched off. Effectively this distinction is that between short-term memory and long-term memory. Floppy and hard disks are examples of secondary storage.

A brief description of several basic concepts related to storage devices will support an understanding of the sections that follow:

◆ Storage devices can have varying degrees of functionality in terms of their ability to record data. At one end of the spectrum, a **read-only** device can only be used to access data that is already present on the media. A normal CD-ROM drive, for example, is unable to write data to a compact disc. A **WORM** (write once – read many) storage device allows data to be written only once. Once the data has been written, it can not be changed or erased. Fortunately, the majority of storage devices allow data to be written, erased and rewritten as often as required.

Units of measurement

The capacity of a storage device is often measured in terms of kilobytes, megabytes and gigabytes. The following may help readers understand these units:

◆ A **bit** is a single binary digit and represents a zero (0) or a 1. The bit is the smallest unit of measurement.

◆ A **byte** is made up of eight bits and represents a value between 0 and 255. A byte can be thought of as the amount of space required to hold a single character.

◆ A **kilobyte** (Kb) is approximately 1000 bytes, or the equivalent of 1000 characters.

◆ A **megabyte** (Mb) is approximately 1000Kb, or the equivalent of one million characters.

◆ A **gigabyte** (Gb) is approximately 1000Mb, or the equivalent of one billion characters.

◆ A **terabyte** (Tb) is approximately 1000Gb, or the equivalent of one thousand billion characters.

Primary storage

Data and instructions are loaded into memory such as Random Access Memory. Such storage is temporary.

Secondary storage

Floppy disks and hard-disks are secondary storage which provides permanent storage.

Read-only

A device that can only be used to access data that is already present on the media and is unable to write data.

Write once – read many (WORM)

A storage device allows data to be written only once. Once the data has been written, it cannot be changed or erased.

Bit

A single binary digit representing a zero (0) or a 1.

Byte

Made up of eight bits and represents the amount of space required to hold a single character.

Kilobyte (Kb)

Approximately 1000 bytes, or the equivalent of 1000 characters.

Megabyte (Mb)

Approximately 1000Kb, or the equivalent of one million characters.

Gigabyte (Gb)

Approximately 1000Mb, or the equivalent of one billion characters.

Terabyte (Tb)

Approximately 1000 Gb, or the equivalent of one thousand billion characters.

◆ The media used to hold data can be fixed or removable. Removable media, such as floppy disks, tend to be portable. Fixed media, such as a hard disk drive, have limited storage capacity but often allow speedy access to data.

▶ Secondary storage – floppy disk

Floppy disk

Consists of a plastic disk, coated with a magnetic covering and enclosed within a rigid plastic case.

Early **floppy disks** were enclosed within a cover made of thin card, hence the term 'floppy disk'. A modern floppy disk consists of a plastic disk, coated with a magnetic covering and enclosed within a rigid plastic case. Floppy disks are available in a number of different sizes and with varying capacities. At present, the most common type is the high density 3.5" floppy disk.

The two main advantages of the floppy disk are as follows:

◆ It is a common, standardised means of storing data and floppy disk drives can be found on the majority of personal computers.

◆ Floppy disks are portable between computer systems, allowing users to transfer relatively small amounts of data between machines.

Some of the main disadvantages of the floppy disk include:

◆ Floppy disks are relatively delicate, being susceptible to dust, magnetic fields, liquid spills and other forms of accidental damage.

◆ The storage capacity of the floppy disk is considered small. A standard 3.5" disk is capable of storing 1.44Mb of data, the equivalent of approximately 350 pages of text.

◆ The floppy disk drive is considered relatively slow; it can take several minutes to read or write data to a disk.

▶ Secondary storage – hard disk drive

Hard disk

A magnetic media that stores data upon a number of rigid platters that are rotated at very high speeds.

Hard disk drives are a standard feature of a modern personal computer. They are used to store the computer's operating system, application software and data.

A hard disk drive stores data on a number of rigid platters that are rotated at very high speeds. Since the magnetic read/write heads float above the surface of the platter at a distance of a few microns, the drive mechanism is enclosed within a vacuum to protect against dust and other contaminants.

The main advantages of the hard disk drive are as follows:

◆ Hard disk drives tend to have large storage capacities, typically varying from 850Mb to more than 6Gb, equivalent to between approximately two million and fourteen million pages of text.

◆ A hard disk drive is considered a fast means of storing and retrieving data, for example a modern drive can be hundreds of times faster than a floppy disk drive.

◆ The hard disk drive is a standard component of a personal computer system. As such they are relatively inexpensive to purchase or replace.

The main disadvantages of the hard disk drive are as follows:

◆ Hard disk drives are seen as delicate devices that are easily damaged. They are particularly susceptible to damage from sudden shocks and excessive vibration.

◆ In general, a hard disk drive is considered to be a fixed part of a computer system and is not portable. However, it should be noted that removable hard disk drives exist and that these are rapidly becoming popular.

▶ Secondary storage – removable disk

Removable disk drives have become popular in response to the need for portable storage devices with larger capacities than the traditional floppy disk. A removable disk drive combines some of the advantages of the hard disk drive and the floppy disk drive. An example is the Iomega Zip drive now provided as a standard component on many new computer systems.

Some of the features of removable disk drives include the following:

◆ Removable disks tend to have relatively large capacities and are often capable of storing 100Mb of data or more. New disks are relatively inexpensive, allowing for an almost unlimited storage capacity.

◆ Although drives can be installed permanently they are often portable, featuring their own power supplies and connecting cables.

◆ Although removable disk drives tend to be many times faster than a floppy disk drive, they are considered relatively slow when compared to other devices, such as hard disk drives.

▶ Secondary storage – CD-ROM

The first compact disc players were launched in 1982 but did not become established in Europe until the mid-1980s. The compact disc was originally marketed as a replacement for vinyl records and audio cassettes. One of the advantages of the compact disc was that data was stored in digital form. This ensured that music recordings could be played back at a very high quality, far higher than traditional vinyl recordings and audio cassettes.

The **CD-ROM** drive arose from the audio compact disc player and began to gain popularity during the late 1980s. The acronym CD-ROM stands for compact disc – read only memory, denoting the fact that CD-ROM discs are read-only devices; data cannot be written to a CD-ROM by a conventional player.

The data on a **compact disc** is encoded as a series of dips and raised areas. These two states represent binary data – the same number system used by microprocessors. The player shines a laser beam on to the surface of the disc and measures the light that is reflected back. The intensity of the light enables the player to distinguish individual binary digits.

The two main advantages of the compact disc are:

◆ A compact disc has a very high storage capacity. A standard disc is able to store 650Mb of data. This is equivalent to approximately 2 million pages of text or 74 minutes of high-quality music.

◆ The costs associated with CD-ROM storage are typically very low. CD-ROM drives are inexpensive and can be repaired or replaced easily.

Some of the disadvantages of CD-ROMs include:

◆ Compact discs are relatively fragile. They are easily damaged, for example by accidental scratches or exposure to heat.

◆ CD-ROM drives are relatively slow in comparison to other storage devices, such as the hard disk drive.

CD-ROM

A computer storage device offering a relatively high capacity. The acronym CD-ROM stands for Compact Disc – Read Only Memory, denoting the fact that CD-ROM discs are read-only devices.

Compact disc (CD)

The media used by CD-ROM players. The data on a compact disc is encoded as a series of dips and raised areas.

◆ CD-ROM is a read-only medium. Although listed as a disadvantage, this can sometimes be seen as an advantage, since unauthorised changes and accidental erasure of data can be prevented. It should be noted that drives capable of recording on to blank compact discs are available but are more expensive.

CDR (CD-recordable)

Can read both conventional compact discs but also write data to special 'gold' discs.

A variation on the traditional CD-ROM drive is the **CD-recordable (CDR)** drive. These drives can not only read conventional compact discs but can also write data to special 'gold' discs. Compact discs produced in this way are known as *write-once* discs, that is, once data has been stored on the disc it cannot be altered or erased.

A more recent development is the **CD re-writable (CDRW)** drive. In addition to providing the functionality of the CDR drive, the CDRW drive also allows the use of special compact disc media that can be written and erased many times. However, discs produced in this way are not compatible with standard CD-ROM drives and can only be used with a CDRW unit.

CDRW (CD re-writable)

In addition to providing the functionality of the CDR drive, the CDRW drive also allows the use of special compact disc media that can be written and erased many times.

Two other notable variations on optical storage devices are:

◆ *Laserdisc players* provide high-quality playback of sound and video. Playback from some laserdisc players can be controlled via a personal computer. This enables specific audio and video sequences to be located and played automatically. This ability means that laserdisc players are often used in training and educational applications.

◆ *WORM (write once – read many)* drives exist in a variety of forms and can be compared to CDR drives. Data can only be written to the media once and cannot be altered or erased. WORM drives are often used for archiving and backup applications.

▶ Secondary storage – DVD

Digital versatile disc (DVD)

Similar to CD-ROM but with higher storage capacities, typically between 4Gb and 7Gb which is accessed at higher speeds.

Digital versatile disc (DVD) players began to gain in popularity in 1997 and are now fitted as a standard component of many new personal computers. Although superficially similar to CD-ROM, DVD offers two important benefits to users. First, the discs used by a DVD player offer extremely high storage capacities, typically between 4Gb and 7Gb. Second, data held on DVD can be accessed at very high speeds. One of the most common applications for DVD is as a distribution medium for full-length feature films.

▶ Secondary storage – magnetic tape

Magnetic tape has been a common storage medium for more than three decades. The most common form of storage device based on magnetic tape is the **tape streamer**. A tape streamer is normally installed as an internal device, similar to a floppy disk drive or CD-ROM drive. The tape streamer uses small plastic cartridges filled with magnetic tape. Since each cartridge tends to have a relatively small storage capacity, it is often necessary to use several in order to store large data files.

Tape streamer

A common form of storage device that uses magnetic tape as a storage medium.

The main characteristics of magnetic tape include:

◆ Magnetic tape allows only sequential access – data can only be accessed in strict order.

◆ The costs associated with the use of magnetic tape as a storage medium are extremely low.

- Storage devices based on magnetic tape are considered extremely slow. In view of this, they are mainly used for archiving and backup applications.
- Magnetic tape is relatively fragile and is easily damaged.

A range of new devices based on magnetic tape have begun to appear over the past few years. The majority of these devices make use of **digital audio tape (DAT)** or ordinary video cassettes. Digital audio tape couples higher storage capacities with improved speed. However, at present storage devices based on DAT remain costly and are often beyond the reach of small organisations. As alternatives to DAT there are a number of storage devices based on domestic video cassette recorders. These inexpensive units often consist of little more than a small expansion card designed to allow communication between the computer system and the video cassette recorder.

▶ Primary storage – memory

Computer memory can take a number of different forms and is found within many of the devices that form part of a computer-based information system. Computers, printers, graphics cards, modems and many other devices all make use of various kinds of memory 'chips'. Although relatively expensive, memory is the fastest form of storage available.

There are two broad categories of computer memory: volatile and non-volatile. The contents of **volatile memory** are lost when the power to the device is switched off. On the other hand, **non-volatile memory** retains its contents until changed in some way.

Random access memory (RAM) is used as working storage, holding instructions and data that are waiting to be processed. The contents of RAM are volatile, that is, any data held is lost when the power to the computer system is switched off. A typical computer system will feature 16Mb, 32Mb or 64Mb of RAM. In general, the more RAM a computer system is equipped with, the faster it will operate and the more powerful it will be in terms of the complexity of the programs it can run. RAM is also found in a number of other devices, for example in a printer RAM is used to store an image of the document to be printed.

The contents of **read-only memory (ROM)** are fixed and cannot be altered. ROM is also non-volatile, making it ideal as a means of storing the information needed for a device to function properly. In a computer system, for example, the basic information needed so that the computer can access disk drives and control peripherals is stored in ROM. This in known as the PC's BIOS (p 83). This prevents users from accidentally deleting or altering information essential to the computer's operation.

Some other forms of computer memory include the following:

- An **EPROM** (eraseable programmable read-only memory) is a type of ROM that retains its contents until they are changed using a special device (known as a 'burner').
- **VRAM** (video random access memory) is a type of memory that has been optimised in order to speed up operations that involve graphics.
- **CMOS, NMOS** and **PMOS** memory is used as a semi-permanent means of storage in a variety of different devices. Similar to EPROMs in many ways, a major difference is that a special device is not needed to alter the contents of the memory. As an example, this kind of memory is generally used in computer systems as a means of

Digital audio tape (DAT)

A storage medium that combines some of the characteristics of magnetic tape and compact disc.

Volatile memory

Anything held in memory is lost once the power to the computer system is switched off. However, non-volatile memory retains its contents until altered or erased.

Non-volatile memory

Non-volatile memory retains its contents until altered or erased.

Random access memory (RAM)

RAM is used as volatile, working storage by a computer, holding instructions and data that are waiting to be processed.

Read-only memory (ROM)

The contents of ROM are fixed and cannot be altered. ROM is non-volatile.

Eraseable programmable read–only memory (EPROM)

This is a form of ROM memory that retains its contents until changed using a special device known as a 'burner'.

storing any special settings needed to control the operation of the computer or a peripheral. This approach allows users to add or remove devices quickly and easily.

It is worth highlighting the wide range of ways in which computer memory is used. In a domestic environment, for example, one might find memory chips in television sets, satellite receivers, video cassette recorders, burglar alarm systems, alarm clocks, washing machines, microwave ovens, hi-fi equipment and a variety of other devices. In terms of a computer-based information system, the following examples illustrate the range of applications to which computer memory can be put:

◆ In a modem, ROM is used to store the commands used to control communications and any special settings the user has specified.

◆ In a laser printer, special ROM cards can be used to expand the printer's range of typefaces. Additional RAM can also be added to speed up printing or allow the printing of more complex documents.

Cache memory

Used to improve performance by anticipating the data and instructions needed by the processor. The required data is retrieved and held in the cache, ready to be transferred directly to the processor when required.

◆ In a computer system, **cache memory** is used to improve performance by anticipating the data and instructions that will be needed by the processor. The required data is retrieved and held in the cache, ready to be transferred directly to the processor when required. By removing the need for data to be retrieved from the computer's much slower main memory (RAM), the overall speed of the system is improved. The *hit rate* describes how often a correct prediction has been made in terms of the data needed by the processor. In general, the higher the hit rate, the greater the increase in performance.

▶ SELECTING STORAGE DEVICES

The selection of a storage device will normally be based on speed, storage capacity and cost. However, the importance of these factors will vary according to the function being performed, for example speed might be considered of little importance when making a backup of data overnight. Table 3.3 summarises some of the characteristics of several typical storage devices.

▶ Speed

Many of the tasks carried out by a computer-based information system require large quantities of data to be processed quickly and efficiently. In many cases, the overall time taken to complete an action will depend on the speed of the storage device used.

Table 3.3 Typical storage devices

Storage medium	Speed	Cost	Capacity	Permanent
Magnetic tape	Very slow	Very low	Very high	No
Floppy disk	Slow	Low	Very low	No
Hard disk drive	Fast	Low	High	No
CD-ROM	Slow	Low	Very high	Yes
Memory	Very fast	High	Low	Sometimes

The speed of a storage device is usually measured in terms of its access time (sometimes known as seek time) and data transfer rate.

The **access time** refers to the average time taken to locate a specific item of data. Access times are normally given in milliseconds, for example a typical hard disk drive might have an access time of 11 ms.

Access time

The average time taken to locate a specific item of data.

The **data transfer rate** describes how quickly the device is able to read continuous blocks of data. This figure is normally expressed in terms of kilobytes or megabytes. A typical data transfer rate for a CD-ROM drive, for example, might be given as 900Kb per second, while a hard disk drive might transfer more than 3Mb per second.

Data transfer rate

The rate at which a device is able to read continuous blocks of data.

▶ Capacity

The storage capacity of a given device will be measured in kilobytes, megabytes or gigabytes, for example a CD-ROM has a storage capacity of 650Mb. Some storage devices, such as a hard disk drive, will have a fixed storage capacity, while others will use removable media that provide an almost unlimited amount of data storage.

In general, a fixed storage device will operate faster than one that uses removable media. In addition, many applications generate large data files that cannot be stored conveniently on removable media. A database file, for example, can easily exceed the capacity of a floppy disk or removable disk.

▶ Cost of storage

The costs associated with storage devices are normally given in terms of **cost per megabyte**. In some cases, the cost per megabyte is based on the cost of the hardware, in others it is based on the cost of media. Two simple examples should help make this clearer:

Cost per megabyte

A simple means of gauging the costs associated with a given storage device.

- A hard disk drive has a fixed capacity, so the cost per megabyte can be calculated by simply dividing the cost of the hard drive by its storage capacity.
- A floppy disk drive uses removable media with a capacity of 1.44Mb. The cost per megabyte would be calculated by dividing the cost of a single floppy disk by 1.44.

> Using advertisements, price lists or other sources of information, create a table showing the costs associated with a range of common storage devices. Provide cost per megabyte figures for the following: floppy disk, hard disk, magnetic tape cartridges, CD-ROM and CDR.

ACTIVITY

▶ Other factors

A number of other factors should be taken into consideration when selecting a storage device. Among these are the following:

- The *reliability* of a storage device can be an important factor in many circumstances, for example a hardware failure might prevent all access to important business data. Furthermore, errors introduced when storing or reading data might also have serious consequences. For example, a small error on a magnetic tape cartridge might lead to the loss of all the data held on the cartridge.

◆ *Permanence* of storage is important if there is a need to protect data from being deleted or altered. A more permanent form of storage can also be desirable if the data held is unlikely to change often. Reference materials, for example, are often distributed on CD-ROM.

◆ It may often be necessary to take *security* measures to prevent data from being stolen or damaged. Removable media, such as floppy disks, can easily be transported from one location to another. While this can provide added security, it can also increase the risk of theft. Fixed devices, such as hard disk drives, are less vulnerable but also less versatile.

▶ ## PROCESSOR

Processor

Uses instructions from software to control the different components of a PC.

Complex instruction set computer (CISC) processor

A type of microprocessor which has a wide range of instructions to enable easy programming and efficient use of memory.

Reduced instruction set computer (RISC) processor

Designed so that it has to perform fewer instructions than a CISC processor and it can then operate at a higher speed.

The **central processing unit** (CPU) – or processor – found within a computer consists of two components: a control unit and an arithmetic logic unit (ALU). The control unit fetches commands from memory, decodes them and then executes them. It controls the operation of all hardware, including all input/output operations. The ALU carries out arithmetical calculations, for example addition, and can also make comparisons between values. The **processor** uses instructions from software to control the different components of a PC.

When a computer is first turned on, the microprocessor receives the first instruction from the Basic Input/Output System (BIOS). Following that, the operating system is loaded, followed by the application programs the user selects and the microprocessor performs the instructions it is given by these programs.

The technology used in processors (referred to as processor architecture) is continually evolving. Early versions of the Pentium processor contained 3.1 million transistors which regulate the flow of current in the chip, a Pentium II now contains over 5 million transistors. A microprocessor architecture, or the way in which it is structured and designed to process instructions varies between different types of computer.

The two best known architectures are known as CISC (**complex instruction set computer**) and RISC (**reduced instruction set computer**).

Web reference: http://www.intel.com

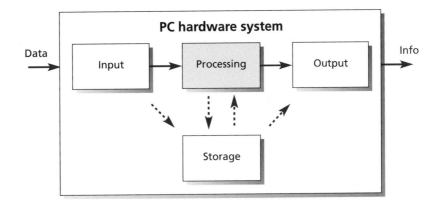

Fig 3.7 **A processor**

▶ COMPONENTS OF A PERSONAL COMPUTER

The preceding sections have already described a wide variety of the input, output and storage devices that can form part of a computer system. In this section, we look at a range of other components found in a typical personal computer.

▶ Microprocessor

The speed of a processor will depend on a number of different factors. Two such factors are clock speed and bandwidth. The **clock speed** determines how many instructions per second the processor can execute. The **bandwidth** describes how many pieces of data can be transmitted at one time. In both cases, the higher the value, the more powerful the processor. Clock speed and bandwidth values can be helpful when attempting to compare processors in order to select the most appropriate. For example, clock speeds for Pentium processors have varied from 60MHz in early versions through 90, 133, 166 to 266MHz.

Most IBM-compatible personal computers are based on a series of processors manufactured by Intel and several of its competitors. Older systems may feature 80386 and 80486 processors, while more up-to-date computers will use a Pentium-class processor such as a Pentium II. Over recent years, Intel has faced increasing competition from rivals such as AMD and Cyrix. These companies manufacture processors that are compatible with the various types of Pentium processors but tend to market them at lower prices. Both the K6 (AMD) and M2 (Cyrix) processors, for example, are compatible with Pentium processors operating at 166MHz or more.

It is important to recognise that all of a computer's actions are governed by the processor. As a general rule, the faster the processor, the faster and more efficient the computer.

Clock speed

Measured in MHz (megahertz, or millions of pulses per second). The clock speed is governed by a quartz-crystal circuit.

Bandwidth

Describe how many pieces of data can be transmitted or received at one time by the bus connecting the processor to other components of the PC.

▶ Graphics card

A graphics card enables a computer to display text or graphics on a monitor. The graphics card prepares and stores the image in memory prior to showing it on the screen. When the image is complete, it is transmitted to the monitor and displayed. A graphics card may produce and display images more than 60 times per second.

The amount of memory available to a graphics card determines the maximum resolution of the image and how many colours can be displayed. All graphics cards support the VGA (video graphics array) standard which specifies a maximum image size of 640 by 320 pixels, displayed in 16 colours. A VGA display can be achieved with just 256Kb of memory, but larger images with more colours can require 1Mb of memory or more. Many graphics cards are supplied with 4Mb or even 8Mb of memory, allowing them to display very complex images at large sizes, for example 4Mb of memory allows images to be displayed at 1600 by 1200 pixels in 256 colours.

Table 3.4 illustrates some of the most common graphics standards, indicating the highest resolution and maximum number of colours possible. Note that the table is arranged in approximate order of age, from oldest to newest.

Many graphics cards contain a graphics coprocessor that is used to carry out graphics calculations. This can help improve the speed of the computer, as some of the burden on the CPU is removed. Graphics cards that use a graphics coprocessor are often called **graphics accelerator cards**.

Video graphics array (VGA)

A common standard for graphics cards. All graphics cards support the VGA (video graphics array) standard which specifies a maximum image size of 640 by 320 pixels, displayed in 16 colours.

Graphics accelerator card

A type of graphics card containing its own memory and featuring a coprocessor.

Table 3.4 Graphics standards

Standard	Highest resolution	Maximum colours
MDA	Text only	2
Hercules	720 by 348	2
CGA	640 by 200	2
EGA	640 by 350	16
VGA	640 by 480	16
XGA	1024 by 768 (800 by 600)	65 000 (16 million)
SVGA	1600 by 1200 (1280 by 1024)	16 million

3DFx graphics card

A type of graphics card that features a sophisticated coprocessor used to manipulate an image so that it appears more realistic.

A growing trend towards more detailed graphics has spurred development of 3DFx graphics cards. A 3DFx card features a sophisticated coprocessor that manipulates an image so that it appears more realistic. Complicated calculations are required in order to perform actions such as smoothing jagged shapes or showing the shadows that an object might cast. The quantity and complexity of these calculations are such that they are beyond the abilities of a conventional graphics card and can place an unacceptable processing burden on the CPU. In view of this, the 3DFx card is normally supplied as a separate unit that is installed in addition to a standard graphics card. Both cards work together to process graphics information before it is passed to the screen.

ACTIVITY

Choose the most appropriate monitor for each of the following types of applications:

◆ Home use: basic wordprocessing

◆ Business use: CAD or DTP

◆ Business use: accounts packages and spreadsheets

Fill in on Table 3.5 the most appropriate size, resolution and colour depth given a limited budget.

Table 3.5 Monitors for various applications

Feature	Home	CAD/DTP	Accounts
Size (inches)			
Resolution (pixels)			
Colour depth (max colours)			

Motherboard

The motherboard is the main circuit board within a computer and houses the processor, memory, expansion slots and a number of connectors used for attaching additional devices, such as a hard disk drive.

▶ Motherboard

The **motherboard** is the main circuit board within a computer and houses the processor, memory, expansion slots and a number of connectors used for attaching

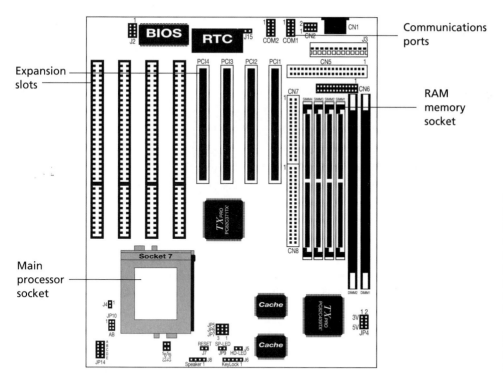

Expansion slots

Communications ports

RAM memory socket

Main processor socket

Fig 3.8 A typical personal computer motherboard

additional devices, such as a hard disk drive (*see* Fig 3.8). Any device that forms part of the motherboard is able to communicate directly with the processor.

On a personal computer, the motherboard will contain a ROM chip that holds the computer's BIOS. The **BIOS** (basic input/output system) contains software that controls all of the computer's most basic activities. It is the BIOS that allows the keyboard, display, hard disk drives, serial ports and other devices to function. The BIOS is stored in ROM so that it is always available and cannot be accidentally damaged or erased.

Storage devices, such as hard disk drives, are attached via the motherboard's I/O (input/output) connections. At least two **serial ports** are also supported, allowing a mouse, modems, printers and a range of other devices to be connected. In addition, a **parallel port** is normally used to connect a printer, scanner or other device.

Expansion slots allow additional devices to be connected to the computer. They are described in more detail in the next section.

▶ Expansion slots

As mentioned above, a computer's capabilities can be extended by adding special circuit boards (known as **expansion cards**) to the motherboard (*see* Fig 3.9). Common expansion cards include graphics cards, modems and sound cards. A typical computer will feature up to eight expansion slots and will accept large 'full-length' or smaller 'half-length' expansion cards.

Basic input/output system (BIOS)

Housed in a memory chip on the computer's motherboard, the BIOS contains software that controls all of the computer's most basic activities.

Serial port

A type of connector that allows various devices to be attached to a computer system. Examples of common serial devices might include a mouse, modem or printer.

Parallel port

A type of connector that allows various devices to be attached to a computer system. Examples of common parallel devices include printers and external storage devices.

Expansion slot

A slot on the computer's motherboard which can accommodate expansion cards.

Expansion card

Expansion cards can be used to extend a computer's capabilities by adding new devices to the system.

Industry standard architecture (ISA)

This describes a common standard governing the way in which an expansion card interacts with a computer's motherboard and CPU.

Extended industry standard architecture (EISA)

Supersedes the 16 bit interface of ISA, with 32 bit data transfer between CPU and Motherboard.

Peripheral component interconnect (PCI)

This describes a common standard governing the way in which an expansion card interacts with a computer's motherboard and CPU. PCI devices often support the Plug and Play installation of devices. *See* Expansion card, Plug and Play and Motherboard.

Plug and play (PnP)

This describes a means by which expansion cards can be added to a computer system and configured automatically without the user needing to enter settings or make other changes. *See* Expansion card.

Small computer system interface (SCSI)

This describes a common standard governing the way in which an expansion card interacts with a computer's motherboard and CPU. Up to seven separate devices can be attached to a single SCI interface simultaneously. Connecting several devices in sequence is known as daisy chaining. *See* Expansion card, Plug and Play and Motherboard

Universal Serial Bus (USB)

This describes a relatively new standard that governs the way in which an expansion card interacts with a computer's motherboard and CPU.

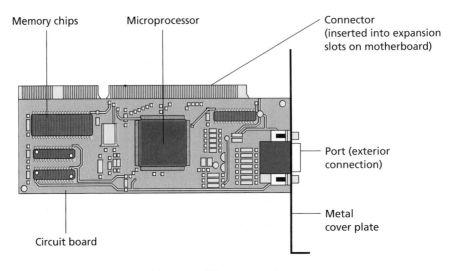

Fig 3.9 A typical expansion card for use with a personal computer

A motherboard will normally support expansion cards conforming to several different data bus standards, such as PCI or USB. Some of the most common standards include the following:

◆ The ISA (Industry Standard Architecture) and EISA (Extended Industry Standard Architecture) standards were the first to be widely adopted by manufacturers. Expansion cards based on these standards tend to offer relatively poor performance. However, since both ISA and EISA are well established, expansion cards are easily obtainable and often available at low cost.

◆ The PCI (Peripheral Component Interconnect) standard allows devices to communicate with the processor at high speeds. PCI expansion cards can also support **plug and play** (PnP), where new devices can be configured automatically without the user needing to enter settings or make other changes. Almost every new computer system features at least two PCI expansion slots.

◆ SCSI (Small Computer System Interface) devices are able to transmit data at very high speeds. In addition, up to seven separate devices can be attached simultaneously to a single SCSI interface. Connecting several devices in sequence is known as **daisy chaining**. Common SCSI devices include scanners, hard disk drives, CDR units and printers.

◆ The USB (Universal Serial Bus) port is a relatively new means of connecting devices to a computer. In addition to offering very high data transmission speeds, USB also supports plug and play, the connection of up to 127 devices and hot plugging. This describes the ability to add or remove new devices while the computer is running and have the operating system automatically recognise any changes made.

It is worth noting that while a motherboard will normally have up to eight expansion slots, not all will be available for use. Three or more expansion slots may be taken up by items that might include graphics card, sound card and internal modem. Furthermore, some slots may be inaccessible or there may not be enough space within the computer's case to add extra cards.

It should also be pointed out that new devices need not be installed inside the computer. Some expansion cards merely add a new interface, allowing devices to be attached outside of the case via a connecting cable. Furthermore, many devices can be connected to the computer via its serial or parallel ports. An external modem, for example, can be connected to a serial port via a special cable.

▶ Casing

The case used to house the motherboard and other components of a computer system also contains the computer's **power supply unit** (PSU) and cooling fan. The PSU converts AC current into DC current, regulating the amount of power supplied to the motherboard and any other devices installed within the case. The cooling fan ensures an even flow of air through the case so that heat can be dissipated quickly and efficiently.

Cases can be obtained in a range of different shapes and sizes. The three most common types of case are known as desktop, mini tower and full tower cases.

Power Supply Unit (PSU)

All modern personal computers feature a power supply unit used to convert AC current into DC current.

- A *desktop case*, as the name implies, is intended to fit comfortably on top of a desk, typically with the monitor sitting on top of the computer. Although desktop cases can be valuable if space is limited, they can sometimes prevent the installation of expansion devices, such as an additional hard disk drive.
- A *mini tower case* is narrow and tall, designed to placed alongside the monitor or beneath a desk. These cases provide more room for expansion devices but tend to require more space on the desktop.
- A *full tower case* is the largest type of case available and is normally placed on the floor next to a desk or table. Since a typical full tower case is intended to house a large number of expansion devices, it tends to have a larger power supply and can include a more powerful cooling fan.

▶ HARDWARE FOR NETWORKS AND COMMUNICATIONS

The majority of the computer systems purchased by large organisations are intended to form part of a network system. One of the most important benefits gained from introducing such a system is the ability to share hardware, software and data resources. In addition, a network allows users to work collaboratively and improves communication within the organisation.

This section introduces some of the hardware components needed in order to establish a network system. Chapter 5 describes networks and telecommunications in more detail.

Network interface card

A network interface card is an expansion card that allows a personal computer to be connected to a network.

▶ Network interface card

A **network interface card** is an expansion card that allows a personal computer to be connected to a network. The network card deals with all communications between the network and the computer.

▶ Printer sharers

Printer sharer

A printer sharer allows several computers to be attached to a single printer.

A **printer sharer** allows several computers to be attached to a single printer, thus reducing costs. Manual printer sharers are controlled by turning a dial to indicate

Modem (modulator-demodulator)
A modem is a communications device that allows users to send and receive data via an ordinary telephone line.

Digital data
Digital data can only represent a finite number of discrete values of 0 (zero) and 1.

Analogue
Analogue data is continuous in that an infinite number of values between two given points can be represented.

Dial-up networking (DUN)
Allows users to access a network at a remote location via a modem. Most home computer users, for example, access the Internet via dial-up networking.

Remote access
A means of accessing a network from a distant location such as when travelling.

Fax-modem
Combines the capabilities of a modem with the ability to send and receive fax transmissions.

Voice modem
Combining voice, fax and data facilities, at a simple level, a voice modem can be used as a speaker phone or answering machine.

Voice–data integration
Sometimes known as *computer telephony*. A combination of different communications technologies that provide a range of sophisticated facilities, for example automated call-switching, telephone answering services and fax-on-demand.

which computer will be used to send data to the printer. Automatic printer sharers detect any data sent to the printer and configure themselves accordingly.

▶ Modem

A **modem** (modulator-demodulator) is a common feature of many personal computers. It allows users to send and receive data via an ordinary telephone line. A modem works by converting data between digital and analogue form. The modem receives analogue data transmitted via a telephone line and converts this into digital data so that the computer can make use of it. Similarly, the modem converts outgoing digital data into an analogue signal before transmitting it.

> **Digital data** can only represent a finite number of discrete values. For example, at the most basic level, a computer recognises only the values 0 (zero) and 1. Any values *between* 0 and 1, for example 0.15, cannot be represented.
>
> **Analogue data** is continuous in that an infinite number of values between two given points can be represented. As an example, the hands of a clock are able to represent every single possible time of the day.

The main application for the modem is for **dial-up networking** (DUN) facilities. This allows users to access a network at a remote location via a modem. Most home computer users, for example, access the Internet via dial-up networking.

> **Remote access** describes a means of accessing a network from a distant location. A modem and specialised software allow users to send and receive information from home or an office when travelling. A sales representative, for example, might use remote access to review current prices and stock levels before meeting with a client.

A **fax-modem** combines the capabilities of a modem with the ability to send and receive fax transmissions. Incoming fax messages can be displayed on the screen or sent directly to a printer. Outgoing messages can be composed within a wordprocessor or other package and transmitted automatically. Alternatively, an optical scanner can be used to read in an existing document and convert it into a form suitable for transmission.

Voice modems offer greater flexibility by combining voice, fax and data facilities. At a simple level, a voice modem can be used as a speaker phone or answering machine. However, the more sophisticated applications now possible have made **voice–data integration** (sometimes known as computer telephony) extremely popular with business organisations in a very short time. Some examples of common applications include:

◆ Automated call switching allows the modem to intercept all incoming telephone calls and route them to appropriate locations. A fax, for example, might be stored on the computer's hard disk and also printed automatically so that it is available as soon as the user returns.

◆ A variation on answering systems is a **fax-on-demand** service that allows users to select from a range of documents by using the keys on the telephone handset. Once a document has been selected, the system automatically telephones the user's fax machine and transmits the document. Many organisations use fax-on-demand for dealing with common customer support queries, issuing price lists and making product information available to customers.

Fax-on-demand

A service that allows users to select from a range of documents by using the keys on the telephone handset.

The speed of a modem is measured in **baud** or bits per second (bps). Early modems operated at speeds of 1200 baud, the equivalent of approximately 100 characters per second. At present, the highest speed supported by a typical modem is 56 600 bps, equivalent to approximately 4700 characters per second. The speed with which data is transmitted can be improved by making use of data compression techniques that attempt to place data in a form that requires less space than usual. However, the modem that receives the data must use a compatible protocol in order to decompress data sent in this format.

Baud

A simple means of measuring the performance of a modem or other device. Data transmission rates can also be expressed in bits per second (bps) or baud.

A number of applications require high data transfer rates in order to function effectively. Video conferencing, for example, requires large quantities of data to be transmitted simultaneously to several users. However, the limitations of conventional telephone lines restrict the maximum speed with which data can be transmitted. Some of the alternatives to the modem and conventional telephone line include the following:

◆ Digital telephone exchanges support an **integrated services digital network (ISDN)** standard that allows data transfer rates that are up to five times faster than a 56 600 bps modem. An ISDN telephone line provides two separate 'channels' allowing simultaneous voice and data transmissions. Since ISDN lines transmit digital data, a modem is not required to make use of the service. Instead, a special terminal adapter (often called an ISDN modem) is used to pass data between the computer and the ISDN line.

Integrated services digital network (ISDN)

An ISDN telephone line provides two separate 'digital channels' allowing simultaneous voice and data transmissions.

◆ A relatively recent development has been the introduction of systems that make use of satellite communications in order to receive data at very high speeds. The DirecPC service, for example, uses a conventional modem to send requests for data, such as an Internet page. The requested data is received via a satellite link at speeds of up to 400Kbps, approximately four times faster than an ISDN link.

◆ The growing network of fibre-optic cables installed by cable television companies supports digital telephone communications at very high speed. The cable modem, although not yet widely available, offers many of the benefits associated with ISDN but with even higher data transfer rates.

◆ Following successful trials, devices allowing the transmission of data via ordinary electricity cables are expected to appear by the end of the 1990s. The use of the national electricity grid offers the potential for permanent, high-speed communications links at very low cost.

CASE STUDY: TOPIC AREA

FT

Siemens Nixdorf

Technology: the all-in-one hi-tech revolution

Video telephony has come of age. But now, says Clive Cookson, it has to be marketed.

Wanted by Europe's biggest computer company: a 'killer application' to sell millions of its latest device, which brings together personal computing and internet access with television and video telephony.

Siemens Nixdorf, being a conservative German company, is taking a cautious view of its clumsily named new 'PCTV Multimedia Integration Box'. As one of its executives said, when Siemens Nixdorf demonstrated a prototype to journalists at a conference in Athens this month: 'If we were an American company we'd be hyping this to the skies'.

The concept behind the box is far from being unique to Siemens Nixdorf. The explosive growth of the internet – and particularly the world wide web, which enables PC users to surf through a froth of highly illustrated 'pages' – has prompted many electronics companies to find ways of delivering net services on television. Best known is WebTV, a small Californian company that was bought last year for $425m by Microsoft, the US software giant.

But Siemens Nixdorf has gone further than its competitors in bridging the gap between the worlds of information technology and home entertainment. Its device is more than a 'set-top box' that enables people to surf the web on a domestic television – though it does this very well, with technology to simplify web pages by removing extraneous clutter and then displaying them on the screen with unusual brilliance and clarity.

The PCTV also offers video telephony, with a little camera on top of the box, and a vast range of entertainment, communication and online services. The primary component is a PC running Windows software, with an infra-red device that works like a computer mouse. It can be attached to any other home electronics device, such as a CD or DVD (digital video disc) player.

The big question now, says Peter Pagé, Siemens Nixdorf chief technologist, is whether the company and its partners can find the 'killer application' – something that will make millions of people want to use the box, in the way that word processing and spreadsheet packages made PCs popular.

By itself, web surfing on TV will not do the trick. For that you do not need a machine in the $500–$850 price range (depending on accessories) that Siemens Nixdorf is projecting for its PCTV when it reaches the market later this year. A much cheaper and simpler set-top box will deliver adequate internet access.

It is possible, however, that some combination of video telephony with home shopping or electronic commerce could be the killer.

In Athens, Siemens Nixdorf demonstrated a railway enthusiast navigating his way through the web sites of companies and clubs with model trains for sale – and then calling up one of the vendors, who showed him a particular model (a continental crocodile-style electric locomotive) over the videophone. He paid for it with an electronic transfer of funds, using the same box.

The company is taking advantage of an enormous improvement in the quality of video telephony. New 'compression' technology makes it possible to squeeze moving pictures down telephone lines far more effectively than even a couple of years ago, reducing the flickering jerkiness that has so irritated earlier users of videophones.

Siemens Nixdorf is unlikely to sell PCTVs directly to consumers. The company believes it is more likely to find a mass market by working through service providers such as telephone and cable television companies. These would market the whole package – box plus applications – to users. They could subsidise the high initial price of the box for people who sign up for the service, just as mobile phone companies often do for handsets.

To test the water, the company is carrying out a small trial with Deutsche Telekom subscribers in Berlin. 'We want to get it right first in Germany and then elsewhere in Europe,' says Pagé. 'We don't want to go straight into the US; the Americans wouldn't accept something like that from a European supplier.'

Up-market hotels are another promising field for PCTVs – one that Siemens Nixdorf is investigating with Holiday Inns. The idea is that they would enhance the televisions in guests' rooms with the technology, which would enable travellers not only to check local facilities and attractions, but also to log on to their own home or office computer.

Although it is possible to do this today if you take a powerful laptop and plug it into a telephone socket, the PCTV should give a more reliable connection and a far better display. To provide additional security, the box can include a reader of electronic chipcards (smartcards).

Anyone with the interests of the European electronics industry at heart will hope that Siemens Nixdorf can find and then exploit that elusive killer application.

However, for all its technical excellence, the German company has a cautious disposition and a reliance on corporate computing that makes some observers doubt whether it can move boldly enough.

Source: Financial Times, 21 February 1998

Questions

1 Describe some of the business applications for devices such as the Siemens Nixdorf PCTV.

2 What hardware devices are made use of by PCTV?

3 Describe some of the advantages and disadvantages of using PCTV devices in place of a personal computer system.

▶ HARDWARE SELECTION

FOCUS ON

The process of selecting a supplier for hardware is often known as vendor analysis. Here we relate this to a structured means of comparing potential suppliers of hardware in order to select the most appropriate. Chapters 7 and 8 also consider the issue of selection from a different perspective, that of selecting the correct source for an information system.

▶ Tenders

Although the purchase of small items can normally be carried out quickly and easily, larger purchases may involve the organisation in producing a tender document. A **tender document** is an invitation to suppliers, asking them to bid for right to supply an organisation's hardware, software and other requirements. An organisation selects a supplier by examining each response to the *invitation to tender* in detail. When several suppliers compete for the same contract, this is known as *competitive tendering*.

Tender documents will also often ask for important information about potential suppliers. Obtaining this information can be critical in selecting the right supplier. Some of the items requested might include the size of the organisation (staffing, premises, turnover etc.), number of years' experience, details of any major projects undertaken and details of any previous customers who may be willing to provide references.

In general, organisations will invite a number of potential suppliers to compete against one another for the tender. The number of suppliers chosen will depend on several factors, such as the overall size of the project. Choosing too many suppliers can be time consuming and wasteful of company resources; choosing too few does not allow the company to consider all 'good' suppliers.

> **Tender document**
>
> A document used as an invitation to suppliers, asking them to bid for right to supply an organisation's hardware, software and other requirements.

▶ Evaluating proposals

There are three basic criteria for evaluating a supplier's proposals. These are based on technical, cost and support issues.

Technical issues

Technical issues refer to the extent to which the proposal satisfies the hardware/software requirements set out in the tender document or statement of requirements. They include:

◆ *Performance*. It is important to determine whether or not the hardware will perform as specified. The performance of a new computer, for example, may be adequate when used as a standalone machine but may degrade when the machine is used as part of a network.

◆ *Compatibility*. In addition to checking that hardware items actually work properly when used together, it is also important to ensure that equipment is compatible with the company's existing systems, particularly any software packages already in use. Furthermore, compatibility with the organisation's plans for future development is also important, as is the capability to take advantage of changes in technology, for example the introduction of new processors.

Costs

Cost issues describe the overall cost of the project, including installation, ongoing maintenance and factors involving methods of finance.

Consideration must be given to the different costs associated with the purchase of a new computer system. The *initial cost* of a computer system covers the purchase of hardware, installation and training. *Ongoing costs* include insurance and maintenance and are paid over the life of the system. These are known as the total **cost of ownership**. This issue is of great relevance to the manager of end user computing, since it also covers other support costs. It is described in more detail in Chapter 16.

Since most hardware becomes out of date after approximately three years, it is important to consider the initial cost in comparison with the business value of the new system. Simply, the value of the system must be equal to or greater than the costs involved.

Cost of ownership

The cost of ownership describes a range of different expenses incurred by purchasing and maintaining a computer system.

Support issues

These describe the reputation of the supplier in terms of its ability to provide adequate support, training, advice, repairs and maintenance.

Some of the criteria that can be used to evaluate a supplier include the following.

◆ *Training*. Suppliers should be able to offer a range of training courses that cater for mixed abilities and enable users to reach different levels of competence. Training courses should be available at reasonable cost and should take place at a convenient location.

◆ *Maintenance*. Many organisations require suppliers to guarantee that important repairs will be carried out within a fixed time limit. An organisation might require a supplier to guarantee a response time of a few hours for a vital system, but might be willing to allow longer times for less important equipment.

◆ *Implementation*. The extent of the service offered by a supplier may be of importance when purchasing large or complex systems. Instead of placing work with several suppliers, it is often advantageous to select a single supplier which is capable of performing most or all of the work required. The purchase of a network system, for example, will require a number of tasks to be performed, including the installation of network cabling, software configuration, data conversion, training and ongoing maintenance. The use of a single supplier can help ensure that the project runs more smoothly and simplifies the division of responsibilities.

◆ *Backup facilities*. Many suppliers provide a variety of backup and recovery services for their clients. At a basic level, this can involve little more than arranging for copies of important data files to be made on a regular basis. However, many organisations, such as major banks and insurance companies, require more extensive facilities. A **backup or disaster recovery site**, for example, reproduces an organisation's computing facilities in order to provide a measure of protection against a major breakdown. In the event of a breakdown, the organisation's activities can be transferred to the backup site with a minimum of disruption.

▶ Evaluation methods

There are two basic methods for evaluating supplier proposals.

Benchmarking

Benchmarks are the results of a range of tests carried out on hardware/software. As an example, the speed with which a modem can transfer a file might be measured. By carrying out benchmark tests on a range of hardware items, comparisons can be made among specific items of hardware. In turn, this information can be used to select the most appropriate supplier.

Scoring systems

In a **scoring system**, the requirements of the organisation are used to devise a list of criteria for the selection of a given piece of hardware or a supplier. The *relative* importance of each factor is determined by a weighting factor. Each item or supplier is assigned a series of scores based on the criteria in a *weighted ranking table*. The total score for each item or supplier is calculated and used as the basis for final selection. Evaluation methods for information systems are described in Chapter 8.

Backup site

Reproduces an organisation's computing facilities in order to provide a measure of protection against a major breakdown.

Benchmarks

This describes the process of testing the performance of computer equipment. Having carried out a series of benchmark tests, the results can be compared against similar items in order to make the best selection.

Scoring system

A means of selecting hardware, software and suppliers using a point-scoring system.

▶ HARDWARE DEVICES IN THE FUTURE

As a glimpse of the future and to help summarise this chapter, review the case study on retailing – the microchip in the supermarket. This indicates how new and improved input and output technology can change the way we use computer systems.

CASE STUDY: TOPIC AREA

FT

Retailing

Retailing: the microchip in the supermarket

by Peggy Hollinger

It is Saturday morning and Mary Duffy is getting ready to do the weekly grocery shop.

She goes to the kitchen cupboard and has a quick look. The kids have been at the biscuits again and three packets stand half empty. She picks up a pen and runs the point over the bar code on the biscuit packets. The brands are automatically added to an electronic shopping list via the scanner built into the pen.

▶

The list will also include products which, once used, have been thrown into a bin specially adapted to read radio signals emitted by intelligent labels.

She splashed out on the Trashscan just two months ago, but was annoyed to discover there are still some bugs: such as when the baby repeatedly lifts rubbish out of the bin and puts it back in again. Frustrating, but it is simply a matter of adapting the shopping list, which has been downloaded on to the interactive television or the family's personal computer. Both now use a Microsoft-designed Windows navigation system.

Although Mrs Duffy usually has the groceries delivered, this Saturday she decides to shop herself. So after adapting the list on the PC, she sends it to the store. Everything but the fresh fruit and meat will be waiting for her when she gets there. She, like most customers, prefers to choose these items herself.

On the way she remembers at least three things she forgot to put on the list. No problem. The voice-activated personal computer fitted into the dashboard of her car will send an updated list.

Mrs Duffy's shopping trip sounds far-fetched, but all the items she used can be purchased today. The penscanner is available from Symbol Technologies of the UK, interactive television will launch in the UK this year, and leading car manufacturers such as Mercedes and BMW are planning to launch models with voice-activated computer screens.

The only fantasy item might be Trashscan, developed by ICL, the computer services company, two years ago. As Mrs Duffy has discovered, it still has a few bugs and is prohibitively expensive. But it is there and the cost will come down.

Technology is the new battleground of retailing. Through technological innovations such as loyalty cards, which track consumers' shopping habits, retailers hope to get closer to their customers. And it is by building relationships with consumers as individuals, knowing their interests and needs, that retailers hope they will encourage loyalty among the highest spenders.

'The western world is overshopped, planning restrictions are biting and the population is not growing,' says Sion Roberts of ICL. 'The message for retailers is simple: take customers from competitors and hold on to your own. This requires a detailed understanding of customers.'

But retailers have to be careful not to overstep the mark, says David Symonds of Andersen Consulting's Smart Store Europe project. 'Technology that goes into the store must let customers be in control and not the other way round,' he says. 'It takes years to build up trust and loyalty but only a nanosecond to lose it.'

Brian Woolf, author of the book *Customer Specific Marketing*, estimates that the loyal customer is 11 000 times more profitable than the convenience shopper. But customers are a lot less loyal than they were five or 10 years ago.

ICL says that the absence of a single item is enough to tempt 30 per cent of consumers to consider shopping elsewhere. And if that 30 per cent happens to be the third which contributes on average 70 per cent of your sales, the result could be catastrophic.

ICL has launched a virtual store at its Reading headquarters, to display not the headline-grabbing technology of the distant future, but products which are available now and aimed at enhancing customer service. The theory is that by taking the hassle out of the shopping trip with better service, customers will be more loyal.

When Mrs Duffy gets to the supermarket, she could use her loyalty card at one of the interactive screens built into the aisles, to see what customised bargains the store has for her today.

She decides, instead, to insert her microchip loyalty card into her hand-held personal computer, which she attaches to her specially adapted trolley. She bought the PC for a cut price at the supermarket and used her points to get an even greater discount than that offered to less loyal customers.

As she wanders round the store to get ideas for the dinner party tomorrow night, she notices a special offer on compact discs. Pressing the trigger on the keyring given to her by the supermarket chain after she built up 100 000 points, the CD's electronic price tag flashes up a further 10 per cent off just for her.

The price looks good, but just to double check, Mrs Duffy runs the scanner in her mobile phone across the album's bar code. It dials up the bargain hunting search engine on the internet and lists the 10 retailers who sell the CD at the lowest prices. Only one is cheaper than the supermarket's offer, so she decides to buy it.

Passing the clothing aisle, Mrs Duffy notices a silk dress in lime green. But she hates green, so taking the microchip card out of the PC, she slips it into the virtual fitting room kiosk. The screen calls up her picture and she chooses to clothe her image in a red version of the dress.

It is a new technology, even for Mrs Duffy in 2003, but she finds it immensely useful. The card carries the specifications for all the family, as well as for her house, allowing her to try out colour schemes, sofas, or whatever else she is looking for. A virtual mini world in her wallet as she describes it.

The dress ordered, Mrs Duffy now has everything she needs. She has not spent more than 30 minutes shopping and can get home in time for a swim before lunch. Payment is made by typing her password into the hand-held price scanner, which deducts the bill from her supermarket bank account.

Just as she is leaving the store an electronic voice from behind asks her to step aside. Scrubbah, the robot floor cleaner first introduced by the Dutch supermarket group Albert Heijn seven years ago, whizzes past with a polite thank-you. These days even the technology has had to learn manners.

Source: Financial Times, 3 April 1998

Questions

1 Describe the input devices with which Mrs Duffy comes into contact during her trip.

2 Describe the output devices with which Mrs Duffy comes into contact during her trip.

3 Describe the storage devices with which Mrs Duffy comes into contact during her trip.

4 How practical do you think these devices are for everyday use? When do you think we might see them in the shops?

▶ SUMMARY

Figure 3.10 provides a diagrammatic summary of the interrelationship between the different hardware components explained in this chapter.

1 A computer system consists of a number of interrelated components that work together with the aim of converting data into information. In a computer-based information system, processing is carried out electronically, usually with little or no intervention from a human user.

2 Hardware describes the physical components of a computer system. The hardware of a computer system can be said to consist of input devices, memory, central processing unit, output devices and storage devices.

3 Major categories of computers include mainframes, minicomputers and microcomputers.

4 The main hardware components of a computer system are as follows:

◆ Input devices are used to enter data, information or instructions. Typical input devices include mouse, keyboard, optical scanner, trackball, joystick, bar-code reader, touch screen, graphics tablet, video capture card, sound card and digital camera.

◆ Output devices display the results of computer processing. Examples include visual display unit, printer, plotter, microfilm and sound card.

◆ Storage devices are used to store programs, data awaiting processing and the information resulting from computer processing. Examples of secondary storage devices which retain data even when a PC is switched off include floppy disk drives, hard disk drives, CD-ROM, DVD, magnetic tape and digital audio tape. Computer memory provides permanent or temporary storage of data. The contents of volatile memory are lost when the power to the device is switched off. On the other hand, non-volatile memory retains its contents until changed in some way. The two main categories of computer memory are random access memory (RAM) (primary memory) and read-only memory (ROM).

5 A personal computer consists of a number of components, including microprocessor (CPU), graphics card, motherboard and casing. Hardware for networking and communications includes network interface cards, repeaters, hubs, bridges, routers, modems and printer sharers.

6 Tendering is a common method by which organisations select suppliers for hardware. Responses to tender documents are analysed in order to select an appropriate supplier. Other common methods for selecting hardware include benchmarking and scoring systems.

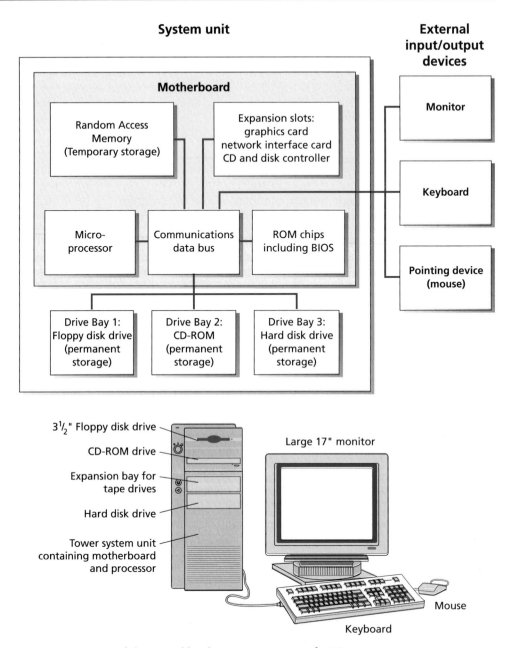

Fig 3.10 Summary of the typical hardware components of a PC

▶ EXERCISES

▶ Self-assessment exercises

1 Which type of printing technology is best suited to the production of the following documents?
   (a) a business letter
   (b) a program listing

(c) a chart or diagram, printed in colour

(d) an internal memorandum

(e) an engineering diagram.

2 Which input device is best suited to the following tasks?

(a) entering the details of bank cheques

(b) entering data from multiple-choice test papers

(c) entering data from labels or price tags

(d) entering a diagram, picture or photograph

(e) entering the text of a letter.

3 Describe some of the main characteristics of mainframes, minicomputers and personal computers.

4 How can network computers help to reduce the cost of ownership?

5 List at least three common pointing devices.

6 What is the meaning of each abbreviation and acronym listed below? Provide a brief explanation for each of the items listed.

(a) MICR   (f) OCR
(b) RAM   (g) COM
(c) BIOS   (h) PDA
(d) CD-ROM   (i) ROM
(e) CPU   (j) DVD

▶ Discussion questions

1 Will network computers make personal computers obsolete? Using relevant examples, make a case for one side of this argument.

2 You intend to purchase a personal computer to help with your studies. You have decided to create a weighted ranking table to help you choose a suitable system. What criteria should be used for selection and how should each item be weighted?

3 Despite still being functional, an obsolete computer system is of little value to a business organisation. Organisations should continually upgrade or replace systems in order to keep abreast of changes in technology. Make a case in favour of or against this argument.

▶ Essay questions

1 IBM's AS/400 series of minicomputers is one of the most popular systems available and is used by an extremely wide range of organisations. Conduct any research necessary to complete the following tasks:

(a) Provide an overview of the costs associated with the purchase and installation of a mini-computer system such as the AS/400.

(b) Provide an overview of the variety of applications for which the AS/400 system is used. Offer relevant examples where necessary.

(c) In your opinion, what features of the AS/400 range may have contributed to its popularity?

2 You have been asked to produce a guide to buying a personal computer for a fellow student on your course. The student has a budget for hardware of £1500. Avoiding technical terms as far as possible, produce a guide that addresses the following:

(a) Produce a detailed specification for a personal computer system. You should describe the system in terms of the input, output and storage devices needed. Justify any choices made and explain any technical terms used.

(b) Select at least two computer systems that meet the requirements specified. Evaluate each of the systems in turn and make a recommendation to the student.

(c) Provide a realistic costing for the chosen system. Ensure that any ongoing costs are included.

3 Voice recognition systems have begun to gain popularity with both business and home users. However, such systems still suffer from a number of limitations that restrict their over-all effectiveness. Conduct any research necessary to produce a report that addresses the following tasks:

(a) Provide an overview of voice recognition technology and describe how such systems operate.

(b) Provide a balanced view of the advantages, disadvantages, strengths and limitations of voice recognition systems.

(c) Explain some of the uses to which voice recognition systems can be put. Pay particular attention to the business applications for this technology.

▶ Examination questions

1 A small business organisation wishes to purchase a number of personal computers and has issued a tender document to several suppliers. Using relevant examples, provide an overview of the technical, support and cost issues that should be considered when evaluating supplier proposals.

2 A modern supermarket will make extensive use of technology to support all of its activities. Considering an organisation such as ASDA or Sainsbury's, describe the range of input, output, storage and processing devices that might be used within a typical branch. For each item iden-tified, provide a brief description of its purpose and any benefits gained from its use.

3 Considering a typical IBM-compatible personal computer, you are required to:

(a) Identify the main components of a personal computer system. For each item identified, provide a brief description of its purpose.

(b) Using relevant examples, describe some of the methods that can be used to assess the performance and quality of key components.

(c) In addition to the initial cost of the personal computer itself, a number of other expenses are likely to be incurred. Using relevant examples, provide an overview of these additional costs.

▶ References

Cookson, C. (1998) 'Technology: the all-in-one hi-tech revolution', *Financial Times*, 21 February.

Foremski, T. (1998) 'The mouse: small but very useful rodent', *Financial Times*, 24 April.

Hollinger, P. (1998) 'Retailing: the microchip in the supermarket', *Financial Times*, 3 April.

▶ Further reading

Botto, F. (1992) *Multimedia, CD-ROM and Compact Disc: a Guide for Users and Developers*, Wilmslow, Sigma Press.

Clifton, H. and Sutcliffe, A. (1994) *Business Information Systems*, 5th edition, Prentice Hall, Hemel Hempstead.
> Chapter 2 deals with a variety of topics including computer architecture, office automation and telecommunications. Chapter 3 considers computer hardware, with particular emphasis on input and output devices.

Emmerson, B. (1995) 'PC communications: computer telephony adds new efficiencies to small and home offices', *BYTE*, November.

Fuori, W. and Gioia, L. (1995) *Computers and Information Systems*, Prentice-Hall, Englewood Cliffs, NJ.
> Chapter 2 provides a comparatively generalised view of computer hardware. Chapter 3 provides extensive coverage of input and output devices. Chapter 5 deals with processing by computer and microprocessors.

Hurwicz, M. (1997) 'Superfast peripherals', *BYTE*, March – USB, FireWire, Fibre Channel and SSA.

Hussain, K. and Hussain, D. (1995) *Information Systems for Business*, Prentice Hall, Hemel Hempstead.
> Chapter 4 describes computer hardware in terms of the major functions of input, output, processing and storage. Chapter 5 deals with networks and communications.

Knight, J. (1995) *Personal Computing for Business*, Financial Times Pitman Publishing, London.
> Chapter 15 provides practical guidelines for selecting a personal computer.

Laudon, K. and Laudon, J. (1995) *Management Information Systems: Organization and Technology*, 3rd edition, Macmillan, Upper Saddle River, NJ.
> Chapter 6 deals with a variety of topics including microprocessors, storage devices and output devices.

Microsoft Press (1997) *Microsoft Press Computer Dictionary*, Redmond, WA.

O'Brien, J. (1993) *Management Information Systems: a Managerial End User Perspective*, 2nd edition, Richard D. Irwin, Boston, USA.
> Part 2 (Chapters 4–7) provides an alternative overview of fundamental Information Technology concepts. Chapter 4 provides a relatively traditional overview of computer hardware.

▶ Web references

http://www.whatis.com   This site is effectively a glossary giving succinct definitions of terms relating to hardware and software.

http://www.tomshardware.com   Despite the name, this site is a detailed, well-laid-out site giving detailed reviews on areas such as RAM and hard disks.

http://www.howstuffworks.com and http://howitworks.com   These sites contain explanations, with animations of how hardware, software and other technologies function.

http://www.pcmech.com   Clear description of hardware components with diagrams and pictures.

http://www.hardwarecentral.com   Further descriptions of hardware components.

Software

INTRODUCTION

This chapter builds on the concepts introduced in Chapter 3 and provides an overview of the common software packages used in business. The material addresses two separate themes: a review of the features common to a range of modern software applications, and the way in which software can be used to support the business activities of an organisation. The final section of the chapter focuses on programming languages as a means of creating software applications.

The topics covered are intended to give readers an understanding of:

◆ categories of computer software;

◆ categories of applications software;

◆ the features found within a range of common software packages;

◆ the ways in which computer software can support the activities of a business organisation.

The chapter focuses on general-purpose applications software such as wordprocessors and spreadsheets, which is sometimes referred to as productivity software. Software for specific business applications is described in detail in Chapter 6.

It is intended that this chapter provides readers with an *overview* of the available features in different categories of applications software, not a user guide! Readers will, of course, obtain experience of the use of the software through practical experience. Jane Knight's book *Personal Computing for Business* provides an excellent guide to the available features and how to use business applications such as wordprocessors and spreadsheets.

▶ Links to other chapters

Chapter 3	describes the computer hardware required to enable the efficient and productive use of computer software.
Chapter 5	provides detailed coverage of computer networks.
Chapter 6	describes functional information systems and applications-specific software, providing a view of how computer hardware and software can be used to support specific business activities.
Chapter 8	contains a review of techniques for evaluating information systems from different suppliers. These techniques can also be applied to types of software described in this chapter and Chapter 6.
Chapter 11	considers data analysis for relational database management systems.
Chapter 12	describes design techniques for relational database management systems.
Chapter 17	contains detailed material related to the Internet and the use of corporate intranets.

▶ SOFTWARE

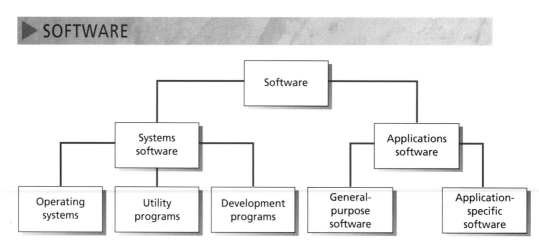

Fig 4.1 Categories of computer software

Software

A series of detailed instructions that control the operation of a computer system. Software exists as programs that are developed by computer programmers.

Systems software

This form of software manages and controls the operation of the computer system as it performs tasks on behalf of the user.

Operating system (OS)

Software that interacts with the hardware of the computer in order to manage and direct the computer's resources.

Software can be defined as a series of detailed instructions that control the operation of a computer system. Software exists as *programs* that are developed by computer *programmers*.

There are two main categories of software: systems software and applications software, illustated in Fig 4.1.

▶ Systems software

Systems software manages and controls the operation of the computer system as it performs tasks on behalf of the user. Systems software consists of three basic categories: operating systems, development programs and utility programs.

Operating systems

The **operating system** interacts with the hardware of the computer by monitoring and sending instructions to manage and direct the computer's resources. Figure 4.2 indicates the relationship between the operating system, the hardware and other types of software for a typical computer system. The components can be considered as different layers, with information being passed between each layer as the user interacts with the application. The operating system functions as an intermediary between the functions the user needs to perform, for example with a spreadsheet, and how these translate to and from the hardware in the form of responding to mouse clicks and displaying information on the screen. For most operating systems such as Microsoft DOS there is a text-based operating system and a GUI (graphical user interface) operating environment such as Windows 3.1. In Windows 95 and Windows 98 the text-based operating system is normally not evident but remains present.

The basic functions of the operating system include allocating and managing system resources, scheduling the use of resources and monitoring the activities of the computer system. Examples of these functions include the following:

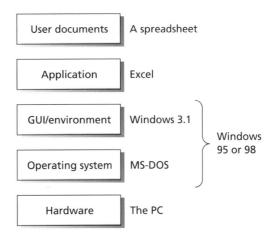

Fig 4.2 Diagram showing the relationships between the different types of software and hardware

- Control access to storage devices, for example disk drives.

- Coordinate and control peripheral devices, for example printers.

- Allow users to input data and issue instructions, for example by allowing data to be entered via keyboard.

- Coordinate and control the operation of programs, for example by scheduling processor time.

- Manage the computer's memory.

- Perform file management, for example by allowing users to create or delete files.

- Deal with errors, for example by displaying a message to the user if a fault is detected within a hardware component.

Operating systems can be described as text based or graphical. A text-based operating system uses a **command line interpreter (CLI)** to accept instructions from the user. Instructions are entered as brief statements via the keyboard, for example COPY C:\AUTOEXEC.BAT A: would instruct the operating system to copy a file called AUTOEXEC.BAT from the computer's hard disk drive to a floppy disk. MS-DOS (Microsoft Disk Operating System) is an example of an operating system that uses a CLI.

An operating system based around a **graphical user interface (GUI)** allows users to enter instructions using a mouse via menus and icons. The term **WIMP (windows, icons, mouse and pull-down menus)** is often used to describe this kind of environment. Examples of operating systems using a GUI are OS/2, GEM, Windows 95 and Windows 98.

Operating systems for PCs such as Windows 98 are normally 'bundled' when a computer is purchased. This is also true for some applications software.

Operating environments describe programs intended to simplify the way in which users work with the operating system. Early versions of Windows, for example, provided a graphical user interface that removed the need for users to work with the more complex aspects of MS-DOS.

Network software (NOS)

In general, the **network operating system (NOS)** used by an organisation will provide the majority of facilities required to support workgroup computing. For example, the NOS will allow a network manager to define a group of users as belonging to a particular workgroup. Some of the typical services provided by the NOS include:

- A centralised storage space can be created on the network system for the exclusive use of workgroup members.

- The security features of the NOS can be used to restrict access to documents and other data by those outside of the workgroup.

- The workgroup can be given network privileges that allow individual members access to resources and facilities that are not normally available to others. For example, many organisations with only limited Internet and e-mail facilities restrict access to key members of staff.

NOS are now often integrated with operating systems such as Microsoft Windows NT and UNIX, but Novell Netware is still commonly used on PC-based networks in conjunction with Microsoft Windows.

Network operating software is described in more detail in Chapter 5.

Command line interpreter (CLI)

Passes instructions from a user to a computer program as instructions from a user in the form of brief statements entered via the keyboard.

Graphical user interface (GUI)

Provides a means for a user to control a computer program using a mouse to issue instructions using menus and icons.

Windows, icons, mouse and pull-down menus (WIMP)

This is often used to describe a GUI environment.

Operating environment

Programs intended to simplify the way in which users work with the operating system. Early versions of *Windows*, for example, provided a graphical user interface that removed the need for users to work with the more complex aspects of MS-DOS.

Network operating system (NOS)

This describes the software needed to operate and manage a network system.

Utility programs

Utility programs provide a range of tools that support the operation and management of a computer system. Programs that monitor system performance or provide security controls are examples of utility programs.

Development programs

Development programs allow users to develop their own software in order to carry out processing tasks. Different types of programming languages are reviewed in the 'focus on' section at the end of this chapter.

▶ Applications software

Applications software can be defined as a set of programs that enable users to perform specific information processing activities. Applications software can be divided into two broad categories: general purpose and application specific.

General purpose

General-purpose applications describe programs that can be used to carry out a wide range of common tasks. A wordprocessor, for example, is capable of producing a variety of documents that are suitable for many different purposes. This type of application is often referred to as **productivity software**, since it helps improve an individual's efficiency.

The next sections in this chapter will describe the use of some general-purpose applications software in more detail for each of the following business tasks carried out in an office:

◆ *Document production and graphics software.* This involves the creation of various internal and external documents, including letters, reports, invoices, notes and minutes of meetings. Various types of software can be used to support these activities, including text editors, wordprocessors and desktop publishing packages.

◆ *Processing numerical information using spreadsheets.* All organisations require the means to store, organise and analyse numerical data. The spreadsheet program represents the most common means of carrying out these tasks.

◆ *Storage and retrieval of information using databases.* All organisations require the means to store, organise and retrieve information. Electronic database packages represent the most common means of carrying out these tasks.

◆ *Multimedia software.* Multimedia involves the user interacting with a computer using media such as text, sound, animation or video. Its main business applications are computer-based training and customer service in retail applications.

◆ *Sending and retrieving information using the Internet and intranets.* This describes activities involving internal and external communications. Significant examples include electronic mail (e-mail) and the use of Web browsers to find information on the World Wide Web.

Application specific

Application-specific software describes programs intended to serve a specific purpose or carry out a clearly defined information processing task. A program designed to carry out payroll processing would be an example of an application-specific program.

Application-specific packages such as software for accounting or marketing are described in Chapter 6.

▶ DOCUMENT PRODUCTION SOFTWARE

One of the most common activities in a business organisation is the production of documents for internal or external use. Internal documents, such as an inter-office memo, are generally used to support communications within an organisation. External documents, such as a sales brochure, are generally used to support communications with customers, suppliers and other agencies.

The requirements for internal and external documents are often very different. The appearance of an internal document, for example, is seldom important, since the document's main purpose is to convey information quickly and efficiently. However, since the appearance of an external document can have an impact on an organisation's image and reputation, a great deal of emphasis is often placed on its presentation.

Internal documents can include inter-office memos, reports and summaries, such as minutes of meetings. External documents can include invoices, sales brochures and correspondence. Using these examples, identify some of the other characteristics of internal and external documents. Are any of the characteristics you have identified common to both internal and external documents?

ACTIVITY

A modern view of document production sees technology as used in three basic ways: wordprocessing, desktop publishing and document management.

◆ *Wordprocessing* is concerned with entering or editing text, with emphasis on the *content* of the document. Wordprocessing allows the production of simple documents but gives limited control over layout.

◆ *Desktop publishing* is concerned with the overall *appearance* of documents, placing a great deal of emphasis on features that provided control over the layout and presentation of a document.

◆ *Document management* involves documents such as company procedures which are circulated to a large number of people in an organisation. It is an important business application which is described in more detail in Chapter 6.

The distinctions between different categories of document production software have become blurred. A modern wordprocessor, for example, will often have much of the functionality of a desktop publishing program. Similarly, many desktop publishing packages now have sophisticated text editing features and no longer rely on users preparing the different elements of a document in advance.

The case study on the paperless office indicates how document management techniques have been integrated with Internet technologies to be applied in company intranets. Note that the paperless office is a concept that has been suggested for more than 20 years, but it has failed to materialise because most individuals still appear to be more comfortable working with paper-based documents.

CASE STUDY: TOPIC AREA

FT

The paperless office

Corporate networks: private intranets help demolish mountains of paperwork

by Geoffrey Nairn

Microsoft's generous employee stock option scheme is famous throughout the IT industry – but administering it has caused real headaches. The company has thus turned to intranet technology to take the paperwork out of the scheme as part of a broader initiative to reduce paper consumption by 40 per cent across a range of internal operations.

Practising what they preach, IT companies are leading the field in intranet use, but other industries are also finding that intranets – corporate networks based on off-the-shelf internet technologies – can provide real benefits, particularly when focused on paper-intensive processes.

The insurance industry, for example, depends heavily on documents and while the retail insurance market has embraced IT to improve customer service with call centres and web sites, the rest of the industry has been slower to change.

'One of the things that dominates this business is paper,' says Alex Gargolinski, group marketing director with McLarens Toplis, a leading UK loss adjuster. 'The way we circulate information at the moment is cumbersome as it depends on people having an efficient filing system.'

McLarens Toplis has the task of inspecting the damage suffered in a particular insurance claim and deciding a financial value for the loss by reference to standard databases of property values and so forth. The company receives up to 200 000 insurance claims a year from retail insurance companies, each of which has its own sets of procedures that McLarens Toplis must follow.

A claim may involve 20 or 30 transactions before it is fully settled and lengthy reports have to be produced. The company has been running the same bespoke claims settlement software for 12 years on a Unix system.

The program, called Portfolio, has been through 14 releases and Mr Gargolinski jokingly compares it to the ageing and accident-prone Mir space station.

'Portfolio has worked well, but we wanted something that could run our business faster and allow us to add more applications,' he says. The company thus turned to intranet technology to implement a new claims and data management solution, which is currently being tested in one of the company's 100 offices.

The new system will provide up-to-the minute 24-hour access to greater detail on the claims process for the loss adjuster's 1500 staff and will be introduced in all its offices, starting from May. The new system will deal with every stage of the loss adjusting process, enabling McLarens Toplis to offer a faster, more efficient service to its customers.

For example, the reporting procedures for adjusters have been largely automated so that they can rapidly assemble the loss report – which largely consists of standard phrases – by clicking 'drop down' boxes in their web browser.

Technicians can access the report before it is complete over the intranet, allowing them to get an earlier start in calculating the scale of damages suffered. One important benefit is the ability to access documents in another office.

'Before, it was not possible to access an adjuster's files in a different office but now staff can sign on to files anywhere in the country,' says Mr Gargolinski.

Another benefit is that insurance companies can be quickly provided with summary reports on claims. 'Previously, we had to consolidate information manually and it took a lot of time,' he says.

Ultimately, McLarens Toplis would like to give the insurance companies access to the claims information via an extranet, so that they can see the progress of each claim.

Starting in May, the Unix systems will be replaced by 90 Microsoft SQL Server databases running the Windows NT operating system, with central support provided by clusters of Digital Alpha servers.

Installation is expected to be completed by September 1998 at which point 'Portfolio will be retired gracefully'.

Mr Gargolinski says it is too early to measure benefits – 'but there are bound to be cost-savings because of the savings in our loss adjusters' time'.

The project is so far running to schedule and on budget. 'Maybe that is due to our strict financial training,' he says, with a smile.

If paperwork is a necessary evil in many businesses, in the technical documentation industry, paper has traditionally been its lifeblood. Nevertheless, that situation is beginning to change with new technology enabling electronic publication to become a viable alternative to paper-based manuals.

Heitmann SAC is a UK technical documentation company specialising in manuals for systems in the automotive, defence, telecommunications and energy fields. When GEC Alsthom, the engineering company, put out tenders for a project to build commuter trains for a new railway link in Sweden, Heitmann SAC saw it as the ideal opportunity to improve on existing on-line manuals by creating a new intranet-based web manual.

Paper-based documentation would typically run to 12 heavy 500-page manuals for such a system and GEC Alsthom was keen to put the documentation on an intranet to reduce its engineers' reliance on paper manuals, which are costly to print and difficult to keep up-to-date.

One particular problem with online documentation is accurately reproducing detailed technical drawings and schematics. Antony Bartlett, technical manager at Heitmann SAC, says this challenge has been overcome using a 'plug in' that allows a standard web browser to view computer-aided design files, produced using the AutoCad package.

The site has been developed using Microsoft FrontPage authoring software with sophisticated search engines that can find a phrase or even a particular drawing.

A 'red lining' tool allows users to comment on the information on the site – when published information seems incorrect, for example – and this feedback is passed to the web site administrator, who is the only person allowed to make changes.

The project will finish this summer and GEC Alsthom expects to achieve cost savings of between 2 per cent and 5 per cent in maintenance activities and depot management by having the manual on the intranet.

Source: Financial Times, 18 March 1998

Questions

1 Referring to the case study, describe some of the problems faced by organisations using 'paper-intensive processes'.

2 What benefits have the companies described in the case study gained by turning towards technology?

3 The case study refers to a number of software applications that can be described as office automation systems. List the applications described in the case study and identify the categories to which they belong.

4 What is the 'paperless office'? Can office automation systems genuinely achieve such a goal?

▶ Wordprocessing

A **wordprocessor** provides the ability to enter, edit, store and print text. In addition, wordprocessing packages allow users to alter the layout of documents and often provide a variety of formatting tools.

Wordprocessor

Provides the ability to enter, edit, store and print text and layout different elements of a document.

Overview

Early wordprocessors produced effects, such as bold or italics, by inserting special codes into the text. This made it difficult to see how the finished document would appear until it was printed. One of the most important features of a modern wordprocessor is the provision of a so-called WYSIWYG display (pronounced 'whizzywig'), where What You See Is What You Get.

▶ Features of a wordprocessor

The sheer range of features provided by a typical wordprocessing program is a reflection of the diverse requirements of modern business organisations (*see* for example Fig 4.3). Many features are underutilised because many packages are so 'feature rich' that it is difficult to be aware of all the features that are available. This section is intended to give an overview of potential features.

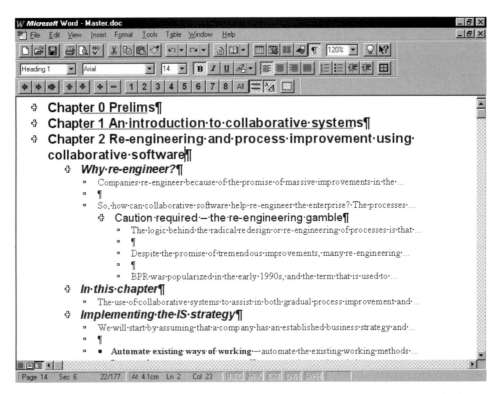

Fig 4.3 Microsoft's Word for Windows 95 showing the use of a master document which can be used to manage large reports, or in this case a book. The user can select which different heading levels are displayed

Editing

The process of entering or correcting text is known as editing.

Word wrap

In a wordprocessor, as users type text and move towards the end of a line, the program automatically moves to the beginning of a new line.

Justification

In a wordprocessor, the alignment of text with the left and right margins can be controlled by specifying the justification.

Editing text

All wordprocessing programs allow users to enter, edit, copy, move and delete text. The process of entering or correcting text is known as **editing**.

Word wrap

As users type text and move towards the end of a line, the program automatically moves to the beginning of a new line. The spacing between words and characters is also adjusted so that the appearance of the text is improved.

Justification

A wordprocessor allows the user to control *text alignment,* that is, the layout of the margins on the page. Text that is flush with the left margin but has a ragged right margin is known as *left justified* (sometimes also known as *unjustified*). Text that is flush with the right margin but has a ragged left margin is known as *right justified*. Text that is flush with both margins is *fully justified* (often referred to as *full justification*).

> This paragraph is *left justified*. Note that the text is flush with the *left* margin but has a ragged *right* margin. In contrast, the text in this book is *fully justified*.

> This paragraph is *right justified*. Note that the text is flush with the *right* margin but has a ragged *left* margin. In contrast, the text in this book is *fully justified*.

Block operations

All wordprocessing packages allow users to manipulate blocks of text in a number of ways. Once a block of text has been marked, it can be moved, deleted, copied or formatted. One powerful feature of a wordprocessor is the ability to *cut and paste* blocks of text. A marked block can be removed from a document (cut) but held in the computer's memory. One or more copies can then be pasted into a new position in the same document. This can be used to move whole sections of a document from one place to another or to make several copies of a block of text.

Search and replace

Programs such as Word for Windows allow the user to search an entire document for a specific word or phrase. Once the text has been located, it can be deleted or replaced with something else. Searches can be *conditional,* where the word or phrase must appear exactly as specified, or *unconditional,* where any occurrence of the text will be found. For example, a conditional search for 'London' would locate only those occurrences where London began with a capital letter. On the other hand, an unconditional search would locate every occurrence of London, even if it began with a lower case 'l'. Text can be replaced *globally,* where every occurrence of the specified text is replaced automatically, or with *confirmation,* where the user is asked whether or not to replace each piece of text as it is found.

Type/font styles

Most wordprocessing packages allow users to specify the style, font and point size of text. *Style* refers to text effects such as bold, italics and underlined. The typeface used in a document is referred to as the **font**. The size of the characters used is referred to as the *point size*. A typical size for the text in the body of a document is 12 points. Titles and headlines tend to be set at between 24 and 36 points. It is worth noting that there are 72 points to a vertical inch.

Font

The typeface used in a document is referred to as the font. The size of the characters used is referred to as the point size.

> This text uses the Arial font, which is similar to the Helvetica used for newspaper headlines.

> `This text uses the Courier font found on typewriters.`

Page layout

The wordprocessor allows users to specify the layout of the pages in the document. This is done by setting the sizes of the top, bottom, left and right margins of the page and by selecting the size of the paper that will be used.

Headers and footers

A header is a piece of text that will appear at the top of every page of the document. Headers are typically used to print a chapter heading or title at the top of each page. A footer appears at the bottom of each page. Footers are typically used to print page numbers at the bottom of every page. Headers and footers can be seen in many publications, including newspapers, books and magazines.

Mailmerge

Packages such as Word for Windows allow sets of personalised letters to be produced by merging information taken from a separate data file with a standard ('form') document. For example, a database could be used to hold the names and addresses of a number of business clients. A standard letter could be produced with blanks where the name and address of the client are meant to appear. When the mailmerge process begins, each name and address would be inserted in the document and printed. Mailmerge is not restricted to names and addresses; any kind of data can be merged into a standard document. This allows mailmerge to be used for applications ranging from the production of invoices to personalised newsletters.

Import/export of data

Many wordprocessors allow documents to be saved in a number of formats. This allows users to produce a document, save it to disk and then load it into, for example, a desktop publishing program for further enhancement. Similarly, many programs allow users to load documents created using other packages without losing any special formatting commands. For example, Word for Windows can save data in a format compatible with packages such as WordPerfect and Ami Pro. Similarly, Word for Windows can also load documents from these packages. In all cases, the layout of the document is preserved, complete with text effects and fonts. The process of saving a file in a format compatible with another package is known as **exporting**. The process of loading a file created with another package is known as **importing**. The ability to import and export data is not limited to wordprocessing documents – most packages are able to share data with a variety of other programs, including spreadsheets and databases.

Exporting

The process of saving a file in a format compatible with another software package is known as exporting.

Importing

The process of loading a file created with another package is known as importing.

Graphics and tables

Most modern wordprocessing packages allow users to incorporate graphics and tables of figures into their documents. As an example, Word for Windows can import pictures from a range of sources. Some of the most common picture file formats are GIF, TIFF, PIC, GEM and PCX.

Columns

Many packages allow users to generate columns within their documents. These can be used in a number of ways, including producing a newspaper-like layout for newsletters and other documents.

Spellchecker and thesaurus

Most packages allow users to check the spelling of every word in a document. When an error is detected, the program can suggest alternative spellings and make any corrections automatically. The thesaurus function found in most modern packages can be used to suggest synonyms and antonyms for a highlighted word or phrase.

Multiple windows

The majority of packages allow users to work on more than one document at a time. Each document is displayed in a window on the screen and the user can move between windows using the mouse or by pressing special keys. This allows users to carry out a number of useful activities, such as copying a block of text from one document to another, without having to open and then close the documents in order.

Macros

A **macro** is a sequence of instructions that can be used to automate complex or repetitive tasks. Macros can emulate a sequence of keys pressed on the keyboard or can be programmed to carry out more complicated processes. For example, consider the phrase: 'I look forward to hearing from you.' The key presses required to produce this sentence could be stored in a macro and recalled using a single key, reducing the amount of typing needed to be done by the user. Modern packages often feature entire programming languages that can be used to handle extremely complex tasks. Word for Windows, for example, contains Visual Basic for Applications – a complete implementation of the Visual Basic programming language which is available in all the Microsoft Office programs described in this chapter.

Macro

A sequence of instructions that can be used to automate complex or repetitive tasks.

Autocorrect

Many recent wordprocessing programs offer an autocorrect feature that attempts to correct spellings as the user types. Common misspellings such as entering 'teh' instead of 'the' are detected and changed automatically by the program. This feature can also be used to expand abbreviations into their correct form, for example a user might enter 'ys' and allow the autocorrect feature to expand this into 'Yours sincerely'.

Tabs

Special markers, known as tabs, can be set so that users can move to specific columns in the document with the use of the TAB key. This allows tables of numbers or columns of text to be created quickly and easily.

Print preview

The **print preview** feature displays a document exactly as it will be printed, enabling users to check and correct the document without making unnecessary printouts.

Print preview

The print preview feature displays a document exactly as it will be printed, enabling users to check and correct the document without making unnecessary printouts.

Drawing and graphics

Many packages provide a variety of drawing tools, allowing users to add lines, shapes or graphic files to their documents.

Tables

Many packages allow users to produce tables containing a specified number of rows and columns. Tables created in this way often provide some of the functionality of a spreadsheet program, although this is often limited.

▶ GRAPHICS PACKAGES

Traditionally, graphics packages have been divided into three basic categories: drawing (or paint) packages, design packages and presentation software. However, it has become common to include two other categories of graphics software: diagramming packages and photo-editing programs.

▶ Drawing programs

Paint programs

Serve the same purpose as a sketch pad or easel and enable users to produce drawings using a variety of different techniques.

Paint programs serve the same purpose as a sketch pad or easel and enable users to produce drawings using a variety of different techniques.

A combination of tools allows users to create drawings made up of freehand lines and regular shapes. Among the tools available are the following:

- ◆ A palette of drawing tools can be used to mimic the effects of drawing with different materials, including pens, spray cans, brushes and charcoal.
- ◆ Selection tools can be used to copy, erase or resize sections of a drawing.
- ◆ Painting tools let users apply shading and colours to areas or shapes.
- ◆ Text tools allow users to add text to a drawing. Users can specify the typeface, size, colour and style of the text.
- ◆ Special tools provide a range of sophisticated features. A colour replacement tool, for example, can be used to change one colour for another within a specific section of the image.

Bitmap image

Small dots (pixels) arranged in a grid to form an image. The finer the grid, the higher the resolution of the image.

Vector image

Image made up of lines and shapes, rather than individual dots. Mathematical formulae determine the size, position and colour of the shapes that make up a given image.

One of the distinctions that can be made between drawing packages involves the type of image that can be produced. In general, paint packages produce bitmap images while drawing packages create vector images.

A **bitmap image** is made of up of small dots (*pixels*) arranged in a grid. The finer the grid, the higher the *resolution* of the image. A newspaper photograph, for example, might offer a resolution of 100 dpi, while a photograph reproduced in a textbook might have a resolution of 1200 dpi. Although bitmap images are suited to certain types of image, such as photographs, they suffer from two main disadvantages. First, the overall quality of the image cannot be maintained if it is resized. Second, bitmap images can require a great deal of storage space, depending on the number of colours contained in the image and its resolution.

Vector graphics are made up of shapes, rather than individual dots. Mathematical formulae determine the size, position and colour of the shapes that make up a given image. Since far less information needs to be recorded about the contents of a vector image, they require comparatively little storage space. In addition, vector images can be resized with great precision and without loss of quality. Since it can be difficult to produce highly detailed images, vector graphics are often used for diagrams and relatively simple drawings.

Diagramming software

The need to produce a wide variety of business-related charts and diagrams has resulted in the emergence of numerous diagramming packages. Aimed at business users, the majority of these packages assume little technical knowledge and rely on menus, icons and palettes of tools in order to construct diagrams.

In order to produce a chart or diagram, users select shapes and symbols from a library of pre-prepared materials. The libraries used by these programs are often called *stencils* or *stamps*, reflecting the idea that users are not expected to draw each required shape manually. Having arranged a number of shapes in order, users can then add text, lines and other elements to complete the diagram.

Diagramming programs such as Visio tend to offer a relatively limited number of stencils from which users can select. However, all packages cater for a range of common business diagrams. A typical package will provide stencils that enable users to produce flow charts, office layouts, organisational charts, network diagrams, project timelines and block diagrams.

Photo-editing software

The growth in the use of optical scanners and video capture devices has resulted in a need for tools that can be used to manipulate photographic images. **Photo-editing packages** enable users to capture, view and edit scanned images.

Although the majority of photo-editing programs provide many of the features found in paint packages, most provide more sophisticated tools intended especially for use with scanned images. Two typical examples include:

◆ Capture features enable a user to acquire images directly from an optical scanner attached to the computer system, removing the need for the user to control two separate programs.

◆ **Filters** can be used to apply a range of special effects to an image. For example, they can sharpen a blurred image or alter brightness and contrast.

▶ PROCESSING NUMERICAL INFORMATION USING SPREADSHEETS

Spreadsheet packages are used for a variety of different purposes. Some examples include the following:

◆ *Financial applications*. Common applications include the production of cashflow forecasts, accounting statements, invoices, purchase orders, sales orders, quotations, managing expenses and project management.

◆ *Modelling and simulation*. In general, **modelling** involves creating a numerical representation of an *existing* situation or set of circumstances, while simulation involves *predicting* new situations or circumstances. In both cases, a model is pro-

---

Photo-editing packages

Photo-editing packages enable users to capture, view and edit scanned images.

Filter

In a spreadsheet or database, a filter can be used to remove data from the screen temporarily. Filters do not alter or delete data but simply hide any unwanted items.

Spreadsheet

A program designed to store and manipulate values, numbers and text in an efficient and *useful* way.

Modelling

Modelling involves creating a numerical representation of an *existing* situation or set of circumstances, while simulation involves *predicting* new situations or circumstances.

duced that provides a numerical representation of the situation or circumstances being studied. A cashflow forecast, for example, is a numerical model that attempts to predict the financial state of a business over a given period. Once a model has been constructed, it can be manipulated so that users can see how changes to parts of the model influence the whole. As an example, a user might change the level of sales in a cashflow forecast to see how overall profit and loss would be affected. This ability to manipulate models is often referred to as **what if? analysis** and is considered one of the spreadsheet's most powerful features.

What if? analysis

This describes the ability to see the predicted effect of a change made to a numerical model.

◆ *Statistical analysis.* All spreadsheet programs provide a wide range of tools that can be used to analyse numerical information in a number of ways. Two simple examples illustrate the range of facilities available.

Goal seeking

In a spreadsheet, goal seeking describes a way of automatically changing the values in a formula until a desired result is achieved.

   (a) **Goal seeking** describes a way of automatically changing the values in a formula until a desired result is achieved. As an example, a user might enter a formula that calculates the profit made on sales of various items. Goal seeking could then be used to calculate the level of sales needed to produce a specified level of profit.

   (b) Many programs offer a descriptive statistics feature that can be used to generate various summaries relating to a block of data. The spreadsheet performs a simple analysis and automatically creates a set of descriptive statistics. The results are presented in table format and include values such as maximum, minimum, mean, average, standard deviation, sum, count and variance.

> The term *formulas* is used to distinguish between traditional mathematical formulae and those used by spreadsheets.

All modern spreadsheet programs originate from the original Visicalc program launched in 1979 by Bricklin, Frankston and Fylstra. The program was originally created as a means of carrying out repetitive calculations for the Harvard Business School. Although created for the Apple II computer system, the program rapidly gained in popularity and became one of the best-selling software products of all time.

   The interest shown in the Visicalc package prompted the Lotus Development Corporation to develop a version of the program for IBM-compatible computer systems. The release of Lotus 1-2-3 in 1982 is often credited as being responsible for the widespread acceptance of personal computers in business.

> Both Visicalc and Lotus 1-2-3 are often held to be the first *killer apps*. This term describes a program that offers a service so valuable that the purchase of a computer system is warranted in order to be able to use the software. More recently, the same term has begun to be used to describe an application that is superior to all similar products.

▶ Spreadsheet overview

We can describe a spreadsheet as a program designed to store and manipulate values, numbers and text in an efficient and *useful* way.

The work area in a spreadsheet program is called the **worksheet**. A worksheet is a grid made up of cells. Each cell is uniquely identifiable by its horizontal (row) and vertical (column) coordinates. A cell can contain text, numbers or a formula that relates to information held in another cell. For example, a cell could contain any of these pieces of data:

```
127
'Cashflow Forecast'
+A12 (a reference to another cell)
```

Figure 4.4 shows how a worksheet is organised. Cell coordinates are traditionally given in the form of column–row, for example the very first cell in a worksheet is A1.

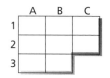

Fig 4.4 Organisation of a worksheet

One of the most important features of a spreadsheet is its ability to update the entire worksheet each time a change is made. For example, imagine that the cell at A1 contains information based on the contents of the cell at B1. Changing the contents of B1 causes the computer to update the worksheet, placing a new value in A1 automatically.

Another important feature of the spreadsheet is that users can manipulate the contents of cells using functions and formulas. A spreadsheet **function** is a built-in command that carries out a calculation or action automatically. As an example, in Microsoft Excel, the PI function returns the value of Pi to 15 decimal places. A **formula** is a calculation that is entered by the user and performed automatically by the spreadsheet program. Formulas can be used to manipulate the values held in cells by referring to their coordinates. As example, if A1 holds 3 and A2 holds 4, then placing the formula =A1+A2 in A3 can be interpreted as 'take whatever is in A1 (in this case, 3), add it to the contents of A2 (in this case, 4) and place the result in A3' – giving a result of 7 in A3.

▶ Features of a spreadsheet

Automatic formulas

Many programs allow users to enter part of a formula, completing the rest of it automatically. The *autosum* feature, for example, is found in a number of different programs and automates the generation of totals. In order to use this feature, the user selects the cells to be added and then chooses the autosum feature. The program then generates the formula needed to add the numbers together automatically.

Formatting

All spreadsheet programs provide a variety of tools that can be used to enhance the appearance of worksheets. A built-in range of *numeric formats*, for example, allows users to display values as currency or to a fixed number of decimal places. Users may

Worksheet

An individual area or sheet for entering data in a spreadsheet program.

Function

In a spreadsheet, a function is a built-in command that carries out a calculation or action automatically.

Formula

In a spreadsheet, a formula is a calculation that is entered by the user and performed automatically by the spreadsheet program.

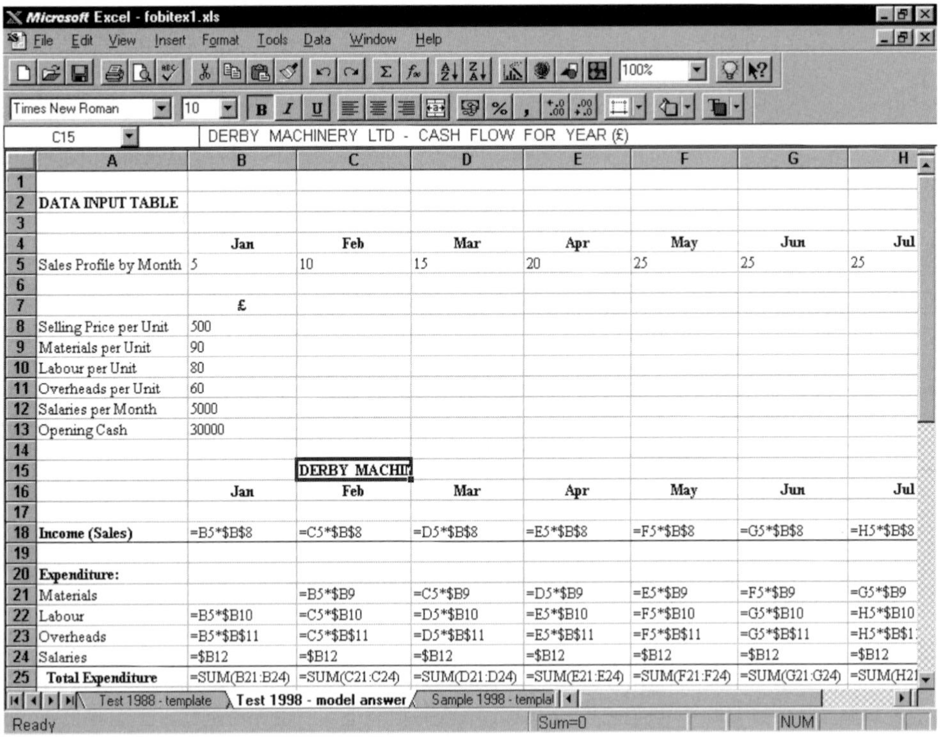

	A	B	C	D	E	F	G	H
1								
2	**DATA INPUT TABLE**							
3								
4		Jan	Feb	Mar	Apr	May	Jun	Jul
5	Sales Profile by Month	5	10	15	20	25	25	25
6								
7		£						
8	Selling Price per Unit	500						
9	Materials per Unit	90						
10	Labour per Unit	80						
11	Overheads per Unit	60						
12	Salaries per Month	5000						
13	Opening Cash	30000						
14								
15			DERBY MACHI					
16		Jan	Feb	Mar	Apr	May	Jun	Jul
17								
18	Income (Sales)	=B5*B8	=C5*B8	=D5*B8	=E5*B8	=F5*B8	=G5*B8	=H5*B8
19								
20	Expenditure:							
21	Materials		=B5*$B9	=C5*$B9	=D5*$B9	=E5*$B9	=F5*$B9	=G5*$B9
22	Labour	=B5*$B10	=C5*$B10	=D5*$B10	=E5*$B10	=F5*$B10	=G5*$B10	=H5*$B10
23	Overheads	=B5*B11	=C5*B11	=D5*B11	=E5*B11	=F5*B11	=G5*B11	=H5*B1
24	Salaries	=$B12	=$B12	=$B12	=$B12	=$B12	=$B12	=$B12
25	**Total Expenditure**	=SUM(B21:B24)	=SUM(C21:C24)	=SUM(D21:D24)	=SUM(E21:E24)	=SUM(F21:F24)	=SUM(G21:G24)	=SUM(H21

Fig 4.5 Microsoft's Excel for Windows 95 showing a worksheet being used for cashflow analysis

also adjust the width and height of rows and columns, use different typefaces and make use of shading, colour and lines.

Other functions can be used to assist users in working with the data held in the worksheet. *Cell protection*, for example, can be used to lock cells so that data cannot be accidentally altered or deleted. Users can also add **annotations** to individual cells in the worksheet so that notes or instructions can be made to appear when the cell is accessed.

Annotation

A note or message that can be attached to a document. Voice annotations are spoken messages that can be embedded within a document.

Functions

All spreadsheet programs contain a number of built-in functions that can be used to simplify the construction of a worksheet. Functions are normally divided into a number of different categories so that users can locate them easily. Some typical categories include:

◆ *Date and time.* These allow users to perform calculations dealing with dates, for example a user might wish to calculate the number of working days between two dates.

◆ *Database.* Typical functions include the ability to sort rows or columns into a specified order.

◆ *Financial.* These provide a variety of financial and accounting functions, for example the ability to calculate loan repayments based on factors such as the interest rate and the amount borrowed.

◆ *Logical*. These allow users to create formulas that perform calculations according to whether or not specific conditions have been met. As an example, a worksheet used to create invoices might generate a different total according to whether or not the customer is required to pay VAT.

◆ *Lookup and reference*. These provide a range of functions that can be used to create more sophisticated worksheets. As an example, a user might wish to create a formula that looks up a value from a table.

◆ *Mathematics*. These include mathematical and trigonometry functions, such as factorials, exponential numbers and square roots.

◆ *Statistical*. These allow users to produce statistical information, such as frequency distributions.

◆ *Text*. These provide various methods for manipulating text, such as converting a piece of text into a value.

Charts

An integral feature of spreadsheet programs is the ability to create a variety of different charts based on the data held in the worksheet. Modern programs provide a range of different chart types, including bar charts, pie charts, line graphs and area charts. Most packages also offer a range of specialist chart types in order to cater for users with particular requirements. A good example is the *combination chart* which can be used to show two or more sets of data in a single diagram.

The charts created by spreadsheet programs are often described as *live* or *dynamic*, meaning that if the data in the worksheet is altered, the chart will be updated automatically in order to reflect the changes made.

Workbooks and multiple worksheets

Early spreadsheet programs allowed users to work with only a single worksheet at a time. In order to make use of information stored on a different worksheet, special commands were needed to access the disk file containing the data required. This often resulted in applications that were unnecessarily complex, slow to operate and prone to errors.

Modern packages enable a user to organise groups of worksheets within a single **workbook**. In addition, several workbooks can be opened at the same time. This facility allows users to carry out large or complex tasks more easily and quickly. Two examples may help to make this clearer:

Workbook

In a spreadsheet program, this describes a collection of worksheets.

◆ An organisation wishes to analyse monthly sales data. The data for each month can be stored on separate worksheets within a single workbook. Although the data held on each worksheet can be analysed separately, users can also employ special formulas and functions to examine the workbook as a whole. The total sales for the year, for example, could be obtained by using a formula that adds together the monthly totals taken from each worksheet in the workbook.

◆ An organisation uses two workbooks to store data on sales and expenses respectively. The data from both workbooks can be combined within a third workbook to produce information related to profitability. Only the third workbook needs to be open in order to carry out any calculations required, but all three workbooks can be open simultaneously if required.

Views and scenarios

An important feature of modern spreadsheet packages is the ability to create *views* on the data held in a worksheet or workbook. The use of views enables users to focus on specific sections of the worksheet by displaying data in a predetermined way. As an example, a manager might wish to view only the summary information held in a worksheet. In order to cater for this, a view could be created that displays only the required information, hiding all other data from sight.

As mentioned earlier, once a worksheet has been constructed it can be used to perform **what if? analysis** by changing some of the values stored. The task of keeping track of the changes made to the worksheet can be simplified by making use of *scenarios*. The user begins by constructing the basic model to be used for the analysis and stores it under a given name. The worksheet can then be altered repeatedly until the user obtains results he or she considers important. Each time a new set of results is obtained, the user can save these by storing the worksheet as a new scenario. The worksheet can then be altered again or the original data can be restored to begin a new analysis. After the analysis has been completed, the user can access any of the scenarios stored and compare these to the original worksheet.

> The sheer size of the workspace available to a spreadsheet user means that functions providing quick and efficient navigation are essential.
>
> Although the capacity of a spreadsheet program will be limited by available memory and storage space, a typical workbook can contain 256 worksheets and a typical worksheet can contain 16 384 rows by 256 columns. This means that a worksheet can contain up to 4 194 304 cells and that a workbook can contain up to 1 073 741 824 cells.

Database functions

The way in which data is organised within a worksheet, by rows and columns, means that all spreadsheet programs are capable of being used to perform simple database operations. Although spreadsheet programs are clearly unable to offer the functionality of a specialised database program, all programs offer the basic functions of queries, filters and sorting.

Data analysis tools

The majority of modern spreadsheet packages contain a number of tools designed to automate common data analysis tasks. These tools remove the need for users to memorise complex formulae and perform all calculations automatically.

Examples of common data analysis tools include analysis of variance, correlation, covariance, T-test, Z-test and regression.

Import/export of data

Spreadsheet programs are able to deal with data drawn from a variety of different sources. In many cases, files produced by other packages can be imported directly into a worksheet with no loss of data.

Occasionally, it may be necessary to convert data into a form that can be used by the spreadsheet program. A common file format used to transfer data between spreadsheet packages and other programs is known as **comma separated (or delimited) values (CSV)**. A CSV file is a simple text file made up of items enclosed within quotation marks and separated by commas. The use of commas and quotation marks enables the spreadsheet program to identify individual items.

> ## ▶ STORAGE AND RETRIEVAL OF INFORMATION USING DATABASES

Prior to the introduction of electronic database systems, almost all of the information an organisation needed to store was organised using manual filing systems. Typical methods included filing cabinets and card index records. Although manual filing systems are still used widely, electronic databases are also commonplace and are considered to provide a number of important benefits to business organisations. Since databases are so important in storing data for information systems, the analysis and design need to create databases are covered extensively in Chapters 11 and 12.

We can understand something more about electronic databases by first considering the disadvantages of manual filing systems. Some of the most common disadvantages include:

- The way in which information is organised largely determines the uses to which it can be put. For example, if a list of customers is stored in alphabetical order by name, it is difficult to view customers by location.

- It is often difficult to retrieve specific items of information quickly.

- It might not be possible to add, amend or delete the information held in a manual record without creating a new copy of the record.

- It is sometimes difficult to classify information so that it can be stored in the correct location. This can make it difficult to locate specific items at a later date.

- If the information is used regularly by number of different individuals or departments, multiple copies of manual files may need to be maintained. This alone can introduce a number of difficulties arising from the duplication of data. Some examples include:
  (a) Extra expense is incurred in terms of the additional storage space and labour power required to maintain files.
  (b) Changes made to one set of files may not be reflected in all copies. This can mean that some files contain outdated information, while others may contain new or additional details.
  (c) If a standardised filing system is used, this may not suit the needs of all users. On the other hand, the use of different filing systems creates problems in maintaining files and locating information.

The use of electronic databases can remove all of the difficulties outlined above. An electronic database offers the following advantages:

- A database will allow users to organise information in a variety of different ways. The initial order in which records are placed is often unimportant, as information can be reorganised quickly and easily. This allows an organisation to maximise its usage of the information it holds, through techniques such as **data mining**.

Comma separated values (CSV)

A simple text file made up of items enclosed within quotation marks and separated by commas in order to assist conversion between programs.

Data mining

This involves searching organisational databases in order to uncover hidden patterns or relationships in groups of data.

◆ The powerful search facilities provided by electronic database programs can be used to locate and retrieve information many thousands of times faster than by manual methods.

◆ An electronic database provides facilities for users to add, amend or delete records as required. Additional features simplify data entry and assist in managing the information held. As an example, adding groups of similar records can be simplified by making multiple copies of an existing entry. Each copy can then be edited as needed. This removes the need for the data entry operator to enter the details of each record in full.

◆ Sophisticated indexing features mean that the same basic information can be stored under a number of different categories. This provides great flexibility and allows users to locate, retrieve and organise information as needed.

◆ Databases used throughout a company are usually accessed by many different users across a network system. Some of the advantages of this approach include:

(a) Since the unnecessary duplication of information is minimised, the costs involved in maintaining records are reduced.

(b) Any changes made to the information held in the database are reflected to all users, ensuring consistency at all times.

(c) Although information is held in a structured manner, the database software will normally provide sufficient flexibility to meet the different requirements of individual users and departments.

Database

A collection of related information stored in an organised way so that specific items can be selected and retrieved quickly.

A **database** can be defined as a collection of related information. The information held in the database is stored in an organised way so that specific items can be selected and retrieved quickly. A database need not involve the use of technology – examples of manual databases include telephone directories, address books, diaries and card index files.

Database management system (DBMS)

One or more computer programs that allow users to enter, store, organise, manipulate and retrieve data from a database.

▶ An overview of the types of database

The information held in an electronic database is accessed via a **database management system (DBMS)**. A DBMS can be defined as one or more computer programs that allow users to enter, store, organise, manipulate and retrieve data from a database. For many users, the terms **database** and **database management system** are interchangeable, although the definitions given here demonstrate that this is not the case.

Field

The data in an electronic database is organised by fields and records. A field is a single item of information, such as a name or a quantity.

The data in an electronic database is organised by fields and records. A **field** is a single item of information, such as a name or a quantity. A **record** is a collection of *related* fields and a **table** is a collection of related records. Two examples can be used to illustrate these terms:

Record

In an electronic database, a record is a collection of *related* fields.

◆ An address book typically stores three items of information: a name, an address and a telephone number. Each of these types of information can be thought of as a **field**. Since the name, address and telephone number of a specific person are related to one another, these constitute a **record**. Together, all of the entries in the address book form a **table** and in this case the **database** has a single table.

Table

In an electronic database, data is organised within structures known as tables. A table is a collection of many records.

◆ Consider a filing cabinet used to store information on sales or orders. The cabinet itself is the **database**, since it holds *all* the information on sales. Each drawer represents a **table** in which related information is stored and each document inside the cabinet is a **record**, since each holds details on a particular sales order. The details of the order, such as the customer who has placed it and its value, can be thought of as a **field**.

In order to identify a specific item of information within a database, all records must contain an identifier, normally called the *key field*. The **record key** usually takes the form of an number or code and will be different for each record in the database.

The design of databases is a common business activity. How to approach design is covered in much more detail in Chapter 12, with an example of how a Microsoft Access database can be used for storing sales orders. The role of key fields in managing relational databases is also covered in more detail at this point.

Record key

Identifies a specific record within a database, usually takes the form of a number or code and will be different for each record in the database.

A number of national databases store information on every adult in the country. Each of these systems uses a unique identifier to distinguish between specific individuals. As an example, all UK adults have a unique National Insurance number that can be used to track pension contributions and entitlement to welfare benefits. Other unique identifiers used by national databases include driving licence reference number, passport number and NHS number.

Imagine you are going to catalogue a collection of books. What fields would you use to hold information on each book?

ACTIVITY

▶ Approaches to file processing

Three basic approaches have become popular for the design of electronic databases: file processing, database management systems and relational database management systems. The following provides a brief overview of each of these approaches.

File processing

Early data processing systems were based around numerous files containing large amounts of data related to daily business transactions. As a result, many organisations found themselves in a position where they held large amounts of valuable data but were unable to maximise their use of it. A major problem stemmed from the fact that the data held was often stored in different formats, for example completely different structures might be used to store details of sales and purchases. In order to make use of this data, it was usually necessary to create specialised computer programs, often at great expense.

Some of the characteristics of this *file processing* approach included:

◆ Data was held separately from the programs that made use of it.
◆ Programs were limited in functionality as they were often created to perform a single task – carrying out new tasks often resulted in a need to create a completely new program.

- Since a relatively high degree of technical knowledge was needed to create and operate programs, non-technical users often found it difficult to access the information they needed.

- The process of developing new programs each time new requirements needed to be addressed was considered expensive, time consuming and inefficient.

Flat file database

A self-contained database that only contains one type of record – or table – and cannot access data held in other database files.

This type of database is sometimes described as having a **flat file** structure. A flat file database can be said to be self-contained since it contains only one type of record – or table – and cannot access data held in other database files.

Flat file databases are suited to relatively small applications where the data held does not need to be cross-referenced with other database files. Since the structure of a flat file database tends to be quite simple, data can be processed very quickly.

An address book would be a typical application for a flat file database.

Free-form database

Free-form database

Allows users to store information in the form of unstructured notes or passages of text. Information is organised and retrieved by using categories or key words.

A **free-form database** allows users to store information in the form of brief notes or passages of text. Each item held can be placed within a category or assigned one or more key words. Information is organised and retrieved by using categories or key words.

A modern variation on free-form databases comes in hypertext databases. In a **hypertext database** information is stored as series of objects and can consist of text, graphics, numerical data and multimedia data. Any object can be linked to any other, allowing users to store disparate information in an organised manner.

Hypertext database

Information is stored as series of objects that can consist of text, graphics, numerical data and multimedia data. Objects are linked allowing users to store disparate information in an organised manner.

Both free-form and hypertext databases provide great flexibility in terms of the type and content of the information stored. However, they are unsuitable for certain applications, for example those involving complex data from across an organisation.

A good example of a free-form database is in the help files found within most software packages. An example of a hypertext database could be the pages available via the World Wide Web.

Database management systems

The introduction of database management systems altered the way in which organisations managed their data resources. Although data was still held separately from the programs that made use of it, this new approach offered greater flexibility while reducing development and operating costs. Some of the major characteristics of the **database management system** (DBMS) approach included:

- Programs included a range of general-purpose tools and utilities for producing reports or extracting data. This meant that comparatively little development was needed in order to undertake new tasks.

- The availability of general-purpose tools enabled non-technical users to access data. Users were able to analyse data, extract records and produce reports with little support from technical staff.

- The use of DBMS encouraged organisations to introduce standards for developing and operating their databases. As an example, many organisations developed standards governing the structure of any new data files created.

We will now review the main types of database management system.

Relational database management systems

The popularity of the **relational database management system (RDBMS)** approach grew from a need to share data resources across the entire organisation. In the past, it had been normal to concentrate resources in a small number of specific areas. For example, an organisation's accounting and stock-control functions often dealt with the largest number of business transactions and were seen as having the greatest need for the organisation's information technology resources. In the same way, these functions were also seen as having the greatest need for the organisation's data resources. However, as companies aimed to become more efficient and reduce costs, it became essential to ensure the widest possible access to organisational data resources. In addition, organisations were also beginning to receive increased demands for information from users and managers.

The RDBMS approach placed great emphasis on the careful design of new systems for two main reasons. First, in order to satisfy the diverse needs of many different users, it was important to allow information to be combined from numerous sources. Second, since information might be used in a wide variety of ways, it was necessary to ensure that all systems offered high levels of flexibility. As an example, greater care had to be taken in designing the structure of tables used to store data, since a poorly designed table would result in an inability to meet the needs of some users.

The RDBMS approach can be seen as an extension of the DBMS approach, with the additional benefits to be gained by sharing data across an organisation and the ability to combine data from several different sources. As an example, it is possible to reduce stockholding costs by linking together an organisation's production and stock-control functions. Such an approach would allow stock levels to be adjusted continuously by examining production levels. In this way, stocks of raw materials can be increased or decreased according to actual usage. In the same way, production scheduling might be improved by inspecting stock levels at regular intervals.

Relational databases enable data to be stored within a number of different tables. They are the most widely used type of database. Separate record designs can be used to store data dealing with different subjects. For example, a database used for stock control might use separate record designs to store information concerning items stocked, re-order levels and supplier details.

The tables within a relational database can be linked together using one or more record keys. As mentioned earlier, all database records must contain a unique record key that can be used to identify a specific record. In a relational database, this is often called the **primary key**. However, records can also contain other keys to help locate data stored in another table. The record keys contained in each table can be used to establish one or more **relationships** between tables. By using record keys in combination – called a **compound key** – it is possible to retrieve data from several tables at once.

Figure 4.6 illustrates how records can be linked together using record keys. The diagram illustrates a simple relational database containing two tables: one holding details of an employee's pay, the other holding personal information, such as the employee's address. The database is to be used to generate payslips for all employees. In order to accomplish this, the DBMS would carry out the following actions for each record in the Personal Details table:

1 Locate a record within the Personal Details table. The unique primary key can be used to identify a specific employee.

2 Extract any information required from the Personal Details record, such as the employee's name and address.

Relational database management system (RDBMS)

An extension of a DBMS and allows data to be combined from a variety of sources.

Relational databases

Data is stored within a number of different tables with each dealing with different subjects that are related (linked) using key fields.

Primary key

The tables within a relational database can be linked together using one or more record keys. All records must contain a unique record key called the primary key.

Relationship

In a relational database, data can be combined from several different sources by defining relationships between tables.

Compound key

In a relational database, it is possible to retrieve data from several tables at once by using record keys in combination, often known as a compound key.

Fig 4.6 An example of how key fields are used to link information from different database tables

3 The secondary key identifies a unique record in the Pay Details table. Since the secondary key in the Personal Details table matches the primary key in the Pay Details table, the DBMS can locate the specific record required.

4 The information required from the Pay Details table is extracted and the payslip is printed.

A more detailed explanation of database terminology and applications based on a case study is provided in Chapter 12.

Object-oriented databases

Object-oriented database

The database is made up of objects combining data structures with functions needed to manipulate the object or the data it holds.

An **object-oriented** approach to database design employs the concept of reusable objects in order to develop sophisticated or complex applications. An *object* combines data structures with any functions needed to manipulate the object or the data it holds. As an example, an object called Employee might be created to store details of staff. The object would contain a data structure that allowed basic details such as name, address, age etc. to be stored. In addition, the object would also contain facilities that allow various actions to be performed, such as changing an employee's address.

This object-oriented approach offers several important advantages:

◆ Since objects are self-contained, they are easy to manage, for example changes can be made to an individual object without necessarily altering any other part of the system.

◆ New objects can be created quickly and easily from existing ones. Continuing with the example given previously, the Employee object might be used as the basis for a new object entitled Manager. Only minor changes would be needed to complete the new object, since it would already share all of the features of Employee.

◆ Objects can be copied or transferred into new systems with little difficulty. Since the object already contains any functions needed to make use of it, it can be used immediately within the new system.

Object-oriented approaches to design are described in Chapter 12 and the adoption rate of these techniques is described in Chapter 19.

Network and hierarchical models of databases

Mention of these types of databases is included for completeness. These are alternatives to the relational model which were its competitors in the 1980s. In the 1990s, the vast majority of business applications are based on RDBMS, but with object-oriented techniques being used increasingly. Owing to the widespread usage of RDBMS, the coverage of data analysis and database design in Chapters 11 and 12 is directed to RDBMS. The network or hierarchical model may be used for some high-performance applications such as data warehouses (although many of these are based on RDBMS). The interested reader can read an overview of the network and hierarchical database in Curtis (1998).

▶ Features of relational database management systems

All database programs enable users to create and edit tables or record structures. In addition, all packages allow users to enter, modify, delete, sort and extract records. The majority of packages also enable users to print data in a variety of different formats. Microsoft Access is the best-known database used on the PC (Fig 4.7). Others include Borland Paradox, Lotus Approach, Microsoft FoxPro and dBase. These databases are mainly for personal or departmental use by a small number of users. Where databases are used by a large number of users, they are hosted on a mainframe or on a UNIX or Microsoft Windows NT server. These databases for 'mission critical' applications include Oracle, Informix, Sybase, Microsoft SQL Server and IBM DB2.

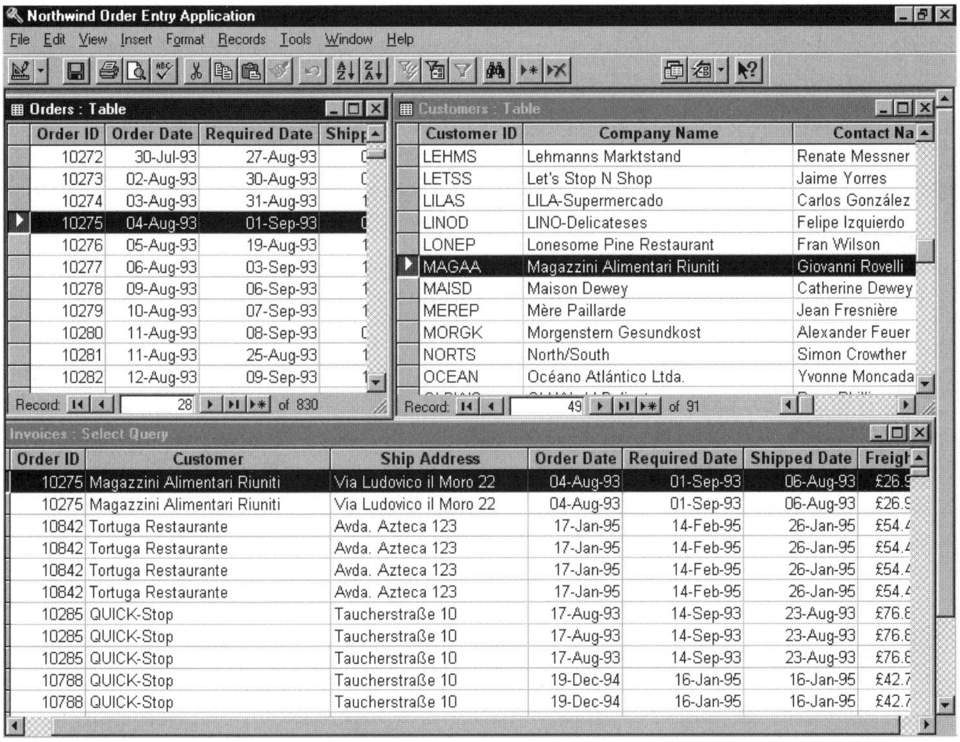

Fig 4.7 Microsoft's Access for Windows 95 showing a query (bottom window) which is formed out of the two highlighted records from the two tables in the Windows above

Multiple tables

The majority of modern database programs support the creation of relational databases containing several linked tables. Although tables can be used in isolation, they can also be used to combine together information drawn from one or more other tables.

Many programs also provide the ability to link tables together automatically. Microsoft Access, for example, provides an interactive facility to analyse one or more tables and create any required relationships.

Forms

Data entry form

In an electronic database, a data entry form provides a convenient means of viewing, entering, editing and deleting records.

All major database programs enable users to create and modify **data entry forms**. A data entry form provides a convenient means of viewing, entering, editing and deleting records.

Indexes

Index

Stores information concerning the order of the records in the database. The index lists the locations of records but does not alter the actual order of the database.

An **index** stores information concerning the order of the records in the database. The index lists the locations of records but does not alter the actual order of the database. This can be made clearer by using the index of a book as a simple analogy: the index allows users to find a specific piece of information quickly and easily, regardless of how the material in the book is organised.

Indexes are commonly used to increase the speed with which records can be located or sorted. Multiple indexes can be created so that the records in the database can be sorted in a variety of ways.

Security

All modern database programs provide a range of sophisticated security features. Examples of some of the most common features available include:

- ◆ *Encryption*. Data can be encoded so that it appears meaningless until decoded. Passwords provide control over the encryption and decryption process.
- ◆ *Recovery*. Many programs contain tools that allow damaged database files to be repaired. In the event that a file cannot be repaired, additional tools may be available that allow users to retrieve as much data as possible from the damaged file.
- ◆ *Passwords*. Access to specific files or tables can be restricted through the use of passwords. Several passwords can be used to limit what parts of the database different users can view or alter. As an example, a data entry clerk might be assigned a password that prevents changes being made to the structure of a table or the format of a report.

Reports

All major database packages allow users to generate a wide variety of reports. Many programs are capable of creating simple reports automatically. In addition, many programs allow users to perform calculations and other actions as the report is produced. This enables additional information, such as subtotals, to be calculated and included in the report whenever required.

Queries

A **query** enables a user to locate, sort, update or extract records from the database. Users design a query by specifying the conditions that must be met in order for a record to be selected. In many programs, the creation of a query is an interactive process, where users respond to a series of questions in order to generate the required design.

There are two basic types of query – selection queries and update queries:

◆ A *selection query* can be used to locate and display any records meeting a set of specified conditions. None of the data held in the database is altered; any records not meeting the conditions set are simply hidden from view temporarily.

◆ An *update query* can be used to modify records in a variety of ways. Records are selected for alteration according to a set of conditions specified by the user. Common actions performed by update queries include:
  (a) updating values held in fields, for example by carrying out a calculation;
  (b) deleting any records no longer required;
  (c) appending new records to the database;
  (d) generating new tables containing selected records or summary information.

It is worth noting that the majority of database programs make use of a special structured query language (SQL) in order to create queries. SQL is described in more detail below.

Query
Extracts data according to a set of conditions specified by the user.

Filters

A **filter** allows users to view the information held in a database in a variety of ways. Filters can be used to sort data into different orders, display only selected fields or display only selected records. In many ways, filters can be thought of as combining some of the features of both indexes and selection queries. It is worth noting that filters do not alter any of the data held in the database.

Structured query language

Structured query language (SQL) provides a standardised method for retrieving information from databases. Although traditionally used to manage large databases held on mainframes and minicomputers, it has become a widely used and popular tool for personal computer database packages. One of the reasons for this popularity is that SQL supports multi-user databases that operate across network systems.

SQL programs are created by producing a series of statements containing special key words. The example below shows a simple SQL query designed to search the Student Record table and display records for students with a last name of 'Jones':

Structured query language (SQL)
A form of programming language that provides a standardised method for retrieving information from databases.

```
SELECT DISTINCTROW [Student Record].[Last Name]
FROM [Student Record]
WHERE (((([Student Record].[Last Name])='Jones'));
```

Users are often unaware that queries created using the interactive design tools provided by many modern database packages are converted into SQL programs before being executed. In Microsoft Access, for example, a mouse is used to design a query on the screen. However, the query is translated into equivalent SQL statements before it is executed.

Macros

In common with many other types of application software, most modern database packages include a macro language or a programming tool that can be used to handle extremely complex tasks.

Data analysis tools

The majority of modern database programs contain a number of tools designed to automate common data analysis tasks. The ability to generate charts and graphs, for example, is a common feature.

Import/export of data

Database programs are able to deal with data drawn from a variety of different sources. In many cases, files produced by other packages can be imported directly into a database with no loss of data. In addition, some programs are capable of producing table designs automatically, based on the content of the file being imported.

The ability of a database program to export data in a variety of formats is used extensively in a variety of applications. Mailmerge operations, for example, often make use of data drawn from customer records held in an organisation's sales database.

▶ MULTIMEDIA SOFTWARE

Multimedia is the term used to describe software which (together with appropriate hardware) can interact with the user through different techniques such as text, sound, animation or video. The type of hardware required to support multimedia was briefly described in Chapter 3. It includes sound and video cards and capture using microphones and video cameras.

Multimedia software is most common in home computers, but also has business applications. These include training courses and product promotions which are distributed on CD-ROM. Multimedia or computer-based training (CBT) have been demonstrated to be more effective than simple presentations since studies show that we remember:

◆ 10 per cent of what we see;
◆ 30 per cent of what we see and hear;
◆ 50 per cent of what we see, hear and do (through interaction or role plays).

Multimedia functions can be incorporated into both general-purpose software and application-specific software. For example, a wordprocessor or e-mail can incorporate multimedia elements such as a commentary or video from a manager who has reviewed a document.

An example of a business application of multimedia is the CBT system used by Andersen consulting in the US. This company has developed an interactive training package which provides the consultant with different challenges according to the particular client. Video images and audio of the client describing their requirements are shown and the trainee has to use these and supporting documentation to recommend the best solution. CBT is also used in more hazardous environments such as for rail or construction site workers to reduce the cost and risk of such training.

Information kiosks are used for retail applications in shops or supermarkets. They usually consist of a PC mounted in a stand which is accessed by a touch screen and will often make use of multimedia. They have the appeal that they can be consulted when sales staff are not available, and they are used to provide information rather than giving a 'hard sell'. It remains to be seen whether they become widely used, since many customers may still prefer to speak to a member of staff. It is estimated that there are over 100 000 kiosks in the US. The mini case study on information kiosks illustrates several instances where information kiosks are used by retailers in Europe.

Information kiosks

A multimedia system usually integrated with a touch screen to provide information for retail or community applications.

Information kiosks – a retail application for multimedia

MINI CASE

This case study reviews various information kiosks to indicate the range of applications for which they can be used.

Argos – product purchase

Catalogue retailer Argos uses information kiosks to enable a customer to select any product from its catalogue and then pay using a credit or debit card. This gives customers the opportunity to avoid queues if they are comfortable with the technology.

IKEA – product design and selection

IKEA use a multimedia kiosk to give customers the opportunity to select a fabric for furniture and then view how it will appear on the particular item. The chosen combination can then be ordered.

B & Q – product selection

B & Q has trialled information kiosks in its DIY stores in Wandsworth and Cambridge. The idea of these kiosks is to give customers advice and guide them through selection of products with a range of options. The kiosks feature power drills from Black and Decker and Bosch and involve a dialogue with the customer in which they are asked what they will be using the tool for. In about ten seconds the system will display pictures, features and pricing of the recommended tool from each manufacturer.

Daewoo use kiosks to sell cars without salespeople!

Daewoo uses kiosks in car showrooms (see Fig 4.8) and encourages customers to use them rather than talking to salespeople, since research has shown that customers can be afraid of car salespeople. In common with the other applications described above, the kiosks provide information on products which are matched against a customer's requirements. Daewoo has committed to the kiosks to the extent that it has at least one in every outlet and between 200 000 and 300 000 customers using them each year.

Financial services

Banks such as NatWest and Lloyds use kiosks to give assistance on accounts available or share investment decisions.

▶

Fig 4.8 Daewoo's information kiosk

BT Touchpoint scheme

This is a different type of scheme in that the kiosks are not devoted to a single retailer. BT locates them in shopping centres and then customers can use them for a range of services, such as information on 'what's on', where to eat and holiday prices.

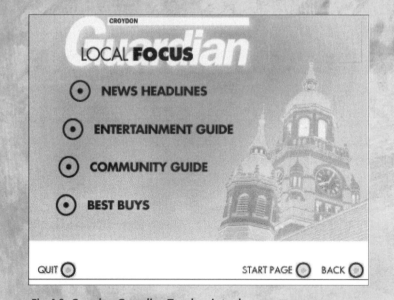

Fig 4.9 *Croydon Guardian* Touchpoint scheme

The new media magazine *Revolution* (July 1997) offers the following advice about designing kiosks:

1 Keep it simple – no one will use a complex kiosk.
2 Put as little information on each screen as you can. Make it as clear and readable as possible.

3 Make it quick. The process of selecting and selling a product shouldn't take too many stages and the machine should respond quickly to commands.

4 Think about positioning. It should be easy to find and in a place where people are likely to spend some time.

5 Make it obvious what the kiosk is, otherwise people will ignore it.

6 Make it logical. Customers will need their hands held. Don't expect them to show any initiative.

7 Make sure you get the height right. You don't want to alienate potential customers.

These guidelines, in particular 1–3, are relevant to the design of many information systems. Aspects of user interface design are described in Chapter 12.

▶ SENDING AND RETRIEVING INFORMATION USING THE INTERNET AND INTRANETS

This section introduces the importance of the Internet to modern business organisations. Additionally, we consider briefly how software is used to access the Internet. Business applications of the Internet are considered in detail in Chapter 17.

Development of the Internet and intranets

The simplest way in which the **Internet** can be described is as a global network system made up of smaller systems. Estimates suggest that it is composed of approximately 2.5 million individual network systems distributed across the world. Since the Internet is growing at a tremendous rate, it is difficult to offer more accurate estimates of how many users and systems there are. Some estimates place the total number of users at only 20 million, while others suggest that there are more than 200 million users in the US and Europe alone.

Internet

A global network system made up of many smaller systems.

The Internet was conceived by the Defense Advanced Research Projects Agency (DARPA), a US intelligence organisation, in 1969. It began to achieve its current form in 1987, growing from systems developed by DARPA and the National Science Foundation (NSF).

A variety of tools are available to exchange information over the Internet, of which e-mail is the best known. The others, such as telnet, gopher and WAIS, are summarised in Chapter 17. They are not used sufficiently widely by business people or students to warrant further study. Although the Internet has existed for around 30 years, it is only since 1989 when the Web browser was developed that the use of the Internet by business has grown dramatically. Given this, in this chapter and in Chapter 17 we focus on the use of the World Wide Web by businesses. A more recent development using the tools and techniques of the Internet is the *intranet*, which can be thought of as an internal, private company Internet used for sharing information. Business applications of intranets are also described in Chapter 17.

▶ The World Wide Web and Web browsers

World Wide Web (WWW)

Interlinked documents on the Internet made up of pages containing text, graphics and other elements.

The **World Wide Web**, or Web for short, is a medium for publishing information on the Internet in an easy-to-use form. If we take the analogy of television, then the Internet would be equivalent to the broadcasting equipment such as masts and transmitters, and the World Wide Web is equivalent to the content of different TV programmes. The medium is based on a standard document format known as **HTML (Hypertext Markup Language)**, which can be thought of as similar to a wordprocessing format. It is significant since it offers hyperlinks which allow users to move readily from one document to another – the process known as 'surfing'.

Hypertext Markup Language (HTML)

WWW pages are mainly created by producing documents containing HTML commands that are special tags (or codes) to control how the WWW page will appear when displayed in a Web browser.

The World Wide Web (WWW) is accessed using a **Web browser**. Since they have been designed for ease of use, WWW pages feature sections of text that include hypertext links and graphics. Figure 17.4 on page 602 shows the Microsoft Explorer Web browser being used to access a search engine to find information. The other main browser is Netscape Navigator.

▶ Features of a Web browser

Hypertext

Web browser

A Web browser program enables users to navigate through the information available and display any pages of interest.

The interface used by a Web browser makes use of hypertext linking techniques. A **hypertext** is a document that includes highlighted words or phrases. These highlighted sections represent links to other documents or sections of the same document. Clicking the mouse above one of these links causes it to be activated. A link can be used to move to another document, transfer a file, view a section of video, listen to a sound file or carry out a number of other actions.

Hypertext

Hypertext is highlighted words or phrases that represent links to other documents activated by clicking the mouse.

As users move through a hypertext document, their actions are recorded automatically by the program being used. Users can access the history of their movements and jump backwards or forwards through all of the documents they have viewed.

Navigation

Navigating

The act of moving from one section of the Internet to another.

All Web browsers provide users with a variety of tools that enable them to **navigate** through often complex collections of WWW pages. Some of the most common tools include:

- *Navigation buttons*. These enable users to move backwards and forwards through the list of pages previously viewed. Additional command buttons include:
  - **(a)** *Stop*. This cancels the action currently being taken.
  - **(b)** *Home*. Users are able to designate a specific WWW page as a 'home page' that is displayed each time the Web browser runs. The user can return to the page at any time by using the appropriate command button.

Search engine

Key words are entered to locate information stored on the Internet.

  - **(c)** *Search*. Many pages provide access to **search engines** that can be used to locate specific information on the Internet. This command causes the Web browser to load a WWW page that provides access to one or more search engines.
- *History*. All Web browsers maintain a list of pages previously viewed by the user. The user is able to display the list and can revisit any of the pages previously viewed.
- *Address bar*. Users are able to enter the location of a WWW page or file via the address bar.

Cache

In order to increase the speed and efficiency with which a Web browser functions, a temporary storage space is used to store copies of any pages that the user has viewed. If the user returns to a given location, the Web browser retrieves the required page from the temporary storage space, rather than transferring a fresh copy from the remote computer. The use of a **cache** improves the speed with which previously viewed pages can be displayed.

Channels

Channels (sometimes described as netcasting) enable users to subscribe to particular sites on the Internet, in much the same way that one might subscribe to a newspaper or magazine. The use of channels allows both the user and the information provider to select the information to be sent and schedule its transmission.

> The transmission of information across the Internet is often described as being based around either pull or push technology. **Pull technology** describes information sent out as a result of receiving a specific request, for example a page is delivered to a Web browser in response to a specific request from the user. **Push technology** describes information that is sent without a user specifically requesting it, for example a customised news service received by subscribing to a channel.

Bookmarks

All Web browsers allow users to maintain a directory of WWW sites. The directory will enable users to add, edit, delete and organise addresses in the form of **bookmarks**.

Security

As organisations seek to apply the Internet to business applications, renewed emphasis has been placed on matters concerning security and privacy. As an example, many users and organisations cite security concerns as a reason for not taking up developments such as e-commerce. In order to address these concerns, many Web browsers now provide a range of security features that can be used alone or in combination to offer varying levels of security. Some common features include the following:

◆ *Digital ID*. A **digital ID** provides a means of confirming the identity of a specific user through the use of a small data file called a **personal certificate**. The certificate contains encrypted information relating to the user's identity. Since the user's Web browser is able to transmit or receive personal certificates, it is possible to verify the identity of a third party or confirm a user's own identity to that party.

◆ *Certificates*. A **site certificate** contains information regarding the identity of a particular site on the Internet. As with personal certificates, the site certificate is encrypted to protect the information it contains. Web browsers automatically maintain a list of certificates concerning sites designated as being trustworthy by the user or organisation. When the Web browser accesses a given site on the

---

Cache
A temporary storage space is used to store copies of any pages that the user has viewed for rapid access if the user revisits a site.

Channels
Users subscribe to particular sites which allows both the user and the information provider to select the information to be sent and schedule its transmission.

Pull technology
Information sent out as a result of receiving a specific request, for example a page is delivered to a Web browser in response to a specific request from the user.

Push technology
Information that is sent without a user specifically requesting it, for example a customised news service received by subscribing to a channel.

Bookmarks
All Web browsers allow users to maintain a directory of WWW sites. The directory will enable users to add, edit, delete and organise addresses in the form of bookmarks.

Digital ID
Provides a means of confirming the identity of a specific user through the use of a small data file called a personal certificate.

Personal certificate
A data file containing encrypted information relating to the user's identity.

Site certificate
Contains information regarding the identity of a particular site on the Internet. The site certificate is encrypted to protect the information it contains.

Internet, the corresponding certificate is checked to ensure the authenticity of the site. If the information in the certificate is invalid or out of date, a suitable warning is issued.

◆ *Ratings.* Many browsers support the use of **ratings** in order to restrict access to inappropriate content, for example pornography. The majority of ratings schemes are voluntary and are based on four basic criteria: language, nudity, sex and violence. When a Web browser is used to access a site belonging to a given scheme, the site's ratings are checked against the list of criteria set within the browser. If a site does not meet the criteria specified within the browser, access to the site is denied.

◆ *Applets.* WWW pages can contain small programs that are activated when a page is accessed. Such programs can take a variety of forms and can include complete, self-contained applications known as **applets**. As an example, a page may have been created to display an animation sequence by activating an appropriate applet after the page has finished loading. Although such programs are generally considered harmless, they can represent a potential security risk to an organisation or individual. As a result, all Web browsers provide control over the operation of any applets embedded in a WWW page.

Plug-ins

A **plug-in** is a small program or accessory that can be used to extend a Web browser's capabilities. For example, a number of different plug-ins exist that allow a Web browser to display video or animation sequences.

The use of plug-ins offers two main advantages. First, users are able to select which plug-ins they require and can install only those needed to meet a specific requirement. This acts to reduce storage space requirements and prevents unnecessary or unwanted changes being made to the user's computer system. Second, the functionality of some plug-ins can be extended to the user's computer system as a whole. Controls created using Microsoft's OCX and ActiveX formats, for example, can be used within a variety of other applications. From the point of view of a company hosting the Web page, it has the major disadvantage that its customers will not be able to view the content unless they go through the process of downloading and setting up the plug-in.

Scripts

All modern Web browsers are capable of executing special commands that have been embedded within the body of a WWW page. These **scripts** can be used to control the appearance of the page or can provide additional facilities, such as on-screen clocks and timers. Many scripts are produced using special programming language known as **VB Script** or **Java Script**.

Java, a derivative of the C++ programming language, can be used to create small applications that run when users display a WWW page or activate a control shown on the screen. One of the main advantages of Java is that applications are *platform independent*, meaning that they can be used with any system equipped with the correct software. This allows applications created using one particular kind of system to work on other systems without modification. Note that although Java shares some features with Java Script, the former is a much more sophisticated language.

Ratings

Used restrict access to certain content. If a site does not meet the criteria specified within the browser, access to the site is denied.

Applets

Small programs with limited functions typically running from within a Web browser.

Plug-in

A small program or accessory that is installed permanently to extend a Web browser's capabilities.

Script

Program instructions within a web page used to control the appearance of the page or provide additional facilities.

Java

Java is a derivative of the C++ programming language and can be used to create small applications that run when users display a WWW page or activate a control shown on the screen.

Page design

Many Web browsers provide facilities that allow users to construct their own WWW pages using a special authoring language known as **Hypertext Markup Language (HTML)**. HTML documents use a series of special tags (or codes) to control how a page will appear. The example below shows a section of an HTML document containing a single heading and a single line of text:

```
<H1>HTML Example</H1>
<HR>
<P>
HTML Sample
</P>
<HR>
```

▶ E-MAIL

E-mail – electronic mail – can be defined as the transmission of a message over a communications network. Messages can be entered via the keyboard or taken from files stored on disk. In general, e-mail communications take the form of brief text messages with little or no formatting. More sophisticated e-mail software packages can allow a user to send messages that contain different typefaces, graphics and other elements intended to enhance the presentation of the message. In addition, messages can be accompanied by data files, such as spreadsheet files. Including a data file with an e-mail message is known as adding a *file attachment*.

Although messages are usually composed of text alone, additional files can be 'attached' to an e-mail message so that users can send programs, data files and other materials with their messages.

E-mail messages can be composed online or offline. They can also be posted immediately or can have delivery deferred. When a message is composed **online**, the user's connection to the Internet is active. When a message is composed **offline**, the user's connection to the Internet is inactive. This allows the user to take more time and care over the content of the message.

Immediate delivery means that a completed message will be transmitted via the Internet immediately. If the user is working online, the message is queued for delivery and sent as soon as possible. If working offline, messages will only be transmitted when the user specifically chooses to send them. *Deferred delivery* allows a user to compose a number of messages and then store them so that they can be transmitted all at once later on. This tends to be the most efficient way of working, since sending a batch of messages is quicker and easier than sending large numbers of messages individually.

Electronic mail (e-mail)

The transmission of a message over a communications network.

Online

When a user is connected to their Internet account, usually by a modem link, they are said to be online.

Offline

When a user is not connected to their Internet account, they are said to be offline.

▶ Overview

In a business organisation, e-mail can be used to support both internal and external communications. Examples of two typical applications for e-mail are as follows:

◆ *Internal communications*. Many organisations use e-mail instead of internal memos or telephone calls. One of the advantages of using e-mail in this way is that messages are stored automatically until the user comes to access them. In addition, a great deal of information, such as the date and time of the message, can automatically be included in the message.

◆ *Teleworking*. It is estimated that as much as 5 per cent of the UK workforce uses **teleworking**. E-mail enables people to stay in contact with clients, colleagues and employers. In addition, it allows teleworkers to send or receive work-related materials quickly and easily. Teleworking is considered further in Chapter 19.

Teleworking

A teleworker is a person who works from home, using technology as a means of communicating with employers, clients and other persons.

> A teleworker is a person who works from home, using technology as a means of communicating with employers, clients and other persons. Teleworkers send or receive materials using a variety of different methods, including e-mail and fax.

▶ Advantages of e-mail

Some of the major advantages of e-mail can be summarised as follows:

◆ *Speed*. E-mail messages can be transmitted very quickly. A typical message containing 400 words, for example, can be transmitted in under a second. As a means of communication, e-mail is considered extremely fast, with some messages able to reach their destinations in a matter of minutes. Since e-mail is considered to be an extremely fast method of communication, users often use the derisory term 'snail mail' to refer to the conventional postal system.

◆ *Cost*. The cost of sending or receiving messages is considered very low. Hundreds of messages can be sent or received for the cost of a brief telephone call, making e-mail far cheaper than the postal service.

◆ *Multiple copies*. E-mail allows multiple copies of the same basic message to be created and transmitted. As an example, Eudora, a leading e-mail package, uses a special directory to hold the names and e-mail addresses of friends and colleagues. Using some of the functions of the directory, groups of people can be assigned an **alias** (sometimes known as a nickname), for example the name of a department might be used as an alias for all of the people working there. A message can be created in the usual way and addressed to the alias. When the message is transmitted, copies are sent automatically to each of the people belonging to the group.

Alias

The process of sending e-mail messages to specific individuals or groups of users can be simplified by making use of an alias or nickname.

◆ *Auditing*. Even the simplest e-mail package will provide a number of features that allow users to audit their messages. Most programs allow users to keep copies of any messages they produce, automatically marking them with the date and time they were created. Some programs can automatically create receipts that can be used to check if a message sent to another user has been received, or even if the message has been read.

◆ *Sharing data*. E-mail messages can be used to transmit data files to other users. Files can be *attached* to messages and transmitted in the usual way. All types of data can be sent in this way, including wordprocessor files, spreadsheet data, graphics and database files.

◆ *Multimedia*. The latest e-mail packages allow users to include multimedia elements in their messages. Messages can include a variety of different elements, including graphics, video, hyperlinks to information on the Internet and sound files.

◆ *Groupwork*. E-mail supports groupwork and remote working. *Groupwork* involves several people working on the same project, using IT to help them communicate with each other and share data files. *Remote working* (teleworking) involves people working away from a central office – perhaps at home – but staying in contact through e-mail and other methods.

◆ *Flexibility*. The hardware and software used for handling e-mail can also be used for a variety of other purposes. A typical modem, for example, can also be used to send or receive fax messages.

▶ Disadvantages of e-mail

Some of the main disadvantages of e-mail can be summarised as follows:

◆ *Routing*. E-mail messages seldom take the most direct route to their destinations. A message sent from Manchester to London, for example, might travel through Leicester, Birmingham and Nottingham before reaching its final destination. This can lead to a number of difficulties:
  (a) the time taken to receive the message can be very long;
  (b) there are more opportunities for the message to become lost or garbled;
  (c) there are more opportunities for messages to be intercepted.

◆ *Cost*. In order to send or receive e-mail, organisations must have access to the correct hardware and software. The expense of buying new equipment, such as a PC with modem, can mean that it is beyond the reach of smaller companies. Organisations needing to deal with large volumes of data may need to invest in fibre-optic cabling or microwave transmitters.

◆ *Technical issues*. Since using an e-mail service requires a certain level of technical knowledge, novice users may find it difficult to operate the hardware and software involved. This can place a burden on an organisation in terms of training and technical support requirements.

◆ *Spam*. Unwanted messages, such as advertisements, are received by most e-mail users. The act of sending out these messages is usually called **spamming**. Dealing with unwanted or unnecessary e-mail messages can place a great burden on an organisation's resources.

> **Spam**
> Unwanted messages, such as advertisements, are received by most e-mail users. The act of sending out these messages is usually called spamming.

> Independent research commissioned by Novell in 1998 suggests that unwanted e-mail messages cost UK businesses more than £5 billion each year. Up to 15 per cent of workers may spend as much as an hour each day dealing with unwanted or nuisance e-mail.

◆ *Security*. Unless they are encrypted, e-mail messages can be intercepted relatively easily. This makes e-mail unsuitable for sending confidential information unless special precautions are taken.

▶ Features of an e-mail package

Message editor

All packages provide a facility that allows users to enter the text of a new message. More sophisticated programs will have many of the features of a wordprocessor, for example spell checking.

Message reader

All e-mail programs are designed to collect new messages and allow users to view them on the screen. Most programs also enable users to print the contents of a message or copy the text into another program, such as a wordprocessor.

Replying to messages

Most packages will automatically include the e-mail address, subject and the text of the message being replied to. This enables a user to annotate a message that has been received and return their comments to the sender.

Filters

Filters provide the ability to mark messages for special attention. A filter searches for key words or phrases in a message. Any messages matching the filter conditions can be dealt with automatically. Filters can be used to highlight messages for special attention, delete messages automatically, copy or move messages to another location or reply to incoming messages automatically.

Mail boxes

Most packages provide facilities for archiving, copying, moving, deleting and grouping messages. Mail boxes can be created to hold messages from certain people or concerning a particular subject.

Encryption

Many programs provide the facility to encode messages so that only intended recipients can read them.

File attachment

E-mail messages can be used to transmit data files to other users. Files can be attached to messages and transmitted in the usual way.

File attachments

Data files, such as wordprocessing documents, can be attached to messages and sent to other users. Many packages have the ability to encode and decode files automatically so that they can be sent and received with little difficulty.

Address book

A way of grouping e-mail addresses in a similar way to a phone book.

Aliases and address books

As described earlier, the process of sending messages to specific individuals or groups of users can be simplified by making use of **aliases**. An alias usually consists of a description and the e-mail addresses of those grouped under the alias.

Groups of aliases can be stored within the **address book** tool found within most e-mail packages. The address book enables users to create, delete, edit and organise aliases. In addition, different address books can be used for different purposes, for example a user might create separate address books for customers and suppliers.

Signature file

Information such as an address and phone number that can be automatically added to the end of an e-mail message.

Signatures

A **signature file** contains information that can be automatically added to the end of an e-mail message. The signature file is normally a simple text file that can be created or edited using a text editor or similar program. Most e-mail programs allow users to have a number of different signature files.

An e-mail address identifies an individual or organisation. At its simplest, an e-mail address can be thought of as being the equivalent of the address written on an envelope. The contents of an e-mail address can be used to identify a great deal of information concerning its owner. As an example, the final section of an e-mail address (the domain type), normally ends with an identifier that describes the organisation to which the owner belongs. Common identifiers include the following:

◆ .com denotes a US or multinational company;

◆ .co.uk denotes a UK company;

◆ .ac.uk denotes an academic institution such as a university;

◆ .fr, .de denotes other countries such as France and Germany.

▶ MANAGEMENT APPLICATIONS OF PRODUCTIVITY SOFTWARE

General-purpose applications aim to support users in performing a variety of common tasks. In addition to the productivity applications considered above, more specialist management applications are also possible.

▶ Managing time and projects

One of the principal activities of a business organisation is managing resources so that tasks are completed as quickly and efficiently as possible. It can be argued that the most important organisational resources are the skills and abilities of employees. For this reason, a significant category of business applications is devoted to maximising the use of employee time. This type of software can be subdivided into a number of other categories:

◆ *Packages for managing tasks and projects.* These programs allow managers to schedule tasks, allocate resources and monitor progress. Typical applications include project management programs and scheduling software. How they are applied is described in Chapter 9.

◆ *Packages for individual time management and organising personal information.* These programs help managers to make more effective use of their time by facilitating scheduling appointments, organising meetings and recording important information. Typical applications include personal information managers (PIM) and contact management software.

Personal information manager (PIM)

A program that allows users to store, organise and retrieve personal information.

◆ A **personal information manager** can be thought of as an electronic personal organiser. The program allows users to store, organise and retrieve personal information such as appointments, personal expenses, telephone numbers and addresses, reminders and to-do lists. Generally, a PIM is made up of several individual applications that are linked together by a menu system. Typical applications include diary, calendar, address book, notebook, to-do list, personal expenses and calculator.

◆ **Contact managers** can be used to maintain lists of information relating to customers, suppliers and other important individuals or organisations. Such programs are commonly used by sales organisations to assist in building and maintaining business relationships between customers and individual members of staff.

Contact manager

This describes a software application that can be used to maintain lists of information relating to customers, suppliers and other important individuals or organisations.

The contact manager can store notes and other information for each of the contacts recorded. This allows, for example, a user to review the details of a previous meeting before telephoning a particular contact. Many contact managers provide additional features, such as the ability automatically to dial a telephone number selected by the user. In some cases, the program will also create a new record containing the date and time of the telephone call so that the user can make notes regarding the conversation. Other common features include printing address labels, protecting the information held via a password system or encryption and printing directories of names, telephone numbers and addresses.

▶ Office automation systems and groupware

Office automation systems

For automating many of the activities carried out within a typical office, organisations seek to improve efficiency, reduce costs and enhance internal communications.

In business organisations, productivity software is often used to reduce the time needed to complete routine administrative tasks, such as producing documents or organising meetings. By attempting to automate many of the activities carried out within a typical office, organisations seek to improve efficiency, reduce costs and enhance internal communications. Computer-based information systems used in this way are generally referred to as **office automation systems**. Applications of these systems and the software used to support them are described in Chapter 6.

The functions of office automation systems are commonly provided by groupware. **Groupware** can be defined as a category of software used to support the activities of workgroups. In general, groupware applications fall into two basic categories:

Groupware

A category of software used to support the activities of workgroups.

◆ *Network software.* This describes the software used to establish workgroups on an organisation's network system. The programs used provide the basic infrastructure for workgroup computing.

◆ *Scheduling software.* This describes programs that help to organise the activities of the workgroup. Typical applications include calendars, scheduling programs and workflow software.

Workgroup

A group of individuals working together on a given task.

A **workgroup** can be defined as a group of individuals working together on a given task. Each member of the workgroup will be attached to the organisation's network system so that tasks can be organised and information can be shared with other members.

Office automation systems can be divided into five basic categories, desribed below.

Electronic publishing systems

This describes a category of Office Automation Systems that supports the production of documents, such as letters, reports and catalogues.

Electronic publishing systems

Electronic publishing systems support the production of documents, such as letters, reports and catalogues. Some of the typical programs used include wordprocessors and desktop publishing packages.

Electronic communications systems

Electronic communications systems support internal and external communications by providing facilities such as e-mail and voice mail. This is a function of groupware and workflow applications that is described in Chapter 6.

Electronic meeting systems

This describes a category of Office Automation Systems that facilitates business meetings.

Electronic meeting systems

Electronic meeting systems seek to improve communications between individuals and groups. Examples of these systems are provided by groupware that supports teleconferencing, teleworking and groupwork.

Image processing systems

Image processing systems allow users to create, edit, store and retrieve documents in electronic format. **Document image processing (DIP)** is an example of an image processing system.

Office management systems

Office management systems assist users in scheduling projects and tasks. Examples of office management systems include personal information managers (PIM) and project management software.

▶ PRESENTATION PACKAGES

Interactive presentations are commonly used for a number of purposes, including staff training, briefings and as sales tools. **Presentation software** enables users to create, edit and deliver presentations via a computer system. At a simple level, presentations can consist of nothing more than a series of simple slides displayed on a computer monitor (*see* Fig 4.10). More sophisticated presentations can incorporate multimedia, such as video sequences, and can allow users to interact with the material presented. Although primarily concerned with the creation of slides, many programs also support the creation of speaker notes, handouts and overhead transparencies.

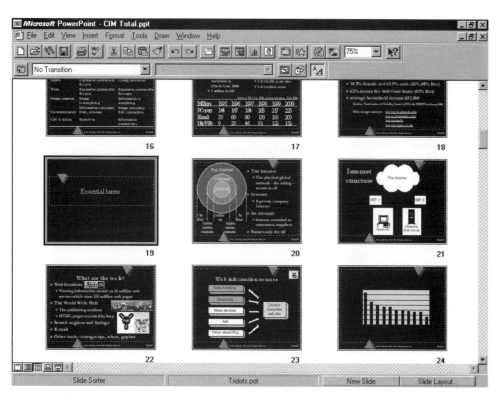

Fig 4.10 Microsoft's Powerpoint for Windows 95 showing the 'Slide Sorter' view which can be used when preparing a presentation

Image processing systems

This describes a category of Office Automation Systems that allows users to create, edit, store and retrieve documents in electronic format.

Document image processing (DIP)

DIP systems are used in industry to convert printed documents into an electronic format so that they can be stored, organised and retrieved more easily.

Office management systems

A category of Office Automation Systems that assists users in scheduling projects and tasks.

Presentation software

Enables users to create, edit and deliver presentations via a computer system.

The case study 'User documents support corporate intelligence' suggests how the information that is saved in users' wordprocessors, spreadsheets and databases can contribute to the pool of knowledge within an organisation, but only if it is managed adequately.

CASE STUDY: TOPIC AREA

FT

User documents support corporate intelligence

Effective use of information is often the vital factor in determining whether a company will succeed, stagnate or die. Demand for new ways to strategically track, manage and manipulate corporate information – and maximise its use – has given birth to a whole new sector of the computer industry aimed squarely at providing such services to 'the enterprise'.

According to the London-based PA Consulting Group, the solution to properly implementing distributed data and connectivity solutions lies not only in choosing the right technology: it suggests that a strong set of 'best practices' needs to be developed alongside the technology, which create a situation in which:

Information is treated as a shared business resource and, through appointed stewards, is actively and strategically directed.

Users understand what information is available within the company and what their own further data needs are likely to be.

The company works to continuously improve the quality of its information resources and formally audit its information resources.

Information storage, security, availability and accessibility are managed efficiently, effectively and economically.

All information is openly and easily accessible to those who need it.

Employees have the necessary capability to manage, use and exploit those resources in accordance with goals for improved business excellence and continued business success.

Innovation in using and enriching information is encouraged and rewarded.

There is strong evidence that these ideas apply more widely across more sectors of the economy than ever before. A global study released by Microsoft, in conjunction with McKinsey & Company, suggests that a growing percentage of the world's workforce is primarily knowledge workers. This, in turn, means that the way in which staff use and manage and access information is fundamental to their jobs.

According to Steve Ballmer, Microsoft executive vice president, the results of the survey show that in 'semi-developed' economies, about 47 per cent of people are knowledge workers.

'It's clear that those numbers are higher in advanced economies such as the US or Germany, while the figures

are lower in developing economies,' he says. 'But certainly there's a shift in the workforce as economies develop, where for more and more of the people, their fundamental job is working with information.'

Bob Muglia, vice president of server applications at Microsoft, suggests that the challenge now lies in making this 'knowledge' as useful and relevant as possible.

'A key problem is that corporations have so much information, created by staff in so many different formats, that taking that information, and creating useful, easy-to-find documents and a valuable knowledge-base is a major challenge,' he says. 'And it's something in which the right technology can make a very great difference.'

It appears that corporations everywhere are taking this message to heart for both their employees and their customers. The impact of this need to use and work with distributed information was recently demonstrated in a decision by British Airways to develop and run a serviced technology centre for its frequent flyers.

At the airline's new business centre in London Heathrow's Terminal One, BA's Silver and Gold Club Members, as well as Club Europe passengers, can access the World Wide Web and check their e-mail.

Hewlett-Packard and Computacenter developed the centre for BA.

The airline reports that, so far, accessing the internet has been one of the most popular services used by travellers, along with the sending of 'last minute' e-mails and faxes.

Source: Financial Times, 18 March 1998

Questions

1 On a modest scale, the need to 'strategically track, manage and manipulate corporate information – and maximise its use' can be addressed by making use of productivity software. Describe some of the ways in which the applications described in the chapter could be used to support 'corporate intelligence'.

2 Why is it important to develop a strong set of 'best practices' alongside the technology? What best practices would be most suited to making use of the productivity applications described in this chapter?

▶ PROGRAMMING LANGUAGES

Programming languages enable users to develop software applications in order to carry out specific information processing tasks. In order to understand more of the nature of programming languages, this section examines some of the different ways in which they can be classified.

Programming language

Enables users to develop software applications in order to carry out specific information processing tasks.

▶ Generations of programming languages

Programming languages can be described in terms of their historical position in the development of computer programming systems. The five generations of programming languages provide a good overview of how user requirements and technological changes have changed over the past six decades.

First generation

Early computer systems were programmed using **machine language** that consisted of strings of binary digits. Programmers required advanced technical skills in order to develop and enter their programs. Programs were considered expensive to develop as they took extremely long periods to design, code and test.

Machine language

This describes the natural language of a computer. Machine language instructions are made up of binary digits and use only the values of 0 (zero) and 1.

Second generation

Assembly language represented an attempt to simplify the process of creating computer programs. Symbols and abbreviations were used to create sequences of instructions. An *assembler* was used to translate a completed assembly language program into the machine code required by the computer.

Although assembly language provided a number of advantages over machine language, it also suffered from two major disadvantages. First, since assembly programs did not run as quickly as their machine language counterparts, they were unsuitable for certain tasks, such as those involving large-scale data processing. Second, since programmers were still working at a very low level with the computer's hardware, it remained difficult to create large or complex programs using assembly language.

Assembly language

Symbols and abbreviations were used to create sequences of instructions.

Third generation

Third-generation programming languages provided a more natural means of developing programs by enabling users to create programs made up of English-like statements. Such programming languages are still in use today and are known as **high-level languages**. Languages such as COBOL allowed users to develop programs quickly and easily, although the resulting applications were sometimes slow and inefficient.

Fourth generation

A drive towards even greater ease of use resulted in the development of new programming systems designed to allow even non-technical users to develop their own applications. The focus of such tools was on ease of use and the rapid development of applications. Examples of common programming tools include report generators, query languages and application generators.

Fifth generation

Artificial Intelligence (AI)

Attempt to make a computer system behave in the same way as a human being.

Fifth-generation languages are likely to be based around a number of different technologies and techniques. As an example, **artificial intelligence** (AI) methods attempt to make a computer system behave in the same way as a human being. One application for AI is in *natural language processing*, where users can communicate with a computer system using English-like statements. Developments in this area may result in programming systems that accept a spoken question from a user and then generate a computer program intended to produce the required information.

▶ Classifications of programming languages

We can classify programming languages using three basic approaches. The first approach describes a programming language as being either high level or low level. This indicates the level of interaction between the programmer and the hardware of the computer system.

Low level vs high level

Low-level language

Requires the programmer to work directly with the hardware of the computer system. Instructions are normally entered in machine code or assembly language.

A **low-level language** requires the programmer to work directly with the hardware of the computer system. Instructions are normally entered in machine code or assembly language. Programmers must have detailed knowledge of the computer hardware being used in order to construct programs. One of the main characteristics of low-level languages is that applications tend to run very quickly.

A **high-level language** allows programmers to issue instructions in a more natural form. Programs are normally created using English-like statements that can be organised to form a clear, logical structure. In addition, high-level languages provide programmers with a variety of tools that assist in the process of creating the program and locating errors. Although simpler to use than machine code or assembly language, applications developed using high-level languages are considered slow. Java, C++ and Visual Basic, three of the most popular languages currently, are all high-level languages.

Machine-oriented

A programming language produced in a form that suits the way in which the microprocessor functions.

Machine oriented vs problem oriented

It can be argued that all computer programs are created to serve a specific need. In most cases, programs are constructed in order to solve a particular problem or meet a clearly defined set of information processing requirements. The way in which programming languages allow a problem or set of information processing requirements to be expressed provides a second means of classification.

Problem-oriented

A problem-oriented language focuses on the expression of a problem or a set of information processing requirements. The language will provide a variety of features that allow programmers to express their requirement in a natural form.

A **machine-oriented** language focuses on the requirements of the computer hardware being used, where programs are produced in a form that suits the way in which the microprocessor functions. In order to create a program, a programmer may often need to translate a problem or set of requirements into a new format that is suitable to the way in which a particular microprocessor operates.

A **problem-oriented** language focuses on the expression of a problem or set of information processing requirements. The language will provide a variety of features that allow programmers to express their requirements in a natural form. The language will also provide the facility to translate the program into a form suitable for the computer's microprocessor. Effectively, problem-oriented languages allow programmers to focus on the problem to be solved, rather than on the operation of the computer's hardware.

Compiled vs interpreted

The instructions contained within any computer program must be converted into machine language before they can be executed. The way in which instructions are translated into machine language provides a third way of classifying programming languages:

◆ *Compiled.* The instructions that make up a computer program are often stored as a simple text file, usually called a *source code* file. The instructions held as source code cannot be executed directly by the microprocessor since they must first be converted into machine language. Although this is a somewhat simplistic description, a **compiler** produces an *executable program* by converting instructions held as source code into machine language. If the source code is altered in any way, it must be compiled again so that a new executable program can be produced.

◆ *Interpreted.* An **interpreted** program can be run directly, without the need for compilation. As the program runs, each instruction is taken in turn and converted into machine language by a *command interpreter*. Since the process of converting each instruction into machine language can take a great deal of time, interpreted programs operate much more slowly than compiled programs.

Having described some of the ways in which a programming language can be classified, an example may help clarify some of the points made. The Pascal programming language is widely used in UK schools, colleges and universities as a means of introducing students to programming concepts. The extract below represents a simple Pascal program designed to convert temperatures in Fahrenheit to an equivalent value in Centigrade.

Compiler

A compiler produces an executable program by converting instructions held as source code into machine language.

Interpreted

An interpreted computer program can be run directly, without the need for compilation since each line is converted as required.

```
PROGRAM temperatures (OUTPUT);
VAR
  fahrenheit, centigrade: REAL;
BEGIN
    Writeln ('Please enter temperature in fahrenheit');
    Readln (fahrenheit);
    centigrade:=(fahrenheit-32)*(5/9);
    Writeln (fahrenheit:0:2,' Fahrenheit is ',centigrade:0:3,'
Centigrade.');
END.
```

When the program runs, the output displayed on the screen might appear as follows:

```
Please enter temperature in fahrenheit
144
144.00 Fahrenheit is 62.222 Centigrade.
```

The terms used to structure a program are discussed further in Chapter 13, which covers the build phase of a systems development project in which programming or 'coding' is one of the main activities.

▶ Categories of high-level programming languages

The majority of modern programming languages can be classified as high-level languages. In terms of the applications that high-level languages serve, we can define six basic categories.

Commercial languages

Commercial languages are intended to create applications that meet the basic information processing requirements of business organisations. In general, such languages are geared towards activities that involve processing data files. An example of a commercial language is COBOL.

Commercial languages

This category of programming languages is intended to create applications that meet the basic information processing requirements of business organisations.

Scientific languages

Scientific languages are designed to serve scientific and mathematical applications. In general, these languages provide an extensive range of features to support complex mathematical calculations. An example of a commercial language is FORTRAN.

Scientific languages

Scientific programming languages are designed to serve scientific and mathematical applications.

Special-purpose languages

The majority of special-purpose languages are geared towards database applications. Such languages often provide an extensive range of features for working with database files and records. **Structured Query Language (SQL)** is an example of a special-purpose language.

Applications generators

Applications generator

An applications generator creates a computer program without the need to be a programming expert.

An **applications generator** performs an action or creates a computer program based on a set of requirements given by the user. Many applications generators allow users to define a series of actions or requirements by arranging icons on a specially designed screen. The resulting design is then converted into a series of instructions or an executable program. Realizer is an example of an applications generator that can be used to construct relatively complex database applications.

Genetix

Building blocks: modular approach

Mark Ward on an inspired approach to writing and running software

A 60-year-old thought experiment has inspired a novel approach to writing and running software that could one day make operating systems and memory intensive applications obsolete.

In 1935 Cambridge undergraduate Alan Turing – the mathematical genius who later helped to crack the German Enigma code – came up with the idea for a universal computer that could perform the functions of any other, more specialised, computer.

This device worked by scanning a tape fed into it and reacting on the basis of the symbols printed on the tape. Mr Turing never intended the machine to be built, but worked on it because he was interested in what problems were and were not computable.

Now Bernard Hodson of Genetix Software in Ottawa, Canada has taken Mr Turing's ideas and used them to inspire an approach to software writing that could lead to smaller, more robust computer programs and faster application development.

Existing computer programs act like arrogant snobs – they do nearly everything their own way, rarely sharing computer code even if they are doing the same thing (such as displaying text on screen) as another program. Some Microsoft and Apple Macintosh programs do call on the same bit of computer code for some functions, on PCs and Macs respectively, but only for a fraction of what they are capable of carrying out.

In contrast, Genetix software programs share everything. Unlike Mr Turing's theoretical machine their instructions are not written on a tape, they are contained in what Mr Hodson has dubbed 'genes'. The most basic genes are written in machine code and when they are called on to perform they talk directly to the processor in the computer. This saves space and removes the need for an operating system.

Higher functions are built out of lower level genes. Creating an application is relatively straightforward. The genes that already exist can be used for most of the functions, but some new ones may have to be written for any functions unique to a particular application.

'We take an application and see what genes it needs,' says Mr Hodson, 'Then we build the genes if there is something that we have not previously written.' He says this is one of the main advantages of his approach: the more programs written using Genetix software the bigger the pool of genes and the fewer new genes are needed to emulate other programs.

One thing Genetix software does share with Mr Turing's machine is a single reading head that works out what to do. This tiny program calls up the genes from a common pool that do what the user of the program wants to.

Using this approach Mr Hodson believes it would be possible to do many things larger programs such as Microsoft Word do, but in far less memory, possibly only a few hundred kilobytes.

For the moment though, Mr Hodson is concentrating on more specialist applications. He is working on using the Genetix approach to make the processors on smart cards more powerful and to send video down telephone lines.

Next year he hopes to produce a version of Genetix that can run programs written in Sun's Java computer language. He is also planning a European conference next year to present the latest work.

Robin Bloor, a UK-based computer consultant, says he is impressed so far by what he has seen of Mr Hodson's work. He believes the Genetix approach will find its first uses in smart cards, embedded processors and for programs currently being written in Java.

Mr Hodson, a retired computer professional, says he has been thinking about the ideas for the Genetix software for years, but only now does he have the spare time to develop them. Although he started later than Mr Turing his legacy could be just as long-lasting.

Source: Financial Times, 23 December 1997

Questions

1 In terms of a business organisation, what benefits might be achieved by 'smaller, more robust computer programs and faster application development'?

2 Why is machine code used to create basic 'genes'?

3 Given the way in which computer programs are currently developed, how likely is the Genetix approach to become successful?

▶ SUMMARY

1 Software can be defined as a series of detailed instructions that control the operation of a computer system. There are two main categories of software: systems software and applications software.

2 Systems software manages and controls the operation of the computer system as it performs tasks on behalf of the user. Operating systems interact with the hardware of the computer at a very low level in order to manage and direct the computer's resources.

3 Applications software can be defined as a set of programs that enable users to perform specific information processing activities. Applications software can be divided into two broad categories: general-purpose productivity software and application specific.

4 Productivity software describes general-purpose applications that aim to support users in performing a variety of common tasks. In business organisations, productivity software is often used to reduce the time needed to complete routine administrative tasks, such as producing documents or organising meetings. Computer-based information systems used in this way are generally referred to as office automation systems.

5 The three main types of productivity software are as follows:
   ◆ A wordprocessor provides the ability to enter, edit, store and print text. In addition, wordprocessing packages allow users to alter the layout of documents and often provide a variety of formatting tools.
   ◆ Spreadsheet programs are designed to store and manipulate values, numbers and text in an efficient and useful way.
   ◆ The data in a database is organised by fields and records. A field is a single item of information, such as a name or a quantity. A record is a collection of related fields. A database can be defined as a collection of related information. The information held in an electronic database is accessed via a database management system (DBMS). A DBMS can be defined as one or more computer programs that allow users to enter, store, organise, manipulate and retrieve data from a database. A relational database can consist of numerous record designs – tables – and can combine information drawn from several tables. A key field can be used to identify individual records within an electronic database or to create relationships between different tables.

6 The Internet provides a variety of opportunities for organisations to carry out business activities. These include competitor research, product research, customer support, advertising and promotion and e-commerce. The World Wide Web (WWW) is a part of the Internet that can be accessed using a Web browser. A Web browser provides the means to search for and retrieve information quickly and easily.

7 E-mail (electronic mail) can be defined as the transmission of a message over a communications network. Messages can be entered via the keyboard or taken from files stored on disk. E-mail programs provide the ability to create, edit, organise, transmit and receive e-mail messages.

8 Office automation systems consist of five basic categories: electronic publishing systems, electronic communications systems, electronic meeting systems, image processing systems and office management systems.

9 Management applications consist of personal information managers (PIM), project management software, contact managers and groupware applications.

EXERCISES

▶ Self-assessment exercises

1 Produce your own definitions of the following terms:
  (a) software;
  (b) operating system;
  (c) graphical user interface;
  (d) productivity software;
  (e) personal information manager.

2 Describe the five basic categories of office automation systems.

3 What is data mining and how can it bring benefits to a business organisation?

4 In an electronic database, what are the differences between queries and filters?

5 Describe the different approaches to file processing. What are the main characteristics, advantages and disadvantages of each?

▶ Discussion questions

1 In recent years the developers of encryption programs have been placed under pressure to provide government agencies with a means of decrypting messages sent by e-mail. In both the US and the UK it has been argued that such facilities are essential in order to combat terrorism and organised crime. However, civil liberties organisations feel that government agencies may abuse their power and begin to monitor e-mail traffic on a massive scale. Prepare a case for one side of this argument.

2 A wide range of factors should be considered before purchasing applications software. Construct a list of selection criteria and place these in order of importance. Justify each item on the list.

▶ Essay questions

1 Select two competing software packages as the basis for a detailed comparison. Produce a report that addresses the following tasks:
  (a) Using relevant examples, describe the main features of each package.
  (b) Considering the range of features offered by each package, indicate how these might be of benefit to a business organisation.
  (c) Which package would be most likely to meet the needs of a business organisation? Provide a detailed rationale for your choice.

2 Conduct any required research and produce a report that addresses the following tasks:
  (a) Provide an overview of how organisations can conduct business transactions over the Internet.
  (b) Discuss the advantages and disadvantages of using the Internet as a business tool.

(c) Issues related to security are of great concern to many organisations. Discuss the main security problems faced by organisations conducting business over the Internet.

3 As a student, you are required to produce essays and reports containing graphics, diagrams and charts. You may also be required to take part in seminars and presentations. As your course progresses you are likely to recognise a need to store information obtained through research. Produce a report that addresses the following areas:

(a) Considering the tasks described above, identify a range of applications software that can be used to support your studies.

(b) Discuss the ways in which the applications you have identified can help improve your studies or enhance the quality of your work.

(c) Identify and discuss any other ways in which the applications identified may be of benefit.

▶ Examination questions

1 Interest in commercial uses for the Internet has grown rapidly over the past five years. You are required to carry out the following tasks:

(a) Using relevant examples, describe the range of business applications to which the Internet can be applied.

(b) Using relevant examples, discuss the costs, technical problems and organisational issues associated with making use of the Internet as a business tool.

(c) Using relevant examples, discuss the potential benefits to an organisation of using the World Wide Web as a business tool.

2 You have been approached for advice by the manager of a small company. The manager wishes to purchase a number of software packages in order to improve the productivity of staff. Prepare a guide that can be used by the manager when selecting appropriate applications.

3 Groupware improves productivity, enhances communication and reduces costs. Using relevant examples, provide a balanced discussion of this statement.

▶ References

Curtis, G. (1998) *Business Information Systems: Analysis, Design and Practice*, 3rd edition, Addison Wesley, Harlow.

Knight, J. (1995) *Personal Computing for Business*, Financial Times Pitman Publishing, London.

▶ Further reading

Bocij, P. (1994) *Introduction to CD-ROM and Multimedia*, Capall Bann Publishing, Chieveley, Berkshire.

Clifton, H. and Sutcliffe, A. (1994) *Business Information Systems*, 5th edition, Prentice Hall, Hemel Hempstead.
    Chapter 5 deals with operating systems and computer programming.

Fuori, W. and Gioia, L. (1995) *Computers and Information Systems*, Prentice-Hall, Englewood Cliffs, NJ.
    Chapter 6 describes telecommunications hardware and software in detail. Chapter 11 provides highly detailed coverage of programming and programming languages. Chapter 7 deals with the functions of operating systems. Chapters 8 to 10 give detailed and practical coverage of common software applications, including wordprocessing, spreadsheets, databases and graphics.

Hussain, K. and Hussain, D. (1995) *Information Systems for Business*, Prentice Hall, Hemel Hempstead.
Chapter 3 provides coverage of microprocessors, computer programming and programming languages.

Knight, J. (1995) *Personal Computing for Business*, Financial Times Pitman Publishing, London.
Part 1 deals with the theoretical principles of personal computing, covering areas such as document production and numerical analysis. Chapters 8 to 12 provide detailed and practical coverage of common software applications, including wordprocessing, spreadsheets, databases and presentation graphics. Chapters 7 and 14 provide coverage of operating systems and operating environments, with particular emphasis on MS-DOS and Windows.

Krivda, C. (1995) 'Data-mining dynamite', *BYTE,* October.

O'Brien, J. (1993) *Management Information Systems: a Managerial End User Perspective*, 2nd edition, Richard D. Irwin, Boston, USA.
Chapter 5 provides general coverage of computer software. Chapter 6 deals with telecommunications hardware and software. Chapter 7 covers topics related to database management. Chapter 8 provides a detailed overview of office automation software and workgroup computing.

Wayner, P. (1997) 'Who goes there?' *BYTE*, June.

Zorkoczy, P. (1994) *Information Technology: an Introduction*, Financial Times Pitman Publishing, London.
A detailed and varied introductory text that includes areas such as human–computer interaction.

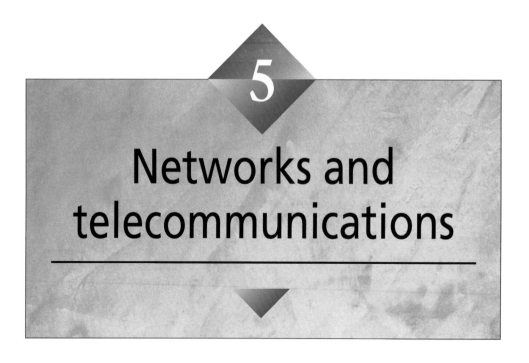

Networks and telecommunications

INTRODUCTION

For the modern business to operate effectively, the links connecting its people and their computers are vital. The network links provide the channels for information to flow continuously between people working in different departments of a company, or in different companies. This allows people to collaborate much more efficiently than before the advent of networks when information flow was irregular and unreliable. These links also allow hardware such as printers and faxes to be shared more cost effectively.

As with many aspects of technology, jargon is rife when describing the different parts of and types of network. As an example, of the many three-letter acronyms (TLAs), networks of different scales are referred to as LAN, WAN, VAN, VPN and PBX! Here, we will try to filter out the jargon to highlight which terms you need to know when understanding and specifying information systems for a business.

> ▶ Learning objectives
>
> After reading this chapter, readers will be able to:
>
> ◆ specify which components of a communications system are necessary to exchange information within and between businesses;
>
> ◆ identify the benefits available through the introduction of computer networks;
>
> ◆ identify the advantages and disadvantages of the client/server architecture in comparison with traditional approaches;
>
> ◆ specify a suitable structure for a network;
>
> ◆ identify and act on an awareness of the problems and constraints associated with the introduction of communications systems.

> ▶ Links to other chapters
>
> The chapter focuses on the physical components of networks and how they can be structured.
>
> Chapter 1   describes the qualities of the business information shared and transported via networks.
>
> Chapter 3   covers software for network management including network operating systems, and also software that makes use of networks such as groupware and e-mail.
>
> Chapter 16   shows how networks and end-users can be managed once they have been created.
>
> Chapter 17   explains the importance of intranets and the Internet to a business.

In this chapter, we trace the use of computer networks from small local networks through to the global network of the Internet. We look at the components which form a network and how to specify a suitable architecture for the modern business.

▶ INTRODUCTION TO COMPUTER NETWORKS

▶ What are computer networks?

We can describe the links that exist between different parts of an information system on different scales. At the smallest scale, links are etched in silicon between the different components of a microchip. At a larger scale, all the components of a PC, such as the hard disk, CD-ROM and main processor, are connected by internal cables. In this chapter, we consider links at a larger scale still, that is, between computers and other hardware devices such as printers, scanners and separate storage devices. These links between computers and other hardware form a computer network.

A **computer network** can be defined as: 'a communications system that links two or more computers and peripheral devices and enables transfer of data between the components'.

As we shall see, computer networks are themselves constructed on different scales. Small-scale networks within a workgroup or single office are known as **local area networks (LAN)**. Larger-scale networks which are national or international are known as **wide area networks (WAN)**.

A simple network that links three PC workstations with a shared server and printer is shown in Fig 5.1. Here the computers and the printer are the main components of the network, with the cables and network cards forming other components. We will explain servers in more detail later. For now, consider them as a more powerful computer which is used to store data and help the other PCs communicate. The final component needed to make the network function, which is not shown on the diagram, is the communications software which enables all the components to work together.

Computer network

A computer network can be defined as: 'a communications system that links two or more computers and peripheral devices and enables transfer of data between the components'.

Local area network (LAN)

A computer network that spans a limited geographic area, typically a single office or building.

Wide area network (WAN)

Networks covering a large area which connect businesses in different parts of the same city, different parts of a country or different countries.

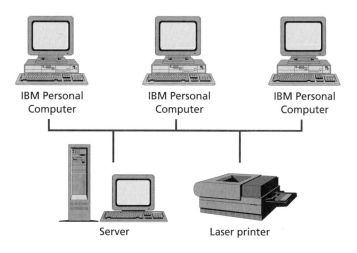

Fig 5.1 A small workgroup network connecting a single server to three PCs and a laser printer

This small-scale or workgroup network gives the following benefits by enabling:

◆ workers to share common information which is typically stored on the server;

◆ communication between workers, perhaps through e-mail or a shared diary system;

◆ sharing of various facilities such as printing, hard disk storage or software applications on the server.

The capability to share devices and applications also gives another major benefit of cost reduction.

▶ Telecommunications

Telecommunications

The method by which data and information are transmitted between different locations.

On a national or global scale, communications technology such as satellite and microwave transmissions are important in linking businesses. To transfer information electronically, companies create **telecommunications** systems. These systems consist of both the hardware and the software necessary to set up these links. Telecommunications enable a business which operates from different locations to run as a single unit. This means that the same information and control structures do not need to be repeated at each company office. Instead, information can be managed centrally and control maintained from a central location. As well as improving internal communications in a company, telecommunications also allow companies to collaborate using electronic data interchange with partners which are suppliers. This technique is described later in the chapter. Similarly, customers can contact the company using the Internet. The details of these business benefits are described later on page 154.

▶ The evolution of networking technology

It is instructive to examine the progression of how networks have been used in industry. The trends illustrate why networks are important and some of the issues

that govern their structure. Terms are introduced which are explained in more detail later in the chapter.

The 1960s – mainframes and dumb terminals

In the 1960s those companies that had computer systems were using mainframes. A central mainframe was connected to terminals by a simple network. The main function of these aptly named 'dumb terminals' consisted of the display and input of character information. Limited information was transmitted over the network.

Characterised by being: cost driven and technology limited.

The 1970s – minicomputers

In the 1970s the trend to downsizing was underway and cheaper minicomputers such as the DEC PDP-11 and VAX became popular. It was during this period that wide area networks started to be used for specialist functions such as air travel reservation and banking.

Characterised by being: cost driven, technology enabled through use of microchips.

The 1980s – the IBM PC and Apple Macintosh

With the introduction of the PC in the early 1980s, networking faced a setback. PCs were often deployed as standalone, non-networked machines. While this often gave the user more freedom to develop applications such as spreadsheet models, it meant that information sharing was limited, with a failure to add value to the business through information. This was known as the period of the 'trainer net', as file sharing occurred by people walking from one machine to the next. The opportunities for sharing devices such as printers and storage devices were also often missed.

Characterised by being: led by technology and by the desire for increased user autonomy.

It was not long before these limitations were realised and a rapid increase in the adoption of the PC LAN occurred. Managed by early versions of network operating systems such as Novell Netware and IBM LAN Manager, these gave all the benefits of printing, file sharing and security which had been lost with the standalone PC.

Characterised by being: driven by cost and by the desire for e-mail and file sharing.

In the 1980s large numbers of companies were starting to communicate with their suppliers and overseas operations via wide area networks.

The 1990s – the client/server architecture and global networks

As the popularity of LANs increased, the benefits of a client/server architecture became clear and the introduction of first-generation **client/server** architecture with centralised data and mainly local processing occurred. This gradually became more sophisticated with the introduction of second-generation client/server with a distributed architecture where data and processing are shared between several computers over a LAN or WAN.

The latest phase, which we are currently in, is the age of the intranet and Internet. Intranets are secure networks within a company which use relatively low-cost Internet technology such as Web servers and browsers to share company information. With increasing concerns about the cost of PC ownership, we are now seeing a reversion to centralisation of processing power and administrative functions with the

Client/server

The client/server architecture consists of client computers such as PCs sharing resources such as a database stored on more powerful server computers.

introduction of network computers (NCs) and Net PCs (*see* Chapters 3 and 16) which have lower specifications than PCs.

Characterised by being: collaboration and cost driven.

▶ The role of communications in business

Communications technologies are vital to a business. They are important for the cost savings and improved communications that arise from an internal network. Beyond this, they are truly vital, because they help a business reach out and connect with its customers, suppliers and collaborators. Through doing this a company can order new raw materials quickly and cheaply from its suppliers and can keep in touch with the needs of its customers.

Figure 5.2 indicates the links that may exist between different partners. In some industries, such as the travel industry, travel agents and suppliers (such as the airlines) have made use of telecommunications links for over 20 years. In other sectors, however, most communications have been over the phone or in person, until more recently. The Internet is changing this by driving down the cost and complexity of linking companies.

▶ What benefits do networks give a business?

When computers and telecommunications are integrated, they can provide many advantages. Take the simple example of a humble e-mail sent to a colleague over the Internet. This costs only a few pence and can be sent to any location in the world in a few minutes. As well as the low cost and fast delivery, it can be integrated to work with the users' other information needs, perhaps by supplying a spreadsheet as an attachment.

We will now look at the benefits that networks provide in more detail.

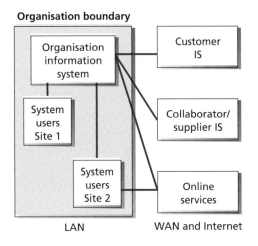

Fig 5.2 Communications links between different stakeholders in an industry

1 *Reduces cost compared to traditional communications.* Costs can be reduced in various ways depending on the type of communication required. If information has to be sent to another location, the cost of sending is very low compared to using a letter or even a fax. If face-to-face communication is needed to exchange information or solve a problem, then the traditional approach would be to jump into a car or on to a plane. Telecommunications now make this less necessary. Meetings can be conducted by conferencing, which not only includes video conferencing, but also sharing ideas through writing on whiteboards or running shared software. Money is saved on transport and accommodation but, perhaps more significantly, the time it takes for people to travel to the meeting is also saved.

2 *Reduces time for information transfer.* The benefits of shorter times for messages to arrive are obvious, but more subtle benefits can also occur through the rapid transfer of information. It is now possible for the global company to operate 24 hours a day by taking advantage of people working in different time zones. If someone is working on a product design in New Zealand, for example, they can dispatch it for review in Europe at the end of their working day. The review can then be conducted in Europe while the other team members are asleep and will be ready for review the next morning. Using this simple method product designs could be accelerated significantly. Customer service queries can also be turned around more quickly through the use of telecommunications.

The healing power of global communications

MINI CASE

A medical example reported in *Computer Weekly* in August 1997 involved an unusual pattern in the X-ray of a boy's knee in Turkey. The surgeons looking after him were unfamiliar with this type of injury, so they posted it via the Internet to a medical newsgroup. It was identified by specialists in the US as being a rare type of tumour which was then successfully operated on. In a business context, such discussion areas can be used to give customers details of problems with products and how to overcome them, which can be accessed at any time of the day or night.

In May 1998 the Internet prevented the suicide of a young woman in Leeds, UK when a message she had posted to an Internet discussion group was read by someone in the US who alerted the British authorities. They found her before she died and she was successfully treated.

3 *Enables sharing and dissemination of company information.* Opportunities to share information are lost when it is locked in a filing cabinet or stored on an individual's PC. By placing information on a server, either as a file or within a database, it can be made accessible to all departments who need it and the flow of information in the company improved. This has proved to be one of the big benefits of intranets. A company selling through agents worldwide can provide information such as prices or technical specifications over an intranet. This information is always up to date, as there is no delay while price lists are reproduced and transported to the agents. Of course, this approach also helps in reducing costs. Intranets are described in detail in Chapter 17.

4 *Enables sharing of hardware resources such as printers, backup, processing power.* An obvious benefit of setting up a network is that it enables the cost of equipment such as printers, faxes, modems or scanners to be shared between members of a workgroup. Printers are the most obvious item that can be shared within a business. Workgroup printers may be shared between small teams of three or four up to 20 or so people, but a more powerful printer would be required in the latter case. For a printer shared by many people, it is usual to use a print server to schedule the jobs and store them while they are pending. Through storing information on a server, the security of the users' data can be increased by attaching a tape or optical backup device to the server and performing regular backups. Other administrative tasks are also made easier by centralising more complex equipment.

5 *Promotes new ways of working.* As well as the tangible benefits, introducing networks can enable a different approach to running a business. Setting up an internal network makes it possible to use group-working tools. Setting up a wide area network makes electronic data interchange with suppliers possible.

6 *Operate geographically separate businesses as one.* Through using wide area communications technology, it is possible to rationalise the operations of a company that originally operated as separate business units in different geographic locations, perhaps with their own working practices, procedures and reporting mechanisms. Linked business units can use common ways of working. Sharing of information on best practices can also occur.

7 *Restructures relationships with partners.* In the same way that different groups or businesses within a company can work more effectively together, different companies can also collaborate better. This may occur, for example, when new products are being designed or when a manufacturer is ordering goods from its suppliers. These types of business-to-business communication are often assisted by electronic data interchange or EDI, discussed on page 158.

To balance against the many benefits, there are, of course, disadvantages with introducing networks. The main disadvantages are:

1 The initial setup cost may be high, and there may be a considerable period before the costs are paid off.

2 When implementing or updating the network there may be considerable practical difficulties. Deploying cabling can be very disruptive to staff doing their daily work.

3 In the long term, companies become reliant on networks and breaks in service can be very disruptive. For this reason investment in network maintenance is vital.

4 Security is reduced through introducing a network, since there are more access points to sensitive data. Data may also be intercepted when it is transferred from one site to another.

Despite these disadvantages, most companies still proceed with implementation and take care to reduce the risks of disruption and security breaches. In doing so, further costs will be introduced. Table 5.1 summarises the advantages and disadvantages of networks.

Table 5.1 A summary of the key advantages and disadvantages of network technology

Advantages	Disadvantages
1 Improved sharing of information and hardware resources	1 Overreliance on networks for mission-critical applications
2 Reduced costs through sharing hardware and software	2 Cost of initial setup and administration
3 Reduced time for communication compared with traditional methods such as postal mail	3 Disruption during initial setup and maintenance
4 Increased security of data which is backed up on file servers. Increased security through restricting access via user names and passwords	4 Reduced security due to more external access points to the network on wide area networks and the Internet

Federal Express turns IS 'inside out' using communications technology

MINI CASE

To a global company such as Federal Express, communications are an integral part of the business operation. FedEx makes use of the Internet to allow customers to arrange a delivery and then track its progress to its destination (see Fig 5.3). In 1997 its site (http://www.fedex.com) was receiving over 300 000 'hits' or accesses a day from its customers.

To enable progress monitoring and to schedule delivery of a package, FedEx makes use of satellite communications to link its many offices around the world.

Fig 5.3 The FedEx parcel tracking page

These developments demonstrate how FedEx and now many of the other parcel companies have turned their information systems 'inside out' to face their customers. The original system involved FedEx customers phoning a call centre where staff used various IS to assemble an answer and, if necessary, phone back. Now the *customer* operates the new IS and this has cut transaction costs significantly from $25 to 25 cents in round figures. Similarly, United Parcel Services reports that it has saved on a staggering 500 000 phone calls per month.

▶ Business applications made possible by networks

Networks make possible a wide range of business solutions which we now take for granted. Different types of software application have been developed to assist communication within and between businesses. The success of these software applications has further boosted the adoption of the networks on which they are based. For example, the growth of LANs has encouraged the use of e-mail and, in turn, the need to have e-mail as a business tool has encouraged companies to set up LANs. Software to support communication and collaboration has become widespread in the 1990s as all medium to large companies have a network over which these tools can be usefully applied. Let us now look at some examples of the applications that can be provided by networks connecting different parties.

▶ Collaboration and management within a business

Groupware tools can help collaboration within or between organisations. They include:

◆ electronic mail (e-mail);

◆ workgroup software enabling collaboration, e.g. on a bid document or using a shared office diary;

◆ voice mail;

◆ facsimile (fax servers for desktop fax);

◆ teleconferencing and video conferencing.

Within the retail sector, electronic point of sale (EPOS) systems allows information about sales in each branch to be collected and analysed at head office, as is the case with the national lottery system.

Office automation systems and collaboration tools are introduced in Chapter 3 and described in more detail in Chapter 6.

Business-to-business collaboration – electronic data interchange

Electronic data interchange (EDI)

The electronic exchange of structured information between businesses using wide area network.

Electronic data interchange (EDI) is the electronic exchange of information between businesses using wide area networks. EDI includes transactions of structured data such as electronic payment and documents. It is defined by a specific International Standard ANSI X12/EDIFACIT.

EDI is now widespread in supporting collaboration between different business partners. It provides a reliable method of electronic transactions between companies. The transactions cover a range of information, often relating to supply chain interactions. Figure 5.4 shows the typical information transfer between two companies

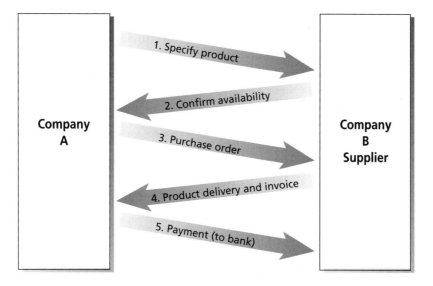

Fig 5.4 Communications in a purchase that can be facilitated by EDI

when a product is purchased. Once Company A has confirmed the availability and price of the item it needs, a request for the item (a purchase order) will be sent to Company B (the supplier) using EDI. The supplier will confirm the date of delivery and send an electronic invoice with another message. Payments between companies are also made electronically, using a bank as intermediary. Another application of EDI is the exchange of design documents for a new product. In the past, EDI has mainly been based around private leased networks. Increasingly, it is making use of secure transactions over the Internet. The use of the Internet reduces the barrier of cost of entry to many companies.

Although significant cost savings are possible through EDI, the main driver for its introduction is to be able to perform existing processes faster. This can give companies a competitive advantage over rivals who have not adopted EDI. Time is reduced when purchasing from suppliers, both that taken for purchase requests and for confirmations to arrive. This is possible since the transactions no longer occur by mail or fax and there is no need to rekey information. Another plus point is that if there is a problem with a customer order, perhaps through late delivery of a component, it is much easier to find the status of the delivery by looking at the system. Furthermore, the whole process can be automated and the risk of human error reduced. Companies working together on a product design can achieve reduced lead times and better quality through close collaboration.

EDI is now conducted using the cheaper communications made available by the Internet. Chapter 17 describes how retailer Tesco uses EDI to communicate with suppliers.

Companies may start by automating part of the supply chain, such as ordering new supplies. This can be extended by linking up this part of the EDI system to internal systems for stock control. The stock control can be linked in turn to a sales order processing system. Software systems such as SAP R/3 enable all of these parts of the business to be seamlessly integrated, and are often referred to as enterprise resource planning systems (ERP), which are reviewed in more detail in Chapters 6 and 19.

Business-to-customer interactions

For catalogue companies, phone links and the Internet provide what is now an essential means of obtaining sales and providing customer services. 'Call centres' provide an integrated phone and computer network for answering customer queries or taking orders. Auto-teller machines (ATMs) used by bank customers are made available by a country-wide or international network.

Call centres have been introduced by many companies selling financial services. They integrate computers, networks and telephony to assist teams of customer service representatives who take customer phone enquiries. In the UK, First Direct, one of the main 'phone banks', has its main call centre in Leeds. Call centres are described in more detail in Chapter 19.

MINI CASE

The virtual organisation

The virtual organisation is now touted by many authors as the shape of the future business. A virtual organisation makes use of networking to set up communication between its employees, suppliers and customers in such a way that there are no physical boundaries or constraints on the company. Employees may work anywhere in the world and customers are able to purchase tailored products from any location. The absence of any rigid boundary or hierarchy within the organisation should lead to a more responsive and flexible company. This extends to 'virtual products' where mass production is replaced by the ability to tailor the product to the customer's need.

A hypothetical example is of a 'virtual shoe company' which contracts seven other companies to:

◆ research the shoe market;
◆ design shoes;
◆ make shoes;
◆ advertise shoes;
◆ transport to retailers;
◆ sell shoes;
◆ do the accounts.

The Internet and a wide area network are used to set up the links between the players in the virtual organisation. Software such as e-mail, groupware and workflow are used to aid collaboration between people in the organisation.

Virtual organisations are referred to in more detail in Chapter 19.

▶ ALTERNATIVE STRUCTURES FOR COMMUNICATIONS NETWORKS

When specifying computer networks, it is useful to distinguish between networks which are used within a single office of a company and more extensive networks which connect different offices of the same company or different companies. The former is known as a local area network (LAN) and the latter a wide area network (WAN). Definitions of these, and how they vary, are described opposite.

▶ Local area networks (LAN)

A LAN consists of a single network segment or several connected segments which are limited in extent, hence local. A network segment defines a group of clients which are attached to the same hub or network interface card linked to a single server. The term local can be interpreted in different ways. LANs are usually limited to a company occupying a single building, but would equally apply to a network connecting several buildings across a larger company site. Faster, higher-capacity links such as fibre-optic cables connecting different LANs or network segments are sometimes referred to as 'backbones'. Such networks may just have a single server if the company is of fewer than, say, 20 people. Larger companies with hundreds of employees are very likely to have several central servers and possibly departmental servers also. A LAN is used to share computer resources between different members of a company or workgroup.

An example of a LAN which might serve a workgroup or a small company is shown in Fig 5.5.

Local-area network (LAN)

A computer network that spans a limited geographic area, typically a single office or building.

▶ Peer-to-peer networking

This is a simple type of local area network which provides sharing of files and peripherals between PCs.

Peer-to-peer refers to the capability of any computer on a local area network to share resources, in particular files and peripherals, with others. It is particularly appropriate for small workgroups where central control from a server is less necessary. Both Windows for Workgroups and Windows 95 provide these capabilities. For example, a user can, with permission, share across the network a file stored on another user's hard disk. With a peer-to-peer arrangement, data will be distributed and therefore difficult to backup and secure.

PCs can also be connected with a serial cable using the serial ports on each machine. This enables files to be transferred between, for example, a laptop and a desktop PC. This facility is available through Windows 95 or 98 or through specialised software such as Laplink.

Peer-to-peer network

A simple type of local area network which provides sharing of files and peripherals between PCs.

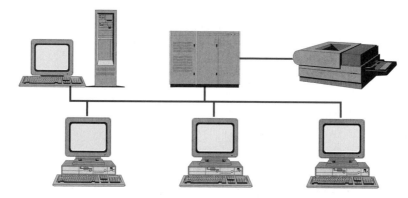

Fig 5.5 A workgroup LAN

**Wide area
network (WAN)**

Networks covering a
large area which
connect businesses in
different parts of the
same city, different
parts of a country or
different countries.

▶ Wide area network (WAN)

These are large in extent and may connect offices in different parts of the same city, different parts of a country or even different countries (Fig. 5.6). The WAN will connect many servers at each site. When we connect from a PC at one site to a server at another site, we talk about connecting to a 'remote' server across a WAN. If there is a large international coverage, it will be referred to as a global network. If the WAN enables communication across the whole company, it is referred to as the 'enterprise network' or 'enterprise-wide network'. Companies usually pay for their own 'leased lines' or communications links between different sites. Virtual private networks and value-added networks, which are described later, provide cheaper alternatives where the communications links are shared.

Often the public telephone network is used to connect remote sites, referred to as POTS or 'Plain Old Telephone System'. A company can also lease private or dedicated lines from a telecommunications supplier to connect sites, or can set up links using microwave or satellite methods.

Other terms are also used to refer to the extent of a network. Many colleges and universities will have campus networks which connect different buildings making up the campus. Large cities such as London or New York often have a high-speed metropolitan area network to connect businesses within the city. Singapore has developed the concept of the 'intelligent island' in which businesses of the city are connected by a very high-speed network.

▶ The Internet

The Internet is clearly significant as a method of improving communications on a global scale. It is made up of many other national and international wide area networks and is loosely referred to as the 'information superhighway'. The Internet helps business communications by enabling e-mail or EDI to be conducted between companies throughout the world.

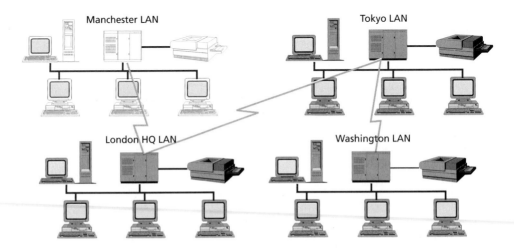

Fig 5.6 A wide area network (WAN)

The profile of the Internet has been increased recently by the growth in use of the World Wide Web, or Web for short. This provides a method of storing, accessing and transmitting information which is very easy to use and cost effective. For example, a company can place marketing information on the Web promoting its products, or can arrange for its products to be ordered and paid for via the Web. The potential market for the company's products is global given the extent of the Internet.

The Internet is covered in greater detail in Chapter 17; as an important business tool it warrants its own chapter.

For an example of how governments are using communications networks to give their economies a competitive advantage, the mini case study on two of the 'Asian tiger' economies shows how two governments intend to make sure they are not 'left behind' as technology develops.

Asian tigers innovate through major communications initiatives

MINI CASE

The Singapore 'intelligent island' concept and Singapore ONE (One Network for Everyone)

The Singapore government believes that for the country to maintain a competitive edge it must take advantage of communications technology to connect its businesses and citizens. The National Computing organisation is tasked with achieving this. Two initiatives have been started.

At the end of 1997 the number of applications on what is described as 'the world's first nationwide broadband network' was 103. Some 5000 homes and businesses have been connected, accessing Singapore ONE's applications that range from leisure and entertainment to health information, services for businesses, banking, education and distance learning.

Some of the most recent applications on Singapore ONE include:

◆ an online medical service linking medical professionals in the healthcare community;
◆ an online ticket booking system for events such as film festivals;
◆ concerts, musical performances and family entertainment shows;
◆ an online, one-stop system enabling O-level students to register for admission to colleges and polytechnics;
◆ a video mail system that enables audio/video messages to be transmitted and broadcast via electronic mail using video streaming technology;
◆ an interactive, multimedia-based educational software that teaches young children how to recognise and read simple Arabic scripts;
◆ a Web-based game, Xiang Qi, that allows remote players from around the world to come together for a cordial game of Chinese chess.

Malaysia launches multimedia super corridor

In 1996 Malaysia launched an ambitious 'multimedia super corridor' linked by a $2 billion network of fibre-optic cable which was projected to cost up to $15 billion and will be funded by both private and public sources. The corridor is a 15 km-wide area that runs from Kuala Lumpur in the north, past the international airport to Sepang, 50 km to the south.

▶

Owing to the scope of the project, construction could take 10 years. The multimedia super corridor will include:

◆ a new multimedia university;
◆ research labs;
◆ a futuristic cybercity for 240 000 people, which will be wired with the latest technology.

People living in the new cybercity will use smartcards for buying products and services and hospitals will provide telemedicine. It will also be a site for the new multibillion-dollar paperless government capital, which will be named Putrajaya. The Malaysian Prime Minister is personally endorsing the project. Major foreign companies are investing in the multimedia super corridor, including Sun, IBM, delivery company DHL and Siemens AG. New employment laws have been passed that make it easier for foreigners to gain employment in the country, to give an employment market with virtually no restrictions.

Value-added networks (VANS)

Value-added networks (VANS) give a subscription service enabling companies to transmit data securely across a shared network.

▶ Value-added networks (VANs)

Value-added networks (VANS) are so named since they allow a company to minimise its investment in wide area communications while still receiving all the benefits this can bring. The cost of setting up and maintaining the network is borne by the service provider, which then rents out the network to a number of companies. This works out more cheaply than if a company had leased its own point-to-point private lines, but it is not as secure.

A similar concept to VAN are **virtual private networks (VPNs)**. This is a data network that makes use of the public telecommunications infrastructure and Internet, but information remains secure by the use of which is known as a 'tunnelling protocol' and security procedures such as 'firewalls', which are described in Chapter 17. A virtual private network can again be contrasted with a system of owned or leased point-to-point lines that can only be used by one company.

Virtual private network (VPN)

A data network that makes use of the public telecommunication infrastructure and Internet, but information remains secure by the use of security procedures.

▶ Private branch exchange (PBX)

A PBX enables switching between phones or voice and data using existing telephone lines. This can be used for printer sharing, for example.

Private branch exchange (PBX)

Enables switching between phones or voice and data using existing telephone lines.

▶ Layouts for company networks

The physical layout of a LAN is known as a **network topology**. Bus, star, ring and combinations are most common.

There are a number of alternative arrangements for connecting the clients to the server in a local area network. These are known by the description of the layout or topology: namely bus, star or ring. The layouts of the alternatives are shown in Fig 5.7. When building a network for a company, the topology adopted will form part of the specification for the company performing installation of the network. The topology chosen and the media used to implement it will affect the network cost and performance, so these aspects are referred to in the description below. The advantages of the different types of topology are summarised in Table 5.2.

Network topology

The physical layout of a LAN is known as a network topology. Bus, star, ring and combinations are most common.

Table 5.2 Summary of the advantages and disadvantages of the main local area network topologies

Topology	Advantage	Disadvantage
Bus or linear	Easy to install and manage for small workgroup	Breaks in the cable disrupt the whole network
Star	Provide protection from cable breaks	Dependent on central host
Ring	Suitable for large data volumes and mission-critical applications	Higher initial cost and time for installation

Bus or linear topology

The bus topology provides one of the simplest arrangements of networked computers. It consists of a serial or 'daisy-chain' arrangement of nodes. This is often the cheapest type of network to set up using co-axial thin ethernet (10Base-2) cable (*see* page 174). Twisted pair 10Base-T ethernet can be used but is more expensive and less easy to handle, although it is more robust. At each end of the network segment there is a terminator block and at each node there is a T-shaped connector for attaching the cable to the 'stub' or port on the network card which is installed in the PC. These terminators and connectors are often referred to as BNC connectors. To join two ethernet trunks a repeater device is needed to boost the signals across the greater extent of the network.

When planning LANs using thin ethernet there are some physical constraints, since the maximum segment length is 186 metres and there is a maximum of 30 nodes per trunk. Although suitable for a small network, the bus topology is prone to disruptions to service caused by a break in the links. If there is a break in the cable, then the PCs on either side of it will not be able to communicate. Breaks in the links can be quite common if the cable is exposed, since it is not very robust. All nodes in a bus topology will receive each packet of information broadcast from the server, although the information is only acted on by the node if it is intended for that node.

Star topology

For larger networks, the star topology is easier to manage than the bus, since if new PCs are added it is not necessary to break the existing cable. In a star topology, each PC is connected via a cable to a central location. Each PC is not usually connected directly to the server, but to a hub which is in turn connected to the server. If this cable is damaged then only one PC will be affected. Because there is more cabling, most companies will invest in plastic ducts to hide the cables. You should check that the cost of networking includes this structured cabling. Twisted pair cable or 10Base-T ethernet cable is normally used in a star topology. Twisted pair cable in turn uses another type of connector, the RJ-45, which is similar in appearance to a telephone cable and socket. Hubs typically provide 12 or 24 ports into which the cables are plugged. These hubs can be daisy chained together to give a larger capacity.

Star-configured bus

This configuration is used to connect two or more star configurations together. Often the star will be connected to a hub which is connected to the other star by linear buses.

Ring topology

In this topology there is a continuous ring of network cable. The most common form of this technology is token ring. Physical ring topologies are rare, since network managers set up a star arrangement with PCs attached to a hub or MAU (multistation access unit) containing a logical ring configuration. Confusingly, token ring is often referred to as 'star-configured ring'.

The 'token' refers to a packet of data which is passed from one node to the next. If it contains an identifier indicating that it is destined for that node, its contents are read and it is marked as empty. To send a message, the node will use an empty packet by adding a message and a destination address. Token ring topologies use twisted-pair or fibre-optic cable.

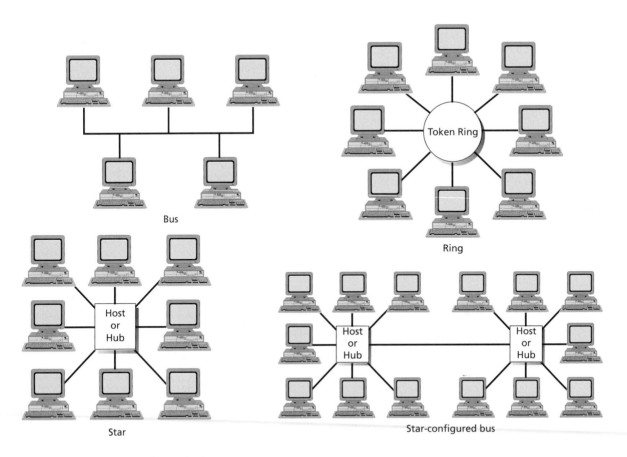

Fig 5.7 Local area network topologies

▶ COMPONENTS OF NETWORKS

In this section we will examine how to specify the often confusingly named components that are necessary to set up a network. We start by looking at the big picture: the client/server architecture of the modern information system and why this has been adopted by businesses. We will then examine each of the components in turn and look at how they fit together and the important factors in their selection.

▶ The client/server model of computing

The **client/server** architecture consists of client computers such as PCs sharing resources such as a database stored on more powerful server computers. Processing can be shared between the clients and the servers.

Client/server architecture is significant since most modern information systems are based on this structure. The client/server model involves a series of clients, typically desktop PCs, which are the access points for end-user applications. As is shown in Fig 5.8, the clients are connected to a more powerful PC or UNIX server computer via a local area network within one site of a company, or a wide area network connecting different sites and/or companies. The network is made up of both telecommunications processors to help route the information and the channels and media which carry the information.

The server is a more powerful computer which is usually used to store the application and the data shared by the users. When a user wants to run a program on a PC in a client/server system, the applications, such as a wordprocessor, will usually be stored on the hard disk of the server and then loaded into the memory of the client PC, running or 'executing' on the processor of the client. The document the user creates would be saved back to the hard disk of the server. This is only one alternative. One of the benefits of client/server is that there are many choices for sharing the workload between resources. The system designers can decide to distribute data and processing across both servers and client computers, which is described in Chapter 12. There it is also explained how different functions can be partitioned between client and server and the merits of using 'thin' or 'fat' clients, applications on the former being smaller and easier to maintain.

Client/server

The client/server architecture consists of client computers such as PCs sharing resources such as a database stored on more powerful server computers.

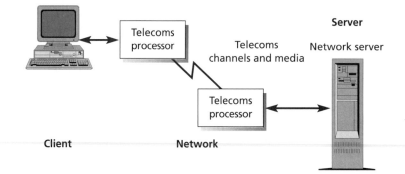

Fig 5.8 Components of a client/server system

To summarise, the main components of a client/server system are shown in Fig 5.8 and can be defined as follows:

◆ Client software, the interface by which the end-user accesses the software. It includes both the operating system, such as Windows 95, and the applications software, such as wordprocessors. Increasingly, Web-based browsers are being used as clients on a company intranet.

◆ Server software, used to store information, administer the system and provide links to other company systems. Again, this may be a Web server or a database server.

◆ The application development environment, which provides interactive programming tools to develop applications through the application programming interface (API) of the package.

◆ The infrastructure or plumbing of the system. This is based on local and wide area networking techniques and consists of the telecommunication processors and media.

Why use client/server?

The adoption of the client/server architecture was part of a trend to 'downsize' from large mainframes with arrays of user terminals which had limited functionality. This latter type of architecture was widespread in businesses during the 1970s and 1980s. The client/server model represented a radically new architecture compared to the traditional, centralised method of a mainframe, with its character-based 'dumb terminals' which dated back nearly to the birth of computers. Rather than all the tasks involved in program execution (other than display) occurring on the mainframe, client/server gives the opportunity for them to be shared between a central server and clients. This gives the potential for faster execution, as processing is distributed across many clients.

Cost savings were originally used to drive the introduction of client/server. PC-based servers were much cheaper than mainframes, although the client PCs were more expensive than dumb terminals. The overall savings were dramatic. These savings were coupled with additional benefits of ease of use of the new clients compared with the older terminals. The clients used new graphical user interfaces which were easier to use thanks to a mouse, and the graphics could improve analysis of business data. Customisation of the client is also possible – the end-user is empowered through being able to develop their own applications and view data to their preference. With queries occurring on the back end, this reduces the amount of network traffic that is required. Centralised control of the user administration and data security and archiving can still be retained.

With these advantages, there are also a host of system management problems which were not envisaged when client/server was first adopted. These have been partly responsible for the reduced costs promised with this 'downsizing' not materialising. To some extent there is now a backlash, in which the new network-centric model is being suggested as a means of reducing these management problems. These disbenefits include:

1 *High cost of ownership.* Although the purchase price for a PC is relatively low, the extra potential for running different applications and modifications by end-users means that there is much more that can go wrong in comparison with a dumb ter-

minal. More support staff are required to solve these problems resulting from the complex hardware and software. The annual cost of ownership of a PC is now estimated by the Gartner Group to be $8000, which is about four times the purchase price. The cost of ownership of a dumb (text-based) terminal is approximately $2000. The issue of reducing what is known as the total cost of ownership is considered further in Chapter 16.

2 *Instability.* Client/server technology is often complex and involves integrating different hardware and software components from many different companies. Given this, client/server systems may be less reliable than mainframe systems. EuropCar suffered three days of system downtime in the early 1990s, which was thought to have led to the loss of $300 000 of rental business. This downtime occurred after migration from a mainframe to a client/server system.

3 *Performance.* For some mission-critical applications, a smaller server cannot deliver the power required. In a travel agency business, for example, this will give rise to longer queues and poorer customer service. For this reason, many banks and travel agents have retained their mainframe-based systems where performance is critical. The use of a PC can also cause delays at the client end, as the screen takes a long time to redraw graphics compared to a teletext terminal.

4 *Lack of worker focus.* Although PCs can potentially empower end-users, the freedom of choice can also lead to non-productive time wasting, as users rearrange the colours and wallpaper on their desktop rather than performing their regular tasks!

Despite these difficulties, the compelling arguments of ease of use and flexibility of client/server still remain. The empowerment of the end-user to develop their own applications and to use and share the data as they see fit is now considered to be the main benefit of client/server.

▶ Servers

Servers are vital to an information system, since they regulate the flow of information around the network in the way that a heart controls the flow of blood around the body. Network servers run the network operating system (NOS), the software that is used to manage the network, and are often used to store large volumes of data. The server and NOS together perform the following functions:

Server

A server is a powerful computer used to control the management of a network. It may have a specific function such as storing user files or a database or managing a printer.

◆ *Maintain security* – access to information in files is restricted according to the user name and password issued to users of the network.

◆ *Sharing of peripheral devices* connected to the network, such as printers and tape drives. These are often attached directly to the server.

◆ *Sharing of applications* such as wordprocessors, which do not then need to be stored on the hard drive of the end-user's computer. The cost of buying applications can be reduced through buying a 'site licence'.

◆ *Sharing of information* – access to this data is maintained by the NOS and it is stored within the hard drive of a server as files or as part of a database.

Both applications and data can be managed better when they are stored on a managed server. It is easier to audit who uses which applications and to ensure the security of the data. Data quality can also be managed more effectively.

For the larger network of perhaps 20 people or more, the functions described above may be split between several servers to share the load. There may be a separate file server, print server, password server and database server. In very large companies there will be many servers used for data storage. These will all be linked by the network to ensure that the data is accessible by everyone. They will also be responsible for ensuring through a process known as **replication** that the same version of data exists on different servers. With the use of many servers, an opportunity exists to spread the computing workload across these servers rather than overloading a single central machine, which is what happened in the days of the mainframe. When functions are shared across several computers this is known as distributed computing. An example of distributed computing is given in Chapter 19.

The different types of server are summarised in Table 5.3.

Replication

Ensures that the versions of data stored on different servers are consistent. Software is used to check changes made to data on each server. Changes are transmitted to all other servers.

Table 5.3 Types of server

Type of server	Purpose
Network	Contains functions to manage the network resources and control user access
File	This term is sometimes used to refer to network server functions. It can also indicate that users' files such as documents and spreadsheets are stored on the network server
Print	Dedicated print servers have a queue of all documents for which print requests have been made, often combined with file or network servers
Fax	Used to route incoming and outgoing faxes received and sent from the users' desktop
Mail	Stores and forwards e-mail messages
Database	Used to store data and provide the software to process data queries supplied by users, often accessed by Structured Query Language (SQL)
Application	Used to store programs such as spreadsheet or bespoke applications run by end-users on their PCs. This removes the need to store each application on every user's hard disk
Communications	Manages connections with other networks in a WAN configuration. Sometimes known as gateways and attached to other gateway devices such as routers and firewall servers.

When creating an information system, there are a number of critical functions which must be designed in to the server. These are important requirements which must be checked with server vendors, database vendors and operating systems vendors. They are:

◆ *Performance.* The server should be fast enough to handle all the requests from users attached to the network. A margin should be built in to accommodate future growth in users and network traffic. This means specifying a suitable amount of

memory (for example, a PC server might need 512 Mb RAM minimum on a PC-based server), a fast hard disk and, less importantly, a fast processor.

◆ *Capacity.* When initially specified, the hard disk capacity should be large enough that it will not need to be upgraded in the near future.

◆ *Resilience/fault tolerance.* If there is a problem affecting the hardware, such as a power surge or a problem with the hard disk, it is important that the whole network does not 'crash' because of this. Preventive measures should be taken, such as installing a uninterruptible power supply or running two disks in parallel (disk mirroring or RAID (Redundant Array of Inexpensive Disks)).

◆ *Clustering* is used to spread the load across different servers, so improving reliability and performance. It involves linking several servers together via a high-speed link such as fibre-optic cabling. This can enable parallel processing, where tasks are shared between processors, and also storage mirroring, where duplicate copies of data are stored on different servers to improve performance and reduce the risk of one server failing.

Servers can be specified as powerful PCs running an operating system such as Windows NT or Novell Netware, or they can run the UNIX operating system, from companies such as Sun, IBM or Hewlett-Packard.

▶ End-user computers or terminals

The access points for users of a network are known variously as clients, nodes, workstations or, most commonly, plain PCs. It is best to use the term 'client PC', as this helps distinguish clients from servers which may also be PC based. To work on the network each client must have networking software such as Novell Netware or TCP/IP installed. TCP/IP stands for the Transmission Control Protocol/Internet Protocol. It is a networking standard that controls the transmission of data packets from clients connected to the Internet or an intranet. Of course, a physical connection to the network is also required. For a PC on an office LAN, this is provided by a *network interface card* in one of the PC's slots. The card is then attached to the network cabling. For a PC at home which is linked to the Internet, the network card is replaced by a modem. Specialised systems software known as Windows sockets, or 'Winsock' for short, is required to connect to the Internet via an Internet service provider.

▶ Data communications equipment or telecommunications processors

As well as the physical cables that link the computers, there are also other important components of the complete telecommunications system which have to be purchased by a business. These are the pieces of hardware which are used to link the servers and clients and different networks together. These devices can be thought of as connectors located between client computers and servers which join the transmission media. Collectively, these processors can be called telecommunications processors or gateways, but they are usually referred to by their specific names, such as hubs, multiplexers, bridges and routers. In a company that needs to use gateway devices, a specialist is required to maintain them. Modems and network interface cards also fit into this category.

Modems

Modem is short for modulator-demodulator. Its function is to convert the digital signal sent from a computer to the analogue signal which is transmitted along the phone lines. On receiving a transmission the modem will reverse the translation and convert from analogue to digital.

Modems often need to be selected for small office or home computers, so we will spend a while looking at the factors involved in their purchase.

The first choice is whether to choose an internal modem card or an external modem attached via a port on the back of the PC. If you purchase a home PC with a modem, it is very likely to be pre-fitted with an internal card. If you purchase a modem, it is probably best to opt for an external modem as this is easier to fit and transfer between PCs.

The next option is then the speed supported by the modem: the faster the better. The transmission rate is measured in bits per second or bps. Bits per second are still occasionally referred to as baud. Basic models offer 14 400 or 28 000 bps, with 33 600 and 56 000 bps offered in more expensive models. This is the limit of speed possible with analogue phone lines. This is not fast enough for frequent business use, where modems may be connected by other technologies such as ISDN (64 000 or 128 000 bps). More advanced models now support voice as well as fax and data transfer. Other standards exist with modems, but it is not necessary to be aware of these as long as you check that the modem is compatible for PC use with Windows over analogue phone lines.

Hubs

Hubs are used to connect up to 20 PCs to a network in a convenient way using patch cables (which look similar to phone cables and sockets) running between the back of each PC and the hub. A hub may then be attached to a server or a backbone connection leading to the server.

Bridges and routers

These are used to connect different LANs and transfer data packets from one network to the next. They can be used to connect similar types of LAN. They also offer filtering services to restrict local traffic to one side of the bridge, thus reducing traffic overall. Routers can select the best route for packets to be transmitted and are also used on the Internet backbones and wide area network to achieve this. Although these devices used to be distinct, they are now produced as hybrids which share functions.

Companies attached to the Internet usually use a router as a gateway to attach their internal network to the Internet. This is often combined with a 'firewall', which is intended to reduce the risk of someone from outside the company gaining unauthorised access to company data. Firewalls are described in more detail in Chapter 17.

Repeaters

Over a long transmission distance, signal distortion may occur. Repeaters are necessary to increase transmission distances by regenerating signals and retransmitting them.

Data service units and channel service units

These devices are used to connect to digital communications lines by converting signals received from bridges, routers and multiplexers.

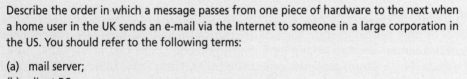

> Describe the order in which a message passes from one piece of hardware to the next when a home user in the UK sends an e-mail via the Internet to someone in a large corporation in the US. You should refer to the following terms:
>
> (a) mail server;
> (b) client PC;
> (c) modem;
> (d) hub;
> (e) network cable;
> (f) network card;
> (g) gateway server (telecommunications processor);
> (h) router.
>
> Treat the Internet transmission as a single stage.

ACTIVITY

▶ Telecommunications channels

Telecommunications channels are the different media used to carry information between different locations. These include traditional cables and wires known as *guided media,* and wires and more recent innovations such as satellite and microwave which are *unguided media.*

We will now examine the benefits and applications of these different media. When doing this, the main factors that need to be considered are the physical characteristics, data transmission method, performance and cost.

Telecommunications channels

The media by which data is transmitted. Cables and wires are known as guided media and microwave and satellite links are known as unguided media.

Characteristics of guided media

The main types of cabling used in LANs are based on copper cabling. Data is transmitted along this by applying a voltage at one end, which is received at the other. A positive voltage represents a binary one and a negative voltage represents a binary zero. There are two main types of twisted copper cabling used in networks. Insulated straight cabling is not suitable except for very short distances such as between a computer and a printer. The two types are:

◆ *Twisted-pair (often used for 10Base-T Ethernet).* Twisted-pair cabling consists of twisted copper wire covered by an insulator. The two wires form a circuit over which data can be transmitted. The twisting is intended to reduce interference. Shielding using braided metal may also be used to reduce external interference. A cable may have more than one pair. Twisted-pair cabling was traditionally used for telephones.

◆ *Co-axial (used for Thin 10Base-2 Ethernet).* Co-axial cable consists of a single solid copper core surrounded by an insulator and a braided metal shield. 'Co-ax' can be used to connect devices over longer distances than twisted pair. It is possibly best known as the means used to connect an antenna to a television set. However, it has largely been superseded for office LAN environments, since twisted pair has now been refined to offer faster speeds than co-axial.

Fibre-optic is a relatively new transmission medium, and consists of thousands of fibres of pure silicon dioxide. Packets are transmitted along fibre-optic cables using light or photons emitted from a light emitting diode at one end of the cable, which is detected by a photo-sensitive cell at the other. Fibre-optic cables give very high transmission rates since the cable has very low resistance. This is well known as a method by which cable-TV is delivered to homes. A method proposed for increasing the speed of home access to the Internet is to use 'cable modems' for homes which receive cable TV. Fibre-optic cables are also better for security, since it is less easy to tap into them.

Characteristics of unguided or wireless media

For wide area network cables are still commonly used, but they are being superseded by the use of unguided media. This method uses signals transmitted through air and space from a transmitter to a receiver. It tends to be faster than wired methods. Wireless transmissions can be used for different business applications at different scales:

◆ *Wireless infra-red transmission* can be used for sending data between a portable PC or personal digital assistant (PDA) and a desktop computer. This saves download-ing files by floppy disk or serial cable. It is useful for sales people or engineers who are away from base frequently but need to upload the data they have collected in the field from their mobile computer to their desktop computer. Recent laser printers from Hewlett-Packard can now also receive documents for printing via wireless infra-red transmission from desktop or laptop computers that do not need to be connected to the printer.

◆ *Wireless transmission* can also be used locally to form a wireless LAN. Here a microwave or narrow-band radio transmitter and receiver may be used to connect different buildings. Wireless LANs are often used across college campuses. These have the benefit that the cost of laying cabling is not incurred. This makes them particularly suitable where it is not clear whether a link is needed in the long term.

◆ *Microwave transmission* can be used to beam information through the atmosphere. The maximum distance that can separate microwave transmitters is 45 km, since the signal follows a straight line and the curvature of the earth limits transmission distance. This can make microwave an expensive method of transmitting data, but the cast can be reduced if it is combined with satellite methods.

◆ *Satellite transmission* operates at two orbit levels, high orbit at 22 300 miles in a geostationary orbit and at a lower orbit. Messages are sent from a transceiver at one location on the earth's surface and are bounced off the satellite to another transceiver. Because of the distances involved, this can give a time delay of up to a quarter of a second, which is evident in interviews conducted by satellite. A range of frequencies can be used. Satellite applications include television, telephone and data transmission.

▶ Transmission methods

Transmission of data can be achieved in a variety of ways. Of those methods given below, the difference between analogue and digital signals is the important one to grasp.

Signal type

The two alternate methods of transmission are analogue and digital. An **analogue** signal represents a message by using a continuous wave-form which is carried by a cable such as a phone line. Here analogue transmission is used to carry voice, data or fax. Analogue is less suitable for higher capacity needs such as video, since its 'bandwidth' is limited (*see* below). A **digital** signal is not continuous, consisting of binary data sent in pulses of ones and zeros. This is achieved by varying the voltage of the line from a high to a low state. Digital transmissions are used where higher bandwidth is available. They have the dual advantages that no conversion from digital to analogue is necessary before sending, and the quality is better since distortion does not occur when the signal is boosted when long-distance transmission is required.

Analogue

Analogue transmissions send data in a continuous wave-form.

Digital

Digital transmissions send binary data as a series of ones and zeros.

Communications method

Data transmission can occur in different modes according to how the individual characters are transmitted. Asynchronous communication occurs when transmission of data occurs one character at a time with control bits to either side. Synchronous communication occurs when groups of characters are sent as **packets** and both the sending and receiving device synchronise data using a timer.

Packets are units of data that are exchanged between different devices over communications media. The entire message to be sent is broken down into smaller packets, since if an error occurs in transmission, only the packet with the error needs to be retransmitted.

Packets

Units of data that are exchanged between different devices over communications media. An entire message is broken down into smaller packets.

Transmission modes

When all end-user computers were character-based terminals, the terms 'simplex' and 'duplex' were commonly used to refer to the transmission mode. Today, these terms are unimportant to end-users or business managers. For the record, the differences are:

◆ *Simplex* refers to a one-way transmission.

◆ *Half-duplex* refers to a two-way transmission, but only one way at a given time.

◆ *Full-duplex* refers to a simultaneous two-way transmission.

The terms have now dropped out of common usage since LANs became predominant and most digital networks achieve full-duplex mode with simultaneous data flow in both directions.

Transmission speed

The speed at which data can be transferred from A to B is governed by the channel capacity, which is measured in bits per second (bps). Transmission of a single bit in a second is equivalent to one baud, a binary event. Rates are usually measured in terms of thousands of bits/second (Kbit/sec), millions of bits/second (Mbit/sec) or billions of bits per second (Gbit/sec).

A general term often used for describing capacity is **bandwidth**. The technical definition of bandwidth is that it is a measure of capacity given by the difference between the lowest and highest frequencies available for a given medium. This range of frequencies is measured in Hertz. For example, bandwidths in the 500 to 929 MHz range are used for TV and radio broadcasts.

Bandwidth is commonly used in a general sense to describe the data transfer rate. A good way to think of bandwidth as a measure is that it is similar to the diameter of a pipe along which a fluid is flowing. The larger the width of pipe, the higher capacity of water or data that can be transmitted. So the bandwidth of a 10 Mbit/sec LAN is much higher than the bandwidth available over analogue lines with a 28.8 Kbit/sec modem.

Table 5.4 summarises the characteristics of the different transmission media that we have considered.

Bandwidth

Bandwidth indicates the data transfer rates that can be achieved using a given media. It is measured in bits-per-second.

Table 5.4 A summary of characteristics for different transmission media

Characteristic	Twisted pair	Co-axial	Fibre-optic	Microwave radio	Satellite
Maximum data transfer rate	4 Mbit/sec	140 Mbit/sec	10 000 Mbit/sec	100 Mbit/sec	100 Mbit/sec
Installation	Easy	Moderate	Difficult	Difficult	Difficult
Cost	Low	Moderate	High	High	High
Maintenance	Moderate	Low	Low	Low	–

ACTIVITY

Rank the following in terms of their data transmission speeds:

(a) Ethernet LAN (10 Mbit/sec);
(b) modem attached to a phone line (28 800 baud);
(c) ISDN2 link to the home operating at 128 Kbit/sec;
(d) fibre-optic cable used for video conferencing at a speed of 10Gbit/sec.

▶ Network operating systems

The final component that is needed to make all the other components work in unison is a **network operating system (NOS)**. This is systems software necessary to control the access to and flow of information around a network. It is used to implement the different levels in the *OSI models*. It provides the following functions:

- ◆ Access control or security through providing user accounts with user names and passwords.
- ◆ File and data sharing of data stored on a database server or file server.
- ◆ Communication between users via e-mail, diary systems or workgroup software such as Lotus Notes.
- ◆ Sharing of devices, enabling, for example, the backup to tape of data on the server, or printer sharing.

The most widely used NOS for a PC-based LAN are Novell Netware and IBM LAN Manager. However, NOS features are now being built into standard operating systems such as Microsoft Windows NT, and this is increasingly being adopted by companies. For UNIX-based servers the NOS is a component of the operating system. Unix is used by many medium and large companies operating servers from companies such as Sun Microsystems, Hewlett-Packard and IBM. It is often thought to offer better stability than Windows NT since it is a long-established NOS.

Network operating system (NOS)

The software necessary to control the access to and flow of information around a network. It is used to implement the different levels in the OSI model.

▶ Middleware

Middleware is a specialised type of software which allows different software applications to communicate. It acts as a layer between other software to assist in data transfer between incompatible systems. It acts as a layer between other software to assist in data transfer between incompatible systems. It is often described as the 'glue' that binds the software applications with systems software. It is important in a networked world, since it provides translation services between software running on different types of computer systems in different companies. An example of middleware is gateway software which enables an internal e-mail system such as Lotus cc:Mail to send messages to other e-mail systems via the Internet. Middleware is also necessary to enable a single software application such as sales order processing to access different types of database, such as Oracle, Informix or Microsoft SQL Server, which a large company may use. Middleware to assist in communications can be categorised according to a seven-layer model known as the OSI model.

Middleware

A type of software that acts as a layer between other software to assist in data transfer between incompatible systems.

Open Systems Interconnection (OSI) model

The **OSI model** is an international standard defining connectivity of links between computers created by OSI to assist in ensuring compatibility between network components from different manufacturers in different countries. It emerged as part of an industry trend to 'open systems'. The idea behind open systems and the OSI model is that information can be exchanged across networks between different computers regardless of the manufacturer. Before this standard, systems from different manufacturers were often incompatible. The OSI reference model is based on a layered

Open Systems Interconnection (OSI) model

An international standard defining connectivity of links between computers at different levels.

Protocol

A definition of
the method of
communication
between network
components which
forms part of a
standard.

approach, with each network service having its own standard rules, known as **protocols**, for each layer. A protocol is a definition of the method of communication between network components which forms part of a standard.

Often network managers and engineers will refer to setting up the 'protocol stack' correctly for a PC client. By this they mean checking that all the correct software standards are installed to enable the client to communicate with the server. When a message such as an e-mail is dispatched from a client computer, the message will pass down all seven layers starting with the applications layer and finishing at the physical layer. When the message is received at the server, this sequence will be reversed. At the application level the server will identify who is the recipient of the e-mail and will dispatch it to the relevant person by looking up the directory services standard.

The seven layers of the OSI model are shown in the box below. When reviewing these, remember that it is not the understanding of the details in each layer which is important, but the capability that the OSI model gives for systems from different vendors in different companies to communicate.

The OSI model for connectivity

7 Application layer (application services)

The application layer describes how user programs will access the network services available to them by other layers. Application protocols include the Message Handling System (X.400) and Directory Services (X.500). These are important for messaging applications such as e-mail.

6 Presentation layer (application services)

The presentation layer is implemented in the operating system and the application and defines the formatting for display of information.

5 Session layer (application services)

At the session level, standards define how the exchange of information will occur when the session is created.

4 Transport layer (network services)

As would be expected, the transport layer defines a method for controlling the movement of information between different systems. This is the TCP component of the well-known TCP/IP protocol used by the Internet.

3 Network layer (network services)

The network layer is a lower-level standard defining the details of data transmission at the packet level. The IP component of TCP/IP determines how information is routed between servers.

> **2 Data link layer (network services)**
>
> This layer specifies rules for sending data across the physical links between systems.
>
> **1 Physical layer (connection and transmission)**
>
> This defines the physical characteristics of the interface. A well-known example is the RS-232 standard for serial cables used by personal computers.

Specific networking standards

Other network standards define transmission for particular types of network. These are briefly covered in this section for reference purposes, since they are used frequently in industry when new communications facilities for a company are being installed. These standards include:

◆ *ISDN (Integrated Services Digital Network).* This is used for sending digital data over telephone networks. In the UK speeds of 64 or 128 Kbps are possible, making it suitable for exchange of voice, data, images and short video sequences.

◆ *SMDS (Switched Multimegabit Data Service).* This provides a higher speed than ISDN. It is often used in metropolitan areas of Europe for linking branches of shops or financial service providers with the regional office. It provides an extension of LAN communication methods across a city.

◆ *ATM (Asynchronous Transfer Mode).* ATM is applicable to both local and wide area networks and has been touted as the way forward for providing the high-speed services required by businesses for supporting multimedia such as video conferencing. It achieves this by accommodating bursts in traffic and so more packets. To provide the bandwidth needed, ATM is coupled with fibre-optic cables.

◆ *X.25.* X.25 is a packet-switching network allowing communication across a wide area network. Although it is well established for use in light traffic between remote sites, it is not practical for real-time data or video. The maximum speed of the standard is 2 Mbit/sec, compared to a maximum of 600 Mbit/sec with ATM.

◆ *Ethernet network.* The Ethernet standard was developed jointly by Xerox, Digital and Intel in the 1980s. It is implemented most commonly using 10Base-T twisted-pair or 10Base-2 co-axial cable to implement a bus or star LAN topology.

◆ *X.400.* This message handling system standard is important in allowing different types of e-mail systems to interoperate. This is particularly important for large companies which have many incompatible mail systems, each of which would require a gateway product to talk to the others. With X.400, gateways are no longer required.

◆ *X.500.* This defines a standard for directory services. For the global organisation, this is important as it defines a hierarchy for locating staff and equipment efficiently. Once implemented it will effectively give a global phone directory which will make finding a person's e-mail address easier. The information most relevant to each site is stored locally to make it quicker to access.

CASE STUDY: TOPIC AREA

Communications technology of the UK National Lottery

The National Lottery has one of the most advanced computer and communications networks in the world. There are two computer centres used to operate The National Lottery. Racal Network Services have created an X25 data network and a VSAT (satellite) network to link our computers with retailers. Over 1000 concentrators at specially located sites around the country link up the whole system, including individual connections to each retailer terminal.

State of the art software was developed to enable vast volumes of transactions to be handled quickly and securely. The software used represents the equivalent of over 300 man years of development and is believed to have a larger capacity than the air traffic control system at Heathrow airport. The whole network can handle 400 000 plays a minute processing six megabytes of information, the equivalent of two encyclopedias' worth of information, every second. The security of the system is paramount and many hours are spent testing to ensure that the highest levels of performance and integrity are maintained.

What happens to your National Lottery game ticket

An 'on-line' play follows a definitive path through the computer system from the point the lottery entry is created until the entry is finally removed from the operating system files. Although the time frames may vary, the life cycle of a ticket follows a few basic steps:

Play

A lottery entry is created when a ticket is purchased at a National Lottery retailer. Tickets are usually purchased and the numbers recorded using a playslip; however, your numbers can be entered directly into the terminal by asking your retailer. These numbers are then transmitted via the private National Lottery communications network to the central computer system. When your numbers are received and recorded by the central computer the terminal in the retailer prints out the ticket which is given back to you. The communication from the retailer's terminal to the central computer system and back again takes less than five seconds at busy times; less for quieter periods.

Recording transmission

The central computer system keeps a record of all daily play transactions. It also stores information on cancellations and winning cashes (people who have cashed winning tickets).

Close of play

At 11.00 pm every day the central computer system closes and programs are run to separate all the play transactions from the cancellations and winning cashes into files for each day. These daily files are then scanned on a draw day to select the winning tickets.

Draw time

At 7.30 pm on Saturday and 7.30 pm on Wednesday entries for that evening's particular draw close. As the numbers are drawn live on the TV, they are entered into the central computer system. Then all plays entered for that draw are scanned, not forgetting multi-draw plays, and then the number of winners for that draw and the consequent prizes are calculated.

Winning cashes

The winning plays for every draw are transferred to a new file. When a winning ticket is claimed and validated at a retailer, the information on the ticket is cross-referenced with this file for verification. The central computer system then sends a message to the retailer's terminal to confirm that the ticket is a winner and the amount that should be paid.

Purging

Once a winning ticket has been claimed, the central computer system changes the status of the ticket to indicate that it has been paid. After a short period of time these paid tickets are cleared out of the file. Unclaimed winning tickets are kept in the file for 180 days for you to claim. After 180 days the unclaimed winnings, together with any interest earned, are paid to The National Lottery Distribution Fund and the winning ticket record is purged.

The computerised Lottery today

During the last 20 years, the advance of technology has significantly helped the operations of lotteries around the world. Previously, lotteries operated using labour intensive manual methods for ticket printing, distribution and winner selection. Today, however, lottery games are being converted to on-line systems, like The UK National Lottery, which take advantage of high speed computer processing capabilities and high levels of security. The private National Lottery communications network in the UK provides fast transmission of the lottery entry using a combination of satellite links, leased private telephone lines and fibre optics cables. The specially developed computer software which records the plays, maintains accounting records, integrates security features and provides reporting capabilities is provided by GTECH who are the world leader in lottery technology and the only company to focus their attention solely on computerised lottery systems. They are involved in over 80% of the world's lotteries. To ensure that the lottery computer operates everyday between 6.00 am and 11.00 pm three separate back up systems are available at two separate locations, all of which constantly receive the same transaction information so that any one can take over at short notice if another one fails. Additionally there is a team of thirty people responsible for looking after the lottery systems working twenty four hours a day, seven days a week, three hundred and sixty five days a year.

Source: © Camelot (Web site). http://www.camelot-lotteries.co.uk and www.national-lottery.co.uk

Questions

1 What type of communications technology is used for the National Lottery?
2 Make notes summarising the capacity of the National Lottery and how long it took to develop.
3 Which computing operations are real time and which are batch? You may need to refer to Chapters 6 and 12 to answer this question.
4 What 'fail-safe' mechanisms are used to make sure that no data is lost?

▶ SPECIFYING AND BUILDING NETWORKS

There are three key factors in deciding which network system to purchase. These are the performance or speed that the system can deliver, how stable it is and the cost. Most network managers receive frequent complaints about network downtime and slow performance when loading applications or data across the network. Naturally, when upgrading or specifying a new network, these will be targeted as the most important areas to improve.

When implementing communications systems, one of the main factors is the extent of the disruption to staff who are already working. This is usually minimised by making the changes out of working hours, over the weekend or during the night. A further problem is the lead time for all the different hardware and software to be delivered. This needs advanced planning. Once the new network has been installed, there may also be a lengthy period when the stability of the links is checked and optimised.

▶ SUMMARY

1 Computer networks are built on different scales, from those limited to a single location (LAN) to national or international wide area networks known as WAN. Table 5.5 summarises the different types.

2 Most PC-based networks are based on a client/server architecture in which there are a number of PC clients which share resources and communicate via a more powerful server computer. Client/server networks can be arranged in a number of different topologies, such as bus, star and ring.

3 The main components of a network are the server and client computers which are linked to peripheral devices such as printers. The hardware is connected by guided media such as cables or, on a larger scale, unguided satellite and microwave. Telecommunications processors or gateways are required to translate information as it is passed from the hardware devices to the media. A network operating system such as UNIX, Windows NT or Novell Netware is necessary to control the hardware and provide facilities such as security and file and printer sharing.

Table 5.5 Summary of the applications of different scales of network

Scale of network	Description	Business application
Peer-to-peer	A simple network enabling sharing of files and devices	Small company or local work-groups in a single department
Local area network	One or several servers accessed by client computers and used for sharing peripheral devices such as printers	Network at a single company site
Wide area network	LANs at different sites are linked via leased lines which will often use microwave or satellite transmission	National company with several offices or multinational company; company wanting to perform EDI with its suppliers
Internet	A global arrangement of wide area networks	Companies needing to communicate with many other companies via e-mail or accessing Web servers

4 Through using networks, companies can exchange information more rapidly and reduce costs by removing the need for human resources. The advantages of faster communication are not only internal, but extend to improving links with customers, suppliers, collaborators and even competitors.

▶ EXERCISES

▶ Self-assessment exercises

1 Specify the components required for a client/server based LAN for a company of 10 people.

2 Distinguish between a local area network (LAN) and a wide area network (WAN).

3 What are the main business benefits delivered by a local area computer network?

4 Explain the concept of a value-added network.

5 What are the main components of a telecommunications system?

6 Why have many companies adopted a client/server architecture for their information systems?

7 What is the difference between digital and analogue signals? Over which telecommunications medium are analogue signals most commonly used?

8 What is the purpose of a network operating system?

▶ Discussion questions

1 Do you think that the introduction of client/server systems has been worthwhile to businesses?

2 There are many possible benefits of company-wide networks. Is it possible for them to be achieved without changing working practices?

▶ Essay questions

1 You are a newly installed IT manager in a company of 100 staff. You want to convince the directors of the benefits of adopting a local area network across the whole company. How would you present your case?

2 Explain the benefits that a company deciding to downsize to a client server/architecture as part of its IT strategy could derive. What management initiatives will be necessary to ensure that the introduction of the new system is a success?

▶ Examination questions

1 Name three ways in which installing a local area network can reduce costs. Explain how this is achieved.

2 Which features would you need to specify for a company network for a company of 100 people working at a single site?

3 Computer networks exist on different scales. Distinguish between the following types:
   (a) local area network;
   (b) wide area network;
   (c) metropolitan area network;
   (d) value-added network.

4 Explain, with the aid of diagrams, the difference between the following network topologies:
   (a) star;
   (b) bus;
   (c) ring.

5 Distinguish between the following different types of servers:
   (a) network;
   (b) applications;
   (c) database.

6 What are the advantages of the following types of media? Is each more likely to be found in a local or wide area network?
   (a) copper cable;
   (b) fibre-optic;
   (c) satellite;
   (d) microwave.

7 Networked communications in business occur through wide area networks and local area networks.
   (a) How do the two types of network differ?
   (b) What is the difference between a local area network and an intranet?

▶ Further reading

Hawyrszkiewycz, I. (1997) *Designing the Networked Enterprise*, Artech House, Boston USA.
> This book explains how networks can be implemented and describes the impact on the organisation at operational and strategic levels. It focuses more on the human and organisational issues rather than giving technical details.

Held, G. (1998) *Understanding Data Communications: from Fundamentals to Networking*, 2nd edition, John Wiley, Chichester.
> This book complements that by Hawyrszkiewycz since it has comprehensive coverage of different communications technologies.

Laudon, K. and Laudon, J. (1995) *Management Information Systems: Organization and Technology*, 4th edn, Prentice Hall International, London.
> A summary of how telecommunications are used in business is given in Chapters 9 and 10.

Sheldon, T. (1994) *LAN Times Encyclopedia of Networking*, Osborne-McGraw-Hill, Berkeley.
> Useful summaries of networking terms, with good use of diagrams. Comprehensive.

▶ Web references

http://www.ncb.gov.sg The Singapore National Computer Board, which is responsible for managing the Singapore ONE and 'intelligent island' initiatives, has a great deal of information related to these projects.

http://www.whatis.com This site has good definitions for different terms related to networks and further references to other sites.

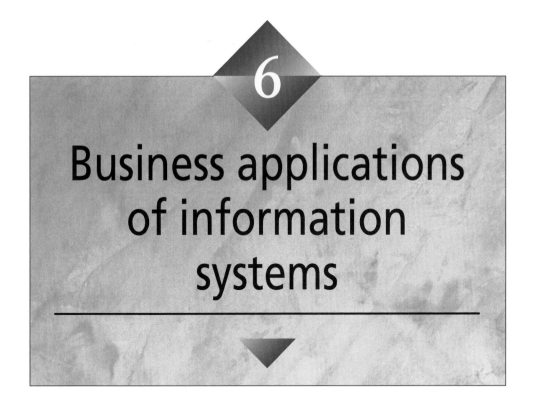

6

Business applications of information systems

INTRODUCTION

In Chapters 1 and 2 we introduced the role of information in decision making and in Chapters 3 to 5 we showed how the hardware and software components of information systems are necessary to turn this information into a useful business resource. In this chapter we consider in more detail how information and different information systems are used in different parts of organisations and in organisations of different types, such as manufacturing and service industries. The chapter is structured in three parts, based on the different management levels at which decisions are taken in an organisation. In the first part, different types of *operational* information systems are described. These include those used for manufacturing and office automation and the common function of managing business transactions. In the second part, we look at how decision support systems can be used for tactical and strategic planning and review decision-making models. In the third part, we consider how different types of software are used in different functional areas of a business, such as finance and accounting, human resources and marketing.

The way in which software is applied across different industries is quite complex. Figure 6.1 hints at this complexity. It shows that information systems for business can be broken down by:

1 *Industry segment.* These are referred to as vertical markets, such as manufacturing or retail.

2 *Industry subsegment.* Each industry segment can be subdivided into further vertical markets (not shown on the diagram). For example, manufacturing will have electronics and automobile subsegments and retailing will have food and clothing subsegments.

Manufacturing	Energy and chemical	Retail	Financial services	Local and central government	
EIS	EIS	EIS	EIS	EIS	**Strategic and tactical**
Business intelligence	Business intelligence	Business intelligence	Business intelligence	Business intelligence	
Decision support	Decision support	Decision support	Decision support	Decision support	
Transaction processing	Transaction processing	Transaction processing	Transaction processing	Transaction processing	
Process control	Process control	Process control	Process control	Process control	**Operational**
Office automation	Office automation	Office automation	Office automation	Office automation	

Fig 6.1 Matrix showing vertical divisions of software by industry and horizontal division of software by type of application used to support the different levels of decision making

3 *Level of decision making.* These are operational, tactical and strategic. It is often difficult to distinguish systems used to solve strategic and tactical problems, so these are grouped together.

4 *Type of business information system.* These relate to the different levels of decision making. At the operational level there are office automation, transaction processing and process control systems. At the strategic and tactical level there are different types of system used for supporting decision making. These are sometimes referred to as management information systems and include information reporting tools, expert systems, business intelligence or data warehouses and executive information systems (EIS). These types of systems are described later in the chapter. The type of business information system can also be broken down by department or function in an organisation. At the end of the chapter we consider applications in the three areas of human resources, marketing and accounting.

Note that each type of system such as TPS or EIS is repeated, occurring once in each vertical sector. This is to indicate that the type of system required for each vertical market may be from a different vendor or have different options to suit the needs of the market. For example, the transactions involved in financial services are quite

---

▶ Learning objectives

After reading this chapter, readers will be able to:

◆ appreciate the importance of transaction processing systems, process control and office automation systems to the operational management of a business;

◆ select an appropriate system for decision support at tactical and strategic levels of an organisation;

◆ evaluate the potential for using information systems in different parts of an organisation.

> **Links to other chapters**

Chapter 1   provides an introduction to how information can be used for decision making.

Chapter 2   introduces the different types of information systems.

                 Some of the technologies in this chapter are introduced briefly in Chapter 4, which provides an introduction to the different types of software.

Chapter 19   considers the future potential of some of these technologies.

different from those in the energy industry. However, common systems can be used across the vertical markets. For example, the groupware system Lotus Notes could be used in each of the sectors and tailored as required.

▶ OPERATIONAL SYSTEMS

Operational systems are used for the tasks involved in the daily running of a business. Their performance is often vital to an organisation and they are sometimes described as mission critical or strategic information systems. We consider three types of operational systems:

1 *Transaction processing systems (TPS).* These are used to manage the exchange of information and funds between a company and third parties such as customers, suppliers and distributors.

2 *Office automation systems (OAS).* OAS are used to manage the administrative functions in an office environment and are often critical to service-based industries.

3 *Process control systems.* These are important in manufacturing industries for controlling the manufacture of goods.

▶ Transaction processing systems (TPS)

Transaction processing systems (TPS) perform the frequent routine external and internal transactions which serve the operational level of the organisation. Transactions involve recording events within or between a business and third parties which incorporate the exchange of information regarding different services. Examples of these transactions include:

◆ customers placing orders for products and services from a company, such as making a holiday booking;

◆ a company placing orders with a supplier for components from which to make its products;

◆ payment for goods or services received by a third party;

◆ a customer visiting a supermarket to shop (see the mini case study on retail applications of TPS by Sainsbury's);

◆ a customer ringing a call centre of a bank to pay her bills;

◆ a withdrawal of money from an auto-teller machine.

> **Transaction processing systems (TPS)**
>
> Manage the frequent external and internal transactions such as orders for goods and services which serve the operational level of the organisation.

Although the functions undertaken by the TPS are routine and repetitive, they usually perform a vital function in the organisation.

Figure 6.2 shows the typical components of a transaction processing system. Data is usually input by being keyed in to onscreen data entry forms such as those used when orders are placed by phone. For retail applications, customer transactions are recorded through bar-code technology.

Storage and retrieval are often handled by a database management system, except where high performance is required. Here, a transaction monitor linked to a native file system may be used. Transactions will typically occur across a local area network within a retail branch or bank environment, with real-time processing and data transfer occurring across a wide area network with a central mainframe computer. Sometimes data on transactions such as loyalty card purchases is stored locally in the supermarket on a local server in real time and then uploaded by a batch system (when the store is closed) to head office. This arrangement is shown in Fig 6.3. Other information such as supply requests may be transmitted on demand in real time. Links with suppliers occur through EDI, which is described in Chapter 5.

There are two main types of transaction systems in operation. Batch systems, as the name suggests, collect information on transactions in batches before it is processed at times of lower transaction rates (such as overnight). Real-time systems process information immediately. These two design alternatives are compared in Chapter 12.

Information from the transaction processing system is accessed in the branch and in the head office using online reporting, for example to find stock availability, or offline reporting where information is stored in a separate system for detailed analysis. This is the approach used for data warehouses, which are described later in the chapter.

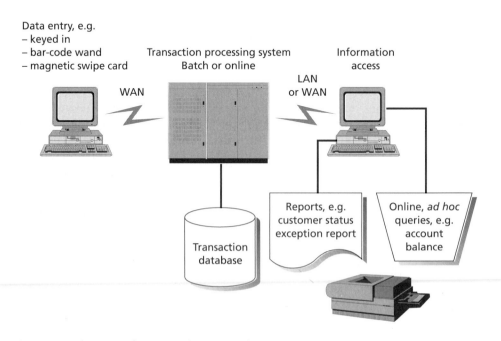

Fig 6.2 Key elements of a transaction processing system

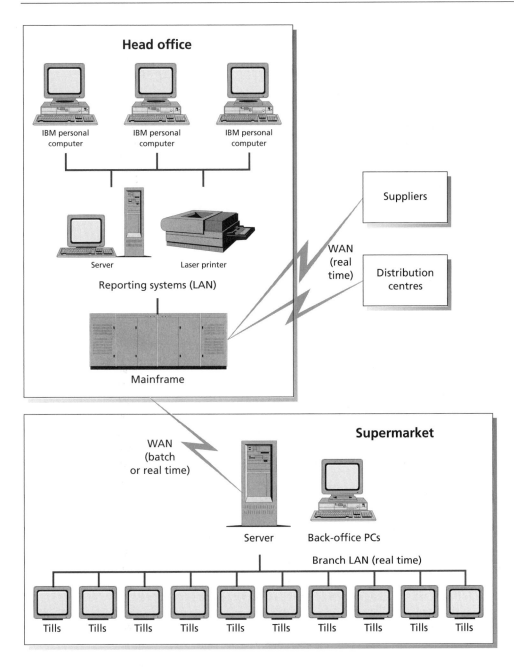

Fig 6.3 Network architecture for a retail transaction processing system

Because the TPS gives direct contact with customers and suppliers beyond the boundary of an organisation, if it fails it becomes immediately apparent to the organisation's customers (think about the consequences of a failure of an airline reservation system!). Therefore these are often mission-critical systems which must be reliable and secure. Another reason for such applications being mission critical is that data captured by the TPS is used to monitor the performance of the organisation.

The mini case study on *retail applications of TPS by Sainsbury's* shows that for some organisations there will be many TPS in operation which have become essential to the needs of the organisation.

MINI CASE

Retail applications of TPS by Sainsbury's

This case study of UK retailer Sainsbury's considers the different ways in which a retailer may make use of TPS.

The company and its customer service objectives

- 17 000 commodities.
- Aim is for no more than five to be unavailable at any one time.
- Order lead time 24–48 hours.
- Distribution centres manage deliveries of 11 million cases to 335 stores.

How is Sainsbury's helped by TPS technology?

- Improved customer service through more choice, lower prices, better quality of produce and full shelves.
- Improved operational efficiency by automatic links to suppliers and better information on product demand and availability.
- Assessment of the effectiveness of product promotions through availability of better information.
- Marketing through customer loyalty schemes.

How does Sainsbury's use technologies?

- At the till – EPOS and EFTPOS.
- On shelves – auto price-changing LCDs.
- On trolleys – 'self-scanning systems'.
- At home – direct wine sales from the Internet BarclaySquare site.
- At warehouses – EDI links between stores, warehouses, suppliers and banks.
- For banking – TPS are vital to providing customer statements and cash withdrawals.
- In the marketing department – the effectiveness of marketing campaigns and loyalty card schemes can be assessed using information on transactions stored in data warehouses. This type of system is covered in more detail later in the chapter.

Questions

1 Draw a diagram summarising the links between all the parties who access Sainsbury's TPS.
2 What benefits will Sainsbury's gain compared to the time before the introduction of TPS?
3 Can you think of any problems with using TPS so extensively? What can be done to counter these problems?

▶ OFFICE AUTOMATION SYSTEMS (OAS)

FOCUS ON

Office automation systems (OAS) are information systems intended to increase the productivity of office workers. Examples include groupware, workflow and general-purpose applications such as wordprocessors and spreadsheets.

Laudon and Laudon (1996) state three critical organisational roles for office automation systems:

Office automation systems (OAS)

IS intended to increase the productivity of office workers. Examples include groupware, workflow and general-purpose applications such as wordprocessors and spreadsheets.

◆ They coordinate and manage the work of local, professional and information workers within the organisation.

◆ They link the work being performed across all levels and functions of the organisation.

◆ They couple the organisation to the external environment, including to its clients and suppliers; when you call an organisation, you call an office.

These roles emphasise the fact that the office should be seen as more than a typing area but rather as a centre for the exchange of organisational knowledge. Activities undertaken in offices include document management, collaborative work and the management of project activities. These types of activities are important to support the reengineered processes in a company which are discussed in Chapter 14.

Personal OAS technologies have been introduced in Chapter 4. These applications included desktop publishing (DTP), for producing, for example, drafts of promotional marketing material such as brochures and flyers; personal information managers (PIM), for managing tasks and contacts; and project management software, to assist the management and control of projects. In this coverage we focus on groupware and workflow management systems, which are most significant in office automation systems, involving teams of people.

Groupware

Groupware is software that enables information to be shared by people collaborating on solving problems. This could include activities such as the scheduling and running of meetings, sharing documents and communicating over a distance. It is often used together with workflow management systems for reengineering of companies, as described in Chapter 14.

Groupware

Software which enables information and decision making to be shared by people collaborating within and between businesses.

Groupware assists teams of people in working together because it provides the 'three Cs' of communication, collaboration and coordination:

◆ *Communication* is the core groupware feature which allows information to be shared or sent to others using electronic mail. Groupware for conferencing is sometimes known as computer-mediated communication (CMC) software.

◆ *Collaboration* is the act of joint cooperation in solving a business problem or undertaking a task. Groupware may reduce some of the problems of traditional meetings, such as finding a place and a time to meet, a lack of available information or even dominance by one forceful individual in a meeting. Groupware improves the efficiency of decision making and its effectiveness by encouraging contributions from all group members. As a result, the study of groupware is known as computer-supported collaborative work (CSCW).

◆ *Coordination* is the act of making sure that a team is working effectively and meeting its goals. This includes distributing tasks to team members, reviewing their performance or perhaps steering an electronic meeting.

When people exchange information simultaneously, as is the case with real-time chat or a telephone conversation, this is known as **synchronous**. When collaborators send messages which can be accessed at a later time, these are known as **asynchronous**. Asynchronous exchange occurs with e-mail or discussion groups.

A further reason that groupware has become a useful business tool is that it can be used for collaboration within and between companies when face-to-face contact is impossible. Employees can continue to communicate and work on joint projects even when they are in different locations or in different time-zones. The asynchronous use of groupware is one of its key benefits. When considering the benefits of collaborative systems, it is useful to categorise them according to the quadrant in which they lie on a grid showing how people can work together in time and space (Table 6.1).

Synchronous

When people exchange information simultaneously as is the case with real-time chat or a telephone conversation this is known as synchronous.

Asynchronous

When collaborators send messages that can be accessed at a later time these are known as asynchronous. Asynchronous exchange occurs with e-mail or discussion groups.

Table 6.1 Different uses of collaborative systems classified in time and space

	Synchronous	Asynchronous
Same location	Same time, same place Example: meeting support software	Different time, same place Example: workflow systems
Different location	Same time, different place Example: video conferencing	Different time, different place Example: e-mail and discussion groups

Software associated with groupware includes electronic calendars that allow individuals to keep track of appointments, but also may permit other group workers to inspect each other's workload to allow scheduling of meetings. E-mail allows messages to be transmitted over long distances cheaply and quickly. It also enables messages to be sent to large groups of employees in an organisation, so facilitating groupworking. Video conferencing software allows meetings to take place between people who are a great distance apart. Each participant may be viewed on a visual display by the other group members, so allowing the exchange of visual cues from people's faces. Although the cost of video conferencing is reducing, it is still relatively high enough to restrict its use to meetings on such topics as business strategy, company collaborations, project management reviews and product design seminars for engineers.

Table 6.2 summarises the main functions available in groupware systems.

Normally, applications such as electronic calendars and e-mail are purchased as separate software packages. However, some software provides an integrated package of groupware functions. One such package is Lotus Notes, which is based on a database that allows the sharing of text, graphics, sound and video data. The system can run on a local area network (LAN) or a wide area network (WAN) and so allows infor-

Table 6.2 Main groupware functions

Groupware function	Application
E-mail and messaging	E-mail, electronic forms processing
Document management and information sharing	Improved information dissemination
Collaborative authoring	Team development of documents
Conferencing	Text conferencing, video conferencing, whiteboarding
Time management	Calendar and group scheduling
Groupware management and decision support	Remote and distributed access facilities including replication and access control
Ad hoc workflow	Loosely coupled collaboration
Structured workflow	Structured management of tasks

mation to be shared over distance. Communication between users is automatically logged by Notes for reference. This facility can be used to increase customer service by retrieving previous interactions between organisational members and customers in a variety of formats in response to a customer request. The other main integrated groupware packages are Novell Groupwise and Microsoft Exchange. These are similar to e-mail software in that they have an in-box of messages (Fig 6.4), but they also provide calendar and worklist facilities and document management.

The use of groupware applications has been revolutionised by the adoption of intranets in companies, as described in Chapter 17. Many groupware products are now available through Web browsers which enable e-mail, for example, to be sent and reviewed.

The next categories of office automation software described are sometimes considered to be groupware-type functions of products such as Microsoft Exchange and Lotus Notes, but they can rightly be considered in their own right.

Calendar and scheduling software

Calendar programs help organise meetings by allowing workgroup members to synchronise schedules. As an example, a user wishing to call a meeting can view the schedules of all other workgroup members. Having picked a convenient date, time and location, the user enters this information into the calendar program. The program can then automatically complete the rest of the process, for example by reserving resources, such as a meeting room, and issuing e-mail messages to remind users of the date of the meeting.

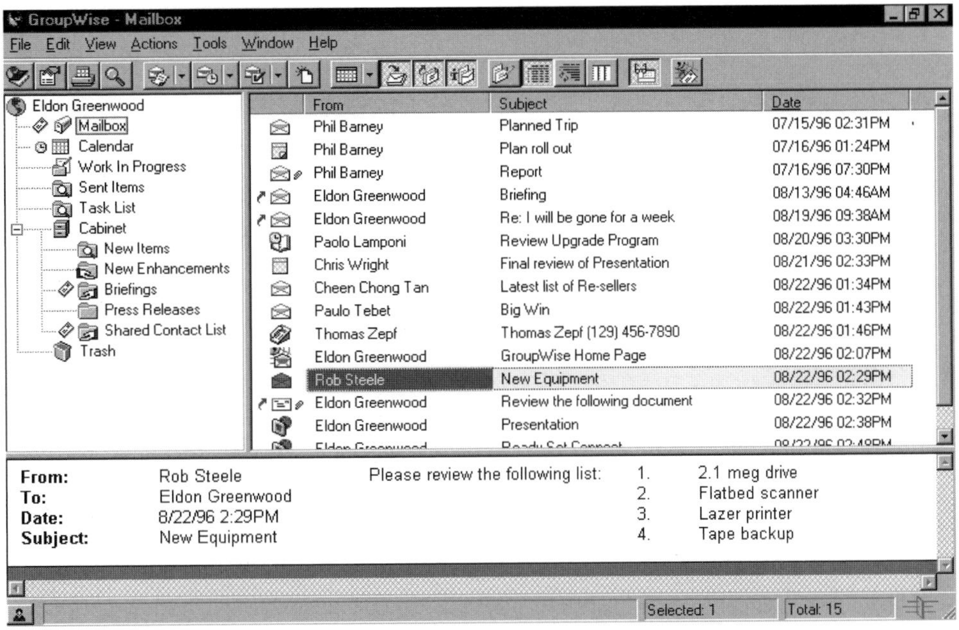

Fig 6.4 Universal in-box of Novell Groupwise groupware product

Document conferencing software

This type of software allows the members of a workgroup to work simultaneously on a given project. The program automatically updates each user's view of the document each time a change is made. In addition, the program will maintain a log containing the details of any changes or additions made by individual users. Users are also able to make annotations or send additional information to each other as work on the document progresses.

Document imaging processing (DIP)

Document image processing (DIP)

DIP systems are used in industry to convert printed documents into an electronic format so that they can be stored, organised and retrieved more easily.

DIP systems attempt to alleviate the problems caused by paper-based systems, including the cost of handling large amounts of paperwork and the time wasted searching for paper documents. DIP systems convert documents (and images) into a digital format which allows storage, retrieval and manipulation of the document on computer. The document is converted using a scanner which can be either handheld and passed over a document, or a flat-bed type where a document is placed on a glass sheet and a scanner reader passes under it. Because the document is stored as a digital image, it will consume a large amount of disk space. Often compression software is used to minimise the size of the file created, but if many images are stored they are likely to be held on an optical storage medium and retrieved using database software. Optical storage has slower retrieval times than a conventional PC hard disk, but a much greater capacity. The main components of a DIP system are shown in Fig 6.5.

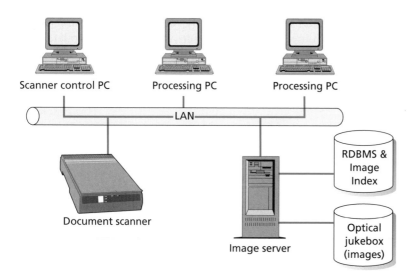

Fig 6.5 Components of a document image processing system

Electronic document management systems (EDMS)

EDMS are used for the management of large procedural documents which are required in organisations for managing their products and services. For example, the aircraft manufacturer Boeing has a service manual for each aircraft containing thousands of pages (*see* case study). To write and update this is a significant undertaking because of the volume of material and the number of authors. EDMS are intended to help in the task of managing the document lifecycle of:

◆ write;
◆ review and annotate;
◆ modify;
◆ publish;
◆ distribute;
◆ update and repeat the cycle.

Electronic document management software (EDMS)

Systems that convert documents into a digital format which allows storage, retrieval and manipulation of the document on computer.

Boeing uses EDMS for managing technical information

At Boeing there are 10 500 users of an EDMS system to update and access information about Boeing Standards, each of which defines a design or manufacturing process. There are 70 000 pages of information on over 10 000 processes. Boeing has used the Interleaf EDMS to implement this system by scanning in previous documents and using OCR to convert them to electronic text. The main savings have been:

◆ 31 per cent decrease in time to locate a standards document;
◆ 63 per cent reduction in rework caused by inaccurate or out-of-date documents;
◆ 6 per cent elimination of paper distribution;
◆ return on investment 96 per cent (payback period of five years).

Source: Myers-Tierney, L. and Campbell, I. (1996) *The Business Case for Electronic Document Management*, International Data Corporation, Framingham, MA, USA.

MINI CASE

Similarly, banks and building societies have a large volume of procedural documentation on conditions for issuing loans, for example, which must be updated regularly and distributed throughout the organisation and its agents. The case study on Abbey National gives an example of such an application of EDMS.

CASE STUDY: TOPIC AREA

Abbey National Bank uses EDMS to tackle the documentation plague

Internal documentation is a plague. It needs to be generated, checked, maintained and, above all, distributed, often to thousands of people across an organisation. In a larger company, the documentation procedures manuals, reference material, standards documentation, regulatory compliance requirements can be the main point of on-going contact between central management and the workforce, across the country or across the globe. On it depends the smooth running of any medium to large organisation. Get it wrong, and the customers get the wrong information; regulatory requirements are missed; the company is exposed to litigation or worse.

Abbey National knows this. Two million pages of information are sent out every month to its network of 675 UK branches and support centres. Updates for manuals; new manuals; new product information – all needed in the branches and all imposing a significant management overhead on the organisation. In one month, the company sent out some 268 changes to procedures – changes which (they hoped) were accurately inserted into or used to replace existing publications.

The question was: could technology help? If so, which technology? What would the real impact be? Paul Greenfield, Abbey National's business communications manager, set out to find out. 'We needed to meet a variety of needs with any new electronic document distribution system. It had to be economical; it had to fit in with the introduction of Microsoft Windows into the branches; it couldn't be allowed to impact on the X.25 transaction processing networks and infrastructure currently connecting branches; it had to be easier to use and be more useful than paper.'

The problem could be split into three parts: how to get the documents to the users; how to facilitate access once delivered; and how would the users react to the new method of working. It was known already that staff felt uncomfortable looking up paper manuals in front of customers and there was a worry that this might lead to important procedural or compliance steps being missed.

In the event, Greenfield quite literally looked to the skies for inspiration. As the majority of information had to flow in one direction – from the centre to the branches – it made sense to opt for a unidirectional delivery mechanism. The answer lay in satellite transmission. This brought a number of benefits. First, there was a huge amount of bandwidth available. Abbey National estimates it will use up to 150MB per night (all document updating will be done at night) and more capacity is available if needed. Also, infrastructure costs were a fraction of those involved in upgrading the X.25 network to handle large data flows.

Now, all branch-oriented documentation is to be assembled during the day and transmitted to the satellite service providers. Overnight, they beam the information up to the satellite and down again, simultaneously to every branch equipped with a 'head-end' PC (a PC on the local branch network). The head-end PC receives the data, runs a batch programme to update the local document server and sends an acknowledgement back to the centre around the X.25 network. Any problems with reception are communicated in the same way. 'This means we can send far more data without interfering with transaction information sent over the existing network', said Greenfield.

Security was an issue at first; there is a perception that satellite transmission is easy to intercept and decode. Abbey National's IT staff took a close look at the system used and, while not considering it as secure as the X.25 network for transaction processing, nevertheless were reassured that the company's secrets were safe. In fact, it has been decided to use the satellite route for updating branch

software, as well as for document distribution. 'With the increasing complexity of branch systems and the use of Windows-based software, the volume of data sent in software distribution expands constantly,' said Greenfield. 'The largest transfers might have taken ten days to reach every branch. Now, they will all be reached overnight.'

In the event, actually using the technology has been largely trouble-free. The main problems have been of a non-technical nature: getting planning permission for satellite dishes on branches in conservation areas; agreeing with other tenants and with landlords as to their siting, and so on. Learning times are short and the resistance felt by users towards using paper materials is not evident when accessing its electronic cousin.

A lot of this high acceptance level is down to the care taken by Greenfield and his team. They ran two pilot projects to determine the best working practices and to iron out bugs in the system. The first, in the third quarter of 1995, was a 'proof of concept' project which generated valuable feedback for operational purposes and also provided many of the metrics used to cost-justify the full implementation. Now, the system is being deployed across Abbey National's retail branch network, on the heels of the Windows roll-out. Peter Greenfield expects all 15 000 user licences contracted to be in use by the end of 1996, while the low marginal cost of expanding the network – just a PC, a satellite dish and an interface card – is going to sim-

plify the potentially protracted process of adding new branches, including the recently-acquired National & Provincial branch network.

Despite the £3 million total cost of the system, including infrastructure costs, Abbey National expects a pay-back in less than three years, which period will be shortened as new applications are implemented across the satellite link. Among the immediate savings are lower management costs at the document centre; an appreciable fall in the numbers of calls requesting duplicate copies of lost documentation; and a full £50 000 per month currently spent simply on replacing manuals. Security is also improved: no longer is it possible for manuals to 'walk', while in-built audit trails make compliance inspections much simpler.

Source: Document Manager, June 1996

Questions

1 Explain the information management problem referred to in the case study.

2 Summarise the potential savings and benefits of the new system.

3 What are the software and hardware requirements necessary to implement the system?

4 What potential difficulties does the introduction of electronic document delivery introduce?

The main products for EDMS are Documentum and Interleaf, with products available from other companies such as Filenet, IBM and Xerox. These are all now being enabled for access from the Internet or company intranets. Figure 6.6 shows the Interleaf WorldView product which uses a book metaphor, but with additional navigational tools such as hyperlinks between pages and searching facilities.

Workflow management systems (WFMS)

Workflow management (WFM) is defined by the Workflow Management Coalition as:

> the automation of a business process, in whole or part during which documents, information or tasks are passed from one participant to another for action, according to a set of procedural rules.

Workflow systems are used to automate business processes by providing a *structured* framework to support the process. Workflows helps manage business processes by ensuring that tasks are prioritised to be performed:

as soon as possible
by the right people
in the right order.

Workflow management (WFM)

Systems for the automation of the movement and processing of information in a business according to a set of procedural rules.

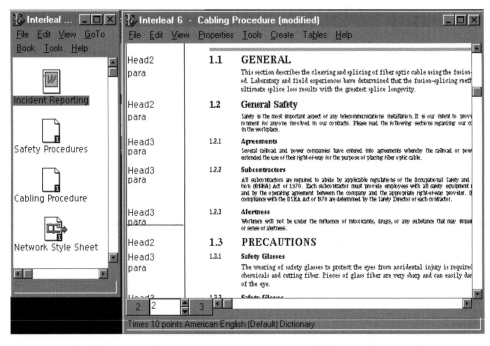

Fig 6.6 Interleaf electronic document management system being used to record company procedures

This gives a consistent, uniform approach for improved efficiency and better customer service. Workflow software provides functions to:

◆ assign tasks to people;

◆ remind people about their tasks which are part of a workflow queue;

◆ allow collaboration between people sharing tasks;

◆ retrieve information needed to complete the task, such as a customer's personal details;

◆ provide an overview for supervisors of the status of each task and the team's performance.

The radical redesign of business process is referred to as business process reengineering (BPR). Workflow and groupware systems such as that referred to in the United Distillers case study are often used to support reengineering. BPR is discussed in detail in Chapter 14.

Workflow is usually used in conjunction with DIP technology to improve efficiency by automatically routing documents to the correct person to deal with it. Each person is given a list of tasks or documents on which to work, from what is known as the workflow queue. Figure 6.7 gives an example of an integrated DIP/workflow system used for a customer service application to action a letter of complaint.

WFMS can be particularly effective when they replace a large, paper-based system and substantial amounts of time can be saved by eliminating lengthy searches for documents. Another improvement area is for customer service applications, such as

Fig 6.7 Example of a workflow application from Staffware

at a call centre when a document can be called up instantaneously in response to a customer request. The drawbacks associated with the technology include the expense of installation and the problem of integration with existing computer network systems. In order to gain the full benefits from WFMS, it is also necessary to reengineer or redesign the paper-based workflow in order to avoid simply automating inefficient processes. The case study illustrates a typical application for workflow.

CASE STUDY: TOPIC AREA

United Distillers uses workflow to manage product diversification

United Distillers' core business of distilling carefully nurtured and much loved tipples is thankfully conservative and not at all prone to wild innovation. However, there have to be frequent changes in the detail of what is now a very wide product range as existing markets change and new opportunities emerge.

United Distillers, part of Guinness, is the most profitable spirits company in the world. With sales of £2.77 billion in 1993, the company produces Johnnie Walker, the world's leading Scotch whisky, and Bell's, the UK brand leader. Its Gordon's label is the best-selling gin internationally, and other leading brands like

Dewar's and Tanqueray are also products of this major UK exporter.

With the drinks business now fully international and highly competitive, with existing markets changing and new opportunities emerging, the company has to be able to respond to the market rapidly, and time to market has become as important here as it is in any of the newer industries.

Underpinning a whole new product change procedure resulting from a substantial BPR exercise in the early 1990s, Workflow Automation, provided by Staffware, has helped reduce process times from as many as 270 days to as few as 40 and there is now close control, monitoring and consistency throughout a highly critical business process.

When UD's Business Analysis Unit began investigating the product change process in 1991, it soon became clear that the change process itself needed to be changed, and radically.

One problem was that the operation was primarily manual and paper based. With so many people and units needing to be involved in authorising and then processing product changes, paper movement alone introduced delays and unpredictability. At one extreme, the unit found changes being processed in 60 days and at the other extreme, 270 days.

Some variation was inevitable, since change proposals could vary between revising the label on a minor product line for one distributor to wholesale revision and repackaging of a mainstream range of drinks for another. However, lack of both well-defined responsibilities and rigorous progress control were clearly significant factors in the wide variations discovered during that BPR investigation.

Defining any business procedure involving the routing of information from one user to another for processing and approval, and the monitoring and managing of that process, are relatively day-to-day jobs for most workflow system vendors.

As an example, nine separate and geographically dispersed business units would be involved; over 150 users would need to be supported and around 3000 cases per year would pass through the system, often requiring processing of some complexity.

The UD units involved in the process include central functions such as finance, planning and purchasing, but also five sales regions and a series of departments within the production plants. The BPR exercise, which was therefore very demanding, finally resulted in a staged authorisation process with all areas of responsibility defined, timescales established, and a strategy put in place to automate and monitor the flow of work.

With its new product change procedures now firmly established and mature on the Staffware platform, UD has a clear idea of the benefits that workflow can bring to a key business process. First and foremost is the contribution that the system makes to achieving an improved and consistent time to market, the original justification for the investment. Those wild variations in timescales for requesting and processing product changes are a thing of the past; 40 days are now the norm.

Management now has much greater control over the whole process. There is cause analysis for any missed deadlines, and performance analysis by time or variance. Information gathering is vastly improved and flexible in its presentation. Service levels can now be guaranteed. UD has also benefited from another often unsung virtue of workflow. As well as providing management with means of monitoring, Workflow encourages self-monitoring as participants now have a much clearer view of their roles and responsibilities.

Source: Staffware plc Workflow Case Study Product Promotion Pack (1997) Maidenhead, Berkshire.

Questions

1　With which business processes is the WFMS used to assist?

2　What is the relationship between the introduction of this software and reengineering?

WFM is most closely associated with large companies such as banks and insurance companies which deal with a large number of complex, paper-based transactions. These transactions need to be dealt with in a structured way and use structured or production workflow systems to manage them.

Small and medium companies are making increasing use of workflow for administrative tasks. These involve fewer transactions and can be managed by less costly software which is based on an e-mail system. Example applications for this administrative or forms-based workflow include authorisation of travel claims or holidays or payment of an invoice. In the latter example, the details of the invoice could be typed into the workflow system by a clerk. The workflow system will then forward the details of the invoice to a senior manager for authorisation. When this has

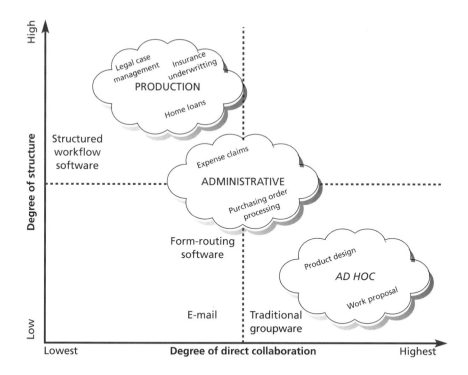

Fig 6.8 Classification of different types of workflow systems

occurred, the authorised invoice will automatically be sent back to the clerk for payment. This process will occur entirely electronically through routing of forms.

Figure 6.8 illustrates the different categories of workflow software according to the degree of structured working they support. *Production* systems are highly structured and are used in call centres, for example, for assessing insurance claims or issuing new policies. *Administrative* workflow is more widely used, for routine administration such as processing a travel claim. *Ad hoc* workflow overlaps with groupware applications, such as in a group design of a new product.

▶ PROCESS CONTROL SYSTEMS FOR OPERATIONS MANAGEMENT

Process control systems

Used to manage manufacturing type processes.

This type of system is used to support and control manufacturing processes. Operations management involves the transformation of inputs, such as raw materials, equipment and labour, into outputs in the form of goods and services. All organisations undertake this process, even if they may not have an identifiable operations function.

Business applications of operations management which need to be supported by information systems include product design, planning for resource requirements, location decisions, layout design, job design, quality control and business planning.

Traditionally, information systems for manufacturing were thought of in terms of automation of *repetitive*, uniform products such as foodstuffs from a production line. While this was true when information systems were first introduced, there is a strong trend to specialised tailoring of products or *mass customisation* to an individual customer's needs (Fig 6.9). The Hi-Life case study on page 208 illustrates this: it has 60 000 different products of which 50 per cent are 'one-off'.

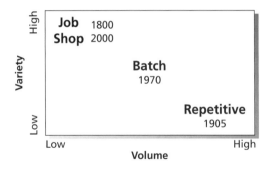

Fig 6.9 Development of manufacturing in terms of volume of production and variety of product

Figure 6.9 shows the three main types of production facility that information systems can be used to support:

◆ *Repetitive*. Production-line-type systems producing a standard product such as the Model T Ford car (this is the equivalent of packaged software).

◆ *Job shop*. Production of individual 'jobs' for individual customers according to their specific requirements (this is the equivalent of bespoke software).

◆ *Batch*. Intermediate between the two, a batch of identical products produced before changing the production setup for the next batch of systems.

Process control information systems have provided the flexibility to enable all three types to be automated.

▶ Application of process control systems

Managing material flows and production management

The receipt of a customer order will trigger a series of information flows through the operations function of a manufacturing company. These are shown as a simplified flow process chart in Fig 6.10. Flow process charts are described in the context of system design in Chapter 12.

The information flow that needs to be supported by an IS begins with the customer order, which will normally provide information on the product required, the quantity and the date when the order is required. An order management system should enable the status of customer orders to be checked continually. Information should be available on the progress of the order through the production process and the reason for any delays (e.g. equipment breakdown, awaiting a raw material shipment).

A production plan determines the sequence in which work generated by orders is performed by the production system. The orders are not processed in the order that they are received but are rearranged according to their required due dates and the amount of resources they require.

A detailed breakdown of the order in terms of its components and an examination of components held in stock provides the information required for activating the ordering of additional components. In addition to material availability, equipment availability must be determined. Maintenance records need to be consulted and the

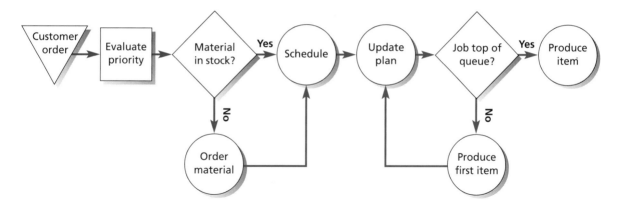

Fig 6.10 Simplified flow process chart for a production management system

equipment may not be available due to routine maintenance or breakdown. Also, special tools may be required to process a particular component.

Scheduling concerns the order and quantity of components that are processed through the production system on a day-to-day or operational basis. In order to form a schedule, information on labour availability and the routing of the order through the system is required. Scheduling issues are usually considered under the three main types of production system which are put into the context of variety and volume in Fig 6.9, repetitive, job shop and batch.

When the goods have passed through the production process they are held as finished goods inventory. Information on finished goods inventory is used to form a shipping schedule for delivery to customers (in service operations, storage of the finished service is not usually feasible).

Materials management

Three approaches to materials management will be described. Materials Requirements Planning (MRP) aims to ensure that just the right amount of each item is held at the right time in order to meet the needs of the manufacturing schedule. Just-in-time (JIT) production uses a 'pull' mechanism which provides a trigger when demand occurs and then attempts to supply that demand. Optimised Production Technology (OPT) focuses on the system bottleneck, that is, the production stage with the lowest level of capacity which is the limiting factor on the speed of the flow of goods to the customer.

MRP requires information from three main sources. The master production schedule (MPS) identifies what products are needed and when they are needed based on customer orders held and a forecast of future demand. The bill of materials (BOM) file provides a list of the components required to create each product, and the inventory status file (ISF) provides information on the current stock level of each component. From this information, the MRP system will indicate when an order should be placed.

The JIT approach implements a 'pull'-type system called the kanban production control system. The idea is that parts are requested in the system only when needed by 'pulling' them from the subsequent operation which requires more work. To implement this system, a kanban (Japanese for 'card' or 'sign') is used to pass information through the production system, such as part identification, quantity and the location of the next work centre. The kanban authorises the production and movement of material through the pull system.

The OPT system is based on the identification of bottlenecks within the production process. The idea is that the output of the whole production process is determined by the output of the bottleneck machine. Thus the bottleneck should pace production and determine the amount of work done at non-bottleneck resources.

Product/service design and development

Good design of products and services is an essential element in satisfying customer needs. The success of the design process is primarily dependent on the relationship between the marketing, design and operations function of the organisation. Information requirements are:

◆ market research to evaluate customer needs;
◆ demand forecasts;
◆ component costings;
◆ technical specification of the product.

In order to reduce time to market for new designs, the concept of concurrent design can be implemented. This replaces the traditional sequential design process when work is undertaken within functional business areas. Instead, the contributors to the design effort work together as a team (groupware can assist in this). This means improved communications and enables different stages of the design process to occur simultaneously. Another concept is design for manufacture (DFM), which aims to improve design and reduce costs through such techniques as simplification, standardisation and modularisation of the product design (Slack *et al.*, 1995).

Facility design

Facility design concerns how capacity will be supplied by the organisation to meet market demand, that is, it involves the design of production facilities, often using CAD/CAM software which is defined in the next section. Information requirements are:

◆ external sources on the state of competition and risks associated with not undertaking a task in-house;
◆ facility location needs to consider long-range demand forecasts and information on the cost of land, the availability of appropriately skilled labour, transportation links and the quality of local education and training services.

▶ Software for operations management

Spreadsheets

Spreadsheets are often used in production planning applications. A spreadsheet template is constructed providing information on work centre capacities and forecast demand. This ensures it is feasible to meet production goals (i.e. customer order due date) with the current available capacity.

Statistical packages

Statistical software can be used for applications such as inventory control and planning production levels using linear programming. It aims to find the solution to the problem of what mix of products to manufacture to maximise profits under current capacity constraints.

Project management software

For project activities (e.g. development of a new product) project management software is useful for tactical management control. The PERT chart indicates the relationships between activities in a project and the GANTT chart indicates the timing of activities. If any activity falls behind schedule, the software can be used to assess strategies for bringing the project back under control (*see* Chapter 9 for further details of project management).

Bar coding

Bar-coding devices are a critical element in a materials flow software system. A barcode reader can scan a bar code on such items as delivered goods and components within the production system. This information can be transmitted to an information system that can provide an assessment of the status of the production system at any particular point in time.

Programmable logic controllers

A programmable logic controller or PLC is a device that remembers a series of instructions and then transmits them to a machine. A dedicated controller is needed rather than a central computer because of speed constraints. For example, to control the speed of a drill as it is being used requires a large amount of data and a near instantaneous response time.

Quality control software

The widespread use of *statistical process control (SPC)* has led to specialist software being produced that provides a graphical display of the level of variances occurring during the production of a good or service. These control charts enable personnel to be able to distinguish normal variations expected in a process due to statistical fluctuations from unexpected variations due to a change in the process which should be investigated. Software is used to warn managers automatically when a significant variance from the quality standard occurs.

Virtual reality (VR) software

Virtual reality (VR) software is defined by consultants Ovum as 'a suite of 3D graphics and simulation tools and technologies which allow users to operate within a computer-generated environment, interactively and in real-time with little or no awareness of the human–computer interface'. It is used in a number of specialist areas. One of the best known is the simulation of design automation, accounting for nearly half of current applications. Visualisation of new products and manufacturing processes can save large sums of money by identifying possible design flaws before a product is put into full production. The other main application of VR software is in computer-based training for hazardous environments such as rail maintenance or mining.

Virtual reality software (VR)

Software defined by consultants Ovum as 'a suite of 3D graphics and simulation tools and technologies which allow users to operate within a computer-generated environment, interactively and in real-time with little or no awareness of the human–computer interface'.

Materials Requirements Planning (MRP) software

Materials Requirements Planning (MRP) software

Used to plan the production of goods in a manufacturing organisation by obtaining components, scheduling operations and controlling production.

Materials Requirements Planning (MRP) software used to plan the production of goods in a manufacturing organisation by obtaining components, scheduling, operations and controlling production. Dedicated MRP software provides input screens, a database and reporting facilities required of a production system. Information required by the system includes the master production schedule which states what needs producing, the bill of materials or component list and the inventory status file (ISF) giving the current component stock levels. A typical structure for a MRP system is shown in Fig 6.11. For large amounts of components a computerised system is essential. The MRP system will automatically generate a series of purchase orders for components along with the timing of their release to the production process, in order to ensure that customer order due dates are met. A development of the MRP system termed MRP II integrates the information system with other functional areas in the business such as finance and marketing; for instance, the incorporation of cost data through integration with the financial accounting system.

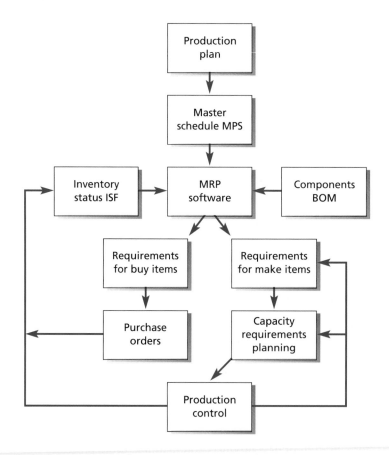

Fig 6.11 Flow of control and information requirements for a typical MRP system

Optimised Production Technology (OPT)

OPT is a computer-based technique which helps schedule production systems to the pace dictated by the bottleneck resource. The development and marketing of OPT as a proprietary software product were originated by Goldratt and Cox (1986).

Computer-aided design (CAD)

CAD provides interactive graphics that assist in the development of product and service designs. It also connects to a database, allowing designs to be recalled and developed easily.

Computer-aided manufacture (CAM)

CAM involves the use of computers directly to control production equipment and indirectly to support manufacturing operations. Direct CAM applications link a computer directly to production equipment in order to monitor and control the actual production process. An example is a computer numerical-controlled (CNC) machine which reads instructions for making parts from tape or disk. Indirect CAM applications include MRP, quality control and inventory control systems.

CAD/CAM

The successful design of a component must consider not only design issues in achieving customer requirements, but also the ability of the production system to manufacture the design. CAD/CAM systems improve the design process by enabling information exchange between the CAD and CAM systems by using a common database containing information on items such as component lists, routings and tool design.

Computer-integrated manufacture (CIM)

CIM aims to integrate information for manufacturing and external activities, such as order entry and accounting, to enable the transformation of a product idea into a delivered product in the minimum time and cost. CIM incorporates design activities such as CAD/CAM and operational activities such as MRP, FMS and inventory control. One of the main challenges in the implementation of CIM is integrating equipment from different manufacturers on a common network. In order to overcome this a data communication standard, called Manufacturing Automation Protocol (MAP), has been evolved. CIM covers all aspects of the overall process of production in a business. Its aims, through process automation, are to simplify production processes and product design, automate using robots and process control computers and integrate inventory holding and stock control and costings through the accounting information system. Table 6.3 summarises some of the tools discussed which form part of CIM.

Flexible manufacturing systems (FMS)

An FMS is a group of machines with programmable controllers linked by an automated materials handling system and integrated by an information system that enables a variety of parts with similar processing requirements to be manufactured. FMS systems are most suited to batch production systems which have intermediate amounts of variety and volume of output. The system aims to use computer control to produce a variety of output quickly.

Computer-aided design (CAD)
Provides interactive graphics that assist in the development of product and service designs. Connects to a database allowing designs to be recalled and developed easily.

Computer-aided manufacture (CAM)
CAM involves the use of computers directly to control production equipment and indirectly to support manufacturing operations.

Computer-integrated manufacture (CIM)
Aims to integrate information for manufacturing and external activities such as order entry and accounting to enable the transformation of a product idea into a delivered product in the minimum time and cost.

Table 6.3 Summary of the relationship between CIM and other tools

Business activities	CAD/CAE	CAM	
		Planning	Control
Procurement	Engineering analysis	Capacity planning	Process control
Accounting	Drafting	Materials planning	Shopfloor control
Order entry	Design review	Process planning	Computer-aided inspection
Payroll		Manufacturing activities	
Billing etc.		Materials handling, fabrication, assembly, inspection	

MINI CASE

Hi-Life Tools uses CIM to slash product development times and increase sales

Why does Hi-Life Tools use CIM?

◆ Aerospace and automotive parts, 200 staff.
◆ 60 000 different products, small batches, 50 per cent output one-off.
◆ Originally competing on cost and quality, but losing orders on delivery time (14 weeks order to dispatch).
◆ Target to reduce lead time through CIM process automation particularly in 'pre-production' and use of cellular manufacturing.

Result:

◆ Now 10 days' dispatch for US market.
◆ Sales increase of 1.3 million in year.

Source: Computer Weekly, 9 December 1993

Simulation modelling

Simulation modelling consists of building a computerised model of a production process and using that model to investigate different design options. Simulation is often used in layout design where the incorporation of an animated display allows material flows to be visualised on the computer screen. In order to build a simulation model, information such as product routing, process durations and resource availability is required. Simulation software available includes the ARENA and PROMODEL systems.

▶ MANAGEMENT INFORMATION SYSTEMS

Management information systems were introduced in Chapter 2 where they were defined as systems used to support tactical and strategic decision making. Here we will consider the application of MIS from a decision-making perspective.

▶ Decision types

The identification of problems according to their degree of structure dates back to Garry and Scott-Morton (1971), but it still provides a useful framework for defining decision types (Fig 6.12).

Figure 6.12 indicates that at the operational level, structured decisions predominate and these are commonly supported by TPS. Decision support systems are mainly used to support the tactical, semi-structured decisions that need to be made as part of the evaluation and planning of the business. Executive information systems are targeted at strategic decision making, which often involves unstructured decisions (*see* the box on examples of decision types).

It should be noted that there is considerable overlap between strategic and tactical and structured and unstructured. Similarly, there is overlap between the types of systems used to support these different levels. For example, decision support systems can also be used in a strategic capacity or in an operational capacity – an example later in the chapter (page 185) shows how they are used to detect fraud in credit card transactions. In this section we will focus on understanding how decision support systems are used at the tactical and strategic level.

▶ Decision-making theory

A **business rule** defines the actions that need to occur in a business when a particular situation arises. For example, a business rule may state that if a customer requests credit and they have a history of defaulting on payments, then credit will not be

Business rule

A rule that defines the actions that need to occur in a business when a particular situation arises. Broken down into an event which triggers a rule with test conditions which result in defined actions.

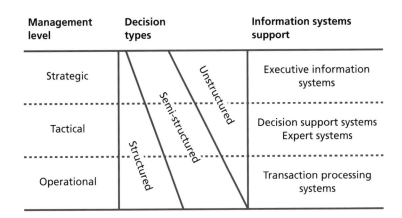

Fig 6.12 Classification of decisions by decision type and their relation to different types of system

---

Example of decision types

Structured decisions: operational planning
How should we process a sales order?
How do we perform quality control? For example, measure conformance of product (is it within quality limits on a control chart?). If outside limits, then system will reject part.

Semi-structured decision: tactical planning
How do we target our most profitable customers and what are their characteristics?
Which foreign markets should we target?
What is the best pricing structure for this product?

Unstructured decision: strategic planning
Which business area should the organisation be in?
How should the organisation be structured?
What should our distribution channels be?

---

issued. A business rule is broken down into an event which triggers a rule with test conditions which result in defined actions.

Decision making involves selecting the correct action from a series of alternative choices. The business rules governing the correct action may be complex, so we use diagrams and tables to help take the decision in a structured way and to ensure the rules are defined correctly for when they are implemented as program code. Consider the example of the business rule for when a company checks credit for a customer. This can be broken down as follows:

1 Name of event or process   Credit request
2 Condition (question when event occurs)   Is credit OK?
3 Alternative results   Yes or No
4 Alternative actions   If Yes: Continue   If No: Refuse order

Decision tree

A diagram showing the sequence of events, decisions and consequent actions that occur in a decision-making process.

Decision table

A matrix showing all the alternative outcomes of different decisions which occur when certain input conditions occur.

The need for a decision typically results from an event such as, in this case, a customer requesting credit. There is then a question that needs to be answered. In this case there are two alternative results: either the customer is creditworthy or not. Different actions will need different actions. In this case, if the customer is creditworthy the order can continue, if not the order will be refused.

In this example there is a single condition or question. However, most business rules will involve several questions and these can be misinterpreted if they are not clearly defined. In more complex cases we use a combination of decision trees and decision tables. **Decision trees** are usually drawn first and then the corresponding **decision table** is then based on the decision tree. This is the approach used in the examples below.

A decision tree is a diagram showing the sequence of events and decisions that occur in a process. It shows the different business rules using flow chart notation. The simple decision tree for the rule above is shown in Fig 6.13.

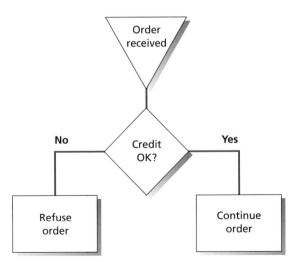

Fig 6.13 Decision tree notation for checking credit

A decision table is a matrix showing all the alternative outcomes of different decisions that occur when certain input conditions are met. It shows the different components of the decision in a tabular form, as in Fig 6.14.

A decision table for the credit checking example is shown in Fig 6.15.

To understand more about the application of decision trees and decision rules, a fuller example is required. The credit checking example above is extended to include other decisions that are required when a sales order is received from a customer. Figure 6.16 shows the decision tree for the sales order process. The first question is whether the customer has sent payment with the order. If they have, then the next question to ask is, are the items in stock? If they are, then the order can be dis-

Condition or rule	Condition entry
Action	Action entry

Fig 6.14 Framework for a decision table

Rule: Is credit OK?	Yes	No
Action: *Continue*: accept order *Terminate*: refuse order	X	
		X

Fig 6.15 Decision table for the credit checking example

patched to the customer. If not, the orders must be put on hold until the items are available. If the customer has not sent payment with the order, then the third question about the customer's credit is asked. If the customer's credit is acceptable, then the order can proceed and the question about the availability of items must be asked.

Table 6.4 shows the decision table for this example. The five rules correspond to the five final outcomes at the end of each branch of the tree in Fig 6.16. The upper part of the table shows the three test conditions and the relevant Yes/No outcomes for each of the rules. The lower part of the diagram shows the corresponding outcomes. For example, for rule 3, the outcome or action will be to refuse the order if the customer has not provided payment with the order and they are not creditworthy.

Once decision tables for the business rules have been produced, these act as a summary for the business rule that will be enacted by the information system. The corresponding program code for this example is shown in the box. Structured English is a method of design described in Chapter 12.

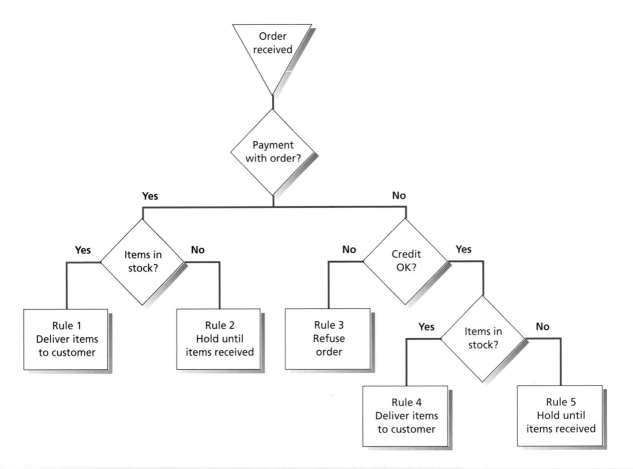

Fig 6.16 Decision tree indicating decisions involved in a sales order processing system

Table 6.4 Decision table for Fig 6.16

| | | Rules | | | | |
		1	2	3	4	5
Test conditions	Payment with order	Y	Y	N	N	N
	Items in stock	Y	N	–	Y	N
	Credit OK?	–	–	N	Y	Y
Actions dependent on conditions	Deliver item to customer	X			X	
	Hold order until items received		X			X
	Refuse order			X		

Structured English program code for implementing the decision table in Table 6.4

```
IF Payment_with order? THEN

        IF items_in_stock? THEN
                Deliver item to customer (Rule 1)
        ELSE
                Hold_until_received (Rule 2)
        ENDIF

ELSE

        IF credit_OK? THEN
        IF items_in_stock? THEN
                Deliver item to customer (Rule 4)
        ELSE
                Hold_until_received (Rule 5)
        ENDIF
        ELSE
                Refuse order (Rule 3)
        ENDIF

ENDIF
```

▶ Decision support systems

Decision support systems (DSS) provide information and models in a form to facilitate tactical and strategic decision making. They are information systems that support management decision making by integrating:

◆ company performance data;

◆ business rules based on decision tables;

◆ analytical tools and models for forecasting and planning;

◆ an easy-to-use graphical user interface.

They are often developed by end-users and are departmental rather than corporate systems. DSS tend to be used for *ad hoc* queries rather than regular reporting. The technology varies particularly rapidly in this area and the newest developments such as data warehouses attest to this. They are frequently used as a marketing tool, with applications such as:

◆ forecasting sales through geodemographic analysis;

◆ optimising distribution networks, using a model to select the best retail locations;

◆ optimising product mixes.

When used by teams of people to make decisions, they are sometimes known as GDSS or group decision support systems. DSS are often implemented as specialised types of information systems such as data warehousing, expert systems, geographical information systems or even spreadsheet models. We will explore some of these in more detail below.

Functions of a decision support system

Sprague (1980) suggests the following main objectives for a DSS:

1 The DSS should provide support for decision making, but in particular semi-structured and unstructured decisions.

2 The DSS should not focus on a single level of management decision making, such as tactical. Rather, it should integrate across all levels in recognition of the overlap between operational, tactical and strategic decisions.

3 The DSS should support all phases of the decision-making process outlined above.

4 The DSS should be easy to use.

Decision support system components

Watson and Sprague (1993) identify three main components in a decision support system. These are:

1 *Dialog.* This component is used for achieving interaction with the user so they can formulate queries and models and review results. Essentially, it is the user interface. It is often difficult to devise an effective user interface for a DSS since there is a trade-off between simplicity and flexibility. Simplicity is needed since some managers may not be frequent users of DSS or other decision support systems. Flexibility is required to allow a range of different questions to be asked and to

enable data to be displayed in different ways. The problem is that as more flexibility and options are built into the system, it becomes more difficult to use.

2 *Data*. Data sources are, of course, critical to DSS. Information may need to be collected from a range of sources such as operational systems (for sales performance), financial accounting systems (for financial performance), or document sources such as internal documents or those available on the Internet.

3 *Model*. The model component provides an analysis capability for the DSS. A financial model, for example, may predict for given inputs what the future profitability of a company will be if it continues on the present course.

Analysis techniques available for a salesforce management problem

MINI CASE

Here, we will briefly review commonly used expressions for describing analysis using DSS in relation to a simple example. A company has recognised that there is a positive correlation between the number of sales staff and revenue generated. Through setting up a simple model in a spreadsheet based on this relationship, it is possible to perform the following types of analysis:

1 *What-if? analysis*. Changing a series of variables to see the effect, e.g. What if we increase our salesforce by 10 per cent? The corresponding forecast increase in sales will readily be calculated by the spreadsheet.

2 *Sensitivity analysis*. This is a structured what-if? analysis where we change a single variable repeatedly to see the effects, e.g. increase salesforce in increments of 1 per cent.

3 *Goal-seeking analysis*. This is the reverse of what-if? Here we change variables governing the value of the goal until it is achieved, e.g. By what percentage do we need to increase the salesforce to achieve a growth in sales of £100 000?

4 *Optimisation analysis and simulation*. Change a number of variables to find the optimal solution through, for example, linear programming, e.g. Which is the best mix of increasing advertising and salesforce to achieve a set increase in sales?

5 *Data mining*. This approach is used with data warehouses (*see* below) to try to identify a relationship between variables in order to assist decision making. It will involve statistical techniques such as multiple linear regression where a number of variables are compared to identify patterns.

Types of decision support system

There is a bewildering array of terms used to describe software developed to help solve unstructured and semi-structured problems. These include artificial intelligence, expert systems, neural networks, fuzzy logic, data mining, knowledge-based systems and intelligent knowledge-based systems. All of these types of software have the same broad aim – to assist decision making by using software to mimic the way decisions are made by experts in their own field.

Artificial Intelligence (AI)

The study into how computers can reproduce human intelligence.

Artificial intelligence (AI) is the term given to research into how computers can reproduce human intelligence. Many of the terms above, such as expert systems and neural networks, are specialist areas of artificial intelligence from which business applications have been produced. Further business applications of AI include voice recognition and security applications such as retinal scanning.

A useful method of considering different types of DSS is to consider the different types of problem they can solve (Luconi *et al.*, 1986). The problems are considered in terms of four elements:

- ◆ the data;
- ◆ the problem-solving procedures;
- ◆ the goals and constraints;
- ◆ the flexibility of strategies among the procedures.

The types of problem are:

- ◆ Type I problems are structured in all of the four elements above.
- ◆ Type II problems have some incomplete data and partly understood goals and constraints.
- ◆ Type III problems are those in which rules can be defined in a knowledge base and the software can then solve problems of a similar type.
- ◆ Type IV problems have aspects of both Type II and Type III problems.

Which types of DSS can be used for solving these types of problems? Type I problems are usually incorporated into operational systems as part of the program logic and do not require a specific DSS. The problem example with credit checking falls into this category. Type III problems can be solved by a classical expert system and Types II and IV require a hybrid approach, which may involve modern techniques such as data mining, neural networks and genetic programming as described by Goonatilake and Khebbal (1995). We will now consider some of these types of system in more detail.

Expert systems

Expert systems

Used to represent the knowledge decision-making skills of specialists so that non-specialists can take decisions.

Expert systems are used to represent the knowledge and decision-making skills of specialists so that non-specialists can take decisions. They encapsulate the knowledge of experts by providing tools for the acquisition of knowledge, representation of rules and their enactment as decisions. They need to contain information relevant to taking the decision. This is often referred to as the *knowledge base* and includes the rules on which the decisions are based. An important distinction between expert systems and other information systems which are used for decision making is that the suggested actions are not based only on rules and algorithms. Instead, they also use heuristic techniques that may involve searching through different 'rules of thumb' which recommend the best action. The different rules are applied using a separate module of the expert system, known as the *inference engine*. This uses specialist techniques such as forward chaining and backward chaining, explained briefly in the box.

The relationship between these different components of the expert system is shown in Fig 6.17. The *user interface* program, sometimes referred to as the expert system shell, is used to build rules and ask questions of the system.

Applications of expert systems include:

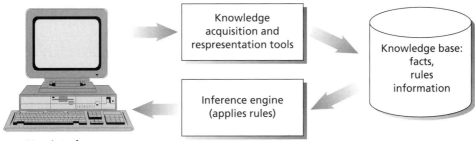

Fig 6.17 Components of an expert system

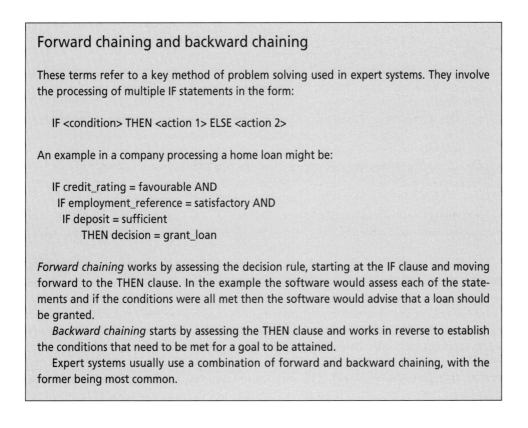

Forward chaining and backward chaining

These terms refer to a key method of problem solving used in expert systems. They involve the processing of multiple IF statements in the form:

IF <condition> THEN <action 1> ELSE <action 2>

An example in a company processing a home loan might be:

IF credit_rating = favourable AND
  IF employment_reference = satisfactory AND
   IF deposit = sufficient
     THEN decision = grant_loan

Forward chaining works by assessing the decision rule, starting at the IF clause and moving forward to the THEN clause. In the example the software would assess each of the statements and if the conditions were all met then the software would advise that a loan should be granted.
  Backward chaining starts by assessing the THEN clause and works in reverse to establish the conditions that need to be met for a goal to be attained.
  Expert systems usually use a combination of forward and backward chaining, with the former being most common.

◆ gold prospecting!
◆ medical diagnosis;
◆ credit decisions and insurance underwriting;
◆ product design, management and testing.

In medicine, expert systems have recorded some success in diagnosing illnesses which might not have been recognised by doctors because of their obscurity. In a medical expert system such as MYCIN which was used to identify the treatment for blood disorders, the symptoms of a condition are entered into the expert system, which then compares them with all the known symptoms of different ailments in a knowledge base and gives a diagnosis. The knowledge base consists of facts or expert knowledge, in this case the symptoms and also a series of rules that match the symptom to the problem.

MINI CASE

Pareto Partners use expert systems to manage over £130 million in global financial markets

Investment company Pareto has invested over £1 million in an expert system which manages many times that amount in investments. The system uses hybrid techniques according to the type of problem that is being solved. It uses fuzzy logic based on reasoning and imprecise values such as low, medium or high. For other scenarios it uses case-based reasoning relating to previous examples and standard forward and backward chaining techniques, employing about 2000 rules based on the expertise of leading financial analysts.

In financial markets, the amount of profit required is usually proportional to the risks that a company is prepared to take. This risk–return ratio is therefore a programmable parameter of Pareto's system.

To date, *Computer Bulletin* reported in March 1998 that the system has achieved a return of 3.4 per cent, which matches the performance of the top quarter of human investment managers. The magazine also notes that such a system is unlikely to succumb to the stress of decision making in this high-pressured situation. It is difficult for a human manager to remember the number of investment opportunities and past trends. If a manager manages funds in 10–15 markets with 10–20 variables for each of three sources of variables, then this is equivalent to millions of combinations.

Expert systems are used quite widely in the financial services industry for assessing the risk of investing in a particular share or futures market (*see* case study) or in personal finance or issuing a loan. For example, if a customer wants a loan they will give personal details about their employment history and where they have lived, and an expert system will assess what the credit risk is based on this pattern of behaviour in their existing customer base. The degree of sophistication of this risk assessment could vary from assessing the individual on a series of rules or a more advanced system using neural networks. The rules-based approach might state, for example, that credit cannot be issued if an individual has not lived in a particular location for less than six months over the last five years or if the amount of the loan is greater than 10 per cent of their salary. With a neural network approach, the software would learn from the history of previous customers what characteristics represented a bad credit risk and assess according to these criteria.

Expert systems (ES) achieved prominence during the 1980s as the result of work summarised by Scott-Morton *et al.* (1991). Since this time they have not been applied as widely as forecast, often only being used in niche applications such as credit broking. Their use to date and predicted future use are described in Chapter 19.

More recent artificial intelligence type systems have been referred to as *intelligent hybrid systems* by Goonatilake and Khebbal (1995). These differ from expert systems in that they are adaptive – they often have the ability to modify their decision-making capabilities as their knowledge base is expanded, in other words they can 'learn'. **Neural networks** are systems that use a similar process to biological intelligence to learn problem-solving skills by 'training' or exposure to a wide range of problems. The learning occurs through interactions between nodes, which are similar to the neurons of the brain. Neural networks work in a similar way to the neurons of the brain, which gives them the capacity to learn through exposure to different patterns. For example, a neural network could be used for a photofit application if it learnt the characteristics of different types of people. As an example of the way in which neural networks can be applied to business applications, consider a bank processing Visa credit card transaction. Of all the transactions that occur, a proportion will be fraudulent. By learning from past transactions, both legal and fraudulent, a neural network will be able to predict the likelihood of fraud on an account. Barclays Bank installed such a system in the UK in 1997, and it was soon recognising over £100 000 of fraudulent transactions each month.

Another type of adaptive system is a *genetic algorithm*. This uses successive iterations of a problem-solving algorithm to improve the quality of decision taken by the software. A further method is known as *fuzzy logic*, often combined with neural networks in a hybrid system.

Expert systems have not been widely adopted in industry, although they are widely used in some areas such as financial risk assessment. Since most business users are unlikely to be involved in the specification or use of expert systems, they are not covered further here. The interested reader should refer to Curtis (1998) for a summary of different techniques for representing and processing knowledge in expert systems, or Turban (1995) for a complete text on expert systems and decision support.

Executive information systems (EIS)

EIS or executive support systems provide senior managers with a system to assist them in taking strategic and tactical decisions. Their purpose is to analyse, compare and highlight trends to help govern the strategic direction of a company. They are commonly integrated with operational systems, giving managers the facility to 'drill down' to find out further information on a problem.

In the US the terms business intelligence and online analytical processing (OLAP) are often used for these types of applications by analysts such as the Garner Group and vendors such as Cognos and Business Objects. These terms and the data warehouses described in the next section are also starting to supersede EIS in the rest of the world.

Business intelligence software is a general term to describe the market for a range of decision support systems, including EIS, DSS and data-warehouse software and including application of expert systems and data-mining techniques to interpret data.

Online analytical processing (OLAP) is a synonym for a data warehouse. It refers to the ability to analyse in real time the type of multidimensional information stored in data warehouses. The term online indicates that users can formulate their own queries, compared to standard paper reports. The originator of OLAP, Dr E. Codd, defines it as the dynamic synthesis, analysis and consolidation of large volumes of multidimensional data.

Neural networks

Systems that use a similar process to biological intelligence to learn problem-solving skills by 'training' or exposure to a wide range of problems.

Executive information systems (EIS)

Provide senior managers with a system to assist them in taking strategic and tactical decisions. Their purpose is to analyse, compare and highlight trends to help govern the strategic direction of a company.

Business intelligence software

A general term to describe the market for a range of decision support systems including EIS, DSS and data warehouse software.

Online analytical processing (OLAP)

Refers to the ability to analyse in real time the type of multidimensional information stored in data warehouses.

EIS are intended as decision support tools for senior managers. Since these strategic decisions are based on a wide range of input information, they always need to be well integrated with operational systems in a business. Some important features of EIS are:

◆ They provide summary information to enable monitoring of business performance. This is often achieved through measures known as critical success factors or key performance indicators (KPIs). These will be displayed in an easy-to-interpret form such as a graph showing their variation through time. If a KPI falls below a critical preset value, the system will notify the manager through a visible or audible warning.

◆ They are used mainly for strategic decision making, but may also provide features which relate to tactical decision making.

◆ They provide a drill-down feature which gives a manager the opportunity to find out more information necessary to take a decision or discover the source of a problem. For example, a manager with a multinational manufacturing problem might find from the EIS that a particular country is underperforming in production. He could then drill down to see which particular factory was responsible for this.

◆ They provide analysis tools.

◆ They must be integrated with other facilities to help manage the solving of problems and the daily running of the business. These include electronic mail and scheduling/calendar facilities.

◆ They integrate data from a wide variety of information sources, including company and external sources such as market and competitor information.

◆ They have to be designed according to the needs of managers who do not use computers frequently. They should be intuitive and easy to learn.

All these facilities require integration with operational data. Since this information is commonly stored in ERP systems (*see* page 239), these are often integrated with EIS or have EIS functions built in.

A further example of an EIS is provided by Comshare Commander, a UK product. Its range of functions is indicated by the following main menu options:

◆ Financial reporting;

◆ Management reporting;

◆ TQM reporting;

◆ Profit management;

◆ Enterprise budgeting;

◆ Executive information.

Focus, from US-based Company Information Builders is also popular, and has been in existence for over 20 years. Other companies producing EIS such as Arbor Essbase and Cognos are now best known for their data warehousing products.

Useful Web sites include:

http://www.ibi.com;
http://www.comshare.com;
http://www.cognos.com;
http://arborsoft.com.

EasyView – an EIS for business-to-business marketing staff

EasyView has the typical features of an EIS, since it has an easy-to-follow user interface which provides an overview of company performance according to an integrated series of measures, and it also alerts managers to specific problems. It is possible to choose any combination of product or geographical area in which a company is operating, including an aggregation of all areas, as is shown in Fig 6.18.

Summary of EasyView performance measures

1 *Bid* shows the company's success rate in winning bids (in this case for organising exhibitions). If bid price > 0, the company bid was too high, if < 0 then too low, and if bid price = 0 the company was successful.
2 *Market* shows the market share and market size for this particular product.
3 *Product and Customer* indicate customer satisfaction levels according to the icon.
4 *Profit* indicates financial performance compared to forecast. In this case the company has not met its targets, as is clearly evident from the gauge.
5 *Market events* provide alerts to highlight particular problems such as a substantial decline in profits. These figures are derived through searching the database for problem performance areas, which would be time consuming to do manually for a company with many products.

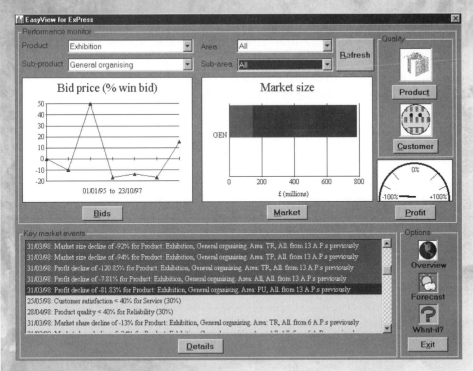

Fig 6.18 Performance measurement using EasyView

Data warehouses, data marts and data mining

Data warehouses

Large database systems containing detailed company data on sales transactions which are analysed to assist in improving the marketing and financial performance of companies.

Data marts

These are small-scale data warehouses which do not aim to hold information across an entire company, rather they focus on one department.

Data warehouses are large database systems (often measured in gigabytes or terabytes (terabytes = 1000 billion bytes)) containing detailed company data on sales transactions which are analysed to assist in improving the marketing and financial performance of companies.

Data warehouses form a category of business intelligence software that has been adopted by many companies for analysis of transactions to help improve their competitiveness. Such is their popularity that the term data warehouse has to a great extent displaced EIS in software purchases for strategic and tactical decision making. Trends in their use and their benefits and disadvantages are described in Chapter 19. **Data marts** are a newer development. This term defines a smaller, departmental version which may be easier to manage than a company-scale data warehouse. Data marts do not aim to hold information across an entire company rather they focus on one department.

William Inmon is often known as the father of the data warehouse. He defines a data warehouse as:

> A subject oriented, integrated, time variant, and non-volatile collection of data in support of management's decision making process.

It is worth considering each of the characteristics of the definition in more detail:

◆ *'subject oriented'*. Examples of subjects that are commonly held in data warehouses for analysis are customer and product.

◆ *'integrated'*. An important principle of data warehouses is that information is collected from diverse sources within an organisation and brought together to enable integrated analysis.

◆ *'non-volatile'*. Data is transferred from operational information systems such as sales order processing systems into a data warehouse where the information is static – it is not updated.

◆ *'in support of management's decision making process'*. This final point emphasises the purpose of the data warehouse.

Keys to success for a data warehouse

In a 1998 White Paper by US analysts IDC, Graham and Notarfonzo listed five keys to success. These are:

1 Ensure end-user's needs are fully defined.
2 Ensure business requirements are fully defined.
3 Develop enterprise-level data models and business rules.
4 Include individuals from affected departments in the development teams.
5 Promote use of the warehouse internally.

The top five pitfalls they identified are:

1 Raising users' expectations higher than you can deliver.
2 Letting the project scope become unmanageable.

---

3 Underusing the warehouse.
4 Letting management interest wane.
5 Not fully developing business requirements.

In a report by analysts The Meta Group, *Data Warehouse Opportunities 1997/98: an In-depth Analysis of the Key Market Trends*, a survey indicated the following key challenges to implementing the data warehouse (by % of respondents):

- ◆ 35–40%: Data quality;
- ◆ 30–35%: Transforming/scrubbing legacy data, managing end-user expectations;
- ◆ 20–25%: Managing management expectations, business rule analysis, managing meta-data (data about data);
- ◆ 15–20%: Database performance tuning/scaling, ROI justification;
- ◆ 10–15%: Time to load/refresh data;
- ◆ 5–10%: Security, maintenance.

Figure 6.19 indicates the structure of a data warehouse. It can be seen that the data warehouse takes information from operational systems (which record sales or trans-actions with customers) and transfers this information into a repository for decision making, which happens across the network via a Web-based client, or a specific client from a BI software vendor such as Cognos Powerplay.

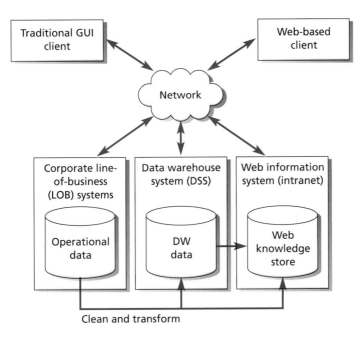

Fig 6.19 Data warehouse architecture

BI and data warehousing software is used in three main ways:

1 For analysing large volumes of product sales information to identify problem areas where sales targets are not being achieved. The data may be 'sliced and diced' by different dimensions to spot particular problems. These include by product segment, by geographical area, by time period (monthly, quarterly, yearly), by sales person and by customer type (for example age and sociodemographic group for retail consumers).

2 For data mining. This identifies trends in the data, allowing marketing managers to optimise the product mix. For example, if a credit card company is experiencing a high 'churn rate' of customers moving to other brands, data mining could be used to identify the characteristics of these customers and then suggest a method or alternative product that could be offered to alleviate this.

3 For forecasting and performing what-if? scenarios. Using this type of software the company can vary the characteristics of its products or the customers it targets and see the likely impacts on future sales.

Data mining

An attempt to identify relationships between variables in data warehouses in order to assist decision making.

Data mining of data warehouses is an attempt to identify a relationship between variables in order to assist decision making. It will involve statistical techniques such as multiple linear regression where a number of variables are compared to identify patterns.

Data mining is used to identify patterns or trends in the data in data warehouses which can be used for improved profitability. The well-known Walmart example shows that these patterns would often not be evident without computer analysis. Rather than asking direct questions such as: 'Who are the top 20 per cent of our customers?', more open questions will be asked such as: 'What are the characteristics of the top 20 per cent' of our customers?'. Through understanding customers better, their needs can be better met.

Examples of data mining products include:

◆ 4Thought from Cognos;

◆ Pilot Discovery Server;

◆ Applix OLAP reporting tool.

MINI CASE

Walmart identifies correlation between beer and nappies using data mining!

Through using data mining of a data warehouse, US retailer Walmart recognised a correlation between sales of nappies and beer. This was accounted for by men with children purchasing both items at their end of weekly shop. By placing both items together in the store, sales of beer increased dramatically.

Major providers of data warehousing solutions are:

http://www.cognos.com (provider of PowerPlay);
http://www.businessobjects.com;
http://www.oracle.com (as an additional module to the Oracle database);
http://www.essbase.com.

CASE STUDY: TOPIC AREA

Data warehouse analysis techniques for describing multidimensional data

Example 1: a car sales data warehouse

Information collected on transactions can often be broken down in different ways. Say that we have data on car sales. We can break this information down by:

◆ time car was sold;
◆ model;
◆ location at which sold;
◆ sales person;

and so on. This type of breakdown is vital for marketing staff to assess the performance of advertising campaigns, sales staff and dealerships. Problems in sales of particular models or particular staff can be identified and then rectified.

Whenever we break information down in this way we are identifying the different *dimensions* of the data. There are usually three common dimensions:

◆ time period;
◆ product or market segment;
◆ geographic location where the product was sold (or where consumers originate).

The example in Fig 6.20 shows how these three dimensions form a cube, with each individual cube effectively representing one combination of data. The small cube represents all four-wheel-drive vehicles in Quarter 1 of 1998 sold into a particular postal sector.

When designing data warehouses, each dimension and its division into categories can be shown on a diagram, as in Table 6.5.

Note that measures such as sales figures and market share, which are all broken down into the different dimensions, are shown along the bottom of the table. This table can also be used to assess the information storage requirements.

Example 2: a retail data warehouse for camping equipment

This example shows two different views on this data. The first (Fig 6.21) tabulates sales for a particular product range – outdoor products in 1996 for the North American market. It can be seen from the categories dialogue box that it is possible to choose different views of the data

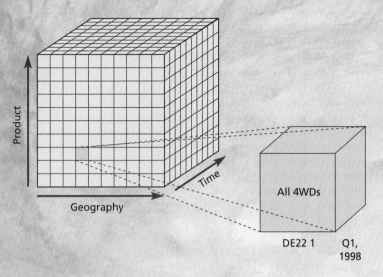

Fig 6.20 Example of multidimensional data cube for vehicle sales

Table 6.5 Designing a data warehouse

	Dimensions					
	All time periods (85)	All locations (4306)	All products (35)	Age groups (8)	Economic groups (6)	All genders (3)
	Year 5	Regions 6	Segments 5	8	ABC1 C2DE 6	3
	Quarter 20	Postal areas 200	Models 30			
Categories	Month 60	Postal districts 1500	(Paint colours 100)			
		Postal sectors 2000	(Plus competitor segments)			
		Dealerships + DARs (plus sales staff not shown) 300 * 2				

Measures:
Forecast sales, Budget sales, Actual sales, Budget variance (calc), Forecast variance (calc), Market share. For each of 6 measures, number of data items are: 85*4306*35*8*6*3 = 1.8 billion. Assume 4 bytes each item 6 * 4 * 1.8 billion. Approx 40 Gigabytes.

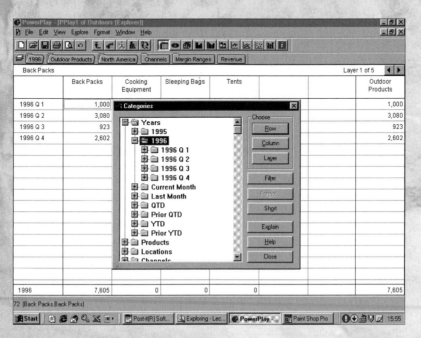

Fig 6.21 Cognos Powerplay showing example data for outdoor products

according to the category. Cognos Powerplay is a widely used tool for analysis of complex, multidimensional data.

The view of the data in Fig 6.22 shows the same data in graphical form. Sales variations in the five products for the five different quarters are clearly evident.

Hammergren (1996) gives a good treatment of some of the techniques of data analysis described in this case study.

Question

For the second example of outdoor equipment, develop a matrix showing the dimensions and categories of information in the same form as that for the car sales matrix. List your assumptions where insufficient information is available.

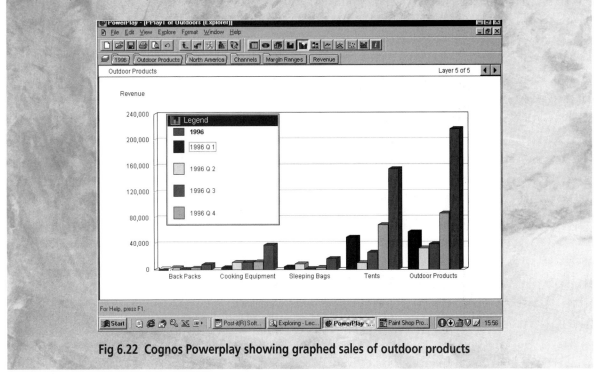

Fig 6.22 Cognos Powerplay showing graphed sales of outdoor products

The case study gives an indication of some of the specialised techniques necessary to deal with analysis of the volume of data stored in a data warehouse, which is referred to as multidimensional data.

Useful Web sites include:

◆ http://www.data-warehouse.com. A resource centre for data warehousing techniques;

◆ http://www.dw-institute.com. the Data Warehousing Institute.

Multidimensional data shows how data is broken down in the analysis used for building a data warehouse, this is often referred to as the different dimensions of the data. For sales data the common dimensions are time period, product types and geographic location. Dimensions are broken down into categories. For time these could be months, quarters or years. Data describing the data is known as **metadata**.

Multidimensional data

Data broken down in analysis for a data warehouse into dimensions such as time period, product segment and the geographical location. Dimensions are broken down into categories. For time these could be months, quarters or years.

Metadata

Reference data describing the structure and content of data in a data warehouse is known as metadata.

▶ BUSINESS APPLICATIONS

In the final section of this chapter we will review how information systems can be used in three key functional parts of an organisation: the human resources, marketing and finance functions. These three examples have been chosen since they usually require applications-specific software. Other functional areas which are part of the value chain, such as production, procurement and logistics, have already been briefly considered in the section on process control systems. The value chain is described in Chapter 14.

▶ Human resource management (HRM) information systems

Human resource management (HRM)

Management that ensures the employees of the organisation have the required skills and tools in order to meet the strategic goals of the organisation.

Human resource management (HRM) is about ensuring that the employees of the organisation have the required skills and tools in order to meet its strategic goals. The management of an organisation's human resources is critical to its success. The development of an organisation's human resources is particularly important in a service company, where employees are more likely to be required to provide customer contact. Human resource decisions and information systems support will be required both within the central human resource function and by managers of the functional areas of the business. Organisations need a supply of trained and qualified personnel in order to achieve their goals. Human resource management (HRM) is about ensuring that the employees of the organisation have the required skills and tools in order to meet its strategic goals.

Objectives of HRM software

The main role of HRM software is to act as a storage and retrieval system maintaining large volumes of data on employee and job specifications. This data will be required for applications such as routine reports for government agencies, information for recruitment and selection and more sophisticated forecasting models for workforce planning. The supply of information related to legislative data is described in Chapter 18.

MINI CASE

IT liberates personnel staff from 'paper shuffling'

Writing in the *Scotsman* newspaper on 11 June 1998, Neil Fitzgerald argues that technology has 'liberated personnel staff from their paper prison'. He describes a conference arranged by the Institute of Personnel Development which demonstrated that 'the long-winded paper shuffling process of job adverts, applications, CVs and interviews was undergoing dramatic change thanks to computer and communications technology'.

As an example of the use of workflow technology, Federal Express introduced a workflow system within its human resources management function. For a large company such as FedEx, managing job applications, contracts and training records is a significant undertaking. PRISM, a workflow system with imaging, has been used since 1991 to scan up to 10 000 images a day. Workflow is used to automate the process of hiring and also to build in checks. If a manager decides to hire, the system checks that the candidate has not worked in any other offices previously, then checks that the position is budgeted, assigns an employee identification number and finally transfers information from the applicant-tracking database to an employee database. This automation does not usually involve human intervention – no onscreen forms need to be filled in and not a single piece of paper is generated.

The screenshot in Fig 6.23 of Staffware, a workflow package, shows how the process of managing many applications, interviews and follow-ups can be partially automated using a workflow system.

Consultant Graeme Wright of Park Human Resources painted a picture of the future at the conference when he described the situation in the US, where leading employers are conducting initial interviews over the Internet, and one retailer asks employers to visit a store where they are interviewed by a computer which scores them electronically.

Questions

1 What are the advantages to the employer of using workflow systems in the HR function?
2 What would your reaction as an interviewee be to your application being in such a system? How would you handle an 'electronic interview'?
3 What checks could be built into such a system to prevent errors?

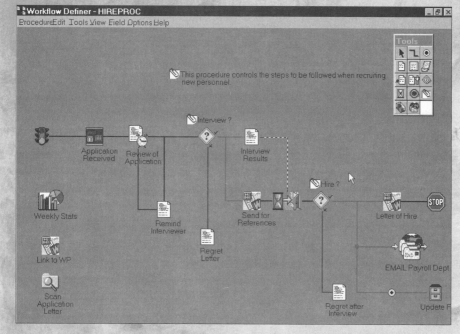

Fig 6.23 Software workflow system showing an HRM application

Information needs for human resources systems

The main activities of the HR function and the information needed to support them are:

◆ *Job analysis and design.* HR systems need to contain job descriptions describing the purpose, tasks and responsibilities of that job and job specifications describing the skills, knowledge and other characteristics required of workers in order to undertake the tasks specified in the job description.

◆ *Job management.* This includes recording of employee development through appraisals, training and salary and benefits planning. The government will also require human resource information to be available from all organisations to comply with laws governing such areas as health and safety legislation, equal opportunities regulations and employee sickness history.

◆ *Recruitment.* In large organisations workflow systems are used for managing the thousands of applications for jobs. Such systems will help structure interviewing and sending out letters.

Software for HRM information systems

A database provides a central feature of HRM systems and will contain information on such areas as name, address, job title and attendance for each employee in the organisation and other information required to construct job description and applicant files. With this information it should be possible to use a database management system to match applicant and current employee details to a job specification. The database could also be used in areas such as the identification of training needs and producing details of employees for government agencies. Unfortunately, some HR databases have been constructed within the HR function and are not compatible with such areas as payroll. This leads to problems of duplication and ensuring that data is up to date. Small companies could develop their own databases, but more often small, medium and large companies will buy an off-the-shelf package based on a database.

Client server UNIX applications used in large companies include:

◆ Oracle HR;
◆ SAP R/3;
◆ Peterborough software.

Unlinked PC software used in smaller companies includes:

◆ standard spreadsheets;
◆ timesheet software;
◆ payroll packages;
◆ job evaluation software;
◆ training packages.

A variety of computer-based training (CBT) software is available, much of this utilising the multimedia capabilities of the personal computer (PC). Computer-based training has the advantage of saving on instructor time, allowing employees to work through the training scheme at their own pace and the ability to run the software at a variety of locations (e.g. training centre, office, home).

An example HRM database

Single *record* per employee in main employee *table*.
  Fields within the employee *table* to include:

◆ surname, forename, next of kin;
◆ date of birth;
◆ address;
◆ National Insurance number;
◆ position – job description;
◆ department;
◆ salary;
◆ tax code;
◆ start date.

Links to other *tables*:

◆ training records;
◆ assessment/performance appraisal details;
◆ payroll.

The terms table, field and record were introduced in Chapter 3. Database design is discussed further in Chapters 11 and 12.

BT Global Communications

MINI CASE

◆ 9000 staff, 2500 outside UK (part of BT).
◆ Uses Oracle database-based HR package – integrates HR, payroll and training functions and replaces six different, unlinked systems – timesheets, payroll, job evaluation and training.
◆ Uses WAN to enable global access to training and skills databases – not just line managers – important for a mobile workforce.
◆ Use of WAN also enables global manpower managing and reporting.

▶ Marketing information systems

The word marketing has two distinct meanings in terms of modern management practice. It describes:

1 The range of specialist marketing functions carried out within many organisations. Such functions include market research, brand/product management, public relations and customer service.

2 An approach or concept that can be used as the guiding philosophy for all functions and activities of an organisation. Such a philosophy encompasses all aspects of a business. Business strategy is guided by an organisation's market and competitor focus and everyone in an organisation should be required to have a customer focus in their job.

The modern marketing concept unites these two meanings and stresses that marketing encompasses the range of organisational functions and processes that deliver products and services to customers and other key stakeholders, such as employees and financial institutions. Increasingly, the importance of marketing is being recognised both as a vital function and a guiding management philosophy. Marketing has to be seen as the essential focus of all activities within an organisation.

Given the importance of marketing to an organisation, many companies make use of information systems to assist in mission-critical activities such as customer sales. These have been described in the section on transaction processing systems earlier in the chapter. In this section we will mainly consider information systems that are used within the marketing department to assist in running the marketing function.

Marketing information systems support decision making at the operational, tactical and strategic levels. At the operational level, distribution information systems and telemarketing systems offer assistance in day-to-day activities and provide information to areas such as inventory and customer credit systems. Tactical marketing systems provide assistance in such areas as product pricing and sales management information systems. At the strategic level, information from sales forecasting, marketing research and competitive tracking systems helps management plan and develop new products.

Marketing information systems

Support the decision making at the operational, tactical and strategic levels necessary to manage the marketing function.

Application areas for marketing information systems

The following types of marketing information system can be identified:

◆ *Sales information systems*. Employees involved in the sales area are required to identify potential customers, negotiate the sale of goods and services with those customers and provide a follow-up service. Systems are available to support each of these tasks. Prospect information systems provide lists of potential customers by categories such as product range or geographic area. The database may be in the form of disks, CD-ROM or be available online through services such as the Internet. Whichever method of delivery is used, it is important that the data is up to date. It is usually possible to obtain updates of the database over time from the software supplier. Databases can also be used to assist in the selling process. Telemarketing and direct mail systems will incorporate a database to enable storage and extraction of the large amounts of required when dealing with extensive client lists.

◆ *Distribution information systems*. Speed of delivery is often an important aspect of service to the customer. In order to ensure this, it is important that tracking systems are in place which can locate products during the distribution process. These tracking systems may incorporate technology such as mobile and satellite communications and pen-based computing.

◆ *Sales order processing (SOP) systems*. The sales order processing (SOP) system is usually based in the financial area and provides a variety of data that can be used for marketing purposes, such as the timing and value of orders from customers. These can be used for applications such as sales forecasting, which is a significant input into the sales planning process. Other data supplied by the SOP system includes inventory levels. If inventory levels are high, then this might trigger a discount programme for a particular product line.

◆ *Sales and campaign management information systems.* The sales management information system provides information in support of decision making at the tactical level. It will hold information on such aspects as sales performance by geographic area, by product group and sales person. This information can be used to determine sales effort in different areas and products and level of bonus payments to an individual sales person. The data can also be used to investigate the strength of relationship between such factors as customer types and product sales. This information can be used as the basis for a marketing plan based around an advertising and promotion scheme aimed at a particular customer segment (e.g. targeting of designer-label drinks at people in the 18–25 age range). Sales management software consists of a specialist package based on database technology that provides information on sales person activity and performance, sales orders and customers.

◆ *Product pricing information systems.* The price of a good will be dependent on a variety of factors, such as the cost of producing the product or providing the service, the required profit margin and the price of competitor goods. The price may also be affected by a marketing strategy to build market share by lowering the price. The product pricing information system will collate information on costs and predicted market demand at different price points and discounts in order to support the pricing decision. More sophisticated software in the form of a pricing model enables the user to input various market and product attributes and, based on relationships formalised in the model, provides a suggested price.

◆ *Sales forecasting information systems.* At a strategic level, it is necessary to provide sales forecast data in order to help form the long-range strategic plan. Sales forecast data is essential so that demand can be met and resource employed in the correct areas. For instance, marketing needs to inform other functions such as operations of predicted demand, so that they can organise their resources to meet this demand. The information system is required because of the range of data that goes into the forecast and the need continually to update the database so the forecast is as accurate as possible.

◆ *Marketing research and analysis information systems.* In order to ensure that there is a demand for the organisation's goods and services, it is necessary to undertake market research. For a new product, this may include information on demographic changes and customer feedback from questionnaires and interviews indicating customer preferences. For existing products, this will involve analysis of sales using **business intelligence** software such as **data warehouses**, described in the section on decision support software.

◆ *Competitive tracking.* Knowledge of competitor prices, products, sales and promotions is an important factor in the development of a marketing strategy. For example, the organisation would need to consider its reaction to a competitor move to build market share.

◆ *Telemarketing software.* This software is designed to dial the telephone numbers of potential customers automatically based on customer files maintained in a database. The software will also allow notes to be stored on customer requests, generate follow-up letters and display information gathered on the customer for reference as the call is taking place. Telephone call centres use computer-integrated telephony (CIT) to sell direct product lines such as insurance and personal

finance. CIT is also used to provide customer service via helpdesk and advice services. The software can be integrated with a workflow system that provides automatic management of customer requests (e.g. automation of activities such as letter generation). Using historical data, the software can also be used to predict workload levels over time and thus aid management in workforce planning.

◆ *Geographical information systems (GIS)*. Geographical information systems (GIS) use maps to display information about different areas. They are comonly used for performance analysis by marketing staff. Performance of distribution channels such as branches can be shown by colour coding them. Colour-coded areas on the map can be used to show variation in the demand of customers for products or the characteristics of people living in different areas, such as average disposable income. Figure 6.24 shows an example of the application of a GIS. The locations of banks are shown – the dark areas indicate where the bank is performing well and lighter areas where the bank is underperforming. The performance ratio here can be thought of as market share. Marketing analysts can review this in an attempt to correct problems in areas of underperformance. For example, there appears to be an opportunity in the south of the area to open a new branch. The mini case study on Blockbuster Video illustrates how a company may use software to support decision making on how best to target a new market.

Geographical information system (GIS)

Uses maps to display information about different geographic locations such as catchments or branches. They are commonly used for performance analysis by marketing staff.

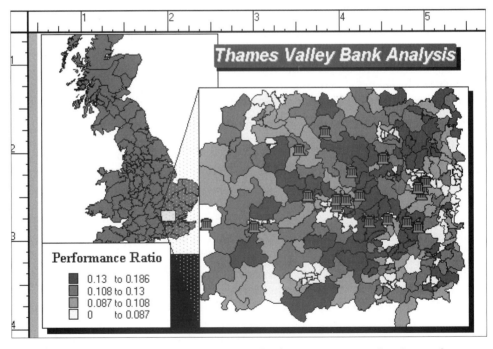

Fig 6.24 Data view from MapInfo geographical information system showing performance analysis for a bank

Blockbuster Video uses GIS and market profiling to locate new branches

Finding the best overseas locations for its retail outlets is a major priority for Blockbuster Video, a successful US video chain. The company has been expanding rapidly into Europe and recognises that the nature of each local market varies widely between countries. It needs a detailed understanding of each market before making investments in new sites.

Using Experian's marketing information system, MOSAIC Systems, Blockbuster has been able to analyse the make-up of widely differing local communities and to identify the locations with the greatest profit potential. The system has also enabled Blockbuster to target promotional activities at its best prospective customers using the most effective media. According to Ted Kerr, Blockbuster's managing director of developing territories: 'Experian has provided us with an excellent tool for evaluating potential store locations. It has enabled us to invest in markets such as Spain, Germany, Austria, Denmark and the Netherlands with much greater confidence.'

Source: Experian Web site, http://www.experian.com

▶ Accounting information systems

Accounting information systems are used for the financial activities that take place in any organisation. These include the operation of sales order processing systems, payroll, budgeting and reporting of the financial condition of the organisation. Other functions include the management of capital investment and general cashflow management.

Operational accounting systems focus on daily recording of business transactions, that is, the flow of funds through an organisation. All businesses require this basic information. In larger businesses these systems will be linked to other operational functions, such as sales order processing and inventory.

Management accounting systems enable planning and control of business finance. These are sometimes referred to as financial information systems and will be linked to executive information systems.

Application areas for accounting information systems

Most companies use an integrated accounting system that covers a number of application areas, as shown in Fig 6.25. The essential modules are accounts receivable, accounts payable and the general ledger. Many companies will look to extend these to related areas such as sales order processing and payroll.

◆ *Sales order processing.* The SOP system is particularly important, as it records sales transactions and supplies documents to other areas such as stock control and manufacturing. There might also be links to payroll to calculate such elements as bonus payments to sales people on receipt of a customer order. The accounts receivable system contains customer information such as sales made, payments made and account balances for overdue payments. These can be used to halt the

Accounting information system

Provides functions for the numerous financial activities that take place in any organisation.

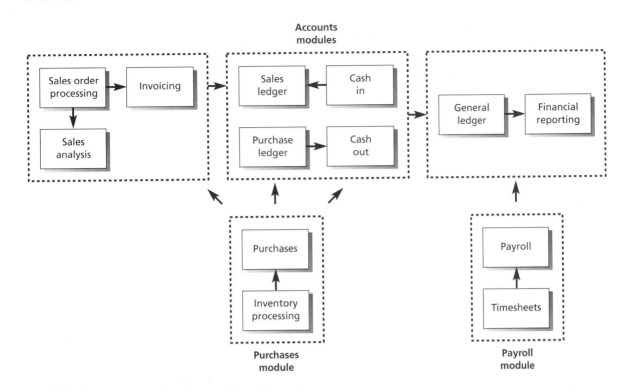

Fig 6.25 Modules of a standard accounting system, plus additional purchasing, sales order processing and payroll modules

extension of further credit until the balances have been cleared. The system may also be searched to identify lists of customers who have purchased certain items, which is then used as the basis for a mailing list for promotional purposes. The accounts payable system contains information regarding the firm's creditors (as opposed to customers for the accounts receivable). The system provides information on which a schedule of supplier payments can be made and thus ensures that payments can be made as late as possible (to optimise cashflow) without losing discounts offered from suppliers for prompt payment.

◆ *Inventory*. The inventory system maintains stock levels by recording when stock is used for sales orders. A reorder point (ROP) system will generate an order for stock once the level of a stock item falls below a number of units. Other time-based systems will replenish stocks after a predetermined time interval.

◆ *Payroll*. The payroll system processes payments to employees, including deductions for such items as National Insurance and income tax. Many organisations will have electronic links to banks for direct deposit to employee accounts rather than issuing pay cheques.

◆ *Budgeting systems*. Budgets are an important control tool for management. A predetermined budgeted amount is periodically compared to the actual expenditure and any difference noted as a variance. This comparison of allocations (budgeted amounts) against actuals (amounts spent or received) can be reported to management. The identification of a variance will normally instigate a discussion and

may lead to corrective action being taken to eliminate any adverse variance. Budgets for areas or departments can be aggregated or brought together to form a functional or organisational budget statement for higher-level decision making.

◆ *Cashflow reporting.* A major cause of business failure is inadequate cash reserves to keep the organisation functioning. Cashflow reporting is necessary to keep track of the organisation's cash reserves. Cash is needed for working capital (day-to-day expenses) and for the purchase of long-term assets such as plant or machinery. A cashflow report will contain a running total of the cash balance from information on cash inflows and outflows for each reporting period. An adverse cash position may necessitate the deferring of a planned acquisition. The report can be used as a planning tool by incorporating different cost and revenue scenarios and studying the results.

◆ *Capital budgeting system.* The financial system should contain tools which allow for the evaluation of capital spending plans. Major investments are compared to the financial return that the organisation could have gained from placing the cash in a bank account and accruing interest. The investment evaluation may also inform the decision to buy or lease equipment. Financial measures often used to assess an investment include net present value (NPV), internal rate of return (IRR) and pay-back period.

◆ *Financial analysis system.* Financial analysts use a variety of performance measures to gauge the financial position of an organisation. These include such measures as the current ratio, inventory turnover and earnings per share (Dyson, 1997). An information system can be used to generate these values automatically using figures stored in a database of such items as current assets and current liabilities.

◆ *Forecasting systems.* By projecting budget statements into the future, an organisation is able to forecast the potential financial state of the organisation. These forecasts will need to incorporate economic and market forecasts in order that sales and cost data can be estimated.

▶ Accounting information systems software

Spreadsheets

Owing to their flexibility in numerical analysis and the incorporation of built-in facilities for statistical and numerical analysis, spreadsheets are an ideal medium in which to conduct financial analysis. For instance, a budget can be compiled by the addition of relevant items under income and expenses headings. If a spreadsheet template is constructed, consisting of the headings for the relevant items to be included, it is simply a matter of the user entering the appropriate amounts into the spreadsheet cells.

Once the cashflow statement has been entered, any values can easily be changed and the spreadsheet cell values will be updated to reflect the new cash position.

Accounting packages

A vast number of accounting software packages are available which can produce invoice statements, monthly budget statements and other financial items needed to run a small to medium-sized organisation.

PC packages are segmented according to the size of company for which they are intended. Package cost tends to vary from £500–£15 000 for five users. Examples include:

◆ Sage (Sovereign), top-selling UK package;

◆ Pegasus (Opera, EDItion, OPERAtions, Senior, Capital, Solo);

◆ Tetra (Chameleon, Legend), strong for distribution and manufacturing;

◆ SBS (Exchequer);

◆ TAS Books, originally released in 1991, low end;

◆ Intuit Quicken, Microsoft Money, Dynamics and other US packages.

The requirements for accounting information systems will differ from other types of system in which issues such as ease of use and performance will usually be considered important. In accounting systems, accuracy and reliability are paramount. This is highlighted by the box on *what accountants look for in accounts packages*.

What are accountants looking for in accounts packages?

A survey of 500 UK accountants in October 1995 by Interactive Software and the Hyperion Group showed that the following were the most important features:

◆ reliability (45 per cent);
◆ ease of use (19.5 per cent);
◆ functionality (18.2 per cent);
◆ performance (17.3 per cent).

A further factor not mentioned is that the system must fit in with country-specific or local practices. Many accounting packages are therefore produced in the country in which they are purchased. This is probably the reason for Sage and Pegasus being the best-known packages in the UK.

In the survey, 46 per cent of respondents were expecting to use new technologies over the next 12 months, with 28 per cent using MS Windows, increasing to 56 per cent and 17 per cent using Unix increasing to 22 per cent PC vs UNIX minicomputer or UNIX/mainframe.

Other detailed factors (not mentioned in the survey) that accountants may consider are:

1 Is it accurate and reliable?
2 How well does it cover the basics – accounts receivable and payable plus general ledger? Does it produce appropriate reports?
3 Can it integrate with other functions: sales/production/costing/payroll functions?
4 How well does it support several users (multi-user support)?
5 Does it support undo and roll-back (to reverse transactions)? Is special security built in to prevent this?
6 What analysis tools are available? For example, can accountants drill down to find the detailed transactions of a particular debtor?
7 Is it easy to learn and use?

High-end packages cashing more than £50 000 include:

◆ Oracle Financials based on RDBMS features;
◆ Computer Associates MasterPiece;
◆ Dun and Bradstreet SmartStream financials;
◆ SAP R/3, 'most reliable and robust'.

The higher cost of the systems is considered worthwhile by the companies purchasing them because they will excel in the areas of:

◆ accuracy (well tested);
◆ security;
◆ integration with other systems;
◆ scalability;
◆ bespoke features.

Financial modelling packages

While accounting packages tend to be restricted to operational systems, financial modelling packages are also available for decision making at the strategic and tactical levels of an organisation. These provide the following types of facilities for strategic planning:

◆ corporate financial forecasting models;
◆ merger and acquisition strategy.

Facilities for tactical planning include:

◆ annual budgets – cashflow, capital, tax planning;
◆ new product assessments – ROCE.

They can also be used for operational financial management issues such as:

◆ funds management – cash and securities, shares;
◆ cost accounting/project cost monitoring;
◆ tax accounting.

Systems to provide these functions tend to be available as modules of the high-end accounting packages. Software such as IFPS allows the decision maker to hold financial models of the organisation in order to construct 'what-if?' analysis. It has the advantage of providing the decision maker with more guidance than a spreadsheet on building financial models.

▶ Enterprise resource planning applications

Enterprise resource planning (ERP) software provides integrated functions for major business functions such as production, distribution, sales, finance and human resources management. It is normally purchased as an off-the-shelf package which is tailored by a consultant. A single package typically replaces many different previous packages.

ERP software is a single system which gives functions for all the major business functions discussed in this chapter, such as production, distribution, marketing and sales, finance and human resources management. It is normally purchased as an off-the-shelf

Enterprise resource planning applications (ERP) software

Provides functions for managing business areas such as production, distribution, sales, finance and human resources management.

package, with modules for each major business process or business function which are then tailored by a consultant. A single package typically replaces many different previous packages. The benefits of this approach are clear:

◆ Reduced cost of buying from a single supplier.

◆ Better transfer of information within the organisation since all modules of the system are compatible.

◆ Simplified support and maintenance through a single supplier.

◆ Use of 'best-of-breed' solutions applied by other companies.

Many companies have also introduced ERP applications to solve the problem of the millennium bug by discarding their legacy applications which will not work in the Year 2000.

The use of Enterprise Resource Planning (ERP) software is a major trend in deployment of business information systems during the 1990s which is described in Chapter 19. ERP software originates with the idea of extending the basic modules of an accounting system to other functions such as sales order processing and human resources.

ERP software is produced by companies such as the German company SAP, the Dutch company Baan and American companies such as JD Edwards and Peoplesoft. The database manufacturer Oracle also operates in this area, with separate modules Oracle Financials and Oracle Human Resources.

Potentially, a single ERP system can replace all of the functions in a vertical market, as shown in Fig 6.1. Some packages such as Peoplesoft originate in human resources, while others such as JD Edwards originate in manufacturing and tend to be best suited to these areas. Companies such as SAP will modify their basic ERP solution with versions appropriate for the different vertical markets.

The main disadvantage of ERP systems seem to be the high costs charged by suppliers due to the demand for this type of system. This high demand has also given rise to skills shortages. The other disadvantages of ERP systems are shared with all off-the-shelf systems, namely that the business often has to change its processes or way of working in order to fit the way the software operates. This may not present a problem if a company is looking to reengineer its processes, since then the ERP software can provide a framework.

Owing to the high cost of ERP solutions, only large companies can afford the software and the consultants, which will often be a total cost of millions of pounds. Smaller companies can take advantage of the features of integrated accounting packages which now provide modules beyond those of the basic accounting package.

▶ SUMMARY

1 Operational information systems are often critical to the success of a business, since their efficiency directly affects customer experience, profitability and cashflow. Operational systems include:

◆ transaction processing systems for managing transactions such as customer orders, supplier purchases and payment;

◆ office automation systems such as groupware and workflow systems, which enable office workers to collaborate on administration and customer service;

◆ process control systems for manufacturing.

2 Decision support systems are tools for assisting decision making at tactical and strategic levels within an organisation. The main tools available are:
- expert systems which enable non-specialists to take unstructured decisions outside their area of expertise;
- executive information systems for giving senior managers an overview of the business, with monitoring facilities to alert them to a problem and then provide drill-down to find the source of a problem;
- data warehouses providing a repository for transaction data with analysis tools for marketing-driven optimisation of company performance.

3 Business applications have traditionally served the functional areas of an organisation, such as:
- human resources;
- accounting;
- production;
- inbound and outbound logistics;
- marketing and sales.

4 In large companies, applications in these functional areas are gradually being replaced by enterprise resource planning applications that provide functionality applicable across the organisation.

5 In smaller companies, accounting systems are being extended to use in other areas such as payroll, purchase ordering and inventory management.

▶ EXERCISES

▶ Self-assessment exercises

1 Describe the main elements of groupware.

2 Discuss the relationship between workflow management and document image processing software.

3 Evaluate the role of transaction processing systems in an organisation.

4 How can information systems support the manufacturing process?

5 Which features identify a decision support system?

6 What is the difference between an expert system and a data warehouse?

7 Which information systems tools can be used to support the marketing function?

8 What is a decision tree?

9 Why have enterprise resource planning packages become popular?

▶ Discussion questions

1 How should spreadsheet database, statistical and specialist software packages be used to support the accounting function?

2 Data warehouses are only the latest in a long line of reporting tools. They will not make a significant impact on business. Discuss.

3 Workflow systems are currently mainly in large organisations. This is likely to remain the case. Discuss.

4 Neural networks, fuzzy logic and genetic programming are some of the latest artificial intelligence ideas. Are they likely to remain lab-based products, or is there potential for their use in industry?

5 Enterprise resource planning software is likely to replace packages used in a single area of the organisation, such as accounting, logistics, production and marketing. Discuss.

▶ Essay questions

1 Review the changing tools available for decision making at a strategic level within the organisation. What does this mean for senior managers?

2 Has the promise of expert systems in the 1980s been delivered in the 1990s? Justify your answer.

3 How must transaction processing systems be managed given their mission-critical role in many organisations?

4 Critically assess the importance of data warehouses to large organisations. Are they relevant for the small to medium enterprise?

5 Do you believe that the advantages of enterprise resource planning applications outweigh their disadvantages? Illustrate your answer with reference to company examples.

▶ Examination questions

1 Define an expert system.

2 What is the purpose of data warehouses?

3 How can workflow software and groupware assist in reengineering an organisation?

4 Explain the relationship between a decision tree and a decision table, using an example.

5 What special precautions need to be taken when using IT for managing human resources?

6 What is the difference between a batch and a real-time system? Which would be most appropriate for each of the following situations:
   ◆ periodic update of a data warehouse from an operational database;
   ◆ capturing information on customer sales transactions.

7 Company decision making is dependent on fixed business rules that specify which actions should occur given a particular input or situation. Explain using an example how such rules operate in the programming IF statement featured in expert systems, spreadsheets and programming languages.

8 What are the main modules of an accounting system? How could these be integrated with other business functions?

9 Define an enterprise resource planning application. Name two main disadvantages of this type of approach.

▶ References

Curtis, G. (1998) *Business Information Systems, Analysis, Design and Practice*, 3rd edition, Addison Wesley.

Dyson, J. (1997) *Accounting for Non-Accounting Students*, Financial Times Pitman Publishing, London.

Garry, A.G. and Scott-Morton, M. (1971) 'A framework for Management Information Systems', *Sloan Management Review*, 12, 55–70.

Goldratt, E.M. and Cox, J. (1986) *The Goal – beating the competition*, Creative Output, Middlesex.

Goonatilake, S. and Khebbal, S. (1995) 'Intelligent hybrid systems: issues, classifications and future directions', in Goonatilake, S. and Khebbal, S. (eds) *Intelligent Hybrid Systems*, John Wiley, New York.

Gore, C., Murray, K. and Richardson, B. (1992) *Strategic Decision Making*, Cassell, London.

Hall, A. (1995) *Accounting Information Systems*, West Publishing, London.

Hammergren, T. (1996) *Data Warehousing: Building the Corporate Knowledgebase*, Thomson Computer Press, London.

Inmon, W.H. (1996) *Building the Data Warehouse*, 2nd edition, John Wiley, New York.

Laudon, K. and Laudon, J. (1995) *Management Information Systems: Organization and Technology*, 3rd Edn, Macmillan, Upper Saddle River, NJ.

Luconi, F.L., Malone, T.W. and Scott-Morton, M. (1986) 'Expert systems: the next challenge for managers', *Sloan Management Review*, 27, 3–14.

Scott-Morton, M. (1991) *The Corporation of the 1990s: Information Technology and Organisational Transformation*, Oxford University Press.

Slack, N., Chambers, S., Harland, C., Harrison, A. and Johnston, R. (1995) *Operations Management*, Financial Times Pitman Publishing, London.

Sprague, R.H. (1987) 'DSS in context', in Sprague, R.H. and Watson, H. J. (eds) *Decision Support Systems: Putting Theory into Practice*, 3rd edition, Prentice Hall, Hemel Hempstead.

Sprague, R. (1980) 'A framework for the development of decision support systems', *MIS Quarterly*, vol. 4, no. 4.

Tapscott, D. and Caston, A. (1993) *Paradigm Shift: the New Promise of Information Technology*, McGraw-Hill, New York.

Turban, E. (1995) *Decision Support and Expert Systems*, 4th edition, Macmillan, Englewood Cliffs, NJ.

Watson, H.J. and Sprague, R.H. (1993) 'The components of an architecture for DSS', in Sprague, R.H. and Watson, H.J. (eds) *Decision Support Systems: Putting Theory into Practice*, 3rd edition, Prentice Hall, Hemel Hempstead.

Zuboff, S. (1988) *In the Age of the Smart Machine: the Future of Work and Power*, Heinemann, Oxford.

▶ Further reading

Bentley, R. (1997) *Groupware and the World Wide Web*, Kluwer Academic, London.

Chaffey, D.J. (1998) *Groupware, Workflow and Intranets: Reengineering the Enterprise with collaborative software*, Digital Press, Woburn, MA.

Coleman, D. (1995) *Groupware: Technologies and Applications*, Prentice-Hall, Englewood Cliffs, NJ.

Dudman, J. (1998) 'So you want a data warehouse? Boardroom briefing', *Computer Weekly*, 14 May.

Georgakopoulos, D., Hornick, M. and Sheth, A. (1995) 'An overview of workflow management: from process modelling to workflow automation infrastructure, *Distributed and Parallel databases*, vol 3, 119–53.

Krooenke, D. and Hatch, R. (1993) *Business Information Systems*, McGraw-Hill, New York.

O'Brien, J. (1993) *Management Information Systems: A Managerial End User Perspective*, 2nd Edition, Richard D. Irwin Inc., Boston, USA.
    Part 3 (Chapters 8–12) provides good detail on business applications of different types of information systems.

O'Hicks, J. (1993), *Management Information Systems: A User Perspective*, 3rd Edition, West Publishing Company, St. Paul (Minneapolis), USA.

Workflow Management Coalition (WfMC). 1996a. Reference model. Version 1. In *The Workflow Management Coalition Specification. Terminology and glossary.* Workflow Management Coalition, Avenue Marcel Thiry 204, 1200 Brussels, Belgium.

Zhang, H. and Alton, L. (1994) *Computerized manufacturing process planning systems*, Chapman & Hall, London.

▶ Web references

http://www.ed.ac.uk/WfMC This Workflow Management Coalition site contains extensive technical papers explaining how workflows are defined. It also contains introductory papers on the purpose and components of workflow systems.

http://www.waria.com WARIA is another significant industry body which again has good industry support and is active promoting conferences and sharing of experience and documentation. It has been less active in promoting standards.

http://www.aiim.org The Document Management Alliance (DMA) is a task force created by AIIM in April 1995 attempting to create a uniform approach to the design, implementation and management of enterprise-wide Document Management Systems.

PART 2

INFORMATION SYSTEMS DEVELOPMENT

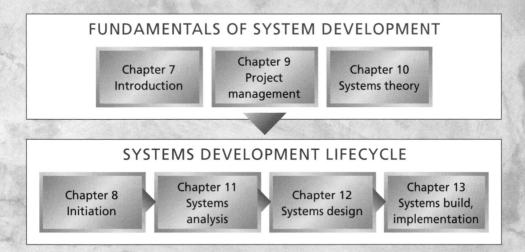

FUNDAMENTALS OF SYSTEM DEVELOPMENT

Chapter 7
Introduction

Chapter 9
Project
management

Chapter 10
Systems theory

SYSTEMS DEVELOPMENT LIFECYCLE

Chapter 8
Initiation

Chapter 11
Systems
analysis

Chapter 12
Systems design

Chapter 13
Systems build,
implementation

Part 2 focuses on how information systems (IS) are acquired and built. An understanding of building IS is important to users and managers who are responsible for, or are involved in, a systems development project. Such managers need to understand the activities involved with different stages of systems development to help plan the project or work with the developers of the system. They will also need to be aware of the alternatives for sourcing IS such as buying a pre-written off-the-shelf system or a specially written bespoke system, in order to decide which is best for their company or department.

To build a good quality IS, a company will follow a process which has defined stages with clear objectives and deliverables at each stage. Part 2 describes the typical activities involved when a new system is built. These stages form what is commonly referred to as the systems development lifecycle:

◆ *Initiation*: a startup phase which usually occurs in response to a business problem or opportunity;

◆ *Feasibility*: an attempt to determine whether the proposed systems development will be viable;

◆ *Systems analysis*: to determine what the system is required to do;

◆ *Systems design*: to specify how the system will deliver the stated requirements;

◆ *Systems build*: the design is transformed into a physical system by programming, testing and creation of databases;

◆ *Systems implementation and changeover*: the organisation moves from installing and testing the information system to operating in a live business environment;

◆ *Review and maintenance*: the success of the system is measured against the original requirements and modifications are made over its lifetime.

Note that as errors are found, or new requirements arise, it is necessary to revisit previous stages. Iterative models such as the spiral model are used to show the cyclical nature of system development where several prototypes may be built which involve repeating the analysis, design and build phases.

The unique nature of systems development projects, which is in part due to the speed of technological and business change and the iteration referred to above, make it very difficult to develop a system which satisfies the three key constraints of:

1 Does it meet the requirements of the business and end-users?

2 It is delivered on time?

3 Has it been produced within the allocated budget?

Part 2 involves reviewing each stage systematically to consider what action can be taken to ensure the project objectives are met.

An introduction to acquiring and developing information systems

INTRODUCTION

This chapter provides the foundation for subsequent chapters in Part Two by taking a broad look at the main activities involved in acquiring and building new computer-based information systems. The word 'acquire' is used deliberately here, since 'development' implies the writing of a system. However, since many business applications can be purchased off the shelf without the need for any development activity, 'acquisition' more precisely defines the process we are going to outline here.

This chapter will start by considering alternative approaches to the acquisition of new computer-based information systems, ranging from purchasing off-the-shelf applications through to creating new bespoke systems.

Information Systems acquisition describes the method of obtaining an information system for a business. The main choices are off the shelf (packaged), bespoke applications developed by an in-house IT department or a software house, or end-user developed systems.

We will then review the traditional **systems development lifecycle (SDLC)**, sometimes known as the waterfall model of systems development. This defines the different stages involved in developing a new system. The stages will be summarised in this chapter in preparation for a more detailed description in subsequent chapters.

Any information systems project follows a logical series of development phases. These are known as the systems development lifecycle. Typical stages are: initiation, feasibility study, analysis of business requirements, systems design, system build and implementation and finally review and maintenance.

Finally, we will look at different methodologies for building systems to establish which are the most appropriate for different types of business and system. The methodologies to be covered include traditional structured methods (using the example of structured systems analysis and design methodology (SSADM)) through to more modern approaches involving prototyping and rapid applications development (RAD).

▶ Learning objectives

After reading this chapter, readers will be able to:

- ◆ evaluate the different alternatives for acquiring information systems;
- ◆ distinguish between the typical stages involved in building an information system;
- ◆ explain the purpose of each stage in building a system;
- ◆ select the best alternative type of approach or methodology for building an information system.

▶ Links to other chapters

This chapter provides a framework for all subsequent chapters in Part Two.

Chapter 8   describes the startup or *initiation* phase of an information systems development project.

Chapter 9   reviews methods for controlling the progress of the development through *project management* techniques.

Chapter 10   covers basic *systems theory* as a preparation for the study of systems analysis and design.

Chapter 11   describes techniques for *analysis* of system requirements.

Chapter 12   covers techniques for systems *design*.

Chapter 13   examines the final phases of system development – *build and implementation*.

Chapter 16   describes the end-user development method of acquisition in more detail.

▶ METHODS OF SOFTWARE ACQUISITION

Many texts deal admirably with the range of tools and techniques available to the systems analyst for bespoke systems development. However, bespoke development is only one method of software acquisition. In fact for many businesses, especially small and medium-sized enterprises, bespoke applications development is not a viable option because of the costs and practical difficulties involved. It is necessary, therefore, to begin by looking at the range of acquisition methods and consider which is most appropriate for the needs of a particular business.

There are three main methods for acquiring the information system necessary to

support a particular business need. These are bespoke development, off-the-shelf software and end-user development.

▶ Bespoke development

Bespoke development is the term for when an information system is developed 'from scratch' by an information systems professional to suit the business requirements of the application.

Here a new information system will be developed from scratch by a team of information systems professionals. The IS professionals will either work for the business, in which case we refer to this as 'in-house' bespoke development, or for a third party such as a software house, in which case we say that the software development has been 'outsourced'. Bespoke development has the benefit of producing software tailored to the precise requirements of the business. On the downside, there are a number of difficulties:

◆ *Expense*. Bespoke development is the most expensive way of developing new information systems.

◆ *Time*. Bespoke development, especially when using formal structured development methodologies, is notorious for time overruns, with delays of months or years not uncommon.

◆ *Quality*. Bespoke software is not usually free from bugs; software bugs can range from the trivial to the catastrophic, the latter often attributable to poor analysis of requirements.

Bespoke development

An IS is developed 'from scratch' by an IS professional to suit the business requirements of the application.

▶ Purchase 'off-the-shelf' software

Off-the-shelf purchase of packaged software is an acquisition method which involves direct purchase of a pre-written application used by more than one company.

This type of software is pre-written and is available for a whole variety of hardware platforms from PCs to mainframes. Off-the-shelf software is written to offer a broad functionality which will suit a wide range of different businesses. This broad range of functions has the benefit of fitting the requirements of a large number of businesses. It also may offer too many features for any particular business, which may then feel that it is paying for things it will not use. At the same time, it may require businesses to process information in a particular way which is at odds with the way they normally do business. Alternatively, a certain off-the-shelf software package may not offer sufficient features. For example, a well-known accounting package in the UK only offers an eight-character code for the customer's order number, when it would appear that some 50 per cent of UK companies use longer order number codes. The major benefit, however, of off-the-shelf software packages is their low cost when compared with acquiring bespoke software with the same level of functionality. In addition, because packaged software has been developed for a commercial market, it is less likely to suffer from the bugs that afflict bespoke software.

In a tailored off-the-shelf purchase, pre-written software is purchased from a supplier, but it is possible to configure it to be specific to the company. In a component off-the-shelf purchase, different modules may be purchased from different suppliers and built together. Visual Basic controls for graphing is a good example of a component that can be added to an off-the-shelf application.

Off-the-shelf purchase or packaged software

An acquisition method that involves direct purchase of a pre-written application used by more than one company.

▶ End-user developed software

End-user developed software is software written by non-IS professionals, i.e. the business users.

Writing in 1989, Senn estimated that 50 to 75 per cent of all computing applications will be classed as end-user applications (as distinct from institutional applications) and that many of these systems will be developed by end-users (i.e. non-IT professionals).

Enterprise resource planning or institutional applications are those that affect general corporate activities, cut across more than one department or functional area, or systems that involve organisational data held in corporate databases. Examples include accounting systems, sales order processing systems and materials requirements planning.

End-user applications are more limited in scope. Applications may be departmental or personal in nature and are usually output or report oriented rather than input driven. These applications may either be written by IT professionals or by the end-users themselves. If the latter is the case, they are often referred to as *end-user developed applications*.

Such systems may be simple (e.g. a spreadsheet or a small PC database) or less commonly they may be more sophisticated (e.g. a production planning system based on sales forecast data from several branches of the same organisation). Such applications are typically for individual or departmental use, although in the case of the second example above the system may have company-wide relevance. The main benefit of end-user developed software is that it is normally used by those who develop it and so the requirements are not subject to mistranslation or the provision of over-sophisticated solutions. The negative side to this is that in some cases inappropriate software development tools might be used (such as complicated spreadsheets instead of the construction of a database). A further significant concern with end-user development is that software may be riddled with bugs as a consequence of corner cutting (poor or non-existent design, little or no testing and no documentation). The end-user development approach is described in more detail in Chapter 16.

There are also a number of hybrid approaches to acquisition. A group of organisations in the same business or activity area may have information systems requirements which individually may be very expensive to develop. A solution may be for a bespoke system to be developed by a third party, which allows the development costs to be spread among all the organisations involved. Good examples here are a university student records system and various systems used in police forces across the UK.

Similarly, an off-the-shelf package may provide 80 per cent of the required features, but others may need to be added through some bespoke development by either IS/IT professionals or by end-users.

▶ Factors affecting software acquisition

There are a number of factors that will influence the choice of acquisition method. The first of these are time, cost and quality considerations.

If an organisation has a pressing problem that requires a new information system quickly, it is probable that a package or tailored package will be sought. An example here is a business which may have been operating an old legacy system and in order to

Table 7.1 Alternatives for procurement of software

Acquisition option	Delivery time	Cost	Quality: Bugs	Quality: Fits business needs
Bespoke in-house	Poor	Poor	Poor	Good
Bespoke software house	Good	Very poor	Medium	Medium
End-user development	Poor	Medium	Poor	Good
Tailored – off the shelf	Good	Good	Good	Medium
Standard – off the shelf	Very good	Very good	Very good	Poor

become Year 2000 compliant saw 'buying' rather than 'making' as the only realistic solution. Similarly, an organisation which needs a 'quality systems solution' may well consider the packaged software route, especially if its requirements are straightforward.

The different acquisition options have different strengths when considered in terms of these three critical criteria. Table 7.1 shows how the alternatives compare in terms of these three criteria. Quality of the delivered product is considered from two respects: the number of bugs or errors found and the suitability of the software in meeting the requirements of the business user. Note that good quality in terms of the number of bugs which typically occur for packaged software may coincide with poor quality in terms of the business fit.

The benefit of packaged software occurs because the cost of developing and debugging the software is shared between more than one company. This results in lower costs and fewer bugs than bespoke development for a single company. The use of packaged software by more than one company is also its greatest weakness, since its features must suit the typical company. As a consequence, it may not meet the needs of an individual company.

Other factors affecting software acquisition include the following:

◆ *Organisation size.* A small to medium-sized business will inevitably have relatively limited resources for the purchasing of information systems and information technology (IS/IT). This suggests that there will be a tendency for such organisations to favour the purchase of off-the-shelf packages or possibly end-user applications development.

◆ *In-house IS/IT expertise.* Where little in-house IS/IT expertise exists, either in the form of IS/IT professionals or experienced end-users, there will be a need to use third parties in the acquisition of new business information systems. These may include software vendors for off-the-shelf software packages, the use of consultants and/or software houses. Precisely what form of third party is used will depend on the other factors discussed here.

◆ *Complexity of the required information system.* Where a business information system requirement is particularly complex, or for an unusual application not available as a packaged solution, it is possible that one may view bespoke software (either developed in-house or by a third party) as the only viable solution. However, complexity does not necessarily equate to 'uniqueness'. For example, one could regard a materials requirements planning system or a complete accounting system as complex, but many packages exist for a variety of hardware platforms. Therefore, complexity is not necessarily an indicator that an off-the-shelf package should be ruled out.

◆ *Uniqueness of the business or business area to be supported.* The higher the degree of uniqueness which exists in the area to be supported, the less likely it is that a suitable off-the-shelf package can be found. This is clearly an indicator, therefore, for bespoke development of some kind. As before, we must not confuse uniqueness with complexity. It may well be feasible for a non IS/IT specialist to develop a solution using tools available to end-user developers. Of course, if the required system is both complex and carries a high degree of uniqueness, then bespoke development by IS/IT professionals is probably the best acquisition method.

◆ *IS/IT expertise among end-users.* A certain degree of IS/IT literacy and expertise is necessary if end-users are to be able to develop information systems. In addition, such literacy is desirable when selecting suitable off-the-shelf packaged software, as it can help the business focus more clearly on its precise requirements both from a functional and a technological perspective. If an organisation has little end-user IS/IT expertise of its own, but has its own IS/IT department, it will be very much dependent on solutions provided by IS/IT professionals with or without third-party support.

◆ *Linkages with existing applications software.* Where new business software needs to integrate very tightly with existing information systems, there is a higher probability that at least some bespoke development work will need to be done to integrate the two systems. Also, a high degree of integration may imply that the new information system has to be developed in a bespoke fashion in order to achieve the desired level of integration. Having said that, many software vendors supply packages for different business areas which integrate very well with each other. For example, on the IBM AS/400 hardware platform alone, it is possible to find single vendors such as JD Edwards or JBA which will supply a sales order processing system, an accounting system, a warehouse management system, a payroll and personnel system and a manufacturing system, all of which can be purchased separately or together and which operate in a fully integrated manner as enterprise resource planning applications (Chapters 6 and 19).

By looking at combinations of the above, it is possible to come up with a 'best-fit' acquisition method. Figure 7.1 illustrates the relationship between the complexity of the required application (as driven by the business needs) and the uniqueness of the application under consideration. The reader should note that bespoke development may be performed either by in-house IS/IT specialists or by a third party.

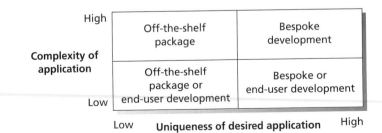

Fig 7 .1 Application complexity versus uniqueness

Similar relationships can be established with other pairs of selection acquisition factors. For example, when comparing the expertise of end-users in developing applications with the complexity of the desired application, a relatively simple information system may need professional IT staff involvement if the end-users do not have sufficient IS/IT capability.

▶ THE TRADITIONAL WATERFALL MODEL

The 'Waterfall model' outlines the series of steps that should occur when building an information system. These steps usually occur in a predefined order with a review at the end of each stage before the next can be started. It is possible to read half a dozen different texts on this topic and come across six different ways of describing the elements within this model. Not only will there be a different number of steps in each alternative model, but there will also be differences between the names given to each of the stages. For example, in one text the term 'implementation' may refer to the process of programming, testing and data conversion, while in another the same term may refer to the process by which a developed and tested system becomes a live, operational system. During the course of this chapter, therefore, a consistent and clear approach to the naming of the individual elements will be adopted and reference will also be made to other terms that the reader might encounter when reading additional texts.

The purpose of the waterfall model of systems development is to divide the development process up into a series of manageable parts that relate to each other in an organised way. In addition, some tasks will have to be completed before others can commence. For example, it will not be possible for a programmer to start writing a program until the design specification for that program is complete. The waterfall model is a simple representation of what actually happens during a systems development, project, but it provides a good framework for introducing information systems development, since all of the activities that are identified in the model occur in a typical project. We will examine more realistic models later in the chapter.

We will now summarise the basic steps that most systems development projects follow.

▶ Initiation (Chapter 8)

Initiation phase is the initiation or startup phase and is the first phase in an information systems development project. Its aims are to establish whether the project is feasible and then prepare to ensure the project is successful.

Input: creative thought and/or systematic evaluation of IS needs.

Output: idea for initiation of a new information system.

The initiation phase contains the stimulus from which the need to develop a new information system arises. This stimulus may come about as a result of some external event such as a change in legislation, or it may arise from a desire internally to develop an information system that better supports the business needs of the organisation. The source of this initiation process may be one of the following:

◆ *Managing director or other senior management.* Systems initiated from this point are likely to have the support necessary for successful development.

Waterfall model

Outlines the series of steps that should occur when building an information system. The steps usually occur in a pre-defined order with a review at the end of each stage before the next can be started.

Initiation phase

The startup phase in an IS development project. Its aims are to establish whether the project is feasible and then prepare to ensure the project is successful.

Initiation phase context

Input: creative thought and/or systematic evaluation of IS needs. Output: idea for initiation of a new information system.

◆ *Information systems department.* A system may be initiated here as part of the organisation's overall IS/IT strategy; to maximise the chances of success the system will still need high-level management support.

◆ *Functional business area.* A system initiated here will be competing for attention with all other development projects then being undertaken; often an organisation will have a steering committee to decide on development priorities.

In terms of the size of the likely systems development project that follows, the larger the project, the more important it is to divide the project up into easily managed parts. Once the need for a new information system has been clearly established, it then becomes necessary to assess whether it is feasible to acquire a computerised solution.

▶ Feasibility assessment (Chapter 8)

Feasibility assessment

An activity at the start of the project to ensure that the project is a viable business proposition. The feasibility report analyses the need for and impact of the system and considers different alternatives for acquiring software.

Feasibility assessment context

Input: idea for initiation of a new information system. Output: feasibility report and recommendation to proceed.

The **Feasibility assessment** is the activity that occurs at the start of the project to ensure that the project is a viable business proposition. The feasibility report analyses the need for and impact of the system and considers different alternatives for acquiring software.

The feasibility assessment can be considered to be part of the initiation phase. It will establish whether a computer-based information system fits certain feasibility criteria. Three criteria are usually cited:

1 It must be established whether the information system is *technically feasible*. To be technically feasible, either the technology exists or it can be created to support the required system.

2 To be *economically feasible*, an information system must generate more in the way of benefits than the cost needed to produce it. One of the problems here is that benefits are often difficult to quantify in monetary terms, while costs are far easier to estimate. The problem of assessing the time value of money must also be taken into consideration (costs now, with benefits later). Discounted cashflow methods for countering this are described in Chapter 8.

3 Assuming that a proposed information system is both technically and economically feasible, an assessment must be made of whether the project is *operationally and organisationally feasible*. By operationally feasible, we mean that the system must be capable of performing within the required speed, volume, usability and reliability parameters. Also, to be feasible for the organisation, the proposed information system must either be capable of running alongside work patterns or existing work patterns must be capable of being adapted or reengineered to run alongside the new information system. Organisational feasibility will involve a review of how the potential users' skill sets and attitudes will affect the system.

Part of the feasibility process may be the invitation to tender for some or all of the information system elements. These may include application software, hardware, communications technology or systems software. Different alternatives from different vendors will then be assessed.

The output from this step (and, therefore, the input to the next step of the model) is a stage review and a feasibility report, which will recommend either that the project proceeds or that the project is reassessed in some way.

The topic of feasibility will be discussed in more detail in Chapter 8.

▶ Systems analysis (Chapter 11)

Systems analysis is the capture of the business requirements of a system from talking to or observing end-users and using other information sources such as existing system documentation.

Once a proposed information system is agreed to be feasible, it is necessary to carry out the detailed work of assessing the precise requirements which the intended users have for the new system. Note that the *systems analysis* step is sometimes referred to as the requirements determination step or the systems study step. There are three main tasks within this phase.

First, it is necessary to gain an understanding of how the *current* information system (computerised or paper based) works. Second, a diagrammatic model of the current system workings is produced to ensure that IT professionals and system users are in agreement. Finally, a set of requirements for the new information system is produced. The requirements specification will define:

◆ the features which the new system is required to contain (e.g. the ability for end-users to be able to design their own reports);

◆ the scope of the system under consideration (for example, is the system intended for just one functional area of the business or is it to embrace all business activities?);

◆ the intended users of the new system;

◆ system performance standards, including response times, batch processing times (if required) and reliability needs;

◆ environment requirements such as physical working environment, operating system and hardware on which the system will run.

In this last task, it may be desirable to produce another diagrammatic model, this time of the *required* information system.

If at any point it is discovered that the requirements of the system as articulated by the prospective users appear to be unfeasible in some way, it will be necessary to revisit the feasibility step and perform an additional analysis of the possible options.

The output from this step in the model will be a user requirements analysis document which details *what* the proposed system must do. Chapter 11 will deal with the subject of systems analysis in more detail.

▶ Systems design (Chapter 12)

The Systems design phase defines how the system will work in key areas of user interface, program modules, security and database transactions.

The input to this stage is a breakdown of the requirements that the proposed information system is to deliver. The task of the systems design stage is to convert those requirements into a number of design alternatives from which the best will be selected. The design step therefore deals with *how* the proposed information system will deliver what is required.

Systems analysis
The capture of the business requirements of a system from talking to or observing end-users and using other information sources such as existing system documentation. Defines *what* the system will do.

Systems analysis context
Input: terms of reference in feasibility report describing outline requirements. Output: detailed requirements specification summarising system functions. Supported by diagrams showing the information flow and processes that are required.

Systems design
Defines *how* the system will work in key areas of user interface, program modules, security and database structure and transactions.

Systems design context
Input: requirements specification. Output: detailed design specification.

Some texts and methodologies make a distinction between 'systems design' and 'detailed design'. Systems design is broader in scope and will deal with such matters as:

◆ choosing an appropriate database management system;

◆ establishing general systems security standards;

◆ deciding on methods of system navigation (e.g. menu systems and graphical user interfaces);

◆ general standards for printed report production;

◆ screen design standards for input and output;

◆ data capture requirements;

◆ data storage requirements.

Detailed design, on the other hand, will result in a blueprint for individual system modules which will be used in the systems build phase that follows. Detailed design will further define some of the aspects of system design referred to above.

If at any point during the design step it becomes obvious that the requirements as presented in the analysis step do not have a design solution (e.g. because of conflicting or incomplete requirements), it will be necessary to revisit the analysis step and determine more precisely what the new information system is to do in those particular respects.

The various elements which go to make the systems design step will be discussed in more detail in Chapter 12.

▶ Systems build (Chapter 13)

Systems build is the creation of software by programmers. It involves writing the software code (programming), building release versions of the software, constructing and populating the database and testing by programmers and end-users. Writing of documentation and training may also occur at this stage.

The term systems 'build' is one that we shall be using in addition to the more usual and ambiguous term 'implementation' which is found in many texts and methodologies. This step embraces three substeps: physical database construction, programming and testing.

Physical database construction involves the conversion of the database design from the previous step into the required tables and indexes of a relational database. The programming substep involves the construction of a computer code that will handle data capture, storage, processing and output. In addition, it will be necessary to program various other operational attributes of the required system (e.g. those which stem from control design). Alongside and subsequent to the programming substep, various forms of testing will take place.

The output from the build stage will be an information system that has been tested and is available for final data conversion or take-on and live operation.

If during the build phase it appears from testing that the system does not meet the original requirements as determined during the analysis step, then it will be necessary to revisit the design step to see whether any errors were made in interpreting the systems requirements. If the design brief was correctly interpreted but the system still

System build

Describes the creation of software by programmers. It involves writing the software code (programming), building release versions of the software, constructing and populating the database and testing by programmers and end-users. Writing of documentation and training may also occur at this stage.

System build context

Inputs: requirements and design specification. Outputs: working software, user guides and system documentation.

contains errors in the delivery of the perceived requirements, it will be necessary to revisit the analysis to determine the systems requirements more precisely.

The systems build step will be discussed in more detail in Chapter 13.

▶ Systems implementation and changeover

System implementation covers practical issues such as making sure the hardware and network infrastructure for a new system are in place; testing of the system; and also human issues of how best to educate and train staff who will be using or affected by the new system. Implementation also involves the transition or changeover from the old system to the new.

Input: working system, not tested by users.

Output: signed-off, operational information system installed in all locations.

This step in the waterfall model deals with preparing for and making the change from old to new information systems. As one might expect, the systems implementation step is fraught with difficulties. Here, it will be discovered whether all the previous steps have combined to deliver an information system which delivers what the users actually want and which also works properly. Data will be converted from old information systems or directly entered into the new database. Finally, the new system will become operational either straight away, in phases, or after a period of parallel running. If errors are encountered at the live running stage it may be possible for the system to continue in operation while the errors are corrected. Alternatively, it may be necessary to suspend the operation of the new system while the most significant errors are fixed. Such error correction may require any of the previous steps to be revisited, depending on the nature and severity of the error(s).

It will be clear from this short discussion that the later in the systems development process errors are discovered, the higher the cost of putting them right. The worst-case scenario is probably for a system to have reached the live running stage only to discover that the required system was never really feasible in the first place. Recent cases bear this out, including the London Ambulance Service and the early version of the London Stock Exchange electronic trading system. Many millions of pounds were spent on developing systems that had to be abandoned because they proved unworkable in a live running situation.

A more detailed discussion of this step will take place in Chapter 13.

▶ Review and maintenance (Chapter 13)

Once an information system is operating under live running conditions, it will be inevitable that changes will be required over time. The maintenance phase involves two different types of maintenance. The first, known as unproductive maintenance, stems from errors or oversights in the original systems development which, while not preventing the system operating to an acceptable level, are still necessary to correct for it to conform with the original specification. The second form of maintenance involves the addition of new features and facilities which extend the scope and functionality of the information system. In the early days, these may take the form of 'nice-to-haves' or 'bells and whistles' which were not deemed to be essential to the system at changeover time. Over the longer term, the system will be adapted and modified to meet changing business requirements.

System implementation

Involves the transition or changeover from the old system to the new and the preparation for this such as making sure the hardware and network infrastructure for a new system are in place; testing of the system and also human issues of how best to educate and train staff who will be using or affected by the new system.

System implementation context

Input: working system, not tested by users.
Output: signed off, operational information system installed in all locations.

System maintenance

Maintenance occurs after the system has been signed off as suitable for users. It involves reviewing the project and recording and acting on problems with the system.

Post-implementation review

A meeting that occurs after a system is operational to review the success of the project and learn lessons for the future.

Systems maintenance

Maintenance occurs after the system has been signed off as suitable for users. It involves reviewing the project and recording and acting on problems with the system.

Also during the maintenance step, an activity known as the **post-implementation review** should be undertaken. This should take place about six months after the system changeover and should review what was planned for the information system against what actually happened. Lessons learned from this exercise will be extremely valuable when the next system is developed.

Issues relating to maintenance and change control will be discussed in more detail in Chapter 13.

▶ The sequence of phases in the waterfall model

At each stage in the development process we have seen a number of activities that need to take place and also opportunities for things to go wrong! It is important, therefore, to emphasise the importance of the review which takes place at the end of each stage. Work should not commence on the next stage unless it can be shown that the current stage has been satisfactorily completed.

The waterfall model can now be summarised using Fig 7.2.

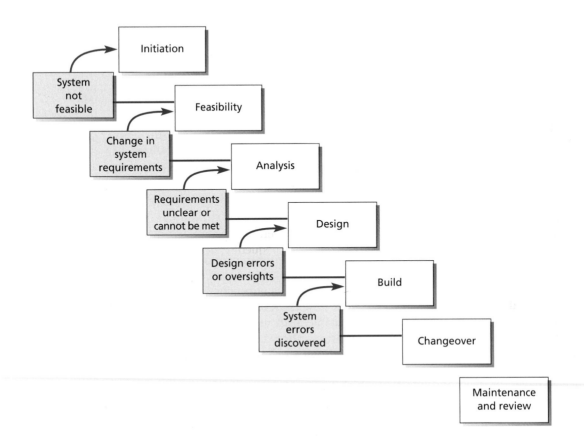

Fig 7.2 The traditional waterfall model of information systems development

It will be seen that each step follows in sequence from the one above. Each step, apart from the first and last, also has a link back to the previous stage, to correct problems discovered at an earlier stage. If during a development project it frequently becomes necessary to revisit a previous stage, it may be a sign that a stage has not been properly reviewed before the next one is started.

Sometimes, if a major problem is discovered it may be necessary to revisit several stages. For example, consider if the user acceptance testing at the changeover or implementation phase identifies a significant user requirement that has been over-looked. This will need each of the analysis, design and build phases to be revisited. Potentially, the feasibility will also need to be reassessed. In 1998 managers of a new UK air traffic control system which has been installed to manage the busy sector for Heathrow airport faced this situation. This forms the subject for a case study in Chapter 13.

The need to revisit previous phases has given rise to alternative models of systems development, such as Boehm's spiral model and rapid application development which are described later in this chapter.

▶ THE TRADITIONAL WATERFALL MODEL AND IS ACQUISITION

The traditional waterfall model as described above implies that the system is being acquired using a bespoke development approach. Bespoke development, whether in-house or by a third party, traditionally follows all the steps described in that section. However, as we have seen, there are methods of information system acquisition that do not require the development of bespoke solutions. Which steps within the tradi-tional waterfall model are required for these alternative methods of software acquisition? We will consider each acquisition method in turn.

▶ Bespoke development

It is in this form of business information systems acquisition that the traditional waterfall method is most evident. Different information systems development methodologies have different approaches to achieving the same overall objective, that is, the acquisition of business information systems that deliver real business benefits by providing the information needed to make better business decisions.

In this chapter, it is not proposed to discuss the waterfall model in any detail with respect to this acquisition method. This is because subsequent chapters will deal with each step of the model in much more detail than is appropriate here. However, it is worth making the following points:

◆ Bespoke development is much more expensive than alternative software acquisi-tion methods – the software that is produced is unique and must be tailored to the precise needs of the users.

◆ The time taken to develop a new, bespoke computer-based information system is significantly longer than the period needed to purchase an off-the-shelf software package. This is especially so if traditional programming languages rather than more modern fourth-generation ones are used. That said, there have been recent develop-ments in a method known as 'rapid applications development' (see page 268) which claims to reduce substantially the time taken to develop bespoke software.

Bespoke development

An IS is developed 'from scratch' by an IS professional to suit the business requirements of the application.

◆ There will be situations where bespoke development provides the only realistic way of producing the required software – high degrees of organisational or application uniqueness or the need to integrate a new information system very tightly with existing applications are common reasons for this.

▶ Purchase of an off-the-shelf package

◆ *Initiation.* This step clearly applies regardless of the acquisition method: there must be some kind of stimulus which creates the notion that a computer-based information systems is needed to respond to a business opportunity or problem.

◆ *Feasibility.* Again, this step must be followed. Indeed, it is during the feasibility step that an investigation will be undertaken into the technical aspects of the required system and a make-or-buy decision will be made. A 'buy' decision indicates that a solution is probably available off the shelf; a 'make' decision indicates that a bespoke solution is probably required because of a combination of factors, as discussed above.

◆ *Analysis.* This is as important a step in the acquisition of off-the-shelf software as it is in building bespoke software solutions. System requirements must be determined and catalogued so that they can be compared with the features offered by the package.

◆ *Design.* It is here that significant differences are found when compared with bespoke software design. An off-the-shelf package will have been designed with many different businesses in mind and will offer a range of features to satisfy most requirements. The 'how' aspect of software acquisition has, therefore, already been determined and the system subsequently built. The task for the purchaser of an off-the-shelf package is to compare the design features required (e.g. menu systems, database design or user interface design) against those offered by different packages.

◆ *Build.* With an off-the-shelf package, the system has already been built by the vendor. As part of the feature set offered by a package, there may be an ability to customise aspects of the software product by setting certain parameters. For example, an accounting package may be set up either to interface with a sales order processing system from the same vendor, or to offer the ability to interface with a package offered by another supplier or with a bespoke system. There will also need to be a testing phase where all the relevant features of the package are run in a simulated live environment. This might, for example, be done in parallel with existing information processing activities.

◆ *Implementation/changeover.* As with a bespoke software solution, data will have to be converted or entered from old computer or paper-based information systems. One of the benefits of purchasing off-the-shelf software is that the product should be free from major bugs and errors. The purchaser should be confident, therefore, that the software product will work as specified from the outset.

◆ *Maintenance and review.* Maintenance and enhancements of the software will differ from a bespoke solution. Whereas bespoke software can be enhanced over time by the developer (either in-house or third party), an off-the-shelf package will differ in a number of ways. Enhancements to the package will normally be made available by the vendor as a new release. Sometimes it is possible for a business organisation to build its own enhancements or 'add-ons' to the package. There is a danger that

such bespoke amendments to standard packages may be lost if the organisation buys a new release of the software. In addition, maintenance is usually covered by a separate maintenance agreement after the original guarantee period. Annual maintenance costs can vary from 10 to 20 per cent of the original software purchase price. There may be differential pricing depending on whether the maintenance agreement is to cover simply 'bug fixing' or whether it is to entitle the user to the latest version of the software at no or little additional cost. As with the bespoke solution, a post-implementation review should be undertaken.

▶ End-user development

End-user applications development is in line with the steps normally covered during the bespoke development process. The main difference is that end-user developed applications are usually on a much smaller scale than those developed for corporate use. However, many of the tools and techniques associated with large-scale corporate bespoke development still have a role, albeit a more limited one, in end-user developed information systems. As before, each step in the waterfall model will be discussed separately. The advantages and disadvantages of end-user development are described in detail in Chapter 16.

End-user developed software

Software written by non-IS professionals, i.e. the business users.

- *Initiation.* The stimulus for end-user information system development will typically come from a personal or departmental requirement which can be satisfied by employing easy-to-use end-user development tools. Such systems may either be standalone with no linkages to any other end-user or corporate system, or they may use databases and database extracts from corporate information systems (perhaps with additional database tables created by the user) and manipulate the data in order to produce information not previously made available. In the latter case, the data may already exist in the corporate database, but the processing necessary to produce the information has not been included as a core part of the application.

- *Feasibility.* Part of the feasibility exercise is for the user to be sure that the necessary and appropriate end-user development tools exist or can be acquired in order to proceed with the development. A second aspect is an analysis of the cost involved in end-user developed software: while an end-user is producing software, their 'normal' tasks either remain undone or have to be done by someone else. Therefore, end-user applications development needs to be justified on economic grounds.

- *Analysis.* One of the benefits is that an end-user need not present information systems requirements to an IS/IT specialist for subsequent development. This therefore reduces the risk of mistranslating information systems requirements and increases the probability that the developed system is what the user actually wants. The end-user may still find it useful to apply some of the tools associated with the analysis phase such as those discussed in Chapter 11, although clearly they will be used on a much smaller scale.

- *Design.* End-user developed software has a tendency to be developed more on a 'trial and error' basis than through the use of formal design techniques. When it works well, this can result in the faster development of applications software. The downside is that poor design may result in a system which at best does not work quite as it should and at worst a system which actually results in incorrect information being produced. Incorrect information can have various results ranging

from short-term irritation to corporate decision-making errors with large financial consequences. One of the most useful tools in end-user design is entity relationship modelling, which should be used in conjunction with logical and physical database design. The probability is that if the database design and associated data validation rules are correct, then the system is more likely to produce the information that is required.

◆ *Build*. Recent improvements in the availability of inexpensive development tools such as Visual Basic for the PC have made it much easier for the end-user developer to build systems without recourse to difficult programming techniques. As end-user development is now much easier than it was five years ago, emphasis can be placed on the functionality which the system is to offer. Also, development times are speeded up and this provides for the effective use of iterative prototyping in this step.

◆ *Implementation/changeover*. This step is less critical than for company-wide information systems. Data is either locally generated or extracted from central databases, where it can be assumed that the data is validated and verified as correct. In fact, the term changeover is probably not a good one in this context – 'live running' may be a better one. It is quite possible that an end-user developed system is capable of producing useful information even before it becomes a 'live' product. A risk is that end-user developed software may not have been tested sufficiently thoroughly and this raises an important question of the management of such software. We will deal with this in Chapter 16.

◆ *Maintenance and review*. All software has to be maintained in some way. In many respects, the maintenance of end-user developed software is more problematic that other forms of software acquisition. This is because end-user developed systems are often not documented and they may employ obscure techniques in their construction.

End-user development is discussed in more detail in Chapter 16.

FOCUS ON

Systems Analysis and Design Method (SSADM)

A methodology that defines the methods of analysis and design that should occur in a large-scale software development project. It is used extensively in the UK, particularly in government and public organisations.

▶ THE WATERFALL MODEL AND SSADM

Systems Analysis and Design Method (SSADM) is a methodology that defines the methods of analysis and design that should occur in a large-scale software development project. It is used extensively in the UK, particularly in government and public organisations.

Structured Systems Analysis and Design Methodology (SSADM) is one of over 1000 brand-name methodologies (Jayaratna, 1994). We will focus on SSADM because it is one of the most widely used formal methodologies in the UK today. Indeed, SSADM must be used for any government systems development projects, usually alongside the PRINCE project management method (Chapter 9).

SSADM focuses on the feasibility, analysis and design aspects of the systems development lifecycle. It provides fewer guidelines on the changeover and maintenance aspects of an IS project.

Describing SSADM in some detail highlights the methodical approach required for large-scale projects which some may refer to as bureaucratic. It also illustrates the contrast with alternative techniques such as RAD.

In its latest incarnation (version 4) SSADM has a five-module framework within which are seven stages. Each stage has its own activities and the required deliverables are clearly mapped out for each. It is not possible to go into a large degree of detail here. Texts such as Eva (1992) and Weaver (1993) deal with the methodology in a comprehensive manner. However, we will discuss the essentials of each module and associated stage(s) in turn.

▶ Feasibility study

Stage 0 – Feasibility

The project will already have been through a planning or initiation stage, so it is necessary at this point to determine whether it is technically and economically feasible. The feasibility study is broken down into four steps:

- *prepare for feasibility study* by assessing the scope of the project;
- *define the problem* (what should the new system do which the present one does not);
- *select the best feasibility option* from those available (typically up to five business options and a similar number of technical options);
- *assemble the feasibility report*, including a rationale for the selected option.

The output from this stage, the feasibility report, now provides the input for the next module – requirements analysis.

▶ Requirements analysis

This module is broken down into two stages: investigation of current environment and business system options.

Stage 1 – Investigation of current environment

This stage is critically important because it is used to gain a full understanding of what is required of the new system. Any errors or omissions made at this stage will be reflected in the rest of the systems development process. The following steps are taken:

- *Establish analysis framework.* The scope of the project is reassessed and then planned accordingly.
- *Investigate and define requirements.* Broad requirements will have been defined at the feasibility stage: these are now expanded into a detailed catalogue of systems requirements.
- *Investigate current processing.* The feasibility study will have created an initial data flow diagram which is now expanded to embrace all the existing processes.
- *Investigate current data.* A logical data model is developed so that the organisation can obtain a clear picture of which attributes the data entities contain and how they relate to each other. Entity and attribute are defined in Chapter 12.
- *Derive logical view of current services.* This involves the revision of the logical data model so that it reflects the business logic of the system under consideration rather than its current physical implementation.

◆ *Assemble investigation results*. This is the last step in the analysis of the current system environment. The analysts will check for consistency and completeness before proceeding to the next stage.

Stage 2 – Business systems options

This stage comprises two steps, the objective of which is to agree what the functionality of the new system should be. A number of possible systems solutions for the perceived business requirements are formulated and the impacts and benefits of each will be evaluated. The solution selected will be the one which most closely matches the requirements of the business. The two steps are:

◆ *Define business systems options*. Activities here will include the establishment of minimum systems requirements, the development in skeleton form of alternatives, the production of a short list of options, and finally a full evaluation of each alternative short-listed option, including a cost–benefit analysis, impact analysis and system development and integration plan for each.

◆ *Select business system option*. The precise way in which this is done will vary between organisations. The objective is the same, however: for appropriate user managers to select the business system option from the evidence presented by the analysis team.

▶ Requirements specification

This module has one stage which in turn is split into eight discrete steps.

Stage 3 – Definition of requirements

◆ *Define required system processing*. Here, the features of the existing system that are to remain a part of the new system are added to the details contained in the requirements catalogue.

◆ *Develop required data model*. Redundant elements from the data model of the existing system are removed (if any exist) and additional required elements are added. In addition, the relationships between old and new entities are reviewed.

◆ *Derive system functions*. Here, the processes which will have been identified and incorporated in the data flow diagrams are identified more precisely and properly documented.

◆ *Enhance required data model*. The required data model developed earlier is now enhanced by carrying out relational data analysis and normalisation (Chapter 12); the result should be a set of tables which can be implemented using a relational database management system.

◆ *Develop specification prototypes*. This involves the creation of prototypes for selected parts of the specification so that precise requirements can be validated with the intended end-users; such elements as menus, sample data entry screens and reports may be constructed.

◆ *Develop processing specifications*. The analyst at this stage is concerned with illustrating the effect of time on data subjected to various actions (i.e. creation, reading, updating and deleting); two tools which are used here are entity life history analysis and effect correspondence diagrams. These are tools used by the professional systems analyst and it is beyond the scope of this book to deal with them in detail.

◆ *Confirm system objectives*. The penultimate task is to carry out a formal review of the system requirements to ensure that the final requirements specification which follows is complete and fully understood by users and developers alike.

◆ *Assemble requirements specification*. Finally, the various components (including the required system logical data model, function definitions, requirements catalogue and other items) are assembled into the final requirements specification document, which then provides the input into the next module and stage.

▶ Logical system specification

Stage 4 – Technical system options

◆ *Define technical system options*. Here, any constraints on the choice of technical environments are established (e.g. security, performance, ease of upgrade).

◆ *Select technical system options*. The appropriate technical option is selected; it must conform with the required strategic and operational criteria which have already been established.

Stage 5 – Logical design

This stage can take place at the same time as Stage 4. Here, the process of developing the systems specification is continued, with the outcome being a set of implementable components. The individual steps are as follows:

◆ *Define user dialogues*. This is concerned with defining the ways in which the user will interact with the system (e.g. menus and systems navigation).

◆ *Define update processes*. Here, the definition of transactions which will change data are established (entity life histories are used to support this step).

◆ *Define enquiry processes*. In addition to navigation and updating, users will wish to perform enquiries on the data held in the system.

◆ *Assemble logical design*. This is essentially a consistency and completeness check.

Once the logical design is complete and has been 'signed off', the final stage can be tackled.

▶ Physical design

Stage 6 – Physical design

This stage is concerned with the delivery of the final blueprint from which the system can be developed and implemented. There are seven steps to be completed:

◆ *Prepare for physical design*. The implementation environment is studied, applications development standards drawn up and a physical design strategy agreed.

◆ *Create physical data design*. The required logical data model (LDM) is used as a base for this and the business-specific data design is produced.

◆ *Create function component implementation map.* The components of each systems function are drawn up. This includes their relationship with the physical function components (the actual business activities) which they support.

◆ *Optimise physical data design.* The physical data design is tested against the required performance objectives and optimised if necessary.

◆ *Complete function specification design.* This will be for any function components which required programming.

◆ *Consolidate process data interface.* The process data interface is located between the physical database design and the process design. This helps the mapping of the database to the processing requirements (especially important when the database has been altered or the processing requirements have been modified).

◆ *Assemble physical design.* This stage and the whole SSADM lifecycle are completed with this step. A number of products are delivered including the function definitions, the optimised physical data design, the requirements catalogue and space and timing estimates.

▶ SSADM and the waterfall model – a summary

Although complex, SSADM as a methodology only covers part of the systems development process (as the name of the methodology suggests, the emphasis is on analysis and design). However, given the importance of having systems requirements determined correctly before further development takes place, this is perhaps understandable. It is left to other methodologies to provide a more comprehensive approach to the waterfall model as a whole. Meanwhile, we will now turn our attention to what the traditionalists would regard as the very antithesis of a 'proper' structured methodology, that is, rapid applications development.

CASE STUDY: TOPIC AREA

Lascelles Fine Foods

Lascelles Fine Foods (LFFL) is a fictitious example of a long-established company operating in the food industry. The company has its administrative headquarters in Ashville and manufactures on an adjacent site. All customer deliveries are from the Ashville-based warehouse. In addition, LFFL purchases finished and semi-finished food products from other manufacturers which it then finishes before resale.

The company has enjoyed steady growth in recent years and is now seeking to capitalise on the current fashion for quality and healthy food products. LFFL's turnover is £16 million with net profitability of 6.3 per cent of turnover. It is hoping to gain a competitive edge by providing quality food products which meet all present and anticipated quality standards and to this end will be applying for BS5750 accreditation within the next six months. It is hoping to increase turnover by 10 per cent a per year after inflation over the next five years and increase net profitability to 9 per cent of turnover over the same period.

LFFL's main operations are divided into four main areas:

◆ sales and marketing;
◆ warehousing and distribution;
◆ manufacturing;
◆ finance.

All information recording and internal communication is paper based and relies on a range of preprinted documents which are then used as appropriate.

The sales department

LFFL has a diverse customer base, ranging from small health food shops to major supermarket chains. Orders can be one of two types: standard orders placed in advance for delivery in a specific week or priority orders placed for immediate delivery.

Orders are placed either directly through sales office 'account handlers' or through field sales persons (each customer has one sales person). Each customer is allocated an account handler who acts as the main liaison point within LFFL. Besides receiving orders, the account handler is responsible for cash collection, ensuring satisfactory progress of the order and handling day-to-day queries. Customers are also placed into sales categories based on geographic location, volume of business and type of customer (e.g. specialist store vs supermarket chain). The sales director is apt to change his mind about which category a customer is in and which category means what.

Order processing

Once an order is taken, it is recorded on a preprinted order form. One copy is retained by the sales department and two copies are sent to warehousing and distribution.

Warehousing and distribution sort all order forms into date order. When an order is due to be delivered, products are picked from the warehouse and loaded into the appropriate vehicle.

When an order is delivered, it is accompanied by a consignment note and an invoice. The customer is required to check the delivery against the invoice and note any errors on the consignment note. The delivery driver returns with a signed copy of the consignment note and if any errors are noted a corrected invoice is sent to the customer.

Warehousing and distribution

LFFL stores finished products, bought-in products and raw materials in the warehouse. The warehouse is divided into three areas:

◆ the general zone, comprising a high-rise bulk storage area with a floor-level picking area;
◆ the cool zone, comprising low-level storage at 2 to 4° Centigrade;
◆ the frozen zone, with temperatures held to −18° Centigrade.

In addition to their role in the order processing cycle, other activities are also performed:

◆ internal warehouse movements from high-rise locations to ground-level areas and vice versa;
◆ receiving products and raw materials from suppliers and returned products from customers;
◆ issuing raw materials to manufacturing in response to submitted requisition forms;
◆ receiving finished products from manufacturing and any unused raw materials.

Information about quantities of finished goods and raw materials in stock is recorded in a card file, which has to be searched manually for the appropriate entry when updating is required.

Manufacturing

Manufacturing ranges in complexity from simple repackaging of bulk-purchased materials to complex mixing and cooking activities.

Recipes are recorded on 7" by 5" cards and include details of the required ingredients as well as the processing which is to take place.

Finance

LFFL's finance department is divided into three areas:

◆ accounts payable – when LFFL makes purchases, suppliers will invoice them; LFFL uses a manual purchase ledger to manage these accounts;
◆ financial accounting – management of all monies flowing in and out of the company together with compliance with legal accounting requirements;
◆ management accounting – internal accounting information necessary to manage the business more effectively.

The accounts receivable area is handled by the account handlers who use a manual sales ledger and make a weekly return to the finance department on the state of their customers' accounts.

Specific business issues

There are a number of specific issues which relate to the activities of each department. These are detailed below.

Sales
◆ The status of an order cannot easily be determined without pestering the warehouse.
◆ Many customer complaints occur due to delivery of wrong products, orders delivered too late, incomplete orders and faulty products.
◆ Warehousing does not deliver the most important orders first – small orders are often given priority over larger orders from major retailers.
◆ Orders often cannot be delivered on time because manufacturing produces too late and in insufficient quantity.

◆

Warehousing and distribution
◆ Many items have a limited shelf life – warehousing often fails to rotate the stock properly.
◆ Actual stock levels are rarely in step with the recorded stock levels – this may be due to pilfering, poor update of stock records or both.
◆ The sales department often accepts priority orders for products which are not in stock.
◆ Manufacturing bypasses the normal requisition procedures and simply takes raw materials as required – it also often fails to return unused materials to warehousing.

Finance
◆ The sales returns from the account handlers are often incomplete.
◆ There are several bad debts which cannot be recovered – this is attributed to poor credit control procedures.
◆ Management accounting is very difficult due to a general lack of accurate information from other departments.
◆ Financial accounts are often published late due to lack of accurate information.

Manufacturing
◆ Warehousing is slow to respond to requests for raw materials, thus necessitating correct procedures being bypassed (especially when the sales department is applying pressure).
◆ Lack of accurate forecasting makes it difficult for production to be planned ahead and adequate supplies of raw materials to be secured.

General
◆ There is a rapid turnover of staff, especially in the sales area where the pressure from customers can be intense. In addition, field sales personnel are apt to make promises which cannot be kept and new sales personnel are often thrown in at the deep end with little formal training for their jobs.
◆ There is a high level of sickness in the warehousing and distribution area, due mainly to inadequate provision of lifting equipment.

◆ There is a perceived lack of management and technical support which has resulted in a general lowering of morale.

Future plans

The managing director, Clive Moor, has indicated that he would like to replace the existing paper-based systems with 'computers of some kind'. With such a move, he is hoping to improve on the communication of information at all levels in the organisation. However, Mr Moor knows little about computer hardware or applications software except that it seems to cost rather a lot.

In order to proceed with the computerisation programme, Mr Moor has asked the following senior managers to produce a plan:

◆ Paula Barlow   Finance director
◆ Terry Watson   Sales and marketing director
◆ Peter Jackson   Manufacturing operations director
◆ Frances Clarke   Warehousing and distribution director

However, these directors have varying degrees of enthusiasm for the project, together with a desire to minimise the risk of damage or exposure within their own departments. One of the key decisions which must be made will be how LFFL acquires the necessary applications software. One option will be to hire relevant IT staff and build bespoke applications, while another will be to purchase off-the-shelf packages. Yet another option will be for end-users to develop their own applications. This last option may prove awkward, since there is very little IT expertise among the end-users.

Questions

1 Which method(s) of business systems software acquisition would you recommend to LFFL? Explain and justify your answer.

2 Assuming that LFFL decides to go down the route of purchasing off-the-shelf packages, what steps do you recommend it takes to ensure that the applications which are selected meet their requirements?

▶ RAPID APPLICATIONS DEVELOPMENT (RAD)

The evidence from project failures for projects conducted in the 1980s and 1990s implies that traditional structured methodologies have a tendency to deliver systems which arrive too late and therefore no longer meet their original requirements. Traditional methods can fail in a number of ways:

◆ *A gap of understanding between users and developers.* Users tend to know less about what is possible and practical from a technology perspective, while developers may be less aware of the underlying business decision-making issues which lie behind the systems development requirement.

◆ *Tendency of developers to isolate themselves from users.* Historically, systems developers have been able to hide behind a wall of jargon, thus rendering the user community at an immediate disadvantage when discussing IS/IT issues. While some jargon may be necessary if points are to be made succinctly, it is often used to obscure poor progress with a particular development project. The tendency for isolation is enhanced by physical separation of some computer staff in their own air-conditioned computer rooms. Developers might argue in their defence that users also have their own domain-specific jargon which adds to the problem of deciphering requirements.

◆ *Quality measured by closeness of product to specification.* This is a fundamental difficulty – the observation that 'the system does exactly what the specification said it would do' hides the fact that the system may still not deliver the information that the users need for decision-making purposes. The real focus should be on a comparison of the deliverables with the requirements, rather than of deliverables with a specification that was a reflection of a perceived need at a particular point in time.

◆ *Long development times.* A glance back at the previous section on SSADM and the waterfall model will reveal that the processes of analysis and design can be very laborious and time consuming. Development times are not helped by the fact that an organisation may be facing rapidly changing business conditions and requirements may similarly be changing. There is a real risk of the 'moving goal-posts' syndrome causing havoc with a traditional approach to systems development.

◆ *Business needs change during the development process.* This is alluded to above. A method is needed where successive iterations in the development process are possible so that the latest requirements can be incorporated.

◆ *What users get isn't necessarily what they want.* The first a user may see of a new information system is at the testing or training stage. At this point, it will be seen whether the system as delivered by the IS/IT professionals is what the user actually needs. An appropriate analogy here is the purchase of a house or car simply on the basis of discussions with an estate agent or a garage, rather than by actually visiting the house or driving the car. It is unlikely that something purchased in this way will result in a satisfied customer and there is no reason to suppose that information systems developed in a similar way will be any more successful.

Not only is there pressure from end-user management for faster systems development, IS/IT departments themselves increasingly recognise the need to make more effective use of limited human resources within their departments while at the same time delivering systems quickly which confer business benefits. All this is in a climate of rapid business change and, therefore, rapidly changing information needs. **Rapid applications development (RAD)** is a possible solution to these problems and pressures. This uses **prototyping** to involve users and increase development speed.

Rapid applications development (RAD) is a method of developing information systems which uses prototyping to achieve user involvement and faster development compared to traditional methodologies such as SSADM.

Prototyping produces a preliminary version of part or a framework of all of an information system which can be reviewed by end-users. Prototyping is an iterative process where users suggest modifications before further prototypes and the final information system are built.

Rapid applications development (RAD)

A method of developing information systems which uses prototyping to achieve user involvement and faster development compared to traditional methodologies such as SSADM.

Prototyping

A prototype is a preliminary version of part or a framework of all of an information system which can be reviewed by end-users. Prototyping is an iterative process where users suggest modifications before further prototypes and the final information system is built.

The case study on RAD a Lloyds Bank Insurance Services illustrates the benefits that can be derived from a RAD approach. It also hints at some disadvantages, such as the lack of a methodology to support RAD which can lead to a casual approach to a project. A later section on the dynamic systems development method (page 273) shows how this deficiency is being made good.

CASE STUDY: TOPIC AREA

RAD – Lloyds Bank Insurance Services implements a brand new system for scratch in five weeks with the help of a second-generation client/server toolset and rapid applications development

When marketing people spot a business opportunity, it is often IT people who have to think and act the fastest.

Systems have to be put in place that meet the stipulated deadline, that work first time, and that fulfil the expectations of users. Otherwise the opportunity could be lost forever.

That was the situation facing the computer team at Lloyds Bank Insurance Services when a new product called MUDI (Mortgage Unemployment Disability Insurance) required a telesales quotation system that had to be fully operational by October 2nd.

Yet it was already mid-August when David Jacklin, IT Development Manager, LBIS, was informed of the need for a new application. It was a moment he remembers well. 'I faced the classic dilemma of no available resource within my team and an immovable deadline,' he recalls.

However, in spite of that initial reaction and against some unexpected odds, the race against time was won. The insurance broker's objective was achieved with the help of a hard-working software house, a development environment toolset, and a fast-track approach called RAD (Rapid Application Development). In fact, the entire development took just five weeks.

Reason for the urgency at the LBIS headquarters in Haywards Heath, West Sussex was a government decision to amend the rules relating to the payment of mortgage cover out of social security in the event of a house-owner being made redundant. This opened a new insurance window which the company was determined to exploit.

LBIS, a subsidiary of Lloyds Bank and Abbey Life, is a firm of independent brokers dealing in life assurance, pensions and general insurance. Annual turnover is £100 million and 800 people are employed at Haywards Heath and six regional offices. A significant proportion of the company's business is generated through a business unit called Lloyds Bank Insurance Direct.

This is essentially a telemarketing organisation based in Bournemouth. About 70 per cent of its business comes via branches of Lloyds Bank, where advisors take an enquirer's details and ring LBID for a quote. The remaining 30 per cent is from people responding to direct mail of advertisements and telephoning in direct.

A simple version of MUDI was, in fact, available at the bank branches. But there were no facilities for accurate underwriting and anyone taking up the policy paid a straight £6.50 per £100 of cover (i.e. if the monthly mortgage payment was £300, the premium was £19.50). The new system would incorporate a complex screen replacing the existing simple paper form, providing the flexibility to quote premiums appropriate to the enquirer ranging from £4.40 to £9.40 per £100 of cover.

But first the new system had to be built. There already existed another application at Bournemouth – BIQS (Building Insurance Quotations Service) – but this ran under DOS, so what would almost certainly be a Windows system could not merely be tagged on.

Jacklin and his team had been looking at development toolsets and the RAD concept earlier in the summer. They had been particularly attracted by a RAD specialist, MDA Computing, and had already met the Croydon-based software house at the end of July.

Suddenly, with the new business-critical requirement looming, the need for RAD became urgent. 'We had no hesitation going back to MDA. They obviously knew what they were talking about and we were in urgent need of a system,' says Jacklin.

Some of the main attractions of RAD included the delivery of a workable first version within a very short timescale, testing that is integrated within the development cycle, flexibility of the specification, and user involvement throughout the whole process.

Within days, Jacklin and his colleagues had agreed with MDA the RAD methods to be used. The software house underlined the need for an appropriate development environment, and recommended Enterprise Developer. This versatile toolset from Symantec had all the advanced features of a second generation client/server development system, and this was precisely what the LBIS team sought.

Such systems are repository-based and scaleable, and – specially important according to Jacklin – are driven by business rules so that future changes are easily made as business needs change. MDA evaluates every tool that comes on to the client/server market and felt that Enterprise Developer offered the best set of second generation facilities.

Next step was a demonstration of the Symantec toolset at MDA, 'The demo convinced us. We had looked at other development tools but they did not seem meaty enough for our needs. And although MDA had never built anything with Enterprise Developer they were clearly keen to do so.' Following that demo and an agreement of project scope, work began on August 24th.

The key requirement was for a front-end system that would enable telesales staff at 30 screens to capture a caller's details and generate an immediate MUDI quotation. The system would be in Windows 3.1 and GUI based, essentially a classic PC LAN application. It would run a Compaq server using Novell.

However, MDA's first task was systems analysis. At the early stage, LBIS had not formulated all their needs – not even the design of the 'forms' that would appear on the screen. So MDA used RAD techniques to work out what the requirements would be, and spent three days at LBID in Bournemouth prototyping the forms on screen using Enterprise Developer. The software house also had to allay fears, among a user-team with little experience of Windows, about mouse-driven systems.

In order to get the project started, the use of a Watcom database was assumed. However, following discussions within LBIS, it was decided that for strategic and operational support reasons the use of Oracle was preferred.

MDA had to accommodate a new database in already tight development cycle. The ability to adapt to the fresh circumstances and still deliver the system on time was a big tribute to the software house's RAD methods and the

Symantec toolset. (In fact, there were minor compatibility problems which disappeared when LBIS upgraded to Enterprise Developer 2.5 at the beginning of November.)

The system was delivered in the last week of September for final testing in readiness to go live the following Monday. By then, LBIS' own technical team had adjusted the BIQS system so that the telesales people could flip to it from MUDI, depending on the caller's needs, with a simple keyboard Alt/Tab depression.

On 'live' day, the telesales team processed 200 customer quotations with scarcely a hitch. Jacklin, MDA and Symantec had every right to feel pleased with themselves. A business need had demanded IT support, and that support was implemented on time.

Now the end-users, equipped with telephone headsets, enter personal details which affect ratings, such as sex, post code and occupation, on to a GUI screen. The quotation then appears on the same screen. There are five other, supporting screens labelled status, comments, letter print, rating and search for existing customer.

A happy Jacklin concludes, 'Here was a software house that gave us what we needed. They were always confident they could do something with Enterprise Developer and within time. There was no slippage despite it being their first real use of the Symantec product and despite the change in database midway through. I think that says something for Enterprise Developer too. And we went live on the big day.

'We like RAD and we shall use it again. In a market-oriented organisation like LBIS, we always have a need to react to business changes quickly, and I suspect that within 18 months we could need a system to handle all six of our insurance products.'

He adds, 'The system has allowed LBIS to launch a more competitive product than would otherwise have been possible, and we have sold more than we would have done. It had to be in at the right time or we would have missed the boat. From a technical point of view, it forced us to go to Windows which was always our eventual intention. All this, and the system will pay for itself before Christmas!'

Source: This case study was taken with permission from the DSDM Web site.

Questions

1 Why and how did the company choose the RAD approach used for this project?

2 What disadvantages of the RAD method can you identify from the study?

3 Do you think that Lloyds can be confident that future RAD projects will be successful?

▶ The spiral model

The spiral model

An iterative systems development model developed by Boehm (1988) in which the stages of analysis, design, code and review repeat as new features for the system are identified.

The Spiral model is an iterative systems development model developed by Boehm (1988) which incorporates risk assessment.

The spiral model was developed in recognition of the fact that systems development projects tend to repeat the stages of analysis, design and code as part of the prototyping process. Each spiral consists of four main activities, as shown in Fig 7.3 The activities are:

1 *Planning.* Setting project objectives, defining alternatives.

2 *Risk analysis.* Analysis of alternatives and the identification and solution of risks.

3 *Engineering.* Equivalent to the build phase of the SDLC with coding and testing.

4 *Customer evaluation.* Testing of the product by customers.

It can be seen from Fig 7.3 that the model is closely related to RAD, since it implies iterative development with a review possible after each iteration or spiral, which corresponds to the production of one prototype or incremental version. Before the first spiral starts the requirements plan is produced, so it can be seen that the spiral model does not detail the initiation and analysis phase of the SDLC, focusing on design and build.

Although the spiral model has not been applied widely in industry, proponents of this model argue that it includes the best features of both the classic SDLC and the prototyping approach. It also adds validation of requirements and design, together with risk analysis which is often overlooked in RAD projects.

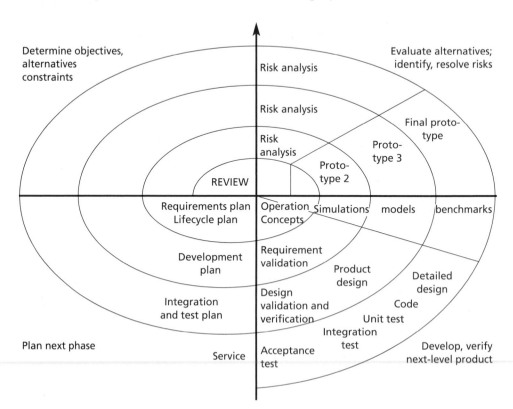

Fig 7.3 Boehm's spiral model of systems development

▶ Dynamic Systems Development Methodology (DSDM)

The ideas behind RAD have been around for several years, but a methodology which encapsulates its principles has only recently emerged. In the UK, an organisation known as the DSDM Consortium has put together a set of underlying principles (the latest being Version 2). These are given in full below, together with a commentary provided by the consortium. In total, **DSDM (Dynamic Systems Development Methodology)** has nine key principles, shown in the box.

Dynamic Systems Development Methodology (DSDM)

A methodology which describes how RAD can be approached.

The nine principles of the Dynamic Systems Development Methodology (DSDM)

I   *Active user involvement is imperative.* DSDM is a user-centred approach. If users are not closely involved throughout the development life-cycle, delays will occur as decisions are made. Users no longer sit outside the development team acting as suppliers of information and reviewers of results but are active participants in the development process.

II   *DSDM teams must be empowered to make decisions.* DSDM teams consist of both developers and users. They must be able to make decisions as requirements are refined and possibly changed. They must be able to agree that certain levels of functionality, usability, etc. are acceptable without frequent recourse to higher level management.

III   *The focus is on frequent delivery of products.* A product-based approach is more flexible than an activity-based one. The work of a DSDM team is concentrated on products that can be delivered in an agreed period of time. This enables the team to select the best approach to achieving the products required in the time available. By keeping each period of time short, the team can easily decide which activities are necessary and sufficient to achieve the right products.

IV   *Fitness for business purpose is the essential criterion for acceptance of deliverables.* The focus of DSDM is on delivering the business functionality at the required time. The system can be more rigorously engineered later if such an approach is acceptable. Traditionally the focus has been on satisfying the contents of a requirements document and conforming to previous deliverables, while losing sight of the fact that the requirements are often inaccurate and the previous deliverables are flawed.

V   *Iterative and incremental development is necessary to converge on an accurate business solution.* DSDM allows systems to evolve incrementally. Therefore the developers can make full use of feedback from the users. Moreover partial solutions can be delivered to satisfy immediate business needs. Iteration is inherent in all software development. DSDM recognises this and, by making it explicit, strengthens the use of iteration. When rework is not explicitly recognised in a development life-cycle, the return to previously 'completed' work is surrounded by controlling procedures which slow development down. Since rework is built into the DSDM process, the development can proceed more quickly during iteration.

VI   *All changes during development are reversible.* Backtracking is a feature of DSDM. However in some circumstances it may be easier to reconstruct than to backtrack. This depends on the nature of the change and the environment in which it was made.

▶

VII *Requirements are baselined at a high level.* Baselining high-level requirements means 'freezing' and agreeing the purpose and scope of the system at a level which allows for detailed investigation of what the requirements imply. Further baselines can be established later in the development.

VIII *Testing is integrated throughout the life-cycle.* Testing is not treated as a separate activity. As the system is developed incrementally, it is also tested and reviewed by both developers and users to ensure that the development is moving forward; not only in the right business direction, but that it is technically sound. Early in DSDM, the testing focus is on understanding the business needs and priorities. Towards the end of a project, the focus is on assuring users and developers that the whole system operates effectively.

IX *A collaborative and co-operative approach between all stakeholders is essential.* The nature of DSDM projects means that low-level requirements are not necessarily fixed when the developers are originally approached to carry out the work. Hence the short term direction that a project takes must be quickly decided without recourse to restrictive change control procedures. When development is procured from an external supplier, both the vendor and the purchaser organisations should aim for as efficient a process as possible while allowing for flexibility during both the pre-contract phase and when the contracted work is carried out.

Source: http://www.dsdm.org

Avison and Fitzgerald (1995) outline an approach to rapid applications development which embraces many of the principles outlined above. For them, the RAD approach:

◆ is based on evolutionary/prototyping rather than the traditional lifecycle approach;
◆ identifies key users and involves them in workshops at the early stages of development;
◆ obtains commitment from the business users;
◆ requires the use of CASE (Computer-Aided Software Engineering) tools for system building.

Typical RAD activities include:

◆ Joint requirements planning (JRP) to determine high-level management requirements.
◆ Joint applications design (JAD) using prototyping tools to explore processes, interfaces, screens, reports, dialogues etc., which are then developed and modelled using entity modelling, dataflow diagrams, action diagrams and function decomposition diagrams.
◆ Transformation of user designs to detailed design and code generation, often with the assistance of CASE tools.
◆ A cutover phase involving more testing, functional-level training, training for organisational change and adaptation, conversion, parallel running and, finally, live running.

The result of the rapid applications development approach should be new information systems which more closely meet the requirements of the intended users, not least because the requirements will not have changed significantly over a relatively short development timescale.

▶ SUMMARY

1 This chapter has taken a wide-ranging look at the whole area of information systems acquisition and some of the methodologies, tools and techniques which support it.

2 While some of the methodologies have been dealt with in some detail, many of the individual tools and techniques have been dealt with in outline only. It is now necessary to explore these in more detail in the chapters which follow.

▶ EXERCISES

▶ Self-assessment exercises

1 Explain what the main similarities and differences are between bespoke development and end-user development.

2 Why would a small business be more constrained in its choice of software acquisition method than a large one?

3 What are the main differences between the analysis and design steps of the traditional waterfall model of systems development?

4 What are the main components of the systems build stage?

5 Explain how the application of the waterfall model differs between (a) the purchase of an off-the-shelf package and (b) an end-user developed application.

6 Briefly review the main advantages and disadvantages of bespoke development when compared with off-the-shelf packages.

7 Identify the main stages involved in SSADM. Which stages of the traditional waterfall model do they relate to?

8 How does rapid applications development differ from SSADM as a means of producing 'quality' software?

▶ Discussion questions

1 The rise of rapid applications development is mainly a response to the failure of traditional systems development methodologies to deliver the right system at the right price and at the right time. Discuss.

2 End-user applications development would be far less popular if central IS/IT departments did not have such a large applications development backlog. Discuss.

3 Do you think it is true that the existence of so many information systems problems attributed to the 'millennium bug' is primarily a reflection of poor systems development techniques?

▶ Essay questions

1 What do you believe to be the main differences between large and small organisations in deciding the best approach for information systems acquisition?

2 In what circumstances do you think that SSADM would be (a) appropriate and (b) inappropriate when carrying out systems analysis and design?

3 In what circumstances do you think that rapid applications development would be (a) appropriate and (b) inappropriate when carrying out systems analysis and design?

4 Is the end-user development approach to business software development something which you think should be encouraged, or do you believe that applications software for business is best left to information systems professionals?

▶ Examination questions

1 Explain the terms 'bespoke development', 'off-the-shelf package' and 'end-user computing'. Illustrate your answer with some of the reasons cited in favour of each of these methods of application software acquisition.

2 Give three advantages usually associated with prototyping.

3 During a bespoke development project, the systems development lifecycle will include a number of steps from requirements analysis, design and system. Which of these steps is relevant to an off-the shelf system? Which activities might be involved?

4 Explain how the spiral model of systems development which can be applied to RAD differs from the traditional waterfall model. Which do you believe represents the best method of developing information systems?

▶ References

Avison, D.E. and Fitzgerald, G. (1996) *Information Systems Development: Methodologies, Techniques and Tools*, Blackwell, Oxford.

Boehm, B. (1988) 'A spiral model of software development and enhancement', *IEEE Computer*, 21, 5, May, 61–72.

Eva, M. (1992) *SSADM Version 4: a User's Guide*, McGraw-Hill, London.

Jayaratna, N. (1994) *Understanding and Evaluating Methodologies NIMSAD, a Systematic Framework*, McGraw-Hill, London.

Senn, J. (1995) *Information Technology in Business Principles, Practices and Opportunities*, Prentice-Hall, Englewood Cliffs, NJ.

Weaver, P.L. (1993) *Practical SSADM Version 4: a Complete Tutorial Guide*, Financial Times Pitman Publishing, London.

▶ Further reading

Curtis, G. (1998) *Business Information Systems: Analysis, Design and Practice*, 3rd edition, Addison Wesley, Harlow, Essex.

Kendall, K.E. and Kendall, J.E. (1995) *Systems Analysis and Design*, 3rd edition, Prentice-Hall, Englewood Cliffs, NJ.

Kerr, J. and Hunter, R. (1996) *Rapid Development: Taming Wild Software Schedules*, Microsoft Press, Redman, WA.

Lewis, P. (1994) *Information-Systems Development*, Financial Times Pitman Publishing, London.

Martin, J. (1990) *Rapid Applications Development*, Macmillan, London.

Stapleton, J. (1998) *DSDM: the Method in Practice*, Addison Wesley, Harlow, Essex.

INTRODUCTION

Many information systems projects fail. Often they may overrun in time or budget, or they may not deliver the benefits expected. A 1995 Coopers & Lybrand survey for 76 UK companies showed that:

♦ 61 per cent of projects had significant cost overruns or failed to meet deadlines;

♦ 42 per cent of projects did not achieve business benefits.

These failures are often the result of errors made during the development project, but other systems projects are set to fail right from the start because the planned systems are unnecessary or not capable of delivering what the business needs. This is often the case if a feasibility study has not been carried out as part of the **initiation or startup phase** of the project. This chapter describes all the activities that need to occur at the start of a project to minimise the risk of failure later in the project.

The initiation phase is the first phase in an information systems development project. Its aims are to establish whether the project is feasible and to prepare to ensure that the project is successful.

The **Feasibility study** is the activity that occurs at the start of the project to ensure that the project is a viable business proposition. The feasibility report analyses the need for and impact of the system and considers different alternatives for acquiring software is normally considered to be part of the initiation phase.

A feasibility study normally occurs as part of the initiation phase (or as a separate phase after initiation) as a preliminary investigation intended to establish whether a business opportunity or problem can be solved through introducing a new information system. It is often also referred to as defining the 'terms of reference' for the project.

Initiation phase

The first phase in an information systems development project. Its aims are to establish whether the project is feasible and prepare to ensure the project is successful.

Feasibility study

The activity that occurs at the start of the project to ensure that the project is a viable business proposition. The feasibility report analyses the need for and impact of the system and considers different alternatives for acquiring software.

▶ Activities involved in project initiation

The purpose of the initiation stage is to assess whether an information systems development project will have a successful outcome. The key activity in a feasibility assessment is a cost–benefit analysis to check that the benefits provided by the system will outweigh the costs. Other factors such as the effect on staff will also be considered and the scope of the project defined. The activities that occur during the initiation stage are summarised in Table 8.1.

Table 8.1 Principal activities during the initiation phase of an IS project

Activity	Purpose
1 Assess feasibility	This is the most important aspect of the initiation stage. It involves performing a cost–benefit analysis and considering non-monetary considerations such as the effect that the new system will have on staff. An overall feasibility study may be conducted to establish the business reasons for proceeding, followed by a comparison of alternative technical solutions from different suppliers.
2 Define business objectives and outline systems requirements	Check that the system is aligned with business needs by defining critical success factors (CSFs) that must be achieved by incorporation of particular features.
3 Evaluate acquisition alternatives	This evaluation will cover different aspects such as cost, suitability and performance of systems from different suppliers, which may be either bespoke or 'off the shelf'.
4 Define scope	This involves specifying system boundaries describing which parts of the organisation will be affected by the system. Will it be used in a single department, across the whole organisation or beyond with suppliers?
5 Define responsibilities	Since a large input to a project in areas such as defining the requirements and undertaking testing is from managers and users of the final system, time for their input must be set aside. Responsibilities of the system developers will also be specified.
6 Assess risks	Identify potential problems which may cause the project to fail, such as skills shortages or changes to the company's market. What precautions can be taken to ensure that the project doesn't fail?
7 Identify constraints and develop project plan	Use estimating and planning to develop an initial project plan. This will preview project size and complexity to establish a preliminary budget and timescale, which will be refined once the go-ahead for the project is given.

Note that the initiation phase may involve two separate phases of feasibility analysis. In the first, overall feasibility may be established by establishing the needs and objectives for the system. If it is decided that the project is worthwhile, a more detailed evaluation of available solutions from different vendors will occur.

Figure 8.1 shows a typical sequence of activities that occur at the initiation stage of a project. For a large-scale project the feasibility report will normally be considered by a panel comprising senior staff in the company, such as the managing director, finance director, IS director or manager, and representatives of departments or processes which will use the system. For a smaller-scale project the departmental manager may be the only person involved if he or she holds the budget. This should be discouraged, since there may be other systems already in the organisation that meet the needs or conflict with the proposed system. Someone with an overview, such as the IS manager, can avoid this problem.

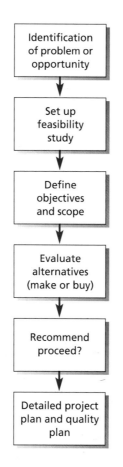

Fig 8.1 Sequence of main activities involved with project initiation

> ### ▶ Learning objectives
>
> After reading this chapter, readers will be able to:
>
> ◆ understand the importance of conducting a structured initiation phase for an information systems development project;
>
> ◆ identify typical tangible and intangible costs and benefits associated with the introduction of an information system;
>
> ◆ discuss the merits of outsourcing system development and some of its related problems;
>
> ◆ use different techniques to select the most appropriate options from different software, hardware and supplier alternatives;
>
> ◆ realise the importance of contracts to a successful outcome to information systems projects.

> ### ▶ Links to other chapters
>
> The chapter focuses on the startup phase of systems development projects.
>
> Chapter 7   describes alternative acquisition methods such as bespoke and off-the-shelf development.
>
> Chapter 9   describes how to manage a project to ensure that the quality of the system is maintained throughout the project.
>
> Chapter 14   also considers cost–benefit analysis in relation to the overall investment that a company makes in IS rather than individual systems. Critical success factors for the new system are described in more detail. Outsourcing of information systems development and management is also described.

▶ REASONS FOR PROJECT INITIATION

A project is usually initiated by a company in response to a business problem or opportunity in order to gain competitive advantage. Some examples of such benefits were introduced in Chapter 2. When a company is considering the benefits that can arise through implementing an information system, a useful framework is provided by the '5Cs' mentioned by Senn (1989) and updated to include customer service as another important factor. This framework covers the following benefits:

1 *Competitive advantage.* Information systems can often give a company the edge over its rivals. For example, a travel agent may have developed an Internet booking service which its competitors do not have. This advantage can be delivered in different ways related to the other factors in this list, such as giving a new capability or improving customer service.

2 *Customer service.* Customer service can be directly improved by introducing 'customer-facing' systems which are used directly by customers or in their presence. A bank might use these to reduce the length of queues, and so improve customer service. Customer service can also be enhanced indirectly. A company could purchase an improved sales order processing system that reduces the time taken to order and deliver a product to the customer.

3 *Capability.* A new information system can provide a new capability to achieve something that has not previously been possible. For example, establishing an Internet presence through a Web site gives a new sales channel capability. Information systems can also be enhanced to improve an existing capability where capacity has become limited. For example, business expansion may produce workloads with which current systems cannot cope – a growing company may find that its existing systems can no longer handle the quantity of orders received. An improved capability can be provided by increasing the amount of storage of an existing system or upgrading the software to a version with new features.

4 *Communication.* Companies which do not currently have a network can improve communication through introducing a local area network within an office or by creating a wide area network between offices. Communications can also be enhanced with suppliers to improve the speed of product delivery of parts or raw materials. Installing the network has to be coupled with installing software to improve communication. E-mail is an obvious example of this. Groupware such as Lotus Notes, Domino and Microsoft Exchange provides tools to help teams of workers collaborate.

5 *Control.* Control can be improved through better information delivery for managers. A sales manager who has weekly reports on the performance of his or her sales force is in a better position to exercise control than a manager who receives the figures monthly.

6 *Cost reduction.* Cost reduction is often the key driver for the introduction of new systems. This factor is relatively easy to quantify and is readily understood by the managing director and finance manager. Different aspects of quantifying cost are given in the section on cost–benefit analysis (page 283).

A further useful measure of the need for the system is to ask:

What would be the consequence of not having the proposed information system?

A summary of the types of benefit that a company can achieve is given in Table 8.2. This gives examples of how a car manufacturing company might use information technology to gain benefits.

It is evident from Table 8.2 that any new information system will give multiple benefits. In addition to the benefits given in the table, other benefits include better decision making and reduced error and wastage in existing manual processes through automation.

Table 8.2 Common benefits of introducing information systems, with examples of how they might assist a car manufacturer

Benefit	Achieved through
1 Competitive advantage	Reduced time to market and improved build quality can be delivered through automation
2 Customer service	Through integrated manufacturing a customer can specify his or her exact requirements for a car which will then be produced within a week
3 Capability	A new capability to build specific cars for customers
4 Communications	A network can be set up linking the head office of the company and dealerships to assist in ordering new cars and monitoring the sales performance of the individual dealership
5 Control	Improved information can be delivered for management decision making and to assist control
6 Cost reduction	'Deskilling' or using information systems and robots to reduce the number of staff required. Computer-aided design and manufacture can help reduce the time and cost from concept to production

ACTIVITY

Select a company or organisation with which you are familiar. Rank in order of importance the benefits that developing a particular new information system could deliver to the business or a particular department. You should give an explanation of why you have placed each benefit factor where you have.

▶ ALIGNMENT OF INFORMATION SYSTEMS WITH THE BUSINESS STRATEGY

When undertaking the feasibility study, as part of the initiation phase it is important to check that there is a strong alignment between the benefits that the new information system will provide and the overall business strategy. This may seem an obvious point, but it is stressed since the culture and structure of many organisations do not support this. If some departments such as marketing have a strong influence on the board, then their systems may be more likely to be accepted from those from another area such as production.

Another reason that poor alignment may occur is when the IS department has sole responsibility for which systems are developed. Traditionally most companies have an area with responsibility for IT, but it is often seen as a support service in the same

way as, for example, estates management. Owing to this, the IT department does not integrate with or understand other business functions and tends to be isolated. This problem is compounded if there is no IT director on the board of the company (or at least another director with responsibility for IT).

Many companies are now changing this situation and this enables the IS strategy to support and be responsive to the business strategy. Developing a culture where the other functions of the business represent internal customers to the IT function also helps in this transition. The main techniques for achieving this alignment include a top-down approach to IS strategy, where the mission and objectives of the company are translated into a portfolio of information systems required by the company. Whether alignment occurs should be assessed as part of the feasibility to the organisation. The feasibility review panel should also ask the question:

Is this system consistent with and supportive of the mission and objectives of the company?

Other techniques such as the application of critical success factors are also relevant. The issue of aligning systems with objectives and choosing systems to affect the organisation is discussed in more detail, from a strategic viewpoint, in Chapter 14.

John Browning, writing in *The Economist* in 1990, acknowledged that IT had gone far beyond being a support service when he wrote:

Information Technology is no longer a business resource; it has become the business environment.

▶ Critical success factors

The use of critical success factors (CSFs) is valuable to help align the new system with the business objectives. CSFs are quantifiable, measurable business objectives in relation to business requirements. Such objectives which may be part of a company's mission statement might include:

◆ reduce time to market by 20 per cent;

◆ increase market share by 5 per cent;

◆ improve quality of product by 30 per cent.

After identification of the CSFs, development of the system is targeted specifically at meeting these objectives at all stages. For example, the analysis stage will question which features the system requires to meet these objectives. The testing stage will involve benefits-based testing to check that the system has the features to deliver the intended benefits. CSFs are covered in more detail in Chapter 14.

▶ ECONOMIC FEASIBILITY – THE COST–BENEFIT ANALYSIS

Assessing costs and benefits is not an exact science. A fundamental problem is that it is not easy to measure each benefit and cost accurately. Even where the benefits and costs are quantifiable, the figures used are only based on an estimate predicting several years into the future. This section describes how cost–benefit analysis occurs at the start of a project to implement a new information system. (Note that cost–benefit

analyses are also conducted when trying to determine a company's strategic IS investments. These are described in Chapter 14.)

All feasibility assessments for information systems development should include a cost–benefit analysis. Although this may seem obvious, some companies miss out this stage because other factors are driving the development. For example, it is currently difficult for a retailer to cost-justify establishing an Internet store (*see* the case study of Tesco in Chapter 17). The cost of setup and maintenance is likely to be greater than the revenue achieved through increased sales. The marketing manager may, however, want to proceed with such a strategic initiative to gain experience aimed at ensuring success in the future when this form of channel becomes more widely used.

Tangible costs

A measure of cost can be calculated for each tangible cost.

Intangible costs

A monetary value cannot be placed on an intangible cost.

Tangible benefits

A definite measure of improvement can be calculated for each tangible benefit.

Intangible benefits

It is not possible to measure an intangible benefit.

The business analyst undertaking a cost–benefit analysis will identify both **tangible and intangible costs and benefits**. When a cost or benefit is tangible, it is possible to set a definite numeric value against an item such as the cost of installing a new network. It is not possible to place a numeric value on intangible costs and benefits. Note that for some factors it may be difficult to establish whether the benefit is tangible or intangible. For example, although it is difficult to measure the benefit of general improvements in data quality, it would be possible to measure specific aspects of quality such as the time the new system takes to deliver information to the users.

Tangible costs are a measure of cost can be calculated for each tangible cost. For example, the purchase price of new hardware needed to run new software is a tangible cost. For intangible costs a monetary value cannot be placed on an intangible cost. The disruption and possible user resistance that will occur due to implementing a new system will have an effect on overall company performance, but they are difficult to measure.

A definite measure of improvement can be calculated for each tangible benefit. A reduction in customer waiting time in a bank due to a new information system is an example of a tangible benefit. For intangible benefits it is not possible to measure an intangible benefit. For example, the improved decision making capability provided by a decision support system would be difficult to cost.

▶ Assessing costs

A range of costs must be included in the feasibility study. These include:

◆ hardware and software purchase costs;

◆ software development costs if a bespoke or tailored solution is chosen;

◆ installation costs including cabling, physically moving equipment and bringing in new furniture to house the computers;

◆ migration costs such as transferring data from an existing system to the new system or running the new and original systems in parallel until the reliability of the new system is established;

◆ operating costs including maintenance costs of hardware such as replacing parts or upgrading to new versions of software. Staff costs in maintaining the hardware and software and troubleshooting any problems must also be factored in. Operating costs may also include an environmental audit of the amount of energy and consumables used;

◆ training costs;

Assess where each of the following examples of costs and benefits should lie in the grid below:

- Software purchase cost
- User resistance
- Reduction in working hours
- Improved decision making
- Hardware purchase cost
- New working practices
- Sales increase
- Broader planning horizons
- Implementation costs
- Disruption during implementation

- Training costs
- Reduction in customer complaints
- Better data integration
- Reduction in maintenance costs
- Better data quality
- Hardware and software maintenance and consumable costs
- Reduction in inventory levels
- Better cash flow

ACTIVITY

| Costs | | Benefits | |
Tangible	Intangible	Tangible	Intangible

◆ wider organisational costs, for example redundancy payments may need to be made if computerisation leads to loss of jobs.

Note that these costs include not only the initial cost of purchase, but also the ongoing maintenance cost. These are considerable for information systems and will often exceed the initial cost of purchase.

It is worth noting that there is a growing realisation that the cost of ownership of a software or hardware product is potentially much higher than the purchase cost. This is mainly due to the cost of troubleshooting software bugs and hardware faults, phone support, installing upgrades and paying for support and/or upgrades from the vendor. Gartner Group figures show that the cost of ownership for a PC may be as high as $8000 per year, reducing to $2000 per year for a simpler thin client such as a network computer. The cost of ownership of your selected software/hardware combination should obviously also be factored in to your cost–benefit analysis. The cost of training and education and documentation of staff should also be included with standard development costs of paying analysts and programmers. Total cost of ownership is described further in Chapter 16.

▶ Assessing benefits

While information systems costs are relatively easy to identify, the benefits are harder to quantify since they are often intangible and will occur in the future. Benefits from a new system can be considered in terms of improvements to business processes and the quality of information used to support these processes. Common benefits include reduced costs of operating processes and greater efficiency leading to faster completion of tasks such as serving a customer. Of course, these benefits are included in the reasons for initiating projects referred to on page 280.

Parker and Benson (1988) recommend a structured approach to identifying tangible benefits. This involves considering the cost of performing a business process *before* introduction of a new system and comparing this to the cost *after* implementation. Costs may include staff time, materials and equipment. This result will indicate either a tangible benefit through cost reduction or an added cost of using the new system.

Intangible benefits will include improvements to the quality of information as described in Chapter 1. A new information system should enable information quality to be improved in some of the following ways:

◆ improved accuracy;

◆ improved availability and timeliness;

◆ improved usability (easier to understand and then act on information);

◆ improved utilisation;

◆ improved security of information.

▶ Using financial measures to assess the viability of a new system

The balance between costs and benefits can be considered using a variety of financial measurements. These techniques may be familiar from the study of accounting, since these measures can be applied to the assessment of the return on any investment. The techniques are reviewed briefly here and the reader is referred to an accounting text or the coverage in Robson (1997).

Once the costs and benefits have been identified and quantified, it is normal to calculate their value in present-day monetary terms since the costs and benefits will be incurred in the future. This is achieved through using a discounted cashflow calculation such as net present value or internal rate of return. In this the future benefits are discounted assuming a fixed or variable level of interest rate. These techniques are described in Robson (1997) and measurement of costs and benefits is described in more detail in Remenyi (1995).

Return on investment (RoI)

An indication of the returns provided by an IS. Calculated by dividing the benefit by the amount of investment. Expressed as a percentage.

Return on investment (RoI)

This is the simplest measure and it is widely used in IS feasibility assessments. The RoI is calculated by dividing the benefit by the investment amount and is expressed as a percentage:

$$RoI = 100 * \frac{Benefit...value}{Investment...value}$$

Benefit value = (Return − Cost)

The Gartner Group suggests that a RoI of more than twice the current cost of borrowing is usually viable. Currently RoIs of 20 per cent or more are usually viable (this is of course dependent on the prevailing interest rate).

Although this appears to be a simple measure that is easy to calculate, there is no standard of how it is applied over the duration of the investment. To counter this, Robson (1997) suggests that the RoI should be calculated using the annual benefit value. Analysts such as the Gartner Group calculate the RoI over an arbitrary four-year period, while others calculate it over the expected lifetime of the project.

Net present value (NPV)

A further problem with the RoI measure is that it is often (but not always) calculated without considering how the future value varies through time. For the calculation to be meaningful, the future value should be discounted so that it is expressed in terms of its value today. This is known as a discounted cashflow (DCF). The NPV can be calculated with a standard spreadsheet function:

$$NPV = \sum_{i=1,n} \frac{Value^i}{(1 + rate)^n}$$

Value = cashflows, starting with investment as negative cashflow.
n = number of periods (usually years).
Rate = company cost of capital (discount rate).

If the NPV is positive, the estimate suggests that the company will achieve a return and it may decide to invest. A NPV which is negative suggests no return on the investment and the project is unlikely to go ahead.

Internal rate of return (IRR)

IRR is also a discounted cashflow technique, considering the NPV from a different perspective. The IRR calculation yields the *interest rate that will produce an NPV of zero*. Robson suggests that this method can be used to compare different potential projects. Project A with an IRR of 15 per cent is more favourable than Project B with an IRR of 5 per cent. In this example, 10 per cent might be set as the cutoff rate for feasible projects.

Payback period

This metric is also usually considered together with ROI, NPV and IRR, since it provides additional information not available in these other measures. The payback period is the period in which, after the initial investment, the company has not achieved a net benefit. This is apparent from Fig 8.2, which shows through the dashed curve that it will be after the benefits start accruing that the payback will be achieved. Information systems often have payback periods of the order of several years, when the initial development and investment may take over a year. Two alternatives may have a similar RoI or NPV, but one project could have a much shorter payback period, so it is important to use a combination of the methods covered here.

Before leaving this topic, it should be noted that the measures reviewed are purely financial and should not be used in isolation. It is important to consider other factors, such as the intangible benefits and the risks expected for the different alternatives. Parker and Benson (1988) coined the term 'information economics', which provides a methodology for evaluating these other factors.

Net present value (NPV)

A measure of the return from a system which takes into account the variation in monetary value through time.

Internal rate of return (IRR)

A discounted cashflow technique used to assess the return of a project by considering the interest rate which would produce an NPV of zero.

Payback period

The period, after the initial investment before the company achieves a net benefit.

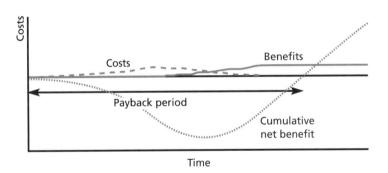

Fig 8.2 Graph showing the relationship between systems development cost and benefit value through time and their effect on cumulative net benefit

▶ Different types of feasibility

As well as considering the costs and benefits of a project, the feasibility study will also consider other aspects of feasibility. These factors will usually be reviewed for each of the possible solutions that have been proposed. The alternative solutions may be from different hardware or software vendors, or they may be different technical solutions that have been proposed.

The different aspects of feasibility are commonly referred to as economic, technical, operational and organisational.

Economic feasibility

Economic feasibility

An assessment of the costs and benefits of different solutions to select that which gives the best value. (Will the new system cost more than the expected benefits?)

Economic feasibility describes the analysis of the different costs and benefits of implementing the new system, as described above.

Economic feasibility. An assessment of the costs and benefits of different solutions to select the one that gives the best value. (Will the new system cost more than the expected benefits?)

Technical feasibility

Technical feasibility

Evaluates to what degree the proposed solutions will work as required and whether the right people and tools are available to implement the solution. (Will it work?)

Technical feasibility refers to the analysis of possible technical problems in the different solutions and who is appropriate to solve them. Technical feasibility can involve asking a series of questions to determine whether a computer system is the right tool for solving a problem. Some tasks may only be conducted using a human operator. The types of questions which are asked are:

◆ Can the system deliver the performance required? For example, a transaction processing system such as a national lottery must be able to deliver thousands of transactions a second.

◆ Can the system support the type of decision making required (particularly support for semi- or unstructured decisions)?

◆ Does the system deliver the necessary level of security?

A technical feasibility assessment will aim to determine whether the proposed solution will work at all. In some cases, such as for an accounting system, there will be an obvious product which will fulfil the outline requirements. In others, such as for a specialised manufacturing facility, a fairly detailed analysis of requirements and a high-level design of the system may be necessary to assess alternatives before it is possible to decide on the feasibility. If this is the case then the initiation stage will be protracted and costly.

Sometimes the technical feasibility will be assessed for different levels of expenditure and according to the skills of staff available to work on the system. A problem that is impossible using basic tools may become possible if a more expensive solution is chosen using outside consultants to implement it. Of course, this decision is also related to economic feasibility.

Operational feasibility

Operational feasibility will review how the introduction of the new system will affect working practices on a day-to-day basis. For example, detailed estimates will be made of whether the system usability and response times are sufficient for the expected volume of customer transactions. At this stage, a check will be made as to whether the proposed system will be able to deliver the features and functions required.

Operational feasibility

An assessment of how the new system will affect the daily working practices within the organisation. (Is the system workable on a day-to-day basis?)

Organisational feasibility

Organisational feasibility considers how closely the solution matches the needs of the organisation and identifies problems that may arise in this area. Organisational feasibility will involve a review of how the potential users' skill sets and attitudes will affect the system. Problems may include resistance to change from end-users, particularly those who don't have experience of using computer systems. If resistance to change from staff is anticipated, then steps should be taken to ensure that this does not happen. Such measures include training and educating staff by explaining why the system is being introduced (Chapter 13). If potential users are not familiar with using computers, then training must occur.

How a system affects the responsibilities and power of different functional parts of the organisation may also be included. A new system may well affect the communication channels and control mechanisms within an organisation and any detrimental effects on these should be established.

Organisational feasibility will also assess how well the proposed system fits in with the company's overall business and IS strategy. This may involve portfolio analysis – considering the purchase in relation to the four main investment categories for information systems that provide a framework within which the strategic value of the investment to the company can be placed. It is useful to identify in which category a new system lies in order to assess its importance and allocate resources to it accordingly. The investment categories are: strategic systems, key operational systems, support systems and high-potential projects. These are described in Chapter 14.

Note that since operational and organisational feasibility are not technical factors, they are sometimes ignored, which can cause a failure in implementation of what is a technically sound solution.

Organisational feasibility

Reviews how well the solution meets the needs of the business and anticipates problems such as hostility to the system if insufficient training occurs. (Considers the effect of change given a company's culture and politics.)

ACTIVITY

> ## Lascelles Fine Foods
>
> This activity is based on the case study in the last chapter where acquisition alternatives were considered for this company.
>
> Produce a feasibility analysis of the alternative methods of acquiring application software as they relate to LFFL. You should pay particular attention to the operational, organisational, economic and technical feasibility of each one. You should conclude with a recommendation on how LFFL should best proceed to the next phase of the information systems acquisition process.

▶ Risk management

Risk management

Risk management aims to anticipate the future risks of an information systems project and to put in place measures to counter or eliminate these risks.

Risk assessment can be used at the start of a project to determine the level of risk and develop plans for reducing this risk. **Risk management** involves the following stages:

1 Identify risks, including their probabilities and impacts.

2 Identify possible solutions to these risks.

3 Implement the solutions, targeting the highest-impact, most likely risks.

Risk assessment has been considered in detail by Boehm (1991). Boehm views risk identification as listing possible factors which might jeopardize a project's success.

Risks can be placed into six broad categories, according to Ward and Griffiths (1996). These can be used as a framework for identifying risk within a project. Each will have a different impact depending on the nature of the system being developed.

1 *Project size.* A large, complex project will be more difficult to manage and complete on time than a small one; this will be owing to its having a larger number of individual tasks and interdependencies within the project and the need to have more individuals working on the project (thus increasing the level of coordination required). In addition, with a large project there is more to be lost if the project fails since it is expected to deliver major business benefits (or it would never have been undertaken in the first place!).

2 *Project complexity.* Complexity may also cause the project to overrun. Note that although a project may be large, the business problem and/or the technology involved may be quite straightforward even in a large project. Complexity will be dependent on:

◆ the variety of business functions that are going to be affected (with implications for the organisational change management process);

◆ integration with other information systems (with implications for the technical change management process);

◆ technical complexity within the system itself (perhaps due to the need to use only recently developed technology that has not been used before within the organisation).

3 *People issues*. These relate to the extent to which senior management are committed to and involved in the project. The right blend of business and technical skills must be found and effective communication between business users and systems deliverers must occur. An example of risk in this category is whether there may be a skills shortage – programmers with the right skill set are not available and there is a lack of input from the end-users.

4 *Project control*. This refers to the rigour with which the time, cost and quality aspects of the project are controlled. Elements in this will include the setting of project milestones, IS/IT standards, systems development and project management methodologies, budgetary control and change management. A rigidly planned project may fail to accommodate unexpected changes, so flexibility is important. Risk will lie in the accuracy of the planning process and extent to which changes can be accommodated. Risks in this category are if sample data is unavailable or hardware ordered late. These may be the responsibility of others, but is still up to the project manager to make these things happen.

5 *Novelty*. If a large amount of business change is needed to allow the project to be implemented or the technical solution contains a great deal of innovation, the risks can become very high. A further potential risk to be aware of is the 'moving goalposts syndrome'– the business needs or the technologies to be used are changing so rapidly that the system may not deliver what is required. However, if the project under consideration is intended to deliver significant competitive advantage, it may be necessary to incur such risks. This is the common problem of the balance between risk and reward.

6 *Requirements stability*. The greater the degree of certainty (business and technical), the lower the level of risk associated with the project. A situation where requirements are fluid or hard to pin down means that the project will be harder to cost and the anticipated benefits harder match against those costs. In addition, a dynamic business environment may mean that fundamental business needs change relatively quickly and this will be reflected in changing systems requirements.

In summary, risk assessment will involve balancing the risks and costs likely to be incurred against the likely business benefits. Ward and Griffiths (1996) provide a summary of techniques to help balance risks against benefits.

► ACQUISITION CHOICES AND METHODS

Part of the feasibility stage is to decide on the method of acquisition. This will usually occur after the need and requirements for the system have been established. The make-or-buy decision will occur, and different suppliers of either off-the-shelf or bespoke solutions will be evaluated, as has been described in Chapter 7. The economic, technical and operational feasibility will be evaluated for each of the suppliers after a tender or request for proposals has been sent out to the suppliers. If a company decides to use a third party to develop its information systems or provide other IS services, this is known as outsourcing. This is usually a strategic initiative which involves the outsourcing company in developing more than one system. The merits of this method of systems acquisition is described in detail in Chapter 14.

▶ Summarising system requirements

Request for proposals (RFP)

A specification drawn up to assist in selecting the supplier and software.

If we decide to go ahead after the initial feasibility study, the next stage for a major implementation for a large organisation will be to issue an invitation to tender document or request for proposals – an RFP. The RFP is a specification drawn up to assist in selecting the supplier and software. An example structure of an RFP is shown in the box 'standard request for proposals'. The purchaser will fill in the first four sections and different vendors fill in the last two sections. For a smaller company or system, alternative suppliers will also need to be assessed, but the effort spent on selection will be scaled down.

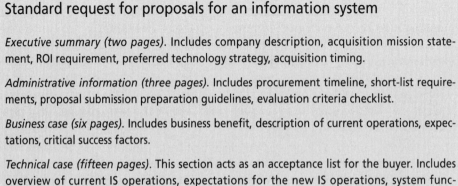

Standard request for proposals for an information system

Executive summary (two pages). Includes company description, acquisition mission statement, ROI requirement, preferred technology strategy, acquisition timing.

Administrative information (three pages). Includes procurement timeline, short-list requirements, proposal submission preparation guidelines, evaluation criteria checklist.

Business case (six pages). Includes business benefit, description of current operations, expectations, critical success factors.

Technical case (fifteen pages). This section acts as an acceptance list for the buyer. Includes overview of current IS operations, expectations for the new IS operations, system functional specs, expected system response time, document management requirements, integration requirements, exception handling, hardware requirements, software requirements, mass storage specifications.

Management (three pages). Can be reserved for short-list vendors to complete. Includes system acceptance criteria; project management plan; site preparation plan; training plan and schedule; delivery and installation plan and schedule; systems maintenance plan; documentation (description and pricing); qualification and experience (number of installations etc.); customer references; financial report.

Agreement (one page). Asks for vendor's pricing breakdown, itemised by definitions, so you can easily compare vendor to vendor.

FOCUS ON

▶ TECHNIQUES FOR MAKING PRODUCT COMPARISONS

When purchasing a system, structured decision making is required to ensure that the best option is selected. Three simple methods for making product or supplier decisions are given below.

▶ Feature checklist – first-cut exclusion

Use this initially to exclude products that are perhaps missing a key function or do not support the operating system you use. The humble feature checklist is the most easily applied and useful tool. This is much abused by marketeers who use it selectively, perhaps missing out one of the main contenders or features for which their product does not rank well. If you use your own checklist or one drawn up by one of the industry magazines such as *Byte*, *Datamation* or *PC Magazine*, then they are a good, reliable guide. The case study shows a typical checklist which would be available in one of these magazines comparing three off-the-shelf software products.

MINI CASE

Feature checklist for comparing three different groupware products

Three products are compared according to

◆ features provided;
◆ operating systems supported for the server platform;
◆ operating systems supported for the client (end) user.

These systems are compared using Table 8.3. Price for different options could also be shown in a table such as this, together with more detailed features, such as does the e-mail have an address book for the whole company or does it support file attachments?

From inspection of the table, it can be seen that Product A and Product C fulfil most of the criteria. Product B would be unsuitable for a company that had a range of existing computers running different operating systems. Since Products A and B are similar and cannot be distinguished using this table, a more detailed evaluation of these two could then occur after excluding Product B. A different example of a more detailed evaluation for a business system is described below.

Table 8.3 Feature comparison

Criteria	Product A	Product B	Product C
Server platforms			
Windows NT	Yes	Yes	Yes
Novell Netware	Yes	No	Yes
OS/2	Yes	No	Yes
Sun Solaris (UNIX)	Yes	No	No
Client platforms			
Windows 95	Yes	No	Yes
Windows 3.1	Yes	Yes	Yes
OS/2	Yes	No	Yes
Features			
E-mail	Yes	Yes	Yes
Scheduling	Yes	No	Yes
Document management	Yes	No	Yes
Internet access	Yes	No	Yes

Sources: http://www.byte.com, www.datamation.com, www.pcmag.com

▶ Feature checklist – detailed ranking

The main deficiency of simple checklists is that they do not attach relative importance to features. To extend them, give each feature a weighting of, say, between 0 and 100 points for each factor and then add up the scores for the different products. The mini case study shows a detailed analysis using a range of factors to decide on which supplier to use.

MINI CASE

Detailed weighted analysis of three products for managing a large vehicle fleet

Table 8.4 shows a real analysis for three products from different suppliers that were compared across many factors to establish which was most suitable. This type of detailed analysis is usually conducted when a new system costs tens or hundreds of thousands of pounds. The grand total shows that Supplier 3 is the clear winner and this is the project which was chosen and successfully implemented.

Table 8.4 Detailed weighted analysis

Decision criteria	Weighting factor	Supplier 1 Score	Supplier 2 Score	Supplier 3 Score
A Individual module functionality (summary)				
Fleet maintenance job control	100	80	86	98
Schedule of rates	100	79	84	85
Stores/purchasing	100	72	71	86
Subtotal	**300**	**231**	**241**	**269**
General functionality				
Fully integrated core modules	100	60	60	60
Integrated job ticket and stores	100	30	40	80
Data maintained online	80	56	56	56
Flexibility to accommodate SOR	80	40	40	68
Data take-on from existing systems	80	64	64	64
Powerful *ad hoc* reporting	70	28	56	56
Performance monitoring	60	30	36	42
Links to office automation systems	60	42	42	42
Interface with financial ledger	60	32	40	42
Training manuals and documentation	60	30	36	36
Subtotal	**750**	**412**	**470**	**576**
B Technical considerations				
Effective data security procedures	80	56	56	56
Runs in an open environment	80	56	56	56
Ease of use and performance	80	48	48	56
Subtotal	**240**	**160**	**160**	**168**
C Other considerations				
Financial considerations	60	36	48	54
Support maintenance	60	36	30	42
Local government user base	50	30	30	30
Confidence in supplier	50	25	25	35
Subtotal	**220**	**127**	**133**	**161**
Grand total	**1510**	**930**	**1004**	**1174**

▶ Final selection using benchmarking

Once you have narrowed down your selection of software using feature checklists to two or three contenders, a number of possibilities are available to make the final decision. These can be quite costly for both purchaser and supplier. First, it is possible to benchmark against other organisations who are performing similar tasks to you – what are their experiences, what performance is the software achieving, are they an independent reference site?

Second, if it is a large order, you can ask the suppliers to provide the software and test important functions using example process scenarios from your company. Table 8.5 gives some example business scenarios for using a groupware product.

Table 8.5 Five example scenarios for selecting a software package

Function to test	Scenario
1 Administration. Add new user.	How readily can a new user be added to system or their personal details changed? How easy to set up the client (end-user) PC?
2 All staff or workgroup e-mail broadcast.	How easy is it to set up a list of all staff, or those in a workgroup you need to e-mail and then reuse?
3 Create a new document using a structured form giving name of company, attendees, date of meeting and report of meeting	A report database containing a summary of all meetings with a key client needs to be updated by a sales person.
4 Circulate minutes of meeting to participants.	How easy is this to achieve?
5 Information query and retrieval.	You have your customer contacts stored in a groupware system. A customer rings reporting a problem with their sales person. How quick is it to find the customer and sales person and retrieve the information required?

▶ Which factors should be used when selecting software?

When comparing software, cost is an obvious constraint on any purchase, but since this is often a fixed constraint we will be looking here at the technical merits of products and how they vary. (You will note from the case study in the previous section that financial considerations were given a relatively low priority, presumably since each product was of a similar cost.) Eight key factors in deciding on software are shown in the box.

Eight key factors in selecting software

1 *Functionality*. Does the software have the features described to support the business requirements?

2 *Ease of use*. For both end-users and initial setup and administration.

3 *Performance*. For different functions such as data retrieval and screen display. If used in a customer-facing situation, this will be a critical factor.

4 *Compatibility or interoperability*. How well does your solution integrate with other products? This includes what you are using now and what you will be using based on your strategic direction.

5 *Security*. This includes how easy it is to set up access control for different users and the physical robustness of methods for restricting access to information.

6 *Stability or reliability of product*. Early versions of products often have bugs and you will experience a great deal of downtime and support calls, hence the saying 'never buy one dot zero' (Version 1.0).

7 *Prospects for long-term support of product*. If the vendor company is small or likely to be taken over by a predator, will the product exist in three years' time? Is the company responsive in issuing patches and new features for the product? Is the company forming strategic alliances with other key vendors which will improve the product's features and interoperability?

8 *Extensibility*. Will the product grow? Are the features available to accommodate your future needs? Are the features available in the initial purchase or will you have to integrate with software from another vendor? As a rule of thumb, it is best if you can single-source software, or use as few vendors as possible: the system will have greater reliability than making different modules interoperate.

Functionality

A term used to describe whether software has the features necessary to support the business requirements?

Compatibility

Software compatibility defines whether one type of software will work with another. For example, will a word processor run in Windows 3.1 or Windows 95. Data compatibility defines whether data can be exported from one package and imported for use into another. For example can a word-processor file from one package be used in another?

Interoperability

A general term used to describe how easily different components of a system can be integrated.

▶ Assessing products from different suppliers

Some businesses make the mistake of limiting an assessment of new software to its technical merits or features. This is unwise, since software purchase is a long-term commitment and a company is reliant on the support provided by the vendor. A small, 'startup' company may provide a good range of features in its products, but it is likely to have fewer staff responsible for ensuring quality of the software and providing aftersales support.

In an article in *Computing* (8 May 1988), Simon Rigden, general manager of ERP specialist JD Edwards, claimed:

> People need to move away from ticklists and start looking more closely at the credibility of the vendor.

The article also suggested that many companies take too long in deciding because they evaluate too many suppliers. Some should be excluded early on, based on basic criteria such as their track record or financial stability. A survey of 200 UK companies by consultants Tate Bramald showed that three-quarters listed up to eight vendors and half of them then spend more than six months deciding.

A further risk is that the vendor may fail or be taken over by a larger company and no support or upgrade versions will be available. A classification of companies and their products which recognises the variation in suppliers is shown in the box on the Gartner Group.

▶ Contract negotiation

An appropriate contract is vital when outsourcing to a third party systems development or any information systems function. This may include custom or bespoke software, amendments to off-the-shelf software and outsourcing/facilities management (FM). In essence, contracts define which activities should happen and when, and who is reponsible for them. For example, the supplier should deliver prototype 1 by 1 October, and review should be completed by 28 November. Both the customer and the suppliers benefit from a reduced risk of failure.

The value of having a well-defined contract is illustrated by failures that have occurred when they are not in place. For example, the UK police terminated a fingerprint system development after two years in development, claiming £10 million in costs. The supplier IBM then counter-claimed £19 million on the basis of the client not making their requirements clear. A protracted legal battle followed before agreement was reached.

Contracts should define the following main parameters:

1 Business requirements and features of system.

2 Deliverables such as hardware, software and documentation.

3 Timescales and milestones for different modules.

4 How the project is managed.

5 Division of responsibilities between different suppliers and the customer.

6 Costs and method of payment.

7 Long-term support of system.

Contracts are particularly difficult to establish for information systems projects for the following reasons:

◆ It is difficult to specify the requirements in detail at the outset of the project when the contract is signed. Varying functional requirements can lead to project overruns.

◆ Establishing acceptable performance at the outset is difficult because this depends on the combination of hardware and software.

◆ Many different suppliers are involved and it is often not clear where responsibilities for fixing problems may lie.

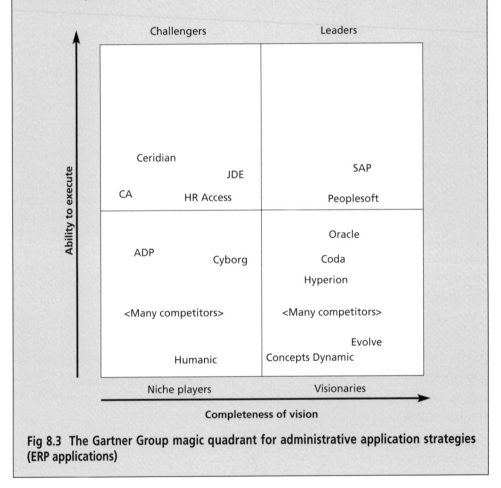

The Gartner Group magic quadrant

The Gartner Group conducts assessment of different products and bases this both on technical evaluation of the products and assessment of the support provided by their producers. Figure 8.3 shows its 'magic quadrant', which categorises suppliers according to their ability to execute (based on financial soundness, management, customer support, marketing and product delivery) and their vision or strategic development plans. It can be seen that SAP and Peoplesoft are the leaders, since they are large, sound companies which operate in a range of industries. JDE, for example, is a challenger since, although it is a large company that is able to execute, it tends to operate in the financial services and engineering industries, although it is diversifying. The ERP packages shown in the grid are discussed in more detail in Chapter 19.

Fig 8.3 The Gartner Group magic quadrant for administrative application strategies (ERP applications)

◆ After the project is finished, critical errors can potentially occur and a support contract is required to ensure that they are remedied rapidly.

◆ If a supplier's business fails, the system may be unmaintainable without the software program, which may need to be put into safekeeping with a third party in a source code escrow agreement.

▶ Contents of a typical IS product contract

A typical contract will be made up of the following sections or schedules, as well as general clauses on confidentiality, intellectual property (who owns the rights to the software), indemnity, law and jurisdiction.

Schedule 1 Product specification and acceptance

This is usually the most involved section, since it will detail the features of the software and acceptance criteria. These will include the completion of all key features with an acceptable level of error and ensure that functions such as reporting occur rapidly enough.

Schedule 2 Input to project from client

This information is sometimes omitted since most activities are conducted by the provider. The activities essential to the completion of the project may include time for writing and reviewing requirements and prototypes; time for user acceptance testing (UAT); time for training; supply of test data; possibly supply of hardware and systems software (if purchased by buying department of company); support from internal IS function and project management.

Schedule 3 Services to be supplied by contractor

Each deliverable should be linked to a milestone and payment to help avoid slippage in the project. Milestones should include deliverables from both client and supplier. Frequent monthly milestones should be set.

Schedule 4 Support of system and warranty

A service-level agreement should state how problems are escalated between suppliers and define acceptable times for response according to the severity of the problem. The fault-logging system and contact points such as a helpdesk may also be defined.

Schedule 5 Project plan

An outline project plan showing key deliverables and milestones should be part of the contract. Responsibility for project management will be identified for both parties and regular meetings defined.

Schedule 6 Payment method

The two main methods of payment are fixed price, which tends to be favoured by the client since it has better visibility of costs, and time and materials, which is usually preferred by the supplier. Timing of payments should be tied into milestones (when they are known as phased payments). Suppliers may prefer regular monthly payments. Penalty clauses or liquidated damages may be stipulated where the supplier loses part of its payment if it delivers it late or risk and reward clauses which provide financial incentives if it delivers early.

CASE STUDY: TOPIC AREA

Blue Circle assesses alternative Enterprise Resource Planning Systems

Industrial giant Blue Circle Industries is taking its first steps towards creating a single pan-European IT and business infrastructure, with a £4.6 million investment in Enterprise Resource Planning (ERP).

Yet despite the importance of the project, its Swedish supplier, Intentia, is virtually unknown in the UK. Blue Circle Industries (BCI) IT director Roger Ellis says that until last year he'd never heard of the company.

So what persuaded one of the UK's leading industrial conglomerates to invest in Intentia's Movex suite and, in the process, to put critical business systems for its heating and boiler manufacturing divisions into the hands of a low-profile ERP supplier?

Ellis says that Intentia's commitment to BCI's business plan was crucial: 'Intentia may not be the largest or best-known of the many vendors we reviewed, but it has grasped the business issues and has an unparalleled enthusiasm to work closely with us.'

Blue Circle's heating division comprises three companies in France, Germany and the UK: Finimetal, Broetgae and Potterton Myson. Acquired over a number of years, each company has its own IT infrastructure, a mixture of mainframes, Micro-VAX, Alpha and outsourcing services, none of which had previously communicated effectively.

'The main reason for investing in new software and hardware was to get these systems to talk to each other, making data sharing easier and more cost-effective,' says Ellis.

'The commercial rationale is to run the companies as pan-European centres of excellence, rather than autonomous business units.

'When we decided to change the business structure, it had a significant impact on IT, while the year 2000 issue was also a key element. We had to do something to make the systems compliant, more effective, and to achieve a lower cost of ownership.'

The change involves moving to the AS/400 platform with E 640 machines installed in the UK and Germany and an E 620 in France. Apart from the central servers, 24 9402-model AS/400s will be installed in each warehouse across Germany to deal with the demands of BCI's wholesale business.

'When our French subsidiary suggested Intentia as a supplier, I was sceptical,' admits Ellis. 'I felt it was fine for France, but had doubts about rolling the Movex suite across the rest of Europe. But we talked with Intentia, which has a high profile outside the UK, and decided to undertake a two-month review. The more I looked at the company, the more I liked it,' he adds.

Ellis acknowledges that choosing an ERP supplier isn't easy, especially as functionality is broadly similar across all suppliers. So what convinced him to take the Intentia route and install a raft of AS/400s?

'We were more concerned about getting the right product than focusing on a single platform. The only technical requirement was the ability to run under NT, now or in the near future,' says Ellis.

'In talks with Intentia, Baan and JD Edwards, we concluded that all three had very good products, but Intentia had the edge. It is big enough to engender confidence, but small enough to develop a close working relationship,' Ellis says.

Intentia took the initiative, according to Ellis. 'The other companies would have done the same things, but I would have had to get them to do it. For example, we said we wanted this to be a pan-European project, so each of Intentia's managing directors attended our discussion meetings.

'They all demonstrated top-level commitment to the pan-European aspect from the start. Bjorn Algkvist – Intentia's founder and chief executive – also took a personal interest in the deal and attended many meetings.'

Ellis says Intentia's track record of long-term client relationships and its accessible chief executive helped during contract negotiation.

'We got lots of detail into the contract and found that Intentia was very flexible,' he adds.

Intentia UK managing director Mike Nutter stresses that Intentia's contracts often run for '15 years or more'.

'Unlike many of our competitors, we don't have several partners per country or region. We focus on building a one-partner relationship per country, rather than working with a host of consultants and integrators,' says Nutter.

'Our business strategy is to invest in research and development, rather than high-profile marketing, and most of our business comes through recommendation. It's a different business model, but we now have over 4000 sites worldwide.'

Intentia's commitment to the project and the fact that it is undertaking all implementation and modification were other key factors in BCI's decision, says Ellis.

'They're not bringing in consultants or third-party integrators, and they're working directly with our project managers,' he adds.

BCI's French and German subsidiaries are installing Movex modules – logistics, production, finance, marketing, sales and personnel administration – and Intentia is customising the system for the German wholesale business.

The UK is installing everything except the sales module, preferring to keep its in-house sales system. Intentia will handle all system modifications, providing extra function for Potterton Myson's spares and services business.

Nutter makes no bones about the nature of an ERP installation: 'Customer resource is a real issue with ERP and when we put in one hour's work, we expect three or four hours' work from the customer. They must be committed, and that must come from the top. It's the customer's project, not ours.'

Costing ERP projects is always a thorny issue, and Ellis says that there was some hard negotiating by both parties. Nutter advocates target pricing rather than fixed pricing, arguing that benefits and penalties should be shared between the vendor and customer.

In BCI's case, Ellis explains that target pricing means that 'payment schedules are dependent on how well the product performs. We have agreed a pricing structure for the overall purchase and mandatory modifications in Germany, but local modifications and issues like training will be negotiated in situ.'

The sheer diversity of IT across BCI is a reflection of growth by acquisition. Until recently, BCI companies were autonomous units servicing their own markets.

The three national subsidiaries intend to collaborate much more closely, targeting the wider European market. To do this effectively, all subsidiaries must access each other's product lead times and schedules to create improved information flows for business efficiency and manufacturing.

The chief executive of the heating division, Frank McKay, was brought in to improve performance levels of the company. He says that a central theme of the restructuring programme is to 'secure superior cost, quality and service levels through greater integration of the companies'.

McKay adds: 'It is essential to meet European and global competition, and the creation of a single IT infrastructure is vital to support this integrated business approach.'

ERP systems are somewhat notorious for running late, and consultants stress that time spent detailing the project and defining its objectives in advance can save money further down the line.

Ellis says that the review and decision periods were not easy: 'We had the thankless and challenging task of building consensus across three countries. We spent a lot of time in discussion and arguments, which delayed us for about four or five months.

'What didn't help was that Intentia's competitors realised they probably weren't going to get the contract and attempted to spoil the deal, which created more debate.

'It's the first time BCI has undertaken a multinational project like this, and it was a complicated negotiating process, both internally and with Intentia and IBM.'

The review-to-decision process ran from May to October. 'Most of this was internal soul-searching characterised by robust debates and negotiations,' comments Ellis.

The French subsidiary kicked off implementation in November 1997. The UK and Germany subsidiaries aimed for a January 1998 start.

'It was a bad month to start,' says Ellis, 'because of year-end issues, and realistically it was February before we were very focused. It's still early days. Part of the system will be complete by the end of 1998, and the implementation should be finished by May 1999 at the latest, which allows us some time for slippage.'

BCI has established a pan-European steering group which will monitor and review the project. Ellis says: 'We have three levels of management and plan to build in a fourth. Apart from the steering group, each country has a full-time project manager, along with a part-time manager from Intentia. The monthly steering group meetings are attended by the main players from each company, including the managing and financial directors.

'We have local business co-ordinators with IBM and Intentia, so that if any issues need urgent attention, I can call the nominated contacts directly.

'The top-level management committee is not in place yet, but we plan to have senior review meetings every four months, attended by myself, our financial director and chief executive, and Intentia's chief executive. Hopefully, it will be no more than a rubber-stamp committee, but the point is that it's staffed by real heavyweights.'

Ellis says that he's hugely impressed by Intentia's software and its commitment to BCI's business. He would be 'very surprised' if the system were to fall down, but it's a business project and BCI has 'contractual clauses defining actions and responsibilities', Ellis adds.

The next phase in BCI's restructuring involves developing a wider communications strategy. Ellis says: 'We don't have dedicated lines between countries, but the UK has an extensive network built on our other business interests.

'We might look at using the Internet, but we're not ready to get into phase two yet, and we need to consider many issues before making any moves on the communications front,' adds Ellis.

ERP vendors have a poor reputation for delivering all their promises, but Ellis is pretty confident that Intentia software will deliver significant business benefits for BCI. He does, however, have one reservation: 'I wish Intentia would do more to get its name known in the UK.'

Source: *Computing*, 16 April 1998

Questions

1 Into which category of acquisition does Blue Circle fit?

2 Why did Blue Circle choose the Intentia solution rather than one of the better-known solutions?

3 What best practices can you identify for successful acquisition and implementation?

4 Can you identify any problems with this approach? Which source for the system would you have chosen if supplied with this information?

▶ SUMMARY

Stage summary: initiation

Purpose: Determine viability of systems and technique used to acquire it
Key activities: Feasibility study
Input: Idea for new system or problem with existing system
Output: Feasibility study, recommendation to proceed

The case study on Blue Circle illustrates the type of feasibility assessment that can occur when political factors are also considered during feasibility analysis. Other key points are:

1 The initiation phase is the first stage of the system development lifecycle.

2 The initiation phase is generally considered to consist of two main activities: the generation of the idea for a new system and assessing the feasibility of introducing a new system. Feasibility assessment should occur for all projects, whatever the acquisition method.

3 Feasibility assessment will involve comparing different alternatives in terms of their:
   ◆ economic feasibility – the cost–benefit analysis;
   ◆ technical feasibility – evaluation of the merits of different alternatives in terms of practicality;
   ◆ operational feasibility – will the system meet the needs of the business and end-users?
   ◆ organisational feasibility – do the staff have the skills to use the system and how will their attitudes affect the acceptance of the system?

4 There is a range of financial measures for assessing the financial viability of a new system. These should take into account the time-varying nature of costs and benefits by using discounted cashflow techniques. Non-financial measures should not be neglected.

5 A contract for the supply of the system should be negotiated at the outset which minimises the risk of project failure and provides adequate support for when the system becomes operational.

▶ EXERCISES

▶ Self-assessment exercises

1 What is the purpose of the initiation phase of a project?

2 What is meant by the terms 'intangible' and 'tangible benefit'?

3 Identify each of the following as tangible or intangible benefits or costs:
   (a) Purchase of a server for data storage with a new information system.
   (b) Reduced waiting time for customers when querying the progress of an order.
   (c) Disruption caused by installation of a new company network.
   (d) Reduced inventory holding period resulting from a new stock management system.

4 Summarise the differences between economic, operational, technical and organisational feasibility.

5 What do you understand by the term 'risk assessment' and how can it be applied to assist an information systems development project?

6 What is the purpose and outline contents of a 'request for proposal' or 'invitation to tender' document?

7 What are the key factors that a company will consider when choosing software from different suppliers?

8 What are the main items that should be specified in an information systems contract?

▶ Discussion questions

1 To what extent is the failure of many information system projects a consequence of too little time being spent on the initiation stage?

2 The techniques that are available for comparing different software packages or systems from different suppliers must be applied rigorously. Discuss.

▶ Essay questions

1 Examine the main consequences for an information systems project if the initiation stage is omitted.

2 A company is intending to purchase accounting software for 100 staff and is considering three different packages. It is currently using a Microsoft Windows 3.1-based application, but want to move to using a Microsoft Windows NT-based application. Give a full account of the factors it should consider when making the comparison. Which do you consider are the most important factors?

3 Risk assessment is a valuable tool for the project manager. What does this technique involve and which future risks might be identified at different stages in the software project?

▶ Examination questions

1 What is the purpose of establishing the following types of feasibility:
   (a) operational feasibility;
   (b) organisational feasibility;
   (c) technical feasibility;
   (d) economic feasibility.

2 Give three reasons for a company initiating an information systems project. Give a brief example of each.

3 Define information systems outsourcing.

4 Give examples of two tangible costs and two intangible costs that may be incurred during an information systems development project.

5 What are the most important factors you would consider when comparing different alternative software packages?

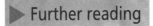 References

Boehm, B. (1991) 'Software risk management: principles and practices', *IEEE Software*, 8, 1, January, 32–41.

Parker, M. and Benson, R. (1988) *Information Economics: Linking Business Performance to Information Technology*, Prentice-Hall, Englewood Cliffs, NJ.

Remenyi, D. (1995) *The Effective Measurement and Management of IT Costs and Benefits*, Butterworth–Heinemann, Oxford.

Robson, W. (1997) *Strategic Management and Information Systems: an Integrated Approach*, Financial Times Pitman Publishing, London.

Senn, J. (1995) *Information Technology in Business Principles, Practices and Opportunities*, Prentice-Hall, Englewood Cliffs, NJ.

Strassmann, P.A. (1985) *The Information Payoff*, Free Press, New York.

Ward, J. and Griffiths, P.M. (1996) *Strategic Planning for Information Systems*, John Wiley, Chichester.

▶ Further reading

Sandison, H. (1992) 'Introduction to software development contracts', in Allen, D. and Davis, K. (eds) *Allen and Davis on Computer Contracting: a User's Guide with Forms and Strategies,* Prentice Hall.

Systems project management

INTRODUCTION

Projects

Projects are unique, one-time operations designed to accomplish a specific set of objectives in a limited timeframe.

Projects are unique, one-time operations designed to accomplish a specific set of objectives in a limited timeframe. Examples of projects include a building construction or introducing a new service or product to the market. In this chapter we focus on providing the technical knowledge that is necessary to manage information systems projects. Large information systems projects like construction projects may consist of many activities and must therefore be carefully planned and coordinated if a project is to meet cost, time and quality targets. The quality target is to implement the desired features with as few errors as possible.

Successful project management for information systems is very difficult to achieve. A recent extensive study reported by Bicknell (1998) has confirmed the parlous state of systems development projects. The US consultancy group Standish has analysed 23 000 projects of a range of sizes completed in 1997 and 1998 and found that:

◆ 28 per cent failed to complete

◆ 46 per cent were 'challenged' by cost and/or time overruns

◆ 26 per cent completed within the constraints of cost/time and delivering and anticipated benefits.

This clearly indicates a serious problem that shows the difficulty in IS project management and the need for effective project managers. On a more positive note it can be pointed out that this was an improvement compared to the survey in 1996 when failures ran at 40 per cent. This suggests that the situation can be improved when projects are managed competently.

The three key objectives of project management are shown in Fig 9.1. The job of project managers is difficult since they are under pressure to increase the quality of the

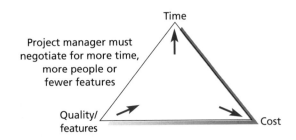

Fig 9.1 Three key elements of project management

information system within the constraints of fixed costs, budget and resources. Often it is necessary to make a compromise between the features that are implemented and the time and resources available – if the business user wants a particular new feature, then the cost and duration will increase or other features will have to be omitted.

While it is difficult to control and plan all aspects of an information systems development project, the chance of success can be increased by anticipating potential problems and by applying corrective strategies. The PRINCE methodology is reviewed since it is used to assist in the delivery of information systems projects to time, cost and quality objectives. Network analysis techniques are also reviewed in this chapter, since they can be used to assist project planning and control activities by enabling the effects of project changes to be analysed.

▶ Learning objectives

After reading this chapter, readers will be able to:

◆ understand the main elements of the project management approach;

◆ relate the concept of project management to the creation of information systems;

◆ understand the significance and tasks of the project manager;

◆ understand the main elements of the project management process;

◆ evaluate the PRINCE project management methodology;

◆ understand the main network analysis techniques and their benefits and limitations.

▶ Links to other chapters

The preparation of a preliminary project plan will occur during the initiation phase of a systems development project which was described in Chapter 8. After the project has been given the go-ahead, a more detailed project plan will be generated using the techniques described in this chapter.

The project plan will specify the activities and the resources needed to complete the subsequent stages of the project lifecycle. These are analysis (Chapter 11), design (Chapter 12) and build and implementation (Chapter 13).

▶ THE PROJECT MANAGEMENT PROCESS

When undertaking an information systems project, the project manager will be held responsible for delivery of the project to the traditional objectives of time, cost and quality. Many information system (IS) applications have the attributes of a large-scale project in that they consume a relatively large amount of resources, take a long time to complete and involve interactions between different parts of the organisation. To manage a project of this size and complexity requires a good overview of the status of the project in order to keep track of progress and anticipate problems. The use of a structured project management process can greatly improve the performance of IS projects, which have become well known for their tendency to run over budget or be late (Bicknell, 1996; Kaye, 1997; Mouler, 1996; Warren, 1996).

▶ Context: where in the SDLC does project planning occur?

Project managers need to control projects and to achieve this they tend to use frameworks based on previous projects they have managed. The systems development lifecycle (SDLC) or waterfall model introduced in Chapter 7 provides such a framework. The majority of project plans will divide the project plan according to the SDLC phases.

An *initial project plan* will usually be developed at the initiation phase (Chapter 8). This will usually be a high-level analysis which does not involve the detailed identification of the tasks that need to occur as part of the project. It may produce estimates for the number of weeks involved in each phase, such as analysis and design, and for the modules of the system, such as data entry and reporting modules. If the project receives the go-ahead, a more *detailed project plan* will be produced before or while the project starts. This will involve a much more detailed identification of all the tasks that need to occur. These will usually be measured to the nearest day or hour and can be used as the basis for controlling and managing the project. The detailed project plan will not be produced until after the project has commenced for two reasons:

1 It is not practical to assess the detailed project plan until the project starts, since the cost of producing a detailed project plan may be too high for it to be discarded if a project is unfeasible.

2 A detailed project plan cannot be produced until the analysis phase has started, since estimates are usually based on the amount of work needed at the design and build phases of a project. This estimate can only be produced *once the requirements for the system have been established at the analysis phase*.

These points are often not appreciated and, we believe, are a significant reason for the failure of projects. Project managers are often asked to produce an estimate of the amount of time required to finish a project at the analysis phase when insufficient information is at their disposal. Their answer should be:

> I can give you an initial estimate and project plan based on similar projects of this scale at the initiation phase. I cannot give you a detailed, accurate project plan until the analysis is complete and the needs of the users and the business have been assessed. A detailed estimate can then be produced according to the amount of time it is likely to take to implement the users' requirements.

▶ Why do projects fail?

Lytinen and Hirschheim (1987) researched the reasons for information systems projects failing. Unfortunately, the reasons remain common today. They identified five broad areas:

- *Technical failure* stemming from poor technical quality – this is the responsibility of the organisation's IS function.

- *Data failure* due to (a) poor data design, processing errors, and poor data management; and (b) poor user procedures and poor data quality control at the input stage. Responsibility for the former lies with the IS function, while that for the latter lies with the end-users themselves.

- *User failure* to use the system to its maximum capability – may be due to an unwillingness to train staff or user management failure to allow their staff full involvement in the systems development process.

- *Organisational failure*, where an individual system may work in its own right but fails to meet organisational needs as a whole (e.g. while a system might offer satisfactory operational information, it fails to provide usable management information). This results from senior management failure to align IS to overall organisational needs.

- *Failure in the business environment.* This can stem from systems that are inappropriate to the market environment, failure in IS not being adaptable to a changing business environment (often rapid change occurs), or a system not coping with the volume and speed of the underlying business transactions.

It is apparent that a diverse range of problems can cause projects to fail, ranging from technical problems to people management problems.

It is the responsibility of the project manager to ensure that these type of problems do not occur, by anticipating them and then taking the necessary actions to resolve them. This will involve risk management techniques, described in Chapter 8. The case study 'Falling at the final hurdle' shows the type of problems that occur, the reasons behind them and the attributes the project manager must possess to be able to manage projects successfully.

CASE STUDY: TOPIC AREA

Falling at the final hurdle

IT projects continue to run over time and over budget, resulting in systems that do not match business or end-user requirements, or stall before they are finished. The only possible fault one can call common to all failures is inadequate, to a greater or lesser extent, management of those projects. And that in turn means blame must be laid fairly and squarely on the shoulders of the project manager responsible. In mitigation, the design and implementation of IT systems is horrendously complicated, involving a highly complex matrix of technologies and business interdependencies, which are shifting at different rates across several management planes. But that is still no excuse for such failures. The reasons IT projects fail, to whatever extent, remain the same as always: the inability to specify user requirements, manage the number of requested changes, or limit the scope of change as the project progresses. There are many other issues behind failed projects, including in-house politics, deadline-centric cultures and new legislation emerging during the project.

Good project management, however, is about taking account of change up-front, and building in risk management and contingency planning buffers. It is about setting realistic duration and cost estimates, and not being afraid to tell the chief executive that his pet project cannot be finished in the six months he expects, even if being so honest puts your job at risk. Since none of this is rocket science, it begs the question as to why IT projects continue to fail. 'It's because there's too often a lack of an agreed requirements specification,' says Dennis Gower, a founding member of the Association of Project Managers. 'At least 50% of the time of the contract should be to find out precisely what users and departments require, it's that important.'

Anne Bentley, a business consultant with project management software house Artemis agrees: 'The actual specification of what's wanted by the department is often not concise or clear, which means costs won't be clear, estimated timescales will be out, and soon the whole thing goes wrong.' In addition, says John Pocock, commercial director at software implementation specialist Druid: 'A lot of the failure is down to the fact that users aren't fully aware of the change that the company has embarked upon on their behalf. Pressure on any project manager to change the scope is fierce, and while there may be formal change management processes in place, he can still get swamped.'

If that all sounds obvious, it is because the people explaining the issues are all project management professionals. Many of those managing end-to-end IT projects, however, are not. Not only that, but the companies they work for have no sense of project management on a corporate basis, spanning all business operations. This state of affairs is changing. With the onset of recession at the start of the decade, corporate minds were focused on monetary constraint and efficiency improvements in existing systems. The number of new projects lessened, and those that were given the go-ahead were, often for the first time, highly scrutinised from a non-IT perspective.

Focus was sharpened on professional project management skills, regardless of whether they came from outside the organisation through consultants, or through in-house training and development programmes. During the past three years, institutes and groups, such as the Association of Project Managers, have emerged. 'The use of project management hasn't been good in the past,' admits James Baker, responsible for setting up the BCS's project management group. 'But in the past five years there's been a dramatic upturn in training, qualifications

and attention to project control, and its role in organisations as a whole.'

Unfortunately, this trend has taken 30 years to arrive, with relatively recent disasters such as those at the Stock Exchange, the London Ambulance Service and British Gas still fresh in the mind. One of the key reasons for this, believes Baker, has been the huge divide between users and IT shops, the latter delivering what it thought the user required, and users naively expecting systems the IT department could not deliver. With IT systems now very much a business issue, adds Baker, those gaps may be closing, but there remain crucial issues regarding managing projects. 'There's an argument that technology always has a solution to technology problems, but you can't necessarily find solutions to people problems, the management of which accounts for perhaps 80% of successfully managed projects.'

If the right people are involved, the chances of success increase exponentially. But what constitutes an ideal project manager is debatable. To some, it is a combination of having a listening ear with the ability to rule with a rod of steel, while having the requisite project management skills. For others, such as long-time project manager Ervin Munir, now projects director with AMS, there is much emphasis on imperturbability. 'In some firms personal success is based on meeting dates, and if slippages are perceived, it leads to situations where the project manager is unwilling to tell the truth.' Munir relates an instance in his career, which has featured Currys, Dixons and Burger King, when he was given six months to complete a project which his own analysis showed would take a year. 'I had to decide whether to keep quiet or tell the truth,' he recalls. 'In the end I stuck to my guns, and the users were pleased with the final result. And that's what all project managers should be able to do.'

For Neil McEvoy, a director at consultancy Hyperion, a key attribute is the ability to manage expectations and balance resources and skills against those expectations. 'When things go wrong because business requirements change, that's when the real skill of project managers come in.' With more project management courses and certification schemes, the prospect of an improved UK base of skilled professionals seems certain. 'Certification', says McEvoy, 'can arm people with a basic toolkit. But most problems are about managing relationships, so all the training in the world will be of little use if the project manager has no instinctive feel for people.'

And there is more, adds Druid's Pocock: 'Project managers need to be methodical, but also intuitive and able to understand real issues. It's an art and a skill.' But UK organisations have shown historically that they are not particularly adept at mixing those attributes. At least with a growing body of professional project managers to call on, the prospects for doing so successfully are enhanced.
Source: Computer Weekly, 8 May 1997

Before the planning process can commence, the project manager will need to determine not only the business aims of the project but also the constraints under which they must achieve these aims. Major constraints include the overall budget for project development, the timescale for project completion, staffing availability, and hardware and software requirements for system development and running of the live system. These questions form the framework for the project and it is important that they are addressed at the beginning of the project planning process. It is usual, however, to only prepare detailed plans of the early stages of the project at this point.

The project management process includes the following main elements:

◆ estimate;

◆ schedule/plan;

◆ monitoring and control;

◆ documentation.

Estimation

Estimation allows the project manager to plan for the resources required for project execution through establishing the number and size of tasks that need to be completed in the project.

Work breakdown structure (WBS)

This is a breakdown of the project or a piece of work into its component parts (tasks).

Project constraints

Projects can be resource-constrained (limited by the type of people, monetary or hardware resources available) or time-constrained (limited by the deadline).

▶ Estimation

The first task in project management is to identify the activities involved in the project. **Estimation** allows the project manager to plan for the resources required for project execution through establishing the number and size of tasks that need to be completed in the project. This is achieved by breaking down the project repeatedly into smaller tasks until a manageable chunk of work of one to two days is defined. Each task is given its own cost, time and quality objectives. It is then essential that responsibility is assigned to achieving these objectives for each particular task. This procedure should produce a work breakdown structure (WBS) that shows the hierarchical relationship between the project tasks. **Work breakdown structure (WBS)**. A breakdown of each piece of work that needs to be done into its component parts. It is an important part of estimation. Figure 9.2 shows how the work on producing a new accounting system might be broken down into different tasks. Work on systems projects is usually broken down according to the different modules of the system. In this example, three levels of the WBS are shown for the accounts receivable module down to its printing function. All the other five modules of the system would also have similar tasks.

At the start of the project in the initiation or startup phase, an overview project plan is drawn up estimating the resources required to carry out the project. It is then possible to compare overall project requirements with available resources.

Projects can be **resource constrained** (limited by the type of people or hardware resources available) or **time constrained** (limited by the deadline).

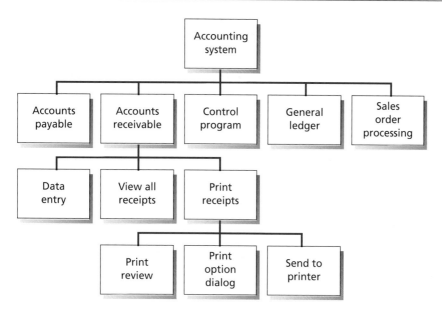

Fig 9.2 Work Breakdown Structure (WBS) for an accounting system

The next step, after the project has been given the go-ahead, is a more detailed estimate of the resources needed to undertake the tasks identified in the work breakdown structure. If highly specialised resources are required (e.g. skilled analysts), then the project completion date may have to be set to ensure that these resources are not overloaded. This is a **resource-constrained** approach. Alternatively, there may be a need to complete a project in a specific timeframe (e.g. due date specified by customer). In this case, alternative resources may have to be utilised (e.g. subcontractors) to ensure timely project completion. This is a time-constrained approach. This information can then be used to plan what resources are required and what activities should be undertaken over the lifecycle of the project.

Effort time and elapsed time

When estimating the amount of time a task will take, it is important to distinguish between two different types of time that need to be estimated. **Effort time** is the total amount of work that needs to occur to complete a task. The **elapsed time** indicates how long in time (such as calendar days) the task will take. Estimating starts by considering the amount of effort time that needs to be put in to complete each task. Effort time is then converted into elapsed time, which indicates how long the task will take through real-time measures such as months or days. Effort time does not usually equal elapsed time, since if a task has more than one worker the elapsed time will take less time than the effort time. Conversely, if workers on a task are also working on other projects, then they will not be available all the time and the elapsed time will be longer than the effort time. An additional factor is that different workers may have different speeds. A productive worker will need less elapsed time than an inexperienced worker. These constraints on elapsed time can be formalised in a simple equation:

Elapsed and effort time

Effort time is the total amount of work that needs to occur to complete a task. The elapsed time indicates how long in time (such as calendar days) the task will take (duration).

$$Elapsed\_time = Effort\_time * \frac{100}{Availability~\%} * \frac{100}{Work~rate~\%}$$

The equation indicates that if the availability or work rate of a worker is less than 100 per cent, the elapsed time will increase proportionally, since availability and work rate are the denominators on the right-hand side of the equation. The equation will need to be applied for each worker, who may have different availabilities and work rates. These factors can be entered into a project management package, but to understand the principles of estimation better the activity on project planning should be attempted (*see* page 314).

From the example in the activity, it can be seen that several stages are involved in estimation:

1 Estimate effort time for average person to undertake task.

2 Estimate different work rates and availability of staff.

3 Allocate resources (staff) to task.

4 Calculate elapsed time based on number of staff, availability and work rate.

5 Schedule task in relation to other tasks.

Yeates (1991) provides the following techniques for estimating the human resource and capacity requirements for the different stages of an IS project:

1 *Estimating the feasibility study*. This stage will not usually be estimated in detail, since it will occur at the same time or before a detailed project estimate is produced. The feasibility stage consists of tasks such as interviewing, writing up interview information and report writing in order to assess the financial, technical and organisational acceptability of the project. The estimate will depend greatly on the nature of the project, but also on the skills and experience of the staff involved. Thus it is important to keep records of previous performance of personnel for this activity in order to improve the accuracy of future estimates.

2 *Estimating analysis and design phases*. The analysis phase will typically involve collection of information about the operation of current systems and the specification of requirements for the new system. This will lead to the functional requirements specification, defining the new system in terms of its business specification. The design phase will specify the new computer-based system in terms of its technical content. This will need to take into account organisational policies on design methodologies and hardware and software platforms. In order to produce an accurate estimate of the analysis and design phases, it is necessary to produce a detailed description of each task involved. As in the feasibility stage, time estimates will be improved if timings are available for previous projects undertaken.

3 *Estimating build and implementation*. This stage covers the time and resources needed for the coding, testing and installation of the application. The time taken to produce a program will depend mainly on the number of coding statements required and the complexity of the program. The complexity of the coding will generally increase with the size of the program and will also differ for the type of application. A lookup table can be derived from experience that gives the estimated coding rate dependent on the complexity of the project for a particular development environment. This is discussed in more detail below.

Estimating tools

Statistical methods can be used when a project is large (and therefore complex) or novel. This allows the project team to replace a single estimate of duration with a range within which they are confident the real duration will lie. This is particularly useful for the early stage of the project when uncertainty is greatest. The PERT approach described later in this chapter allows optimistic, pessimistic and most likely times to be specified for each task, from which a probabilistic estimate of project completion time can be computed.

The most widely used economic model is the **constructive cost model (COCOMO)**, described by Boehm (1981) and first proposed by staff working at US consultancy Doty Associates. The Constructive cost model (COCOMO) model is used to estimate the amount of effort required to complete a project on the basis of the estimated number of lines of program code. Based on an analysis of software projects, the model attempts to predict the effort required to deliver a project based on input factors such as the skill level of staff. A simplified version of the model is given below.

Constructive cost model (COCOMO)

A model used to estimate the amount of effort required to complete a project on the basis of the estimated number of lines of program code.

$$WM = C * (KDSI)^K * EAF$$

where

WM = number of person months

C = one of three constant values dependent on development mode

KDSI = delivered source lines of code $\times$ 1000

K = one of three constant values dependent on development mode

EAF = effort adjustment factor

The three development modes or project types are categorised as organic (small development teams working in a familiar environment), embedded (where constraints are made by existing hardware or software) and semi-detached, which lies somewhere between the two extremes of organic and embedded. For a small project the equation is:

$$\text{person months} = 2.06 * (KLOC)^{1.047} * EAF$$

In order to increase the accuracy of the model, more detailed versions of COCOMO incorporate cost drivers such as the attributes of the end product and the project environment. The detailed version of the model calculates the cost drivers for the product design, detailed design, coding/unit test and integration/test phases separately.

These techniques may take a considerable amount of time to arrive at a reasonably accurate estimate of personnel time required. However, since the build phase will be a major part of the development budget, it is important to allocate time to undertake detailed estimation.

Function point analysis

A method of estimating the time it will take to build a system by counting up the number of functions and data inputs and outputs and then comparing to completed projects.

A problem with the COCOMO model is that the time estimates it produces are in turn dependent on an estimate of the number of lines of programming code to be written. To counter this problem, a method of estimating the number of lines of code was developed by Alan Albrecht of IBM (Albrecht and Gaffney, 1983). Function point analysis is based on counting the number of user functions the application will have. It is possible to do this in detail after the requirements for the application have been defined. The five user function categories are:

1 Number of external input types.

2 Number of external output types.

3 Number of logical internal file types.

4 Number of external interface file types.

5 External enquiry types.

Each of these types of input and output are then weighted according to their complexity and additional factors applied according to the complexity of processing. The function point estimate can be compared to the function point count of previous completed information systems to give an idea of the number of lines and code and length of time that are expected.

Note that both the COCOMO and function point analysis techniques were developed before the widespread use of applications with graphical user interfaces, interactive development environments for 'graphical programming', rapid applications development (RAD) and client/server databases to store information. These new techniques have made it faster to develop applications and the original data sets and principles on which these models are based have been updated to account for this.

ACTIVITY

Project planning exercise

The scenario

You are required to construct a project plan for the following information system development project. Your objective is to schedule the project to run in the shortest time possible. The plan should include all activities, the estimated, elapsed and effort time and who is to perform each activity. In addition, it is necessary to indicate the sequence in which all the tasks will take place. The programs can be scheduled in any order, but for each program the design stage must come first, followed by the programming and finally the documentation.

Within the context of the exercise, you can assume that the detailed systems analysis has already been carried out and that it is now necessary to perform the design, programming and documentation activities. For the purposes of this exercise, we will not include the testing and implementation phases.

Present your project plan in the form of a GANTT chart showing each task, the sequence in which tasks will be performed, the estimated effort and elapsed time and the resource allocated to each task.

The activities

There are five programs in the system. Each has a different level of difficulty:

◆ Program 1   Difficult
◆ Program 2   Easy
◆ Program 3   Moderate
◆ Program 4   Moderate
◆ Program 5   Difficult

For each level of difficulty, the design, programming and documentation tasks take different amounts of effort time:

Design
- ◆ Easy programs   1 day
- ◆ Moderate programs   2 days
- ◆ Difficult programs   4 days

Programming
- ◆ Easy programs   1 day
- ◆ Moderate programs   3 days
- ◆ Difficult programs   6 days

Documentation
- ◆ Easy programs   1 day
- ◆ Moderate programs   2 days
- ◆ Difficult programs   3 days

Resources

In order to complete the project plan, you need to know what resources you have available. For each resource, there are two variables:

- ◆ *Work rate*. This describes the speed at which the resource works (i.e. a work rate of 1.0 means that a task scheduled to take one day should only take one day to complete satisfactorily; a work rate of 1.5 means that a task scheduled for three days should only take two days etc.)

- ◆ *Availability*. Each resource will be available for certain amounts of time during the week. 100 per cent availability = 5 days per week, 50 per cent availability = 2.5 days per week etc.

In planning your project, work to units of half a day. For simplicity, any task which requires a fraction of half a day should be rounded up (e.g. 1.6 days should be rounded up to 2 days). Also, a resource can only be scheduled for one task at any one time!

Resource availability

System Designer 1 (SD1)
- ◆ Work rate   1.0
- ◆ Availability   100%

Systems Designer 2 (SD2)
- ◆ Work rate   1.5
- ◆ Availability   40%

Systems Designer 3 (SD3)
- ◆ Work rate   0.5
- ◆ Availability   50%

Programmer 1 (P1)
- ◆ Work rate   2.0
- ◆ Availability   40%

▶

Programmer 2 (P2)
◆ Work rate   1.0
◆ Availability   100%

Programmer 3 (P3)
◆ Work rate   0.5
◆ Availability   60%

Technical Author 1 (TAl) (to do the documentation)
◆ Work rate   1.0
◆ Availability   60%

Technical Author 2 (TA2)
◆ Work rate   0.5
◆ Availability   100%

Technical Author 3 (TA3)
◆ Work rate   2.0
◆ Availability   40%

Tips

1 This exercise will be easier if you structure the information well. You could do this by producing three matrices for the design, programming and documentation tasks. Each of them should show across the columns three different tasks for easy, moderate and difficult programs. Each row should indicate how long the different types of workers will take to complete the task.

2 To calculate the length of elapsed time for each cell in the matrix, it is easiest to use this relationship:

$$Elapsed\_time = Effort\_time* \frac{100}{Availability\%} * \frac{100}{Work\ rate\%}$$

3 A calculator may help!

4 When drawing the Gantt chart, you may want to put your best people on the most difficult tasks, as you would on a real project.

Scheduling

Scheduling involves determining when project activities should be executed. The finished schedule is termed the project plan.

Resource allocation

This activity involves assigning a resource to each task.

▶ Scheduling and planning

Scheduling is determining when project activities should be executed. The finished schedule is termed the project plan.

Resource allocation is part of scheduling. It involves assigning resources to each task. Once the activities have been identified and their resource requirements estimated, it is necessary to define their relationship to one another. There are some activities that can only begin when other activities have been completed. This is termed a serial relationship and is shown graphically in Fig 9.3.

The execution of other activities may be totally independent and thus they have a parallel relationship, as shown graphically in Fig 9.4. Here, after the design phase, three activities must occur in parallel before implementation can occur.

Figu 9.3 Serial relationship of activities

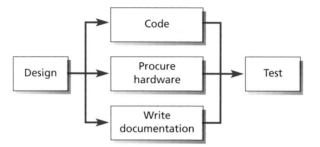

Fig 9.4 Parallel relationship of activities

For most significant projects there will be a range of alternative schedules which may meet the project objectives.

▶ Software for project management

For commercial projects, computer software will be used to assist in diagramming the relationship between activities and calculating network durations. From a critical path network and with the appropriate information, it is usually possible for the software automatically to generate Gantt charts, resource loading graphs and cost graphs, which are discussed later in the chapter.

Project management software, such as Microsoft Project, CA SuperProject and Hoskyns Project Manager Workbench, can be used to assist in choosing the most fea-

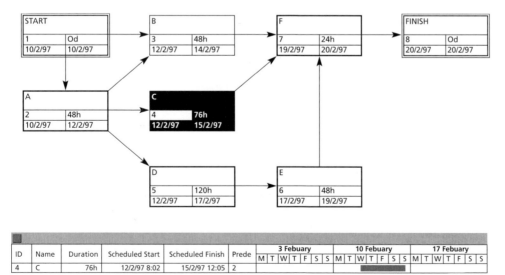

Fig 9.5 Network Chart generated by Microsoft Project

sible schedule by recalculating resource requirements and timings for each operation. The network analysis section of this chapter provides more information on project scheduling techniques.

A screen display for a Microsoft Project network chart is shown in Fig 9.5. This illustrates sequential activities such as from the START to activity A and parallel activities such as C, D and E which occur simultaneously. Note that activity A is on the critical path, since this is the activity that takes the longest time to complete. The critical path is shown by the bold lines for the arrows and dependencies.

▶ Monitoring and control

When a project is underway, its objectives of cost, time and quality against targets must be closely **monitored**. Monitoring involves ensuring that the project is working to plan once it has started. This should occur daily for small-scale tasks or weekly for combined activities. **Control** or corrective action will occur if the performance measures deviate from plan. It is important to monitor and assess performance as the project progresses, in order that corrective action can be taken before it deviates from plan to any great extent. Milestones or events that need to happen on a particular date are defined for which performance against objectives can be measured (e.g. end of analysis, production of first prototype).

Computer project management packages can be used to automate the collection of project progress data and production of progress reports.

Achieving time, cost and quality objectives

As stated earlier, the project should be managed to achieve the defined objectives of time, cost and quality. The time objective is met by ensuring that the project is monitored in terms of execution of tasks within time limits. Corrective action is taken if a variance between actual and planned time is observed. The cost objective is achieved by the use of human resource and computing resource budgets and, again, variation between estimated and actual expenditure is noted and necessary corrective action taken. To ensure that quality objectives are met it is necessary to develop a quality plan which contains a list of deliverable items to the customer. Each of these will have an associated quality standard and procedure for dealing with a variance from the required quality level defined in the quality plan.

Project structure and size

The type of project structure required will be dependent on the size of the team undertaking the project. Projects with up to six team members can simply report directly to a project leader at appropriate intervals during project execution. For larger projects requiring up to 20 team members, it is usual to implement an additional tier of management in the form of team leaders. The team leader could be responsible for either a phase of the development (e.g. analysis, design) or a type of work (e.g. applications development, systems development). For any structure it is important that the project leader ensures consistency across development phases or development areas as appropriate. For projects with more than 20 members, it is likely that additional management layers will be needed in order to ensure that no one person is involved in too much supervision.

Reporting project progress

The two main methods of reporting the progress of a project are by written reports and verbal reports at meetings of the project team. It is important that a formal statement of progress is made in written form, preferably in a standard report format, to ensure that everyone is aware of the current project situation. This is particularly important when changes to specifications are made during the project. In order to facilitate two-way communication between team members and team management, regular meetings should be arranged by the project manager. These meetings can increase the commitment of team members by allowing discussion of points of interest and dissemination of information on how each team's effort is contributing to the overall progression of the project.

▶ DOCUMENTATION

Ensuring adequate **project documentation** is a key aspect of the role of the project manager. Software development is a team effort and documentation is necessary to disseminate design information throughout the team. Good documentation reduces the expense of maintenance after project delivery. Also, when members of the team leave the department or organisation, the coding they have produced must be understandable to new project members. Often a development methodology will require documentation at stages during the project in a specific format. Thus documentation must be an identified task in the development effort and a standard document format should be used throughout the project (this may be a standard such as BS5750 or ISO9001).

Documents which may be required include the following:

◆ *Workplan/task list.* For each team member a specified activity with start and finish dates and relevant coding standard should be defined.

◆ *Requirements specification.* This should clearly specify the objectives and functions of the software.

◆ *Purchase requisition forms.* Required if new software and hardware resources are needed from outside the organisation.

◆ *Manpower budget.* A running total of personnel costs, including expenses and subsistence payments. These should show actual against predicted expenditure for control purposes.

◆ *Change control documents.* To document any changes to the project specification during the project. A document is needed to highlight the effect on budgets and timescales of a change in software specifications.

Project documentation

Documentation is essential to disseminate information during project execution and for reference during software maintenance.

▶ A PROJECT MANAGEMENT METHODOLOGY: PRINCE

PRINCE is a project management methodology that has been developed to be compatible with the system development methodologies used in government IT projects, such as SSADM. It has become the standard project management methodology used for the UK government and is also being increasingly used in commercial organisations in the UK. It will be evident that it offers a structure for a project which is only applicable to large projects involving teams of at least 10 people. Many of the in-built quality assurance checks are, however, appropriate to smaller projects.

PRINCE defines four main project aims:

1 To deliver the required end-product(s).

2 To meet the specified quality.

3 To stay within budget.

4 To deliver on schedule.

Thus the PRINCE methodology is built around the idea that a project is required to deliver a product(s) within the time, cost and quality constraints imposed. The products are defined not just in the sense of the technical product of the delivered IT system, but including management products such as project plans and quality products such as quality reviews.

The planning process under PRINCE involves defining a list of products required to produce the end-product of the project and defining the sequence in which these products must be produced. From this can be derived the activities required to generate these products in terms of management tasks, technical requirements and quality criteria. In order to ensure that the aims of cost, time and quality are met, PRINCE provides controls that enable the progress of the project management and product management activities to be monitored against plan.

In order to ensure user involvement in the project, PRINCE provides an organisational structure and set of job descriptions that define responsibility for activities in a project and ensure a user role in major decisions during the project. The following sections summarise the PRINCE approach to project organisation and the planning and control functions.

▶ Project organisation

PRINCE attempts to ensure user involvement and communication between members of the project by defining an organisational structure and standard set of job descriptions. PRINCE provides a precise definition of the organisational structure and the roles within it. Note that one individual may undertake multiple roles or a single role may be undertaken by several people at different stages of the project.

PRINCE identifies different steering committees to guide the project. These are:

◆ The *information systems steering committee (ISSC)*, which defines and assesses the feasibility of IS projects.

◆ The *information technology executive committee (ITEC)*, which is responsible for the implementation of these projects and resource allocation.

◆ The ITEC appoints a *project board (PB)*, which has the task of managing the implementation of the project. The PB is the top level of management defined within the PRINCE framework and so is defined in more detail in terms of the following roles.

The *senior user* role is to represent the department(s) affected by the project. This involves an understanding of the user issues, human factors and the implementation of change. The *senior technical* role mirrors the user role in that it represents the interests of the IS departments implementing the project. This role requires a knowledge of technical, user and quality issues. The *project manager* role assumes responsibility for the day-to-day management of the project throughout its stages, while *stage managers* who have specialist skills can manage particular stages or work packages. This means that a stage manager need only be associated with a project at a particular time when his or her skills are required. The actual activities of the project and the technical products of each stage are undertaken by stage teams under the supervision of a *team leader*. Finally, the project manager is supported by a *project assurance team* with the following roles:

◆ *Business assurance coordinator* – to monitor progress against financial plan.

◆ *Technical assurance coordinator* – to monitor and report on technical aspects of the project.

◆ *User assurance coordinator* – to monitor and report on user aspects of the project.

▶ Project plans

The planning structure

There are three levels of plan in PRINCE, each of which consists of a technical plan (detailing which activities are required) and a resource plan (giving which resources are needed). The three levels of plans are:

1 *Project plan.* This shows the main activities within the project, providing an overall schedule and identifying resources needed for project implementation.
2 *Stage plan.* A stage plan is produced at the end of each previous stage in the project. The project board reviews all progress against the plan and takes corrective action as necessary.
3 *Detailed plan.* If a project is already broken down into stages, a detailed plan may not be required. However, for large projects with few stages, a series of detailed plans may be needed.

There are also two additional types of plan to complete the planning structure:

4 *Individual work plan.* This provides the allocation of work of a project. This information is extracted from tasks listed in the stage plan or detailed plan.
5 *Exception plan.* Exception plans enable 'out-of-control' behaviour within a stage plan to be reported to the project board. This is required if the project moves outside tolerance margins set by the project board. The exception plan replaces the stage, detailed and individual work plan for that stage.

The idea of the planning structure is to ensure that control activities can be undertaken at a specific level. The project plan is created during the project initiation stage and provides an overall assessment of the cost, time and resources necessary to undertake the project. The stage, detailed and individual work plans are more detailed and provide a basis for day-to-day control of project activities. If the actions within the exception plan are accepted, then it will replace the stage plan for the remainder of that stage.

The planning process

The traditional method of developing a plan is to list the activities involved and arrange them in a work breakdown structure (WBS). However, the PRINCE approach begins with a list of the products or deliverables that will be produced from the project. Activities will then be described from these products. There are three main products, defined as:

1 Management products.

2 Technical products.

3 Quality products.

Figure 9.6 shows how each class of product can be broken down into a number of elements called the product breakdown structure (PBS).

The technical products are defined as follows. Starting from the final product to be delivered, this is broken down into the products that are required to produce the final product. These are then broken down further until a list of products required to

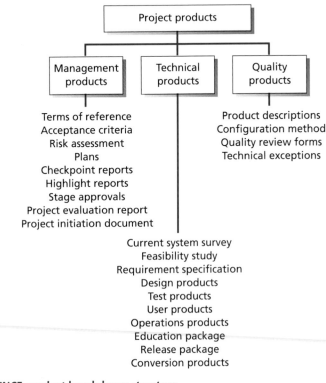

Fig 9.6 PRINCE product breakdown structure

produce the final product is generated. When this has been completed, the management and quality products can be defined. Management products will include such items as the project terms of reference, project plans and progress reports, while quality products will include the product descriptions and quality plans.

For each identified product, it is then necessary to create a product description which defines the finished product and can provide a guide to the resources needed to create the product. The next step is to develop a technical and a quality strategy for the project. The technical strategy may identify a standard software development methodology (e.g. SSADM) to be used for the project, while the quality strategy will consider the resources and techniques used to ensure that quality is maintained.

Once the technical, management and quality products have been identified for a particular project, a product flow diagram is developed which shows the sequence in which products are required over time (Fig 9.7). Any products external to the project are shown in ellipses, while products created by the project are shown in boxes. Management and quality products will need to be examined to see if they should be brought into the flow as well as technical products. Any additional products contained within the product flow need to be added to the product breakdown structure.

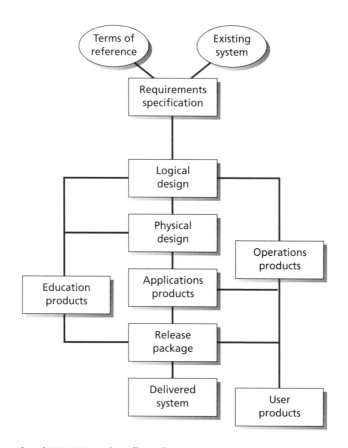

Fig 9.7 A top-level PRINCE product flow diagram

Defining the activities

The lines joining the products in the product flow diagram represent the processes or activities that are needed to transform one product into another. Identification of these activities, their duration and dependence on other activities will allow the production of an activity-on-node (AON) network diagram, as described in the network analysis section of this chapter. This permits the identification of the network critical path and slack times for non-critical activities. The activity network also provides the earliest and latest start and finish times for each activity and the total elapsed time for the project.

Defining the plans

The next stage is to produce a bar chart (termed a Gantt chart in network analysis) which allows the incorporation of resource constraints into the network and forms the basis of the technical plan. Resource allocation will need to take account of the availability of team members during the project. Their 100 per cent availability should not be assumed and other necessary activities should be taken into account (e.g. telephone, administration, unplanned meetings etc.). Once actual availability of resources has been determined, they can be allocated to activities in the project. Allocation should be to critical activities first (i.e. activities for which there is no slack time) and then to other parallel activities. The availability of individual resources can be measured over time using a capacity loading graph (*see* network analysis section). It may be found that due to the duration of activities or the fact that a resource is needed for more than one activity at a time (i.e. parallel activities), the project cannot be completed in the time shown by the activity network chart. This requires either the allocation of extra resources or an adjustment to the project completion time.

The previous resource allocation charts are supplemented by a plan description document to form the technical plans that are submitted to the project board. The plan description contains information regarding the proposed plan, assumptions made on aspects such as resource availability, skill levels and an assessment of risk at each plan level.

▶ Project control

Project control is the activity of ensuring that a project meets planned objectives. PRINCE attempts to ensure this by the use of what is termed business and technical integrity:

- *Business integrity* involves ensuring that the work is carried out to the schedule agreed within resource and cost constraints imposed.
- *Technical integrity* involves ensuring that the development system (i.e. the product) meets the goals of quality, reliability and maintainability.

Control is exercised by comparing performance to plan and taking action on any deviation that is outside the agreed tolerance. Management tolerances measure deviation from planned cost or schedule, while technical tolerances measure deviation in quality as defined by the user requirements and objectives.

▶ Management control

PRINCE provides management controls in the form of meetings of project staff that produce a set of predefined documents. These allow senior management to assess the status of the project before providing further expenditure.

The main control points in a PRINCE project are project initiation, stage assessment and project closure.

Project initiation

The outcome of this stage is a project initiation document that will include a high-level plan for the project and confirmation of the responsibilities of project members. There will also be a more detailed plan of the first stage of the project. The project manager, the first stage manager and members of the project assurance team prepare the document. The project initiation document should include the following elements:

◆ Project organisation diagram.

◆ Job descriptions.

◆ Project brief including project definition and scope of work.

◆ Project terms of reference.

◆ Business case including cost–benefit analysis and risk assessment.

◆ Project plan estimating development cost and duration (*see* planning section) at a high level, to include the following:
   (a) Project technical plan.
   (b) Project resource plan.
   (c) Project quality plan.
   (d) Configuration management plan.
   (e) First-stage plan.

For each stage of the plan the following is required:

◆ Stage technical plan.

◆ Stage resource plan.

◆ Stage resource graphical summary.

◆ Stage plan description.

◆ Stage quality plan.

In addition, the following supporting documents for each stage are recommended:

◆ Stage product breakdown structure.

◆ Stage product flow diagram.

◆ Stage activity network.

Stage assessment

There are *checkpoint meetings* held on a regular (e.g. weekly) time-related basis to review progress against plans, particularly in connection with individual work allocations. They are held at a team level and are usually run by the stage manager or team leader.

Highlight reports provide a regular (e.g. monthly) summary of progress to date to the project board.

The *end-stage assessment (ESA)* is not time based but is triggered by the end of each project stage. Participants should include the project board, project manager, project assurance team, current team manager and next stage manager. The meeting's aims are to confirm delivery of the current stage of the project to specification and to ensure that a viable business case still exists for the project, as well as considering and approving the plan for the next stage. If this is not the case, corrective action must be taken or, if this is not thought possible, the project terminated.

The *mid-stage assessment (MSA)* is an optional event and may be triggered by the following:

◆ A need to check progress during a lengthy project stage.

◆ When stage tolerance levels have been exceeded.

◆ When it is felt necessary to begin the next stage before the end-stage assessment can be held for the present stage.

The mid-stage assessment is attended by and follows the format of the end-stage assessment.

Exception plans

If a stage cannot be completed within its tolerances, the project manager must advise the project board immediately and present an exception plan as a mid-stage assessment. An exception plan consists of the technical plan covering remaining stage activities, a matching resource plan and additional information to describe the exception. This should include the impact of options considered in the stage plan, project plan and business case. If the project board agrees the exception plan, it becomes the stage plan for the remainder of that stage.

Project closure

The project closure meeting replaces the final end-stage assessment and confirms the signing of the system, user, operations, security and business acceptance letters by the appropriate board members. The acceptance criteria should have been clearly stated in the project initiation document.

The last act of a PRINCE project is a business assessment of the system provided by the project after a period of use, called a *post-implementation review*.

Product controls

Product controls ensure that quality is built into the development of the products during the project. Tasks involved include agreeing quality criteria for products with users, planning quality reviews and detecting and correcting quality problems as early as possible. The measurement criteria for a product's quality are contained within the product description and as such are created during the planning stage, thus building in quality to the product design.

Quality reviews

The purpose of the quality review is to identify errors through a planned and documented process as early as possible in the development cycle. The quality review consists of three phases:

1 *Preparation.* This includes setting up a review team and distribution of appropriate documentation.

2 *Review.* The meeting is held and actions are listed and allocated to individuals.

3 *Follow-up.* This covers the correction of actions listed.

Every project managed using the methodology has a quality file containing details of all quality reviews and requests for changes.

The PRINCE methodology uses the following ways to document changes:

♦ *Project issue reports (PIR)* – used by anyone to raise a quality issue.

♦ *Off-specification reports (OSR)* – when systems fail to meet specification.

♦ *Requests for change (RFC)* – propose a change following from a PIR or OSR.

If an RFC causes project budgets to exceed tolerance, an exception plan is created which is considered by the project board. The control document will probably be created by members of the maintenance team and system users and will be sent to the ITEC for signing.

Configuration management

Configuration management is needed because of the dependence between components within a project. Each component will have its own development cycle and during this development any of the components may be changed, which could make them incompatible with other components. Configuration management identifies each hardware, software or documentation component used and records the status of that component. The authorised version of each item is then issued for use. A configuration librarian is used to manage and control configuration management activities.

ACTIVITY

An assessment of PRINCE

An important function of a company's information systems manager is to review which methodologies should be employed to improve the quality of its systems development processes. Some methodologies may add a structure to a company process which improves its efficiency. Others may enforce restrictions which reduce the efficiency of the process and increase the cost and duration of the project.

You are a project manager in a medium to large company of 400 people. The company has a history of developing systems which meet the needs of the end-users well, but can sometimes be over six months late. The managing director has decided that the project will be conducted by internal IS development staff. Your role as the owner of the system in which the project will be implemented is to manage the project using other resources, such as the IS department, as you see fit.

Question

From the information given in the preceding section and using any relevant books, decide whether to use a formal project methodology such as PRINCE or a different approach. Justify your answer, giving a brief evaluation of what you perceive as the advantages and disadvantages of PRINCE.

▶ A PROJECT MANAGEMENT TOOL: NETWORK ANALYSIS

Critical path

Activities on the critical path are termed *critical activities*. Any delay in these activities will cause a delay in the project completion time.

PERT

Sometimes used to refer to a critical path network diagram (PERT charts), but more accurately PERT replaces the fixed activity duration used in the CPM method with a statistical distribution which uses optimistic, pessimistic and most likely duration estimates.

Critical path diagrams are used extensively during scheduling and monitoring to show the planned activities of a project and the *dependencies* between these activities. For example, network analysis will show that activity C can only take place when activity A and activity B have been completed. Once a network diagram has been constructed, it is possible to follow a sequence of activities, called a *path*, through the network from start to end. The length of time it takes to follow the path is the sum of all the durations of activities on that path. The path with the longest duration gives the *project completion time*. This is called the **critical path** because any change in duration in any activities on this path will cause the whole project duration to become shorter or longer. Activities not on the critical path will have a certain amount of slack time in which the activity can be delayed or the duration lengthened and not affect the overall project duration. The amount of *slack time* is the difference between the path duration the activity is on and the critical path duration. By definition, all activities on the critical path have zero slack. Note that there must be at least one critical path for each network and there may be several. The significance of the critical path is that if any node on the path finishes later than the earliest finish time, the overall network time will increase by the same amount, putting the project behind schedule. Thus any planning and control activities should focus on ensuring that tasks on the critical path remain within schedule.

PERT charts are sometimes used to refer to a critical path network diagram. PERT also has a technical meaning, described in detail in a later section.

▶ The critical path method (CPM)

Once the estimation stage has been completed, the project activities should have been identified, activity durations and resource requirement estimated and activity relationships identified. Based on this information, the critical path diagrams can be constructed using either the activity-on-arrow (AOA) approach or the activity-on-node (AON) approach. The issues involved in deciding which one to utilise will be discussed later. The following description of critical path analysis will use the AON method.

Critical path method (CPM)

Critical path diagrams show the relationship between activities in a project.

The **critical path method (CPM)** uses critical path diagrams uses to show the relationships between activities in a project.

The activity-on-node (AON) method

In an activity-on-node network, the diagramming notation shown in Fig 9.8 is used. Each activity task is represented by a node with the format shown in the figure.

Thus a completed network will consist of a number of nodes connected by lines, one for each task, between a start and end node, as shown in Fig 9.9.

Once the network diagram has been drawn using the activity relationships, the node information can be calculated, starting with the earliest start and finish times. These are calculated by working from left to right through the network, termed the forward pass. Once the forward pass has been completed, it is possible to calculate the latest start and finish times for each task. This is achieved by moving right to left along the network, backward through time, termed the backward pass. Finally,

Earliest start	Duration	Earliest finish
Activity number/letter Activity description		
Latest start	Slack/float	Latest finish

Fig 9.8 Activity on node notation

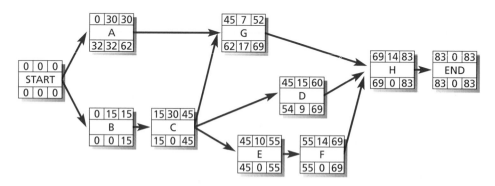

Fig 9.9 Activity on node network diagram

the slack or float value can be calculated for each node by taking the difference between the earliest start and latest start (or earliest finish and latest finish) times for each task.

The activity-on-arrow (AOA) method

The format for the activity-on-arrow method will now be described. The symbol used in this method is as shown in Fig 9.10.

Rather than considering the earliest and latest start and finish times of the activities directly, this method uses the earliest and latest event times, as below:

◆ *Earliest event time.* This is determined by the earliest time at which any subsequent activity can start.

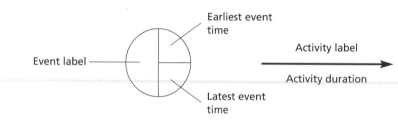

Fig 9.10 Activity-on-arrow notation

Fig 9.11 Calculating event times for a AOA network

◆ *Latest event time.* This is determined by the latest time at which any subsequent activity can start.

Thus for a single activity the format would be as shown in Fig 9.11.

Comparison of activity-on-arrow and activity-on-node methods

There has historically been a greater use of the activity-on-arrow (AOA) method, but the activity-on-node (AON) method is now being recognised as having a number of advantages, including the following:

◆ Most project management computer software uses the AON approach.

◆ AON diagrams do not need dummy activities to maintain the relationship logic.

◆ AON diagrams have all the information on timings and identification within the node box, leading to clearer diagrams.

An example of the use of activity-on-node in Microsoft Project is shown in Fig 9.12. This illustrates *sequential activities* such as from the START to activity A and *parallel activities* such as C, D and E which occur simultaneously. Note that activity A is on the critical path, since this is the activity that takes the longest time to complete. The critical path is shown by the bold lines for the arrows and dependencies.

▶ Gantt charts

Gantt charts

Show the duration of parallel and sequential activities in a project as horizontal bars on a chart.

Although network diagrams are ideal for showing the relationship between project tasks, they do not provide a clear view of which tasks are being undertaken over time and particularly how many tasks may be undertaken in parallel at any one time. **Gantt charts** are used to summarise the project plan by showing the duration of parallel and sequential activities in a project as horizontal 'time bars' on a chart. The Gantt chart provides an overview for the project manager to allow them to monitor project progress against planned progress and so provides a valuable information source for project control.

Figure 9.12 shows a typical Gantt chart produced using Microsoft Project. Note that some phases such as 'Phase 1 – software evaluation' have *subactivities* such as 'consult and set criteria' and 'evaluate alternatives – report'. Each of these subactivities has a certain number of days and a corresponding cost assigned to it. **Milestones** are activities that are planned to occur by a particular day, such as 'Purchase hardware by 17/06'. These are shown as triangles. They are a significant event in the life of the project, such as completion of a prototype.

Milestone

This denotes a significant event in the project such as completion of a prototype.

To draw a Gantt chart manually or using a spreadsheet or drawing package, follow these steps:

ID	Task Name	Duration	Cost	1995 Q2	Q3	Q4	1996 Q1	Q2	Q3	Q4	1997 Q1	Q2	Q3	Q4	1998 Q1	Q2	Q3
1	**Project startup**	**33d**	**£4,500.00**														
2	Business plan/detailed proj plan	5d	£0.00														
3	Project authorisation/start	0d	£0.00														
4	Recruit, brief and train author	20d	£500.00														
5	Purchase hardware	0d	£4,000.00														
6	**Phase 1 – Software evaluation**	**29d**	**£4,050.00**														
7	Consult & set criteria	5d	£100.00														
8	Evaluate alternatives->report	24d	£600.00														
9	Purchase software	0d	£3,350.00														
10	**Phase 2 – Design**	**80d**	**£8,500.00**														
11	Generic publishing framework	45d	£3,000.00														
12	Document database	30d	£2,000.00														
13	Modify groupware engine mechanics	15d	£1,500.00														
14	Design from template for Phase	20d	£2,000.00														
15	Phase 3 – Implement pilot email exercise	30d	£1,000.00														
16	Phase 4 – Implement IT assignment	35d	£1,000.00														
17	Phase 5 – Publish material for 4 UBF	60d	£2,000.00														
18	Phase 6 – Evaluation	60d	£500.00														
19																	

Figure 9.12 Gantt chart showing activities and milestones

1 Draw a grid with the tasks along the vertical axis and the timescale (for the whole project duration) along the horizontal axis.
2 Draw a horizontal bar across from the task identifier along the left of the chart, starting at the earliest start time and ending at the earliest finish time.
3 Indicate the slack amount by drawing a line from the earliest finish time to the latest finish time.
4 Repeat steps 2 and 3 for each task.

If the network analysis is being conducted using project management software, then the Gantt chart is automatically generated from information in the network analysis.

▶ Capacity loading graphs

The basic network diagram assumes that all tasks can be undertaken when required by the earliest start times calculated from the node dependency relationships. However, resources required to undertake tasks are usually limited and the duration of an individual task or the number of parallel tasks may be limited. In order to calculate the capacity requirements of a project over time, the capacity requirements associated with each task are indicated on the Gantt chart. From this, a **capacity loading graph** can be developed by projecting the loading figures on a time graph. The capacity loading graphs show the resources required to undertake activities in a project. If the network analysis is being conducted using project management software, then the capacity loading graph is automatically generated from information in the network analysis.

Capacity loading graphs

Capacity loading graphs show the resources required to undertake activities in a project.

▶ Project costs

Project cost graphs

Shows the financial cost of undertaking the project.

The previous discussion has concentrated on the need to schedule and control activities in order to complete the entire project within a minimum timespan. However, there are situations in which the project cost is an important factor. If the costs of each project are known, then it is possible to produce a **project cost graph** which will show the amount of cost incurred over the life of the project. This is useful in showing any periods when a number of parallel tasks are incurring significant costs, leading to the need for additional cashflow at key times. In large projects it may be necessary to aggregate the costs of a number of activities, particularly if they are the responsibility of one department or subcontractor. As a control mechanism, the project manager can collect information on cost to date and percentage completion to date for each task to identify any cost above budget and take appropriate action without delay.

▶ Trading time and cost: project crashing

Within any project there will be a number of time–cost trade-offs to consider. Most projects will have tasks which can be completed with an injection of additional resources, such as equipment or people. Reasons to reduce project completion time include:

◆ Reduce high indirect costs associated with equipment.

◆ Reduce new product development time to market.

◆ Avoid penalties for late completion.

◆ Gain incentives for early completion.

◆ Release resources for other projects.

Project crashing

Refers to reducing the project duration by increasing spending on critical activities.

The use of additional resources to reduce project completion time is termed **crashing** the network. The idea is to reduce overall indirect project costs by increasing direct costs on a particular task. One of the most obvious ways of decreasing task duration is to allocate additional labour to a task. This can be either an additional team member or through overtime working. To enable a decision to be made on the potential benefits of crashing a task, the following information is required:

◆ The normal task duration.

◆ The crash task duration.

◆ The cost of crashing the task to the crash task duration per unit time.

The process by which a task is chosen for crashing is by observing which task can be reduced for the required time for the lowest cost. As stated before, the overall project completion time is the sum of the task durations on the critical path. Thus it is always necessary to crash a task that is on the critical path. As the duration of tasks on the critical path are reduced, however, other paths in the network will also become critical. If this happens, it will require the crashing process to be undertaken on all the paths that are critical at any one time.

▶ PROJECT EVALUATION AND REVIEW TECHNIQUE (PERT)

PERT replaces the fixed activity duration used in the CPM method with a statistical distribution which uses optimistic, pessimistic and most likely duration estimates.

The critical path method (CPM) described above was developed by DuPont during the 1950s to manage plant construction. The PERT approach was formulated by the US Navy during the development of the Polaris Submarine Launched Ballistic Missile System in the same decade (Sapolsky, 1972). The main difference between the approaches is the ability of PERT to take into consideration uncertainty in activity durations.

The PERT approach attempts to take into account the fact that most task durations are not fixed by using a beta probability distribution to describe the variability inherent in the processes. The probabilistic approach involves three time estimates for each activity:

◆ *Optimistic time*. The task duration under the most optimistic conditions.

◆ *Pessimistic time*. The task duration under the most pessimistic conditions.

◆ *Most likely time*. The most likely task duration.

As stated, the beta distribution is used to describe the task duration variability. To derive the average or expected time for a task duration, the following equation is used:

Expected Duration = Optimistic + (4 * Most Likely) + Pessimistic

The combination of the expected time and standard deviation for the network path allows managers to compute probabilistic estimates of project completion times. A point to bear in mind with these estimates is that they only take into consideration the tasks on the critical path and discount the fact that slack on tasks on a non-critical path could delay the project. Therefore the probability that the project will be completed by a specified date is the probability that all paths will be completed by that date, which is the product of the probabilities for all the paths.

▶ Project network simulation

In order to use the PERT approach, it must be assumed that the paths of a project are independent and that the same tasks are not on more than one path. If a task is on more than one path and its actual completion time was much larger than its expected time, it is obvious that the paths are not independent. If the network consists of these paths and they are near the critical path time, then the results will be invalid.

Simulation can be used to develop estimates of a project's completion time by taking into account all the network paths. Probability distributions are constructed for each task, derived from estimates provided by such data collection methods as observation and historical data. A simulation then generates a random number within the probability distribution for each task. The critical path is determined and the project duration calculated. This procedure is repeated a number of times (possibly more than 100) until there is sufficient data in order to construct a frequency distribution of project times. This distribution can be used to make a probabilistic assessment of the actual project duration. If greater accuracy is required, the process can be repeated to generate additional project completion estimates which can be added to the frequency distribution.

PERT

PERT replaces the fixed activity duration used in the CPM method with a statistical distribution which uses optimistic, pessimistic and most likely duration estimates.

▶ BENEFITS AND LIMITATIONS OF THE NETWORK ANALYSIS APPROACH

The main benefit of using the network analysis approach is the requirement to use a structured analysis of the number and sequence of tasks contained within a project, so aiding understanding of resource requirements for project completion. It provides a number of useful graphical displays that assist understanding of such factors as project dependencies and resource loading, a reasonable estimate of the project duration and the tasks that must be completed on time to meet this duration (i.e. the critical path) and a control mechanism to monitor actual progress against planned progress on the Gantt chart. It also provides a means of estimating any decrease in overall project time by providing extra resources at any stage and can be used to provide cost estimates for different project scenarios.

Limitations to consider when using network analysis include remembering that its use is no substitute for good management judgement in such areas as prioritising and selecting suppliers and personnel for the project. Additionally, any errors in the network such as incorrect dependency relationships or the omission of tasks may invalidate the results. The tasks' times are forecasts and are thus estimates that are subject to error. PERT and simulation techniques may reduce time estimation errors, but at the cost of greater complexity which may divert management time from more important issues. Finally, time estimates for tasks may be greater than necessary to provide managers with slack and ensure that they meet deadlines.

▶ SUMMARY

1 Projects are unique, one-time operations designed to accomplish a specific set of objectives in a limited timeframe with a limited budget and resources.

2 The function of the project manager is to provide clearly defined goals and ensure that adequate resources are employed on the project.

3 A work breakdown structure splits the overall project task into a number of more detailed activities.

4 Critical path analysis shows the activities undertaken during a project and the dependencies between them.

5 The critical path is identified by making a forward then a reverse pass through the network, calculating the earliest and latest activity start/finish times respectively.

6 The activity-on-node (AON) method provides a number of advantages over the activity-on-arrow (AOA) method of network construction.

7 Gantt charts provide an overview of what tasks are being undertaken over time.

8 Capacity loading graphs provide an indication of the amount of resource needed for the project over time.

9 Cost graphs provide an indication of monetary expenditure over the project period.

10 Project crashing consists of reducing overall indirect project costs (e.g. by reducing the project duration) by increasing expenditure on a particular task.

11 The PERT approach provides a method of integrating the variability of task durations into the network analysis.

▶ EXERCISES

▶ Self-assessment exercises

1 What are the main elements of the project management process?

2 What are the main project aims of the PRINCE methodology?

3 What information is required for the construction of a critical path diagram?

4 What information do the Gantt chart and PERT chart convey?

5 Define the term critical path.

6 What is the difference between effort and elapsed time?

▶ Discussion questions

1 Draw a Gantt chart for the following AON network.

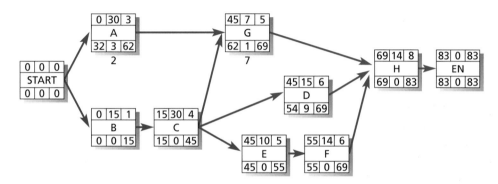

Fig 9.13 AON network

2 One of the most difficult parts of project management is getting the estimates right. Discuss.

▶ Essay questions

1 Explore the features of a project management computer package such as Microsoft Project. Evaluate its use in the project management process.

2 Compare the different alternatives that are available for the critical path method of network analysis.

3 What is the most effective method of estimating the duration of an information systems development project?

▶ Examination questions

1 What are the main elements in the project management process?

2 Evaluate the use of the PRINCE project management methodology.

3 Explain the difference between portraying a project plan as a Gantt chart and as a PERT chart.

4 What is the importance of conducting monitoring and control when managing a project?

5 Why is it difficult and often impossible for a software project manager to balance the three constraints of time, budget and quality? You should relate your answer to two different aspects of the quality of the delivered information system.

6 What is the difference between elapsed time and effort time? How are the two factors related in terms of the availability and work rate of different staff? Describe this in words, or using an equation or an example.

▶ References

Albrecht, A.J. and Gaffney, J. (1983) 'Software function, source lines of code and development effort prediction', *IEEE Transactions on Software Engineering*, SE-9, 639–48.

Bicknell, D. (1996) 'Managers blamed for record project failures', *Computer Weekly*, 18 January.

Bicknell, D. (1998) 'Clark Kent holds keys to project success', *Computer Weekly*, 9 July, p. 14.

Boehm, B.W. (1981) *Software Engineering Economics*, Prentice-Hall, Englewood Cliffs, NJ.

Bradley, K. (1993) *PRINCE: a Practical Handbook*, Butterworth-Heinemann, Oxford.

Johnston, A.K. (1995) *A Hacker's guide to Project Management*, Butterworth-Heinemann, Oxford.

Kaye, J. (1997) 'Falling at the final hurdle', *Computer Weekly*, 8 May.

Lytinen, K. and Hirscheim, R. (1987) 'Information systems failures: a survey and classification of the empirical literature', *Oxford Surveys in IT*, 4, 257–309.

Mouler, J. (1996) 'UK tops project failure league', *Computing*, 8 February.

Sapolsky, H.M. (1972) *The Polaris System Development: Bureaucratic and Programmatic Success in Government*, Harvard University Press, Boston, MA.

Warren, L. (1996) 'Tales of the unexpected', *Computing*, 8 February.

Yeates, D. (1991) *Project Management for Information Systems*, Financial Times Pitman Publishing, London.

▶ Further reading

Boehm, B.W. (1984) 'Software engineering economics', *IEEE Transactions on Software Engineering*, SE-10, 10–21.

Brooks, F.P. (1995) *The Mythical Man-month: Essays on Software Engineering – Anniversary Edition*, Addison-Wesley, Reading, MA.

Button, K. (1996) 'Thou shalt not. . . ', *Computing Weekly*, 2 May.

Dingle, J. (1997) *Project Management: Orientation for Decision Makers*, Arnold, London.

Leung, L. (1996) 'Leading a project', *Computing*, 6 June.

Maylor, H. (1996) *Project Management*, Financial Times Pitman Publishing, London.

Whitten, N. (1990) *Managing Software Development Projects*, John Wiley, New York.

10

Systems theory

INTRODUCTION

An understanding of systems theory is an important background to undertaking systems analysis and design for information systems. A systems theory approach to analysis and design is beneficial since it provides principles for good system design. For example, a well-designed system will have clearly defined subsystems or modules for which the data transfer is clearly defined. However, the systems approach is also applied more widely in society and business and is relevant to the study of organisational structure and behaviour.

The systems approach has become particularly relevant in the past 50 years when it has been used to help deal with the complexity generated by technological and scientific advances. In particular, the development of processes in isolation, with little or no consideration for their effect on the system in which they operate, has led to problems such as environmental destruction, energy wastage, and water, soil and air pollution. The systems approach emphasises that a complex system cannot be reduced to an analysis of its parts alone, since its primary properties derive from the *interactions* between these parts. This concept emphasises the interdependence of both living and non-living systems.

> ▶ Learning objectives
>
> After reading this chapter, readers will be able to:
>
> ◆ understand the concept of systems theory;
>
> ◆ recognise different types of system such as open and closed, close-coupled and decoupled and their strengths and weaknesses;
>
> ◆ apply systems theory to the analysis and design of information systems.

> ▶ **Links to other chapters**
>
> This chapter provides background information for the analysis and design phases of the software development lifecycle. These are described in Chapters 11 and 12. This chapter also relates to the different types of system that were described in Chapter 6.

▶ ALTERNATIVE APPROACHES TO SYSTEMS THEORY

The systems approach has been used since the 1930s. The biologist Ludwig von Bertalanffy is associated with establishing systems theory as a scientific movement. He derived his ideas from biology and was convinced that organisms should be studied as complex wholes, where the whole is more effective than the sum of its constituent parts (von Bertalanffy, 1950). Von Bertalanffy's work helped establish a *general systems theory* (GST), which was developed to deal with general properties of systems, regardless of their form. The theory was later related to organisations by Katz and Kahn (1966), who viewed organisations as open systems with their own goals (in close inter-relationship with their environment). The following sections provide an introduction to different ways of describing systems and aims to show the relationship between general systems theory and information systems and the organisation.

Different approaches to problem solving and the design of information systems have been developed based on systems theory. 'Hard' systems thinking has been defined by Checkland (1978) as:

> the assumption that the problem task they tackle is to select an efficient means of achieving a known and defined end.

'Hard' approaches include systems engineering (Hall, 1962) and systems analysis (Miser and Quade, 1985; 1988). Jackson (1991) also includes operational research (Ackoff and Sasieni, 1968) in this category. The cybernetics approach (Ashby, 1956; Beer, 1959) is an interdisciplinary approach dealing with the general laws that govern control processes. Soft systems thinking (Checkland, 1981) was an attempt to deal with poorly defined and structured problems. Systems dynamics, invented by Forrester (1961, 1969), attempts to study the behaviour of systems through the modelling of dynamic feedback processes. This approach has become popular due in part to its use by Senge (1994) in the study of learning organisations. The main elements of the systems dynamics approach are described later in this chapter.

▶ WHAT IS A SYSTEM?

System

A system can be defined as a collection of interrelated components that work together towards a collective goal.

A system can be defined as a collection of interrelated components that work together towards a collective goal. The function of a system is to receive inputs and transform these into outputs. Figure 10.1 illustrates the organisation of the input, process, output model.

An example might help illustrate this concept and aid understanding. In Chapter 1, the concept of a transformation process was used to explain how data can be converted into information. Using the model shown in Fig 10.1, it can be said that data is used as the *input* for a **process** that creates information as an *output*.

However, this model illustrates a system that is essentially static. The performance of the system cannot be adjusted and there are no checks to ensure that it works correctly. In order to monitor the performance of the system, some kind of **feedback mechanism** is required. In addition, **control** must be exerted to correct any problems that occur and ensure that the system is fulfilling its purpose. An example of such a system was reviewed in the previous chapter, where a project manager will monitor the progress of a project against the plan and then exert control to try to correct any variance from the plan. Corrective action may take the form of varying the inputs such as the number or type of resources used to complete the task. The concepts of feedback and control are described in a later section of this chapter.

If these additional components are added to the basic model of the system, it can be illustrated as in Fig 10.2.

The model shown in this diagram is sometimes referred to as an **adaptive system**, in order to signify that it has the ability to monitor and regulate its own performance.

At this point, it can be argued that a generic system includes five components: input, process, output, feedback and control. Each of these components can now be described in more detail.

◆ The *input* to a system can be thought of as the raw materials for a process that will produce a particular output. Inputs can take many forms and are not necessarily purely physical in nature. Examples of inputs might include data, knowledge, raw

Process

Inputs are turned into outputs by using a transformation process.

Feedback

A feedback mechanism provides information on the performance of a system. An example of feedback might include quality control measurements taken on a production line.

Control

If alterations are needed to the system, adjustments are made by some form of control mechanism. The function of a control mechanism is to ensure that the system is working to fulfil its objective.

Adaptive system

In general, an adaptive system has the ability to monitor and regulate its own performance. In many cases, an adaptive system will be able to respond fully to changes in its environment by modifying its behaviour.

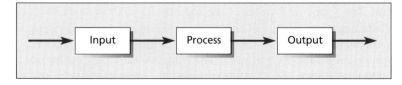

Fig 10.1 A basic model of the systems transformation process

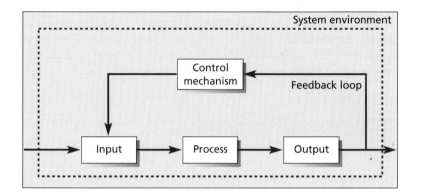

Fig 10.2 A generic model of a system

materials, machinery and premises. Input design is a major element of information systems development (Chapter 12).

◆ Inputs are turned into outputs by subjecting them to a transformation *process*. The concept of a transformation process was described in Chapter 1. Information systems design will need to incorporate the design of processing input into output.

◆ The *output* is the finished product created by the system. Again, the outputs produced by a system can take many forms. Examples might include information, products and services. All system will generate output and output design will be an important element of information systems development.

◆ Information on the performance of the system is gathered by a *feedback mechanism* (sometimes known as a feedback loop). An example of feedback might include quality control measurements taken on a production line which are used to correct the production process when beyond the tolerance limits.

◆ If alterations are needed to the system, adjustments are made by some form of *control mechanism*. In general, control is exerted as the result of feedback information regarding the performance of the system. The function of the control component is to ensure that the system is working to fulfil its objective (which is normally the creation of a specific output). Control occurs by adjusting the process and input components of the system until the correct output is achieved.

The components of a system work towards a collective goal. This is known as the system's *objective*. The objective of a system is normally very specific and can often be expressed in a single sentence. As an example, the objective of a car might be expressed as simply as to transport people and goods to a specified location.

It should also be recognised that systems do not operate in complete isolation, they are contained within an **environment** that contains other systems and external agencies. The scope of a system is defined by its **system boundary**. Everything outside of the boundary is part of the system's environment, everything within the boundary forms part of the system itself. The boundary also marks the **interface** between a system and its environment. The interface describes exchanges between a system and the environment or other systems. For an organisation, the subsystems such as marketing and finance would lie within the systems boundary, while the following elements would lie outside as part of the business environment:

◆ customers;

◆ sales channel/distributors;

◆ suppliers;

◆ competitors;

◆ partners;

◆ government and legislation;

◆ the economy.

Environment

Systems do not operate in complete isolation, they are contained within an environment that contains other systems and external agencies.

Systems boundary

This describes the interface between a system and its environment. Everything within the boundary forms part of the system, everything outside the boundary forms part of the external environment.

Interface

In terms of systems, the interface describes the exchanges between a system and its environment or the system and other systems. In the field of Information Technology, the interface describes ways in which information is exchanged between users and computer software or hardware.

An organisation will interact with all these elements which are beyond the system boundary in the environment. We refer to this as an **open system**. Most information systems will fall into this category, since they will accept input and will react to it. Totally **closed systems** which do not interact with their environment are unusual.

Systems can be extremely complex and can be made up of other, smaller systems known as **subsystems**. Systems composed of one or more subsystems can be referred to as *suprasystems* (but are usually still referred to as systems). The objective of a subsystem is to support the larger objective of the suprasystem. Consider the example given earlier, that of a car. The car can be considered as a suprasystem that is made up of numerous subsystems, including the engine, the steering mechanism, the brakes and so on. Each of the subsystems has an objective that supports the overall objective of the car, for example the objective of the engine might be to move the car in a specified direction at a specified speed. By fulfilling this objective, the engine supports the overall objective of the car, to transport people and goods from one location to another.

Subsystems in an organisation might include:

◆ manufacturing;

◆ marketing and sales;

◆ distribution;

◆ finance;

◆ human resources.

Subsystems in an information system interact by exchanging information. This is known as the *interface* between systems. For information systems and business systems, having clearly defined interfaces is important to an efficient organisation. For example, sales orders must be passed from the sales subsystem to the finance subsystem and the distribution subsystem in a clear, repeatable way. If this does not happen, orders may be lost or delayed and customer service will decline.

Note that the subsystems can be divided further. For example, the marketing function can be broken down into presales, promotion and customer service subsystems. These could be referred to as subsubsystems!

The car example can be used to introduce several additional concepts that are important in understanding systems. If a subsystem pursues its own objectives at the expense of the higher goals of the suprasystem, a condition of *suboptimality* is said to exist. However, when all of the components of a system work together correctly, a state of **synergy** (or holism) can occur. Simply, synergy means that the whole is greater than the sum of the parts. In other words, combining the parts together produces a new result that the parts alone could not achieve. In the case of a car, for example, supplying the engine with fuel results in the combustion that eventually generates movement.

Open system

Interaction occurs with elements beyond the system boundary.

Closed system

No or limited interaction occurs with the environment.

Subsystem

A group of related activities which are part of an overall system. Each subsystem has clearly defined inputs and outputs. Most business systems can be divided into subsystems.

Synergy

Synergy means that the whole is greater than the sum of the parts.

Hierarchical systems

Systems are hierarchical in nature, being made up of subsystems that may themselves be made up of other subsystems.

Interdependence

Interdependence means that a change to one part of a system leads to or results from changes to one or more other parts.

It should also be recognised that systems are hierarchical in nature, being made up of subsystems that may themselves be made up of other subsystems. Once again, the example of a car can be used to illustrate this concept. As mentioned earlier, one can argue that a car is a suprasystem made up of numerous subsystems, such as the engine. In turn, the engine will be made up of other subsystems, such as an ignition mechanism. In its turn, the ignition mechanism will be made up of a number of subsystems, and so on. From this, one should realise that the parts of a system are dependent on one another in some way. This interdependence means that a change to one part of a system leads to or results from changes to one or more other parts.

▶ CONTROL IN ORGANISATIONAL SYSTEMS

Figure 10.3 shows the relationship between different parts of an organisation and how they are related according to systems theory. The control mechanism is indicated by the arrowed line from the output back to the input.

The role of the information system is to provide information to management which will enable them to make decisions which ensure that the organisation is controlled. The organisation will be in control if it is meeting the needs of the environment. The elements of the environment which are relevant to an organisation are termed its stakeholders. These include customers, competitors and suppliers. In this model, the organisation is seen as a mechanism for exchanging inputs and outputs with the environment. The next section will provide more detail on different types of control mechanisms in systems.

One of the characteristics of a system is that its behaviour is directed towards some objective or goal. It does this by means of a control mechanism, which is termed either open loop or closed loop.

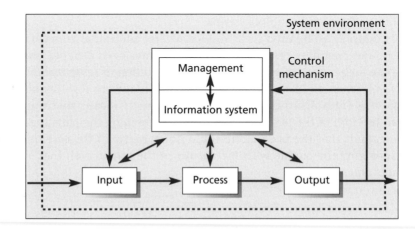

Fig 10.3 Information Systems as an organisational control mechanism

▶ Open-loop control systems

Figure 10.4 shows a generic open-loop system. An **open-loop control system** is one in which there is an attempt to reach the system objective, but no action is taken to modify the process or its input to achieve the targets once the process has begun. Open-loop systems have no mechanism for ensuring that goals are met once the process is underway. Take for example a decision to manufacture to a predicted market demand. In an open-loop system, no changes would be made in reaction to, for example, a decision by a major competitor to cut its price. In order to improve the likelihood that the system objectives will be met, a closed-loop system is employed.

Open-loop control system

An open-loop control system is one in which there is an attempt to reach the system objective, but no control action to modify the inputs or process is taken once the process has begun.

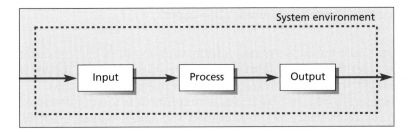

Fig 10.4 A generic open-loop system

Open-loop systems are inadequate in an organisational context because of the complexity of organisational systems and their environments. In other words, open-loop systems would only be successful in attaining the system objectives in cases were we could plan with certainty the events that would take place during the systems process. A legal system is a good example of an open system. The way in which legislation is amended, created and applied is often influenced by a variety of factors, such as public opinion. However, it can also be argued that the introduction of legislation can influence public opinion and behaviour.

▶ Closed-loop control systems

Two types of control mechanism that can be employed in this situation are:

1 *Feedback control*. The output achieved is monitored and compared to the desired output and corrective action is taken if a deviation exists. Figure 10.5 shows a generic closed-loop system.

2 *Feedforward control*. The environment and system process are both monitored in order to provide corrective action if it is likely that the system goal will not be met.

Feedback control

In **feedback closed-loop control systems**, the control loop compares the output of the process to the desired output and, if a difference is found, adjusts the input or process accordingly. The mechanism emphasises the fact that in order to control any

Feedback control

In feedback closed-loop control systems the control loop compares the output of the process to the desired output and if a difference is found, adjusts the input or process accordingly.

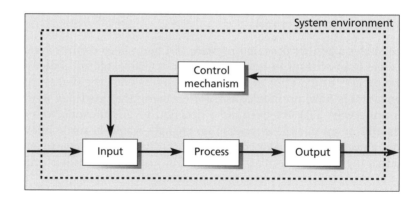

Fig 10.5 A generic closed-loop feedback control system

system, such as a business system, information about its current output state is needed in order that appropriate action can be taken to adjust inputs. If this link between output and input is broken, the process will not be controlled.

Positive and negative feedback. Negative feedback is used to describe the act of reversing any discrepancy between desired and actual output. Positive feedback responds to a variance between desired and actual output by increasing that variance.

The term **negative feedback** is used to describe the act of reversing any discrepancy between desired and actual output. Thus in a business setting a budget overspend would be responded to by actions leading to a reduction in this variance. A business example is rapid sales growth increasing production levels leading to increased sales. A situation of **positive feedback** is unsustainable and some corrective action arising either from within the system or from the environment will occur. For the example of increasing sales and production, the business may meet cashflow problems with expanding too fast, a situation termed overtrading.

The main difficulty with negative feedback systems is the potential for delays in the feedback control loop. Thus the effect of a change in input to bring about a change in output may not be observed until after a period of time. This can lead to an output level which oscillates around the desired output because of overcorrection of input values during the feedback delay period. For example, the delay between the setting of interest rates and their effect on the output goal of a level of inflation can lead to a situation of overcompensation in either direction.

Feedforward control

Positive and negative feedback

Negative feedback is used to describe the act of reversing any discrepancy between desired and actual output. Positive feedback responds to a variance between desired and actual output by increasing that variance.

Feedforward control

Feedforward incorporate a prediction element in the control feedback loop.

Feedforward control systems attempt to overcome the overcorrection and time-delay disadvantages of feedback systems by incorporating a prediction element in the control feedback loop. This process can be summarised in a systems diagram such as Fig 10.6. Thus action is taken based on not only the current state of the system but also a prediction about its future state. Feedforward systems are not as common as feedback systems in business settings. Examples include inventory control systems which work to a planned sales level of material usage rate. Elements of project man-

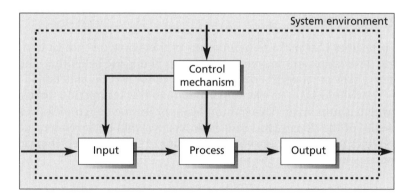

Fig 10.6 A generic closed-loop feedforward control system

agement can also be seen as feedforward control where plans are made for resource requirements over time.

Feedback control systems generally provide a relatively cheap method of control and are an effective method of bringing a system back under control. However, feedforward systems provide a way of overcoming the timing delays associated with feedback systems but depend on the accuracy of the plans on which they are based. A combination of both methods can potentially deliver the benefits of the proactive feedforward approach and the reactive feedback control method.

▶ BEHAVIOUR OF SYSTEMS

The behaviour of a system can be described in a number of ways. The following definitions can usefully be related to information systems.

▶ Holism

The concept that a whole is more than the sum of its parts is called *holism*. This implies that the entire system should be defined before the subsystems which make up that system are examined. In Chapter 11 systems analysis diagramming methods such as dataflow diagrams are introduced. These describe a system at a high level and are then broken down into their constituent parts.

▶ Entropy

This is the amount of disorder or randomness present in any system. All non-living systems tend towards disorder. For an organisation this would represent an inability to transform inputs into outputs. Information systems can provide a vital role in obtaining inputs (information) and providing information to ensure that objectives are met.

▶ Emergent properties

These are properties that make sense in terms of the whole but not in terms of individual parts. This relates to the concept of holism and is the belief that 'the whole is more than the sum of its parts'. Thus a system cannot best be understood by breaking down the whole into its elements, but it is the interaction between these elements which is important. This has implications for the design of software, where the complexity of the design (and thus maintenance) will be dependent not just on its size (e.g. lines of code) but also on the amount of links between the various software subsystems that make up the software.

▶ Equifinality

Systems theory does not assume that there is only one method of achieving a particular output. The characteristic of *equifinality* means that there may be many different configurations of process or system structures which may achieve the same result. This means for activities such as coding and design that the choice of approach could have a significant effect on the quality of outcome, in terms of maintainability for example, even though the finished product may achieve the same results.

▶ Law of requisite variety

An important law relating to systems control is Ashby's law of requisite variety, which implies that the central elements in the system must be flexible enough to cope with all the variations in input that could feasibly occur. This has many important consequences for business and information systems. For instance, it is essential that computer-based information systems can respond to the variety of inputs that they could be expected to encounter (this is referred to as range checking in Chapter 12). Thus the complexity or feasibility of implementing computer-based systems can be partly attributed to the range of possible system inputs encountered.

Ashby's Law is also of relevance to business systems. The range of customer requirements with which an organisation must deal may require a great deal of flexibility in response. Thus consequences for bureaucratic organisations with limited responses who wish to move to a more customer-oriented service may be the introduction of more flexible routines or training of personnel in order for them to be able to respond to a wider range of requests. Many strategic decisions involve matching the flexibility of the organisation with the market in which it is competing.

▶ Deterministic and probabilistic systems

In a *deterministic* system (sometimes known as *mechanistic*), all of the system's outputs can be predicted by examining its inputs. An example of a deterministic system is an electronic calculator, where the results of carrying out a calculation can be predicted with complete accuracy. An example of an information system of this type is a sales order processing system.

In a *probabilistic* system (sometimes known as *stochastic*), the outputs of the system cannot be predicted with complete accuracy. An example of a probabilistic system is a production planning system used to schedule work. Although the system can predict how long the production run is *likely* to take, it cannot provide a precise figure. An example of an information system of this type is a sales forecasting system.

▶ Adaptive systems

An *adaptive system* (sometimes known as *self-organising* or *cybernetic*) responds to changes in the environment and modifies its operation accordingly. The outputs obtained from the system are sometimes uncertain, since the system may respond to the same stimuli in different ways. Examples of adaptive systems include human beings, plants and business organisations and neural networks, an artificial intelligence application (Chapter 6).

▶ Hard and soft systems

A *hard system* has an explicit objective and is governed by fixed rules and procedures, such as those encountered for structured decision making (Chapter 6). The conditions in the system's environment tend to be stable and therefore more predictable. In turn, the system's outputs can be predicted more easily and its performance can be measured objectively. An example of a hard system is a production line.

A *soft system* operates in a relatively unpredictable environment where conditions may be uncertain or liable to rapid change. Soft systems usually involve people or socio-technical situations. The next section describes a specific methodology which can be used for this type of analysis.

Different methods of dealing with hard and soft properties are needed for information systems development. Hard properties are generally easier to process by computers, but soft properties usually contain a human element and there is often a need to consider the interaction between the information and management system of which they are a part.

▶ Differentiation/specialisation

A characteristic of all complex systems is that specialised units perform specialised tasks. This relates to information systems, where a software package will be broken down into a hierarchy of software components. This hierarchy can be based in the notion of a number of parts of a whole or in object-oriented programming components belonging to a class (Chapter 12).

▶ SOFT SYSTEMS METHODOLOGY

Soft systems methodology is a methodology which emphasises the human involvement in systems and models their behaviour as part of systems analysis in a way that is understandable by non-technical experts.

This methodology has its origins in Peter Checkland's (1981) attempt to adapt systems theory into a methodology which can be applied to any particular problem situation. From an information systems development perspective, it is argued that systems analysts often apply their tools and techniques to problems that are not well defined. In addition, it is also argued that since human beings form an integral part of the world of systems development, a systems development methodology must

Soft systems methodology

A methodology which emphasises the human involvement in systems and models their behaviour as part of systems analysis in a way which is understandable by non- technical experts.

347

embrace all the people who have a part to play in the development process (users, IS/IT professionals, managers etc.). Since these people may have conflicting objectives, perceptions and attitudes, we are essentially dealing with the problems caused by the unpredictability of **human activity systems**.

Human activity systems are 'notional system (i.e. not existing in any tangible form) where human beings are undertaking some activities that achieve some purpose' (Patching, 1990).

Proponents of soft systems methodology (SSM) claim, therefore, that true understanding of complex problem situations (and in our case this means information systems development) is more likely if 'soft systems' methods are used rather than formal 'hard systems' techniques. This is not to say that 'hard' methods do not have a place. Rather, it is to suggest that the more traditional tools and techniques will have a greater chance of being used effectively if they are placed within a soft systems perspective.

Soft systems methodology has seven stages. They should be regarded as a framework rather than a prescription of a series of steps that should be followed slavishly.

Human activity system

A human activity system can be defined as a 'notional system (i.e. not existing in any tangible form) where human beings are undertaking some activities that achieve some purpose' (Patching, 1990).

▶ Stage 1 The problem situation: unstructured

This stage is concerned with finding out as much as possible about the problem situation from as many different affected people as possible. Many different views about the problem will surface and it is important to bring out as many of them as possible. The structure of the problem in terms of physical layout, reporting structure, formal and informal communication channels will also be explored.

A soft systems investigator will often find that there is a vagueness about the problem situation being investigated and what needs to be done. There can also be a lack of structure to the problem and the situation that surrounds it.

▶ Stage 2 The problem situation: expressed

The previous stage was concerned with gathering an informal picture of the problem situation. This stage documents these findings. While there is no prescribed method for doing this, a technique that is commonly used is the drawing of 'rich pictures'. A rich picture can show the processes involved in the problem under consideration and how they relate to each other. The elements which can be included are the clients of the system (internal and external), the tasks being performed, the environment within which the system operates, the owners of the 'problem' and areas of conflict that are known to exist.

Rich pictures can act as an aid to discussion, either between problem owner and problem solver or between analysts and users or both. From a rich picture it then becomes possible to extract problem themes, which in turn provide a basis for further understanding of the problem situation. An example of a rich picture is shown in Fig 10.7. Such a diagram can be used in systems analysis to indicate the flows of information, the needs of staff and how the physical environment – the office layout – affects the current way of working. This summary of the existing situation provides a valuable context for systems analysis and design.

Fig 10.7 An example of a rich picture for an estate agency showing the needs and responsibilities of different staff

▶ Stage 3 Root definitions of relevant systems

Checkland describes a root definition as a 'concise, tightly constructed description of a human activity system which states what the system is'.

A root definition is created using the CATWOE checklist technique. CATWOE is an acronym that contains the following elements:

◆ *Clients or Customers* – the person(s) who benefit, or are affected by or suffer from the outputs of the system and its activities that are under consideration.

◆ *Actors* – those who carry out the activities within the system.

- *Transformation* – the changes which take place either within or because of the system (this lies at the heart of the root definition).

- *Weltanshaung or Worldview* – this refers to how the system is viewed from an explicit viewpoint; sometimes this term is described as assumptions made about the system.

- *Owner* – the person(s) to whom the system is answerable; the sponsor, controller or someone who could cause the system to cease.

- *Environment* – that which surrounds and influences the operation of the system but which has no control over it.

The main use of the root definition is to clarify the situation so that it can be summed up in a clear, concise statement. An example of a root definition for a university might be:

> To provide students with the maximum opportunity for self development, while at the same time safeguarding academic standards and allowing the university to operate within its budgetary constraints.

An alternative root definition might be:

> A system to maximise revenue and the prestige of academic staff!

If there are many different viewpoints to be represented, it is possible that a number of different root definitions may be constructed. These in turn will provide a basis for further discussion, so that a single agreed root definition can be produced. A single root definition that is hard to produce is indicative of sharp divisions between the CATWOE elements. From an information systems development perspective, if it is not possible to agree on a single root definition, then the systems development process is likely to be fraught with difficulties.

▶ Stage 4 Building conceptual models

A conceptual model is a logical model of the key activities and processes that must be carried out in order to satisfy the root definition produced in Stage 3. It is, therefore, a representation of what must be done rather than what is currently done.

Conceptual models can be shown on a simple diagram where activities and the links between them can be shown. Figure 10.8 shows a simple conceptual model of a student records system.

Where several alternative root definitions have been produced, it is usual to draw a conceptual model for each one. Successive iterations through the alternative models can then lead to an agreed root definition and conceptual model. When this has happened, it is possible to move on to the next stage.

▶ Stage 5 Comparing conceptual models with reality

Different alternative conceptual models that represent what should happen can be compared with the reality of what actually happens, as represented by the rich picture produced in Stage 2.

The purpose of this step is not to alter the conceptual models so that they fit more closely with what happens in reality. Instead, it is to enable the participants in the

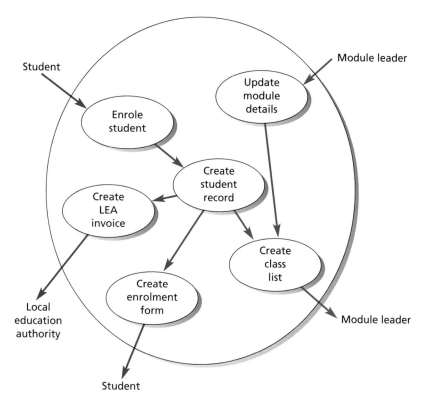

Student

Module leader

Enrole
student

Update
module
details

Create
LEA
invoice

Create
student
record

Create
class
list

Create
enrolment
form

Local
education
authority

Module leader

Student

Fig 10.8 Conceptual Models – a simple example

problem situation to gain an insight into the situation and the possible ways in which the change to reality can take place.

▶ Stage 6 Assessing feasible and desirable changes

From the output of Stage 5, an analysis of the proposed changes can be made and proposals for change drawn up for those which are considered feasible and desirable. Such changes may relate to information systems, but there is no restriction on the type or scope of the change.

▶ Stage 7 Action to improve the problem situation

It is perhaps here that the application of the model is most evident. SSM does *not* describe methods for implementing solutions – this lies outside the scope of the methodology. What it *does* do is to provide a framework through which problem situations can be understood. In fact, there is no reason that SSM should not be used as a tool for assisting the implementation of the required solution – the steps can be repeated, but this time the problem situation under consideration is the implementation of the required solution. This in turn may throw up alternative methods such as SSADM or rapid applications development (Chapter 7) as the best approach to information systems development. Indeed, SSM has often been used as a 'front end' to more traditional structured development methodologies.

▶ COUPLING

The degree of **coupling** defines how closely linked different subsystems are. It is a fundamental design principle for software that it should be loosely coupled. Loose coupling means that the modules pass only the minimum of information between them and do not share data and program code. If there is sharing of code and data, this is referred to as close coupling. Loose coupling leads to less complex links between modules, giving fewer errors and easier maintenance. This principle is also true for information systems.

▶ Close-coupled systems

Systems or subsystems that are highly dependent on one another are known as close-coupled systems. In such cases, the outputs of one system are the direct inputs of another. As an example, consider the way in which an examination system might operate. The letter that confirms a student's grade could be said to be the result of two subsystems working together very closely. One subsystem ensures that all examination scripts are marked and that a list of final results is produced. The second subsystem produces the letter of confirmation as its output. However, the letter of confirmation can only be produced once all marks have been confirmed and recorded. Thus, the output of the marking subsystem becomes the input to the subsystem that creates the confirmation letter.

To take another example, the volume of production of perishable goods such as fruit from a farm must be closely coupled with sales, since otherwise the produce will be wasted. The 'just-in-time' method used by a number of manufacturing organisations also illustrates a close-coupled system. This method involves holding as few parts or raw materials as possible. In order to ensure that production is not halted, parts must be supplied 'just in time' to be used in the manufacturing process. Unless the manufacturing organisation has very close links with its suppliers, this approach cannot work effectively. This approach contrasts with the traditional method of production where material is held 'in hand' as inventory. In this arrangement it is not necessary for production to match sales so closely, so this is an example of a decoupled system (Fig 10.10).

At this point, it is worth considering manufacturing organisations in a little more detail. The close-coupled production systems typically used in such organisations must be monitored and controlled carefully in order to prevent *bottlenecks* from occurring. Figure 10.9 illustrates a simple manufacturing process that involves three stages in the production of a given item. A similar situation could occur in a project management context: if Step C is not completed, then the staff who are ready to work on different aspects of Step B may not be usefully deployed. The diagram shows how a bottleneck can arise when one part of the manufacturing process is unable to keep pace with the rest.

Notice that there are two points at which a bottleneck can occur:

◆ If the people and machinery at Step C cannot produce enough parts to supply those at Step B, then the manufacturing process will slow or stop altogether. Note that a bottleneck at this point will also affect the people and machinery at Step A, since their part of the process depends on receiving parts from Step B.

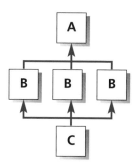

Fig 10.9 How bottlenecks can occur in a manufacturing system

◆ If too many items are supplied to Step A of the process, then the production of finished items will slow or halt. In addition, a backlog of unfinished items will begin to build up.

▶ Decoupled systems

Decoupled systems (or subsystems) are less dependent on one another than coupled systems and so are more able to deal with unexpected situations or events. Such systems tend to have higher levels of autonomy, being allowed more freedom to plan and control their activities. Although decoupled systems are more flexible and adaptive than close-coupled systems, this very flexibility increases the possibility that suboptimality might occur. In the production to sales example (Fig 10.10), the suboptimality results in higher costs of holding inventory.

In manufacturing organisations, a number of techniques can be employed to decouple systems so that overall efficiency can be improved. Some examples include the following:

◆ Careful monitoring and control of stocks can help ensure a steady flow of work. This allows problems caused by inadequate supplies of parts to be reduced or eliminated.

◆ Existing systems can be reorganised in order to improve the parts of the manufacturing process that are prone to bottlenecks.

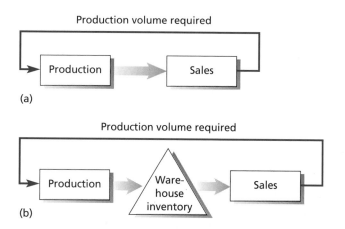

Fig 10.10 Examples of (a) close-coupled and (b) decoupled systems

◆ Additional capacity can be added to existing manufacturing systems. Although relatively expensive to implement, this approach allows a steady flow of work to be maintained more easily and can help minimise losses sustained due to stoppages.

▶ SYSTEMS DYNAMICS

Systems dynamics

Based on the view that the world can be regarded as a set of interdependent systems, it usually uses simulation models to try to understand why systems behave as they do.

This section describes the technique of systems dynamics, which provides an approach to studying the effect of information flows within systems.

Systems dynamics can be used to study systems in either a quantitative or qualitative manner. It is based on the view that the world can be regarded as a set of interdependent systems and usually employs the building of a computer-based simulation model to try to understand why systems behave as they do. Systems dynamics stresses the appearance of certain structural features in human-based systems, such as feedback control and delay mechanisms. The appearance of positive and negative feedback as a control mechanism has been discussed earlier in this chapter. Systems dynamics states that the presence of these loops usually makes the behaviour of human activity systems harder to understand. Another feature of these systems is the delays that occur between the transmission and receiving of information. These tend to make the system much harder to control as overcompensation tends to occur (e.g. overordering to make up for late delivery leading to overproduction).

The following terms are used in systems dynamics:

◆ resources and information;
◆ levels (stocks) and rates (flow).

Resources are the physical items in the system that are the main objective of the transformation process. An example of a resource would be a raw material that is transformed into finished product or a client who is transformed into a satisfied customer. Resources can be classified into consumable (depleted as the process occurs, e.g. raw material) or non-consumable (use to enable the process, e.g. machine).

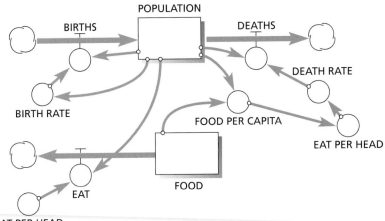

Fig 10.11 Example of a systems dynamics model constructed using Stella software

Information is a non-physical resource that is used to make decisions within the model, e.g. a decision to increase production to match sales demand.

Levels or *stocks* are the accumulation of resources within the system (e.g. work in progress in a manufacturing plant). *Rates* are the movement of resources, which may lead to a change in the level amount (e.g. a production rate increase may lead to an increased level of components in the system).

In systems dynamics the transformation of resources and information is modelled as a series of linked levels and rates. Levels represent the state of the system at any point in time. *Flows* represent rates of changes of resources or of information. Computer software such as Stella II and I Think allows the systems dynamics diagram to be placed on the computer screen, using icons for elements such as stocks and flows. Figure 10.11 shows an example of a Stella diagram.

Systems dynamics is one approach to studying the effect of delayed and distorted information which forms the basis of feedback control in organisational systems.

▶ SUMMARY

1 Systems theory is relevant to the study of information systems because:
   - ◆ it provides a unified framework for the study of business and information systems;
   - ◆ it provides understanding of organisational control issues;
   - ◆ it reveals the many interactions between a system such as an information system and its environment.

2 Important principles of systems theory are:
   - ◆ All systems comprise an input, transformation process and output.
   - ◆ Systems can be broken down into subsystems. The whole system is known as the suprasystem.
   - ◆ In a deterministic system, all of the systems outputs are constrained by its inputs. In a stochastic (probabilistic) system, this is not possible.
   - ◆ Decoupling of subsystems is preferred to close coupling in systems design.

3 Different types of system control are as follows:
   - ◆ Information on the performance of the system is gathered by a feedback mechanism, which can be used to control the system by adjusting its inputs.
   - ◆ Open-loop control systems have limited control in comparison with closed-loop control systems in which feedback or feedforward control occurs.

4 The soft systems methodology (SSM) is intended to adapt systems theory into a methodology that can be applied to any particular problem situation. SSM emphasises the human involvement in systems and models their behaviour as part of systems analysis in a way that is understandable by non-technical experts.

▶ **EXERCISES**

▶ Self-assessment questions

1 Answer the following questions in relation to your college or university:
  (a) What are the institution's objectives?
  (b) Identify a range of typical inputs, processes and outputs.
  (c) What feedback mechanisms are in place and what kinds of information do they produce?
  (d) What control mechanisms exist?

2 Draw a diagram summarising the system defined in Question 1.

3 Match each term to the correct statement.
  (a) input   1 Provides information concerning the performance of a system.
  (b) process   2 Describes exchanges between the system and its environment.
  (c) output   3 Converts raw materials into a finished product.
  (d) feedback   4 Contains everything outside of the system.
  (e) control   5 Defines the scope of the system.
  (f) boundary   6 Examples include raw materials, energy or labour power.
  (g) environment   7 Examples include information, a product or service.
  (h) interface   8 Adjusts the performance of the system.

4 Discuss why determining the system boundary is important in systems analysis and design.

5 Describe how a business could be divided into a number of subsystems.

6 Explain the concept of coupled and decoupled systems with reference to:
  (a) a hi-fi system.
  (b) a standard PC.
  (c) local and national government.

7 Where would you normally place soft systems analysis in the systems development process and why?

▶ Discussion questions

1 Can each of the following be described as a system? For each item, try to identify at least *two* inputs, processes and outputs. In addition, what feedback and control mechanisms exist?
  ◆ a human being;
  ◆ a plant;
  ◆ a house;
  ◆ a country;
  ◆ a computer.

2 When designing business information systems, an important design objective is that the sub-systems of the modules will be decoupled or loosely coupled. Discuss this statement with regard to:
  (a) enterprise resource planning systems;
  (b) just-in-time manufacturing systems.

▶ Essay questions

1 Summarise how an understanding of systems theory can be applied to systems analysis and design.

2 Use business examples to illustrate the importance of control in a business system where a system is used to represent the whole organisation. Which types of control are most appropriate to a business?

3 Draw a diagram illustrating the subsystems occurring in a hospital. Label the inputs and outputs of each subsystem. Which subsystems are most closely coupled?

4 What are the subsystems of a personal computer? Define the interfaces between each subsystem.

▶ Examination questions

1 Distinguish between feedback and feedforward control.

2 Define decoupled and close-coupled subsystems. Give an example of each.

3 Draw a diagram illustrating the main components of a generic system.

4 Explain why feedback and control are important in business information systems.

▶ References

Ackoff, R.L. and Sasieni, M.W. (1968) *Fundamentals of Operations Research*, John Wiley, Chichester.

Ashby, W.R. (1956) *An Introduction to Cybernetics*, Methuen, London.

Beer, S. (1959) *Cybernetics and Management*, EUP, London.

Checkland, P.B. (1978) 'The origins and nature of "hard" systems thinking', *Journal of Applied Statistical Analysis*, 5, 2.

Checkland, P.B. (1981) *Systems Thinking, Systems Practice*, John Wiley, New York.

Forrester, J.W. (1961) *Industrial Dynamics*, John Wiley, New York.

Forrester, J.W. (1969) *Principles of Systems*, MIT Press, MA.

Hall, A.D. (1962) *A Methodology for Systems Engineering*, D. Van Nostrand Co., Princeton, New York.

Jackson, M.C. (1991) *Systems Methodology for the Management Sciences*, Plenum Press, New York.

Katz, D. and Kahn, R.L. (1966) *The Social Psychology of Organisations*, John Wiley, New York.

Miser, H.J. and Quade, E.S. (eds) (1985) *Handbook of Systems Analysis: Overview of Uses, Procedures, Applications and Practice*, John Wiley, Chichester.

Miser, H.J. and Quade, E.S. (eds) (1988) *Handbook of Systems Analysis: Craft Issues and Procedural Choices*, John Wiley, Chichester.

Senge, P. (1990) *The Fifth Discipline: The Art and Practice of the Learning Organization*, Currency/Doubleday, New York.

von Bertalanffy, L. (1950) 'The theory of open systems in physics and biology', in Emery, F.E. (ed.) *Systems Thinking*, Penguin, 70–85.

▶ Further reading

Harry, M. (1997) *Information Systems in Business*, 2nd edition, Financial Times Pitman Publishing, London.

Martin, C. and Powell, P. (1992) *Information Systems: a Management Perspective*, McGraw-Hill, Basingstoke.

Patching, D. (1990) *Practical Soft Systems Analysis*, Financial Times Pitman Publishing, London.

Senge, P. (1990) *The Fifth Discipline: The Art and Practice of the Learning Organization*, Currency/Doubleday, New York.

Skyttner, L. (1996) *General Systems Theory: an Introduction*, Macmillan, Basingstoke.

Tricker, R.I. and Boland, R.J. (1982) *Management Information and Control Systems*, 2nd edition, John Wiley, Chichester.

Wilson, R.M.S. and Chua, W.F. (1993) *Managerial Accounting: Method and Meaning*, 2nd edition, Chapman & Hall, London.

Systems analysis

INTRODUCTION

Once it has been determined that it is desirable to proceed with the acquisition of a new computer-based information system, it is necessary to determine the system requirements before any design or development work takes place. **Systems analysis** is about finding out *what* the new system is to do, rather than *how*. There are two basic components to the analysis process:

- *fact-finding* – an exercise needs to take place where all prospective users of the new system should contribute to determining requirements;
- *documentation* – detailed systems design follows the analysis stage and this needs to be based on documentation and diagrams from the analysis stage which are unambiguous.

Systems analysis involves the investigation of the business and user requirements of an information system. Fact-finding techniques are used to ascertain the user's needs and these are summarised using a range of diagramming methods.

Factors that will influence the use of fact-finding techniques and documentation tools will include:

- *The result of the 'make-or-buy decision'.* Made during the feasibility stage, a 'make' decision where bespoke software is developed will need more detailed analysis than a 'buy' decision where packaged software is purchased off the shelf, especially when the results of the analysis process are fed into the design stage.
- *Application complexity.* A very complex system or one where there are linkages to other systems will need very careful analysis to define system and subsystem boundaries and this will lead to use of more formal techniques when compared with a simple or standalone application.
- *End-user versus corporate development.* End-user development does not lend itself to extensive use of formal analysis tools. However, basic analysis is required and

Systems analysis

The investigation of the business and user requirements of an information system. Fact-finding techniques are used to ascertain the user's needs and these are summarised using a requirements specification and a range of diagramming methods.

there are certain analysis tools that end-user developers can use which increase the probability of success. Similarly, where application development by IS/IT professionals occurs there will be a need for a more formal approach, especially where systems cut across functional boundaries.

Any errors in systems development which occur during the analysis phase will cost far more to correct than errors which occur in subsequent stages. It is therefore essential that maximum thought and effort are put into the analysis process if unanticipated costs are not to arise in the later stages of development.

▶ Learning objectives

After reading this chapter, readers will be able to:

◆ choose appropriate techniques for analysing users' requirements for an information system;

◆ construct appropriate diagrams which assist in summarising the requirements as an input to the design phase;

◆ realise the importance of conducting the analysis phase to the overall success of the system.

▶ Links to other chapters

This chapter is directly related to Chapter 8, which describes the preceding stage of information systems development (initiation), and Chapter 12, which describes the next phase (systems design).

▶ IDENTIFYING THE REQUIREMENTS

The first task in analysis is to conduct a fact-finding exercise so that the information systems requirements can be determined. The methods which an organisation uses in the analysis phase will depend, at least in part, on two factors:

◆ *Levels of decision making involved.* A new information system will be under consideration either to resolve a problem or to create an opportunity. In either case, the objective is to improve the quality of information available to allow better decision making. The type of system under consideration may include a transaction processing system, a management information system, a decision support system, a combination of these or some other categorisation of system (Chapter 6). So, for example, an information system that is purely geared towards the needs of management will require a different approach to fact-finding (for example, using one-to-one interviews with senior managers) to one which mainly involves transaction processing (for example using observation of the existing process).

◆ *Scope of functional area.* A new information system may serve the needs of one functional business area (e.g. the HRM function), or it may cut across many functional areas. An information system that is restricted in scope may be faced with fewer of the problems that can affect new systems designed to meet the needs of many different areas. As before, the techniques of fact-finding may be similar, but how they are used and the findings presented may be radically different. Organisational culture, structure and decision-making processes will all have a part to play in selling the systems solution to all the affected parties.

Regardless of the scope and organisational levels involved, the objective of the fact-finding task is to gather sufficient information about the business processes under consideration so that a design can be constructed which will then provide the blue-print for the systems build phase. We will now turn to a consideration of a number of fact-finding methods.

Although it might be thought that finding out the requirements for a system is straightforward, this is far from the case. Dissatisfaction with information systems, referred to in Chapter 9, is often down to the requirements for the information system being wrongly interpreted. Figure 11.1 shows an oft-quoted example of how a user's requirements for a swing might be interpreted, not only at the requirements analysis stage but throughout the project.

▶ Interviewing

When **interviewing**, a range of staff are interviewed using structured techniques to identify features and problems of the current system and required features of the future system.

Analysis technique – interviewing

Recommended practice: a range of staff are interviewed using structured techniques to identify features and problems of the current system and required features of the future system.

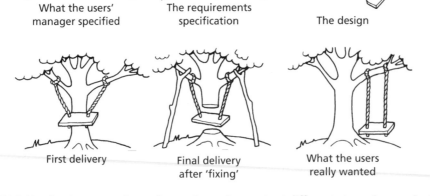

| What the users' manager specified | The requirements specification | The design |
| First delivery | Final delivery after 'fixing' | What the users really wanted |

Fig 11.1 Varying interpretations of a user's requirements at different stages in a project
Source: Johnston, 1995.

Interviewing is one of the most widely used fact-finding methods. Success with this method involves careful planning, proper conduct of the interviews themselves and finally accurate recording of the interview findings. We can expand each of these to provide more detail.

Planning

◆ Clear objectives need to be set which will identify what needs to be achieved at the end of the interviewing process.

◆ Interview subjects must also be carefully selected so that the information gained will be relevant to the system being developed. For example, there may be little use in interviewing all the shopfloor workers in a manufacturing company if the system being developed is an executive information system to assist with decision making at senior levels within the business. There may still be some merit in interviewing certain key personnel involved in operation decision making, since data produced may be useful in the proposed EIS.

◆ Customers should be involved in analysis if the use of a system affects them directly. For example, a customer of a phone-based ordering system or a telephone bank may well give an insight into problems of an existing system.

◆ The topics which the interview is to cover need to be clearly identified and the place where interviews are to take place must be determined.

◆ Finally, it is necessary to plan how the interviews are to be conducted and the types of questions to be used.

Conduct

◆ The interviewer must establish a control framework for the interview. This will include the use of summarising to check the points being made and appropriate verbal and non-verbal signals to assist the flow of the interview.

◆ Interviewers must be good listeners. This is especially important when dealing with complex business processes which are the object of the systems development project.

◆ The interviewer must select a mix of open and closed questions which will elicit maximum information retrieval.

◆ Finally, the interview must be structured in an organised way. There are three main approaches to structuring an interview. The first is the *'pyramid structure'*, where the interview begins with a series of specific questions and during the course of the interview moves towards general ones. The second is the *'funnel structure'*, where the interviewer begins with general questions and during the course of the interview concentrates increasingly on specific ones. The third approach is the *'diamond structure'*, where the interview begins with specific questions, moves towards general questions in the middle of the interview and back towards specific questions at the end.

Regardless of which approach is taken, it will still be necessary to document carefully the findings of the interview.

Interviews should use a mixture of open and closed questions. **Open questions** are not restricted to a limited range of answers such as Yes/No (closed questions). They are asked to elicit opinions or ideas for the new system or identify commonly held views

Open questions

Not restricted to a limited range of answers such as Yes/No (closed questions). Asked to elicit opinions or ideas for the new system or identify commonly held views among staff. Open questions are not typically used for quantitative analysis, but can be used to identify a common problem.

among staff. Open questions are not typically used for quantitative analysis, but can be used to identify a common problem.

Closed questions have a restricted choice of answers such as Yes/No or a range of opinion on a scale of strongly agree to strongly disagree (Likert scale). This approach is useful for quantitative analysis of results.

Closed questions

Closed questions have a restricted choice of answers such as Yes/No or a range of opinion on a scale of strongly agree to strongly disagree (Likert scale). Approach is useful for quantitative analysis of results.

Recording

During the course of the interview, the interviewer will need to make notes to record the findings. It may also be useful to draw diagrams to illustrate the processes being discussed. Some interviewers like to use a tape-recorder to be sure that no points are missed. Whichever methods are used, the requirement is to record three main attributes of the system under consideration:

◆ *Business processes*. A business process exists when an input of some kind (raw materials, for example) is transformed in some way so that an output is produced for use elsewhere in the business.

◆ *Data*. Data will be acquired and processed and information produced as a consequence of carrying out business processes. Data must be analysed so that data acquisition, processing needs and information requirements can be encapsulated in the new information system.

◆ *Information flows*. Functional business areas do not exist in isolation from each other and neither do different business processes within the same business function. It is necessary, therefore, to identify how data and information within one business process are necessary for other business processes to operate effectively.

We will look at some relevant tools and techniques which help to record the findings later in this chapter.

As an information-gathering tool, interviews have a number of advantages and disadvantages. On the positive side they include:

✓ the ability to gather detailed information through a two-way dialogue;

✓ the ability for candid, honest responses to be made;

✓ an open, spontaneous process which can lead to valuable insights, especially when open questions are used;

✓ responses which can easily be quantified, especially when closed questions are used;

✓ being one of the best methods for gathering qualitative data such as opinions, and subjective descriptions of activities and problems.

On the negative side, however, the following points can be made:

✗ The analyst's findings may be coloured by his or her perceptions of how other, similar, business operations work. Interviewers need to be especially skilled if this is to be avoided.

✗ The development of a new information system may represent a threat through the risk of deskilling, redundancy or perceived inability to cope with change. Interviewees may, therefore, not cooperate with the interview process, either by not taking part or by giving vague and incomplete replies.

✗ The interviewee may tell the analyst what he or she thinks should happen rather than what actually happens.

✗ An interview at lower organisational levels may not yield as much information as some other methods if staff in this area are not capable of articulating with sufficient clarity.

On balance, interviewing is an essential part of the information-gathering process. For maximum benefit, interviewing should be used in conjunction with other techniques and we will turn to these now.

▶ Questionnaires

Analysis technique – questionnaires

Used to obtain a range of opinion on requirements by targeting a range of staff. They are open to misinterpretation unless carefully designed. They should consist of open and closed questions.

Questionnaires are used to obtain a range of opinion on requirements by targeting a range of staff. They are open to misinterpretation unless carefully designed. They should consist of open and closed questions.

Questionnaires can be a useful addition to the analyst's armoury, but are not of themselves enough to gather sufficient information for the later stages of the systems development process. That said, questionnaires can be very useful when used with other fact-finding methods, either to confirm the findings obtained elsewhere or to open up possible further areas for investigation. Typically, they are used before more detailed questions by interview.

Successful questionnaires have a number of characteristics:

✓ The questions will be framed by the analyst with a clear view of the information which is to be obtained from the completed questionnaires.

✓ The target audience must be carefully considered – a questionnaire designed for clerical or operational personnel should not contain questions that are not relevant to their level of work.

✓ The questionnaire should only contain branching (e.g. 'if the answer to Question 3 was 'No', then go to Question 8') if it is absolutely necessary – multiple branches create confusion and may lead to unusable responses.

✓ Questions should be simple and unambiguous so that the respondent does not have to guess what the analyst means.

✓ Multiple-choice, Likert-scale-type questions make the questionnaire easier to fill in and allow the results to be analysed more efficiently.

✓ The questionnaire should contain the required return date and person to whom the questionnaire should be returned.

Difficulties that can be encountered with questionnaires include:

✗ the inability of respondents to go back to the analyst to seek clarification about what a question means;

✗ difficulty in collating qualitative information, especially if the questionnaire contains open-ended questions;

✗ the inability to use verbal and non-verbal signals from the respondent as a sign to ask other or different questions;

✗ low response rates – these can be lower than 20 to 25 per cent when sent to other organisations or customers, which means that a large sample size is needed if the results are to carry any weight. Response rate is not such a problem for internal staff.

By contrast, the questionnaire process also has a number of benefits:

✓ When large numbers of people such as customers or suppliers need to be consulted, a carefully worded questionnaire is more efficient and less expensive than carrying out large numbers of interviews.

✓ Questionnaires can be used to check results found by using other fact-finding methods.

✓ The use of standardised questions can help codify the findings more succinctly than other tools.

In summary, questionnaires can have a useful role to play in certain circumstances, but they should not be used as the sole data-gathering method.

▶ Documentation review

Documentation reviews target information about existing systems, such as user guides or requirements specifications, together with paper or on-screen forms used to collect information, such as sales order forms. They are vital for collecting detail about data and processes which may not be recalled in questionnaires and interviews.

All organisations have at least some kind of documentation which relates to some or all of the business operations carried out. A documentation review can be carried out at a number of different stages in the analysis process. If carried out at the beginning of a requirements analysis exercise, it will help provide the analyst with some background information relating to the area under consideration. It may also help the analyst construct a framework for the remainder of the exercise, and enable interviews to be conducted in a more effective way since the analyst has some idea of current business practices and procedures. If document review is carried out later, it can be used to cross-check the actual business operations with what is supposed to happen. The kinds of documentation and records that can be reviewed include the following:

✓ Instruction manuals and procedure manuals which show how specific tasks are supposed to be performed.

✓ Requirements specifications and user guides from previous systems.

✓ Job descriptions relating to particular staff functions which may help identify who should be doing what.

✓ Strategic plans both for the organisation as a whole and the functional areas in particular, which can provide valuable background data for establishing broad functional objectives.

While documentation review can provide a very useful underpinning for other fact-finding tasks, there are still a number of problems:

✗ There can be a large quantity of data for an analyst to process. This is especially true in large organisations and it may take the analyst a long time to identify the documentation that is useful and that which can be ignored.

✗ Documentation is often out of date. If there is an old computerised system, it is quite possible that the documentation has not been changed for years, even though the system may have changed considerably over that period. The same can be said for the documentation of activities and procedures.

Analysis technique – documentation review

Use information on existing systems such as user guides, or requirements specifications together with paper or on-screen forms used to collect information such as sales order forms.

▶ Observation

Observation is useful for identifying inefficiencies in an existing way of working, either with a computer-based or a manual information system. It involves timing how long particular operations take and observing the method used to perform them. It can be time consuming and the staff who are observed may behave differently to normal.

This fact-finding method involves the analyst in directly observing business activities taking place so that they can see what is *actually* taking place rather than looking at documentation which states what *should* be taking place. One of the benefits of observation is that the analyst can see directly how something is done, rather than relying on verbal or written communication which may colour the facts or be the subject of misinterpretation by the analyst. Other benefits include:

✓ the ability to see how documents and records are actually handled and processed;

✓ observation may give a greater insight into actual business operations than simple paper documentation;

✓ identification of particular operations that take a long time;

✓ the opportunity to see how different processes interact with each other, thus giving the analyst a *dynamic* rather than a *static* view of the business situation under investigation.

On the downside, there are a number of difficulties associated with the observation technique:

✗ It is an extremely time-consuming exercise and therefore needs to be done as a supplementary rather than a principal fact-finding method.

✗ While observation allows an organisation to be dynamically assessed, it still does not allow attitudes and belief systems to be assessed. This can be a very important issue if the proposed information system is likely to encounter resistance to change among the workforce.

✗ Finally, there is the issue of the 'Hawthorne effect', where people tend to behave differently when they are being observed, thus reducing the value of the information being obtained. Of course, for the analyst, the problem is in determining whether those being observed are behaving differently or not!

This effect was first noticed in the Hawthorne plant of Western Electrics in the United States. Here, it was noted that production increased not as a consequence of actual changes in working conditions introduced by the plant's management but because management demonstrated an interest improving staff working conditions.

Despite these difficulties, it is desirable for the analyst to conduct at least some observation to ensure that no aspect of the system being investigated is not overlooked.

▶ Brainstorming

Brainstorming uses the interaction between a group of staff to generate new ideas and discuss existing problems. It is the least structured of the fact-finding techniques.

This is the final fact-finding technique we will consider. The methods which we have looked at so far are either passive or conducted on a one-to-one basis, or both.

The brainstorming method involves a number of participants and is an active approach to information gathering. While the other methods allow for many different views to be expressed, those methods do not allow different persons' perceptions of the business processes and systems needs to be considered simultaneously. Brainstorming allows multiple views and opinions to be brought forward at the same time. If the proposed systems user community participates actively, it is more likely that an accurate view of current business processes and information systems needs will be reached.

Brainstorming sessions require careful planning by the analyst. Factors to consider include:

◆ which persons to involve and from which functional business areas;

◆ how many people to involve in the session – too few and insufficient data may be gathered; too many and the session may be too difficult to handle;

◆ terms of reference for the session – there may need to be more than one session to identify clearly areas of agreement and those that need further discussion;

◆ management involvement – a session for shopfloor workers, for example, may be far less successful if management personnel are involved than if they are not. It would be appropriate, however, for management groups to have their own brainstorming session so that tactical and strategic issues can be tacked rather than simply operational ones.

The main benefit of the brainstorming approach is that, through the dynamics of group interaction, progress is more likely to be made than from a simple static approach to information gathering. Brainstorming sessions, if they are handled properly, can result in the productive sharing of ideas and perceptions, while at the same time cultural factors, attitudes and belief systems can be more readily assessed. Also, when the outcomes are positive ones, a momentum for change is built among those who will be direct users of the new information system. Change management is therefore more easily facilitated.

The main danger of the approach is that in the hands of an inexperienced analyst, there is a risk that the sessions may descend into chaos because of poor structure, bad planning, poor control or a combination of all three.

However, if used properly, this fact-finding method can generate the desired results more quickly than by any other information-gathering method. Even so, it still needs to be supplemented by one or more of the other methods discussed above.

Yeates *et al.* (1994) explains how structured brainstorming can be used to identify different options for a new system. This technique involves the following stages:

◆ Invite ideas which are written by individuals on separate sheets of paper or called out spontaneously and then noted on a whiteboard.

◆ Identify similarities between ideas and rationalise the options by choosing those which are most popular.

◆ Analyse the remaining options in detail, by evaluating their strengths and weaknesses.

It is important when brainstorming is undertaken that a facilitator is used to explain that a range of ideas is sought with input from everyone. Each participant should be able to contribute without fear of judgement by other members. When such an atmosphere is created this can lead to 'out-of-box' or free thinking which may generate ideas of new ways of working.

Brainstorming and more structured group techniques can be used throughout the development lifecycle. Brainstorming is an important technique in reengineering a business, since it can identify new ways of approaching processes. Taylor (1995) suggests that once new business processes have been established through analysis, they should be sanity checked by performing a 'talk-through, walk-through and run-through'. Here, the design team will describe the proposed business process and in the talk-through stage will elaborate on different business scenarios using cards to describe the process objects and the services they provide to other process objects. Once the model has been adjusted, the walk-through stage involves more detail in the scenario and the design team will role-play the services the processes provide. The final run-through stage is a quality check in which no on-the-spot debugging occurs – just the interactions between the objects are described. This method is similar to the class responsibility collaboration model proposed by Kent Beck and also described by Kavanagh (1994).

Once the analyst has completed the requirements investigation, it will be necessary to document the findings so that a proposal can be put forward for the next stage of the project. Some of the documentation tools discussed below may be used at the same time as the fact-finding process. For example, information flow diagrams may be used by the analyst to check with the end-user that points have been properly understood.

▶ Pictures and brainstorming

Research has shown that new ideas and recall are improved by the use of pictures, which tend to prompt thought better than text. This point is well made by Buzan (1995), who describes a technique known as mindmapping to record information and promote brainstorming. Mindmaps are a spontaneous means of recording information which are ideally applied to systems analysis, since they can be used to record information direct from user dialogues or summarise information after collection.

Another graphical technique which is useful to the system analyst is the rich picture. The rich picture is an element of the soft systems methodology which was described in Chapter 10. It can be used to describe the context of the current system using pictures which are more easily understood by end-users. An example is given in Chapter 10. They are described in the books by Checkland (1981) and Patching (1990).

▶ DOCUMENTING THE FINDINGS

In this section we will concentrate on three main diagramming tools: information flow diagrams (IFDs), dataflow diagrams (DFDs) and entity relationship diagrams (ERDs). These techniques are used by professional IS/IT personnel, partly as documentation tools and partly as checking tools with the user community. It is important, therefore, for non-IS/IT personnel to understand the fundamentals behind these diagramming tools so that communication between functional personnel and IS/IT experts is enhanced. Furthermore, tools such as ERDs can be applied by end-users to assist them in developing their own personal or departmental applications. As well as these tools, the requirements specification will also contain a text description of what the functions of the software will be. We will consider this first, and then consider the documentation tools.

▶ The requirements specification

The **requirements specification** is the main output from the systems analysis stage. Its main focus is a description of what all the functions of the software will be. These must be defined in great detail to ensure that when the specification is passed on to the designers, the system is what the users require. This will help prevent the problem referred to in Fig. 11.1.

The scope of the requirements specification will include:

◆ *data capture* – when, where and how often. The detailed data requirements will be specified using entity relationship diagrams and stored in a data dictionary. Dataflow diagrams will indicate the data stores required;

◆ *preferred data capture methods* – this may include use of keyboard entry, bar codes, OCR etc. (it could be argued that this is a design point, but it may be a key user requirement that a particular capture method is used);

◆ *functional requirements* – what operations the software must be able to perform. For example, for the maps in a geographic information system, the functional requirements would specify: the ability to zoom in and out, pan using scroll-bars and the facility to change the features and labels overlaid on the map;

◆ *user interface layout* – users will want access to particular functions in a single screen, so the requirements specification will define the main screens of an application. Detailed layout will be decided as part of prototyping and detailed design;

◆ *output requirements* – this will include such things as enquiry screens, regular standard and *ad hoc* reports and interfaces to other systems.

It is possible to categorise user requirements into three: the A list, the B list and the C list (or Priority 1 to 3). The A list should comprise all those requirements that the proposed system *must* support and without which it would not function. For example, an accounting system which does not produce customer statements may be seriously deficient. The B list would contain those requirements which are very desirable but which are not vital to the successful operation of the system. For example, it may be very desirable for a sales order processing system to produce a list of all customers who have not placed an order for the last six months, but it is not essential. The C list would contain those things which are nice to have (the 'bells and whistles') but which are neither essential nor very desirable. It might be nice in a stock control system, for example, if a screen 'buzzed' at the user if a certain combination of factors were present. However, it would not be classified as essential.

The requirements catalogue can be used to prioritise the 'very desirables' and the 'bells and whistles' so that at the design stage, most attention can be paid to those items that are perceived as having the highest priority. It may be, however, that if a low-priority item is seen to be very easy to implement, and a higher-priority item less so, the lower-priority item would be included in the development in preference.

It may be that in the case of a 'very desirable but hard to implement' feature, a simpler item might be included as an imperfect substitute. This would be more readily apparent at the design stage and it may be necessary to revisit the requirements catalogue at this point and consult the functional personnel again.

Requirements specification

The main output from the systems analysis stage. Its main focus is a description of what all the functions of the software will be.

▶ Information flow diagrams

Information flow diagram (IFD)

A simple diagram showing how information is routed between different parts of an organisation. It has an information focus rather than a process focus.

The **information flow diagram** (IDF) is one of the simplest tools used to document findings from the requirements determination process. They are used for a number of purposes:

◆ to document the main flows of information around the organisation;

◆ for the analyst to check that s/he has understood those flows and that none has been omitted;

◆ the analyst may use them during the fact-finding process itself as an accurate and efficient way to document findings as they are identified;

◆ as a high-level (not detailed) tool to document information flows within the organisation as a whole or a lower-level tool to document an individual functional area of the business.

The information flow diagram is a simple diagram showing how information is routed between different parts of an organisation. It has an information focus rather than a process focus.

An information flow diagram has three components, shown in Fig 11.2.

The ellipse in the diagram represents a source of information, which then flows to a destination location. In a high-level diagram, the source or destination would be a department or specific functional area of the business such as sales, accounting or manufacturing. In a lower-level (more detailed) diagram, one might refer to subfunctions such as accounts receivable, credit control or payroll (as you would normally find in an accounts department). The name of the source or destination should appear inside the ellipse. The source or destination is sometimes referred to as an internal or external entity according to whether it lies inside or outside the system boundary. This term is used frequently when constructing entity relationship diagrams and is described more fully later.

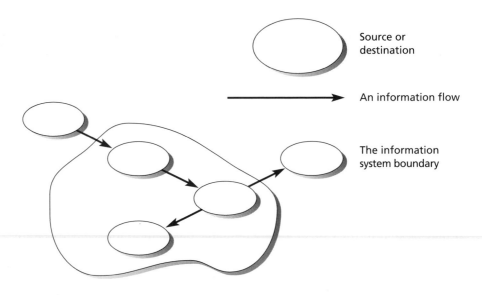

Source or destination

An information flow

The information system boundary

Fig 11.2 Information flow diagrams – the basic building blocks

Fig 11.3 An illustration of a simple information flow

The information flow, as represented by the arrowhead line, shows a flow of information from a source location to a destination. In an IFD the line should always be annotated with a brief description of the information flow. So, for example, if a sales department sends a customer's order details to the accounts department for credit checking, the resulting flow might look like Fig 11.3.

Sources or destinations lying within the systems boundary imply that this information will be used directly by the system. The concept of the system boundary is explained further in the example that follows.

We now need to give a more detailed example to illustrate how an IFD could be used in practice.

CASE STUDY: TOPIC AREA

IFD drawing – a student records system

Suppose that a university wished to move from a manual, paper-based student records system to one which was computerised. The analyst would need to create a clear picture of the required information flows to help the system designer with the blueprint for the proposed system. We include some sample narrative to demonstrate the possible result of an interview between the analyst and the head of admissions.

'When a student enrols for the first time, they are required to fill in a form which has the following details:

◆ Forename.
◆ Surname.
◆ Date.
◆ Local authority.
◆ Home address.
◆ Term-time address.
◆ Home telephone number.
◆ Term-time telephone number.
◆ Sex.
◆ Course code.
◆ Course description.
◆ Module code (for each module being studied).
◆ Module description (as above).

'When the forms have been completed, they are passed to the student information centre. A series of actions follows:

◆ The student information centre (SIC) allocates the student a unique code number which stays with the student until they complete their studies.
◆ The SIC creates a card index of the student's details down to and including course description, plus the new student code number.
◆ The SIC also creates a list of all students belonging to each local education authority (LEA).
◆ The SIC sends the LEA list to the finance department, which then invoice the LEAs for the tuition fees relating to the students from their area.
◆ The SIC creates a study record card (SRC), giving the student details and the modules being studied.
◆ The SIC groups the SRCs by course and for each course sorts the cards into student name order; the SRCs for each course are then sent to the department that runs that course.
◆ Each department will take the SRCs for its courses and produce a number of class lists, based around the modules that the student is studying, which are then passed to the relevant module leaders.
◆ The SIC will issue the student with an enrolment form which the student can use to obtain a library card.
◆ Finally, the SIC will pass a list of all new students to the library and the students' union so that the library can issue students with library cards and the students' union can issue students with their NUS cards.'

It is necessary to translate the above into a series of information flows and also define the systems boundary (i.e. the line which separates what is in the system under consideration and what is outside it).

In order to be successful in drawing IFDs, it is helpful to follow a few simple steps, since an attempt to draw a diagram from scratch may prove a little tricky:

Step 1 List all the sources of information for the system under consideration (in other words, places where information is generated).

Step 2 List all the destinations (receivers) of information for the system under consideration.

Step 3 Make a simple list of all the information flows.

Step 4 For each of the information flows identified in Step 3, add the source and destination that relate to it.

Step 5 Draw the IFD from your list that you produced from 3 and 4.

Tips

1 When you have gained experience in doing this, Steps 1 and 2 can be ignored and Steps 3 and 4 can be combined.

2 An information source/destination can appear more than once on an IFD – it can help to eliminate lots of crossed lines (and crossed lines are best avoided since the annotations can look rather jumbled).

3 Use A4 paper, or larger in landscape mode.

The result of your efforts should look something like this:

Step 1 (information generators)
STUDENT
SIC
FINANCE
DEPARTMENT

Step 2 (information destinations)
STUDENT
SIC
LEA
TUTOR
LIBRARY
STUDENTS' UNION

Step 3 (information flows)
Student's personal and course information
LEA list
Invoices
Students on course
Class list
Enrolment form
List of all new students (times two)

Step 4 (adding sources and destinations to the information flows)

GENERATOR	FLOW	DESTINATION
STUDENT	Student's personal and course information	SIC
SIC	LEA list	FINANCE
FINANCE	Invoices	LEA
SIC	Students on course	DEPARTMENT
DEPARTMENT	Class list	TUTOR
SIC	Enrolment form	STUDENT
SIC	List of all new students (1)	LIBRARY
SIC	List of all students (2)	STUDENTS' UNION
STUDENTS' UNION	NUS card	STUDENT
LIBRARY	Library card	STUDENT

Step 5 (the completed diagram)
It is almost certain that if you were to attempt this diagram your results would not be exactly the same. However, provided that all the flows are represented correctly and there are no crossed lines, the result will be perfectly acceptable. Also, note that the student appears twice on the diagram. This is not just because the student is important (which of course s/he is!), but because it helps avoid crossed lines.

What remains now is to consider the systems boundary. If this manual information system were to be replaced by a new computer-based information system, it would be necessary to identify what would be within the systems boundary and what would be external to the system and, hence, outside the system boundary. For the purposes of this example, we will make some assumptions:

◆ *Students* are external to the system – they provide information as an input to the system and receive outputs from the system but are not themselves part of it – students will, therefore, be outside the system boundary.

◆ The *student information centre* is clearly central to the whole system and, therefore, is an integral part of the system under consideration – the SIC will lie inside the system boundary.

◆ The *finance* area needs a further assumption to be made. Let us assume that the finance area operates a computer-based information system for its accounting records and that the proposed system is to interface directly with it; in this case, it would make sense to include the finance area inside the system boundary.

◆ Similarly, suppose that the *library* operates its own computerised lending system. In the new system, it may wish to use an interface between the student records system and its own system for setting up new students' details. Since the library system is a separate one and does not require development itself, we will place the library outside the system boundary.

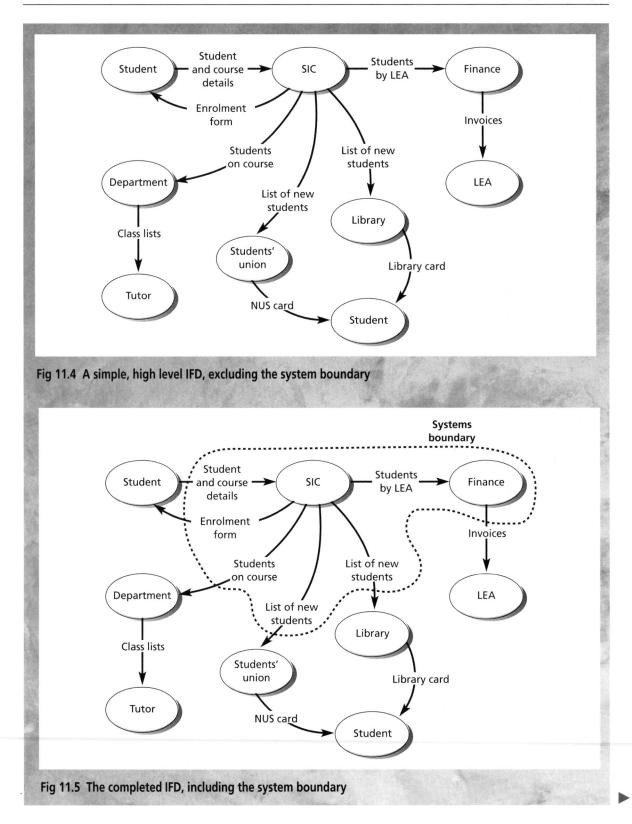

Fig 11.4 A simple, high level IFD, excluding the system boundary

Fig 11.5 The completed IFD, including the system boundary

- As with the library, we need to make an assumption about the *students' union* information systems. The students' union may be able to use an interface file from the student record system to generate NUS cards automatically; but, as with the library, that system would lie outside the scope of the area under consideration. Therefore, we will place the students' union outside the system boundary.
- It is reasonable to assume that the *tutor* is only to receive outputs from the system rather than carry out any processing of the data; it is reasonable, then, for the tutor to lie outside the system boundary.
- Finally, the local education authority is physically external to the university as well as not being part of the university itself; the LEA should, therefore, lie outside the system boundary.

We can see the result of this analysis in the final IFD, with the system boundary included (Fig 11.5).

You will observe that there are three different types of information flow:

- The first crosses the system boundary from outside with its destination inside the boundary – it is thus an input to the system from the external environment.
- The second lies entirely within the system boundary and is, therefore, an output from one area in the system which then forms the input to another.
- The third begins inside the system boundary and its destination lies outside – it is, therefore, an output from the system into its external environment.

What we have now is a diagram which clearly identifies the context for the systems development under consideration. The diagram can be used by the analyst to check with the prospective system users that all areas have been covered. It also helps the user community build a picture of how a new computer system should help to make the processes more efficient. Two separate IFDs are often drawn:

1 System 'as-is' to identify inefficiencies in the existing system.
2 New proposed system to rectify these problems.

What is required is further work to identify the business processes and data needs for the proposed system and this is where the following tools come in.

▶ Context diagrams

Context diagrams are simplified diagrams which are useful for specifying the boundaries and scope of the system. They can be readily produced after the information flow diagram since they are a simplified version of the IFD showing the external entities. They show these types of flow:

1 Flow crosses the system boundary from outside with its destination inside the boundary – it is thus an input to the system from the external environment.

2 Flow begins inside the system boundary and its destination lies outside – it is, therefore, an output from the system into its external environment.

The internal flows which lie entirely within the system boundary are not shown.

Context diagrams provide a useful summary for embarking on dataflow diagrams and entity relationship diagrams, since they show the main entities. The main elements of a context diagram are:

1 A circle representing the system to be investigated.

2 Ellipses (or boxes) representing external entities.

3 Information flows.

Figure 11.6 shows a context diagram for the student loan system described in the previous section.

▶ Dataflow diagrams

Dataflow diagrams (DFD) define the different processes in a system and the information which forms the input and output to the processes. They provide a process

Context diagrams

A simplified diagram which is useful for specifying the boundaries and scope of the system. They can be readily produced after the information flow diagram since they are a simplified version of the IFD showing the external entities.

Dataflow diagrams (DFD)

Define the different processes in a system and the information which forms the input and output datastores to the processes. They may be drawn at different levels. Level 0 provides an overview of the system with levels 1 and 2 providing progressively more detail.

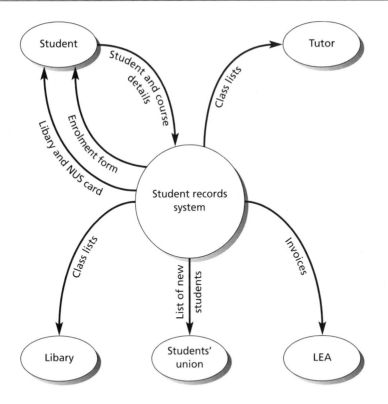

Fig 11.6 Context diagram for the student loan system described in the previous section

focus to a system. They may be drawn at different levels: level 0 provides an overview of the system with levels 1 and 2 providing progressive detail.

Dataflow diagrams of different types are one of the mainstays of many systems analysis and design methodologies. SSADM, for example, makes extensive use of DFDs, not only to document things as they are at the moment but also to document the *required* system. Whether the latter is really of any value is debatable. However, as a tool to document processes, data or information flows and the relationships between them for an existing system (computerised or paper based), they are extremely valuable.

Dataflow diagrams build on IFDs by adding two new symbols as well as subtly redefining others.

The diagram conventions in Fig 11.7 are those which are in most common use in the UK. Differing methodologies adopt different symbols for some items (in particular a circle for a process), as you will see in some of the supplementary texts for this chapter.

Explanations of symbols:

◆ *Sources and sinks.* An information source is one which provides data for a process and is *outside the system boundary*. A sink lies outside the system boundary and is a receiver of information. There is a clear distinction between the use of this symbol in the DFD and the IFD that we looked at before, in that the symbol should not appear inside the system boundary.

◆ *Processes.* Processes convert data either into usable information or data in a different form for use in another process. The data which enters a process can come either from a datastore (*see* below) or from an external source.

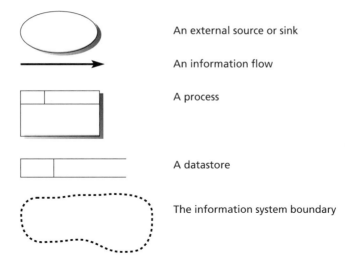

An external source or sink

An information flow

A process

A datastore

The information system boundary

Fig 11.7 Symbols used in Data Flow Diagrams

◆ *Datastores*. A datastore can either provide data as input to a process or receive data which has been output from a process. The amount of time that data would spend in a datastore can vary from a very short time (e.g. fractions of seconds in the case of some work files) or much longer periods (e.g. months or years in the case of master files).

◆ *Dataflows*. A dataflow describes the exchange of information and data between datastores and processes and between processes and sources or sinks. Note that in this context we are using data in a broad sense (to include information) rather than in the narrow sense used in Part One of the book.

◆ *Systems boundary*. This remains the same as for an IFD – it indicates the boundary between what lies inside the system under consideration and what lies outside.

Tips

It is unfortunate that many texts actually contain errors in the DFD examples used. This is mainly through having 'illegal' information flows. In a well-constructed diagram, you will note the following:

◆ Data does *not* flow directly between processes – the data which enters a process will either come from a source or from a datastore, it cannot exist in a vacuum!

◆ Data does *not* flow directly between datastores – there must be an intervening process which takes the input data and converts it into a new form and outputs it either to a datastore or a sink.

◆ Data does *not* flow directly from a datastore to a sink, or from a source to a datastore – there *must* be an intervening process.

To draw a basic high-level DFD, there are *five* steps required:

1 Identify and list all *processes* which take place in the system under consideration. A process is an event where an input of some kind, either from a source or a datastore, is transformed into an output (the output being either to a sink or to a datastore).

2 Identify all the datastores which you think exist in the system under consideration. A datastore will exist wherever a set of facts needs to be stored about persons, places, things or events.

3 For each process identified in Step 1, identify where the information used in the process comes from (this can be either from a *source* or a *datastore* or both) and identify the output(s) from that process (which can be either an information flow to a sink or to a datastore or both).

4 Draw a 'mini' DFD for each single process, showing the process box and any relevant sources, sinks or datastores.

5 Link the mini DFDs to form a single diagram, using the datastores to link the processes together.

Further tips

To help you to construct a diagram, the following tips are useful:

◆ Use A4 paper in landscape orientation.

◆ Aim to have no more than about six or seven processes on a page (ten maximum).

◆ Include the same datastores, sources and sinks more than once if required (to eliminate crossed lines or to make the flows clearer).

Before working through the student records example introduced in the previous section, it is necessary to introduce the concept of 'levelling' in DFDs. For anything other than a very small system with a handful of processes, it would be almost impossible to draw a single diagram with all the processes on it. It is necessary, therefore, to begin with a high-level diagram with just the broadest processes defined. Examples of a high-level process might be 'process customer orders', 'pay suppliers', or 'manufacture products'. Needless to say, each of the processes described can be broken down further until all the fundamental processes which make up the system are identified. It is usual to allow up to three or four levels of increasing detail to be identified. If there are any more levels of detail than this, it suggests that the system is too large to consider in one development and that it should be split into smaller, discrete subsystems capable of separate development.

   To illustrate the levelling concept and also to demonstrate how process boxes should be used, we will take the simple example of checking a customer order. At Level 1, the process box will appear as in Fig 11.8.

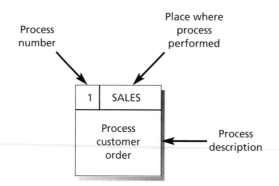

Fig 11.8 An example of a Level 1 process in a DFD

It is desirable to split this process up into smaller components. As an example, suppose the following are identified:

◆ Check customer credit limit – can the customer pay for the goods?

◆ Perform stock check – to see whether the desired goods are in stock.

◆ Create sales order – this may be a special order form that is needed for each order.

◆ Send order to warehouse – the warehouse will need to pick the stock ready for delivery.

◆ Despatch customer order.

◆ Invoice customer.

This will give us six new processes to record at the next level. The process box for the first Level 2 process would be similar to this (Fig 11.9).

Note that the process number is 1.1. This indicates that the process has been decomposed from the higher-level process numbered 1. Subsequent processes would be numbered 1.2, 1.3, 1.4 and so on. Also note that the process name begins with a verb. The choice of verb helps indicate more clearly the type of process that is being performed.

Suppose now that we still need to decompose the new process 1.1 further. For example, the credit check process may involve these steps:

◆ Calculate order value.

◆ Identify current balance.

◆ Produce credit check result.

We need to present the new processes as Level 3 processes, since they have been decomposed from the higher Level 2 process. The first of these would be represented as in Fig 11.10.

The new processes would be numbered 1.1.1, 1.1.2 and 1.1.3. This approach to numbering allows each of the low-level processes to be easily associated with the

Fig 11.9 An example of a Level 2 process in a DFD

Fig 11.10 An example of a Level 3 process in a DFD

higher-level process that generated it. Thus, for example, processes 3.2.1, 3.2.2 and 3.2.3 could be tracked back to process 3.2, and thence to process 3.

We will now return to the student enrolment example. We will concentrate on producing a Level 1 diagram for this procedure, although it will be clear that the example is a somewhat simplified one.

The first task is to identify all the processes which exist. Looking back to page 371, we can identify the following:

1 Allocate unique student code.

2 Create student card index.

3 Create LEA list.

4 Invoice LEA.

5 Create student record card.

6 Create class list.

7 Issue enrolment form.

8 Issue new students list.

Step 2 requires us to identify all the datastores which might exist. Our example reveals the following:

◆ Student card index.

◆ LEA list.

◆ Student record card.

◆ Class list.

◆ New students list.

Step 3 requires us to construct a 'mini' DFD for each of the eight processes identified above. We will restrict ourselves to the first three (*see* Figs 11.11, 11.12 and 11.13).

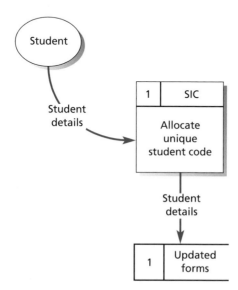

Fig 11.11 Mini DFD for process 1

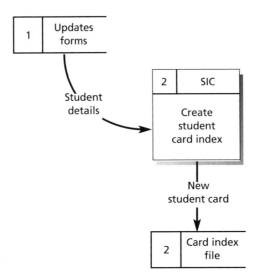

Fig 11.12 Mini DFD for process 2

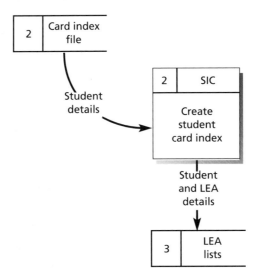

Fig 11.13 Mini DFD for process 3

You will see from these figures that each of the processes we have considered has generated an output which forms an input to the next process. In the full diagram in Fig 11.14 you will see the complete picture, including all processes, datastores, sources and sinks. In this diagram, you will notice that the datastore 'card index file' appears more than once. This does not mean that there are two separate datastores with the same name, but that we have included it for a second time to make the diagram easier to draw. If we did not do this, there would have been either crossed lines or at least very tortuous ones. A system boundary is also included and you will note that sources and sinks lie outside the system boundary, while processes and datastores are inside. Many of the dataflows are inside the boundary, but you see where flows also cross the system boundary.

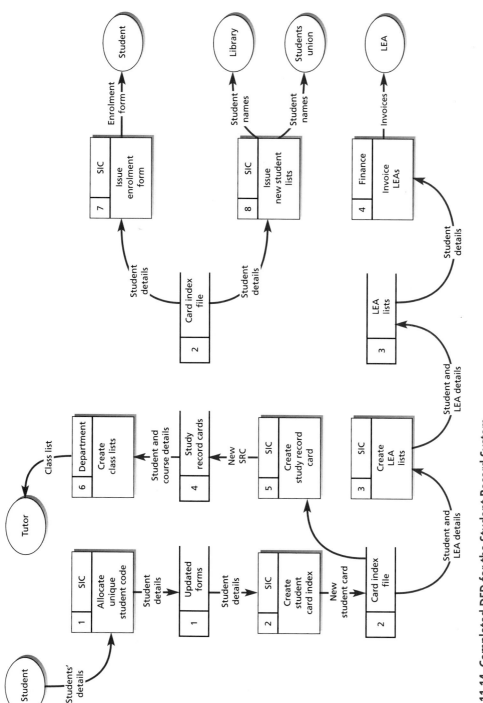

Fig 11.14 Completed DFD for the Student Record System

The final point to note is that a dataflow diagram is *time independent*. This means that we are not trying to show the sequence in which things happen, but rather to show all the things which happen.

The benefits to an organisation of constructing a dataflow diagram can be summed up in the following '3 Cs':

◆ *Communication*. A picture paints a thousand words and DFDs are no exception. A diagram can be used by an analyst to communicate to end-users the analyst's understanding of the area under consideration. This is likely to be more successful than what Ed Yourdon describes as the 'Victorian novel' approach to writing specification reports.

◆ *Completeness*. A DFD can be scrutinised by functional area personnel to check that the analyst has gained a complete picture of the business area being investigated. If anything is missing or the analyst has misinterpreted anything, this will be clearer to the user if there is a diagram than if purely textual tools are used.

◆ *Consistency*. A DFD will represent the results of the fact-finding exercise conducted by the analyst. For the DFD to be constructed at all, the analyst will need to compare the fact-finding results from all the areas investigated and look for linkages between them. If the same processes are portrayed differently by different people, then the DFD will be hard to construct. In such an event, this will be a catalyst for the analyst to return to the fact-finding task, perhaps using brainstorming to get to the real facts.

▶ Entity relationship diagrams (ERDs)

Entity relationship diagrams (ERDs)

Provide a data-focused view of the main data objects or entities within a system such as a person, place or object and the relationships between them. It is a high-level view which does not consider the detailed attributes or characteristics of an object such as a person's name or address.

Entity relationship diagrams (ERDs) provide a data-focused view of the main data objects or entities within a system such as a person, place or object and the relationships between them. It is a high-level view which does not consider the detailed attributes or characteristics of an object such a person's name or address.

In dealing with entity relationship diagrams, we must bear in mind that we are beginning to move away from the analysis stage of the systems development lifecycle towards the design stage. This is because we are beginning to think about how data is represented and how different sets of data relate to each other. For this chapter, we will concentrate on the fundamentals of entity relationships as they exist within a particular business situation, rather than on the detail of database design which follows directly from using this tool. Database design will be covered in much more detail in Chapter 12 where a technique called *data normalisation* will also be covered.

In any business situation, data (be it paper based or computerised) is processed to produce information to assist in the decision-making processes within that business area. Processes may change over time and new ones created to provide new or different information, but very often the types of data that underpin this remain relatively unchanged. Sometimes, data requirements change to allow new processes to be created. For example, a supermarket which moves to a EPOS system from a manual one will generate new data in the form of sales of specific products at specific times and in specific quantities. The data can then be linked to automated stock ordering systems and the like.

In order to produce good-quality information, two things are needed above all others. These are:

◆ accurate data;

◆ correct processing.

If data is inaccurate, correct processing will only result in the production of incorrect information. If data is accurate, but faults exist in the processing, the information will still be incorrect. However, in the second case, the capability exists for producing correct information if the processing is adjusted. With faulty data, it may not be so easy to rectify the situation.

In the analysis context, we need to engage in fact-finding activities that reveal the data which underlies all the relevant business processes, so that it can be captured and stored correctly and then processed to produce the required information. This process will reveal details of certain *entities* which exist within the business. One of the most useful methods that can be used here is the review of records and documentation (for example order forms, stock control cards, customer files and so on).

An **entity** can be defined as *facts about a person, place, thing or event about which we need to capture and store data*. To take the example of a sales department, it would need to know facts about customers, orders, products and stock availability.

Entity

An object such as a person, place, thing or event about which we need to capture and store data. An entity forms a logical grouping for all data about a particular object.

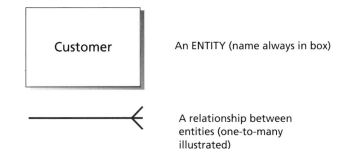

Fig 11.15 Essential symbols in an entity relationship diagram

The essential symbols used in ERDs are very straightforward (Fig 11.15). Note that additional symbols are used in some notations, but they are not necessary for the detail of analysis conducted in this chapter.

There are a number of possible relationships between entities.

One-to-one relationships

For each occurrence of entity A there is one and only one occurrence of entity B.

For example, let us assume that a lecturer may teach on only one module, and that module may be taught by only one lecturer (an unlikely situation) (Fig 11.16).

In Fig 11.16, we have added some additional information. This shows the nature of the relationship between the two entities. This information on the relationship is

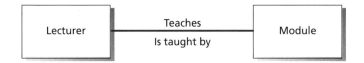

Fig 11.16 A one-to-one relationship

added to the line between the two entities. The relationship can be described in two ways according to which entity we refer to first. The relationships are:

◆ Lecturer *teaches* module.

◆ Module *is taught by* lecturer.

The practice of describing the relationship on the line is recommended since it helps others interpret the ERD more readily. However, the nature of the relationship is omitted on some subsequent diagrams for clarity.

One-to-many relationships

For each occurrence of entity A, there may be zero, one or many occurrences of entity B. For example, a lecturer belongs to a single division, but that division *may* contain many lecturers (it may, of course, have no staff at all if it has only just been created or if all the staff decided to leave) (Fig 11.17).

Fig 11.17 A one-to-many relationship

Many-to-many relationships

For each occurrence of entity A, there may be zero, one or many occurrences of entity B, *and* for each occurrence of entity B there may be zero, one or many occurrences of entity A.

For example, a course MODULE may be taken by zero, one or many STUDENTS and a student may take zero, one or many course modules (Fig 11.18).

Unfortunately, especially in database design, many-to-many relationships can cause certain difficulties. Therefore, they are usually 'resolved' into *two* one-to-many relationships through the creation of a 'linking' entity. The decomposition is shown in Fig 11.19.

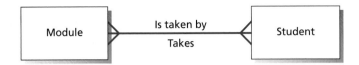

Fig 11.18 A many-to-many relationship

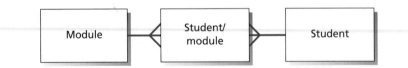

Fig 11.19 A many-to-many relationship decomposed into two one-to-Many relationships

The linking entity will contain an item of data from each of the other entities which allows the link to be made.

The following example shows a simple ERD which illustrates each of the above possibilities in more detail.

Suppose that a nation has a professional hockey league, comprising 16 clubs. Each club may only play in this one league. Each club may employ a number of professional players (although it is also possible for a team to consist completely of amateurs). Each professional player may only be contracted to one club at a time and may also experience periods of unemployment between contracts. Professional players are also eligible to play for their national team, but any one player may only ever play for one national team. Finally, suppose that professionals may have a number of sponsors and that each sponsor may sponsor a number of players.

If we inspect the paragraph, we can identify the following entities:

LEAGUE

CLUB

PROFESSIONAL

NATIONAL TEAM

SPONSOR

Our first-cut ERD is shown in Fig 11.20.

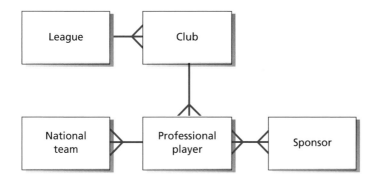

Fig 11.20 First ERD for the professional hockey example

The only obvious difficulty here is the many-to-many relationship between PRO-FESSIONAL PLAYER and SPONSOR. We can resolve this by introducing a linking entity which contains something common to both an individual player and his or her sponsor. This can be seen in the next ERD of Fig 11.21.

We have introduced the linking entity SPONSORSHIP AGREEMENT to resolve the many-to-many relationship. Thus, any one player may have many sponsorship agreements, but any one sponsor agreement will belong to one player and to one sponsor.

This example was pretty straightforward. Others will be less so and it is therefore time to go back to our student records example from earlier in the chapter. In fact, we have already started the process of thinking about entities because the earlier DFD section required us to think about *datastores* – somewhere where we store data, in other words a possible entity! Faced with a more complex set of possible relationships, it is useful to adopt a more structured approach to constructing ERDs.

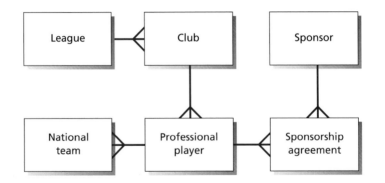

Fig 11.21 Final ERD for the professional hockey players

There are six steps that can be helpful in producing an ERD, especially when one lacks inexperience in drawing them:

1 Identify all those things about which it is necessary to store data, such as customers, orders etc.

2 For each entity, identify specific data that needs to be stored. In the case of a customer, for example, name, address and telephone number are all necessary.

3 Construct a cross-reference matrix of all possible relationships between pairs of entities and identify where a relationship actually exists. To do this, it is very helpful to identify some item of data which is common to the pair of entities under consideration.

4 Draw a basic ERD showing all the possible relationships, but not yet the *degree* of the relationship.

5 On the basic ERD, inspect each relationship and amend it to show whether it is a one-to-one, one-to-many or many-to-many relationship.

6 Resolve any many-to-many relationships by introducing an appropriate linking entity.

Step 1 Identify the entities

By going back to the example on page 371 and the DFD on page 381, it is possible to identify some possible candidate entities. The difficulty here is that the kind of documentation generated from the process obscures what we really need to hold data about. For example, there is a datastore called CARD INDEX FILE. This is hardly helpful! What really needs to be done is ask the question: '*What things do we need to store data about?*' This may yield something rather different from the entities we thought we had before. As a starting point, we will begin with the following entities:

STUDENTS

COURSES

LEAS

DEPARTMENTS

MODULES

Step 2 Identify specific data for each entity

Each entity will be taken in turn, and a number of data attributes suggested.

STUDENTS
name
home address
sex
local education authority name
local education authority code
course code
term-time address
date of birth
next of kin

COURSES
course code
course description
department
course leader

LEAS
name
LEA code
address
contact name
telephone number
fax number

DEPARTMENT
department name
department location
office number
head of department

MODULES
module code
module leader
department
semester run
owning department

Step 3 Construct cross-reference matrix

This part of the process helps novice analysts identify where relationships exist between entities. It is necessary to identify where there is a common data attribute between pairs of entities, so indicating that a probable relationship exists between them. This is the hardest part of the whole exercise. The essence is to ask the question: *'For any occurrence of entity A, are there (now or likely to be in the future) any occurrences of B that relate to it?'* For example, is it likely that for a customer some orders exist that relate to it?

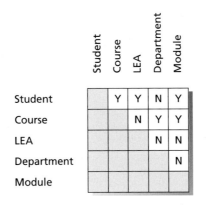

Fig 11.22 Cross reference matrix for student records system

The cross-reference matrix in Fig 11.22 allows each pair of possible relationships to be examined for a link.

In the cross-reference diagram, it is only necessary to identify each possible pair of relationships once. Also, there is no need to examine a relationship that an entity might have to itself. As a result, we are only interested in examining 10 possible pairs of relationship for this small, five-entity example.

Steps 4 and 5 Construct first-cut ERD and add degree of relationship

Steps 4 and 5 will be combined, since there is nothing to be gained here from making separate diagrams. However, when drawing the diagram for the end-of-chapter exercise, it would be wise to split the tasks as suggested.

The diagram in Fig 11.23 is almost correct, but there is still the question of the many-to-many relationship to resolve, so we must move to the final step.

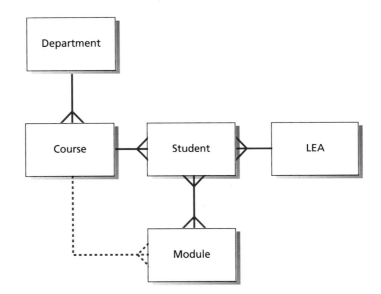

Fig 11.23 Student record system ERD – with many-to-many relationship

Step 6 Resolve any many-to-many relationships

The many-to-many relationship about which we should be concerned is the one between students and modules. A student may enrol for many modules and any modules may be taken by many students. However, what we need to represent is the ability of students to enrol for as many or as few modules as required without causing complications in either the STUDENT entity or the MODULE entity. The many-to-many relationship is therefore resolved by introducing a linking entity which will have one occurrence for each module that one student takes and for the whole student population. So if there were 100 students each studying 8 modules, the new linking entity would contain 800 records. The final diagram is in Fig 11.24.

By working through the student record system example, we have moved from the process of identifying what the data requirements are for the system under consideration (the *analysis* part) and have made substantial progress on how a database might be constructed to hold the required data (which is a *design* task). This exercise is far from complete, however, as database design involves more than just looking at entity relationships. The detailed database design aspects will therefore be covered in the next chapter, when all aspects of system design are considered.

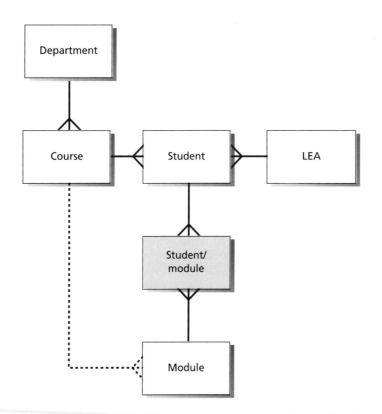

Fig 11.24 Final student record system ERD – with many-to-many relationships decomposed

▶ SYSTEMS ANALYSIS – AN EVALUATION

Any systems development project will be confronted by issues such as system size, complexity and acquisition method. These factors affect the choice of fact-finding and documentation tools. It is appropriate, therefore, to consider three alternative acquisition methods and review fact-finding and documentation needs for each.

▶ Bespoke development

Bespoke software, which can either be developed internally or by a third party, presents the greatest scope for using the full range of analysis tools. Complex systems will require that the analyst gains a very clear and precise understanding of the business processes that take place and all the tools at the analyst's disposal may need to be used. A combination of interviewing, documentation review and observation will yield much of the information that is needed, but if the system is a large one with many users, questionnaires may also need to be used. Brainstorming will be valuable, especially when linkages between different processes and subsystems are being investigated.

Complex projects will also require the use of all of the documentation tools we have discussed. Needless to say, the resulting diagrams will be more detailed and extensive than the ones given as examples in this chapter.

▶ Purchasing packages off the shelf

Even though there is no requirement to produce something from which the system designer can produce a blueprint for the build stage, it is still necessary to gain a clear understanding of user requirements before a package is considered. Therefore, the fact-finding process will still be undertaken, but will be geared towards gaining an understanding of the features which a package must support and those which are desirable.

One benefit of deciding to purchase a package is that a number of candidate packages can be initially selected and used by the analyst as a means of identifying real user needs. It is possible, for example, for a selected group of users to review the features of a small number of packages with a view to compiling an appropriate requirements catalogue. Also, when users actually have an opportunity to experiment with a package, the analyst can gain a much greater insight into what the users' *real* requirements are.

For the analyst, it may still be useful to construct information flow and dataflow diagrams to help ensure that the package that is finally selected will support the required linkages, both between processes in the business area under consideration and to other business areas (from sales to accounts, for example). It will also be useful for the analyst to construct an entity relationship diagram to be sure that the packaged software will support the data requirements of the organisation.

▶ End-user applications development

The situation here is somewhat different from the previous two acquisition methods. The end-user will have a clear idea of what the system is required to do. Also, it is less likely that the system will need to have linkages to other applications. The emphasis

for the user, therefore, should be to identify the data and processing requirements clearly so that an application can be produced which delivers good-quality information. Of the techniques discussed, the most relevant is the entity relationship diagram. By concentrating on data and how it is to be captured and represented, the user increases the probability that the data will be correct, while the use of fourth-generation language tools will help maximise the probability that the processing will also be correct.

Many end-user developed applications suffer from poor database design and, as a consequence, the processing requirements are much more complex and prone to error. By taking care to consider carefully the relationships between the relevant data items, the probability of obtaining successful end-user developed applications is increased.

End-user development is considered in more detail in Chapter 16.

▶ SOFTWARE TOOLS FOR SYSTEMS ANALYSIS

Software tools are available to assist in the analysis phase. These usually focus on the diagramming rather than the enquiry stage, so much of the skill remains with the analyst in interpreting the users', requirements before producing meaningful diagrams showing the information flows and processes.

An important issue in using software tools to help the analyst is the degree to which the diagrams used to summarise processes can be converted easily into the system design and then into the final system. Traditionally, there have been separate tools for the analysis, designer and programmer. The case study on tools to support systems analysis describes some of the tools available. Since there is a strong overlap with the design phase, we will defer the examination of these tools to Chapter 12, which has a section on computer-aided software engineering or CASE tools. Integrated CASE tools are intended to bridge the gap between analysis, design and programming.

CASE STUDY: TOPIC AREA

Tools to support systems analysis

All sites are regularly deluged with adverts for tools and development aids for the programmers; but what about the systems analyst? These are surprisingly thin on the ground. But anyone who has been formally taught systems analysis at the local technical college for RSA or City & Guilds exams as well as for the National Computing Centre's Basic Award in Systems Analysis will remember that iron law of IT that the cost of making changes at the coding stage is at least 10 times the cost of doing them at the analysis stage.

There are plenty of industry veterans who can point to the root of many of the ills of IT being the use of online programming aids and insufficient time or people being allocated to getting the analysis right. In the balmy days of the 1950s and 1960s, when IT didn't take itself too seriously, systems analysts either looked at the business case first or worked very closely with other management services disciplines such as Organisation and Methods or work study. This ensured that no system was over-commissioned if there wasn't a better way of doing it manually and that business logic was very accurately captured.

So just what is available? There are a number of so-called rapid application development (RAD) tools on the market, but most of these tend to assume that the traditional analysis stage has either been skipped or is perfect. One or two of the more enlightened software houses have

developed their own methodologies for trying to auto-mate the analysis stage. For example, Cambridge Technology Partners has customised spreadsheets to help its analysts capture the business processes accurately. Industry giant Texas Instruments offers its Composer range of aids which have their roots in the work done by Dr James Martin in the mid-1980s. Rob Jeahan, TI Software's business development manager, said the tools were based around a repository and gave analysts two levels of granularity. He added: 'The first covers high level planning and allows ana-lysts to take snap-shots of data and the relationships between them. The aim is to prevent scope creep and is heavily user-based as opposed to technology driven. The second covers process analysis and data analysis. This tends to be driven by the data, but upgrades will make this a lot more process driven. What analysts want to do is to be able to look at the business processes end to end and then use this to drive the data model.'

There is no reason, either, why the analyst can't sit down with the user and iterate the business processes online. Any changes which are made and agreed by the user are executed throughout the system automatically. This means that there should never be any bugs in the business analysis once the user has signed it off. This also gives the IT manager a much better idea of how much work is required.

Client/server specialist Concise Software customised another tool originally aimed at RAD to cover the analysis stage. Senior consultant Robin Strong noted: 'You never get the analysis 100 per cent right first time. So you do need feed-back from users and be able to sit down with them and run through the business processes. We have found that using S Designer allows us to get 100 per cent accuracy after up to four iterations. It is much cheaper to make changes at this stage than at the coding stage.' The tools also ensure that any new system is much more closely aligned with actual work practices. You can also use actual objects with business rules. S Designer can also be used to reverse engineer an existing system or database, typically where there is no documentation; this allows analysts to get rid of superfluous data and code and then take back

the revised system to the user. 'We have also found that unless you use the right methodology, the tools won't cap-ture the business processes accurately. Typically using S Designer we capture the business processes and translate these into a logical data model and then a physical model. This is fed into Powerbuilder and typically we can get the new iterations back to the user in 30 minutes,' Strong said.

The final product is one which comes closest to giving fully automated traditional flowcharts. Called Quesheet, it was developed and is marketed by Cambridge-based Quesheet Technology. The product is based on a three-tier model which only looks at business processes and business logic. Managing director Matthew Whitcombe said that installing it on a laptop allowed the analyst to sit down with the business user who was paying the bill and agree all the business processes required for the new system. Whitcombe added: 'The biggest problem for most sites today is that management doesn't understand that 75 per cent of the errors at the development stage are down to faulty analysis'. It is no secret that business users hound their IT directors for computer support and often feel that months later they get something entirely different from what they wanted. Business managers and IT specialists do tend to speak different languages and the aim of Quesheet was to transform business goals (expressed in everyday lan-guage) into designs and working prototypes of the systems the business actually wants. 'There are also plug-in compo-nents which allow analysts to use popular middleware tools and the software also allows the analyst to build up a repository of logical design and be able to attach physical code to it. This encourages much better re-use of objects and management of systems,' Whitcombe concluded.

Source: Computing, 17 January 1997

Questions

1 Why according to the article is it important for analysis to be conducted adequately?

2 Given the limited description of some of the tools avail-able, how would you assess the use of analysis tools in organisations?

▶ CONCLUSION

This chapter has covered a number of fact-finding techniques and documentation tools. The coverage has been far from exhaustive, however. For example, tools such as action diagrams and state transition diagrams have not been included. However, those that have been covered provide a firm foundation for further study should the reader so wish. The methods and tools discussed are in common usage today around the world and they provide a firm basis for the design stage in the next chapter.

CASE STUDY: TOPIC AREA

ABC

Background

The following scenario is typical of many companies in the retail/wholesale business. A number of information flows exist both internally within the organisation and also with people outside. This case study is used for exercises on information flow diagrams (IFDs), dataflow diagrams (DFDs) and entity relationship diagrams (ERDs).

The exercise continues in Chapter 12 when the reader is asked to produce a detailed database design based on the entity relationship diagram produced and the paper form examples.

Questions

1 Using the ABC case study, produce an information flow diagram for the company by following the steps given earlier in the chapter. Does the diagram tell you anything about ABC's operations which may need some attention (such as missing or superfluous information flows)?

2 Using the ABC case study and the information flow diagram that you drew in answer to Question 1, produce a simple Level 1 dataflow diagram for the company by following the steps given earlier in the chapter. Compare your answer with that by one of your colleagues. Are the diagrams the same? If not, is it possible to say which is correct? If not, why not?

3 Using the ABC case study, including the sample forms included below the main text, construct an entity relationship diagram for the company. Make sure that you do a cross-reference matrix before attempting to draw the diagram. When you have drawn your first-cut diagram, check for many-to-many relationships and eliminate any that you find by using the appropriate technique described earlier in the chapter.

ABC case study information

Andy's Bonsai Company (ABC) specialises in selling bonsai kits by mail order. The kits are made up of a number of ele-

ments, including soil, plant pots and seeds. Other products such as mini-garden tools are also sold.

Customers place orders by telephone or by mailing an order slip which is printed as part of an ABC advert. Customers pay either by cheque, credit card or debit card.

When an order is received by ABC, it is directed to a sales clerk. Each sales clerk has responsibility for a particular geographic region. The sales clerk will enter the details of the order onto a preprinted three-part order form. One part is retained by the sales clerk, one copy together with the payment is sent to the accounts department and the other is sent to the warehouse (on confirmation of the customer's creditworthiness).

On receipt of the customer orders and payment details, the accounts department ensures that the customer's payment is valid. If the payment is satisfactory, the department will inform the sales department and the order may proceed. An unsatisfactory payment situation is also communicated to the sales department, which then informs the customer of the problem.

The warehouse keeps a manual card-index system of stock and raw materials held together with copies of customer orders. When an order is despatched to the customer, the relevant order form is marked as having been despatched. The warehouse also needs to keep track of the amount of product in stock and when stock levels are low, it sends a manufacturing order to the manufacturing department.

The manufacturing department is responsible for ordering materials from various suppliers and then packaging them into products for sale to the customer. A three-part purchase order is made out: one part is sent to the supplier, one part is retained by the manufacturing department and the third part is sent to the accounts department. The accounts department holds copies of purchase orders for future matching with delivery notes and invoices. When the supplier delivers the ordered items, together with a delivery note, a check is made to ensure that the delivery matches the order. The supplier will send an invoice to the accounts department on confirmation that the delivery is correct so that payment can be made.

CUSTOMER ORDER FORM

CUSTOMER NUMBER

C234792

ORDER NUMBER

4214

CUSTOMER ADDRESS

26 Vicarage Drive

Thorndyke

West Yorkshire

WF24 7PL

DATE ORDERED

29 March 1999

TELEPHONE NUMBER

01482 737493

CODE	DESCRIPTION	PRICE	QTY	VALUE
1983	MINI-OAK	19.95	2	39.90
0184	MINI-MAPLE	24.50	2	49.00
2984	MINI GARDEN TOOLS (STAINLESS)	29.95	1	29.95
3775	MINI WATERING CAN (COPPER)	17.50	1	17.50

PAYMENT TYPE	Cheque	ORDER VALUE	136.35

WAREHOUSE CARD INDEX

LOCATION   J82   CARD No. 19

PRODUCT CODE   4151

PRODUCT DESCRIPTION   MINI-ASH

START QTY	TRANSACTION QTY	DATE	SIGNATURE
37	−5	2/6/99	RON
28	−3	4/6/99	JEFF
25	−15	9/6/99	LUCY
10	+50	17/6/99	ERIC
60			

MANUFACTURING ORDER FORM

MANUFACTURING ORDER NUMBER   7210

PRODUCT CODE   4151

PRODUCT DESCRIPTION   MINI-ASH

QUANTITY ORDERED   50

DATE ORDERED   3/6/99

DATE REQUIRED   13/6/99

DATE DELIVERED   17/6/99

SIGNATURE   BERYL

PURCHASE ORDER FORM

SUPPLIER NUMBER
    S165

PURCHASE ORDER NUMBER
    214

SUPPLIER ADDRESS

14 Wyke Trading Estate

Heckwhistle

West Yorkshire

WF9 5JJ

DATE ORDERED

29 March 1999

TELEPHONE NUMBER

01637 734679

CODE	DESCRIPTION	PRICE	QTY	VALUE
23	OAK CHIPPINGS	30.00	25	750.00
69	2" POTS	0.03	1000	300.00
84	SILVER SAND	1.77	10	17.70
75	MINI WATERING CAN (STAINLESS)	4.56	20	91.20

ORDER VALUE   1158.90

▶ SUMMARY

Stage summary: systems analysis

Purpose: Define the features and other requirements of the information system

Key activities: Requirements capture (interviews, questionnaires, etc.) diagramming

Inputs: User's opinions, system documentation, observation

Outputs: Requirements specification

1 The analysis phase of systems development is aimed at identifying *what* the new system will do.

2 Analysis will identify the business processes which will be assisted by the software, the functions of the software and the data requirements.

3 The results of the analysis phase are summarised as a requirements specification which forms the input to the design phase, which will define *how* the system will operate.

4 Fact-finding techniques used at the analysis stage include:
   ◆ questionnaires;
   ◆ interviews;
   ◆ observation;
   ◆ documentation review;
   ◆ brainstorming.

5 The results from the fact-finding exercise are summarised in a requirements specification and using different diagrams such as:
   ◆ information flow diagram which provide a simple view of the way information is moved around an organisation;
   ◆ dataflow diagrams which show the processes performed by a system and their data inputs and outputs;
   ◆ entity relationship diagrams which summarise the main objects about which data needs to be stored and the relationship between them.

6 The depth of analysis will be dependent on the existing knowledge of requirements. An end-user development may have limited analysis since the user will have a good understanding of their needs. A software house will need to conduct a detailed analysis which will form the basis for a contract with the company for which it is developing software.

▶ EXERCISES

▶ Self-assessment exercises

1 What is the difference between the 'funnel' and 'pyramid' approaches to structuring an interview?

2 Why can closed questions still be useful in an interview?

3 Assess the relative effectiveness of interviews versus questionnaires when attempting to establish user requirements.

4   In an information flow diagram, why should we not record information flows that lie completely outside the system boundary?

5   What are the main differences between an information flow diagram and a dataflow diagram?

6   What is meant by the term 'levelling' in dataflow diagrams?

7   In a sales order processing system, which of the following are not entities? Customer, colour, size, product, telephone number, sales order, sales person, order date.

8   Why might the construction of an ERD still be useful even if an off-the-shelf package was going to be purchased?

▶ Discussion questions

1   Use a simple example with no more than five processes or ten information flows to examine the differences between the information flow diagram and the dataflow diagram. Which would be most effective for explaining deficiencies with an existing system to:
    (a)   a business manager;
    (b)   a systems designer?
    Justify your reasoning.

2   Compare the effectiveness of 'soft' methods of acquiring information such as interviews and questionnaires and 'hard' methods of gathering information such as document analysis and observation of staff. In which order do you think these analysis activities should be conducted and on which do you think most time should be spent?

3   'For producing a database, the only type of diagram from the analysis phase that needs to be produced is the entity relationship diagram. Dataflow diagrams are not relevant.' Discuss.

▶ Essay questions

1   Compare and contrast alternative fact-finding methods and analysis documentation tools as they might relate to bespoke software development and the purchase of off-the-shelf packages.

2   Errors in the analysis stage of a systems development project are far more costly to fix than those that occur later in the systems development lifecycle. Why do some organisations seem to devalue the analysis process by seeking to get to the systems build as quickly as possible?

3   Compare and contrast the relative effectiveness of the use of information flow diagrams, dataflow diagrams and entity relationship diagrams by a business analyst to demonstrate inefficiency in a company's existing information management processes. Use examples to illustrate your answer.

▶ Examination questions

1   Briefly review the arguments for and against using interviewing as a means of determining system requirements.

2   Explain the relationship between the initiation and analysis phase of the systems development lifecycle.

3 Briefly explain (in one or two sentences) the purpose of each of the following diagramming methods:

(a) information flow diagram;

(b) context diagram;

(c) dataflow diagram;

(d) entity relationship diagram.

4 Draw a diagram showing each of the following relationships on an ERD:

(a) The customer places many orders. Each order is received from one customer.

(b) The customer order may contain many requests for products. Each product will feature on many customer orders.

(c) Each customer has a single customer representative who is responsible for them. Each customer representative is responsible for many customers.

5 The final examination question is based on a case study: Megatoy Ltd.

CASE STUDY: TOPIC AREA

Megatoy Ltd

Introduction

Megatoy Ltd is a long-established, UK-based toy company with an annual turnover of around £50 million. The company employs a total of 230 people at its headquarters in Wellingborough, Northamptonshire. It has enjoyed steady growth over the last 10 years, thanks mainly to its ability to secure licences to manufacture toys based on popular children's television series. However, over the last two years, profitability has declined from a healthy 12 per cent to only 2 per cent of turnover.

Company organisation

Sales

There are two main areas covered by the sales department. First, the company has a total of six sales executives. Two, together with their manager, work on major national customers such as Argos, Woolworths and Toys R Us. The remaining four sales executives, together with their manager, concentrate on a larger number of small to medium-sized retailers. The department is headed by the sales director, Geoff Murphy. In addition to visiting customers on a regular basis, sales executives are responsible, together with their manager, for setting up sales targets and then monitoring actual against forecast performance.

The second part of the sales operation concerns the central sales office (CSO). The CSO is responsible for dealing with customers on a day-to-day basis. This includes taking orders by phone, responding to queries about the progress of particular orders and also managing the collecting of payments by the customers (known as cash collection).

The work of the CSO is carried out by 12 'account handlers'. Each account handler is responsible for a set of customers and uses sales order processing, stock control and accounts systems to help manage the accounts. The system has proved very successful, but it is now recognised that a lack of integration between the computer systems is now a main stumbling block to effective management.

Warehousing and distribution

Warehousing and distribution are responsible for the management of product storage and stock control, picking products from the various storage locations to fulfil customer orders and delivery of orders to customers using the company's fleet of lorries.

The department is managed by Reg Thatcher. He is supported by a transport manager and a warehouse manager. The warehouse operations are carried out by a team of eight warehouse operators.

Finance

The finance department is divided into two main areas: financial accounting and management accounting. The financial area deals with the purchase ledger, costing issues, the general (nominal) ledger and the payroll. The management area is mainly responsible for providing reports for management on the basis of both internal and external data.

Production

Although many products are manufactured in mainland Europe and the Far East, a number of products are manufactured in the UK. The most significant UK-based product is Kiddydoh, a dough-like substance which can be squeezed and shaped using a range of moulds and extruding devices. The current best-selling product range is based on the children's fantasy cartoon series *The Plonkers*. Models and figures from the series are manufactured in the Far East and a board game is produced at an Italian manufacturing plant.

The department raises purchase and manufacturing orders for the various products and in an effort not to under- or overorder uses a sales forecast provided by the sales department.

The MIS department

The management information systems department is managed by Neil Robson. In addition, the following staff are employed: one operations manager; one project leader; seven analyst-programmers and four computer operators. The department is responsible for managing the minicomputer-based applications together with the associated hardware and systems software. The MIS manager also performs the role of business analyst.

Minicomputer systems

Background

Megatoy currently bases its company-wide information systems on an elderly DEC PDP11-43 which was installed in 1979. Various enhancements and additions to the hardware have been made over the intervening period and the existing applications run satisfactorily (given the constraints identified in this case).

The main problem with the existing applications software is its general age and also the lack of integration between the various elements. In addition, 90 per cent of all systems activity is directed towards the existing systems rather than the development of new ones. All mini-based systems, with the exception of the accounting ledgers, are bespoke systems which were either written in-house or by a software house. All recent development and maintenance has been done by the company's information systems department.

Sales order processing (SOP)

This is performed using one of the oldest systems in the company which was originally written by a software house and has since been heavily modified. Sales order details are entered online by the account handlers. At the end of each

day, a batch process identifies all new orders or modifications to existing orders and creates an interface file which is used to update the stock control and despatch system. It is possible for account handlers to enquire about the status of all current orders as they were after the latest batch update from a second interface file from the stock control system (see below). Naturally, once an order has been amended or entered, the details are immediately available for enquiry by the account handlers.

When despatch details have been received from stock control and despatch, a program checks the second interface file and creates an invoice record on the sales ledger system (see finance below). A monthly procedure then takes the invoice records and produces the customer invoices, which are then sent out.

The account handlers may also enquire on the sales ledger in order to check the credit status of a customer before they enter an order. However, this is a time-consuming and often inaccurate process, since no account can be taken of orders already in the system or of invoices yet to be raised.

Stock control and despatch

The stock control and despatch system was written entirely in-house soon after the SOP system was installed. The system keeps track of stock levels for each product sold or by the company. It is also used to manage the picking and despatch of stock to fulfil customer orders. The interface file from the sales department (see above) is used to update the system with any new or modified orders.

A second interface file detailing goods which have been despatched to customers is sent to the SOP system on a weekly basis and this is used to update the status of the sales orders on the SOP system. The timelag caused by the two batch interface file processes can cause problems for account handlers when they attempt to respond to customer queries about the status of a particular order.

Financial ledgers

The financial ledger system is a package purchased by the company at the same time that the SOP system was developed. It comprises three elements: the sales ledger, the purchase ledger and the general ledger. The sales ledger has been modified by the supplying vendor to store and print the invoices as required by the SOP system and the stock control and despatch system. The account handlers are also able to enquire on the current state of a customer account and they enter details of any cash received from customers into the sales ledger.

The purchase ledger is controlled by the finance department and is used to track details of purchases and payments made by the company.

The general ledger is the main financial accounting ledger and is used to prepare periodic accounts for internal and external use.

PC-based applications

Background

All PC-based applications are controlled at departmental level with no central involvement at all. The applications have either been bought in as packages or developed in-house by the users themselves.

Sales

The sales department has developed a sales forecasting system using Microsoft Excel on an IBM PS/2 model 80. The system is used to compare a sales forecast for each category of customer with the actual sales for that period. The data is used to produce sales person performance reports (which can be used to calculate bonuses) and forecast reports which can be used by production to plan manufacturing and purchase orders.

The actual sales data has to be manually keyed into the application using reports produced by the SOP system.

Finance

The Finance department uses an IBM PS/2 model 60 running DBASE 4 and Lotus 1-2-3 version 2.2 to support the management accounting function. Information about sales, payments and inventory levels is obtained from the minicomputer-based packages, rekeyed and then consolidated to produce an overall management report. This task takes one person four days to produce and is done once a week. The management report is used for a regular weekly management meeting at which all departmental heads are present together with the managing director. The meeting often features complaints about the accuracy or otherwise of the information on the management report.

A second IBM PS/2 (model 30) running Quattro Pro version 3 is used by the payroll section to prepare salary and wage details, which are then sent to a payroll service bureau which performs the necessary operations to produce payslips and payments via the BACS system.

Production

Although stock control functions are performed by the minicomputer-based application, an IBM PS/2 model 55 running a Sage manufacturing system is used to keep track of purchase and manufacturing orders. This is an entirely self-contained system, although details of the orders are sent regularly to the finance department for the purchase ledger to be updated.

Miscellaneous

Each department has a secretarial function. IBM PS/2 model 30s running Wordperfect 5.1 for DOS are used together with Epson 24-pin dot-matrix printers.

There is no e-mail facility in the company, so information is exchanged either by telephone, mail or in person.

The marketing department makes no use of any computing facilities. All information is recorded manually. However, the marketing director does receive the weekly management report and attends the weekly management meeting.

Conclusion

A number of problems clearly exist in the way data is handled and processed. There are also problems associated with current business practices and there is no doubt that changes are required.

▶ Questions

(a) From analysis of the case study, produce an information flow diagram which summarises the *current* information flows within the company relating to *sales order processing*.

(b) From the information flow diagram produced in (a), identify problems in the current information flow.

(c) Assuming that Megatoy decides on an in-house developed bespoke solution for an information system to replace the existing system:
   (i) Which suitable fact-finding techniques could be used to implement the system? You should state which are most appropriate and explain why.
   (ii) Explain how a dataflow diagram would be useful to the designers of the system.

(d) Identify the main entities which would be necessary to store information to support the *sales order process*.

Note: Part of the purpose of this exercise is to extract the relevant information from the case study. A common problem for business analysts may be too much information rather than too little. Use a highlighter pen to mark the relevant material.

▶ References

Buzan, I. (1995) *The Mind Map Book*, BBC Books, London.

Checkland, P.B. (1981) *Systems Thinking, Systems Practice*, John Wiley, Chichester.

Kavanagh, D. (1994) 'OMT development process, vintage 1994', in Spurr, K., Layzell, P., Jennison, L. and Richards, N. (eds) *Business Objects: Software Solutions*, John Wiley, New York, 90–105.

Patching, D. (1990) *Practical Soft Systems Analysis*, Financial Times Pitman Publishing, London.

Taylor, D. (1995) *Business Engineering with Object Technology*, John Wiley, New York.

Yeates, D., Shields, M. and Helmy, D. (1994) *Systems Analysis and Design*, Financial Times Pitman Publishing, London.

▶ Further reading

Avison, D.E. and Fitzgerald, G. (1996) *Information Systems Development: Methodologies, Tools and Techniques*, Blackwell, Oxford.

Eva, M. (1992) *SSADM Version 4: a User's Guide*, McGraw-Hill, Maidenhead, UK.

Griffiths, G. (1998) *The Essence of Structured Systems Analysis Techniques*, Prentice-Hall, London.

Flynn, D. (1992) *Information Systems Requirements: Determination and Analysis*, McGraw-Hill, Maidenhead, UK.

Kendall, K. and Kendall, J. (1998) *Systems Analysis and Design*, Prentice-Hall, London.

Lejk, M. and Deeks, D. (1998) *An Introduction to Systems Analysis Techniques*, Prentice-Hall, London.

Robinson, B. and Prior, M. (1995) *Systems Analysis Techniques*, International Thompson Computer, London.

Tudor, D. and Tudor, I. (1997) *Systems Analysis and Design a Comparison of Structured Methods*, Macmillan, Basingstoke.

Weaver, P.L., Lambrou, N. and Walkley, M. (1998) *Practical SSADM Version 4+: a Complete Tutorial Guide*, Financial Times Pitman Publishing, London.

Whitten, J. and Bently, L. (1998) *Systems Analysis and Design Methods*, Irwin/McGraw-Hill, Boston, MA.

Systems design

INTRODUCTION

The **design** phase of information systems development involves producing a specification or 'blueprint' of *how* the system will work. This forms the input specification for the final stage of building the system by programmers and database administrators. The design phase is also closely linked to the previous analysis phase, since the users' requirements directly determine the characteristics of the system to be designed.

The **Systems design** is given in a design specification defining the best structure for the application and the best methods of data input, output and user interaction via the user interface. The design specification is based on the requirements collected at the analysis stage.

Design is important, since it will govern how well the information system works for the end-users in the key areas of performance, usability and security. The design specification will include the architecture of the system, how security will be implemented and methods for entry, storage, retrieval and display of data.

Systems design

The design phase of the lifecycle defines how the finished information system will operate. This is defined in a design specification defining the best structure for the application and the best methods of data input, output and user interaction via the user interface. The design specification is based on the requirements collected at the analysis stage.

> ▶ Learning objectives

After reading this chapter, readers will be able to:

♦ appreciate the difference between analysis and design and the essential overlap between them;

♦ appreciate the relationship between good design and good-quality information systems;

♦ describe the way relational databases are structured;

♦ explain the need for database normalisation and follow the process to achieve it;

♦ evaluate the importance of the different elements of design.

> ▶ Links to other chapters
>
> This chapter is closely linked to Chapters 11 and 13, since the design phase receives input from the requirements specification of the analysis phase and the design specification acts as input to the implementation phase.

▶ AIMS OF SYSTEMS DESIGN

In systems design we are concerned with producing an appropriate design which results in a good-quality information system which is:

◆ easy to use;

◆ provides the correct functions for end-users;

◆ rapid in retrieving data and moving between different screen views of the data;

◆ reliable;

◆ secure;

◆ well integrated with other systems.

These factors are all likely to be important to the end-users. As well as these factors, we must think forward to future releases of the software. When the software is updated in the maintenance phase, it is important to have a system that can be easily modified. Good documentation is important to this, but equally important is that the design is flexible enough to accommodate changes to its structure. To enable flexibility, simplicity in design is a requirement. Many designers and developers adopt the maxim 'KISS' or 'Keep It Simple Stupid!'.

Whitten *et al.* (1994) point out that design does not simply involve producing an architectural and detailed design, but is also an evaluation of different alternative implementation methods. For example, an end-user designing an application will consider whether to implement a system within an application such as Microsoft Access or develop a separate Visual Basic application. However, it is usually possible to take the 'make-or-buy' decision earlier in the software lifecycle, even when the detailed design constraints are unknown. The acquisition method is described in more detail in Chapters 7 and 8 on the startup phases of a project.

▶ CONSTRAINTS ON SYSTEM DESIGN

The system design is directly constrained by the user requirements specification, which has been produced as a result of systems analysis. This will describe the functions that are required by the user which must be implemented as part of the design. As well as the requirements mentioned in the previous section, there are environmental constraints on design which are a result of the hardware and software environment of implementation. These include:

◆ hardware platform (PC, Apple Macintosh or UNIX workstation);

◆ operating system (Windows 3.1, Windows NT Mac OS 7/8 or UNIX);

- data links required between the application and other programs or a particular relational database such as Oracle or MS SQL Server;
- design tools such as CASE tools;
- methodologies or standards adopted by the organisation such as SSADM;
- system development tools such as programming languages (some of which may not offer all the interface elements such as tables or may be of relatively poor performance, for example the native Java language);
- number of users to be supported and the performance required.

▶ THE RELATIONSHIP BETWEEN ANALYSIS AND DESIGN

As Yeates *et al.* (1994) point out, there is considerable overlap between analysis and design. To help ensure completion of the project on time, preliminary design of the architecture of the system will start while the analysis phase is progressing. Furthermore, the design phase may raise issues on requirements which may require further analysis with the end-users, particularly with the prototyping approach.

The distinction is often made between the *logical* representation of data or processes during the analysis stage and the *physical* representation at the design stage. Consider, for example, data analysis: here the entity relationship diagram of the analysis phase will be transformed into a physical database table definition at the design stage. A logical entity 'customer' will be specified as a physical database table 'Customer' in which customer records are stored. Similarly, the dataflow diagram will be transformed into a structure chart indicating how the different submodules of the software will interact at the design stage. This is described further on page 414.

▶ ELEMENTS OF DESIGN

The different activities which occur during the design phase of an information systems project can be broken down in a variety of ways. In this section we consider different alternatives for approaching system design. These alternatives are often used in a complementary fashion rather than exclusively.

A common approach to design is to consider different levels of detail. In the next main section we start by considering an overall design for the architecture of the system. This is referred to as system design. Once this is established, we then design the individual modules and the interactions between them. This is known as module design. Through using this approach we are tackling design by using a functional decomposition or top-down approach, similar to that referred to in Chapter 9 on project management as the 'work breakdown structure'.

▶ Top down or bottom up?

Since many systems are made from existing modules or prebuilt components that need to be constructed, the design approach that is most commonly employed is a top-down strategy. In this approach, it is best to consider the overall architecture first and then perform the detailed design on the individual functional modules of the system. The 'divide and conquer' approach can then be used to assign the design

Top-down design

The top-down approach to design involves specifying the overall control architecture of the application before designing the individual modules.

and implementation tasks for each module to different development team members. The description here will follow this approach by looking at the overall design first and then the detailed module design.

The **bottom-up** approach to design starts with the design of individual modules, establishing their inputs and outputs and then builds an overall design from these modules.

Bottom-up design

The bottom-up approach to design starts with the design of individual modules, establishing their inputs and outputs and then builds an overall design from these modules.

▶ Validation and verification

An aspect of the design which is quite easy to overlook and which is stressed by Budgen (1994) is testing that the design we produce is the right one. Checking the design involves validation and verification.

In **validation** we will check against the requirements specification and ask '*Are we building the right product?*' In other words, we test whether the system meets the needs of the end-users identified during analysis.

When undertaking **verification** we will walk through the design and ask '*Are we building the product right?*' Since there are a number of design alternatives, designers need to consult to ensure they are choosing the optimal solution. Verification is a test of the design to ensure that the one chosen is the best available and that it is error free.

These two questions should be considered throughout the design process and also form the basis for producing a test specification to be used at the implementation stage.

Validation

This is a test of the design where we check that the design fulfils the requirements of the business users which are defined in the requirements specification.

Verification

This is a test of the design to ensure that the design chosen is the best available and that it is error free.

▶ Scalability

Scalability is the potential of an information system, piece of software or hardware to move from supporting a small number of users to a large number of users without a marked decrease in reliability or performance.

When designing information systems, the design target must always be for the maximum anticipated number of users. Many implementations have failed, or have had to be redesigned at considerable cost, because the system used in the development and test environment with a small number of users does not **scale** to the live system with many more users. If the system does not scale, there may be major problems with performance which make the system unusable. Volume testing (Chapter 13) in which the anticipated workload of the live environment is simulated, can help foresee problems of scalability.

The increased popularity of three-tier client/servers considered later in the chapter results from their ability to scale better from departmental to enterprise-level systems. When purchasing or designing applications for the enterprise, it is necessary to check with vendors and other adopters on the scale of their implementations – what are the maximum number of users and transaction rates that are supported?

Scalability

The potential of an information system, piece of software or hardware to move from supporting a small number of users to a large number of users without a marked decrease in reliability or performance.

▶ Data modelling and process modelling

Another common approach to design is to consider data modelling and process modelling separately. The design of the data structures required to support the system, such as input and output files or database tables, are considered in relation to information collected at the analysis stage as the ERD and data requirements. In SSADM a separate stage is identified for data design which is followed by process design, although as Downes *et al.* (1992) point out, the two are often combined.

Process modelling is the design of the different modules of the system, each of which is a process with clearly defined inputs, outputs and a transformation process. Dataflow diagrams are often used to define system processes.

Data modelling considers how to represent data objects within a system, both logically and physically. The entity relationship diagram is used to model the data and a data dictionary is used to store details about the characteristics of the data, which is sometimes referred to as metadata.

The processes or program modules which will manipulate this data are designed based on information gathered at the analysis stage in the form of functional requirements and dataflow diagrams. This approach is used, for example, by Curtis (1996). While this is a natural division, there is a growing realisation that for a more efficient design these two aspects cannot be considered in isolation. Object-oriented techniques, which are increasing in popularity, consider the design of process and model as unified software objects. These are considered in more detail at the end of this chapter.

Other elements of design are required by the constraints on the system. To ensure that the system is easy to use we must design the user interface carefully.

To ensure that the system is reliable and secure, these capabilities must be designed into the system. User interface and security design are elements of design which will be considered both at the overall or system design phase and the detailed design phase.

▶ What needs to be designed?

We will review the different elements of design in the following way:

1 *Overall design or system design*. What are the best architecture and client/server infrastructure? The overall design defines how the system will be broken down into different modules and how the user will navigate between different functions and different views of the data.

2 *Detailed design of modules and user interface components*. This defines the details of how the system will operate. It will be reviewed by looking at user interface and input/output design.

3 *Database design*. How to design the most efficient structure using normalisation.

4 *User interface design*. How to design the interface to make it easy to learn and use.

5 *Security design*. Measures for restricting access data and safeguarding data against deletion.

▶ SYSTEM OR OUTLINE DESIGN

System design involves specifying an overall structure for all the different components which will comprise the system. It is a high-level overview of the different components that make up the architecture of a system and how they interact. The components include both software modules which have a particular function such as a print module, but also hardware components which may be part of the system. Hardware will include specifying the characteristics of the client PC and servers, plus any additional hardware such as an image scanner or specialised printer.

Process modelling

Involves the design of the different modules of the system, each of which is a process with clearly defined inputs, outputs and a transformation process. Dataflow diagrams are often used to define processes in the system.

Data modelling

Data modelling involves considering how to represent data objects within a system, both logically and physically. The entity relationship diagram is used to model the data.

System or outline design

A high-level definition of the different components that make up the architecture of a system and how they interact.

Designing the overall architecture involves specification of how the different hardware and software components of the system fit together. To produce this design, a good starting point is to consider the business process definition which will indicate which high-level tasks will be performed using the different components of the system. These functions can be summarised using a flow process chart as shown in Fig 12.1. This example shows how workers use a workflow system to manage the workflow associated with processing new mortgage applications.

MINI CASE

Use of flow process charts for design of workflow systems

Flow process charts are a tool commonly used in operations management applications to help in identifying the bottlenecks in manufacturing plants. They can also be usefully applied to some information systems applications to help represent the flow of information in an organisation. They represent a hybrid between information flow diagrams and dataflow diagrams.

Flow diagrams have been used for a long time in the design of programs. Recently, they have waned in popularity and tend to have been replaced by dataflow diagrams as a method of displaying structure, since this is less ambiguous and supports different levels of abstraction (detail). However, flow diagrams are described since they offer an alternative analysis method which helps in system design and is easy to understand for business users.

In this example, mortgage (loan) applications are received by post. It is then necessary to identify *new applications* and supporting documentation for applications already received. (This is a decision point indicated by a diamond-shaped decision box.) New applications are keyed into the workflow system as a new *case* and the original form scanned in for reference (these are processes shown as circles on the chart). Supporting material such as ID (driving licences) and letters from employers are also scanned in. A team member will then assign or associate all scanned images of material which have been scanned into a particular case. Assigning new documents (*assignment tasks*) is always the most important task, so these need to be placed by the software automatically at the head of the workflow queue. Once assigned, the documents will need to be actioned (*action tasks*) by the operator, so according to the type of document and when it needs to be chased, the workflow system will assign a priority to the task and place it on the workflow queue. Team members will then have to action tasks from the workflow queue which are prioritised according to date. Processing an action task will usually involve phoning the customer for clarification or writing a letter to request additional information. After this has been achieved, the operator will mark the item as complete and a new workflow task will be created if necessary: for example, to follow up if a letter is not received within ten days.

This diagram is useful to system designers since they can identify different modules of a system and the hardware and software necessary to support these modules. In this case some of the modules are:

◆ scan document (scanner and scanning software);

◆ associate document to customer case (link to customer database);

◆ prioritise document (specialised workflow module);

◆ review document (link to customer database);

◆ contact customer (link to phone system and letter printer).

From these modules, a system architecture will be developed as shown in Fig 12.3 on page 413.

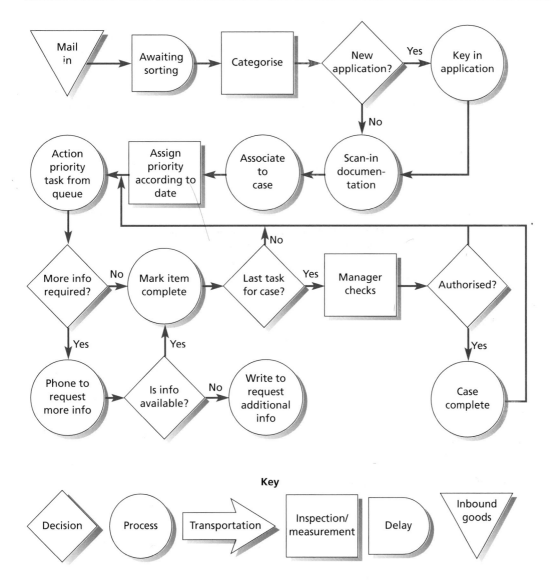

Fig 12.1 Flow process chart showing the main operations performed by users when working using workflow software

The overall architecture description will also include details of the navigation between the main screens or views of data in the application which can be based on this type of diagram.

Screen functions needed in this software are to categorise the type of mail received, associate it with a particular 'case' or customer and review items of work in the workflow queue, marking them as complete where appropriate. Table 12.1 summarises what is achieved during the different types of design.

Table 12.1 Comparison between the coverage of system and detailed design

Design function	System design	Detailed design
Architecture	Specification of different modules and communication between them; specification of hardware components and software tools	Internal design of modules
User interface	Flow of control between different views of data	Detailed specification of input forms and dialogues
Database	Data modelling of tables	Normalisation
File structure	Main file types and contents	Detailed 'record and field structure'
Security	Define constraints	Design security method

▶ The client/server model of computing

Client/server model

This describes a system architecture in which end-user computers access data from more powerful server computers. Processing can be split in various ways between the server and client.

The majority of modern information systems are designed with a client/server architecture. In the **client/server model**, the clients are typically desktop PCs which give the 'front-end' access point to business applications. The clients are connected to a 'back-end' server computer via a local or wide area network. When introduced, the client/server model represented a radically new architecture compared with the traditional centralised processing method of a mainframe with character based 'dumb terminals'. The client/server model was introduced in Chapter 5.

Client/server is popular since it provides the opportunity for processing tasks to be shared between one or more servers and the desktop clients. This gives the potential for faster execution, as processing is shared between many clients and the server(s), rather than all occurring on a single server or mainframe. Client/server also makes it easier for end-users to customise their applications. Centralised control of the user administration and data security and archiving can still be retained. With these advantages, there are also system management problems which have led to an evolution in client/server architecture from two to three tier as described below. The advantages and disadvantages of client/server are discussed in Chapter 5.

When designing an information system for the client/server architecture, the designer has to decide how to divide tasks between the server and the client. These tasks include:

◆ data storage;

◆ query processing;

◆ display;

◆ application logic including the business rules.

In 1995 the Gartner Group produced a report defining five different ways in which application logic, data management and presentation could be partitioned between client and server. These include:

1 Distributed presentation (three-tier client/server).
2 Remote presentation (three-tier client/server).
3 Distributed logic (three-tier client/server).
4 Remote data management (two-tier client/server).
5 Distributed database (two-tier client/server).

Since this time, descriptions of client/server design have followed just two main approaches: two-tier and three-tier client/server. Two-tier client/server is sometimes referred to as 'fat client', the application running on the PC is a large program containing all the application logic and display code. It retrieves data from a separate database server. Three-tier client/server is an arrangement in which the client is mainly used for display, with application logic and the business rules partitioned on a server as a second tier and the database server the third tier. Here the client is sometimes referred to as a 'thin client', because the size of the executable program is smaller. It is important to understand the distinctions between these, since they involve two quite different design approaches which can have significant implications for application performance and scalability. These are the 'thin client' approach where the client only handles display and the 'fat client' approach where a larger program runs on the client and handles both display and application logic. In the 'fat client' model the client handles the display and local processing, with the server holding the data (typically in a database) and responsible for handling processing of queries on the back end. This model, which is known as two-tier client/server, is still widely used, but more recently the three-tier client/server is becoming widespread due to problems with unreliability and lack of scalability with two-tier systems. Examples of recent successful three-tier implementations are described in the book by Edwards and DeVoe (1997). These include:

◆ UK Employment Service record system.
◆ Peoplesoft enterprise resource planning.
◆ 3M Patient Care management system.
◆ Wells Fargo Internet banking.
◆ EUCARIS European car registration scheme.
◆ MCI telecommunications customer transaction management systems.

Figure 12.2 shows a simple two-tier client/server arrangement. In this, a client application directly accesses the server to retrieve information requested by the user, such as a report of 'aged debtors' in an accounting system. In many systems, this is mediated through SQL, with an SQL request being passed to the server as a parameter which is processed by the server and the result of the query returned to the client. In this two-tier model, the client handles all application logic such as control flow, the display of dialogues and formatting of views. Typically, the business rules will also be contained in the 'fat client' application, although these could also be held on the database as stored procedures. The two-tier model has the advantage of simplicity, but it has the main problem that the business rules become bound in with the

Two-tier client/server

Sometimes referred to as 'fat client', the application running on the PC is a large program containing all the application logic and display code. It retrieves data from a separate database server.

Three-tier client/server

The client is mainly used for display with application logic and the business rules partitioned on a second tier server and a third-tier database server. Here the client is sometimes referred to as a 'thin client', because the size of the executable program is smaller.

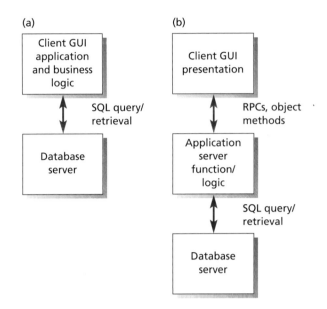

Fig 12.2 (a) Two-tier and (b) three-tier client/server architecture compared

user interface code. This makes maintenance difficult. It has also been found that two-tier client/server did not scale very well to larger implementations.

In a three-tier client/server model (Fig 12.2), the GUI or 'thin client' forms the first tier, with the application and function logic separated out as a second tier and the data source forming the third tier. In this model there may be a separate application and database server, although these could reside on the same machine. Two-tier client/server may be the most rapid to develop in a RAD project, but it will not be the most efficient at runtime or the easiest to update. Through separating out the display coding and the business application into three tiers, it is much easier to update the application as business rules change (which will happen frequently). It also offers better security through fine-tuning according to the service required.

Returning to our example of mortgage processing from earlier in the chapter, the overall system architecture of such an arrangement will be specified to show all the different hardware elements that will form the system. The architecture for this system is shown in Fig 12.3.

▶ Program and module structure

The module and program structure will also be outlined at the system design stage. There are various notations used by programmers to indicate the structure that will be used. The best known is the structure chart which is used in the design methodology JSD (Jackson System Design (Jackson, 1983)). An example of a structure chart is illustrated in Fig 12.4. A structure chart shows how the software will be broken down into different modules and gives an indication of how they will interact. Here the main control module is calling a variety of other modules with different functions. The interaction or exchange of data items between procedures is also shown. For

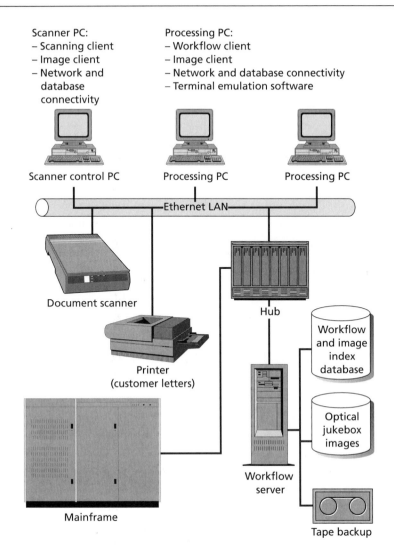

Scanner PC:
- Scanning client
- Image client
- Network and database connectivity

Processing PC:
- Workflow client
- Image client
- Network and database connectivity
- Terminal emulation software

Scanner control PC   Processing PC   Processing PC

Ethernet LAN

Document scanner

Hub

Printer (customer letters)

Workflow and image index database

Optical jukebox images

Mainframe

Workflow server

Tape backup

Fig 12.3 System architecture for the example workflow processing system

example, the 'edit customer' module is passed the name (or customer code) of the customer to edit and if the user changes the data a 'flag' (True or False) parameter is passed back to the control module, indicating that the data was updated. Similarly, the credit check module is passed the name of the customer and a flag indicates whether the customer is creditworthy or not.

The interactions between modules will normally be defined at this stage rather than at the detailed design stage. For example, there may be a function to produce a customer report of credit history. Here, the function will need to know the customer and the time period for which a report is required. Thus the system design will specify the function with three parameters as shown in Fig 12.5.

Function: Print_Credit_history
Parameters: Cust_id, Period_start, Period_end
Return value: Print Successful

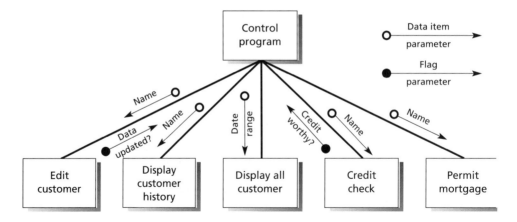

Fig 12.4 Example of a program structure chart

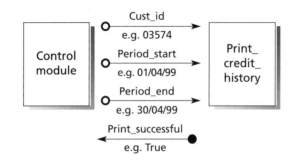

Fig 12.5 Part of a structure chart showing how parameters are passed from a control module to a module to print a credit history

▶ DETAILED DESIGN (MODULE DESIGN)

Detailed or module design

Detailed design involves the specification of how an individual component of a system will function in terms of its data input and output, user interface and security.

Detailed design involves considering how individual modules will function and how information will be transferred between them. For this reason, it is sometimes referred to as module design. A modular design offers the benefit of breaking the system down into different units which will be easier to work on by the team developing the system. It will also be easier to modify modules when changes are required in the future.

Module design includes:

◆ how the user interface will function at the level of individual user dialogues;

◆ how data will be input and output from the system;

◆ how information will be stored by the system using files or a database.

Detailed design is sometimes divided further into external and internal design. The external design refers to how the system will interact with users, while the internal design describes the detailed workings of the modules.

▶ RELATIONAL DATABASE DESIGN AND NORMALISATION – THE CLOTHEZ EXAMPLE

Business users are often involved in the design of relational databases, either in an advisory capacity (specifying what data they should contain) or when building a small personal database, perhaps of customer contacts. For this reason, the terminology used when working with databases and the process of producing a well-designed database are described in some detail.

Relational database terminology was introduced in Chapter 4, but it is restated here since understanding the terms is important to understanding the design process. This section uses the example of a sales order processing database for a clothing manufacturer, 'Clothez'.

▶ Fundamental terms

The terms defining the structure of a relational **database** can be considered as a hierarchy or tree structure. A single database is typically made up of several **tables** which contain many **records** and several **fields**. These terms can be defined in relation to the Clothez example as follows:

1 *Database*. All information for one business application (normally made up of many tables). Example: *Sales order* database.

2 *Table*. Collection of records for a similar entity. Example: All *customers* of the company within the sales order database. Other tables in the database are *product* and *order*.

3 *Record*. Information relating to a single entity (comprised of many fields). Example: single customer such as *Poole*.

4 *Field*. An attribute of the entity. Example: *Customer name* or *address* for a particular customer such as *Poole*.

This structure is represented as a diagram in Fig 12.6 for the Clothez database. It can be seen that the sales order processing database for Clothez could be designed and implemented as three tables: customer, order and product. Each table such as customer is made up of several records for different customers and then each record is divided down further into fields or attributes which describe the characteristics of the customers such as name and address.

Note that this example database is simplified and this structure only permits one product to be ordered when each order is placed. The reason for this restriction is that the database has not been fully normalised from order table into order-header and order-line tables. The normalisation process is described in a later section.

Database

All information for one business application (normally made up of many tables).

Table

Collection of records for a similar entity.

Record

Information relating to a single entity (comprised of many fields).

Field

An attribute of the entity.

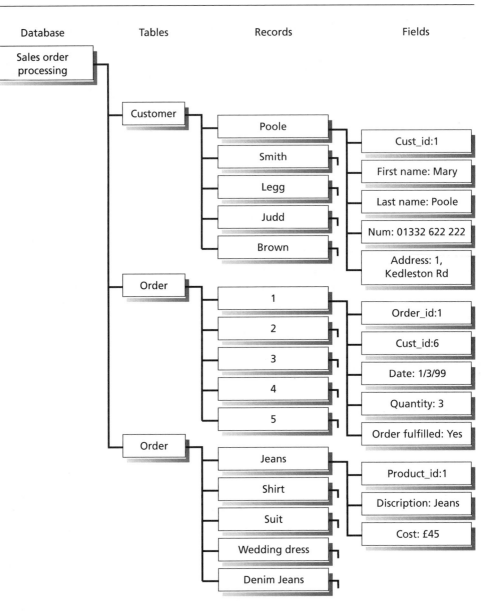

Fig 12.6 Diagram illustrating the tree-like structure used to structure data within a relational database. This example refers to the Clothez database. The fields are only shown for the first record in each table.

Key field

This is a field with a unique code for each record. It is used to refer to each record and link different tables.

If the data was entered into a database such as Microsoft Access, the tables and their records and fields would appear as in Fig 12.7. All three tables are shown. Fields and records for the product table are shown in Fig 12.8.

A further term which needs to be introduced is **key field**. This is the field by which each record is referred, such as customer number. The key field provides a *unique* code such as '001' or '993AXR', comprising either numbers or letters. It is

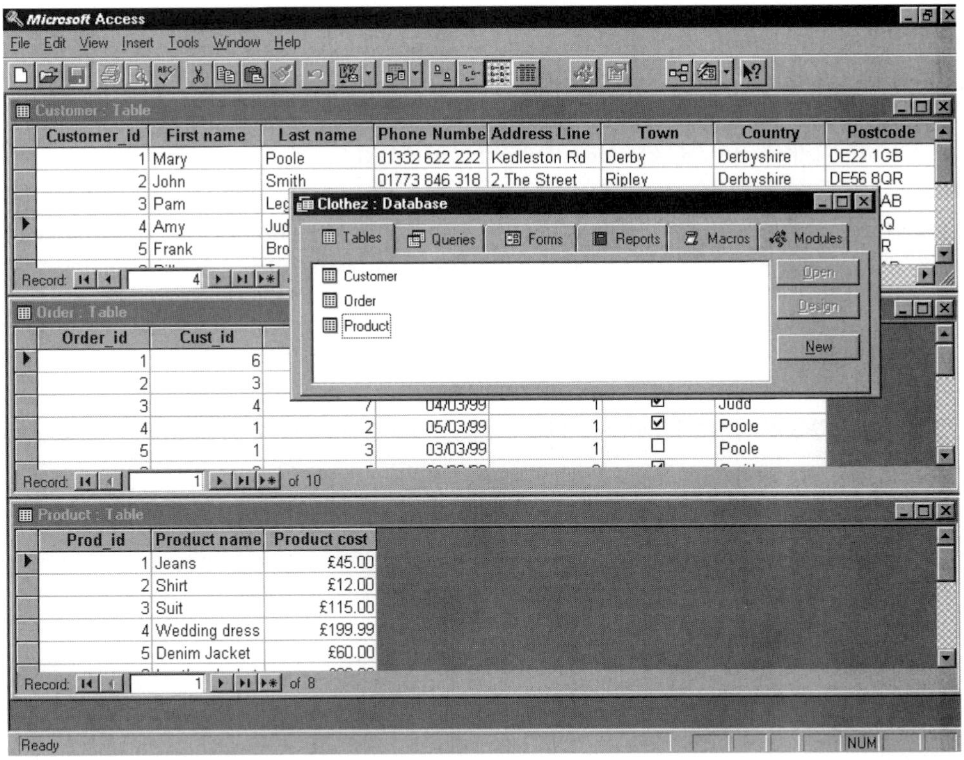

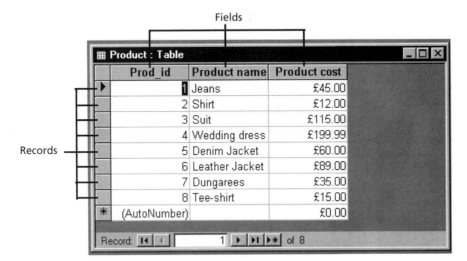

Fig 12.7 Clothez database in Microsoft Access

Fig 12.8 Product table showing records and fields

required to refer to each record to help distinguish between different customers (perhaps three different customers called Smith). Key fields are also used to link different tables, as explained in the next section.

▶ What makes an Access database relational?

The term *relational* is used to describe the way the different *tables* in a database are linked to one another. Key fields are vital to this. In recognition of the importance of key fields, Microsoft uses the key as the logo or brand icon for the Access database.

In the Clothez databases, the key fields are: Customer_id, Product_id and Order_id (id is short for identifier; code, num or number could also be used for these field names). These fields are used to relate the three tables, as is shown in Fig 12.9.

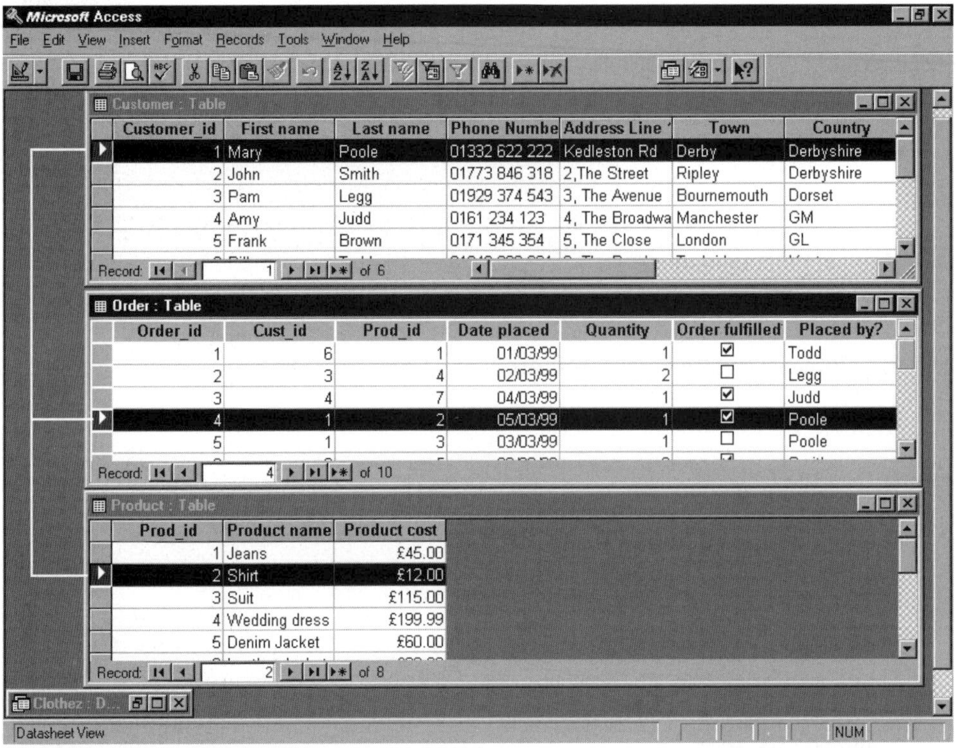

Fig 12.9 Clothez database in Microsoft Access showing how the Order table is related to Customer and Product

Figure 12.9 shows how the highlighted record in the order table (Order_id = 4) uses key fields to refer to the customer, Mary Poole, who has placed the order (Cust_id = 1) and the product (Shirt) she has ordered (Prod_id = 2).

To understand how the key fields are used to link different tables, two different types of fields need to be distinguished: primary and foreign keys.

Primary keys provide a unique identifier for each table which refers directly to the entity represented in the table. For example, in the product table, the primary key is Prod_id. There is only one primary key per table, as follows:

Primary key fields

These fields are used to uniquely identify each record in a table and link to similar secondary key fields (usually of the same name) in other tables.

◆ Customer table: Customer_id
◆ Order table: Order_id
◆ Product table: Prod_id

Foreign or secondary keys are used to link tables by referring to the primary key of another table. For example, in the order table, the secondary key Cust_id is used to indicate which customer has placed the order. The order table also contains Prod_id as a foreign key, but neither of the other tables has secondary keys. There may be zero, one or more secondary key per table.

Foreign (secondary) key fields

These fields are used to link tables together by referring to the primary key in another database table.

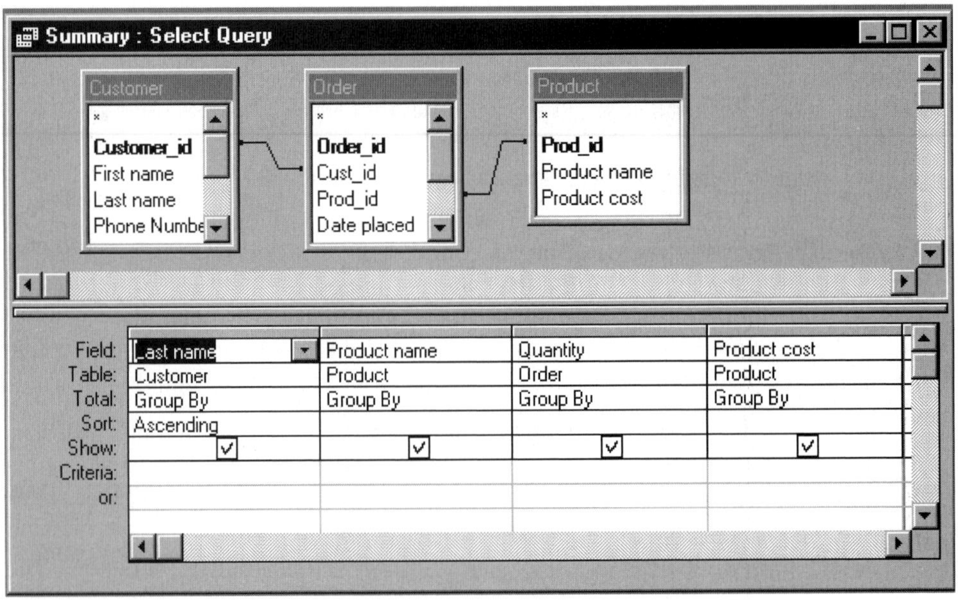

Fig 12.10 Query design screen for the summary query in the Clothez database

Figure 12.10 shows how the primary key fields in the customer and product tables are used to link to their corresponding foreign keys (Cust_id and Prod_id) in the order table when constructing a query in Microsoft Access. This is a summary query which summarises the details of orders by taking data from each table. The result of the query is shown in Fig 12.11.

The highlighted record in Fig 12.11 is the example relationship which was used to illustrate the links between tables in Fig 12.9.

▶ Defining field data types and sizes

A relatively straightforward aspect of database design is deciding on the field definitions. Fields need to be defined in terms of:

◆ field name;
◆ field data type;
◆ field data size;
◆ field validation rules.

Summary : Select Query

Last name	Product name	Quantity	Product cost	Date placed
Judd	Dungarees	1	£35.00	04/03/99
Legg	Wedding dress	2	£199.99	02/03/99
Poole	Shirt	1	£12.00	05/03/99
Poole	Suit	1	£115.00	03/03/99
Smith	Denim Jacket	3	£60.00	02/03/99
Todd	Denim Jacket	1	£60.00	28/02/99
Todd	Dungarees	1	£35.00	05/02/99
Todd	Jeans	1	£45.00	01/03/99
Todd	Leather Jacket	1	£89.00	03/03/99

Record: 3 of 9

Fig 12.11 Summary query for orders placed from Clothez database

Data dictionary

A repository which is used to store the details of the entities of the database. It will define tables, relations and field details which are sometimes referred to as metadata or 'data about data'.

These are defined when the database is created, since storage space for each field is pre-allocated in a database. During analysis and design, the field characteristics are managed in a **data dictionary**. This is often referred to as the metadata or 'data about data', particularly with reference to data warehouses (Chapter 6).

Let us now consider each of the characteristics of a field in more detail:

1 *Field name*. Field names should clearly indicate the content of the field. It is conventional in some databases to use underscores rather than spaces to define the name, since some databases may not recognise spaces (e.g. Order_fulfilled rather than Order fulfilled. In some databases the number of characters is restricted to eight, but this is now rare.

2 *Field data type*. Data types define whether the field is a number, a word, a date or a specialised data type. The main data types used in a database such as Microsoft Access are:

- *Number*. Whole number or decimal. (Most databases recognise a range of numeric data types such as integer, real, double, byte etc.)
- *Currency*. This data type is not supported for all databases.
- *Text*. Often referred to as character, string or alphanumeric. Phone numbers are of this data type, since they may need to include spaces or brackets for the area code.
- *Date*. Should include four digits for the year! Can also include time.
- *Yes/No*. Referred to as Boolean or true/false in other databases.

Key fields can be defined as either number or text.

3 *Field data size*. Field data sizes need to be pre-allocated in many databases. This is to help minimise the space requirements. Field size is defined in terms of the number of digits or characters which the designer thinks is required. For example, a user may define 20 characters for a first name and 40 characters for an address. It is best to overestimate than to risk having to modify the field later.

4 *Field validation rule*. Validation rules are necessary to check whether the user has entered valid data. Basic types of validation are:

◆ Is field essential? For example, postcodes are usually mandatory to help identify a customer's address.

◆ Is field format correct? For example, postcodes or ZIP codes usually follow a set format.

◆ Is value within range? For example, an applicant for a mortgage would have to be more than 18 years of age.

◆ Does field match a restricted list? An entry for marital status would need to be 'married', 'divorced' or 'single'. Restricted list choices can be defined in separate 'lookup tables'.

To maintain data quality validation is an important, but sometimes neglected, aspect of detailed design which is covered in more detail in the section on input design.

Table 12.2 shows how the field definitions for a table can be summarised. Note that setting the key fields to a field size of six allows a maximum number of customers of 999 999.

Table 12.2 Definition of field details for the order table in the Clothez database (with fields added to show range)

Field name	Field type	Field size	Validation rule	Key field
Order_id	Number	6	Mandatory	Primary
Cust_id	Number	6	Mandatory	Foreign
Prod_id	Number	6	Mandatory	Foreign
Date_placed	Date	10	Mandatory, must be valid date	
Order_fulfilled	Yes/No	3	Restricted, must be Yes/No	
Special_instructions	Text	120	Not mandatory	
Total_order_value	Currency	10	Not mandatory	

▶ What is normalisation?

Normalisation a design activity that is used to optimise the logical storage of data within a database. It involves simplification of entities and removal of duplication of data.

One of the most important activities that occurs during database design is referred to as normalisation. The main purpose of data normalisation is to group data items together into database structures of table and records which are simple to understand, accommodate change, contain a minimum of redundant data and are free of insertion, deletion and update anomalies. These anomalies can occur when a database is modified, resulting in erroneous data. They are explained in the next section. Since this activity should be conducted when all databases are designed, and since databases are so widely used in business applications, we consider the process of normalisation in some detail.

Normalisation is essentially a simplifying process that takes complex 'user views' of data (such as end-user, customer and supplier) and converts them into well-structured logical representation of the data.

Normalisation

This design activity is a procedure which is used to optimise the physical storage of data within a database. It involves simplification of entities and minimisation of duplication of data.

Normalisation has its origins in the relational data model developed by Dr E.F. Codd from 1970 onwards and based on the mathematics of set theory. In this section we present a brief, straightforward explanation of the steps involved in normalising data, which can be applied to simple and complex data structures alike. The description of normalisation involves a series of stages which convert unnormalised data to normalised data. There are a series of intermediate stages which are referred to as 1st, 2nd, 3rd and 4th normal form.

▶ Some definitions

Before commencing the steps of normalisation, it is worth providing some key definitions in order to simplify the flow of the following sections. These definitions are summarised in Table 12.3.

Table 12.3 Summary of terms used to describe databases and normalisation

Term	Definition
Normalisation	The process of grouping attributes into well-structured relations between records linked with those in other tables
Table	Used to store multiple records of different instances of the same type of entity such as customer or employee
Relation	Relational database terminology for a record
Attribute	The smallest named unit in a database; other names include 'data item' and 'field'
Update anomaly	The inability to change a single occurrence of a data item in a relation without having to change others in order to maintain data
Insertion anomaly	The inability to insert a new occurrence (record) into a relation without having to insert one into another relation first
Deletion anomaly	The inability to delete some information from a relation without also losing some other information that might be required
Functional dependency	A functional dependency is a relationship between two attributes and concerns determining which attributes are dependent on which other attributes: 'attribute B is fully functionally dependent on attribute A if, at any given point in time, the value of A determines the value of B' – this can be diagrammed as A → B
Determinant	An attribute whose value determines the value of another attribute
Primary key	An attribute or group of attributes that *uniquely* identifies other non-key attributes in a single occurrence of a relation
Foreign key	An attribute or group of attributes that can be used to link different tables; the foreign key will link to the primary key in another table
Composite key	A key made up of more than one key within a relation
Candidate key	A candidate key is a determinant that can be used for a relation; a relation may have one or more determinants; determinants can be either single attributes or a composite key

▶ Unnormalised data

Unnormalised data is characterised by having one or more repeating groups of attributes. Many user views of data contain repeating groups. Consider a customer order form for the Clothez company (Fig 12.12): there might be such information as customer name, customer address and order date recorded at the top of the form; there might also be a section in the main body of the form that allows multiple items to be ordered.

Name:	Mary Poole	**Order date:**	5/3/99	**Order no:**	4
Address:	1 Kedleston Road	**Tel no:**	01332 622 222	**Cust no:**	1
	Derby				
Post code:	DE22 1GB				

Line no	**Product no**	**Product description**	**Quantity**	**Price**
1	2	Shirt	1	£12.00

Fig 12.12 Customer order form for the Clothez company

It is possible to represent the user view described above in diagrammatic form which is equivalent to a physical database table. Note that the example in Fig 12.3 uses a subset of the information shown in the order form example.

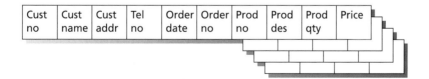

Cust no	Cust name	Cust addr	Tel no	Order date	Order no	Prod no	Prod des	Prod qty	Price

Fig 12.13 Repeating groups for the Clothez database

The possibility of entering multiple lines into a single order form is clearly a repeating group, i.e. order no. is being used to identify multiple order lines within the view and so, therefore, is not a unique determinant of each order line and its details.

It might also be argued that address also represents a repeating group, because there are two address lines. However, in practice a set number of address lines would be given a unique data name for each line and could be identified by a customer number. (Address is an example of a non-repeating 'data aggregate', whereas the line details are an example of a repeating data aggregate.)

By constructing such a diagram, it becomes much easier to identify repeating groups of data and thus pave the way to progressing to first normal form (1NF).

▶ Insertion/update/deletion anomalies

At this stage it is not obvious why repeating groups of data are a bad thing! If Fig 12.13 is transformed into a table, however, updating it could result in errors or inconsistencies. Each of the three different types of anomalies is now explained in turn with reference to Table 12.4.

Table 12.4 Table with example data for the structure shown in Fig 12.13

Cust no	Cust name	Cust addr	Tel no	Order date	Order no	Prod num	Prod des	Prod qty	Price
1	Poole	1, Ked	01332	5/03/99	4	2	Shirt	1	12
2	Smith	2, The	01773	2/03/99	6	5	Denim	3	60
3	Legg	3, The	01929	2/03/99	2	4	Weddin	2	199
3	Poole	1, Ked	01332	3/03/99	5	3	Suit	1	115

Insertion anomaly

It is not possible to insert a new occurrence record into a relation (table) without having to also insert one into another relation first.

Insertion anomaly

If it was desired to enter a new customer into the table, it would not be possible without having an order to enter at the same time.

Update anomaly

It is not possible to change a single occurrence of a data item (a field) in a relation (table) without having to change others in order to maintain the correctness of data.

Update anomaly

An **update anomaly** indicates it is not possible to change a single occurrence of a data item (a field) in a relation (table) without having to change others in order to maintain the correctness of data.

If a customer such as 'Poole' had several orders in the table and that customer moved to a new address, all the entries in the table where that customer appeared would have to be updated if inconsistencies were not to appear.

Deletion anomaly

It is not possible to delete a record from a relation without also losing some other information which might still be required.

Deletion anomaly

A **deletion anomaly** indicates it is not possible to delete a record from a relation without also losing some other information which might still be required.

If a customer such as 'Smith' had only one order in the table and that table entry was deleted, information about the customer would also be deleted.

The way to get round some of these problems is by normalising the data. Stage one of this process is the removal of repeating groups of data, i.e. proceeding to **first normal form (1NF)**.

First normal form (1NF)

Transforming unnormalised data into its first normal form state involves the removal of repeating groups of data.

▶ First normal form (1NF)

In the example above, the repeating group comprises *product number, product quantity and price*. Removing these attributes into a separate table will not suffice, however. For example, how could each entry in the newly created table be related to the order to which it is attached? The answer lies in including a linking attribute (also known as a foreign key) which is present in both the modified table and the new table. In this case, a sensible attribute to use would be *order number*. The first step in normalisation has thus resulted in the transformation of one table into two new ones. The two new tables are shown in Fig 12.14.

The example shows the relationship between fields at the top and example records below.

Removing insertion/update/deletion anomalies

Even though repeating groups have been removed by splitting the unnormalised data into two tables (relations), anomalies of all three types still exist.

Insert anomaly:

◆ In the customer/order relation, an order cannot be entered without also entering the customer's name and address details, even though they may already exist on another order; a customer cannot be added if there is no order to be placed.

◆ In the order/product relation, an item cannot be added without also adding an order for that item.

Customer/order relation

Cust no	Cust name	Cust addr	Tel no	Order date	Order no

Order/product relation

Order no	Prod no	Prod des	Prod qty	Price

☐ Primary key
☐ Foreign key

Customer/order relation

Cust no	Cust name	Cust addr	Tel no	Order date	Order no
1	Poole	1 Ked	01332	5/03/99	4
2	Smith	2 The	01773	2/03/99	6
3	Legg	3 The	01929	2/03/99	2
3	Poole	1 Ked	01332	3/03/99	5

Order/product relation

Order no	Prod no	Prod des	Prod qty	Price
4	2	Shirt	1	12
6	5	Denim	3	60
2	4	Weddin	2	199
5	3	Suit	1	115

Fig 12.14 The revised table structure and example data for two tables

Update anomaly:

◆ In the customer/order relation, a customer's name and address details cannot be amended without needing to amend all occurrences (where the customer has more than one order).

◆ In the order/product relation, an item description could appear on many order lines for many different customers – if the description of the item was to change, all occurrences where that item appeared would have to be changed if database inconsistencies were not to appear.

Deletion anomaly:

◆ In the customer/order relation, an order cannot be deleted without also deleting the customer's details.

◆ In the order/product relation, an order line cannot be deleted without also deleting the item number and description.

It is anomalies of this kind which indicate that the normalisation process needs to be taken a step further – that is, we must now proceed to second normal form (2NF).

ACTIVITY

Identification and removal of insertion, deletion and update anomalies

This activity shows a prototype database that has been produced by an employee of a toy manufacturer relating to its customers and sales activities. The designer, a business user, is not aware of the need for normalisation and has stored all the data in a single table.

Customer number	Customer name	Customer address	Order number	Product code	Product description	Quantity ordered	Price per item	Total cost	Order date	Salesperson number
100	Fred's Toys	7 High Street	10001	324	Action Man	3	13.46	40.38	7/10/99	007
100	Fred's Toys	7 High Street	10001	567	Silly Dog	6	5.15	30.9	7/10/99	007
100	Fred's Toys	7 High Street	10001	425	Slimy Hand	12	1.39	16.68	7/10/99	007
100	Fred's Toys	7 High Street	10001	869	Kiddy Doh	4	0.68	2.72	7/10/99	007
200	Super Toys	25 West Mall	13001	869	Kiddy Doh	12	0.68	8.16	7/17/99	021
200	Super Toys	25 West Mall	13001	637	Risky	3	17.42	52.26	7/17/99	021
200	Super Toys	25 West Mall	13001	567	Silly Dog	2	32.76	43.52	7/17/99	021
300	Cheapo Toys	61 The Arcade	23201	751	Diplomat	24	5.15	123.6	6/21/99	007

▶ Second normal form (2NF)

Second normal form (2NF) states that 'each attribute in a record (relation) must be functionally dependent on the whole key of that record.' To continue the normalisation process to second normal form, it is necessary to explore further some of the terms defined in the introductory section.

Functional dependencies

Within each of the relations produced above, a set of functional dependencies exists. These dependencies will be governed by the relationships which exist between different data items, which in turn will depend on the 'business rules', i.e. the purposes for which data is held and how it is used.

Once the functional dependencies have been established, it is then possible to select a candidate key for the relation.

Candidate keys

The process of analysing the functional dependencies within a relation will reveal one or more possible candidate keys – a candidate key is the minimum number of determinants (key fields) which uniquely determines all the non-key attributes.

Part no	Supplier no	Supplier name	Supplier details	Price

An example

Consider the following record:

Note that this example is different from that given in first normal form, since it illustrates the principles better.

The functional dependencies are as follows:

Part no and supplier no → Price

Supplier no → Supplier name

Supplier no → Supplier details

Second normal form (2NF)

Second normal form states that 'each attribute in a record (relation) must be functionally dependent on the whole key of that record.'

A possible candidate key might be thought to be supplier number. However, supplier number alone cannot be a determinant of price, since a supplier may supply many items.

Similarly, part number alone cannot be a determinant of price, because a part may be supplied by many different suppliers at different prices.

The candidate key is, therefore, a composite key comprising part number and supplier number.

We can express this more clearly by employing a dependency diagram (Fig 12.15).

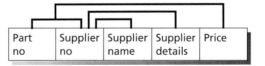

Fig 12.15 Example dependency diagram for supplier example

Two additional properties relating to candidate keys can now be introduced:

1 For every record occurrence, the key must uniquely identify the relation.
2 No data item in the key can be discarded without destroying the property of unique identification.

The dependency diagram in Fig 12.15 indicates a number of problems:

◆ If supplier number is discarded, it will no longer be possible to identify remaining attributes uniquely, even though part number remains.
◆ Details of a supplier cannot be added until there is a part to supply; if a supplier does not supply a part, there is no key.
◆ If supplier details are to be updated, all records which contain that supplier as part of the key must be accessed – i.e. there is redundant data.

This situation is known as a *partial key dependency* and is resolved by splitting the record into two or more smaller records (Fig 12.16).

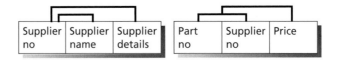

Fig 12.16 Revised dependency diagram for supplier example

A record is, therefore, in *at least* second normal form when any partial key dependencies have been removed.

Removing insertion/update/deletion anomalies

Consider the record structure shown in Fig 12.17. If it is assumed that an employee only works on one project at a time, then employee number is a suitable candidate key, in that all other attributes can reasonably be said to be fully functionally dependent on it.

Note: the record is already in second normal form because there is only one key attribute (therefore partial key dependencies *cannot* exist). However, some problems still exist.

Employee no	Employee name	Salary	Project no	Completion date

Fig 12.17 Example structure diagram – employee details

◆ *Insertion anomaly*: before any employees are recruited for a project, the completion date for a project cannot be recorded because there is no employee record.

◆ *Update anomaly*: if a project completion date is changed, it will be necessary to search *all* employee records and change those where an employee works on that project.

◆ *Deletion anomaly*: if all employees are deleted for a project, all records containing a project completion date would be deleted also.

To resolve these anomalies, a record in second normal form must be converted into a number of third normal form records.

▶ Third normal form (3NF)

Transitive dependency

A data item which is not a key (or part of a key) but which itself identifies other data items is a *transitive dependency*.

Third normal form (3NF). A record is in third normal form if each non-key attribute 'depends on the key, the whole key and nothing but the key.'

> **Third normal form (3NF)**
>
> A record is in third normal form if each non-key attribute 'depends on the key, the whole key and nothing but the key.'

An example

Consider the previous example. To convert the record into two third normal form records, any transitive dependencies must be removed. When this is done the result is the two records in Fig 12.18.

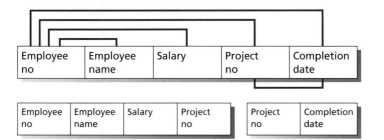

Fig 12.18 Dependency diagram for employee example and revised structure (below)

Removing insertion/update/deletion anomalies

If a record has only one candidate key and both partial key and transitive dependencies have been removed, then no insertion, update or deletion anomalies should result.

However, if a record has more than one candidate key problems can still arise. In this situation we can take the normalisation process still further.

▶ Fourth normal form (4NF) and fifth normal form (5NF)

Further normalisation may be necessary for some applications. In these normalisation can proceed to the fourth normal form and fifth normal form. These are described in

Mcfadden and Hofer (1995): 'In 4NF multi-valued dependencies are removed. A multi-valued dependency exists when there are at least three attributes in a relation and for each value of A there is a well-defined set of values of B and a well-defined set of values of C. However, the set of values of B is independent of set C and vice versa.'

In 5NF it is necessary to account for the potential of decomposing some relations from an earlier stage of normalisation into more than two relations. In most practical applications, decomposition to 3NF gives acceptable database performance and is often more easy to design and maintain.

ACTIVITY

Database design exercise using ABC case study

This activity builds on the ABC case study from Chapter 11. It is not necessary to have completed the Chapter 11 exercise to be able to undertake this one. You should use the extract in Chapter 11 describing ABC and in particular the paper forms of the existing system to identify which fields are required in the database.

Questions

1 Either:
  (a) Use normalisation to third normal form to identify tables and fields for an ABC database; or
  (b) Assume the following entities for the ABC database:
    ◆ customer details;
    ◆ sales person details;
    ◆ sales order header details;
    ◆ sales order line details;
    ◆ item details.

2 For each table in the database, define details of:
  ◆ table names;
  ◆ primary and foreign key fields for each table;
  ◆ name of each field;
  ◆ data type of each field;
  ◆ size of each field;
  ◆ any validation rules which may apply to each field (e.g. a limit on maximum price or quantity etc.).

You may find it most efficient to summarise the database definition using a table (in your wordprocessor).

▶ OTHER SIGNIFICANT DATABASE DESIGN ISSUES

As well as the logical design of the database there are aspects of physical database design which should be taken into account. These are specialised functions performed by a database administrator or DBA. A company which does not employ a specialist risks a poor performance system or, worse still, a loss or corruption of data. These design and database implementation tasks include:

1 *Design of optimal database performance.* Use of specialist techniques such as indexes or stored procedures will accelerate the display of common user views such as a list of all customer orders. Queries can also be optimised, but this is mainly performed automatically by the database engines such as Oracle, Microsoft SQL Server or Informix. To verify the design is good, volume testing is essential to ensure that the system can cope with the number of transactions that will occur.

2 *Designing for multi-user access.* When defining a new system, it is important to consider what happens when two users want to access the same data, such as the same customer record. If access to records is unlimited, then there will be anomalous data in the database if users save data about the customer at a similar time. Since multi-user access will not be frequent, the best method for dealing with it will be to implement record locking. Here, the first user to access a record will cause the database to restrict subsequent users to read-only access to the record rather than read-write. Subsequent users should be informed that a lock is in place and access is read only.

3 *Planning for failed transactions.* Recovery methods can be specified in the design for how to deal with failed transactions which may occur when there is a software bug or power interruption. Databases contain the facility to 'roll back' to the situation before a failure occurred.

4 *Referential integrity.* The database must be designed that when records in one table are deleted, this does not adversely affect other tables. Impact should be minimal if normalisation has occurred. Sometimes it is necessary to perform a 'cascading delete' which means to delete related records in linked tables.

5 *Design to safeguard against media, hardware or power failure.* A backup strategy should be designed to ensure that minimal disruption occurs if the database server fails. The main design decision is whether a point-in-time backup is required or whether restoring to the previous day's data will be sufficient. Frequently, a point-in-time backup will be required. Of course, a backup strategy is not much use if it cannot be used to restore the data, so backup and recovery must be well tested. To reduce the likelihood of having to fall back on a backup, using a fault-tolerant server is important. Specifying a server with an uninterruptible power supply, disk mirroring or RAID level 2 is essential for any corporate system. The frequency of archiving also will be specified.

6 *Replication.* Duplication and distribution of data to servers at different company locations and for mobile users is supported to different degrees by different database vendors. This is covered in more detail by an example in Chapter 19.

7 *Database sizing.* The database administrator will size the database and perform capacity planning to ensure that sufficient space is available on the server for the system to remain functional.

8 *Data migration.* Data migration will occur at the system build phase, but it must be planned for at the design stage. This will involve an assessment of the different data sources which will be used to populate the database.

▶ DESIGN OF INPUT AND OUTPUT FILES

Most modern information systems use relational database management systems for the storage of data. RDBMS provide management facilities which mean that programmers do not have to become directly involved with file management. Owing to this, most business users will not hear these terms unless eavesdropping on systems designers and this section is therefore kept brief. However, some older systems and large-scale transaction processing systems requiring superior performance do not use RDBMS for data storage. Such systems use a terminology which is unfamiliar to most developers of PC-based information systems.

▶ File access methods

File-based systems will access data that is stored in a file using two main methods:

1 *Sequential access.* The program reading or writing a file will start processing the file record by record (usually from the beginning).

2 *Direct (random) access.* Access can occur to any point (record) in the file without the need to start at the beginning.

Sequential, random and direct file access methods

Sequential file access involves reading or writing each record in a file in a set order. Random or direct file access allows any record to be read or written.

Sequential access is often used when batch processing a file which involves processing each record. Sequential file access involves reading or writing each record in a file in a set order. Direct access is preferable when finding a subset of records such as in a query, since it is much faster. Random or direct file access allows any record to be read or written.

▶ Indexing

Index

A file index is an additional file which is used to 'point' to records in a direct access file for more rapid access.

To enable rapid retrieval of data in a random access file (and also a database table), it is conventional to use an `index` which will find the location of the record more rapidly. These are sometimes referred to as indexed sequential files. A file index is an additional file that is used to 'point' to records in a direct access file for more rapid access. An index file for a customer file would contain two fields only for each record – the indexed item such as a customer number and the number of the record in the parent file (also known as the offset or pointer) which contained details on this customer. Indexes are also used to speed access to tables for RDBMS.

▶ File descriptions

In transaction processing systems which use native files rather than RDBMS, there are additional terms that are used to describe the type of files. These types include:

1 *The master file.* This is used to store relatively static information that does not change frequently. An examples would be a file containing customer details. After a customer record has been created it will not need to be updated frequently unless details such as name and address change. New records will only be added as new customers are registered.

2 *The transaction file.* This contain records of particular exchanges, usually related to a transaction such as a customer placing an order, paying for an order or an invoice being produced. This file has records added to it frequently.

3 *Archive file.* To reduce storage requirements and improve performance, transactions that occurred some time ago to which businesses are unlikely to wish to refer are removed from the online system as an archive which is usually stored on a tape or optical disk rather than a magnetic disk. It will be still available for reference, but access will be slower. Depending on the application, archiving may occur for records that are older than one day, one week, one month or one year.

4 *Temporary file.* These provide temporary storage space for the system which might be used during batch processing, when comparing data sets for example. The information would not be of value to a business user.

5 *Log file.* The log file is a system file used to store information on updates to other files. Its information would not be of value to a business user.

▶ File organisation

Information can be organised in file-based systems in a variety of ways, which are not of general relevance to the business user, so the terms are only summarised in tabular form (Table 12.5). Note that the indexed-sequential technique offers the best balance between speed of access to individual records and for achieving updates.

Table 12.5 Methods of file organisation

Organisation method	Access method	Application	Brief description
Sequential	Sequential	Batch process of a customer master file	An ordered sequential access file, e.g. ordered by customer number
Serial	Sequential		A sequential access file, but without any ordering
Random	Random + index	Querying data for decision support; unsuitable for frequent updates due to overhead of updating index	Organisation is provided by index
Indexed sequential	Sequential + index	Querying data for decision support and sequential batch processing	Best compromise between methods above

▶ Batch and real-time processing

When designing information processing systems, designers have to decide which is the most appropriate method for handling transactions:

◆ *Batch* – data is 'post-processed' after collection, usually at times of low system workload.

◆ *Real-time* or online processing – data is processed instantaneously on collection.

Batch system

A batch system involves processing of many transactions in sequence. This will typically occur some time after the transactions have occurred.

Real-time system

In a real-time system processing occurs immediately data is collected. Processing follows each transaction.

Table 12.6 compares the merits of batch and real-time systems according to several criteria.

There is a general trend from batch systems to real-time processing, but it can be seen from the table that batch processing is superior in some areas, not least cost. For a system such as the National Lottery, a real-time system must be used, but it is expensive to set up the necessary infrastructure. Refer to the case study on the Lottery in Chapter 5 to see how both real-time and batch methods are used in this context.

Table 12.6 A comparison of batch and real-time data processing

Factor	Batch	Real-time
Speed of delivery to information user	Slower – depends on how frequently batch process is run – daily, weekly or monthly	Faster – effectively delivered immediately
Ability to deal with failure	Better – if a batch process fails overnight there is usually sufficient time to solve the problem and rerun the batch	Worse – when a real-time system is offline there is major customer disruption and orders may be lost
Data validation	Worse – validation can occur, but it is time consuming to correct errors	Better – validation errors are notified and corrected immediately
Cost	Better – performance is less critical so cheaper hardware can be purchased	Worse – high-specification databases and communications infrastructure are necessary to achieve the required number of transactions per second
Disruption to users when data processing needs to be performed	Better – can occur in slack periods such as at weekends or overnight	Worse – can disrupt customers if time-consuming calculations occur as each record is processed

Batch systems are still widely used, since they are appropriate for data processing before analysis. For example, batch processing is used in data warehousing when transferring data from the operational system to the warehouse (Chapter 19). A batch process can be run overnight to transfer the data from one location to another and to perform aggregation such as summing sales figures across different market or product segments.

As a further example of a batch process, consider the processing that needs to occur to run a loyalty card scheme at a supermarket which was described in Chapter 6.

▶ USER INTERFACE COMPONENT DESIGN

The design of the user interface is key to ensuring that the software is easy to use and that users are productive. User interface design involves three main parts: first, defining the different views of the data such as input forms and output tables; second defining how the user moves or navigates from one view to another; and third providing options for the user.

Each module can be broken down into interface elements such as **forms** which are used to enter and update information such as a customer's details, **views** which tabulate results as a report or graphically display related information such as a 'to-do' list and **dialogs** which are used for users to select options such as a print options dialogue. Figure 12.19 gives an example of these different interface components.

The box on p. 436 summarises some important aspects of user interface design from UK financial services software company AIT.

User interface design is a specialist field which is the preserve of graphic designers and psychologists. This field is often known as **human–computer interaction design (HCI)**. HCI involves the study of methods for designing the input and output of information systems to ensure they are 'user-friendly.' It is covered well in the books by Preece *et al.* (1994) and Yeates *et al.* (1994). Many of the design parameters can be assisted by a knowledge of HCI.

Form

An onscreen equivalent of a paper form which is used for entering data and will have validation routines to help improve the accuracy of the entered data.

Data views

Different screens of an application which review information in a different form such as table, graph, report or map.

Dialog

An onscreen window (box) which is used by a user to input data or select options.

Human-computer interaction design (HCI)

HCI involves the study of methods for designing the input and output of information systems to ensure they are 'user-friendly'.

Dialog box   Report data view   Onscreen form

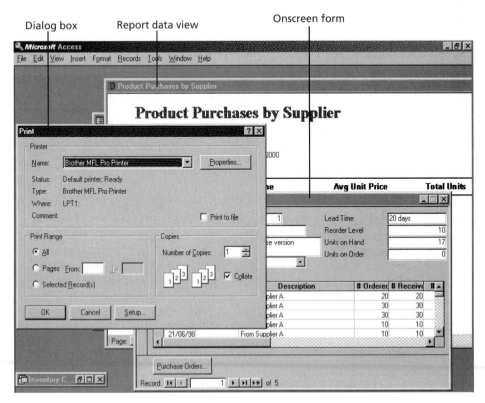

Fig 12.19 Microsoft Access showing key elements of interface design

AIT user interface design principles

1 *Functionality*. The main purpose of the user interface is to allow operators to complete their tasks effectively, quickly, easily and without frustration.

2 *Consistency*. Consistent systems are easier to learn and use because similar operations are performed in a similar manner in different modules. There needs to be consistency in both the presentation of information and operation. Microsoft Windows has consistency between applications which makes it easy to use new applications.

3 *Navigation and control*. The way in which the system works and the way in which tasks and information are structured should be clearly revealed to the user. Users should be guided through the interaction process in the quickest and most efficient manner.

4 *Modes*. A mode is where the system only allows a restricted set of actions. Modes force the users to focus on the way the system works rather than on the task at hand and should be avoided or clearly marked for the user.

5 *Relevancy*. It is important that only relevant and useful information is displayed.

6 *Visual clarity*. Users need to be able to find the information they require easily in order to interact with the system quickly. Each screen needs to be easy to read, uncluttered and the user's attention should be focused on the important information. Important information needs to be highlighted to attract the user's attention.

7 *Feedback*. Informative feedback helps the user to understand what the system is doing and to determine exactly what is required next by the system.

8 *Terminology*. Every word and phrase that appears on the computer screen should be meaningful and helpful in the completion of the user's task. Technical terms and computer jargon should be avoided.

9 *Help*. Users should be encouraged to learn about the system. This will ensure that they are using full functionality. Users needs to be able to use a help facility quickly and easily.

10 *Data input*. The user must be able to enter information easily and quickly. Fields should be formatted to cue the user to the type of information required. This will minimize potential errors. Validation of data input should occur.

11 *Error handling*. The system should be designed to minimize the possibility of user error. All user input should be validated before processing. The system should clearly and promptly inform the user when an error is detected and include information which will enable the reason for the error to be traced.

Source: http://www.ait.co.uk (with permission)

For example, guilelines exist such as:

◆ No more than seven menu options should be allowed at a time since this is the most the brain can absorb.

◆ Limited use of high-contrast colours such as white and blue is better for usability than using many shades of colours which may tire the eyes and be difficult to distinguish.

▶ INPUT DESIGN

User interface design can also be subdivided into **input design** and output design, but input and output design are used more generally to refer to all methods of data entry and display, so they warrant a separate section.

Input design includes the design of user input through onscreen forms, but also other methods of data entry such as import by file, transfer from another system or specialised data capture methods such as bar-code scanning, optical or voice recognition techniques.

Data input design involves capturing data which has been identified in the user requirements analysis via a variety of mechanisms. These have been described in Chapter 3 and include:

◆ keyboard – the most commonly used method;

◆ optical character recognition and scanning;

◆ voice input;

◆ directly from a monitoring system such as a manufacturing process, or from a phone system when a caller line ID is used to identify the customer phoning and automatically bring their details on screen;

◆ input from a data file that is used to store data;

◆ import of data from another system via a batch process (for example a data warehouse will require import of data from an operational system).

Input design

Input design includes the design of user input through onscreen forms, but also other methods of data entry such as import by file, transfer from another system or specialised data capture methods such as bar-code scanning, optical or voice recognition techniques.

▶ Validation

One of the key elements in input by all these methods is ensuring the quality of data. This is achieved through **data validation**. Data validation is a process to ensure the quality of data by checking that it has been entered correctly and prompts to the user informing them of incorrect data entry.

Validation is important in database systems and databases usually supply built-in input validation as follows:

◆ *Data type checking*. When tables have been designed, field types will be defined such as text (alphanumeric), number, currency or date. Text characters will not be permitted in a number field and when a user enters a date, for example, the software will prompt the user if it is not a valid date.

◆ *Data range checking*. Since storage needs to be pre-allocated in databases, designers will specify the number of digits required for each field. For example, a field for holding the quantity of an item ordered would typically only need to vary from

Data validation

Data validation is a process to ensure the quality of data by checking it has been entered correctly.

1–999. So three digits are required. If the user made an error and entered four digits, then they would be warned that this was not possible.

◆ *Restricted value checking.* This usually occurs for text values that are used to describe particular attributes of an entity. For example, in a database for estate agents, the type of house would have to be stored. This would be a restricted choice of flat, bungalow, semi-detached etc. Once the restricted choices have been specified, the software will ensure that only one of these choices is permitted, usually by prompting the user with a list of the available alternatives.

Some additional validation checks may need to be specified at the design phase which will later be programmed into the system. These include:

◆ *Input limits.* This is another form of range checking when the input range cannot be specified through the number of digits alone. For example, if the maximum number of an item that could be ordered is 5, perhaps due to a special offer, this would be specified as a limit of 1–5. Note that the user would not be permitted to enter 0.

◆ *Multiple field validation.* If there are business rules which mean that allowable input is governed by more than one field, then these rules must be programmed in. For example, in the estate agent database, there could be a separate field for commission shown as a percentage of house price, such as 1.5 per cent, and a separate field showing the amount, such as £500. In this situation the programmer would have to write code that would automatically calculate the commission amount depending on the percentage entered.

Checksum digits

A checksum involves the use of an extra digit for ensuring the validity of long code numbers. The checksum digit is calculated from an algorithm involving the numbers in the code and their modulus (by convention modulus 11).

◆ *Checksum digits.* A checksum involves the use of an extra digit for ensuring the validity of long code numbers. The checksum digit is calculated from an algorithm involving the numbers in the code and their modulus (by convention modulus 11). These can be used to ensure that errors are not made in entering long codes such as a customer account number (although these would normally be generated automatically by the computer). They are often used in bar codes.

Checksum digits example

The checksum digit is calculated using the modulus of the weighted products of the number, as follows:

1 Code number without check digit = 293643.

2 Calculate the sum of weighted products by multiplying the least significant digit by 2, the next by 3 and so on. For this example:
$(7*2) + (6*9) + (5*3) + (4*6) + (3*4) + (2*3) = 14 + 54 + 15 + 24 + 12 + 6 = 125$

3 Remainder when sum divided by 11 (modulus 11) = 125/11 = 11 remainder 4.

4 Subtract remainder from 11 to find check digit (11−4) = 7. (If the remainder is 0, check digit is 0; if 1, check digit is X.)

5 New code number with check digit = 2936437.

▶ OUTPUT DESIGN

Output design. Specifies how production of onscreen reports and paper-based reports will occur. Output may occur to database or file for storing information entered or also for use by other systems.

Output data is displayed by three methods:

1 It may be directly displayed from input data.
2 It may be displayed from previously stored data.
3 It may be *derived* data that is produced by calculation.

Design involves specifying the source of data (which database tables and fields map to a point on the report), what processing needs to occur to display data such as aggregation, sorting or calculations and the form in which the information will be displayed – graph, table or summary form. The case study on output design illustrates all the design elements involved in a single report.

Output design

Output design involves specifying how production of onscreen reports and paper based reports will occur. Output may occur to database or file for storing information entered or also for use by other systems.

CASE STUDY: TOPIC AREA

Output design of an onscreen report

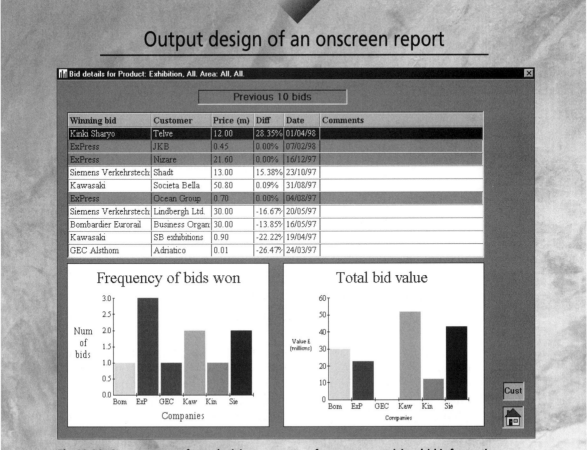

Fig 12.20 Output screen from decision support software summarising bid information

This case study involves a decision support system screen that is used to assess the performance of a company in winning bids against its competitors when it bids to host conferences. To display the table (Table 12.7) the following stages are required:

1 Specification of the source in the database of each of the fields used to display information in the columns is needed. For the 'Difference' field this has to be derived from two other fields, so the calculation needs to be specified.

2 Sorting criteria for the table need to be specified. Here the table is sorted in descending date order (ORDER BY BID_DATE DESC in the SQL query below).

3 Filtering criteria for the table need to be specified. Here only the 10 most recent bids are displayed (SELECT TOP 10 in the SQL query). We are only interested in conferences (other information is also held on the database for exhibitions). Defined by this part of statement: WHERE" + SQLprodpart + SQLareapart+.

4 Query needs to be designed. This is a relatively straightforward query in that all the data is stored in a single table. But note that if programmed the query can still be quite complicated. The query for accessing the information in the table is:

*SQLquery = "Select TOP 10 * FROM BID WHERE" + SQLprodpart + SQLareapart + " BID_DATE < NOW ORDER BY BID_DATE DESC"*

The details of the SQL query are not important to a business user, but note that a specialist programmer with SQL skills will often be required to develop this type of bespoke application.

To display the graphs, the information has already been retrieved using the SQL statement, but we need to specify a further stage of grouping the data by company and aggregating or summing the total number of bids and their value.

Table 12.7 Table for decision support system

Output data	Table	Field	Use of field
Winning bid	BID	BID_SUPPLIER	Column 1
Customer	BID	BID_CUST	Column 2
Price	BID	BID_PRICE	Column 3
Difference	BID	BID_PRICE (BP), BID_WIN_PRICE (WP)	Derived value: 100* (BP–WP)/WP
Date	BID	BID_DATE	Column 4 – used to order table

Output design is important for decision support software to ensure that relevant information can be chosen, retrieved and interpreted as easily as possible. Given that output design involves these three factors, it will also relate to input design (to select the report needed) and database design (to retrieve the information quickly).

▶ DEFINING THE STRUCTURE OF PROGRAM MODULES

The detailed design may include a definition for programmers indicating how to structure the code of the module. The extent to which this is necessary will depend on the complexity of the module, how experienced the programmer is and how important it is to document the method of programming. A safety-critical system (Chapter 4) will always be designed in this detail before coding commences. Structured English is one of the most commonly used methods of defining program structure. Standard flow charts can be used, but these tend to take longer to produce.

▶ Structured English

Structured English

A technique for producing a design specification for programmers which indicates the way individual modules or groups of modules should be implemented.

Structured English is a technique for producing a design specification for programmers which indicates the way individual modules or groups of modules should be implemented. It is more specific than a flowchart. It uses keywords to describe the structure of the program, as shown in the example box. Structured English is sometimes known as pseudocode or program design language. Data action diagrams use a similar notation.

Structured English has the disadvantage that it is very time consuming to produced a detailed design. But it has the advantage that to move from here to coding is very straightforward and the likelihood of errors is reduced.

Example: structured English

This example moves through each record of a database table totalling all employee's salaries. (Note that this could be accomplished more quickly using an SQL statement.)

```
DO WHILE NOT end of table

    IF hours_worked > basic_hours

        SET pay = (hours*basic_rate)+ (overtime_hours*overtime_rate)

    ELSE

        SET pay = (hours*basic_rate)

    END IF

    SET total_pay = total_pay + pay

    move to next record

ENDDO
```

▶ SECURITY DESIGN

Data security is of course a key design issue, particularly for information systems that contain confidential company information which is accessed across a wide area network or the Internet. The four main attributes of security which must be achieved through design are:

1 *Authentication*. Authentication ensures that the sender of the message, or the person trying to access the system, is who they claim to be. Passwords are one way of providing authentication, but are open to abuse – users often tend to swap them. Digital certificates and digital signatures offer a higher level of security. These are available in some groupware products such as Lotus Notes.

2 *Authorisation*. Authorisation checks that the user has the right permissions to access the information that they are seeking. This ensures that only senior personnel managers can access salary figures, for example.

3 *Privacy*. In a security context, privacy equates to scrambling or encryption of messages so that they cannot easily be decrypted if they are intercepted during transmission. Credit card numbers sent over the Internet are encrypted in this way.

4 *Data integrity*. Security is also necessary to ensure that the message sent is the same as the one received and that corruption has not occurred. A security system can use a checksum digit to ensure that this is the case and the data packet has not been modified.

Data must also be secure in the sense of not being subject to deletion, or available to people who don't have the 'need to know'. Methods of safeguarding data are covered in detail in Chapter 15.

▶ DESIGN TOOLS: CASE (COMPUTER-AIDED SOFTWARE ENGINEERING) TOOLS

Computer-aided software engineering (CASE) tools

Software which helps the systems analyst and designer in the analysis, design and build phases of a software project. They provide tools for drawing diagrams such as ERDs and storing information about processes, entities and attributes.

CASE (computer-aided software engineering) tools are software which helps the systems analyst and designer in the analysis, design and build phases of a software project. They provide tools for drawing diagrams such as ERDs and storing information about processes, entities and attributes.

CASE tools are primarily used by professional IS developers and are intended to assist in managing the process of capturing requirements, and converting these into design and program code. They also act as a repository for storing information about the design of the program and help make the software easy to maintain. The use of an engineering approach was intended to impose an engineering discipline on developing software which had been developed in an *ad hoc* way in many companies. CASE tools are based on a user graphically specifying a design using a diagram such as an entity relationship diagram and this logical design is then converted into a physical database structure. CASE tools permit different approaches to the design technique such as dataflow diagrams or object-oriented diagramming techniques. They are often supplied as part of a database package such as Oracle, Informix or Sybase, and in these cases are used for managing the data dictionary.

CASE tools were introduced in the 1980s as part of the need to engineer software products more methodically. The underlying reason behind CASE tools is to provide a software tool which can be used to assist throughout the software lifecycle. Previously there had been some tools to assist with analysis, tools for design and programming tools for the build phase. CASE tools provide a mechanism for architects of systems to use a single tool across all these phases of the lifecycle. Such tools are sometimes described as ICASE or integrated CASE tools, since they can be used throughout the lifecycle and are integrated with databases or programming tools. CASE tools are also useful since they tend to enforce documentation of the detailed design, much of which can be generated automatically.

Different ways in which CASE tools can be used are:

◆ A CASE tool can be used to summarise the requirements of users from the system needed for data modelling. For example, the CASE tool will produce an entity relationship diagram that can be linked to a data dictionary describing the attributes of the entities. This is then used to produce the physical table automatically at the build phase. The Oracle database provides CASE tools that give this facility. A more limited facility also exists in Microsoft Access which enables all the relationships between tables to be defined. These are then used to form queries.

◆ A CASE tool can be used to assist in process modelling. A dataflow diagram can be produced at different levels which relates to a data dictionary and provides a structure to the application, i.e. data can be linked to process and process to program modules.

CASE tools tend to be related to particular methodologies, for example SSADM Select helps users through the stages related to SSADM. Examples of CASE tools include the Oracle CASE/2000 product, Popkin Software System Architect and EasyCASE, which is shown in Fig 12.21.

When first introduced it was thought that CASE tools would dramatically speed up application development and also improve application quality. While they have helped in minimising the risk of project failure, dramatic improvements have not occurred. Intervention is still required by designers to produce a logical design and the need for skilled programmers has not been reduced. Since CASE tools tend to be expensive they are typically used by large companies only on major projects; they are less likely to be used for smaller-scale or end-user developed systems.

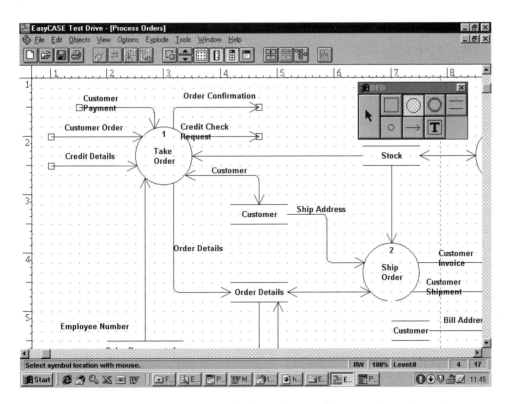

Fig 12.21 EasyCASE case tool showing a dataflow diagram for processing sales orders

▶ ERROR HANDLING AND EXCEPTIONS

The design will include a strategy for dealing with bugs in the system or problems resulting from changes to the operating environment, such as a network failure. When an error is encountered the design will specify that:

◆ Users should be prompted with a clear but not alarming message explaining the problem.

◆ The message should contain sufficient diagnostics that developers will be able to identify and solve the problem.

▶ HELP AND DOCUMENTATION

It is straightforward using tools to construct a Windows help file based on a word-processed document. The method of generating help messages for users will also be specified in the design. Help is usually available as:

◆ An online help application similar to reading a manual, but with links between pages and a built-in index.

◆ Context-sensitive help, where pressing the help button of a dialogue will take the user straight to the relevant page of the online user guide.

◆ ToolTip help, where the user places the mouse over a menu option or icon and further guidance is displayed in the status area.

◆ Help associated with error messages; this is also context sensitive.

▶ OBJECT-ORIENTED DESIGN (OOD)

Object-oriented design

This is a design technique which involves basing the design of software on real-world objects which consist of both data and the procedures that process it rather than traditional design where procedures operate on separate data.

Object-oriented design is a design technique which involves basing the design of software on real-world objects that consist of both data and the procedures that process it, rather than traditional design where procedures operate on separate data. Many software products are labelled object-oriented in a bid to boost sales, but relatively few are actually designed using object-oriented techniques. What makes the object approach completely different?

◆ Traditional development methods are *procedural*, dealing with separate data that is transformed by abstract, hierarchical programming code.

◆ OOD is a relatively new technique involving *objects* (which mirror real-world objects consisting of integrated data *and* code).

Example objects that are commonly used in business information systems include customer, supplier, employee and product. You may notice that these are similar to the entities referred to in Chapter 11, but a key difference is that an object will not only consist of different attributes such as name and address, but will also comprise procedures that process it. For example, a customer object may have a procedure (known as a method) to print these personal details.

SAP uses object-oriented structure for its R/3 ERP product

With its R/3 enterprise resource planning product, SAP provides several hundred standard business process modules for areas such as procurement or finance that can assist in rapid implementation of the system for new users. The business processes are defined as objects that are stored in an object repository. For example, an invoice is defined as an object with the standard methods:

◆ Create (constructor).

◆ Revise.

◆ Release.

◆ Post.

◆ Delete (destructor).

When executed, each of these methods will automatically generate an event that can be used for generating subsequent actions or monitoring workflow status. Although it is possible to tailor the objects somewhat, note that it is not practical to modify the standard objects to any great extent, so a consequence of this approach is that adopters of the SAP system tend to follow the standard processes provided by the software.

The main benefits of using object orientation are said to be more rapid development and lower costs which can be achieved through greater reuse of code. Reuse in object-oriented systems is a consequence of the ease with which generic objects can be incorporated into code. This is a consequence of inheritance, where a new object can be derived from an existing object and its behaviour modified (polymorphism).

Some further advantages of the object-oriented approach are:

◆ Easier to explain object concepts to end-users since based on real-world objects.

◆ More reuse of code – standard, tested business objects.

◆ Faster, cheaper development of more robust code.

Object-oriented design is closely linked to the growth in use of software components for producing systems. Developers writing programs for Microsoft Windows on a PC will now commonly buy prebuilt objects with functionality such as displaying a diary, a project schedule or different types of graph. Such object components are referred to as Visual Basic controls and object controls (OCX). Through using these, developers can implement features without having to reinvent the wheel of writing graphical routines.

An example of a class hierarchy is shown in Fig 12.22. The base class is a person who attends the college. All other classes are derived from this person.

▶ How widely is the object-oriented approach used?

There has been a rapid growth rate in the use of object-oriented techniques in the 1990s, although original research using the Simula language dates back to the late 1960s. This growth in interest is reflected by the increase in the number of jobs advertised by companies looking to develop software using object-oriented methods, such as Smalltalk, C++ and Java which is now one of the main methods for develop-

What are the main characteristics of an object-oriented system?

1 An object consists of *data* and *methods* which act on it. A customer object would contain data such as their personal details and methods to act on it such as 'print customer details'.

2 Objects communicate using *messages* which request a particular service from another object, such as a 'print current balance' service. These services are known as methods and are equivalent to functions in traditional programming.

3 Objects are created and destroyed as the program is running. For example, if a new customer opens an account, we would create a new instance of the object. If a customer closes an account, the object is destroyed.

4 Objects provide *encapsulation* – an object can have private elements that are not evident to other objects. This hides complex details and gives a simple public object interface for external use by other objects. A real-world analogy is that it is possible to use a limited number of functions on a television without knowing its inner workings. In object-oriented parlance the television controls are providing different public methods which can be used by other objects. Abstraction refers to the simplified public interface of the object.

5 Objects can be grouped into classes which share characteristics. For example, an organisation might contain an employee class. The classes can be subdivided using a hierarchy to create subclasses such as 'manager' or 'administrator'. Classes can share characteristics with other classes in the hierarchy, which is known as *inheritance*. This refers to the situation when an object inherits the behaviour of other objects. A specialised part-time staff class could inherit personal details data items from the employee class. If the method for calculating salary was different, then the part-time staff could override its inherited behaviour to define its own method 'calculate salary'. This is known as *polymorphism*, where an object can modify its inherited behaviour.

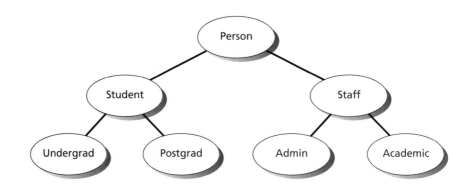

Fig 12.22 A class hierarchy for different types of people at a University

ing interactive Web sites. Specialised methodologies exist for designing object-oriented systems. Some of the most commonly used are the object modelling technique (OMT), described by Kavanagh (1994) and the original text by Rumbaugh (1991), and hierarchical object-oriented decomposition (HOOD), based on work conducted by Booch (1986) relating to the Ada programming language. These share some elements with DFD and ERD, but differ in that a hierarchical class breakdown is an additional perspective on designing the system.

Despite this growth rate, non-object or procedural systems vastly outnumber object systems. So if OOD is nirvana, why doesn't everyone use it? The following are all practical barriers to growth:

◆ Millions of lines of procedural legacy computer code exist in languages as COBOL.

◆ Many programmers' skills are procedural, OOD requires retraining to a different way of thinking.

◆ Methodologies, languages and tools are developing rapidly, requiring constant retraining and making reuse different when using different tools and languages. For example, the most popular object-oriented method has changed from Smalltalk to C++ to Java in just 10 years.

◆ Limited libraries are available for reuse.

◆ When initially designing projects, it is often slower and more costly – the benefits of OOD take several years to materialise.

The experience of early adopters has shown that the benefits do not come until later releases of a product and that initial object-oriented design and development may be more expensive than traditional methods.

MINI CASE

Rover Cars chooses object-oriented design

The Rover Group has based a multimillion-pound client/server dealer information system for customer satisfaction (Discus) on object-oriented technology. Discus enables production of vehicles to match the requirements of buyers, in details of paint colour and trim of the car. An order for a vehicle is either from stock or made to order. Discus has a traditional client/server architecture, with host servers providing information and executing transactions for Windows-based PCs sited at each of Rover's 650 UK dealerships.

The company is now considering delivering Discus to its dealers via a private Internet, or intranet, which would make it substantially easier and cheaper to support the client side of the system. 'Although the application software in an intranet version won't be cheaper, deployment costs will go down,' said Garry Bulmer of system integrators Parallex, which wrote Discus. Discus was written as an object-oriented system, making it very easy to rearchitect and migrate because software modules are reusable.

Source: Computer Weekly, 21 March 1996

Questions

1 The main base classes used for the system are 'vehicle' and 'feature'. Draw a class hierarchy for this system. This should include different types of vehicle and their features.

2 What benefits has the object-oriented system provided to Rover Cars and its customers?

3 What type of architecture has been designed for this system?

▶ SUMMARY

Stage summary: systems design

Purpose:	Defines *how* the system will work
Key activities:	Systems design, detailed design, database design, user interface design
Input:	Requirements specification
Output:	System design specification, detailed design specification, test specification

1 The design phase of the systems development lifecycle involves the specification of how the system should work.

2 The input to the design phase is the requirements specification from the analysis phase. The output from the design phase is a design specification that is used by programmers in the build phase.

3 Systems design is usually conducted using a top-down approach in which the overall architecture of the system is designed first. This is referred to as the systems or outline design. The individual modules are then designed in the detailed design phase.

4 Many modern information systems are designed using the client/server architecture. Processing is shared between the end-user's clients and the server, which is used to store data and process queries.

5 Systems design and detailed design will specify how the following aspects of the system will work:
   ◆ its user interface;
   ◆ method of data input and output (input and output design);
   ◆ design of security to ensure the integrity of confidential data;
   ◆ error handling;
   ◆ help system.

6 For systems based on a relational database and file-based system, the design stage will involve determining the best method of physically storing the data. For a database system, the technique for optimising the storage is known as normalisation.

7 Object-oriented design is a relatively new approach to design. It has been adopted by some companies attracted by the possibility of cheaper development costs and fewer errors, which are made possible through reuse of code and a different design model that involves data and process integration.

▶ EXERCISES

▶ Self-assessment exercises

1 Define systems design.

2 What distinguishes systems design from systems analysis?

3 Describe the purpose of validation and verification.

4 What are process modelling and data modelling? Which diagrams used to summarise requirements at the analysis phase are useful in each of these types of modelling?

5 Explain the client/server model of computing.

6 What parts of the system need to be designed at the detailed design stage?

7 Describe the purpose of normalisation.

8 Explain insertion, update and deletion anomalies.

9 What are the difference between the sequential and direct (random) file access methods? In which business applications might they be used? What is the purpose of a file index?

10 Explain the difference between a batch and real-time system. Which would be the most appropriate design for each of the following situations:
   ♦ periodic updating of a data warehouse from an operational database;
   ♦ capturing information on customer sales transactions?

11 What are the different types of input validation that must be considered in the design of a user input form?

12 Describe the main differences between the analysis and design phases within the systems development lifecycle.

▶ Discussion questions

1 The client/server model of computing has many disadvantages, but these do not outweigh the advantages. Discuss.

2 The distinction between system design and detailed design is an artificial one since a bottom-up approach to design is inevitable. Discuss.

▶ Essay questions

1 Explain, using an example from a human resources management database, the normalisation process from unnormalised data to third normal form (3NF).

2 Table 12.8 from a relational database contains a number of rows and columns. When data is entered into the table, all columns must have data entered. Information about product descriptions, prices, product groups and rack locations is not held elsewhere. Explain how, because of its design, the table contains the potential for insertion, update and deletion anomalies. What is meant by these anomalies and what could be done to prevent them?

Table 12.8 Table from a relational database

Product code	Product description	Product group	Group description	Cost	Retail price	Rack location	Quantity
0942	Small Green	KD	Kiddy Doh	0.19	1.29	A201	16
0439	Large Red	KD	Kiddy Doh	0.31	1.89	W106	35
0942	Small Green	KD	Kiddy Doh	0.19	1.29	E102	0
0902	Small Green	KD	Kiddy Doh	0.19	1.29	J320	56
1193	Spinning Top	PS	Pre-School	1.23	12.49	X215	3
2199	Burger Kit	KD	Kiddy Doh	3.25	17.75	D111	0

▶ Examination questions

1 Explain the difference between validation and verification. Why are they important elements of systems design?

2 What benefits does three-tier client/server offer over two-tier client/server?

3 What are the main elements of system design?

4 Explain normalisation and how it can help remove different types of anomaly when modifying a database.

5 Which criteria are important in deciding whether to use a batch or real-time system?

6 What are the important aspects of user interface design?

7 Which different types of validation need to occur on data input to a system to ensure information quality?

8 What are the four main attributes of information security which need to be attained in an information system?

9 What is meant by the terms 'input design', 'output design' and 'database design'? Illustrate each of them with an example.

▶ References

Booch, G. (1986) 'Object oriented development', *IEEE Transactions on Software Engineering*, SE12.

Budgen, D. (1994) *Software Design*, Addison-Wesley, Wokingham.

Clifton, H.D. and Sutcliffe, A.G. (1994) *Business Information Systems*, 5th edition, Prentice Hall, London.

Curtis, G. (1998) *Business Information Systems, Analysis, Design and Practice*, 3rd edition, Addison-Wesley, Harlow.

Downes, E., Clare, P. and Coe, I. (1992) *Structured Systems Analysis and Design Method: Applications and Context*, 2nd edition, Prentice Hall, London.

Edwards, J. and DeVoe, D. (1997) *3-Tier Client/Server at Work*, John Wiley, New York.

Jackson, M.A. (1983) *System Development*, Prentice Hall, London.

Kavanagh, D. (1994) 'OMT Development Process, Vintage 1994', in Spurr, K., Layzell, P., Jennison, L. and Richards, N. (eds) *Business Objects: Software Solutions*, John Wiley, New York, 90–105.

Mcfadden, F.R. and Hofer, J.A. (1995) *Database Management*, 4th edition, Benjamin Cummings Science, Menlo Park, CA.

Preece, J., Rogers, Y., Sharp, H., Benyon, D., Holland, S. and Carey, T. (1994) *Human Computer Interaction*, Addison-Wesley, Wokingham.

Pressman, R.S. (1997) *Software Engineering: a Practitioner's Approach*, 4th edition, McGraw-Hill, New York.

Rumbaugh, J. (1991) *Object Oriented Modelling and Design (OMT)*, Prentice-Hall, Englewood Cliffs, NJ.

Taylor, D. (1995) *Business Engineering with Object Technology*, John Wiley, New York.

Whitten, J.L. and Bentley, L.D. (1998) *Systems Analysis and Design Methods*, Irwin/McGraw-Hill, Boston, MA.

Yeates, D., Shields, M. and Helmy, D. (1994) *Systems Analysis and Design*, Financial Times Pitman Publishing, London.

▶ Further reading

Galitz, W.O. (1997) *The Essential Guide to User Interface Design: an Introduction to GUI Design*, John Wiley, Chichester.

Heuring, V. (1997) *Computer Systems Design and Architecture*, Addison-Wesley, Menlo Park, CA.

Jacobsen, I., Ericsson, M. and Jacobsen, A. (1994) *The Object Advantage: Business Process Re-engineering with Object Technology*, Addison-Wesley, Wokingham.

Kendall, K. and Kendall, J. (1998) *Systems Analysis and Design*, Prentice-Hall, London.

Skidmore, S. (1996) *Introducing Systems Design*, NCC Blackwell, Oxford.

Stowell, F. and West, D. (1994) *Client Led Design a Systemic Approach to Information Systems Definition*, McGraw-Hill, Maidenhead.

Tudor, D. and Tudor, I. (1997) *Systems Analysis and Design a Comparison of Structured Methods*, Macmillan, Basingstoke.

Yourdon, E. and Constantine, L. (1979) *Structured Design Fundamentals of a Discipline of Computer Program and Systems Design*, Prentice-Hall, Englewood Cliffs, NJ.

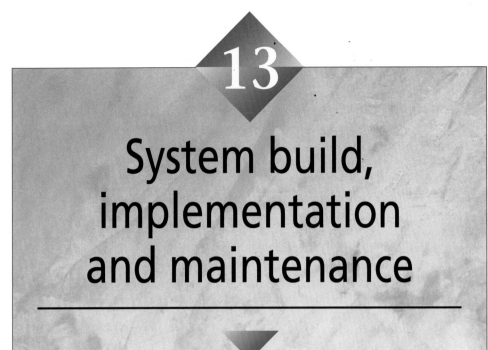

13

System build, implementation and maintenance

System build

The creation of software by programmers involving programming, building release versions of the software and testing by programmers and end-users. Writing of documentation and training may also occur at this stage.

System implementation

Involves the transition or changeover from the old system to the new and the preparation for this such as making sure the hardware and network infrastructure for a new system are in place; testing of the system and also human issues of how best to educate and train staff who will be using or affected by the new system.

INTRODUCTION

System build occurs after the system has been designed. It refers to the creation of software using programming or incorporation of building blocks such as existing software components or libraries. Testing by programmers will occur alongside programming to check for any errors. End-user testing may also occur at this stage as part of prototyping, but it may be delayed until the implementation phase when the complete system can be tested. Writing of documentation to specify the design of the system and end-user documentation also occur during the build stage.

To emphasise the importance of testing in a systems development project, you are referred to the case study on bugs and prolonged testing delaying a new air traffic control system. The number of errors found in this system illustrate that testing can be a significant part of the systems development lifecycle. You should consider whether the thousands of errors or 'bugs' found in a system are inevitable and measures must be taken in the build phase to identify and solve them, or whether there are failures in earlier phases in the lifecycle which are responsible for them.

System implementation follows the build stage. It involves setting up the right environment in which the test and finished system can be used. This may involve setting up a network or purchasing new PCs to run the software. It will also involve preparing new data for the system to run on. This will often involve transferring data from a previous system. Once a test version of the software has been produced, this will be tested by the users and corrections made to the software followed by further testing and fixing until the software is suitable for use throughout the company. This transition is known as the changeover from the existing system to the new system. There are several different alternatives for this which are explored in the chapter.

System build and implementation are just as important as earlier stages in the systems development lifecycle, in that a technically good solution from the earlier stages can still fail if the implementation has not been planned adequately.

A key implementation decision that needs to be taken is how to manage the changeover from the old system to the new system. This decision will always need to be taken, whether a company is moving from an old paper-based system or an existing information system.

We will consider the merits of the different activities of system build first in this chapter, then discuss how to manage change and the maintenance once the system is live.

▶ Learning objectives

After reading this chapter, readers will be able to:

◆ understand the purpose of the build phase, and its difference from changeover and implementation;

◆ understand the basic concepts of programming;

◆ specify the different types of testing required for a system;

◆ select the best alternatives for changing from an old system to a new system;

◆ recognise the importance of managing both the organisational change and software change associated with a new system.

▶ Links to other chapters

This chapter focuses on the build and implementation stage of a systems project before a system goes 'live' within a business. It is indirectly related to previous chapters (7–12) that describe preceding phases of systems development.

CASE STUDY: TOPIC AREA

Bugs and prolonged testing delay new air traffic control system

Passengers on board a Boeing 767 from New York to London last Sunday were convinced they had chosen the right airline when they discovered they had arrived in UK airspace 20 minutes early. But the same passengers were not to know that a lack of computer support for air traffic controllers in the UK is contributing to delays in the air, as planes are sometimes stacked near Heathrow until controllers can be allocated to deal with them.

A new £350m air traffic control centre at Swanwick near Fareham in Hampshire should have been operational by now, easing congestion in the skies. But the Swanwick New En Route Centre has been delayed by four years, partly because of late changes in the specification of a new air traffic control system and also because of the time taken to fix 21 000 bugs.

As the United Airlines flight descended towards Heathrow airport it was ordered to circle, while waiting for air traffic control to give clearance to land. Soon the passengers' high expectations of an early arrival turned to disappointment. The plane eventually landed an hour late, having circled for more than an hour, because of what some passengers were told were 'air traffic control problems'.

It will be of little comfort to those passengers to know that, according to statistics published by the state-owned National Air Traffic Services (Nats) which is responsible for the Swanwick centre, the average delay for each aircraft is only 90 seconds. Nats says it is doing an excellent job. However, the House of Commons environment, transport and regional affairs sub-committee is concerned that it may not be getting reliable information from Nats about the state of the systems. The air traffic organisation has said repeatedly, in public, since 1994 that the systems are sound and has denied that there are any delays, only to admit later that deadlines, and then revised deadlines, have not been met.

This week, however, *Computer Weekly* learnt that Nats is planning to pay Lockheed Martin the remaining 10% of the contract value in the next few weeks. Nats managers say the system supplied by the company meets the acceptance test criteria.

What is less clear is whether the system as specified by Nats in the early 1990s, and delivered by Lockheed Martin, is what is required today. It is still undergoing substantial modifications to meet the needs of air traffic controllers who, by the organisation's own admission, were not consulted adequately when the system was specified.

Complexity is also an issue. In the US, a similar system, which was too complex, was cut from 1.6 million lines of code to 700 000 lines. Meanwhile the Swanwick systems have increased in size from 1.8 million lines of code to more than 2 million. In conclusion the House of Commons report called on ministers and the department to commission a short independent audit to see whether the Swanwick project can be continued or should be abandoned in favour of a simpler system.

The committee's concerns are underlined by evidence that, without Swanwick, increasing reliance has been placed on the London Air Traffic Control Centre at West Drayton near Heathrow. This centre runs IBM 4381 mainframes and software applications that date back to the 1970s. They should by now have been replaced by Swanwick. The London centre is close to its computer capacity.

Source: Computer Weekly News, 16 April 1998

Questions

1 Summarise the scale of the testing part of the build phase for a large information system such as this. Write down the cost of the system, the size of the system, the number of bugs found and the delays that have occurred.

2 What implications does this case study have for the importance of testing smaller information systems?

3 State whether you consider that bugs are inevitable in a large, complex project such as this, or whether good project management can solve these problems.

4 In which stage(s) in the systems development lifecycle do you believe the errors referred to were introduced?

▶ KEY SYSTEM BUILD ACTIVITIES

▶ System development

System development or programing and testing are the main activities that need to occur at the system build phase.

The coverage of programming in this book will necessarily be brief, since the technical details of programming are not relevant to business people. A brief coverage of the techniques used by programmers is given since a knowledge of these techniques can be helpful in managing technical staff. Business users also often become involved in end-user development, which requires an appreciation of programming principles.

Software consists of program code written by programmers that is compiled or built into files known as executables from different modules, each with a particular function. Executables are run by users as interactive programs. You may have noticed *executable files* in directories on your hard disk with a file type of '.exe', such as winword.exe for Microsoft Word, or '.dll' library files.

There are a number of system development tools available to programmers and business users to help in writing software. These have been covered in more depth in Chapter 4 in the Focus on programming languages section. Software development tools include:

◆ Third-generation languages (3GLs) such as Basic, Pascal, C, COBOL or Fortran. These involve writing programming code. Traditionally this was achieved in a text editor with limited support from other tools, since these languages date back to the 1960s. These languages are normally used to produce text-based programs rather than interactive graphical user interface programs that run under Microsoft Windows. They are however still used extensively in *legacy systems*, in which millions of lines of COBOL code exists that must be maintained.

◆ Fourth-generation languages (4GLs) were developed in response to the difficulty of using 3GLs, particularly for business users. They are intended to avoid the need for programming. Since they often lack the flexibility for building a complex system, they are often ignored.

◆ Visual development tools such as Microsoft Visual Basic and Visual C++ and Borland Delphi use an 'interactive development environment' that makes it easy to define the user interface of a product and write code to process the events generated when a user selects an option from a menu or button. They are widely used for prototyping and some tools such as Visual Basic for Applications are used by end-users for extending spreadsheet models. These tools share some similarities with 4GLs, but are not true application generators since programming is needed to make the applications function. Since they are relatively easy to use, they are used frequently by business users.

◆ **CASE or computer-aided software engineering tools** (*see* Chapter 12 for coverage of CASE tools) are primarily used by professional IS developers and are intended to assist in managing the process of capturing requirements, and converting these into design and program code.

Computer-aided software engineering (CASE) tools

Primarily used by professional IS developers to assist in managing the process of capturing requirements and converting these into design and program code.

▶ ELEMENTS OF PROGRAMMING

Programming involves several key elements that will be recognisable to users of spreadsheets, and all managers who are also end-user developers need to be aware of these terms when talking to technical staff.

▶ Functions and procedures

To structure a program so that it is easy to develop and maintain, the lines of programming code (*statements*) are grouped together in functions or procedures. These are blocks or units of code that have a particular purpose. For example, the purpose of a function in a banking program might be to print a letter for a customer when they become overdrawn.

By placing related functions in a module, a program can be broken down into logical parts that are developed by different programmers. A further benefit of functions is that a common function can be reused to avoid duplication of program code.

▶ Variables

Variables are used to store (remember) values during the operation of a program. They are assigned using in this form:

Variable = Value

For example:

total_takings = 100

▶ Parameters

Parameters are variables that are passed or transferred to a function giving further instructions on the processing that needs to occur. For example, the parameters to be passed to a function to print a letter could indicate the customer name and type of letter.

If Then Else statement – definition

These are common within programs since they govern the different actions taken by the program according to a condition.

If Then Else statement – form

IF Condition Then
  Action if condition is
    TRUE
Else
  Action if condition is
    FALSE
End If

▶ Control rules

These are very common within programs, since they govern the different actions taken by the program. These are usually achieved using the IF or '**If Then Else**' statements in a spreadsheet such as Excel. They have the following structure:

=IF('Condition', 'Action if condition is TRUE', 'Action if condition is FALSE')

In Visual Basic this same expression might be written as:

IF Condition Then
        Action if condition is TRUE
    Else
        Action if condition is FALSE
    End If

Consider the example of calculating overtime pay for a worker. To find out whether the worker is eligible for overtime, we need to test whether they have worked more than the basic weekly hours (for example 38 hours/week). This is the condition:

'are hours worked' more than (>) 38

If hours worked are more than 38, the condition is TRUE and overtime payments will be made. If hours worked are less than 38, the condition is FALSE and no overtime payments will be made. A full function to make this test would appear as in the following example.

Example: a function to calculate pay for a worker

```
pay = Set_Pay(48)        ' Call function to set the pay with 48 hours
                         ' The pay calculated is placed in the variable pay

'FUNCTION to calculate pay for a worker
FUNCTION Set_Pay(hours_worked)

Dimension hours_worked, basic_rate, overtime_rate, Pay As Real

' Assign values to variables
basic_hours = 38         ' 38 hours per week
overtime_rate = 5        ' £5 per hour
basic_rate = 7           ' £7 per hour

IF hours_worked > basic_hours ' Test to see whether worker has worked overtime

    overtime_hours = hours_worked - basic_hours
    pay = (basic_ hours*hours*basic_rate)+(overtime_hours*overtime_rate)

ELSE

    pay = (hours*hours*_worked*basic_rate)

END IF

Return(Pay) ' Pass calculated value of pay back to calling statement
```

In a program we may wish to call a function to print an overdraft letter. Here the statement would look as follows:

```
IF balance < 0 Then
        Call Overdraft
End If
```

Further rules can be implemented using a more complex 'nested' If statement or by branches in 'switch' or 'case' statements.

▶ Loops

Loops are used to repeat a certain operation. If, for example, we wish to add the takings of a store across the seven days of the week, the program code might look as follows:

```
FOR day = 1 TO 7
        total_takings = total_takings + day_takings(day)
NEXT
```

Here we are looping through the seven days of the week and repeatedly adding the takings of each day into a variable total_takings. Alternatively, a loop could be used to access each record in a database and total up sales figures.

▶ Assessing software quality

Software or systems quality

Measured according to its suitability for the job intended. This is governed by whether it can do the job required (does it meet the business requirements?) and the number of bugs it contains (does it work reliably?)

Software metrics are used by businesses developing information systems to establish the quality of programs in an attempt to improve customer satisfaction through reducing errors by better programming and testing practices. **Software quality** is measured according to its suitability for the job intended. This is governed by whether it can do the job required (does it meet the business requirements?) and the number of bugs it contains (does it work reliably?). The quality of software is dependent on two key factors:

1 The number of errors or bugs in the software.

2 The suitability of the software to its intended purpose, i.e. does it have the features identified by users which are in the requirements specification?

It follows that good-quality software must meet the needs of the business users and contain few errors. We are trying to answer questions such as:

◆ Does the product work?

◆ Does it crash?

◆ Does the product function according to specifications?

◆ Does the user interface meet product specifications and is it easy to use?

◆ Are there any unexplained or undesirable side-effects to using the product which may stop other software working?

The number of errors is quite easily measured, although errors may not be apparent until encountered by end-users. Suitability to purpose is much more difficult to quantify, since it is dependent on a number of factors. These factors were referred to in detail in Chapters 8 and 11 which described the criteria that are relevant to decid-

---

What is a bug?

Software bug

Software bugs are defects in a program which are caused by human error during programming or earlier in the lifecycle. They may result in major faults or may remain unidentified.

Problems, errors or defects in software are collectively known as '**bugs**', since they are often small and annoying! Software bugs are defects in a program which are caused by human error during programming or earlier in the lifecycle. They may result in major faults or may remain unidentified. A major problem in a software system can be caused by one wrong character in a program of tens of thousands of lines. So it is often the source of the problem that is small, not its consequences.

Computing history recalls that the first bug was a moth which crawled inside a valve in one of the first computers, causing it to crash! This bug was identified by Grace Hopper, the inventor of COBOL, the first commercial programming language.

ing on a suitable information system. These quality criteria include correct functions, speed and ease of use.

Software quality also involves an additional factor which is not concerned with the functionality or number of bugs in the software. Instead, it considers how well the software operates in its environment. For example, in a multitasking environment such as Windows 95 or Windows NT, it assesses how well a piece of software co-exists with other programs. Are resources shared evenly? Will a crash of the software cause other software to fail also? This type of interaction testing is known as 'behaviour testing'.

Software metrics

Software metrics have much in common with measures in other industries involved with assessing the quality of a product. For example, in engineering or construction designers want to know how long it will take a component to fail or the number of errors in a batch of products. Most measures are defect based, measuring the number and type of errors. The source of the error or when it was introduced into the system is also important. Some errors are the result of faulty analysis or design and many are the result of a programming error. By identifying and analysing the source of the error, improvements can be made to the relevant part of the software lifecycle. An example of a comparison of three projects in terms of errors is shown in Table 13.1. It can be seen that in Project 3, the majority of errors are introduced during the coding (programming) stage, so corrective action is necessary here.

While the approach of many companies to testing has been that bugs are inevitable and must be tested for to remove them, more enlightened companies look at the reasons for the errors and attempt to stop them being introduced by the software developers. This implies that longer should be spent on the analysis and design phases of a project. Johnston (1995) suggests that the balance between the phases of a project should be divided as shown in Table 13.2, with a large proportion of the time being spent on analysis and design.

Software metrics
Measures which indicate the quality of software.

Table 13.1 Table comparing the source of errors in three different software projects

	Project 1	Project 2	Project 3
Analysis	20%	30%	15%
Design	25%	40%	20%
Coding	35%	20%	45%
Testing	20%	10%	20%

Errors per KLOC
Errors per KLOC (thousands of line of code) is the basic defect measure used in systems development.

In software code the number of errors or 'defect density' is measured in terms of errors per 1000 lines of code (or KLOC for short). The long-term aim of a business is to reduce the defect rate towards the elusive goal of 'zero defects'.

Table 13.2 Ideal proportions of time to be spent on different phases of a systems development project, focusing on details of build phase

Project activities	Suggested proportion
Definition, design and planning	20%
Coding	15%
Component test and early system test	15%
Full system test, user testing and operational trials	20%
Documentation, training and implementation support	20%
Overall project management	10%

Errors per KLOC is the basic defect measure used in systems development. Care must be taken when calculating defect density or productivity of programmers using KLOC of code, since this will vary from one programming language to another and according to the style of the programmer and the number of comment statements used. KLOC must be used consistently between programs, and this is usually achieved by only counting executable statements, not comments or by counting function points.

The technical quality of software can also be assessed by measures other than the number of errors. Its complexity, which is often a function of the number of branches it contains, is commonly used.

Another metric, more commonly used for engineered products, is the mean time between failures. This is less appropriate to software since outright failure is rare, but small errors or bugs in the software are quite common. It is, however, used as part of outsourcing contracts or as part of the service-level agreement for network performance.

A more useful measure for software is to look at the customer satisfaction rating of the software, since its quality is dependent on many other factors such as usability and speed as well as the number of errors.

▶ Data migration

Data migration

Data migration is the transfer of data from the old system to the new system. When data is added to a database, this is known as populating the database.

A significant activity of the build phase is to transfer the data from the old system to the new system. **Data migration** is the transfer of data from the old system to the new system. When data is added to a database, this is known as populating the database. This process is known as data migration or populating the database. One method of transferring data is to rekey it manually into the new system. This is impractical for most systems since the volume of data is too large. Instead, special data conversion programs are written to convert the data from the data file format of the old system into the data file format of the new system. Conversion may involve changing data formats, for example a date may be converted from two digits for the year into four digits. It may also involve combining or aggregating fields or records. The conversion programs also have to be well tested because of the danger of corrupting existing data. Data migration is an extra task which needs to be remembered as part of the project manager's project plan.

During data migration data can be 'exported' from an old system and then 'imported' into a new system.

When using databases or off-the-shelf software, there are usually tools provided to make it easier to import data from other systems.

Import and export

Data can be 'exported' from an old system and then 'imported' into a new system.

▶ Testing information systems

Testing is a vital aspect of implementation, since this will identify errors that can be fixed before the system is live. The type of tests that occur in implementation tend to be more structured than the *ad hoc* testing that occurs with prototyping earlier in systems development.

Note that often testing is not seen as an essential part of the lifecycle, but as a chore that must be done. If its importance is not recognised, insufficient testing will occur. Johnston (1995) refers to the *'testing trap'*, when companies spend too long writing the software without changing the overall project deadline. This results in the amount of time for testing being 'squeezed' until it is no longer sufficient. This type of problem is evident from the mini case on insurance. As an indication of the amount of testing that needs to occur, Cornhill Insurance recently reported that 80 per cent of the budget for its year 2000 project was spent on testing. *Computer Weekly* reported that the project controller, Sue Pellatt, said:

> Testing is often pushed to the end of the project, especially when there is a fixed deadline. But it should be a routine part of any project, especially after this project.

During prototyping, the purpose of testing is to identify missing features or define different ways of performing functions. Testing is more structured during the implementation phase in order to identify as many bugs as possible. It has two main purposes: the first is to check that the requirements agreed earlier in the project have been implemented, the second to identify errors or bugs. To achieve both of these objectives, testing must be conducted in a structured way by using a **test specification** which details tests in different areas. This avoids users performing a general usability test of the system where they only use common functions at random. While this is valid, and is necessary since it mirrors real use of the software, it does not give a good coverage of all the areas of the system. Systematic tests should be performed using a *test script* which covers, in detail, the functions to be tested.

Test specification

A detailed description of the tests that will be performed to check the software works correctly.

Insurance – testing, testing

If Cornhill Insurance has learnt anything from the engineer management project it would be the importance of testing. IT project manager Peter Williamson says given a second chance he would undoubtedly do a lot more testing than he actually did. 'We had some fairly tight, pretty ambitious timescales, and basically the area that got compounded at the end of the day was testing. There were lots of points of failure and I guess what I would have felt more comfortable with is if we could have done a complete and thorough test. We did a lot of unit testing, but the thing we did a bit of a flyer on was the actual overall link testing.'

Source: Computer Weekly, 24 April 1997

MINI CASE

Given the variety of tests that need to be performed, large implementations will also use a **test plan**, a specialised project plan describing what testing will be performed when, and by who. Testing is always a compromise between the number of tests that can be performed against the time available.

The different types of testing that occur throughout the software lifecycle should be related to the earlier stages in the lifecycle against which we are testing. This approach to development (Fig 13.1) is sometimes referred to as the V-model of systems development, for obvious reasons. The diagram shows that different types of testing are used to test different aspects of the analysis and design of the system: to test the requirements specification a user acceptance test is performed, and to test the detailed design unit testing occurs.

Test plan

Plan describing the type and sequence of testing and who will conduct it.

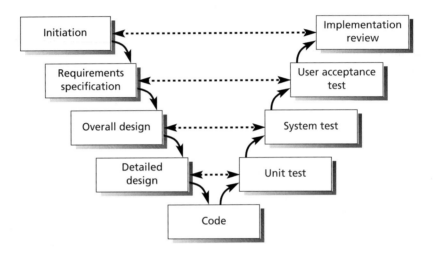

Fig 13.1 The V-model of systems development relating analysis and design activities to testing activities

We will now consider in more detail the different types of testing that need to be conducted during implementation. This review is structured according to who performs the tests.

Developer tests

There are a variety of techniques that can be used for testing systems. Jones (1996) identifies 18 types of testing, of which the most commonly used are subroutine, unit, new function, regression, integration and systems testing. Many of the techniques available are not used due to lack of time, money or commitment. Some of the more common techniques are summarised here.

Module or Unit testing

Individual modules are tested to ensure they function correctly for given inputs.

◆ *Module tests*. These are performed on individual modules of the system. The module is treated as a 'black box' (ignoring its internal method of working) as developers check that expected outputs are generated for given inputs. When you drive a car this can be thought of black box testing – you are aware of the inputs to the car and their effect as outputs, but you will probably not have a detailed knowledge of the mechanical aspects of the car and whether they are functioning correctly. Module testing involves considering a range of inputs or test cases, as follows:

(a) Random test data can be automatically generated by a spreadsheet for module testing.

(b) Structured or logical test data will cover a range of values expected in normal use of the module and also values beyond designed limits to check that appropriate error messages are given. This is also known as boundary value testing and is important, since many bugs occur because designed boundaries are exceeded. This type of data is used for regression testing, explained below.

(c) Scenario or typical test data uses realistic example data, possibly from a previous system, to simulate day-to-day use of the system.

These different types of test data can also be applied to system testing.

◆ **Integration or module interaction testing (black box testing).** Expected interactions such as messaging and data exchange between a limited number of modules are assessed. This can be performed in a structured way, using a top-down method where a module calls other module functions as stubs (partially completed functions which should return expected values) or using a bottom-up approach where a driver module is used to call complete functions.

◆ **New function testing.** This commonly used type of testing refers to testing the operation of a new function when it is implemented, perhaps during prototyping. If testing is limited to this, problems may be missed since the introduction of the new function may cause bugs elsewhere in the system.

◆ **System testing.** When all modules have been completed and their interactions assessed for validity, links between all modules are assessed in the system test. In system testing, interactions between all relevant modules are tested systematically. System testing will highlight different errors to module testing, for example when unexpected data dependencies exist between modules as a result of poor design.

System testing
When all modules have been completed and their interactions assessed for validity, links between all modules are assessed in the system test. In system testing interactions between all relevant modules are tested systematically.

◆ **Database connectivity testing.** This is a simple test that the connectivity between the application and the database is correct. Can a user log in to the database? Can a record be inserted, deleted or updated, i.e. are transactions executing? Can transactions be rolled back (undone) if required?

◆ **Database volume testing.** This is linked to capacity planning of databases. Simulation tools can be used to assess how the system will react to different levels of usage anticipated from the requirements and design specifications. Methods of indexing may need to be improved or queries optimised if the software fails this test.

Volume testing
Testing assesses how system performance will change at different levels of usage.

◆ **Performance testing.** This will involve timing how long different functions or transactions take to occur. These delays are important, since they govern the amount of wasted time users or customers have to wait for information to be retrieved or screens refreshed. Maximum waiting times may be specified in a contract, for example.

◆ **Confidence test script.** This is a short script which may take a few hours to run through and which tests all the main functions of the software. It should be run before all releases to users to ensure that their time is not wasted on a prototype that has major failings which mean the test will have to be aborted and a new release made.

◆ **Automated tests**. Automated tools simulate user inputs through the mouse or keyboard and can be used to check for the correct action when a certain combination of buttons is pressed or data entered. Scripts can be set up to allow these tests to be repeated. This is particularly useful for performing regression tests.

Regression testing

Testing performed before a release to ensure that the software performance is consistent with previous test results, i.e. that the outputs produced are consistent with previous releases of the software.

◆ **Regression testing**. This testing should be performed before a release to ensure that the software performance is consistent with previous test results, i.e. that the outputs produced are consistent with previous releases of the software. This is necessary, as in fixing a problem a programmer may introduce a new error that can be identified through the regression test. Regression testing is usually performed with automated tools.

End-user tests

The purpose of these is twofold: first, to check that the software does what is required; and second, to identify bugs, particularly those that may only be caused by novice users.

For ease of assessing the results, the users should be asked to write down for each bug or omission found:

1 Module affected.

2 Description of problem (any error messages to be written in full).

3 Relevant data – for example, which particular customer or order record in the database caused the problem?

4 Severity of problem on a three-point scale.

Different types of end-user tests that can be adopted include:

Functional testing

Testing of particular functions or modules either following a test script or working through the module systematically.

◆ **Scenario testing**. In an order processing system this would involve processing example orders of different types, such as new customers, existing customers without credit and customers with a credit agreement.

◆ **Functional testing**. Users are told to concentrate on testing particular functions or modules such as the order entry module in detail, either following a test script or working through the module systematically.

◆ **General testing**. Here, users are given free rein to depart from the test specification and test according to their random preferences. Sometimes this is the only type of testing used, which results in poor coverage of the functions in the software!

Multi-user testing

The effect of different users accessing the same customer or stock record is tested. Software should not permit two users to modify the same data at the same time.

◆ **Multi-user testing**. The effect of different users accessing the same customer or stock record. Software should not permit two users to modify the same data at the same time. Tests should also be made to ensure that users with different permissions and rules are treated as they should be, i.e. that junior staff are locked out of company financial information.

◆ **Inexperienced user testing**. Staff who are inexperienced in the use of software often make good 'guinea pigs' for testing software, since they may choose an illogical combination of options that the developers have not tested. This is a surprisingly effective and recommended method of software testing. The staff involved often also like the power of being able to 'break' the software.

User acceptance testing

This is the final stage of testing which occurs before the software is signed off as fit for purpose and the system can go live.

◆ **User acceptance testing**. This is the final stage of testing which occurs before the software is signed off as fit for purpose and the system can go live. Since the customer will want to be sure the software works correctly, this may take a week or more.

◆ **Alpha and beta testing**. These terms apply to user tests which occur before a packaged software product is released. They are described in the section on configuration management.

Benefits-based testing

An alternative approach to testing is not to focus only on the errors when reviewing a system, but rather to test against the business benefits that the system confers. A system could be error free, but if it is not delivering benefits then its features may not have been implemented correctly. This approach can be used with prototyping, so that if a system is not delivering the correct features it can be modified. When undertaking structured testing, the software will be tested against the requirements specification to check that the desired features are present.

Testing environments

Testing occurs in different environments during the project. At an early stage prototypes may be tested on a single standalone machine or laptop. In the build phase, testing will be conducted in a *development environment*, which involves programmers testing data across a network on a shared server. This is mainly used for module testing. In the implementation phase, a special **test environment** will be set up which simulates the final operating environment for the system. This could be a room with three or more networked machines accessing data from a central server. This test environment will be used for early user training and testing and for system testing. Finally, the **production or live environment** is that in which the system will be used operationally. This will be used for user acceptance testing and when the system becomes live.

When a system goes live, it is worth noting that there may still be major problems despite extensive testing. An example of this is provided by the mini case study on a bank network. Here a critical customer-facing banking system failed, apparently due to a problem in the underlying operating system (although this point is disputed by Microsoft).

▶ Documentation

Producing **documentation** occurs throughout the software lifecycle, such as when requirements are specified at the analysis stage, but it becomes particularly important at the implementation and maintenance stages of a project. At this stage user guides will be used as part of user acceptance testing and system developers will refer to design documents when updating the system. The main types of documentation required through the project are referred to in Fig 13.1. The important documentation used at the testing stage includes:

◆ the requirements specification produced at the analysis stage; this is used in the user acceptance test, to check that the correct features have been implemented;

◆ the user manual, which will be used during testing and operational use of the system by business users;

◆ the design specification, which will be used during system testing and during maintenance by developers;

◆ the detailed design, which will be used in module testing and during maintenance;

◆ the data dictionary or database design, which will be used in testing and maintenance by database administrators and developers;

Test environment

A specially configured environment (hardware, software and office environment) used to test the software before its release.

Live (production) environment

The term used to describe the setup of the system (hardware, software and office environment) where the software will be used in the business.

Documentation

Software documentation refers to end-user guidance such as the user guide and technical maintenance documentation such as design and test specifications.

Code error floors bank network

An obscure code error has caused NatWest Bank's brand new Windows NT branch network almost a week's worth of delays and disruptions.

The software glitch prevented the bank from processing customers' queries at all of its 1750 branches, and brought down thousands of branch workstations.

Customers who called branches with basic queries, such as checking account balances, were told the task would take 24 hours and customers were advised to use ATM machines.

The disaster struck after the bank upgraded 5000 PCs and 300 servers with an in-house application, which suffered a handle leak. This type of fault causes an application to repeatedly request services from the server until the system crashes, or the application fails to release system resources such as virtual memory.

According to information on Microsoft's Web site, Windows NT has a history of difficulties operating alongside some third-party applications. Rather than revert to a previous version of the new application, NatWest opted to wait for a quiet period at the weekend to fix the fault. NatWest's head of retail information systems Catherine Doran said the bank had no plans to revamp software testing procedures as a result of the incident.

'There's not a system in the industry that hasn't got problems. You can test and test to destruction,' she said. Microsoft denied the problem was due to a fault in Windows NT itself, but added it had released service packs to solve handle leaks in all versions of the operating system.

Source: Computing, 1 July 1998

◆ detailed test plans and test specifications, which will be used as part of developer and user testing;

◆ quality assurance documents such as software change request forms, which will be used to manage the change during the build and implementation phases.

The writing of documentation is often neglected, since it tends to be less interesting than developing the software. To ensure that it is produced, strong project management is necessary and the presence of a software quality plan will make sure that time is spent on documentation, since a company's quality standard is assessed on whether the correct documentation is produced.

User guides

The user guide has become a less important aspect of systems documentation with the advent of online help such as the help facility available with Windows applications. Online help can give general guidance on the software, or it can give more specific advice on a particular screen or function, when it is known as context sensitive. It is often a good idea to ask business users to develop the user guide, since if programmers write the guide it will tend to be too technical and not relevant to the needs of users. Since business users are sometimes charged with producing a user guide, approaches to structuring these is covered in a little more detail.

Example user guide structure

User guides are normally structured to give a gradual introduction to the system, and there may be several guides for a single system. A common structure is:

1 A *brief introductory/overview guide*, often known as 'Getting started'. The aim of this is to help users operate the software productively with the minimum of reading. The introductory section will also explain the purpose of the system for the business.

2 *Tutorial guide*. This will provide lessons, often with example data to guide the user through using the package. These are now often combined with online 'guided tours'.

3 *Detailed documentation* is often structured according to the different screens in an application. However, it is usually better to structure such guides according to the different functions or applications a business user will need. Chapter titles in such an approach might include 'how to enter a new sales order' or 'how to print a report'. This guide should also incorporate information on troubleshooting when problems are encountered.

4 *Quick reference guide, glossary and appendix*. These will contain explanations of error messages and a summary of all functions and how to access them.

▶ MANAGING CHANGE

▶ Software change management

At each stage of a systems development project, **change requests** or variations to requirements will arise from business managers, users, designers and programmers. These requests include reports of bugs and features that are missing from the system as well as ideas for future versions of the software.

Change (modification) requests
A modification to the software thought to be necessary by the business users or developers.

These requests will occur as soon as users start evaluating prototypes of a system and will continue through to the maintenance phase of the project when the system has gone live. As the users start testing the system in earnest in the implementation phase, these requests will become more frequent and tens or possibly hundreds will be generated each week. This process of change needs to be carefully managed, since otherwise it can develop into *requirements creep*, a problem on many information systems projects. As the number of requirements grow, more developer time will be required to fix the problems and the project can soon spiral out of control. What is needed is a mechanism to ensure first that all the changes are recorded and dealt with, and second that they are reviewed in such a way that the number of changes does not become unmanageable.

The main steps in managing changed requirements are:

1 Record the change requests, indicating level of importance and module affected.

2 Prioritise them with the internal or external customer as *must have, nice to have* or *later release (Priority 1, 2 or 3)*. This will be done with reference to the project constraints of system quality, cost and timescale.

3 Identify responsibility for fixing the problem, since it may lie with a software house, internal IS staff, systems integrator or hardware vendor.

4 Implement changes that are recorded as high priority.

5 Maintain a check of which high-priority errors have been fixed.

When a system is being implemented, it is useful to have a three-way classification of errors to be fixed, since this highlights the errors or missing features which must be implemented and avoids long discussions of the merits of each solution.

When the system is live, a more complex classification is often used to help in deciding how to escalate problems according to their severity. This could be structured as follows:

1 Critical problem, system not operational. This may occur due to power or server failure. Level 1 problems need to be resolved immediately, since business users cannot access the system at all.

2 Critical problem, making part of the system unusable or causing data corruption. These would normally need to be resolved within 12 to 24 hours depending on the nature of the problem.

3 Problem causing intermittent system failure or data corruption. Resolve within 48 hours.

4 Non-severe problem not requiring modification to software until next release.

5 Trivial problem or suggestion which can be considered for future releases.

If the system has been tailored by a systems integrator, these will be their responsibility to fix and this will be specified in the contract or service-level agreement (SLA), together with the time that will be taken for the change to be made. If the system has been developed or tailored internally by the IS department or even within a department, an SLA is still a good idea. If the problem occurs from a problem with packaged software, you will have to hope that an update release that solves the problem is available; if not, you will have to lobby the supplier for one.

Software quality assurance

As we have seen, procedures should be followed throughout the software lifecycle to try to produce good-quality systems. These quality assurance (QA) procedures have been formalised in the British Standard BS5750 Part 1 and its European equivalent ISO9001 (TickIT). These procedures do not guarantee a quality information system, but their purpose is to ensure that all relevant parts of the software lifecycle, such as requirements capture, design and testing, are carried out consistently. Business users can ask whether suppliers have quality accreditation as a means of distinguishing between them. QA procedures would not specify a particular method for design or testing, but they would specify how the change was managed by ensuring that all changes to requirements are noted and that review mechanisms are in place to check that changes are agreed and acted on accordingly.

If a business buys software services from a company that has achieved the quality standards, then there is less risk of the services being inadequate. For a company to achieve a quality standard it has to be assessed by independent auditors and if successful will be audited regularly.

Configuration management: builds and release versions

Configuration management. Control of the different versions of software and program source code used during the build, implementation and maintenance phases of a project.

Throughout the implementation phase, updated versions of the software are released to users for testing. Before software can be used by users it needs to be released as an executable, built up from compiled versions of all the program code modules which make up the system. The process of joining all the modules is technically known as the linking or build process. The sequence can be summarised as:

1 Programmers *write* different code modules.

2 Completed code modules are *compiled* to form object modules.

3 Object modules are *linked* to form executables.

4 Executables are installed on machines.

5 Executables are loaded and run by end-users testing the software.

Each updated release of the software is therefore usually known as a new 'build'. With large software systems there will be hundreds of program files written by different developers that need to be compiled and then linked. If these files are not carefully tracked, then the wrong versions of files may be used, with earlier versions causing bugs. This process of version control is part of an overall process known as **configuration management**, which ensures that programming and new releases occur in a systematic way. One of the problems with solving the millennium bug is that in some companies configuration management is so poor that the original program code has been lost!

During the build phase, updated software versions will become more suitable for release as new functions are incorporated and the number of bugs is reduced. Some companies, such as Microsoft, call these different versions 'release candidates', others use the terminology alpha, beta and gold to distinguish between versions. These terms are often applied to packaged software, but can also be applied to bespoke business applications.

◆ *Alpha releases and alpha testing.* **Alpha releases** are preliminary versions of the software released early in the build phase. They usually have the majority of the functionality of the complete system in place, but may suffer from extensive bugs. The purpose of **alpha testing** is to identify these bugs and any major problems with the functionality and usability of the software. Alpha testing is usually conducted by staff inside the organisation developing the software or by favoured customers.

◆ *Beta releases and beta testing.* **Beta releases** occur after alpha testing and have almost complete functionality and relatively few bugs. Beta testing will be conducted by a range of customers who are interested in evaluating the new software. The aim of **beta testing** is to identify bugs in the software before it is shipped to all customers.

◆ *Gold release.* This is a term for the final release of the software which will be shipped to all customers.

▶ Selecting a changeover method

Choosing the method to be used for migrating or changing from the old system to the new system is one of the most important decisions that the project management

---

Configuration management

Procedures which define the process of building a version of the software from its constituent program files and data files.

Alpha release

Alpha releases are preliminary versions of the software released early in the build process. They usually have the majority of the functionality of the system in place, but may suffer from extensive bugs.

Alpha testing

The purpose of 'alpha testing' is to identify these bugs and any major problems with the functionality and usability of the software. Alpha testing is usually conducted by staff inside the organisation developing the software or by favoured customers.

Beta release

Beta releases occur after alpha testing and have almost complete functionality and relatively few bugs.

Beta testing

Will be conducted by a range of customers who are interested in evaluating the new software. The aim of beta testing is to identify bugs in the software before it is shipped to a range of customers.

Changeover

The term used to describe moving from the old information system to the new information system.

team must make during the implementation phase. **Changeover** can be defined as moving from the old information system to the new information system. Note that this changeover is required whether the previous information system is computer or paper based. Before considering the alternatives, we will briefly discuss the main factors that a manager will consider when evaluating the alternatives. The factors are:

◆ *Cost.* This is of course an important consideration, but the quality of the new system is often more important.

◆ *Time.* There will be a balance between the time available and the desired quality of the system which will need to be evaluated.

◆ *Quality of new system after changeover.* This will be dependent on the number of bugs and suitability for purpose.

◆ *Impact on customers.* What will be the effect on customer service if the changeover overruns or if the new system has bugs?

◆ *Impact on employees.* How much extra work will be required by employees during the changeover? Will they be remunerated for this?

◆ *Technical issues.* Some of the options listed below may not be possible if the system does not have a modular design.

There are four main alternatives for moving from a previous system to a new system. The options are shown in Fig 13.2 and described in more detail below.

Immediate cutover or big bang method

Immediate cutover (big bang) changeover

Immediate cutover is when a new system becomes operational and operations transfer immediately from the previous system.

The **immediate cutover method** involves moving directly from the original system to the new system at a particular point in time. On a designated date, the old system is switched off and all staff move to using the new system. Clearly, this is a high-risk strategy since there is no fallback position if serious bugs are encountered. However,

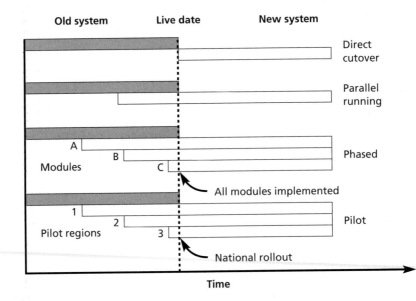

Fig 13.2 Alternative changeover methods for system implementation

this approach is adopted by many large companies (such as Barclays in the case study), since it may be impractical and costly to run different systems in parallel. Before cutover occurs, the company will design the system carefully and conduct extensive testing to make sure that it is reliable and so reduce the risk of failure. The case study shows a relatively successful example of the cutover method and indicates why this is necessary for the implementation of large systems. The success factors of this project are described.

CASE STUDY: TOPIC AREA

Barclays Bank implements customer system using the 'big bang' approach

An example of a company adopting this approach for a major implementation is Barclays Bank, which switched over to a £110 million customer-facing system used in 2000 branches in 1997. This case study is described as an example of a successful implementation in the book *Crash* by Tony Collins and David Bicknell (1977). The bank decided on this approach since it was thought that it would not be possible for the old and new systems to run simultaneously with the hardware available. Furthermore, the cost of running two parallel systems was estimated at millions of pounds, which would reduce the cost savings made by implementing the new system. One of the biggest problems in this implementation, as with all changeovers, was migrating the data from the old system to the new. In this case, it involved transferring 25 million customer names and their account details – all held on various databases in thousands of different locations – into a single IBM DB2 database. One of the benefits of undertaking this migration was that erroneous data such as accounts that had been closed would be removed in this data-cleaning operation. The information from this database was then made available to every branch through nearly 2000 RS/6000 UNIX-based servers.

The day for the system going live was Monday 10 October 1994. This date had been set 18 months earlier and designers and developers from Andersen Consulting had been working towards this target. Transfer of the customer records began on Wednesday 5 October, with a plan to bring 1000 branches online with the new system by noon on Monday 10 October. Compared to many other implementations, this scheme was a great success, with 800 branches going live by noon. The implementation was not without problems and those encountered show the types of errors that can cause big bang implementations to fail.

On the Thursday before the live data, a hard disk head failed and a software bug delayed the schedule by two hours. To recover from this, the bank prevented more than 1000 branches from logging into the branch systems for two hours on the Thursday morning before live Monday, which did cause some disruption to customers. The implications of a more serious error which could not be fixed in two hours are clear.

Collins and Bicknell (1977) consider that the reasons for the success of this system are as follows:

◆ Artificial deadlines were not imposed and all staff were encouraged to be open about problems so that they could be solved.
◆ The scale of the problem was recognised so a realistic budget was set.
◆ Contingency plans were put in place to deal with problems such as the hard disk crash.
◆ Although changeover was targeted for a single day, the process of data migration started almost a week earlier and the whole project over 18 months had focused on a direct changeover through meticulous analysis, design and testing.
◆ Changes to users' requirements were kept under control, with only vital reviewed changes being incorporated.

Questions

1 What benefits and risks do you think Barclays faced by undertaking a big bang implementation?

2 What were the main problems faced in the cutover between the two systems?

3 Why do you think the project was successful? Consider other factors as well as those described in the case study.

Parallel running

With **parallel running** the old and new systems are operated together for a period until the company is convinced that the new system performs adequately. This presents a lower risk than the immediate cutover method, since if the new system fails, the company can revert to the old system and customers will not be greatly affected. Parallel running sometimes also involves using a manual or paper-based system as backup in case the new system fails.

The cost of running two systems in parallel is high, not only in terms of maintaining two sets of software and possibly hardware, but also in the costs of the human operators repeating operations such as keying in customer orders twice. Indeed, the increase in workload may be such that overtime or additional staff may be required. The parallel method is only appropriate when the old and new systems perform similar functions and use similar software and hardware combinations. This makes it unsuitable for business reengineering projects where completely new ways of working are being introduced that involve staff working on different tasks or in different locations.

Phased implementation

A **phased implementation** involves delivering different parts of the system at different times. These modules do not all become live simultaneously, but rather in sequence. As such, this alternative is part way between the big bang and parallel running approaches. Each module can be introduced as either immediate cutover or in parallel. In a modular accounting system, for example, the core accounting functions, such as accounts payable, accounts receivable and general ledger, could be introduced first, with a sales order processing and then inventory control module introduced later. This gives staff the opportunity to learn about the new system more gradually and problems encountered on each module can be fixed as they are introduced.

Although this may appear to be an attractive approach, since if a new module fails the other modules will still be available, it is difficult to implement in practice. To achieve a phased implementation requires that the architecture of the new system and old system are designed in a modular way, and that the modules can operate independently without a high degree of coupling. For all systems, however, data exchange will be required between the different modules and this implies that common data exchange formats exist between the old and the new systems. This is often not the case, particularly if the software is sourced from different suppliers. Designers of systems are using techniques such as object-oriented design to produce modules with fewer and clearer dependencies between each other. This should help in making phased implementations more practical. In the example given for the modular accounting system, modules in the old and new system would have to have facilities to transfer data.

Pilot system

In a pilot implementation, the system will be trialled in a more limited area before it is deployed more extensively. This could include deploying the system in one operating region of the company, possibly a single country, or in a limited number of offices. This approach is common in multinational or national companies with several offices. Such a pilot system usually acts as a trial before more extensive deployment in a big bang implementation.

Using combinations of changeover methods

The different changeover methods are often used in conjunction for different stages of an implementation. For example, in a national or international implementation it is customary to trial the project in a single region or country using a pilot of the system. If a pilot system is considered successful there is then a choice of one of the following:

◆ immediately implementing the system elsewhere using the big bang approach;

◆ running the new and old systems in parallel until it is certain that the new system is stable enough;

◆ if the new system is modular in construction, it is possible for the implementation to be phased, with new modules gradually being introduced as they are completed and the users become familiar with the new system;

◆ parallel running will probably also occur in this instance, in case there is a need to revert to the old system in the event of failure of the new system.

Once the system is proved in the first area, then further rollout will probably occur through the big bang approach.

The advantages and disadvantages of each of these changeover methods are summarised in Table 13.3.

Table 13.3 Advantages and disadvantages of the different methods of implementation

Method	Main advantages	Main disadvantages
Immediate cutover	Rapid, lowest cost	High risk if serious errors in system
Parallel running	Lower risk than immediate cutover	Slower and higher cost than immediate cutover
Phased implementation	Good compromise between immediate cutover and parallel running	Difficult to achieve technically due to interdependencies between modules
Pilot system	Essential for multinational or national rollouts	Has to be used in combination with the other methods

Deployment planning

A **deployment plan** is necessary to get all 'kit' or hardware in place in time for user acceptance testing. A deployment plan is a schedule that defines all the tasks that need to occur in order for changeover to occur successfully. This includes putting all the infrastructure in place such as cabling and hardware. This is not a trivial task, because often a range of equipment will be required from a variety of manufacturers. A deployment plan should list every software deliverable and hardware item

Deployment plan

A deployment plan is a schedule which defines all the tasks that need to occur in order for changeover to occur successfully. This includes putting all the infrastructure in place such as cabling and hardware.

required, when it needs to arrive and when it needs to be connected. The deployment plan will be part of the overall project plan or Gantt chart. A deployment plan is particularly important for large implementations involving many offices, such as the Barclays system referred to earlier in the chapter. Several people may be responsible for this task on large projects.

When planning deployment, advanced planning is required due to possible delays in purchasing and delivery. The burden of purchasing will often be taken by a systems integrator, but it may be shared by the purchasing department of the company buying the new system. This needs careful liaison between both groups.

With installation of new hardware, a particular problem is where changes to infrastructure are required – for example upgrading cabling to a higher bandwidth or installing a new router. This can take a considerable time and cause a great deal of disruption to users of existing systems.

▶ Organisational change management

The implementation of a new system will always cause disruption to staff, because changes to their patterns of working will occur. In some cases staff may be transferred to new roles. The change involved in the introduction of the new system needs management so staff motivation and productivity are not adversely affected.

The best approach to managing this change is to use education to communicate the purpose of the system to the staff, in other words, to sell the system to them. This education should target all employees in the organisation who will be affected by the change. It involves:

◆ explaining why the system is being implemented;

◆ explaining how staff will be affected;

◆ involve users in specification, testing and review: treat them as customers;

◆ training users in use of the software;

◆ above all, listening to users and acting on what they say.

Lewin and Schein suggested a model for achieving organisational change that involves three stages:

1 Unfreeze the present position by creating a climate of change through education, training and motivation of future participants.

2 Quickly move from the present position by developing and implementing the new system.

3 Refreeze by making the system an accepted part of the way the organisation works.

Note that Lewin and Schein did not collaborate on developing this model of personal and organisational change. Lewin developed the model in unpublished work and this was then extended by Edgar Schein who undertook research into psychology based on Lewin's ideas (Schein, 1956). More recently Kurt Lewin has summarised some of his ideas (Lewin, 1972).

Later Schein (1992) concluded that three variables are critical to the success of any organisational change:

1 The degree to which the leaders can break from previous ways of working.

2 The significance and comprehensiveness of the change.

3 The extent to which the head of the organisation is actively involved in the change process.

Change was defined by Kurt Lewin as a transition from an existing quasi equilibrium to a new quasi equilibrium. This model was updated and put into an organisational context by Kolb and Frohman (1970). Although this is now an old model, it remains relevant to the implementation of information systems today.

We will now look at the details of how this can be achieved.

Achieving user involvement

Efforts should be made to involve as many staff as possible in the development. The following types of involvement can occur in a systems development project: (Summarised by Regan and O'Connor, 1994.)

1 *Non-involvement.* Here, users are unwilling to participate or are not invited to.

2 *Involvement by advice.* User advice is solicited through interviews or questionnaires during analysis.

3 *Involvement by signoff.* Users approve the results produced by the project team, such as requirements specifications.

4 *Involvement by design team membership.* Active participation occurs in analysis and design activities (including interviews of other users, creation of functional specifications and prototyping).

5 *Involvement by project team membership.* User participation occurs throughout the project since the user manages and owns the project.

While it will not be practical to involve everyone, representatives of all job functions should be polled for their requirements for the system at the analysis stage. As many user and manager representatives as possible should be involved in the active analysis and design involved in prototyping.

Promotion of the system can also be achieved by appointing particular managers to champion the new system:

◆ Senior managers or board members are used as **system sponsors**. Sponsors are keen that the system should work and will fire up staff with their enthusiasm and stress why introducing the system is important to the business and its workers.

◆ **System owners** are managers in the organisation who will use the system to create the business benefits envisaged.

◆ **Stakeholders** should be identified at every location in which the system will be used. These people should be respected by their co-workers and will again act as a source of enthusiasm for the system. The user representatives used in specification and testing can also fill this role.

◆ **Legitimisers** protect the norms and values of the system; they are experienced in their job and regarded as the experts by fellow workers; they may be initially resistant to change and therefore need to be involved early.

System sponsors

System sponsors are senior managers or board members who are responsible for a system at a senior level in a company.

System owners

These are managers who are directly responsible for the operational use of a system.

Stakeholders

All staff who have a direct interest in the system.

◆ **Opinion leaders** are people whom others watch to see whether they accept new ideas and changes. They usually have little formal power, but are regarded as good 'ideas' people who are receptive to change and again need to be involved early in the project.

▶ Resistance to change

Some resistance to change is inevitable, but this is particularly true with the introduction of systems associated with business process reengineering, since the way work is performed and people's job functions will be changed. If the rationale behind the change is not explained, then all the classic symptoms of resistance to change will be apparent. Resistance to change usually follows a set pattern. For example, Adams *et al.* (1976) have used the transition curve in Fig 13.3 to describe the change from when staff first hear about a system to when the change becomes accepted.

While outright hostility manifesting itself as sabotage of the system is not unheard of, what is more common is that users will try to project blame on to the system and will identify major faults where only minor bugs exists. This will obviously damage the reputation of the system and senior managers will want to know what went wrong with the project. Another problem that can occur if the system has not been introduced well is that avoidance of the system will occur, with users working around the system to continue their previous ways of working. Careful management is necessary to ensure that this does not happen. To summarise the way in which resistance to change may manifest itself, the following may be evident:

◆ *Aggression* – in which there may be physical sabotage of the system, deliberate entry of erroneous data or abuse of systems staff.

◆ *Projection* – where the system is wrongly blamed for difficulties encountered while using it.

◆ *Avoidance* – withdrawal from or avoidance of interaction with the system; non-input of data; reports and enquiries ignored or use of manual substitutes for the system.

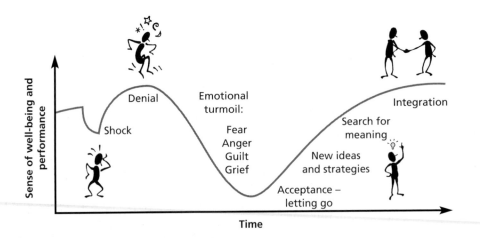

Fig 13.3 Transition curve of showing reaction of staff through time from when change is first suggested

There are many understandable reasons for people to resist the technological change that comes from the development of new information systems. These include:

- social uncertainty;
- limited perspectives and lack of understanding;
- threats to power and influence of managers (loss of control);
- perception that costs of new system outweigh the benefits;
- fear of failure, inadequacy or redundancy.

It is evident that training and education can be used to counter many of these issues. Additionally, other steps can be taken to reduce resistance to change, namely:

- Ensure early participation and involvement of users.
- Set realistic goals and raise realistic expectations of benefits.
- Build in user-friendliness to the new system.
- Don't promise too much and deliver what was promised!
- Develop a reliable system that is easy to maintain.
- Ensure support of the various stakeholders.
- Bring about agreement through negotiation.

Training

Appropriate education and training are important in implementation. Many companies make the mistake of not training staff sufficiently for a new system. This is often because of the cost of training or of taking staff away from their daily work for several days. If companies do provide training, it is often the wrong sort. Practical, operational training in how to use the software, such as which menu options are available and which buttons to press, is common. What is sometimes missing is ideological training: an explanation of why the system is being brought in – why are the staff's existing ways of working being overturned? This educational part of training is very important. Previous projects or examples of how systems have improved the business of competitors may be used here.

Change management and groupware

MINI CASE

Change and senior managers

Aside from the cultural problems that stem from the introduction of a new computer system, some types of software pose their own problems. For example, the introduction of groupware to a company may require a new way of communicating. If there is a tradition of a rigid, autocratic way of working, then groupware will give a more flexible, open way of communicating. This may be resented by senior managers, as they may feel this will erode their chain of command. As a result, it will be the more senior staff members who will find readjustment hardest, so the training and education plan should allow for this. It may also be best to introduce the system first to senior managers so that they can become familiar and comfortable with it, and then they will be better able to use it to manage their workgroups effectively. Companies which already have a relatively flat structure with high information availability and more teamworking will find the transition easier.

▶

The flame-mail phenomenon

Another problem caused by introduction of groupware is the flame-mail phenomenon. Recent research conducted by Novell among over 1000 e-mail users in the UK showed that e-mail can lead to lower productivity and raise stress because of e-mail bullying. 'Flame-mail' or abusive, bullying messages, often from superiors, were said to be experienced by at least half the staff. This shows that a change in culture caused by the introduction of e-mail is not being handled well by some companies. Under time pressure, or when staff want to avoid a face-to-face confrontation, they may lash out using e-mail rather than discussing the problem. This phenomenon highlights the need for training and policies on e-mail use.

The overhead of e-mail

A further problem with e-mail illustrated by this survey is the time it takes to read it: 94 per cent of respondents said that they wasted up to an hour a day reading and replying to messages. The results of the survey were mixed, however, with 70 per cent of respondents saying that they could not now do without e-mail.

Questions

1 What do you think is the best method for managing change when senior managers are involved?

2 Make notes about the problems of e-mail described above and others of which you are aware.

▶ MAINTENANCE

The maintenance phase of a project starts when the users sign off the system during testing and it becomes a live production system. After a system is live, there are liable to be some errors that were not identified during testing and need to be remedied. When problems are encountered, this presents a dilemma to the system manager, since they will have to balance the need for a new release of the system against the severity of an error. It is not practical or cost effective to introduce a new release of the software for every bug found, since each release needs to be tested and installed and fresh problems may exist in the new system. Most systems managers would aim not to make frequent, immediate releases to correct problems because of the cost and disruption this causes. Instead, faults will be recorded and then fixed in a release which solves several major problems. This is known as a **maintenance release** and it might occur at monthly, six-monthly or yearly intervals according to the stability of the system. This is usually a function of the age of the system – new systems will have more errors and will need more frequent maintenance releases.

Maintenance releases will not only fix problems, but may also include enhancements or new features requested by users.

Major and minor releases are denoted by the release or version number. If a system changes from version 1.1 to 2.0, this will be a major release. When moving from version 2.0 to 2.1, some new features might be involved. From version 2.1 to 2.11 would represent a patch or interim release to correct problems.

Maintenance

Maintenance occurs after the system has been signed off as suitable for users. It involves reviewing the project and recording and acting on problems with the system.

Table 13.4 Fault taxonomy described in Jorgenson (1995)

Category	Example	Action
1 Mild	Mispelled word	Ignore or defer to next major release
2 Moderate	Misleading or redundant information	Ignore or defer to next major release
3 Annoying	Truncated text	Defer to next major release
4 Disturbing	Some transactions not processed correctly, intermittent crashes in one module	Defer to next maintenance release
5 Serious	Lost transactions	Defer to next maintenance release; may need immediate fix and release
6 Very serious	Crash occurs regularly in one module	Immediate solution needed
7 Extreme	Frequent, very serious errors	Immediate solution needed
8 Intolerable	Database corruption	Immediate solution needed
9 Catastrophic	System crashes, cannot be restarted – system unusable	Immediate solution needed
10 Infectious	Catastrophic problem also causes failure of other systems	Immediate solution needed

To help make the decision of installing a new release to correct the problem, a scale of severity of the fault is used by companies to govern what action is required. Such a scale may form part of the contract if a company has outsourced its systems development to a third party. An example of such a scale is shown in Table 13.4.

Most systems now have a modular design such that it is not necessary to reinstall the complete system if an error is encountered, rather the module where the error lies can be replaced. This is described in a rather primitive way as applying a **patch** to the system. Patches to off-the-shelf systems are now available for download over the Internet. Because of the competitive pressures of releasing software as soon as possible, a large number of off-the-shelf packages require some sort of patch. For example, Web browser software such as Netscape Navigator and Microsoft Internet Explorer has required frequent patches to correct errors in the security of the browser which permit unauthorised access to the computer on which the browser is running.

Software patch is an interim release of part of an information system that is intended to address deficiencies in a previous release.

▶ Post-implementation review

Post-implementation review

A meeting that occurs after a system is operational to review the success of the project.

A **post-implementation review** or project closedown review occurs several months after the system has gone live. Its purpose is to assess the success of the new system and decide on any necessary corrective action. The review could include the following:

◆ review of faults and suggested enhancements with agreement on which need to be implemented in a future release;

◆ review of success of system in meeting its budget and timescale targets;

◆ review of success of system in meeting its business requirements – has it delivered the anticipated benefits described in the feasibility study?

◆ review of development practices that worked well and poorly during the project.

MINI CASE

Project closure summary for a software house

The form in Table 13.5 shows a real example of the output of a project closure meeting produced after implementation of a small project. It can be seen that the project was completed on time, but needed slightly more effort than estimated to achieve this. This led to a small budget overrun.

Table 13.5 Project closure summary

Project information		
Project	Bespoke module for client A	
Version	1.2	
Release date	18.12.97	

Performance: estimated against actual				
Measure	**Estimated**	**Actual**	**Difference**	**Difference %**
Budget	£7350	£8000	£650	+9%
Date	18/12/97	18/12/97	–	–
Total time (effort)	24.5 days	28 days	3.5 days	+12.5%
Elapsed time	5 weeks	5 weeks	–	–

Learning for next time		
Question	**Answer**	**Improve by?**
What went right?	Completed on time for client	–
What went wrong?	Delays caused by poor procedure for final build from program files	Develop better configuration management plans
	Using existing library code which contained bugs	
What was underestimated?	Greater contingency should have been allowed; 5 per cent was insufficient	15–20 per cent more appropriate contingency
Suggestions for improvement next time?	Keep customer informed more regularly	

An additional reason for performing a post-implementation review is so that lessons can be learnt from the project. Good practices can be applied to future projects and attempts made to avoid techniques which failed.

An example of a post-implementation review is shown in the mini case on project closure summary.

▶ SUMMARY

Stage summary: systems build

Purpose:	To produce a working system
Key activities:	Programming (coding), system and user documentation, testing
Input:	Design specification and requirements specification
Output:	Preliminary working system which can be tested by end-users

Stage summary: systems implementation

Purpose:	To install the system in the live environment
Key activities:	Install computers and software, user acceptance test, changeover, signoff
Input:	Preliminary versions of software
Output:	Tested, release version of software

Stage summary: systems maintenance

Purpose:	To ensure system remains available to end-users
Key activities:	Monitoring errors, reviewing and fixing problems, releasing patches
Input:	Tested, release version of software
Output:	Revised version of software

1 The build stage of systems development involves programming, testing and transferring data from the old system to the new system.

2 The main types of testing are unit testing of individual modules, system testing of the whole system by developers and user acceptance testing by the business. Sufficient time for testing must be built in using a quality assurance system to ensure that the delivered system is of the right quality.

3 The implementation stage involves managing the changeover from the old system to the new system. There are several alternative changeover approaches that can be used together if required:
   ◆ run the old and new systems in parallel;
   ◆ a phased approach where different modules are gradually introduced;
   ◆ cutover immediately to the new system;
   ◆ pilot the system in one area or office before 'rolling out' on a larger scale.

4 Some of the main reasons that information systems projects may fail at the build or implementation stage include:
   ◆ *Forgetting the human issues*. New systems are usually accompanied by a new way of working, so managers need to explain through training why the change is occurring and then train people adequately in the use of the system.
   ◆ *Cutting corners through using RAD*. Some corners cannot be cut, especially design, optimising system performance and testing. If insufficient time is spent on these activities, the system may fail. Documentation may also be omitted, which is vital during maintenance.

- *Computer resources aren't adequate.* The project managers need staff to check, for example, that the server can handle the load at critical times of the day, such as when scanning is occurring or at peak times in a call centre. Checks will also be made to ensure that the system performance does not degrade as the number of users of the systems or customers' records held ramp up.
- *Poor management of change process.* Staff who are involved with the new system should be trained so that they can use the software easily and understand the reasons for its introduction.
- *Lack of support from the top or from stakeholders.* Top management and appropriate stakeholders must support the cultural changes necessary to introduce the new system.
- *Using a big bang method of changeover.* Using this approach is high risk unless there has been extensive testing and methodical design.

5 The maintenance phase is concerned with managing the system once it is live. This will involve responding to errors as they are found. If serious, the problems will have to be solved immediately through issuing a 'patch' release to the system; otherwise they will be recorded for a later release.

6 A post-implementation review will occur which assesses the success of the systems development project and lessons are recorded for future projects.

► EXERCISES

► Self-assessment exercises

1 What are the main activities that occur in the build and implementation phases of a systems development project?

2 What is the difference between unit and system testing?

3 How can resistance to change among staff affect a new information system?

4 What are the most important factors in reducing resistance to change?

5 Why is it important to manage software change requests carefully?

6 What is the difference between the direct changeover method and the parallel changeover method?

7 What is the best option for an end-user to program a system?

8 What is the purpose of a post-implementation review?

► Discussion questions

1 All the different project changeover methods are likely to be used on any large project. Discuss.

2 The most important aspect of software quality assurance is to make sure that bugs are identified during the testing phase.

3 Companies should aim to minimise the number of patch releases, provided that no serious system errors occur.

▶ Essay questions

1 You are a business manager responsible for the successful implementation of a new information system. What problems would you anticipate from staff when the new system is introduced? What measures could you take to minimise these?

2 Discuss the advantages and disadvantages of the different methods of changeover from an old system to a new one. Which is the optimal method?

▶ Examination questions

1 Describe the direct changeover method. How does this differ from phased implementation?

2 What different classes of fault will a user be aiming to identify in a user acceptance test?

3 What are the three classical signs of resistance to change by end-users?

4 Distinguish between system testing and unit testing.

5 What different types of documentation will be used during the implementation phase of a project?

6 What elements of staff training should a new system receive?

7 What is the purpose of volume testing?

8 Which criteria should be used to measure the successful outcome of a systems development project?

9 In the maintenance phase of the systems development lifecycle, why might an information system need to be maintained?

10 Briefly outline the considerations that a company needs to take into account in deciding between the two main methods of changeover to a new information system: direct and parallel running.

▶ References

Adams, J., Hayes, J. and Hopson, B. (1976) *Transitions: Understanding and Managing Personal Change*, Martin Robertson, London.

Collins, T. and Bicknell, D. (1997) *Crash*, Simon and Schuster, London.

Jones, C. (1996) *Software Quality: Analysis and Guidelines for Success*, International Thomson Computer Press, London.

Johnston, A.K. (1995) *A Hacker's guide to Project Management*, Butterworth-Heinemann, Oxford.

Jorgenson, P. (1995) *Software Testing: a Craftsman's Approach*, CRC Press, Boca Raton, FL.

Kan, S. (1995) *Metrics and Models in Software Quality Engineering*, Addison-Wesley, Harlow.

Kolb, D.A. and Frohman, A.L. (1970) 'An organizational development approach to consulting', *Sloan Management Review*, 12, 51–65.

Lewin, K. (1972) 'Quasi-stationary social equilibria and the problems of permanent change', in Margulies, N. and Raia, A. (eds) *Organisational Development: Values, Process and Technology*, McGraw-Hill, New York, 65–72.

Schein, E (1956) 'The Chinese indoctrination program for prisoners of war', *Psychiatry*, 19, 149–172.

Schein, E. (1992) *Organizational Culture and Leadership*, Jossey Bass, San Francisco, CA.

Williams, P and Beason, P. (1990) *Writing Effective Software Documentation*, Scott, Foresman, Glenview, IL.

▶ Further reading

Hallows, J. (1998) *Information Systems Project Management: How to Deliver Function and Value in Information Technology Projects*, Amacom, New York.

Kerzner, H. (1995) *Project Management: A Systems Approach to Planning Scheduling and Controlling*, 5th ed, Van Norstrand Reinhold, New York.

Kit, E. (1995) *Software Testing in the Real World: Improving the Process*, Addison-Wesley, Harlow, Essex.

Lindgaard, G. (1994) *Usability Testing and System Evaluation: A Guide for Designing Useful Computer Systems*, Chapman & Hall, London.

Lucas, H. (1990) *Information Systems Implementation: Testing a Structural Model*, Ablex, Norwood, N.J.

Taylor, D (1992) *Object-oriented Information Systems: Planning and Implementation*, Wiley, Chichester.

PART

3

INFORMATION SYSTEMS MANAGEMENT

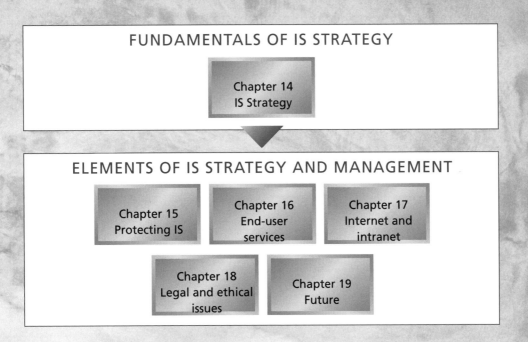

FUNDAMENTALS OF IS STRATEGY

Chapter 14
IS Strategy

ELEMENTS OF IS STRATEGY AND MANAGEMENT

Chapter 15
Protecting IS

Chapter 16
End-user
services

Chapter 17
Internet and
intranet

Chapter 18
Legal and ethical
issues

Chapter 19
Future

Managing information systems within an organisation involves two main elements: strategic planning; and management of systems, to give reliable access to IS for end-users and third-parties such as customers, suppliers and distributors. In Part 3, we start by reviewing approaches to IS strategy and then go on to describe key aspects of IS that need to be managed. These include:

- protecting IS from security breaches;

- providing end-user services;

- providing Internet and intranet based services;

- adhering to moral, legal and ethical constraints;

- managing technical change.

The IS strategy will define the future portfolio of IS that are necessary to support the business objectives of the organisation. The IS strategy will also seek to improve the quality of information used by the company. Since information is an increasingly important asset of the company, it must be managed to ensure it is well protected and of suitable quality for decision making. An IS strategy should also ensure that audits and appropriate follow-up actions occur to be certain that a company is complying with legal and ethical codes relating to the use of information systems. This will involve asking questions such as:

- has the company's applications software been purchased legally?

- is personal information accurate and well protected?

As a conclusion to the book, Part 3 also evaluates how IS is likely to be used in organisations in the future as they apply IS in new ways.

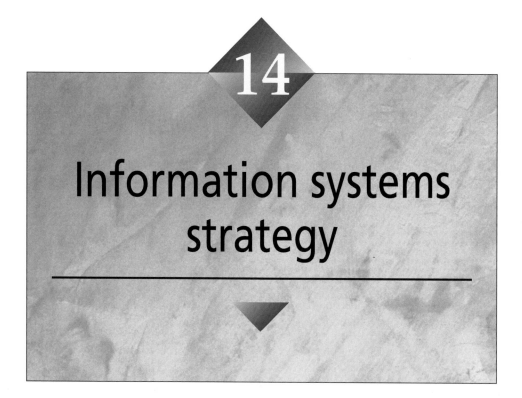

Information systems strategy

INTRODUCTION

Organisations which make the most effective use of information systems (IS) are those which make IS strategy an integral part of their overall business strategy. This chapter looks at how an organisation can develop a strategy for putting information systems in place which will support and enhance its overall business strategy and be consistent with it.

This chapter will cover the following topics:

◆ *Business and IS strategies.* Given that an organisation's IS strategy should have an intimate relationship with its business strategy, it is logical to look at some of the issues, tools and techniques that are involved in the process of strategy formulation and integrating IS with business strategy. Once this is done, we can begin to analyse the various dimensions of IS strategy within the context of an organisation's business strategy.

◆ *Determining IS investment levels.* Too often, decisions about investments in new IS are based on no data or purely quantitative data, without any reference to an assessment of the qualitative costs and benefits associated with the investment. This topic briefly reviews quantitative and qualitative measures and concludes that in many cases what is required before making an investment decision is a 'leap of faith' that the benefits to be obtained will outweigh the costs incurred.

◆ *IS and business process reengineering.* This follows on from the previous section in that we will be looking at the relationship between business processes and how IS can be used to improve their effectiveness.

> ▶ Learning objectives

After reading this chapter, readers will be able to:

◆ recognise the need for a company to possess an information systems strategy that is integrated with its business strategy;

◆ appreciate the need for structured methods of investment appraisal;

◆ apply strategic models to a company which suggest future strategic direction;

◆ relate IS strategy and business process reengineering.

> ▶ Links to other chapters

This chapter introduces some elements of IS strategy. It does not link directly to subsequent chapters in Part 3, since these describe specific aspects of managing information systems which are separate elements of strategy implementation. The aspects of information management covered in Part Three are:

Chapter 15 Managing information.

Chapter 16 Managing end-user services in a business.

Chapter 17 Managing Internet and intranet-based information sytems.

Chapter 18 Professional issues such as data privacy and protection.

Chapter 19 The future of information systems.

Chapter 8 in Part Two covers cost–benefit analysis and investment appraisal for a single information system in more detail than the coverage in this chapter.

▶ BUSINESS AND IS STRATEGIES

This section examines how strategic models can be applied to ensure that there is good congruence between business and IS strategies. The aim is to apply tools that enable us either to *align* the IS strategies with the business needs or use IT/IS to have a favourable *impact* on the business. Aligning techniques are top down in nature, beginning with the organisation's generic business strategy and from this deriving information systems strategies that support business activities. Before these tools can be applied, it is necessary to consider the organisational strategy and the environment in which the business operates.

▶ The foundation of strategy formulation

Any organisation's strategy can be rooted in four areas:

◆ *vision* – an image of a future direction that everyone can remember and follow;

◆ *mission* – a statement of what a business intends to achieve and what differentiates it from other businesses;

- *strategies* – a conditional sequence of consistent resource allocations that defines an organisation's relationships with its environment over time;
- *policies* – guidelines and procedures used in carrying out a strategy.

These areas in turn can be applied at a number of levels within an organisation:

- *corporate strategy* – view of the lines of business in which the company will participate and the allocation of resources to each line;
- *strategic business units (SBU)* – subsidiaries, divisions, product lines;
- *functional strategy* – each functional area within a business unit must develop a course of action to support the SBU strategy.

This straightforward definition masks an underlying complexity of strategy. Indeed, the way in which an organisation can formulate its strategy is the subject of some debate. Claudio Ciborra (Ciborra and Jelassi, 1994) contrasts the mechanistic approach to business strategy with more flexible and eclectic approaches. The former is characterised by such elements as:

- *Conscious and analytical thought,* where strategies emerge from a structured process of human thought and rigorous analysis; it is suggested that implementation can only follow when the strategy has been analytically formulated.
- *Top-down and control orientation,* where strategy is formulated at the peak of the managerial pyramid and responsibility for strategy lies with the organisation's chief executive officer.
- *Simple and structured models* of strategy formulation, where data analysis and internal and external scanning are undertaken so that the resulting model is clear and simple.
- *Separation* between the formulation of strategy and its implementation; diagnosis is followed by prescription and then by action; an organisation structure must therefore follow the formulation of the strategy rather than the other way round.

Flexible and eclectic approaches, on the other hand, are characterised by the fact that gradual changes, muddling through and evolutionary decision-making processes often prevail in organisations that profess to adhere to formal and mechanistic approaches to strategy formulation. Mintzberg (1990), as cited by Ciborra and Jelassi (1994), questions the mechanistic school of thought on three counts:

1 During strategy implementation, surprises occur that question previously developed plans. To be successful, the strategic plan needs to be modified to reflect the new situation and this contradicts the previously stated rationality and rigidity that characterise the mechanistic approach. Organisational learning is also hampered by an unduly inflexible approach.

2 While the mechanistic approach to strategy features the strategist as an impartial and independent observer and participant in the strategy development process, the reality in organisations is that organisational structure, culture, inertia and politics themselves influence the strategy development process. Strategy formulation is therefore profoundly influenced by the environment which it is seeking to affect.

3 The mechanistic approach to strategy formulation is an intentional process of design. However, the reality is that organisations acquire knowledge on a continual basis and this knowledge can have a profound influence on the contents of strategy and, therefore, its formulation process.

Since strategy formulation will always involve the need to react to unforeseen circumstances, resulting in sudden changes to overall corporate objectives, an effective strategy formulation process must embrace adaptation, organisational learning and incremental development that reflect a constantly changing business environment.

▶ TOOLS FOR STRATEGY FORMULATION

This section continues by presenting a variety of tools used in the strategy formulation process. While some of these appear to be mechanistic in nature, it is argued that, provided they are used within a climate of openness and flexibility, they still have a useful role to play in the strategy formulation process and hence an IS strategy that supports it. The tools selected form only a small proportion of those available, but those which are covered provide a firm foundation for further analysis. In addition, each tool will be examined in the context of the way in which it can be used to help derive an IS strategy that is an integral part of an organisation's business strategy.

▶ Porter and Millar's five forces model

Porter and Millar's five forces model

Porter and Millar's five forces model analyses the following competitive forces which impact an organisation: rivalry between existing competitors, threat of new entrants, threat of substitutes, the power of buyers and the power of suppliers.

Porter and Millar's five forces model is a model for analysing the different competitive forces that affect an organisation and how information can be used to counter them. The five forces are: rivalry between existing competitors, threat of new entrants, threat of substitutes, the power of buyers and the power of suppliers.

This model originated in 1985 and has remained one of the classic tools by which an organisation can assess its current competitive position in relation to a number of external factors:

◆ *Rivalry between existing competitors.* This will determine the immediate competitive position of the business and will depend principally on the number of firms already in the industry and the maturity of the industry itself. For example, a mature or declining industry will probably experience a high degree of rivalry, since survival is the key issue at stake.

◆ *Threat of new entrants.* A new entrant to an industry will cause the existing competitive situation to be disrupted. This has been evident in many countries over the last few years, where many of the formerly nationalised industries which were then privatised are now facing competition that they have never faced before.

◆ *Threat of substitutes.* The substitutes in question already exist within the industry, but because of differentiation they are not quite perfect substitutes for each other. The danger here, therefore, is that a company may lose market share if a rival can supply a substitute that more closely matches the needs of certain customers.

◆ *Power of buyers.* The phrase 'the customer is king' is never more true than here where buyers, especially in a business area where there are relatively few of them, can exert power by threatening to switch their purchasing to an alternative supplier. This is also true for businesses where the items being purchased are particularly high-value items (e.g. aero engines).

◆ *Power of suppliers.* This may appear a little odd given the previous point, since a business is going to be the customer to its suppliers. However, there are still competitive pressures to be addressed. For example, in a situation where a material is in short supply, a business is going to be at risk from its competitors bidding up material prices and suppliers selling to the highest bidder. An illustration of this is the worldwide shortage of PC memory chips in the early 1990s, where computer manufacturers effectively had to endure a large hike in prices if they were still to manufacture and sell personal computers.

Figure 14.1 illustrates how the five forces outlined above provide the main external pressure on the successful operation of a typical business.

These five forces can exert a profound influence on how business is conducted. If the model is to be used successfully, it will require a thorough analysis of the industry under consideration. Of itself, the resulting information will not automatically generate a business strategy for the organisation. However, it will create a vivid picture of the market environments within which the organisation is operating and provide some pointers towards avenues of further investigation.

From an information systems strategy perspective, the tool provides further pointers towards how IS can be used to affect one or more of the five forces. Each one of the five forces will be taken and an illustration of how IS can be used to benefit the business will be given:

◆ *Threat of new entrants.* Businesses such as the financial services industry are competing increasingly on the basis of quality and service and information systems are one enabler in this process. Investment in systems that support these two aspects of competition can deter potential entrants if they themselves have to make a significant investment in such systems before they can hope to compete successfully.

◆ *Rivalry between existing competitors.* The greater the extent of rivalry within the industry, the higher the costs that will be incurred by a business as it seeks to com-

Fig 14.1 Porter and Millar's five forces model
Source: Porter and Millar (1985)

pete with its rivals. In addition, industry rivalry will be profoundly influenced by the positioning of its products in both the industry and product lifecycles. In a declining industry, for example, collaborative efforts between industry rivals may help reduce costs or raise the profile of the industry.

◆ *Power of suppliers*. If a supplier believes that its customers will always buy from it because there are few perceived alternatives, it is in a position to exert upward pressure on prices and to dictate trading terms to the customer rather than the other way round. Through external databases and now the Internet, IS can help businesses identify equipment and raw material suppliers much more efficiently than before and so reduce the bargaining power of suppliers. An example of this is provided in Chapter 17 by the BT Trading Places initiative, where the Internet is used to review PC prices from several manufacturers, which reduces the power of the individual supplier.

◆ *Power of buyers*. IS can be used to lock customers into a company's products and so reduce the risk of the customer switching to a rival. For example, a business specialising in organising corporate travel may locate terminals at its main corporate customers so that they will be more likely to book flights, hotels and car hire with that company rather than a competitor.

◆ *Threat of substitutes*. The threat here is greater if the substitute products are a close alternative. In the shape of CAD/CAM and computer-integrated manufacturing, IS can be used to speed up development of new products and therefore reduce the ability of competitors to provide products that are acceptable substitutes.

ACTIVITY

Using Porter and Millar's model to devise strategies for exploiting the Internet and intranets

Using the Internet and intranets as an example of a new information technology, examine how a business could apply these to counter each of Porter and Millar's competitive forces. This provides an easy-to-understand example of how this model can be applied to the competitive use of IS. If you are not familiar with business applications of the Internet, you are referred to Chapter 17.

Applications that you may wish to consider are: sales of existing products by electronic commerce to customers across the Internet; introducing new products available over the Internet; marketing of products across the Internet; reducing the cost and increasing the efficiency of dealing with suppliers through an extranet; and changes in the ease of switching and switching costs through using the Internet. Note that the new technologies may actually improve the power of the company you are dealing with in some instances. State where you feel this is the case.

▶ Porter's competitive strategies

Related to his work on the five forces, Porter proposed three different competitive strategies that could be used to counter these forces, of which the organisation may be able to adopt one (Porter, 1980). Once a competitive strategy has been identified, all marketing efforts can be applied to achieving this and IS can help support the aim. The three competitive strategies are:

◆ *Overall cost leadership*. Firm aims to become the lowest-cost producer in the industry. The strategy here is that by reducing costs, one is more likely to retain customers and reduce the threat posed by substitute products. An example of how this might be achieved is to invest in systems that support accurate sales forecasting and therefore projected materials requirements so that good, long-term deals can be struck with suppliers, thus reducing materials costs.

◆ *Differentiation*. Creates a product perceived industry-wide as being unique. By being able to tailor products to specific customers requirements or by offering an exceptional quality of service, the risk of customers switching is reduced.

◆ *Focus or niche*. This involves identifying and serving a target segment very well (e.g. buyer group, product range, geographic market). The firm seeks to achieve either or both of 'cost leadership' and 'differentiation'.

There is also a possible undesirable outcome:

◆ *'Stuck in the middle'*. The firm is unable to adopt any of the above approaches and, therefore, is ultimately at the mercy of competitors which are able to offer these approaches.

The value of this model is that it encourages an organisation to look at itself in the context of its external environment. It is *not* a methodology that a company can follow to transform itself. It is now appropriate to switch from an externally oriented view to an internal one, again courtesy of Michael Porter.

▶ Value chain analysis

This is an analytical framework for decomposing an organisation into its individual activities and determining the value added at each stage. In this way, the organisation can assess how effectively resources are being used at the various points on the **value chain**. Michael Porter's value chain is a framework for considering key activities within an organisation and how well they add value as products and services move from conception to delivery to the customer. The relevance for information systems is that for each element in the value chain, it may be possible to use IS to increase the efficiency of resource usage in that area. In addition, IS may be used *between* value chain activities to increase organisational efficiency.

Value chain analysis makes a distinction between *primary activities,* which contribute directly to getting goods and services closer to the customer (physical creation of a product, marketing and delivery to buyers, support and servicing after sale), and *support activities,* which provide the inputs and infrastructure that allow the primary activities to take place. Figure 14.2 shows the distinction between these activities.

Primary activities can be broken down into five areas:

◆ *Inbound logistics*. Receiving, storing and expediting materials to the point of manufacture of the good or service being produced.

◆ *Operations*. Transforming the inputs into finished products or services.

◆ *Outbound logistics*. Storing finished products and distributing goods and services to the customer.

◆ *Marketing and sales*. Promotion and sales activities that allow the potential customer to buy the product or service.

◆ *Service*. After-sales service to maintain or enhance product value for the customer.

Value chain

Michael Porter's value chain is a framework for considering key activities within an organisation and how well they add value as products and services move from conception to delivery to the customer.

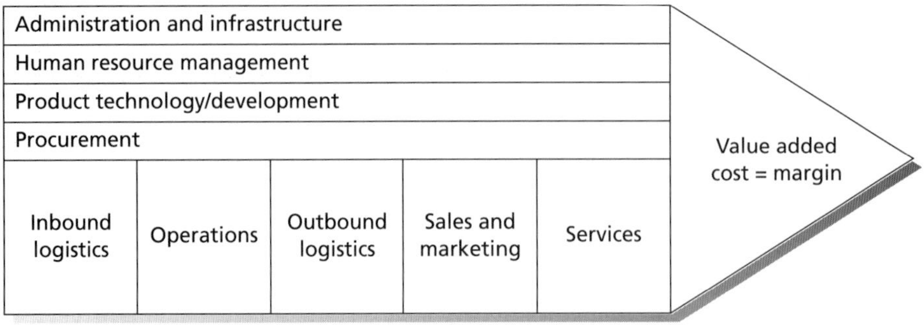

Fig 14.2 Michael Porter's value chain model showing the relationship between primary activities and support activities to the value chain within a company
Source: Porter (1980)

Secondary activities fall into four categories

◆ *Corporate administration and infrastructure.* This supports the entire value chain and includes general management, legal services, finance, quality management and public relations.

◆ *Human resource management.* Activities here include staff recruitment, training, development, appraisal, promotion and rewarding employees.

◆ *Technology development.* This includes development of the technology of the product or service, the processes that produce it and the processes that ensure the successful management of the organisation. It also includes traditional research and development activities.

◆ *Procurement.* This supports the process of purchasing inputs for all the activities of the value chain. Such inputs might include raw materials, office equipment, production equipment and information systems.

It is probably more easy to see how IS can be applied within this model than in the five forces model that we looked at earlier. For example, sales order processing and warehousing and distribution systems can be seen to be very relevant to the inbound and outbound logistics activities. Similarly, accounting systems have an obvious relevance to administration and infrastructure tasks. What is perhaps less clear is how IS can be used between value chain elements. The mini case study on applying the value chain to a manufacturing organisation helps illustrate the use of IS to provide linkages between some of the value chain elements.

How can an organisation have a positive impact on its value chain by investing in new or upgraded information systems? Porter and Millar (1985) propose the following five-step process:

◆ *Step 1.* Assess the information intensity of the value chain (i.e. the level and usage of information *within* each value chain activity and *between* each level of activity). The higher the level of intensity and/or the higher the degree of reliance on good-quality information, the greater the potential impact of new information systems.

◆ *Step 2.* Determine the role of IS in the industry structure (for example banking will be very different from mining). It is also important to understand the information

A toy manufacturer has a range of integrated information systems, including sales order processing (SOP), warehousing and distribution, accounting systems, including sales, purchase and general ledgers, and finally a manufacturing system. The SOP system, which is used to store customer and order details, has a linkage to the accounting system for credit checking and processing accounts receivable. Thus there is an electronic linkage between the sales administration and infrastructure activities. The warehousing and distribution system keeps track of stock levels and actual and projected sales order levels. Information here can be used to generate automatically raw material orders and manufacturing orders. Here is a clear linkage between inbound logistics and operations and also procurement and inbound logistics. Finally, the warehouse and distribution system will generate a 'picking list' that is used to select stock from the warehouse for delivery to specific customers. This illustrates a linkage between the sales and outbound logistics functions. These activities are clearly operational in nature. However, the ability to have related information from a variety of systems also creates the possibility of management information, such as a weekly management report, which draws from all these sources.

Questions

1 Draw a diagram showing the role of information and information technology in assisting the value chain.
2 Give further ways in which the company could apply IT to improve efficiency.

---

linkages between buyers and suppliers within the industry and how they and competitors might be affected by and react to new information technology.

◆ *Step 3*. Identify and rank the ways in which IS might create competitive advantage (by affecting one of the value chain activities or improving linkages between them). High-cost or critical activity areas present good targets for cost reduction and performance improvement.

◆ *Step 4*. Investigate how IS might spawn new businesses (for example, the Sabre computerised reservation system spawned a multibillion-dollar software company which now has higher earnings than the original core airline business).

◆ *Step 5*. Develop a plan for taking advantage of IS. A plan must be developed that is business driven rather than technology driven. The plan should assign priorities to the IS investments (which, of course, should be subjected to an appropriate cost–benefit analysis).

▶ McFarlan's strategic grid

McFarlan's strategic grid model is used to indicate the strategic importance of information systems to a company now and in the future.

This matrix model was developed by McFarlan and McKenney (1993) to consider the contribution made currently by information systems and the possible impact of future IS investments. It is suggested in the original model that any business will occupy one of the segments in the matrix (Fig 14.3):

McFarlan's strategic grid

This model is used to indicate the strategic importance of information systems to a company now and in the future.

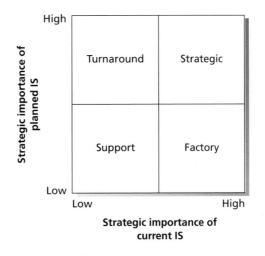

Fig 14.3 McFarlan's strategic grid
Source: McFarlan (1984)

◆ The *strategic* segment indicates that the business depends both on its existing IS and continued investment in new IS to sustain continued competitive advantage.

◆ The *turnaround* segment suggests that, while a business in this position does not currently derive significant competitive benefits from its current IS, future investment in this area has the potential to positively affect the business's competitive position.

◆ On the other hand, a business operating in the *factory* segment, while depending on its current IS to operate competitively, does not envisage further IS investment having a positive impact on its competitive position.

◆ Finally, a business in the *support* segment does not and believes it will not derive significant competitive advantage from information systems.

Note that it is not likely to be the aim for every company to move to a high strategic importance for IS. In some industries such as manufacturing, it is unlikely that IS will ever attain high importance. In others such as retailing, it may become more important. Give the varying significance of IS in different industries, there are a number of ways in which this model can be applied:

◆ Across industries for analysing the strategic importance that particular industries attach to IS.

◆ Within an industry. Different competitors can be plotted according to the relative significance they attach to IS.

◆ Within a company. Different departments within an organisation can be classified and goals set in relation to the future planned importance of IS.

This model has been criticised by Hirschheim *et al.* (1988) as being too simplistic, since most companies have information systems that fall into all four categories. Ward and Griffiths' (1996) modified matrix provides a useful variation on this model by categorising information systems and their business contribution in terms of an applications portfolio. This model recognises that the information systems used by a

single company will not fit into a single quadrant on such a matrix, but rather there will be a portfolio of IS, some of which may lie in different quadrants. The four sectors are shown in Fig 14.4.

The four sectors are:

◆ *Support.* These applications are valuable to the organisation but not critical to its success.

◆ *Key operational.* The organisation currently depends on these applications for success.

◆ *High potential.* These applications may be important to the future success of the organisation.

◆ *Strategic.* Applications that are critical to sustaining future business strategy.

Each of an organisation's application will fall into one of these categories. It is quite feasible that applications will move from one sector to another over time (e.g. today's strategic application may become tomorrow's key operational one). It is quite possible, for example, that a current key operational system needs to be developed to replace an old legacy system that no longer meets all the organisation's requirements (e.g. in respect of year 2000 compliance).

The McFarlan matrix and its variant do not of themselves provide a methodology to assist an organisation with its information systems planning. However, especially in its Ward and Griffiths guise, the matrix can be effective in providing a framework through which an organisation can explore current and planned IS, both from an IS perspective and from that of functional business managers.

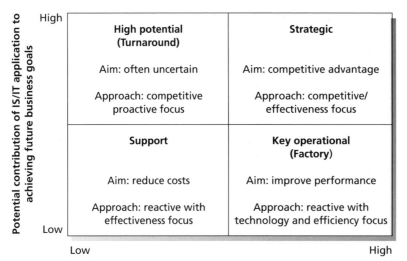

Fig 14.4 Ward and Griffiths' modified strategic grid

Source: Ward and Griffiths (1996)

▶ Nolan's stage model

Nolan's stage model

This model is a six-stage evolutionary model of how IS can be applied within a business.

Nolan's stage model is a six-stage maturity model for the application of information systems to a business.

It must be stressed at the outset that this model dates back to the mainframe era and, therefore, provides a way of looking at an organisation's response to ongoing IS investment and management that is fundamentally influenced by this. However, the model does have value since it is simple to understand, provides an evolutionary view of business use of IS and demonstrates that an organisation's approach to the management of IS will change over time. The model demonstrates that, over time and with experience, an organisation's approach to computer applications, specialist IS personnel and methods of management will evolve to a level of maturity where the planning and development of information systems are embedded into the strategic planning process for the business as a whole.

The six-stage 1979 version of the model is the one on which we will focus here:

1 *Initiation.* The first cautious use of a strange technology, characterised by:
   ◆ low expenditures for data processing;
   ◆ small user involvement;
   ◆ lax management control;
   ◆ emphasis on functional applications to reduce costs.

2 *Contagion.* The enthusiastic adoption of computers in a range of areas:
   ◆ proliferation of applications;
   ◆ users superficially enthusiastic about using data processing systems;
   ◆ management control even more lax;
   ◆ rapid growth of budgets;
   ◆ treatment of the computer by management as just a machine;
   ◆ rapid growth of computer use throughout the organisation's functional areas;
   ◆ computer use is plagued by crisis after crisis.

3 *Control.* A reaction against excessive and uncontrolled expenditures of time and money on computer systems:
   ◆ IS raised higher in the organisation;
   ◆ centralised controls placed on the systems;
   ◆ applications often incompatible or inadequate;
   ◆ use of database and communications, often with negative general management reaction;
   ◆ end-user frustration.

4 *Integration.* Using new technology to bring about the integration of previously unintegrated systems:
   ◆ rise of control by the users;
   ◆ large DP budget growth;
   ◆ demand for database and online facilities;
   ◆ DP dept operates like a computer utility;
   ◆ formal planning and control within DP;
   ◆ users more accountable for their applications;
   ◆ use of steering committees, applications financial planning;
   ◆ DP has better management controls, standards, project management.

5 *Data administration.* There is a new emphasis on managing corporate data rather than information technology:
- ◆ identification of data similarities, their usage and meanings within the whole organisation;
- ◆ the applications portfolio is integrated into the organisation;
- ◆ DP (MIS) department serves more as an administrator of data resources than of machines;
- ◆ the emphasis changes to IS rather than DP.

6 *Maturity.* Information systems are put in place that reflect the real information needs of the organisation:
- ◆ use of data resources to develop competitive and opportunistic applications;
- ◆ MIS organisation viewed solely as a data resource function;
- ◆ MIS emphasis on data resource strategic planning;
- ◆ ultimately users and MIS department *jointly* responsible for the use of data resources within the organisation.

Data processing (DP) department is a term commonly used in the 1970s and 1980s to describe the functional area responsible for management of what is now referred to as information systems and applications development. It is interesting to note that the term focuses on the processing of data rather than the application of information. The head of this department was referred to as DP manager rather than chief information officer or IS manager.

There are a number of implications of Nolan's model which, if taken into account, may help provide a clearer path towards the maturity stage. Both general and IS management must:

- ◆ verify the state of IS development in order to plan for the future;
- ◆ recognise the fundamental organisational transition from computer management to information resource management;
- ◆ recognise the importance of and the future trends in information technology;
- ◆ introduce and maintain the appropriate planning and control devices for the IS function (steering committees etc.).

While it is clear that the model has value, there are clearly a number of shortcomings, particularly in respect of the lack of a human dimension. Galliers and Sutherland (1991) have extended the model so that it is a socio-technical one rather than merely a technical one. They have done this by including reference to the organisation's goals, culture, skills and structure. Nevertheless, we should not dismiss Nolan's model, despite its age, since it can still provide a useful framework for information systems planning. Indeed, the maturity stage implies what all organisations should aspire to: true integration between IS and business planning!

▶ Critical success factors (CSF) analysis

Critical success factors (CSFs) are measures which indicate the performance or efficiency of different parts of an organisation. Good performance of processes measured by these factors is vital to the business unit or organisation.

This technique is one of the most useful for an organisation in pinpointing what are its precise information needs. The essence of CSF analysis is summarised in Fig 14.5.

Data processing (DP) department

Commonly used in the 1970s and 1980s used to describe the functional area responsible for management and implementation of information systems.

Critical success factors (CSFs)

Measures which indicate the performance or efficiency of different parts of an organisation and its processes.

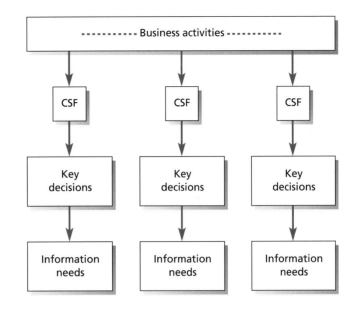

Fig 14.5 Critical success factors and deriving information needs

Critical success factors will exist in every functional area of the business and they indicate those things which must be done right if that functional area in particular and the organisation are to flourish. CSFs will also relate to the level within each functional area. For example, in the sales function, a CSF for an account handler may be the accurate and speedy recording and retrieval of sales data. On the other hand, for a senior manager, a CSF may involve achieving the right mix of products.

Once CSFs have been determined across process and hierarchical levels, it is possible to consider the key decisions that have to be made if those CSFs are to be achieved.

An example of the application of CSFs in sales order processing

When a customer places an order, a number of decisions need to be made, the result of which will determine the processing actions for the order and the effectiveness of the process. The critical success factor for this process will be to achieve a high conversion rate of orders received to orders fulfilled while minimising the risk of bad debts.

One of the first decisions will be whether to accept the customer order at all. Such a decision will hinge on the creditworthiness of the customer. Second, a decision will have to be made about when the customer can receive his or her order. This may be a complex process, depending on the size and importance of the customer, the size and complexity of the order and finally existing stock levels for the ordered items and planned manufacturing or purchasing lead times. If the order is delayed, the customer may seek an alternative supplier.

Having identified the range of key decisions that need to be supported, consideration must turn to the information needed to support the decision-making processes for each relevant functional business area or operational level. To pursue the sales example to its logical

conclusion, one of the first information needs is, therefore, the creditworthiness of the customer as expressed by his or her credit line or limit and the current outstanding amount. Both of these items of information would normally be drawn from a mixture of existing sales and accounts receivable data. The sales account handler needs this information before a decision can be made to continue with the customer order. Second, information relating to order item availability needs to be known before a delivery date commitment can be made to the customer. This information will probably be drawn from:

1 Customer data (for example, is the customer an important one who needs to be looked after?).
2 Stock control data (is there sufficient stock in the warehouse to fulfil this customer's requirements?).
3 Production planning data (if there is currently insufficient stock on hand, will there be sufficient stock in time to meet the customer's requirements?).

Through improving the quality of information available to support decision making, it should be possible to improve the efficiency of sales order processing and achieve the CSF.

▶ Business alignment and impacting techniques

It is useful to consider tools for strategy formulation and implementation in the context of whether they are intended to support an existing business strategy directly (business alignment), or whether they are intended to indicate new opportunities which may have a positive impact on a business strategy (business impacting).

In a business alignment IS strategy the IS strategy will be generated from the business strategy through techniques such as CSF analysis. In a business impacting IS strategy the IS strategy will have a favourable impact on the business strategy through the use of innovative techniques and technologies, often as part of business process reengineering. CSF analysis is fundamentally a business aligning technique rather than an impacting one.

Business impacting could be achieved through the use of value chain analysis where an organisation, through an analysis of the potential for the use of IS within and between value chain elements, may seek to identify strategic IS opportunities. Perhaps the ultimate expression of using IS to impact business performance is through business process reengineering.

Business aligning IS strategy

The IS strategy is derived directly from the business strategy in order to support it.

Business impacting IS strategy

The IS strategy is used to favourably impact the business strategy, perhaps by introducing new technologies.

▶ DETERMINING INVESTMENT LEVELS FOR INFORMATION SYSTEMS IN AN ORGANISATION

Chapter 8 contains detailed coverage of how to assess costs at the initiation phase of a single information systems project. In this chapter, we consider at an organisational level the amount of investment that should occur in information systems.

Managers in many organisations are concerned with the level of investment in information systems and whether they are getting value for money from that investment. One of the difficulties with measuring this is that while costs tend to be tangible in nature, benefits are often more difficult to quantify.

▶ Investment levels

One of the perennial questions surrounding corporate expenditure on IS is how much a business should spend on IS as a proportion of annual turnover. According to report by Spikes Cavell (*Computing*, 19 December 1997), the top 500 companies in the US invested an average of 2.9 per cent of their turnover in IS, while similar companies in Europe spent 2.1 per cent.

The Swedish research company Compass (*Computer Weekly*, 9 April 1998) suggests that as a proportion of total company costs, IS spending has increased from a typical 2–3 per cent in the 1980s to 7–10 per cent in 1998. The same source also suggests that IS spending now makes up 40 per cent of capital investment by businesses in the US, compared to 5–10 per cent twenty years ago. The figures presented here imply that business operations are increasingly dependent on IS.

We consider this topic further in Chapter 19, where we ask the question: 'Are companies getting value for money from these increasing investments in information systems?'

How much an organisation will spend on IS will depend both on the size of the organisation and the nature of its business operations. Spending as a proportion of turnover will also vary over time, depending on the maturity of an organisation's systems and the organisation itself. There is a tendency for the proportion of spending on IS to increase as organisations mature and have to maintain legacy systems. Regardless of any of these considerations, the task facing senior managers remains the same: can we be sure that investment in IS will deliver more benefit than the costs incurred?

The role of legacy systems

Legacy system

A system that an organisation has had for a number of years that has been superseded by new business practices or technologies, but is still required to support business operations.

Legacy systems are those inherited from languages and platforms earlier than current technology. They often serve critical business needs such as processing customer orders.

Today's IS investment is tomorrow's IS legacy system. Unless a new information system is entirely replacing an old legacy system, an organisation is going to experience rising IS costs over time unless the overall level of IS expenditure is fixed. Note that if this latter stance is adopted, the proportion of IS expenditure devoted to developing new information systems is going to fall and the organisation risks losing any competitive advantage that might have come from the original IS investments. This is one of the fundamental reasons for IS investment levels continuing to increase – new systems must be purchased to achieve competitive advantage while old systems must still be maintained.

▶ Information systems costs

As described in Chapter 8, costs can be both tangible and intangible. As you would expect, tangible costs are more easily identified than intangible ones. This leads to the observation that costs can also be classified as *expected* and *hidden*. Research by Keen indicates that there are differences between in-house developed and purchased software in the proportions of expected and hidden costs. This can be compounded by the complexity of the chosen method of software acquisition and the complexity of the system being acquired: the more complex the method and/or system, the more likely costs are to overrun what was anticipated in advance.

Hochstrasser and Griffiths (1990) produced a checklist which can help organisations identify, quantify and evaluate information system costs. The main cost elements include:

◆ hardware costs;
◆ software costs;
◆ installation costs;
◆ environmental costs;
◆ running costs;
◆ maintenance costs;
◆ security costs;
◆ networking costs;
◆ training costs;
◆ wider organisational costs.

Since every information system that is acquired incurs operational and maintenance costs, IS expenditure will always be split between *development* costs and *operational and maintenance* costs.

▶ Information system benefits

While information systems costs are relatively easy to identify, the benefits that accrue from IS investment are harder to quantify. This is because benefits are often intangible in nature and, therefore, harder to ascribe a financial value to. Broadly speaking, benefits from IS investment result from the capability of the organisation to do things that it could not do or did not do very well before. This must be supported by information of good quality, as defined in Chapter 2. This will include:

◆ Information relevance – is the information being provided relevant to the business decisions being made?
◆ Is accurate information available on which business decisions can be made?
◆ Speed of information delivery – does information reach the decision makers when they need it?
◆ The functionality of the IS to support decision making – will the system do what we want it to do?
◆ The reliability of the IS – can we rely on the system to give us the information we want when we want it?

If the above questions can be answered positively, then the investment in IS is providing benefits to the organisation and, therefore, allows it to do things that it could not do before.

In making an IS investment decision, the value that accrues from the above elements must be measured in some way. However, as noted above, value from IS investment can often be intangible in nature and, therefore, harder to measure. Such items of intangible benefit include:

◆ improved customer service;
◆ gaining competitive advantage and avoiding competitive disadvantage;

- support for core business functions;
- improved management information;
- improved product quality;
- improved internal and external communication;
- impact on the business through innovation;
- job enhancement for employees.

Each of these elements has a level of difficulty attached when attempting to determine the value of the benefit. For example, impact on the business through innovation is very hard to measure quantitatively, while the benefit of improved product quality may be easier to measure.

▶ IS investment – balancing costs and benefits

We can deduce from the above discussion that the more accurately we can identify the contribution of IS towards the value of business gain, the more accurately we can identify the value accruing from IS investments. It follows from this that in order to assess the value of future investments in IS, we must come up with a framework that allows us to weigh up the relative costs and benefits and so enable us to make properly considered IS investment decisions.

There are a number of approaches that attempt to evaluate IS investment decisions. In essence, a proposed or ongoing investment should proceed if the benefits from the investment outweigh the costs incurred. However, as Robson (1997) indicates, one of the main difficulties is the intangible benefits, which can amount to at least 30 per cent of all benefits obtained. In addition, even if a benefit can be quantified (e.g. a new system speeds up customer response to queries from an average of 10 minutes to 10 seconds), it is not always easy to put a monetary value on it. This leads to a division in approaches between those that concentrate purely on financial measures and those that attempt a non-monetary evaluation.

Chapter 8 considers the basis of investment decisions taken at the feasibility assessment stage of the initiation of an individual project. It is the role of the IS manager to ensure that individual IS project decisions are consistent with the company's overall IS strategy.

Financial justification methods look at the relationship between the monetary costs of IS investment and the monetary benefits that might be obtained from it. There are a number of techniques which can be used, including:

- return on investment (RoI);
- discounted cashflow (DCF), such as net present value (NPV) and internal rate of return (IRR);
- payback period.

These are described in more detail in Chapter 8, which reviews how they are applied to a proposal for an individual system.

Risk assessment methods, on the other hand, look at a number of factors other than those related to pure financial return. Such considerations include:

◆ the benefits that are designed to accrue from investment in different categories of IS;

◆ the reasons that systems fail;

◆ categories of risk and their likely impact on systems success.

Information systems fail when they do not deliver the benefits they were intended to achieve. Clearly, the greater the investment in IS, the greater the impact of a failed project, especially as that investment could have been made in another part of the business (e.g. investment in additional plant, people or equipment) with much greater effect.

We will now look at each of the above considerations.

Investment categories of the IS applications portfolio

Sullivan (1985) identified four investment categories for information systems that provide a framework within which the strategic value of the investment to the company can be placed. It is useful to identify in which category a new system lies within the IS portfolio, in order to assess its importance and allocate resources to it accordingly. The investment categories are:

1 *Strategic systems.* These are designed to bring about innovation and change in the conduct of business and so bring about a competitive edge. Business processes may need to be designed and relationships with customers and suppliers changed. Risk occurs because of the level of uncertainty associated with these kind of systems (we are dealing with unstructured decision making, the results of which are often hard to quantify).

2 *Key operational systems.* Existing processes are rationalised, integrated or reorganised in order to carry out the activities of business more effectively. The risk occurs in the complexity of the systems in this category and the need to integrate them with other systems (externally as well as internally).

3 *Support systems.* Such systems support well-structured, stable and well-understood business processes (i.e. decisions are usually made in a climate of relatively high business certainty). Benefits derive either from eliminating unnecessary processes or from automating regular and routine procedures. In either case, the aim is to reduce cost and raise efficiency. The risks occur in selecting the right kind of software (often packaged) and implementing it effectively to gain the benefits.

4 *High-potential projects.* These are of research and development orientation and may have the capacity to deliver significant business benefits in the future. They are usually high-risk projects (in the sense that they may not deliver anything at all) and the main business risk lies in committing too much money to the project (i.e. the attitude that if we invest more, we *must* realise some benefits!).

The challenge for the organisation is to channel investment into the areas that are likely to yield the highest level of potential benefit at the lowest level of acceptable risk.

Risk factors

These have been summarised by Ward and Griffiths (1996). They should be considered at the start of a project to attempt to reduce the risk of project failure. Risk management is described in more detail in Chapter 8.

▶ BUSINESS PROCESS REENGINEERING

Business process reengineering (BPR)

Identifying and implementing radical new ways of carrying out work, often enabled by new IT capabilities.

Business process reengineering (BPR) involves identifying radical, new ways of carrying out business operations, often enabled by new IT capabilities.

Business process reengineering has been the subject of much debate in recent years. On the one hand, it has been hailed as one of the most dramatic tools for achieving dramatic improvements in an organisation's performance. On the other hand, others regard it simply as a 'fad' responsible for many large-scale redundancies in the early 1990s, ultimately failing to confer major business benefits while at the same time providing management consultants with a great deal of revenue. It is not the purpose of this section to support either stance! Rather, it presents a review of how IS can fit into the BPR process. Before this is done, we will give an overview of the main BPR concepts and also consider the business framework within which BPR operates.

▶ BPR fundamentals

BPR has its origins at the beginning of the 1990s and is closely associated with the work of Hammer and Champy (1993) and Davenport (1993). The essence of BPR is that there is a recognition that business processes and management structures can be fundamentally altered so that the business itself is better defined, focused, organised and run. Hammer and Champy defined BPR as:

> the fundamental rethinking and radical redesign of business processes to achieve dramatic improvements in critical, contemporary measures of performance, such as cost, quality, service, and speed.

The key words of reengineering are:

◆ *Fundamental rethinking.* Reengineering usually refers to changing significant business processes such as customer service, sales order processing or manufacturing.

◆ *Radical process redesign.* Reengineering is not involved with minor, incremental change or automation of existing ways of working. It involves a complete rethinking of the way in which business processes operate.

◆ *Dramatic improvements.* The aim of BPR is to achieve improvements measured in tens or hundreds of per cent. With automation of existing processes, only single-figure improvements may be possible.

◆ *Critical contemporary measures of performance.* This point refers to the importance of measuring how well the processes operate in terms of the four important measures of cost, quality, service and speed.

Information systems are often central to enabling the changes to take place. As we have seen earlier, IS has a capacity to allow communication within and between functional areas of the business much more quickly and efficiently than traditional manual methods. In *Reengineering the Corporation*, Hammer and Champy have a chapter giving examples of how IS can act as a catalyst for change. These include tracking technology, decision support tools, telecommunications networks, teleconferencing and shared databases. Hammer and Champy label these 'disruptive technologies' that can force companies to reconsider their processes and find new ways of operating.

Business process reengineering is sometimes confused with less radical solutions to business problems. These have the benefit that they may have lower costs and risks, but the potential benefits may also be lower. The potential of each of these alternative strategic approaches is summarised in Table 14.1.

Table 14.1 Alternative terms for using IS to enhance company performance

Term	Involves	Intention	Risk of failure
Business process reengineering	Fundamental redesign of all main company processes	Large gains in performance (>100%?)	Highest
Business process improvement	Targets key processes in sequence for redesign	(<50%)	Medium
Business process automation	Automating existing process	(<20%)	Lowest

A problem with BPR is the historically high failure rate among BPR projects. It has been estimated that some 70 per cent of BPR projects fail, either completely or at least in delivering the benefits that were originally conceived. These figures have even been quoted by the original proponents of BPR such as Hammer. Given this, many companies are now adopting a more conservative approach by more gradually improving key business processes, perhaps one at a time. This is often referred to as business process improvement or BPI – a less radical term than business process reengineering. Note that BPI still involves a redesign of processes, but it does not involve disrupting the entire organisation.

Business process automation is a misnomer that suggests radical change, but actually only involves using IS to automate existing ways of working. The introduction of a sales order processing system that mimics existing ways of working fits into this category. While such projects are likely to be easier to implement, they may not deliver sufficient benefits to pay for themselves.

Business process automation

Automating existing ways of working manually through information technology.

A further observation is that BPR has, in the past, been hampered by the lack of any really coherent methodology for carrying out BPR projects. For a broad framework, Davenport's stage approach to BPR offers a useful guide:

◆ Identify the process for innovation.

◆ Identify the change levers.

◆ Develop the process vision.

◆ Understand the existing processes.

◆ Design and prototype the new process.

◆ *Identify the process for innovation.* Emphasis here should be on major business processes. Commentators differ on how many major processes an organisation may have. It seems reasonable to equate a major business process with those from the organisation's value chain which add most to the value of the finished product or service.

◆ *Identify the change levers.* The main areas where emphasis can be placed include the organisation's information systems and its **organisational culture** and structure. As discussed earlier, BPR activities will be directed towards improving business processes either through better use of information, restructuring the organisation (physically and socially) or both.

Organisational culture

This concept includes shared values, unwritten rules and assumptions within the organisation as well as the practices that all groups share.

The concept of organisational structure includes shared values, unwritten rules and assumptions within the organisation as well as the practices that all groups share. Corporate cultures are created when a group of employees interact over time and are relatively successful in what they undertake.

◆ *Develop the process vision.* Before a BPR project can begin in earnest, it is necessary to generate a view of how and why business processes might be modified. The vision must be communicated to all parties in a way that acts as a motivator to all concerned.

◆ *Understand the existing processes.* Current business processes must be documented. This allows the performance of existing business processes to be benchmarked and so provides a means for measuring the extent to which a reengineered process has improved business performance. In addition, a documented process provides a framework for discussion when process redesign is actually taking place.

◆ *Design and prototype the new process.* Here, the BPR team needs to be creative as it seeks to design the replacement processes – the vision must be translated into practical new processes that the organisation is going to be able to operate. Prototyping the new process operates on two levels. First, simulation and modelling tools can be used to check the logical operation of the process. Second, assuming that the simulation model shows no significant problems, the new process can be given a full operational trial. Needless to say, the implementation must be handled sensitively if it is to be accepted by all parties.

It is now appropriate to consider a possible framework that seeks to clarify how a number of factors can influence the BPR process itself.

▶ Success factors in BPR – the BPR diamond

Figure 14.6 shows a number of dimensions within which BPR must operate to be successful. Of these influences, the most important is the value chain, since BPR often seeks to affect this.

1 *Value chain activities.* BPR attempts fundamentally to alter processes *within* one or more of an organisation's value chain activities in order to improve business performance. It can also seek fundamentally to improve the effectiveness of relationships *between* value chain elements. It follows, therefore, that an organisation must fully understand its own value chain if it is to stand any chance of success with a BPR project. An important point here is the impact on the rest of the value chain of an improvement in one part of it. For example, substantial improvements in one value chain element (e.g. operations) may be pointless if

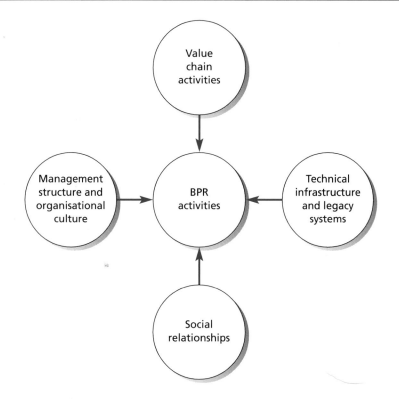

Fig 14.6 The BPR diamond: influences on BPR activities

another (inbound logistics, say) is incapable of expediting the necessary raw materials in time. ERP applications (Chapters 6 and 19) are often used when reengineering the value chain.

2 *Management structure and organisational culture.* This will have a profound impact on the probability of success of a BPR project. Factors that are important here include:

◆ communication of the business vision by managers;

◆ corporate strategy formation;

◆ hierarchical structures – shallow structures may increase the likelihood of success, since they may indicate less bureaucratic management structures;

◆ senior management commitment is essential for success; many BPR projects fail because senior managers are not fully committed to the cause.

3 *Technical infrastructure and legacy systems.* The original proponents of BPR felt that IS was one of the key enablers of radical process redesign, not least because of its ability to transform working relationships within and between value chain elements. The ability of an organisation to act on this will be dependent on its existing IS infrastructure. For example, a business dominated by old mainframe legacy systems may actually be prevented from reengineering business processes because the IS systems are too inflexible or overloaded.

4 *Social relationships.* The efficiency of any organisation is dependent on the complex formal and informal relationships that exist within it. These can be formal in

the sense of hierarchical work relationships within and between functional business areas. Informal relationships are created through people working with each other on a regular basis and will cut across functional boundaries. BPR has the capacity to alter both types of relationships, as it brings about change within and between functional business areas. Project management and a change management program are clearly going to be essential if a BPR project is to succeed.

▶ How to reengineer

Many commentators exhort companies to reengineer, but without giving detailed guidelines on how to achieve this. Nick Obolensky's book (1994) offers detailed guidelines for reengineering with company case studies and is recommended reading. Figure 14.7 shows his recommended stages for reengineering, which are consistent with a generic method of implementing business strategy. The first stages are involved with creating a vision for the company at a senior level and then planning the implementation. There follows the stage of undertaking reengineering, which covers activities such as process analysis, design and implementation. Once the reengineered system is operational, collecting metrics occurs so that the processes of the company can be continuously improved to keep up with or be one step ahead of the competition.

More detailed reengineering methodologies have been developed by management consultancies, for example the Breakpoint BPR methodology developed by Coopers and Lybrand. This has three phases: discover, redesign and realise:

◆ Phase 1 is the initiation, in which the project vision and communications strategy is developed, processes for redesign are identified and teams are built.

◆ In Phase 2 the redesign modules are mobilise, analyse, innovate, engineer and commit.

◆ Phase 3 is mobilise, communicate, act, measure and sustain.

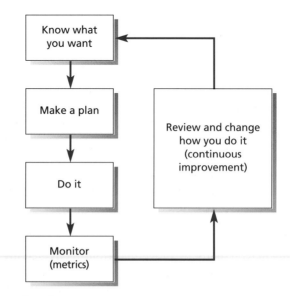

Fig 14.7 Stages in reengineering

Source: adapted from Obolensky (1994)

The ProSci Web site (http://www.prosci.com) also gives detailed methods of undertaking BPR.

The case study on managing the change process reviews the results of reengineering initiatives at companies such as British Airways, SmithKline Beecham and Siemens Nixdorf. It illustrates some of the problems faced by companies on this path and some of the solutions that have been tried.

CASE STUDY: TOPIC AREA

Focus on corporate reengineering – managing the change process

Five reengineering practitioners explain why these factors hold the key to performance improvement.

Turning a vision of radical performance improvement into hard results can test management to the limit. Potential difficulties can be encountered at all stages of the cycle. Targets may be too modest to stimulate breakthrough solutions. But by far the greatest set of problems cluster round the management of change and corporate culture.

'The more projects I have done, the more I have come to realise the importance of change management', says Martin Boiling, a partner with Price Waterhouse with extensive experience of reengineering. 'Once you start tackling major projects you end up with a much more complex programme of change, and that means handling the people problems. It has been a traditional blind spot for most companies', says Boiling.

Typically, it is at the implementation phase that reengineering starts to show the stresses and strains of change. But if diagnosed and treated in time, the symptoms need not be fatal.

In 1993 SmithKline Beecham set itself the goal of establishing a single supply chain process supported by appropriate information technology systems to replace the jumble of incompatible systems and practices that linked its 150-plus trading units worldwide. In the end, its project turned out to be a success. Initial indications are that the group is likely to achieve a 60 per cent improvement in cycle times, 40 per cent improvement in inventory and error rates close to zero. But this was one reengineering project that could easily have been added to the log of failure stories.

'There are always peaks and troughs in projects', says Robert Abel, director and vice president, inter-company trade, SmithKline Beecham. 'But in this case the trough was deeper than anticipated.' The reason why was not immediately clear, although it was apparent the project was lacking the support and commitment it needed to be driven forward.

It was around this time that Abel became aware of the change management concepts and techniques pioneered by ODR, an American-based company that had started out in the 1970s studying success factors in corporate change. Relating their framework to the problem showed where the main problem lay. Executive sponsors had been inadequately involved in the initiative. While he now understood how the reengineering programme should be managed, Abel was saddled with a difficult situation. There had been a change of ownership and senior executives. 'When the new owners asked what was going on, the perception from the business was not very positive', he says. 'It was that much harder to get started again, we had to go back to basics. It was a hard sell.'

By this stage, the project had not entirely fizzled out but had gone underground. 'It was kept going through the personal network, more or less as a favour', says Abel. Its revival hinged on the readiness of the new executive to take up the sponsor's role and provide active support. Abel successfully put the case for continuation by demonstrating that, although patchy, some progress had been made. Given the green light again, Abel applied the ODR tools and techniques to the project. This provided the means for engaging people to play their essential roles. That included senior executives as sponsors and front line staff as change agents, individuals prepared to play an active role in facilitating change over and above their regular commitments. Just as selling sponsorship to senior executives had been difficult, winning others to play their part in the change management process presented challenges.

'Change agents were hard to find', says Abel. 'We did it through education by looking at the issue from the "what's in it for me?" angle, and people signed up for it.'

As a result of getting the project back on track, Abel has now won himself the job of sorting out supply chain issues for the group and its external suppliers.

▶

SmithKline Beecham's experience underlines the high-risk nature of reengineering. 'If you can reach your goal through continuous improvement then this is always preferable because reengineering is disruptive, risky and demands a high level of commitment', says Mark Maletz, managing director of Business Process Design Associates, whose career is rooted in process improvement at Xerox and American Airlines. The choice depends on how wide the gulf is between current and target performance levels. It is this gap that has been key to persuading some companies that reengineering is the only option.

Initially, British Airways Engineering believed poor information flows from the support areas of the business to aircraft maintenance staff was what was holding back performance. But it became apparent that there was a more basic problem to be tackled.

'Reengineering is the vehicle for creating a new way of working within the engineering business', says Ray Claydon, project manager, British Airways Engineering. When the programme is completed, it will affect a workforce of 9500 people. The vision for the reengineered organisation was signed off in June 1995 and work is now well advanced.

'Implementation has been a major challenge', says Claydon. 'It involves project management on a massive scale to coordinate change across the entire business.'

Central to the programme was the restructuring of the business to create a number of cross-functional teams to support and manage aircraft maintenance, component overhaul, design modifications and supply chain logistics. Processes and product groups have replaced departments as the principle for the new organisational structure. Self-sufficient business units will each have their own integrated technical support, production, engineering, planning and other management support facilities.

British Airways Engineering has placed great emphasis on the change management side of the project. Audio-visual presentations for all staff have been a key feature of the structured communications programme. This was followed by an open job forum where staff had the opportunity to find out about the reengineered organisation from the 'new world' managers and the new roles and responsibilities they will be required to take on. To date, the programme has affected 2500 support staff, most of whom have had to apply for these new jobs. Already, says Claydon, there is evidence of performance improvement. The reengineering project deliberately tackled the people and organisational changes first, leaving the systems strategy review until now. 'In this way we can be sure our future systems are designed to support our new ways of working', he says. If strong sponsorship and project management are features of successful reengineering projects, another factor is the close involvement of those most affected by the changes brought about by reengineering.

For Roger Boyes, financial director of the Halifax Building Society, this is an essential ingredient in the society's Finance 2000 project, now about half way through its two-year programme. 'I am asking the people involved to design the new systems. It's not me telling them what to do. I am empowering people to come up with new processes.'

Behind Finance 2000 is recognition that the changes that were begun in the 1980s with the deregulation of financial services require a new mindset and approach to serving the market. In the past, building societies have tended to be inward looking. But continuing rapid changes in financial services call for a different outlook.

'It is no good having a customer-facing branch network, if support does not recognise customers are both internal and external', says Boyes. The primary goal is to reengineer financial processes and services so they support the business unit strategy that will enable the Halifax to develop into a broad-based financial services organisation.

'We will have focused self-accounting business units, responsible for strategy and financial control with upward consolidation into the group', he says. 'This gives you the opportunity to reengineer all those processes.'

The programme of changes is extensive and will involve the introduction of fully loaded P&L reports at the business unit level, the application of leading-edge cost accounting techniques, distribution channel and customer profitability, the use of value engineering and the development of a balanced scorecard. But it is not only processes that will change. 'It doesn't make sense to have a customer-oriented branch network and inward looking support services', says Boyes. 'You've got to have one culture.'

According to Maletz, management should turn their attention to corporate culture to ensure it is aligned with the goals of the transformed organisation before embarking on any transformation programme. 'Unless that happens, you are unlikely to bring about the improvements you want.' In a reengineering context, the values, beliefs and behaviour consistent with the desired changes can include a willingness to take risks and experiment with new ways of working, increased responsibility and accountability among those who deal directly with customers, and a more entrepreneurial approach to business.

Maletz argues it is possible to turn round corporate culture, even in international groups, within two years or so. 'If they are prepared to tackle the three main dimensions of corporate culture: strategic direction, organisational structure and organisational behaviour as part of a timetabled programme of change, then the results can start to come through even faster than that. But it calls for a high level of commitment, time and energy.'

Siemens Nixdorf, one company with which he has been working, has bet its future on achieving a dramatic turn-round in its corporate culture to give it the capacity to compete in the global information technology market.

Inside two years, it started to win new business as a direct result of its transformation into a customer-focused, market-oriented company.

Organisationally, its switch to process-based operations has begun in conditions where the changes have the best chance of taking root.

Siemens Nixdorf, and other companies, are discovering that investing in what has been regarded in the past as the soft side of business pays off. The right corporate culture not only enables performance improvement to work well. It may be the only investment that can guarantee longer term success.

Source: Adapted from David Harvey, *VNU-NET*, 1 October 1996

Questions

1 What are the success factors for the change process referred to in relation to SmithKline Beecham?

2 What new structures were created as part of the British Airways reengineering?

3 Summarise the common solutions to problems faced by all companies in the case study.

IS and BPR

As will have been clear from the preceding analysis, IS is a key enabler in the BPR process. This operates on four main levels:

1 *Potential impact of new IT.* In this context, IT includes hardware, communications technology, systems software and systems development tools (including development languages and database technologies). The ability of the organisation to use this will depend to a large extent on its existing hardware and systems software strategy. For example, a strategy based on preserving an old mainframe environment may create fewer opportunities than one based on a more modern, up-to-date one (such as a client/server architecture). To make the shift away from the mainframe environment will be more involved and therefore costly, not least in respect of old legacy systems.

2 *Potential impact of new information systems.* This will be constrained both by the ability of the information technology infrastructure to support new information systems and by the existence of legacy systems. For example, an information system solution to a requirement that would be enabled by a significant amount of end-user development may be impossible to implement if there is little history of this within the organisation. Similarly, an information systems development that depended on taking advantage of relational database capability would be fundamentally constrained if existing legacy systems used non-database file storage techniques.

3 *Prototyping and IS support for BPR process.* As referred to above, software tools such as simulation and modelling applications make it possible to model both existing systems and the redesigned business processes. Such tools are frequently used in manufacturing applications where, for example, they may model operations and workflow, thus revealing bottlenecks within the production process that can then be removed by reorganising the process.

4 *Organisational culture and the ability to absorb new IS.* The culture of an organisation can have a profound impact on how it approaches IS investment decisions. For example, an organisation that can be categorised as conservative and thus valuing low-risk strategies, may well be reluctant to make IS investments which, although carrying an element of risk, could confer major competitive advantage if successful. Indeed, conflict will almost definitely occur if a dynamic MIS manager has an IS vision that conflicts with a fundamentally conservative organisational culture!

It could be argued, of course, that an organisation in this position is unlikely to make a success of a BPR project even if it embarked on one in the first place. Perhaps this explains why BPR failure rates are so high!

Chaffey (1998) refers to five guidelines for integrating IS strategy with BPR. These are shown in the box. These guidelines indicate the responsibilities that the IS manager has in an organisation for making BPR work. In particular, he or she is responsible for achieving standardisation across the processes and developing systems that are accepted by users, so easing the change process.

Guidelines for supporting process improvement

1 Develop and maintain an IT strategy that is integrated and aligned with the company's business goals

Closely aligned business and IT strategies are necessary so that IT solutions are implemented to support business goals, not so that developers can use 'cool new technology'. Information resources should be made available through collaborative systems to support decision making at all levels within the company: strategic, tactical and operational.

2 Create and foster a customer focus for the IT organisation and personnel

Action Technologies considers customer focus in processes so critical that its workflow process model is defined through specifying a customer and a supplier for each subprocess. This customer–supplier relationship puts the spotlight on customer service and can boost the quality of solutions delivered. Customer focus can apply to both internal or external customers.

3 Design an IT organisation that maximises support for the company's various business groups

This guideline indicates that although processes and their supporting teams may seem to operate independently, it would be a mistake to think there are no links between these processes. Groupware is important in allowing information to be shared between different teams as well as within teams.

4 Use a centralised IT function to set enterprise-wide architecture standards

This is important to ensure the adoption of common applications and standards throughout the company in order to reduce cost, but also to minimise technical problems of incompatibility between applications and promote information exchange throughout the organisation.

5 Develop a clearly communicated process for integrating new technology into the business

The final point emphasises the importance of explaining through training why new collaborative technologies are being introduced and developing a plan so that there are no surprises for employees as new technologies are brought in to support processes. A culture can be established where continuous change is familiar. It will then be no surprise when new technologies are introduced to support changing business needs.

▶ LOCATING THE INFORMATION SYSTEMS MANAGEMENT FUNCTION

There are two basic approaches to locating the information system function in an organisation, which operates at more than one location. These are the centralisation of all IS services at one office (usually head office) and decentralisation. It is unusual for a company to choose one extreme or the other; typically, the approach will vary for the different types of services. The approach chosen is significant, since it will have a direct correspondence to the quality of service available to the end-user departments and the cost of providing this service.

▶ What needs to be managed?

It is useful to make a distinction between information systems and information technology. As has been stated before, we can view IT as the infrastructure and an enabler, while information systems give a business the applications that produce the information for decision-making purposes. IS cannot exist without the IT to support it, but IT on its own does not of itself confer any business benefits.

For information technology the following must be managed:

◆ *Hardware platforms.* These need to be selected and supported (for example, it may be decided only to operate a client/server environment using UNIX workstations).

◆ *Network architectures.* An organisation currently operating a mixture of AS/400 computers and PCs may wish to focus on a particular network architecture for the PCs in order to facilitate easier integration with the AS/400 systems.

◆ *Development tools.* It may be desirable to adopt tools that permit more rapid development of new information systems. Such tools will need to be able to run on the selected hardware platform and also be compatible with chosen database management systems.

◆ *Legacy systems.* These systems may run on old hardware platforms and be difficult to integrate with planned systems development. While strictly an IS issue rather than an IT one, it may still be necessary in the short to medium term to provide the necessary IT support to allow these systems to continue to operate.

◆ *Operations management.* This covers a number of areas, including hardware management, capacity planning, security (backups, access control, error detection, archiving), technical support (for hardware and systems software), telecommunications and network management.

The areas that relate to information systems management are:

◆ *Business systems development.* Applications development falls into two broad categories: those applications which deal with corporate data and those which are departmental or personal in nature.

◆ *Migration and conversion strategy.* While strictly being part of the systems development process, migration from one system to another involves specialists from both IS/IT and functional business areas. For corporate information systems, many functional areas may be involved.

◆ *Database administration.* Today's information systems depend very much on database management systems (such as DB2, Oracle, Informix and Access).

◆ *User support and training.* All applications software users require support at some point. The objective is to get the right support to the right people at the right time.

◆ *End-user application development.* This is becoming increasingly popular, especially in medium to large organisations. Such development will not only require support (e.g. advice on appropriate development tools) but will require explicit management to ensure that wheels are not being invented and bug-ridden software produced.

◆ *Shared services.* Recent innovations such as e-mail and collaborative work systems (*see* the Hamamatsu/Lotus Notes case study in Chapter 19) have both local and corporate application. The objective should be to maximise local flexibility while at the same time ensuring that organisation-wide standards are adhered to (the same could be said of end-user development).

◆ *IS/IT staffing.* While this is more of a human resources issue than an IT one, it is, nevertheless, important to stress that for an IT strategy to be implemented, there need to be staff with expertise in hardware, communications, systems software and development software. Naturally, for a small business this expertise will be limited.

This analysis indicates that there are some aspects of IS/IT that need central control and management, but at the same time there are local needs that have to be addressed within individual functional areas of the business. Therefore, we should now move from *what* needs to be managed to *where* IS/IT needs to be managed and the factors that influence this.

▶ Structuring information systems management

In a large company with several sites, IS/IT management must be organised and located in such a way as to ensure full integration of business and IS/IT strategies, as well as full support for the IS/IT needs of each functional area of the business.

Questions that should be asked when ascertaining the best approach include:

◆ *Is information systems management (ISM) in tune with corporate strategy?* Structures need to exist in such a way that an organisation's information systems strategy is fully embedded within its business strategy. This means that mechanisms must exist that embrace all functional areas of the business as well as the most senior management.

◆ *Is ISM in tune with organisational shape?* A heavily centralised approach to managing all aspects of IS/IT may conflict with a geographically dispersed organisation, or with one where individual functional areas enjoy a high degree of local autonomy.

◆ *Is the focus of ISM inward looking on managing technology)?* If this is the case, it suggests that IS/IT is operating mainly in a support capacity rather than a strategic one. An alternative, less palatable explanation is that the IS/IT department is rooted in the past and does not see IS/IT as being an integral part of business strategy.

◆ *Is the focus of ISM outward looking on helping the business plan the best use of technology)?* A positive answer to this question indicates a modern approach to IS/IT management. One can look at all aspects of IS/IT, from getting the best management information from existing transaction processing systems to implementing a company-wide communications strategy to enable business processes to be reengineered and facilitate better links to customers and suppliers.

There are a number of additional factors that will influence the structuring of information systems management. An organisation that operates in a single geographic location will have different needs from one that is spread over many sites (perhaps over many countries). Similarly, a business that has a diverse range of products and business operations may need an ISM different from that of a single product company. If a large organisation has a number of discrete strategic business units, it may be appropriate to treat each distinct SBU as a separate entity in its own right for ISM purposes.

One must also not ignore the impact of organisational culture and management style on ISM structure. An organisation that has a **decentralised** management philosophy may find it easier to decentralise certain ISM functions than one that is highly **centralised**. King (1983) discusses these issues.

There are two approaches to IS/IT management. The centralised approach will concentrate all aspects of IS/IT management at a single point within the organisation, such as the data processing or management information systems (MIS) department. An MIS department may either report into a single functional business area (traditionally, the accounting department has been a popular choice) or it may report directly at board level. The modern trend is for MIS managers or chief information officers (CIO) to report directly at board level in the same way as heads of functional areas such as HRM, sales and finance.

The decentralised approach recognises that some aspects of IS/IT management are best located close to the point of use. If any degree of decentralisation exists, the inference is that there will be staff located within the parts of the organisation that enjoy a degree of local autonomy. In some cases, the staff will be IS/IT professionals who might otherwise be located in a more centralised structure.

Alternatively, there may be 'hybrid' personnel who have both functional area expertise and good IS/IT skills. Aspects of IS/IT that lend themselves well to a degree of decentralisation are the development of end-user applications, use of report generators with corporate data as the main input, and finally information systems in functional areas that carry out discrete activities not connected with primary business functions (such as plant maintenance or HRM systems).

For centralised and decentralised approaches there are advantages. With the centralised approach, it is suggested that it is possible to:

✓ achieve and control consistent IS/IT strategy without having to worry what individual functional business areas are doing;

✓ coordinate IS/IT activities more easily;

✓ implement simpler control systems, since it will not be necessary to monitor the quality of the distributed IS/IT activities;

✓ allocate resources more efficiently, using the benefit of economies of scale and eliminating the risk of similar applications being developed in different parts of the organisation;

✓ achieve speedier strategic decision making because of fewer parties being involved.

Supporters of the decentralised approach also claim a number of advantages:

✓ The presence of IS/IT expertise at a functional level allows for a rapid response to local problems without the competition for resources that exists with the centralised approach.

✓ Where local decisions can be made about IS/IT that directly affects that area, improved motivation and commitment among staff to their information systems is likely.

Decentralised IS management

Management of some IS services in individual operating companies or at regional offices, but with some centralised control.

Centralised IS management

The control of all IS services from a central location, typically in a company head office or data centre.

✓ The cumbersome overhead associated with purely centralised systems is reduced.

The decentralised approach also has a number of problems associated with it:

✗ Where responsibilities are split (e.g. between operational and strategic matters), they need to be very carefully defined if matters are not to be forgotten.

✗ Central management may become frustrated by what they perceive as an idiosyncratic approach being adopted within the functional business areas (and vice versa).

✗ Split responsibilities may result in complicated control procedures which make decision making more difficult and time consuming. No one location will be correct for all organisations. Indeed, as an organisation moves towards the maturity stage, it will evolve different locations for different areas of information systems management.

For those who get the balance right between centralised and decentralised services, they can expect to enjoy:

✓ rapid information systems development;

✓ harmonious IS and business relationships;

✓ an IS service that is tailored for the user community;

✓ a cost-effective IS/IT function;

✓ development of technology infrastructures that support the required information systems;

✓ business success through successfully implemented IS/IT strategies;

✓ adoption of appropriate IS strategies;

✓ effective change management processes;

✓ encouragement of end-user computing where appropriate;

✓ accurate assessment of IS/IT costs and benefits, thus ensuring value for money from IS/IT investments.

On the other hand, those organisations that fail can expect:

✗ continual conflict between functional business areas and the IS/IT function;

✗ continual complaints about information systems management as a whole;

✗ business decline or inefficient service provision;

✗ lack of interest in information systems by non IS/IT personnel;

✗ skills problems – either shortages in certain areas or wasteful duplication;

✗ high staff turnover;

✗ gaps and overlaps in the provision of IS/IT services.

CASE STUDY: TOPIC AREA

Security Services Limited (SSL)

Introduction

SSL has grown over the last 30 years to be one of the main providers of private security services in the UK. Turnover for the previous financial year was up 17 per cent to £98.4 million from the previous year. Profitability has remained steady at around 9.2 per cent of turnover for three successive financial years. SSL provides a wide range of services to companies, individuals and the public sector. The company has grown due to a combination of factors, including organic growth from the original core business, startups in associated areas of security and finally takeover of and merger with companies providing related services. The range of services offered includes:

◆ armoured transport for conveying substantial amounts of cash and cheques between businesses and banks, cash from banks to businesses for wages and conveyance of high-value items between various parties;

◆ provision of security services for businesses – these will include security guards (day and/or night-time cover), analysis and installation of security devices and regular security sweeps of business premises;

◆ provision of domestic security services – this includes the analysis of domestic security needs and the installation of appropriate security devices.

The most recent addition to the range of services has been the transfer of prisoners between police cells, the courts and prison. This is a contracted-out service sanctioned by the Home Office and carried out to Home Office standards.

Company organisation

Because of the way in which SSL has evolved, the present company structure does not necessarily represent the most effective or efficient way of doing business.

SSL has its corporate headquarters in Milton Keynes, Buckinghamshire. It also has four discrete divisions, each of which represents a key area of the business. The divisions are geographically separate from the corporate headquarters and are organised as follows:

◆ *Private Transport Division (PTD)*. Based in Bedford, it also has offices in the county town of every county in England and Wales.

◆ *Business Security Division (BSD)*. Based in Leicester, it too has offices in the county town of every county in England and Wales.

◆ *Domestic Security Division (DSD)*. Based in Newcastle-upon-Tyne, it has similar provision of offices to the above two divisions.

◆ *Home Office Services Division (HOSD)*. Based in Central London, the precise organisation of this division will be covered later.

None of the divisions shares its premises with any of the other divisions. This is in part due to the way in which the business has evolved (including takeovers and mergers). However, it is also due to the very separate operation of each division.

Divisional responsibilities

The autonomous nature of the PTD, BSD and DSD divisions means that in effect they carry out all the activities associated with an individual business. The way in which each division carries out its business activities varies from division to division.

Private Transport Division (PTD)

◆ *Sales section*. This is charged for in two ways: (a) contract sales, negotiated for various periods and typically relating to regular transport of specific items between two or more locations; (b) once-off sales – for single transportation tasks arranged by customers on an *ad hoc* basis. The sales area is headed by a senior sales manager based at the divisional headquarters. Each area office also has a sales coordinator together with a number of sales executives.

◆ *Marketing section*. This function is performed by a small marketing department of two persons based at the divisional headquarters. Annual marketing spend is small. This division carries out core, well-established business operations with limited scope for growth.

◆ *Transport section*. This is the key area for this division: the business operations depend on scheduling the appropriate vehicle for the appropriate route and with the right security team. In addition, activities such as vehicle maintenance and staff duty rostering have to be managed.

◆ *Information systems section*. This is part of the transport section; the division operates a network of three PCs running the following applications:

◆ financial ledgers (Sage Sovereign);

◆ route planning (Autoroute);

◆ duty rostering (end-user developed spreadsheet).

Payroll processing is contracted out to Midwest Bank Business Services.

Job costing for new and renewed contracts is performed manually, as is once-off business. This is an area where a new information system may be useful.

The IS function in this division is managed by an ex-policeman who gained some IT experience while in the force but who is not an IT specialist. However, he has made judicious use of consultant support since his appointment.

Business Security Division (BSD)

This part of the business has experienced steady growth over the past five years. Recent developments have included a response to increased levels of computer theft in small to medium high-tech companies. An objective of this division is to continue with this organic growth while at the same time increasing its profile in the high-tech marketplace. The management structure is well established and comprises:

◆ *Sales*. This is managed by a team of sales consultants based at each office. At office level, it is managed by a senior sales consultant. The senior sales consultants report into the sales director in Leicester. Sales data is recorded on a PC-based sales ledger and monthly sales figures are sent to Milton Keynes on floppy disk. This department also runs a separate, standalone, PC-based sales tracking and marketing system. A subsection of this department is an installations section that is responsible for supplying and fitting security equipment as ordered by the customers.

◆ *Marketing*. There is no specific section dealing with this: marketing is perceived as being little more than advertising and leaflet drops in each geographic area and it is left to the sales force to accomplish this.

◆ *Finance section*. This division has a separate finance function that runs a range of standalone, PC-based financial ledgers. Purchase and general ledger information is communicated to head office on hard copy – this is because the ledgers are incompatible with the systems used at head office. Payroll processing is also carried out in-house using the Pegasus payroll package on a standalone PC.

◆ *Purchasing section*. This is a subset of the finance section that deals with equipment procurement for the installations section. Manual purchase data is passed to the finance section for processing.

The IS function is now managed by a 24-year-old graduate in business computing who has just replaced a recently retired senior accountant.

Domestic Security Division (DSD)

This is the most recently established division, having been created by the acquisition from the receivers of a nation-wide chain of domestic security specialists within the last six months. SSL has inherited a sound infrastructure of local offices and a reasonable customer base and has been concentrating on turning round a business operation that failed principally due to inadequate financial controls.

The key issues for this division are to expand the customer base by (a) increasing the number of customers; (b) marketing new services (e.g. security audits); and (c) emphasising the need for ongoing maintenance of existing security systems.

This division is devolved to area office level, with each office responsible for the local management of the sales activity, materials procurement and installation. Costs and revenues are therefore managed at the local level, with little current coordination by the divisional head office in Newcastle-upon-Tyne. Currently, the divisional head office is responsible only for collecting financial data from each of the branches (provided by them manually and in a variety of different formats), which it then collates and then passes to SSL headquarters, again in manual paper form. SSL realises that it has to do something about the whole setup in order to establish a strategic and operational direction for this division.

There is no IS investment and no specialist IS staff in this division.

Home Office Services Division (HOSD)

This division was set up some three years ago as a result of a successful tender to manage the transportation of prisoners between police cells, the courts and the Prison Service. In addition to the divisional headquarters in central London, there are six regional offices throughout England and Wales. From these offices, the transport of prisoners and deployment of staff are coordinated. In addition to staff in the transportation vehicles, a number of staff are stationed permanently at police stations in each county.

The divisional headquarters is responsible for:

◆ coordination of the regional offices;

◆ ensuring that the contractual arrangements are adhered to;

◆ accurately costing both the standard service provision and any additional services offered;

◆ processing accounts payable and receivable and providing financial and management accounting information to SSL's headquarters (manual hard copy only).

This division is the best organised in computing terms: the divisional headquarters runs an IBM AS/400 minicomputer that has a set of financial ledgers, budgeting and costing software purchased from KCB Ltd (a specialist in AS/400 financial systems); each regional office has a PC running routing and rostering software; each regional PC is linked to the AS/400 over a WAN; the divisional headquarters also has a number of PCs running business productivity-type packages (e.g. spreadsheet) that are also linked to the AS/400 (thus allowing the download of data to the PCs for further analysis). The division's computing is managed by a 'hybrid' manager with both financial and IT expertise. There is also one analyst/programmer and one operator/programmer.

SSL headquarters

The company has yet to rise to the challenge represented by an increasingly diverse yet related range of business operations. Similarly, its previous underinvestment in IS has meant that the divisional areas can only send information in manual form only where it is rekeyed into relatively old, mainframe-based financial systems.

The divisional nature of SSL means that the activities at headquarters are principally general and financial management oriented.

The IT department is somewhat old-fashioned and certainly less up to date than some of the divisions. In addition to a DP manager, there are six data entry clerks who are responsible for rekeying financial data from the divisions, three programmers, a systems analyst and two

computer operator/systems programmers. The DP manager is about to retire and SSL must consider how it wishes to manage IS both at headquarters and divisional level.

Questions

It is recommended that up to one hour should be spent on each question.

1 Analyse how SSL may identify the value it obtains from its current portfolio of information systems and evaluate the techniques that may be used in assessing future IS investments.

2 In many parts of the company, it is clear that SSL does not have a coherent IS strategy. Analyse how it may construct an IS strategy that is supportive of its business strategy and the benefits that it would derive from this.

3 Analyse the strategic potential for greater investment in information systems and technology at SSL, both from a divisional and company-wide perspective. Could business process reengineering be a useful tool in maximising the potential of IS and IT within the company? Explain and justify your answers.

4 Describe the current location of IS functions within SSL. Recommend the best location for IT services in the future.

▶ OUTSOURCING

Outsourcing occurs when a function of a company, which was traditionally conducted internally by company staff, is instead completed by a third party. The main reasons for doing this are usually cost reduction and to enable focus on the core business. The functions that are commonly outsourced include catering, cleaning, public relations and information systems.

Outsourcing is a major trend in the development and management of information systems. Analysts IDC estimate that the global outsourcing market will exceed $121 billion by the year 2000, with outsourcing exhibiting a compound annual growth rate of nearly 10 per cent through to the end of the century. Major public and private organisations in the UK such as the Inland Revenue and Rolls-Royce have outsourced their IS management to Electronic Data Systems (EDS). Outsourcing is currently most popular in central government and the financial services industries (Table 14.2).

With the growth in popularity of outsourcing it is likely that outsourcing will be increasingly adopted across all sectors. According to an ITnet survey quoted by Sharon Smith (1997), total outsourcing revenue in the UK is over £2 billion, with a growth rate of 40 per cent a year; £2 billion represents nearly 20 per cent of the £11 billion value of the UK software and computing services industry.

Information systems outsourcing

All or part of the information systems services of a company are subcontracted to a third party.

Table 14.2 UK outsourcing market by sector

Market by sector	Percentage of sector
Central government	24%
Financial services	20%
Engineering	14%
Energy and utilities	11%
Local government	8%
Retail and distribution	7%
Health	5%
Other	10%

Source: ITnet survey

▶ Types of outsourcing

There are different degrees of outsourcing, varying from total outsourcing to partial management of services. It is best to consider the types of outsourcing services offered rather than terms such as facilities management and time sharing, which are open to different interpretations. The main categories of services that can be managed include:

Time sharing

The processing and storage capacity of a mainframe computer is rented to several companies using a leasing arrangement.

Facilities management (FM)

The management of a range of IT services by an outsourcing provider. These commonly include network management and associated software and hardware.

1 *Hardware outsourcing.* This may involve renting time on a high-capacity mainframe computer. Effectively, the company is sharing the expense of purchasing and maintaining the network with other companies which are also signed up to an outsourcing contract. This arrangement is sometimes known as a **time-sharing** contract.

2 *Network management.* Network management may also be involved when managing hardware: here a third party is responsible for maintaining the network. This is often referred to as **facilities management** or FM, which may also include management of PC and server hardware.

3 *Outsourcing systems development.* When specialised programs are required by a business, it is necessary either to develop bespoke software or to modify existing systems. This is also a significant outsourcing activity. When EDS undertook its contract with the Inland Revenue in the UK, one of its main tasks was to write the software to deal with changes to the way in which tax forms were submitted.

4 *IS support.* A company help desk can be outsourced to a third party. This could cover answering queries about operating systems, office applications or specific company applications. It could also include fixing problems, in which case an onsite presence would be required. Microsoft outsources much of its support for Windows 95 and 98 to third parties such as Digital.

5 *Management of IS strategy.* Determining and executing the information systems strategy is less common than the other types of outsourcing outlined above, because many companies want to retain this control. A great deal of trust will be placed in the outsourcing partner in this arrangement and it is most common in a total outsourcing contract.

6 *Total outsourcing.* An example of total outsourcing is the 1996 agreement between Thorn Europe and IBM Global Services. This five-year contract involves IBM taking over all IT operations on hardware from five different vendors, managing 90 staff and defining and implementing the IT strategy as well.

A 1996 report by Olivetti on outsourcing among 700 UK MIS managers at large sites (more than 1000 PCs) showed that a mix of in-house and outsourced functions is most common. Only 19 per cent rely exclusively on in-house services. An example of a company that uses a mixed approach is Rolls-Royce and Associates, which has customers in the defence sector. While functions such as accounting and management reporting systems have been outsourced to EDS, the specialised IS functions and confidential work involving mathematical modelling and product design have been kept in-house.

Anglian Water Services Limited and CSC – an outsourcing partnership?

MINI CASE

In October 1995 Anglian Water Services Limited and CSC (Computer Sciences Corporation) signed a contract for 10 years. Under this agreement, Anglian transferred the whole information services operation including staff to CSC with the exception of telemetry (monitoring of water flows). The contract covered the development of new systems for five years. The contract is regarded as a partnership by both parties. Principles agreed by both parties to try to achieve success were:

◆ all investment in IS is aimed at achieving specific business objectives;

◆ objectives must be clearly identified before investment;

◆ business users must justify their case and deliver the benefits;

◆ full lifecycle costs must be identified up front;

◆ investment and legacy systems must be minimised;

◆ business and IS are jointly responsible for development.

At the start of the contract the majority of information systems staff were transferred to Anglian Water, with only 17 IS staff retained within Anglian to manage the contract and work directly with CSC.

One of the first tasks was to standardise on common hardware and software, since the original devolved IS management had resulted in a less standardised arrangement. As part of this standardisation, SAP was implemented as a single ERP application that replaced 13 existing applications and provided services to 1000 users. It is now also possible for staff to hot-desk – they can log in from any computer.

Anglian staff have found that the main difficulty with operating the partnership is that inevitably in cases of disagreement it is necessary to use a formal contract. For example, no service-level agreement was in place initially, but one had to be established later. A further problem for the staff was that they thought that CSC could provide all the answers, but Anglian inputs needed to describe their particular industry and way of working.

Questions

1 What problems can you identify with the partnership arrangement?

2 Can you suggest any additional recommendations to ensure success?

▶ Why do companies outsource?

The main reasons for IS outsourcing are to achieve the following:

◆ *Cost reduction.* An outsourcing vendor can share its assets, such as mainframes and staff, between different companies and achieve economies of scale. It is also argued by outsourcing vendors that lower costs are achieved since they are in a contractual relationship, unlike most internal providers of IT services.

◆ *Quality improvements and customer satisfaction.* Through outsourcing IS functions to a company which is expert in this field, it should be possible to deliver better-quality services to internal and external customers. Better quality could be in the form of systems that are more reliable and have appropriate features, a more reliable company network and better phone support.

◆ *Enables focus on core business.* A company can concentrate its expertise on what it is familiar with, i.e. its market and customers, rather than being distracted by information systems development. This particular argument is weak in some industries such as the financial services sector where information systems are critical to operating in a particular market.

◆ *Reduce risk of project failure.* Owing to the contract, there is more pressure on the supplier compared with internal developers to deliver a quality product on time, hence it is more likely to succeed.

◆ *Implementation of a strategic objective.* To implement a strategic objective may involve considerable risk if it is undertaken internally or resources are not available. For example, in the mid-1990s many companies undertook outsourcing to ensure that the 'millennium bug' could be fixed by using a third party with the expertise to solve the problem (this is true of the Anglian example in the case study). Similarly, in the mid-1990s many companies were undertaking business process reengineering initiatives that often involve major changes to information systems.

Reasons for outsourcing

The top 10 reasons companies outsource (in alphabetical order), according to the Outsourcing Institute:

1 Accelerate reengineering benefits.

2 Access to world-class capabilities.

3 Cash infusion.

4 Free resources for other purposes.

5 Function difficult to manage or out of control.

6 Improve company focus.

7 Make capital funds available.

8 Reduce operating costs.

9 Reduce risk.

10 Resources not available internally.

Source: http://www.outsourcing.com, Outsourcing Institute

Whether these benefits are achievable is currently the subject of a great deal of debate, with the detractors of outsourcing arguing that although costs may be reduced, the quality of the service will also decline. Since outsourcing is a relatively new phenomenon, it is not clear whether the promises are achieved, but the number of companies signing up to outsourcing contracts indicates that it is a major industry trend. Other problems that may occur are that IT staff are likely to be unhappy, as they are transferred to a third-party company with new contracts. To summarise this section, reasons given by companies as to why they have outsourced are given in Table 14.3.

Table 14.3 Main reasons for outsourcing

Reason	Percentage mentioning
Cost savings	57%
Improved quality of service	40%
Access to specialist expertise	37%
Increased flexibility	27%
Strategic business decision	21%
Free management time	19%
Lack of resources	11%
Improved financial control	8%

Examine Table 14.3 and assess which of the reasons for outsourcing would be important to the following:

1 Financial manager (chief finance officer).

2 Information systems manager.

3 Managing director.

4 Departmental manager in human resources, marketing or production.

ACTIVITY

PROBLEMS OF OUTSOURCING

Collins and Millen (1995) cite the following concerns over outsourcing:

◆ loss of control of IS;

◆ loss/degradation of internal IS services;

◆ corporate security issues;

◆ qualifications of outside personnel;

◆ negative impact on employee morale.

In addition to these problems, case studies seem to suggest that the principal objective of undertaking outsourcing, cost reduction, may not be achieved in many cases. Cost reduction is usually thought to occur due to a reduction in the number of staff employed and savings on the cost of acquisition of hardware and software through discounts available due to economies of scale. For example, the UK National Audit Office reported in 1996 that through outsourcing Home Office IT to Sema Group, savings of £23.6 million would occur. However, a survey from the UK National Computing Centre reported that only 15 per cent of managers with experience in dealing with external suppliers thought that outsourcing was a good way to save money, while 46 per cent didn't agree that outsourcing reduced service costs.

Lacity and Hirscheim (1995), in their classic study of outsourcing, identify the following reasons for escalating costs:

◆ Not identifying present and future requirements fully, and leaving loopholes in the contract.

◆ Failing to identify the full costs and service levels of existing in-house operations, with the result that contracts turn out to cost more than originally anticipated because in-house calculations were too low.

◆ Change of character clauses prompting excess fees for any changes in service or functions.

◆ Software licence transfer clauses making customers responsible for fees.

◆ Fixed prices that soon exceed market prices because the cost of IT is decreasing.

◆ Fluctuations in data processing volumes not covered by fixed limits under the contract, and incurring significantly higher fees.

◆ Paying extra for services that the customer assumed were included in the fixed price, because of poor analysis beforehand of services provided by the in-house group leading to a limited fixed-price contract.

◆ Subsidising the vendor's learning curve.

◆ Changes in technology: vendors offer services on existing platforms and subsequent moves into new technology often cost more than anticipated.

These types of problems are illustrated by the *1998 Global Survey of Chief Information Executives* by Deloitte and Touche Consulting Group. This survey seems to suggest that what are perceived as the desired benefits of outsourcing often turn out to be the biggest disappointment, suggesting that in many, but not all, cases, outsourcing fails to deliver the anticipated benefits.

Table 14.4 Summary of perceptions of outsourcing

Objective	% who perceived as most desired benefit of outsourcing	% who perceived as greatest disappointment of outsourcing
Cost reduction	33%	59%
Transition to new technology	41%	42%
Improved quality	47%	51%
Focus on core competencies	49%	41%
Supplier expertise	52%	59%

Source: 1998 Global Survey of Chief Information Executives, Deloitte and Touche Consulting Group

To avoid some of the problems outlined above, the design of the contract is critical to ensure that the supplier provides a full service. For network management this can be achieved through service-level agreements (SLAs) that specify minimum acceptable values for availability of the network, such as 99.8 per cent access or give the maximum number of failures per month. It is more difficult to specify in a contract services to be provided for developing software. As a result of this, the costs of outsourced software development can spiral. Further details on defining contracts for information systems development are given in the final section of this chapter.

The case study on retail outsourcing shows how retailers have embraced outsourcing during the 1990s. It includes examples of several companies and illustrates well the problems they faced and how they attempted to manage them.

CASE STUDY: TOPIC AREA

Retail outsourcing: better out than in?

The main driving force behind outsourcing in the retail sector is the need to find partners that can assist in managing the growing complexity of the IT environment. These partners must embrace new technologies and use IT to drive the business, as opposed to just keeping up with it. The old agenda of cutting costs and reducing headcount remains, but has changed face somewhat.

Chris Tawton, marketing manager for Digital, says, 'Saving money no longer applies. Retailers now want to make the money work harder.' Terry Skodak, account executive for supermarkets at EDS in the US, says, 'When competition hit retailers, they suddenly realised that IT had a strategic role to play. Carnegie Mellon University worked out that they had just 36 months to transform their IT infrastructure.'

So far, 7–11, Smiths Food & Drug, Brunos and Reiser have farmed out to EDS. Richard Young, manager of managed services at ICL, explains, 'Retailers that learnt the hard way by doing things themselves are welcoming outsourcing. Others want to improve their status with the business and see it as a way to take the pressure off them.'

Russell Wolak, services marketing manager at Olivetti, says, 'Retailers are coming to realise the true cost of IT and outsourcing is ideal for reducing the cost of ownership.' Identifying invisible costs – which can be two to five times greater than visible ones – is not easy in a distributed environment, but once they have come to light retailers realise that outsiders can often do a better job.

Hoskyns associate director Alan Glover wonders what took them so long. 'They have got used to outsourcing warehousing, security and distribution, so why not for less controversial, non-core activities like IT?' BhS, Thorn Europe, Granada and John Menzies have all contracted out their IT and now other retailers are beginning to talk seriously about facilities management. John Menzies Retail, a 274-newsagent chain, got the picture and outsourced to CSC in 1995 in a deal valued at $60m (£40m) over 10 years. CSC now manages the company's entire datacentre operations from mainframe to desktop and provides strategic planning as well. The company recruited 30 Menzies staff. Menzies Retail finance director, John McCoach, says, 'Now, all that remains is a very small in-house team which works on strategy and liaises with CSC.' McCoach's explanation of Menzies' reasons for outsourcing bears out the view that retailers are having to revamp their technology to meet competition not only from each other but also from new entrants that are using remote channels to reach customers. 'We were an early adopter of fourth generation languages and Unix so there was nothing wrong with the technology we had.' he says. 'It's just that we wanted to make a giant leap to Oracle and new electronic point-of-sale systems. Not only was the investment massive but also we didn't have the skills in-house. We could have carried on as we were but market forces said we needed to get ahead.'

As at Menzies, the goal at BhS was to make swift changes to the business and build for the future. CSC took over BhS's Luton data centre and now runs the entire information infrastructure. CSC is responsible for purchasing and asset management, and the introduction of new technologies such as neural networking and multimedia. Establishing the reasons to outsource is the easy bit. Choosing a partner is more tricky. McCoach and the IT team at Menzies took a close look at both CSC and EDS in the US and also visited BhS. McCoach says, 'Technically, they were both highly competent but we felt that we had a better fit with CSC. We now work in partnership and accept that, like all relationships, there will be ups and downs.'

◄ 527

Choosing a partner is not always straightforward and this is not the first time that the technology supplier has been judged on cultural as well as technical worthiness. It is said that, at Lucas, EDS had the deal all sown up but at the 11th hour, the retailer signed with CSC after it had seen at first hand how EDS worked.

It is generally said that EDS is prescriptive and less committed to partnerships. This has not prevented it from building a huge business, particularly in the US where retail outsourcing is more mature. In the UK, retailers tend to stress their desire to work closely with partners that understand their business and that can harness diverse technologies into a logical whole.

The beauty parade for retail outsourcing is short but formidable. For total facilities management, the options are EDS, IBM, Hoskyns and CSC. It seems that only the large suppliers can combine resources with the sheer nerve required. On the other hand, recognising impossibly long sales cycles, difficult politics and uncertain outcomes, some suppliers take a step back into selective outsourcing or out-tasking. ICL, Siemens Nixdorf, Olivetti, Unisys and Digital claim to be able to handle full outsourcing but their portfolios are dominated by managed services, covering systems integration, network management and business recovery services.

They accept that deciding what is and what is not IT is the first challenge, particularly in a distributed environment, and that this can make it difficult to create manageable contracts. ICL's Young says, 'It is more risky to do total outsourcing because it is defined in business, not technical, terms.' This comment does seem to be borne out by retailers' experiences. McCoach says, 'The contract process was horrendous. There were troops of solicitors and specialists, mostly American, in and out all the time.'

Skodak says contracts are only complex because retailers cannot start from scratch. He adds, 'The main focus is on what the retailer has to undo, like reallocating resources, working out staff contracts and deciding what stays and what goes.' Whether caused by problems with contracts or with culture, the BhS outsourcing deal with CSC has not always run smoothly, though problems seem largely to have been resolved. The 1993, 11-year deal, valued at $200m (£133m), was supplemented with a nine-month business reengineering contract in 1994 and a further $100m (£66m) last year. However, when the second big tranche of cash was allocated, it was said by some that both BhS and CSC had underestimated the scale of the task ahead. Certainly, CSC has its work cut out. It agreed to a risk–reward clause in the contract by which its compensation is tied to tangible business results. CSC is also trying to slash the time it takes to get merchandise from design to store from as much as eight months to as little as two weeks. One executive involved in the contract says, 'The contract started as facilities management and BhS tried to move it to outsourcing, which hasn't entirely worked. BhS has retained the IT strategy against CSC's wish to add value, drive the business and get involved.' CSC came up with Vision 2000 to inject itself into the forefront, but

according to the executive, 'There was a change of direction and some proposals have been scaled down. Some money was allocated but nothing has yet been signed.'

Retailers will admit that they tend to base their entire view of outsourcing on the latest news from BhS, often fuelled by rumours. One said, 'If the BhS deal doesn't work, then retail outsourcing will die with it.' Difficulties also arise in measuring results, but Jonathan Eales, IT services controller at Woolworths, says, 'We get good service because of who we are but we do manage and monitor the contracts and have tight service level agreements (SLAs).'

Young, in turn, says, 'SLA is an abused term. The business can still collapse even if we stick to our agreement to fix a fault on site by turning up within two hours 95% of the time.' The SLA terms can be so hard to agree that at British Shoe, they have apparently not been signed yet. Skodak worries that the need for tight measurement will commoditise outsourcing. He says, 'Then, the lowest-cost operator will be the winner when outsourcing is all about adding value and making IT make the difference out in the business.'

For Menzies, the results so far have been largely positive. McCoach says, 'We now understand much better where our business is going and CSC puts it into language that anyone can understand. It is also good at training and has made the IT people more end-user friendly.' Ultimately, it is agreed that only a handful of retailers will ever outsource completely, mostly because they fear a loss of control or believe they already have IT taped. Skodak says, 'Very big players have the experience and the scale to manage technology themselves; they are unlikely to outsource.' And some retailers outsource only temporarily. Mothercare contracted out its legacy systems to Hoskyns, leaving it free to downsize and build a new store systems infrastructure. Once that was up and running, central systems were taken in-house again.

On balance, the trend seems to play into the hands of the partial outsourcers. According to Eales, Woolworths has a policy on what it will and will not consider. He says, 'It is important to have rules by which to judge and mainly that covers areas of expertise that we do not have in-house: a need for temporary skills or where we can see economies of scale. By outsourcing tasks that we have not done before, we can get up to speed quickly.'

Having said that, Woolworths has gradually outsourced more and more IT over the years: maintenance, disaster recovery, network systems management and mainframes have all been handed over, mainly to Hoskyns. Meanwhile, retailers continue to look for evidence that outsourcing is able to deliver on its grand promises. The jury is still out, mainly because many retailers remain tight-lipped about the benefits of outsourcing and are certainly not issuing figures. A number of retailers declined to specify the benefits for this report, suggesting that they are not yet comfortable with outsourcing and that it has a long way to go before being regarded as an everyday IT management option.

Source: Christopher Fields, *Computer Weekly,* 26 September 1996

Questions

1 What does the article suggest that companies experienced in outsourcing are now seeking to achieve?

2 What reasons do the managers at Menzies and BhS give for outsourcing?

3 What is an SLA? What is its relevance to outsourcing?

4 What are the views of the retailers on selective outsourcing in comparison to total outsourcing?

▶ Human factors and outsourcing

Outsourcing IS developments will have a direct impact on information systems staff and this needs to be managed. In the worse case staff may be made redundant, but in the majority of cases the outsourcing company will agree to employ existing IS staff while a core of IS staff remain with the company to manage the contract or functions that have not been outsourced. Redundancies tend not to occur, because this is part of the agreement between the company and the outsourcer to avoid resistance to change. Additionally, due to shortages of IS staff it is usually possible for the outsourcing company to redeploy staff if necessary.

Even if staff are not made redundant, transfer of staff will cause major disruption and often resentment. One main cause of this is that staff will be forced to sign a new contract when they transfer. While remuneration may be better, terms and conditions will change. For example, there may be no paid overtime, or staff may be asked to work elsewhere in the country on other outsourcing contracts. The mini case study shows the types of problems that can arise when outsourcing occurs if it is not managed sensitively. As well as disputes on terms and conditions such as remuneration, staff are not happy about the need to relocate. This particular problem has been compounded by the merger of the two banks (TSB and Lloyds).

Lloyds/TSB staff say 'yes' to strike action

MINI CASE

Finance union Bifu has received a unanimous 'yes' response to its postponed strike action ballot of Lloyds/TSB workers outsourced to IT services company Sema. All of the 91 ballot papers received from staff were in favour of action, and armed with that mandate, union official Hugh Roberts met with Sema representatives.

Now it has a yes vote, the Bifu can give Lloyds/TSB bank just seven days' notice before commencing a strike. The ballot of 103 staff at datacentres in Crawley and Andover was originally due to close at the end of February, but was retaken after the union found it had more members at the sites than it previously thought.

It is understood that staff have received improved compensation offers on those made by Lloyds/TSB and Sema two weeks ago. So far Sema has offered staff a goodwill payment of £1200 and a pay rise of 5% on top of the 3.5% received in January.

The bank has offered the staff employment, but cannot confirm which jobs are available or if they would be in Peterborough or London. If Bifu was to launch strike action now it would occur over the Easter period, and could cause severe problems for Lloyds/TSB customers trying to withdraw money from their accounts.

Source: Computer Weekly, 20 March 1997

Positive aspects of outsourcing for staff may include:

◆ improved rates of pay;
◆ better training;
◆ greater career opportunities for improving knowledge and promotion through working in a range of companies.

▶ Making outsourcing work

The critical role of the contract in ensuring that an outsourcing initiative will work has already been mentioned. In addition to this, other factors must be incorporated. These include:

◆ Outsourcing strategy must be consistent with the business and information management strategy.
◆ Level of outsourcing should be appropriate to the business: selective outsourcing for most businesses or total outsourcing where information systems play a mainly supporting role.
◆ A method of retaining control and leverage over the suppliers is necessary. This could include a shorter-term contract, a risk and reward contract, and not including strategic planning in the services to be outsourced.
◆ Human factors involved in outsourcing must be considered in conjunction with the human resources department, particularly where staff may be displaced or made redundant.
◆ If a company does not have previous experience of outsourcing, it may be valuable to get an independent specialist to assist in drawing up the outsourcing agreement.
◆ Allocating time and using measurement systems to manage the outsourcing contract.

Feeny *et al.* (1995) have identified alternative scenarios to help an organisation decide whether to stay in-house or to outsource. These are summarised in Table 14.5.

Table 14.5 Decision matrix for deciding which IS services stay in house

Business characteristic	Outsource	Don't outsource
Business positioning impact	Low	High
Links to business strategy	Low	High
Future business uncertainty	Low	High
Technological maturity	High	Low
Level of IT integration	Low	High
In-house vs market expertise	Low	High

The same authors cite the following statistics from the organisations they surveyed:

◆ 80 per cent had considered outsourcing;
◆ 47 per cent outsourced some or all of their information systems;
◆ 70 per cent did not have formal outsourcing policy in place;

◆ only 43 per cent of organisations that had outsourced actually have an outsourcing policy;
◆ few organisations approach outsourcing in a strategic manner.

▶ SUMMARY

1 Business strategy will embrace business decisions, the broad objectives and direction of the organisation and how it might cope with change – in other words, where the business is going and why. IS has an impact on this and provides potential for competitive advantage.

2 A company needs an information systems strategy that is rooted in business needs, meets the demand for information to support business processes and provides applications for key functional areas of the business.

3 If an organisation does not have a clear picture of what its strategy is, it is difficult to see how the right information systems can be put in place. In turn, if the information needs are unclear, it is difficult to see how the right technology can be put in place to satisfy those needs.

4 Since business strategies have the potential to be subjected to sudden and unpredictable change (or even evolutionary change), the IS and IT strategies that are needed to support changing business strategies must themselves be capable of adaptation and change if they are to continue to reflect the existing business strategy at any time. In reality, IS strategy must be embedded in an organisation's business strategy and be a fundamental part of it. Separation between the two is likely to result in a suboptimal solution, with organisations failing to gain the full benefits that information systems and the technology associated with them can bring.

5 Business process reengineering involves the radical redesign of business processes. It is often supported and enabled by information systems based on groupware, workflow and relational database systems. While many companies have attempted reengineering, the failure rate is high and there is a move to less radical process improvement programmes.

6 The alternatives for structuring or locating IS within an organisation range from centralised to decentralised. A hybrid approach is often used with some aspects of IS management, such as IS strategy and security centralised and others such as user support decentralised.

7 Outsourcing is a significant trend in IS management. It involves a third party undertaking some or all of the following IS activities:
◆ hardware outsourcing;
◆ network management or facilities management (FM);
◆ systems development;
◆ IS support;
◆ management of IS strategy.

When all activities are performed by the external company, this is known as total outsourcing. When some activities are performed, this is known as selective outsourcing. Outsourcing is driven by a desire to reduce costs while improving the quality of IS and user services. The debate on whether this is achieved frequently is still raging!

▶ EXERCISES

▶ Self-assessment exercises

1 When information systems costs are being considered, what kinds of costs would be considered *development* costs and what would be considered *operations/maintenance* costs?

2 How do strategic systems differ from high-potential projects?

3 Why do information systems projects fail?

4 Explain the difference between *project size* and *project complexity* when evaluating information systems risk.

5 Why might the mechanistic approach to strategy formulation be considered inadequate?

6 How might Porter's five forces model be helpful in determining information systems requirements?

7 Explain how a fast-food restaurant may use Porter's value chain analysis to help determine its information systems needs.

8 How might Nolan's stage model be useful to an organisation that is struggling with spiralling IS costs?

9 Identify three critical success factors for the maternity department of a busy hospital. How do those CSFs translate into key decisions and then information requirements?

10 Distinguish between IS as a key enabler of BPR and as a support tool for the BPR process itself.

11 Using the 'Focus on corporate reengineering' case study above, evaluate the importance of the change management process within BPR.

12 What are the main different types of outsourcing?

▶ Discussion questions

1 The millennium bug has demonstrated that organisations, more often than not, take a short-term view in their approach to information systems rather than a strategic one. Discuss.

2 Public-sector organisations such as the police and health service are incapable of delivering good-quality information systems because they are dominated by the need to demonstrate tangible benefits before any investment decisions are made. Discuss.

3 Far from being the 'greatest thing since sliced bread', BPR is simply a vehicle for consultants to sell expensive services that ultimately confer no major business benefits. Discuss.

4 Would you outsource the HRM or accounting functions of a company? If not, what is so different about IS/IT?

▶ Essay questions

1 Why do many new information systems seem to deliver poor value for money?

2 Far from being the ultimate enabler of business performance, BPR in reality is only undertaken by businesses which are desperate to turn round a loss-making situation. Is this view correct or are there wider benefits to be gained?

3 It has been said that when making IS investment decisions, organisations are dominated by organisational politics. Is this really true or are there other, more important issues at stake?

4 Top-down and bottom-up approaches to formulating information systems strategy are fine as far as they go. However, is there a case for a more eclectic or selective approach to the strategy formulation process?

5 What do you see as the main problems with outsourcing and how can they be overcome?

▶ Examination questions

1 Explain the concept of Porter's value chain and how it can be used to identify a company's information needs.

2 What are the two main alternatives for a company's location of its information systems? Summarise the benefits and disadvantages in terms of cost and control.

3 What is a legacy system? What problems do legacy systems present to IS managers?

4 How can McFarlan's strategic grid be used to define an information systems strategy for a company?

5 Explain the difference between a business impacting and business aligning approach to a company's IS strategy. Give examples of strategy tools that can help support each method.

6 Using the potential business applications of the Internet, show how Porter's five forces model can help identify opportunities for deploying information systems.

7 What information systems management activities would occur with a total outsourcing contract?

▶ References

Chaffey, D.J. (1988) *Groupware, Workflow and Intranets: Reengineering the Enterprise with Collaborative Software,* Digital Press.

Cibora, C. and Jelassi, T. (1994) *Strategic Information Systems: a European Perspective,* John Wiley, Chichester.

Collins, J.S. and Millen, R.A. (1995) 'Information systems outsourcing by large American firms: choices and impacts', *Information Resources Management Journal,* Winter, 8,1, 9–14.

Davenport, T.H. (1993) *Process Innovation: Re-engineering Work through Information Technology,* Harvard Business School Press, Boston, MA.

Edberg, D.T. (1997) 'Creating a balanced measurement program', *Journal of Information Systems Management,* Spring, 32–41.

Feeny, D., Fitzgerald, G., Willcocks, L. (1995) 'Outsourcing IT: the strategic implications', *Long Range Planning,* October, 28,5, 59–71.

Galliers, R.D. and Sutherland, A.R. (1991) 'Information systems management and strategy management and formulation: the stages of growth model revisited', *Journal of Information Systems,* Vol 1, No 2, 89–114.

Hammer, M. and Champy, J. (1993) *Reengineering the Corporation: a Manifesto for Business Revolution,* HarperCollins, New York.

Hirscheim, R., Earl, M.J., Feeny, D. and Lockett, M. (1988) 'An exploration into the management of the IS function: key issues and an evolving model', *Proceedings of the Joint International Symposium on IS,* March.

Hochstrasser, B. and Griffiths, C. (1990) *Regaining Control of IS Investments: a Handbook for Senior UK Management,* Kobler Unit.

King, J.L. (1983) 'Centralised versus decentralised computing: organisational considerations and management options', *Computing Survey,* 15, 4, 319–49.

Lacity, M. (1993) *Information Systems Outsourcing: Myths, Metaphors and Realities,* John Wiley, Chichester.

Lacity, M. and Hirscheim, R. (1995) *Beyond the Information Systems Outsourcing Bandwagon – the Insourcing Response,* John Wiley, Chichester.

Lytinen, K. and Hirscheim, R. (1987) 'Information systems failures: a survey and classification of the empirical literature', *Oxford Surveys in IT,* 4, 257–309.

McFarlan, F. and McKenney, J. (1993) *Corporate Information Systems Management,* Prentice Hall, London.

Mintzberg, H. (1990) 'The design school: reconsidering the basic premises of strategic management', *Strategic Management Journal,* 11, 171–95.

Obolensky, N. (1994) *Practical Business Re-engineering: Tools and Techniques for Achieving Effective Change,* Kogan Page, London.

Porter, M.E. (1980) *Competitive Strategy,* Free Press, New York.

Porter, M.E. and Millar, V.E. (1985) 'How information gives you competitive advantage', *Harvard Business Review,* July/August, 149–60.

Remeny, D., Money, A. and Twite, A. (1995) *Effective Measurement and Management of IT Costs and Benefits,* Butterworth-Heinemann, Oxford.

Robson, W. (1997) *Strategic Management and Information Systems: An Integrated Approach,* Financial Times Pitman Publishing, London.

Smith, S. (1997) Outsourcing: Better out than in? *Computer Weekly,* 29 May 1997.

Sullivan, C.H. (1985) 'Systems planning in the information age', *Sloan Management Review,* Winter, 3–12.

Ward, J. and Griffiths, P.M. (1996) *Strategic Planning for Information Systems,* John Wiley, Chichester.

This book provides an excellent review of current thinking on IS strategy. The strategic analysis and planning coverage is mainly restricted to the first eight chapters, with latter chapters dealing with implementation issues:

Chapter 1 offers a strategic overview from a historical perspective.
Chapter 2 outlines important concepts in business strategy with particular relevance to IS.
Chapter 3 describes what is involved in the IS planning process.
Chapters 4 and 5 explore methods of strategic analysis.
Chapter 8 describes management of organisational issues including the management of change and the placement or location of IS within an organisation.
Chapter 9 Information Management
Chapter 10 Investment assessment
Chapter 11 Application of development
Chapter 12 Provision of IT infastructure

▶ Further reading

Callon, D. (1996) *Competitive Advantage through Information Technology,* McGraw-Hill, London.

Curtis, G. (1995) *Business Information Systems: Analysis, Design and Practice,* 2nd edition, Addison-Wesley, Harlow, Essex.

Hammer, M. (1990) 'Reengineering work: don't automate, obliterate', *Harvard Business Review,* July/August, 104–12.

Kendall, K.E. and Kendall, J.E. (1995) *Systems Analysis and Design,* 3rd edition, Prentice-Hall, Englewood Cliffs, NJ.

Lewis, P. (1994) *Information-Systems Development,* Financial Times Pitman Publishing, London.

Patching, D. (1990) *Practical Soft Systems Analysis,* Financial Times Pitman Publishing, London.

▶ Web references

http://www.warwick.ac.uk Business Processes Resource Centre at Warwick University. A good resource for software tools and techniques used for reengineering.

http://www.computer.weekly.co.uk 'The outsourcing tightrope', special focus, 25 June 1998.

http://www.outsourcing.com Outsourcing Institute Web site.

http://www.strassman.com The Web site of Paul Strassman, which includes many of his articles on the Vale of Information and issues such as outsourcing and IS investment.

http://www.prosci.com Consultancy ProSci provides articles and tutorials relating to BPR and process metrics.

http://www.brint.com The business researchers' interests site gives thorough coverage of strategic issues such as business process reengineering, workflow technology, knowledge management and organisational learning.

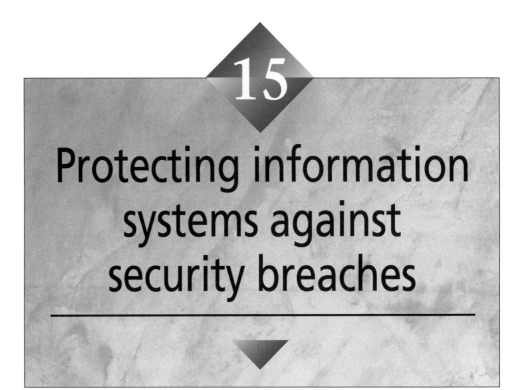

Protecting information systems against security breaches

INTRODUCTION

The importance of information systems and information to organisations is continually increasing. While this is happening, the reliance on the information also increases, as do the consequences of the information being lost or destroyed. This chapter therefore tackles an important subject for business managers and IS managers alike by asking the question: how do we protect our information assets against security breaches? A **security breach** can be defined as any act, deliberate or unintentional, that leads to unauthorised access to or loss or damage to information or an information system. For the IS manager, protecting a company's information will be one of his or her chief concerns. For the business manager, it is important to be aware of the risks so that procedures can be put in place to safeguard information. This is particularly important in the small to medium company where there may not be a person with specific responsibility for IS.

Security breach

A deliberate or unintentional act that leads to unauthorised access to or loss/ damage to information or an information system.

> To give an indication of the extent of the problem of security breaches, a 1997 survey of 1 000 businesses by the Department of Trade and Industry showed that nearly half of UK businesses had experienced at least one security breach of £20 000 or more. Common problems included power failure, network failure, viruses, user errors and theft. DTI minister Barbara Roche was quoted as saying that poor security procedures represented a £1 billion economic liability.

The first section of this chapter discusses the need for controls on information systems, paying particular attention to preventing unauthorised access. Having established some of the threats facing modern computer-based systems, several strategies are introduced for ensuring the integrity of an information system. A description of some of the control strategies is followed by a more detailed examination of two areas of contemporary interest: computer viruses and theft.

This chapter is intended to provide:

◆ an understanding of the need to control information systems;

◆ an overview of the strategies that can be employed in order to maintain the security of an information system, including disaster recovery;

◆ an overview of some methods that can be used to control access to and the operation of information systems;

◆ an understanding of the nature of crime in relation to information technology;

◆ a more detailed understanding of some common forms of computer-related crime.

▶ Learning objectives

After reading this chapter, readers will be able to:

◆ understand and assess potential threats to a computer-based information system;

◆ propose an overall strategy for ensuring the security of a computer-based information system;

◆ identify specific techniques that might be used to protect a computer-based information system against damage or unauthorised access.

▶ Links to other chapters

Chapter 17 deals with managing Internet and intranet-based information systems. Many of the problems referred to in this chapter are a negative consequence of companies connecting themselves to the Internet.

Chapter 18 deals with ethical issues of relevance to the developers and managers of computer-based information systems. It also considers further issues of computer-related crime and theft.

▶ THE NEED FOR CONTROLS

Controls on information systems are based on two underlying principles:

◆ the need to ensure the accuracy of the data held by the organisation;

◆ the need to protect against loss or damage to corporate information or hardware.

Note that the information that computer systems hold is now often a more significant asset than the hardware, which can be more readily replaced. Controls should therefore focus on protecting the information.

Although this chapter is largely concerned with unauthorised access and the physical security of information systems, many of the issues raised are also relevant to the discussion of accuracy and privacy provided in Chapter 18.

The most common threats faced by organisational information systems can be placed in the following categories:

◆ accidents by users or support staff;

◆ natural disasters;

◆ sabotage (industrial and individual);

◆ vandalism;

◆ theft;

◆ unauthorised use (hacking);

◆ computer viruses.

To place these in perspective, refer to Fig 15.1 showing the extent of some of these threats during 1996. This survey found that 59 per cent of companies surveyed had experienced a security breach.

It can be seen that the important threats are either deliberate or accidental, but the end result of information loss is always the same. Malicious internal and external damage is relatively unimportant, but significant enough that measures should be put in place to counter it. Table 15.1 gives some examples of some of the better-known threats that have occurred.

It is notable that many of the problems referred to are, in part, a consequence of inter-organisational networks such as the Internet that enable viruses to be transmitted or Russian hackers to gain access to a bank in the US. The increasing use of such networks is a further reason that companies should pay great attention to security as an element of IS strategy.

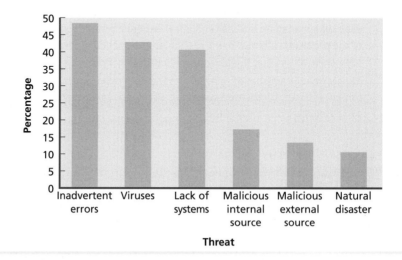

Fig 15.1 Percentage of respondents reporting loss of information in a 1996 Business and Technology Ernst & Young survey amongst UK businesses

---

Table 15.1 Why do we need controls? A catalogue of major computer-related crimes, 1991–6

1991

◆ More than 27 000 copies of the AIDS (computer) virus were mailed out in a huge blackmail attempt. Estimates are that the blackmailer received more than $10 million before being caught.

1992

◆ The Michelangelo virus infected 600 000 machines worldwide.

◆ A Dataquest survey spanning 300 sites and more than 600 000 machines found that 63 per cent of sites had experienced a virus and that 9 per cent had suffered a serious loss of data.

1995

◆ A computer virus spread to over 500 000 sites worldwide in only two hours from its point of origin in Chengdu, China.

◆ A Russian hacker stole $400 000 from Citicorp and transferred $11.6 million into foreign accounts

1996

◆ Lloyds Bank suffered chip theft worth more than £70 000.

◆ IBM's UK headquarters suffered chip theft worth more than £100 000.

◆ An unnamed public utility suffered a chip theft worth more than £750 000.

▶ Accidents

Examples of information loss such as those in Table 15.1 are high profile and well known, but estimates suggest that as much as 65 per cent of all damage caused to information systems or corporate data arises as a result of human error. Some examples of the ways in which human errors can occur include:

◆ *Inaccurate data entry*. As an example, consider a typical relational database management system, where **update queries** by a database administrator are used to change records, tables and reports. If the contents of the query are incorrect, errors might be produced within all of the data manipulated by the query. Although an extreme example, significant problems might be caused by adding or removing even a single character to a query.

Update query

Used to change records, tables and reports held in a Database Management System.

◆ *Attempts to carry out tasks beyond the ability of the employee*. In smaller computer-based information systems, a common cause of accidental damage involves users attempting to install new hardware items or software applications. In the case of software applications, existing data may be lost when the program is installed or the program may fail to operate as expected.

◆ *Failure to comply with procedures for the use of organisational information systems*. Where organisational procedures are unclear or fail to anticipate potential problems, users may often ignore established methods, act on their own initiative or perform tasks incorrectly.

◆ *Failure to carry out backup procedures or verify data backups.* In addition to carrying out regular backups of important business data, it is also necessary to verify that any backup copies made are accurate and free from errors.

▶ Natural disasters

Safety-critical system

Where human lives rely on the correct operation of a computer-based information system.

> Where human lives rely on the proper operation of an information system, this is usually known as a **safety-critical system**. Perhaps a better way of describing a critical system is to suggest that it is an information system that must not fail. A good example of a safety-critical system is an air traffic control system or control system for a nuclear power station.

All information systems are susceptible to damage caused by natural phenomena or so-called acts of God, such as storms, lightning strikes, floods and earthquakes. In Japan and the US, for example, great care is taken to protect critical information systems from the effects of earthquakes. Although such hazards are of less concern within Europe, properly designed systems will make allowances for unexpected natural disasters.

▶ Sabotage

With regard to information systems, sabotage may be deliberate or unintentional and carried out on an individual basis or as an act of industrial sabotage.

Individual sabotage

Logic bomb

Sometimes also known as a time bomb, a logic bomb is a destructive computer program that activates at a certain time or in reaction to a specific event.

Individual sabotage is typically carried out by a disgruntled employee who wishes to exact some form of revenge on his/her employer. The **logic bomb** (sometimes known as a time bomb) is a well-known example of how an employee may cause deliberate damage to the organisation's information systems. A logic bomb is a destructive program that activates at a certain time or in reaction to a specific event. In most cases, the logic bomb is activated some months after the employee has left the organisation. This tends to have the effect of drawing suspicion away from the employee.

Back door

A section of program code that allows a user to circumvent security procedures in order to gain full access to an information system.

Another well-known example is called a **back door**. This is a section of program code that allows a user to circumvent security procedures in order to gain full access to an information system. Although back doors have legitimate uses, such as for program testing, they can also be instruments of sabotage. It should be noted, however, that individual sabotage is becoming more infrequent due to legislation such as the Computer Misuse Act.

Industrial sabotage

Industrial sabotage is considered rare, although there have been a number of well-publicised cases over the past few years. Industrial sabotage tends to be carried out for some kind of competitive or financial gain. The actions of those involved tend to be highly organised, targeted at specific areas of a rival organisation's activities and supported by access to a substantial resource base. Industrial sabotage is considered more serious than individual sabotage since, although occurrences are relatively few, the losses suffered tend to be extremely high. A well-known example concerns the legal battle between British Airways and Richard Branson's Virgin, where it was alleged that BA gained access to Virgin's customer databases and used this information to 'poach' Virgin's customers.

Unintentional sabotage

An intent to cause loss or damage need not be present for sabotage to occur. Imagine the case of an organisation introducing a new information system at short notice and without proper consultation with staff. Employees may feel threatened by the new system and may wish to avoid making use of it. A typical reaction might be to enter data incorrectly in an attempt to discredit the new system. Alternatively, the employee might continue to carry out tasks manually (or with the older system), claiming that this is a more efficient way of working. In such cases, the employee's primary motivation is to safeguard his or her position – the damage or loss caused to the organisation's information systems is incidental to this goal.

▶ Vandalism

Deliberate damage caused to hardware, software and data is considered a serious threat to information systems security. The threat from vandalism lies in the fact that the organisation is temporarily denied access to some of its resources. Even relatively minor damage to parts of a system can have a significant effect on the organisation as a whole. In a small network system, for example, damage to a server or shared storage device might effectively halt the work of all those connected to the network. In larger systems, a reduced flow of work through one part of the organisation can create bottlenecks, reducing the overall productivity of the entire organisation. Damage or loss of data can have more severe effects, since the organisation cannot make use of the data until it has been replaced. The expense involved in replacing damaged or lost data can far exceed any losses arising from damage to hardware or software. As an example, the delays caused by the need to replace hardware or data might result in an organisation being unable to compete for new business, harming its overall profitability.

▶ Theft

As with vandalism, the loss of important hardware, software or data can have significant effects on an organisation's effectiveness. Theft can be divided into two basic categories: physical theft and data theft.

> Between 1995 and 1996, thefts of equipment from government offices in the UK grew by 400 per cent – from £100 000 to £400 000.

Physical theft, as the term implies, involves the theft of hardware and software. **Data theft** normally involves making copies of important files without causing any harm to the originals. However, if the original files are destroyed or damaged, then the value of the copied data is automatically increased.

Chip theft involves removing small but valuable components from computers, such as memory modules and processors.

Chip theft

The removal of small but valuable components from computers, such as memory modules and processors.

Service organisations are particularly vulnerable to data theft, since their activities tend to rely heavily on access to corporate databases. Imagine a competitor gaining access to a customer list belonging to a sales organisation. The immediate effect of such an event would be to place both organisations on an essentially even footing. However, in the long term, the first organisation would no longer enjoy a competitive edge and might, ultimately, cease to exist.

> In 1996, a survey into information security breaches found that the average theft from UK businesses cost £25 000, representing a 325 per cent increase since 1994.

Both data theft and physical theft can take a number of different forms. The case study provides a brief overview of the relatively new phenomenon of 'chip theft', sometimes known as 'RAM raiding'.

MINI CASE

Chip theft

A recent trend with regard to the theft of equipment has become known as 'chip theft'. During the late 1980s and early 1990s, the prices of certain computer components, particularly RAM modules, grew steeply. As prices rose, so too did attempted thefts. By 1994, large consignments of SIMMs being delivered to manufacturers in America's Silicon Valley had to be accompanied by armed guards. Furthermore, a number of attempted and actual armed robberies were reported where, in some cases, SIMM chips worth more than $1 million were stolen during a single raid.

The attraction of stealing SIMMs, processors and other components grew to a point where the normal patterns of equipment theft changed significantly. In the past, thieves had taken the whole machine – usually with the intention of selling it on the second-hand market or breaking it down for spares. Now it was more lucrative simply to remove key components and sell these separately. In the past, thieves had raided company offices and removed as much equipment as possible. This often required the use of a vehicle, increasing the risk of detection. Preparing the machines for sale also increased the chances of detection, particularly since it can be relatively easy to identify a specific machine. Furthermore, selling machines on the second-hand market also incurred expenses; cases needed to be changed, advertising placed and so on.

The new generation of computer equipment thieves quickly learned that chip theft was simple, less risky and potentially far more lucrative. Raids now involved dismantling machines as quickly as possible in order to remove processors and SIMMs. Since a vehicle was no longer necessary, the chances of detection during a raid were reduced. Furthermore, since individual SIMMs and processors are almost impossible to identify, there was little chance of a stolen item being traced back to the thief. Demand was such that the items could be sold quickly and for relatively high prices. In many cases, items were sold as new to unsuspecting manufacturers and the public. Ironically, the anonymity of the SIMM and the processor meant that companies occasionally found themselves buying replacement parts from the very people who had stolen them.

An explanation for the emergence of chip theft as a major form of computer-related crime can be found by examining how the prices of SIMMs and other components grew so dramatically. The sudden increase in the price of RAM chips has been explained as a combination of two main factors:

◆ A fire at a major manufacturing plant drastically reduced the production of SIMMs for a relatively lengthy period, inflating prices by up to 50 per cent. As a result, some manufacturers became fearful of losing their supplies and began to stockpile large quantities of SIMMs. The effect of this was to reduce supplies still further and encourage extra price increases.

◆ During the early 1990s, the release of new, more powerful productivity software prompted many users to increase the amount of memory in their machines. Additionally, this caused a growth in demand for new machines to arrive with 4Mb or 8Mb of RAM as standard. Note that in the late 1990s the manufacturers were able to supply PCs with between 32 Mb to 128 Mb RAM as standard prices of RAM fell dramatically due to a combination of oversupply and cheaper production techniques. Thus, manufacturers suddenly found that they needed up to four times the number of SIMMs they were currently using. A similar effect was observed with the launch of Windows 95 and other products, such as Windows NT. In the case of Windows 95, although it was claimed to run in 4Mb of memory, most users suggested that a minimum of 8Mb is required – and preferably 16Mb or more.

This global shortage in the supply of SIMMs saw prices rise by as much as 200 per cent over a period of less than six months. In the UK, the typical price of a 1Mb SIMM grew from around £20 to £40, although some manufacturers charged as much as £60 per Mb of additional memory.

When measured weight-for-weight, SIMM chips were more valuable than gold and platinum during 1995. Since SIMMs are small, light and almost impossible to trace, it was feared that they would become the new currency of the drugs trade, particularly when it was noted that a briefcase filled with SIMMs could be up to five times more valuable than an identical case filled with heroin or cocaine.

It is likely that incidences of chip theft will become less common by the end of the decade. Supplies of SIMMs are now such that prices have begun to fall significantly. In late 1997, for example, the typical price of a 16Mb SIMM fell from more than £90 to around £40.

SIMM (single inline memory module) chip is the most common form of RAM used in modern personal computers.

▶ Unauthorised use

One of the most common security risks in relation to computerised information systems is the danger of unauthorised access to confidential data. Contrary to the popular belief encouraged by the media, the risk of hackers gaining access to a corporate information system is relatively small. Most security breaches involving confidential data can be attributed to the employees of the organisation. In many cases, breaches are accidental in that employees are unaware that particular sets of information are restricted. Deliberate breaches are typically the result of an employee wishing to gain some personal benefit from using the information obtained. A good example concerns the common myth of the police officer using the Police National Computer to check up on a car he or she wishes to buy. In reality, strict guidelines cover the use of the Police National Computer and a log is kept of all enquiries made.

However, no matter how small, the threat posed by hackers must also be considered. **Hackers** are those who attempt to gain unauthorised access to a computer-based information system, usually via a telecommunications link. In general, most people consider hackers to fall into one of three catgeories:

◆ those who wish to demonstrate their computer skills by outwitting the designers of a particular system;

◆ those who wish to gain some form of benefit (usually financial) by stealing, altering or deleting confidential information;

◆ those who wish to cause malicious damage to an information system, perhaps as an act of revenge against a former employer.

Understandably, the most common crime committed by hackers involves telecommunications fraud. Clearly, the first task carried out by most hackers is to obtain free telephone calls, so that the time-consuming task of breaking into a given system can be carried out without incurring a great deal of expense. However, the growth of digital communications technology means that it is possible to implement countermeasures against hacking.

An excellent example concerns a 1989 case where a hacker managed to access information systems in more than 35 military bases across the US. The hacker's intention was to steal information on the Strategic Defense Initiative (SDI) – the so-called Star Wars project. The hacker was traced on the basis of an anomaly found in telephone records by Clifford Stoll. The unauthorised use of 75 cents of telephone time led to an investigation that lasted more than 18 months. Finally, following a number of failed attempts to trace the hacker via the telecommunications system, he was caught and sentenced to imprisonment.

How to deal with hackers is discussed further in Chapter 18.

▶ Computer viruses

While the use of some methods, such as logic bombs, is beginning to decline, others are becoming more common. The release of 'virus construction kits' and 'virus mutation engines' places the construction of a new computer virus within the hands of most users. Additionally, although methods such as virus scanning provide a degree of protection against virus infection, no completely secure prevention technique has yet been found.

Computer viruses are considered in more detail later in this chapter.

▶ CONTROL STRATEGIES

Control strategies for information systems will need to achieve the following:

◆ control access to information systems;

◆ maintain the integrity of the information held in a computer-based information system;

◆ implement procedures to ensure the physical security of equipment;

◆ safeguard the overall security of an information system.

Of all of these controls, the most important 'golden rule' is:

Always maintain secure backup copies of data.

Organisations usually achieve backups by regularly saving information on servers to magnetic tape or optical disk and then archiving them at another location. Backup copies are usually stored elsewhere in case of fire or other natural phenomena.

After backup, the second most important rule is:

Restrict access to the information system.

Clearly, there is a lower risk to information if people who may want to damage it or steal it will have to work hard to enter a system.

A strategy guideline for information security has been produced as a British Standard that is followed by many large companies. It provides a useful framework for companies which have become aware of security risks and want to check what security measures are necessary.

BS7799: British Standards Institute Code of Practice for Information Security Management

BS7799 is intended to specify best practices for information protection for businesses. It is effectively a checklist to ensure that the correct security measures are in place. BS7799 has been produced in association with companies such as BT, Marks & Spencer, Midland Bank, Shell and Unilever.

Assurance that the standard is adhered to occurs through management controls. Companies can be audited to the standard, when they will have to prove, for example, that user education occurs, virus controls exist and there is a disaster recovery plan. Companies are starting to demand that their trading partners are registered to BS7799, and then they will know there is less chance of their partner being a security risk. The 10 key controls from BS7799 are:

1.1.1   *Information security policy document.* A written policy document should be available to all employees responsible for information security.

2.1.3   *Allocation of information security responsibilities.* Who is responsible for protecting the PC on users' desktops. Who can be called if there is a problem?

4.2.1   *Information security education and training.* Users should be given adequate security education and technical training.

4.3.1   *Reporting of security incidents.* Security incidents should be reported through management channels as quickly as possible.

6.3.1   *Virus controls.* Virus detection and prevention measures and appropriate user awareness procedures should be implemented.

9.1.1   *Business continuity planning process.* There should be a managed process in place for developing and maintaining business continuity plans across the organisation. This process was referred to as disaster recovery planning earlier in the chapter.

▶

10.1.1 *Control of proprietary software copying.* Attention should be drawn to the legal restrictions on the use of copyright material. The company should verify that employees don't have illegal copies of software. An organisational policy to this effect should exist.

10.1.2 *Safeguarding of organisational records.* Important records of an organisation should be protected from loss, destruction and falsification.

10.1.3 *Data protection.* Applications handling personal data on individuals should comply with data protection legislation and principles.

10.2.1 *Compliance with security policy.* All areas within the organisation should be considered for regular review to ensure compliance with security policies and standards.

Source: http://www.bsi.org.uk

In the next sections, strategies for reducing threats to information systems are discussed in more detail. In general, there are four main approaches that can be taken to ensure the integrity of an information system. These are known as containment, deterrence, obfuscation and recovery.

Although each strategy is discussed separately, it is important to note that an effective security policy will draw on a variety of concepts and techniques.

▶ Recovery

A strategy based on recovery recognises that, no matter how well defended, a breach in the security of an information system will eventually occur. Such a strategy is largely concerned with ensuring that the normal operation of the information system is restored as quickly as possible, with as little disruption to the organisation as possible.

Disaster recovery or 'business continuity planning' companies maintain copies of important data on behalf of an organisation. Such facilities are usually provided by a third party which is responsible for the security of the data stored. Disaster recovery usually refers to services required if a company is affected by a dramatic event such as a flood or fire. When bombs have been detonated in the City of London, disaster recovery has enabled companies to continue working. This may occur on alternative premises, sometimes using a mobile computing facility based in a converted lorry. The case study on disaster recovery gives a summary of the types of risks and services available. It also gives practical tips involved in implementing a disaster recovery programme.

The most important aspect of a strategy based on recovery involves careful organisational planning. The development of emergency procedures that deal with a number of contingencies is essential if a successful recovery is to take place.

In anticipating damage or loss, a great deal of emphasis is placed on backup procedures and recovery measures. In large organisations, a **backup site** might be created, so that data processing can be switched to a secondary site immediately in the event of an emergency. Smaller organisations might make use of other measures, such as **RAID facilities** or **data warehousing** services.

Disaster recovery company

Maintain copies of important data on behalf of an organisation and may also provide a service which can immediately supply replacement systems.

Backup site

Houses a copy of the organisation's main data processing facilities, including hardware, software and up-to-date data files. In the event of an emergency, processing can be switched to the backup site almost immediately so that the organisation's work can continue.

Redundant array of inexpensive disks (RAID)

Identical copies of important data files are kept upon a number of different storage devices, often in the same unit.

CASE STUDY: TOPIC AREA

Disaster recovery – be prepared

Disaster recovery: Be prepared . . . or else. It's a little-known statistic that the chances of winning the lottery are similar to those of having a plane crash into your house. And just as the National Lottery is a licence to print money, so some disaster recovery vendors use scare tactics to sell you their products and services.

The threat of terrorism may have receded over the last couple of years, but terrorist incidents have focused organisations' minds on their vulnerability – and the impact on business when an IT disaster occurs.

'A business can just as easily go under as a result of a fire, industrial action, computer breakdown or robbery,' argues Barney Bannington, financial director of Telehouse Europe. 'In terms of frequency, disaster recovery plans are more often invoked due to a computing problem than any major incident – although full relocation will most often be due to a fire.'

For some time now, disaster recovery planning has been essential for front-line offices such as dealing rooms. With the growth of computer users in all departments – ranging from computerised accounting systems to sales leads records – contingency planning has become an essential for all areas of the business.

'As an incentive, insurance companies and auditors are advising organisations to implement effective disaster recovery plans by rewarding them with up to a 40% reduction in premiums,' says Dave Kennington, managing director of recovery specialist, Barron McCann. 'Even though 86% of companies have their technology insured, only 9% assign a monetary value to their business information, which is far more valuable,' he continues.

The growth in computer technology has prompted growth among disaster recovery suppliers. More and more companies are now making a serious commitment to disaster planning to minimise the disruption caused should disaster strike. At the same time, a growing number of organisations are using back-up systems to maximise the efficiency of normal operations.

'The existence of a resilient business continuity plan, or lack of it, may play an important part in the future purchasing policy of many organisations.

'It is not beyond reason to expect that companies may soon be required to include in their audited financial statements whether or not they have a disaster recovery plan in place – as this may affect its credibility as a going concern,' continues Bannington. 'Most companies suffering a disaster will not survive beyond 18 months of the event.'

The potential fall-out from a disaster affects a wide circle of direct and indirect groups, from employees and shareholders, to customers and suppliers. All stand to lose substantially if a business continuity plan is not in place.

Disasters that deny individuals access to their places of work can be big or small, ranging from acts of God and terrorism to careless road diggers. However, that risk not only needs to be avoided but effectively identified, monitored and controlled.

According to Peter Alexander, managing director of the Montal Group, most people's perception of disaster recovery is still based around mainframes, emergency generators, mobile offices and so on. The reality is that companies now rely completely on computers at all levels.

Since most organisations are now online they tend to focus on re-establishing the computer centre with small and portable computers.

'With traditional disaster recovery geared towards the larger user, service providers have had to radically alter their services,' says Alexander. 'The nature of the risk affecting us all is changing.'

Ultimately, disaster recovery is a form of insurance, and one can pay for basic cover or for a number of additional policies ready to be used in the event of an emergency. However, identification of the risks is the essential first step in planning a disaster recovery process. They also need to be prioritised.

Some risks might expose a company to a degree of financial loss; others may fatally damage an organisation.

'Imagine no offices or factories, no phone systems or computer networks. Then the need for an effective disaster recovery strategy appears sound business sense,' says Bannington.

In evaluating risk you must first quantify the probability and maximum threat of each risk exposure. Once identified, these risks can be divided into those that are within the compass of your company's control, and those which are not.

'A business needs to take steps to reduce the effect of exposure to preventable risk, if not eliminate it altogether. However the cost of doing this may well exceed the maximum possible loss arising from the risk,' adds Bannington.

Emphasis should be as much on prevention as recovery. A wide variety of services are available to advise on insurance against business interruption, alternative and mobile sites, off-site data storage and archiving, planning software, restoration and damage limitation and of course, consultancies offering assessment, testing and support.

Unfortunately, as the number of disaster recovery suppliers grows, the threat of sub-standard facilities can arise. This is exacerbated by the intricacies of an IT service. 'Indeed, it is very difficult if not impossible to inspect what is actually available, or planned, or perhaps what is promised without contention,' says Bannington.

'Services need to be checked, diverse routes verified, DR staff vetted, information services contracted, to ensure that the site can distribute data as contracted. The only real measure is a full disaster recovery test,' he adds.

UK companies: the disturbing facts

Business continuity and disaster recovery user group, Survive!, defines a disaster as 'any event causing loss in excess of £10 000, or which inhibits the organisation from achieving its mission. A recent Survive! survey found that 7.5% of UK organisations suffer 'disasters' each year. The Business Information Security Survey '98 reports that half of all respondents have suffered from an information security breach. According to findings in *Corporate UK and the Internet*, just released by the Federation Against Software Theft, research amongst 200 UK businesses shows that 47% openly admit that they do not know how to protect against the misuse of the Internet within their organisation.

Survival tips from top to bottom

Conduct a risk management audit within your company. What is the most likely threat to your business? Is it, for example, fire, flood, power blackout or malicious damage? Identify critical business functions necessary for the short term survival of the business. Then provide back-up facilities for those functions. Consider the human factor. Whatever the incident, you will be expecting people to work over and above their normal contractual obligations.

Select a team of appropriate people to manage a disaster – one person per area of business activity that would be most affected by a disaster (be it the chairman, personnel, operations, finance purchasing and distribution, PR or communications).You should also appoint somebody to lead the disaster recovery team. Stage a mock disaster to check procedures. Formulate a strategy and schedule. Emphasise the process of communication – internally and externally. Ensure that your organisation performs a security review at least every three months. Make sure that access codes are changed regularly. Properly thought out and tested plans can make all the difference. Interruption to a business is often unexpected and even if essential elements are available, people need to know what to do at the time of a crisis. Ensure that your building is protected from unwanted intruders. Install high-security surveillance systems, including video monitoring, 24-hour security and sound detection monitors. Ensure that you have made adequate provision against disaster and that it is regularly reviewed. Find out what the situation is with your insurers for immediate assess damage and make interim payments. Ensure your plan guarantees a full recovery within an acceptable time acceptable to the business – whatever the cause of system discontinuity.

Sources: Computing, 1 July 1998; Guardian Computer Services and Telehouse

Questions

1 List the threats to business information given in the article.

2 What incentives and reasons are there for companies to sign up to a disaster recovery provider.

3 In what ways does the article suggest that disaster recovery has changed?

4 Choose what you think to be the five most important survival tips listed in the article.

▶ Containment

The strategy of containment attempts to control access to an information system.

One approach involves making potential targets as unattractive as possible. This can be achieved in several ways, but a common method involves creating the impression that the target information system contains data of little or no value. It would be pointless, for example, to attempt to steal data that had been encrypted – the data would effectively be useless to anyone except the owner.

A second technique involves creating an effective series of defences against potential threats. If the expense, time and effort required to gain access to the information system are greater than any benefits derived from gaining access, then intrusion becomes less likely. However, defences must be continually improved and upgraded in order to keep up with advances in technology and the increasing sophistication of hackers. Thus, such an approach tends to be expensive in terms of organisational resources.

A third approach involves removing the target information system from potential threats. Typical ways in which this might be achieved include distributing assets across a large geographic area, distributing important data across the entire organisation or isolating important systems.

▶ Deterrence

A strategy based on deterrence uses the threat of punishment to discourage potential intruders. The overall approach is one of anticipating and countering the motives of those most likely to threaten the security of the system.

A common method involves constantly advertising and reinforcing the penalties for unauthorised access. It is not uncommon, for example, to dismiss an employee for gaining access to confidential data. Similarly, it is not uncommon for organisations to bring private prosecutions against those who have caused damage or loss to important information systems. Attempts to breach the security of the information system are discouraged by publicising successful actions against employees or other parties.

A second approach involves attempting to detect potential threats as early as possible, for example by monitoring patterns of information system usage and investigating all anomalies. However, although such a technique can prevent some attacks and reduce the damage caused by others, it can be expensive in terms of organisational resources.

The third technique involves predicting likely areas of attack and then implementing appropriate defences or countermeasures. If an organisation feels, for example, that it is particularly vulnerable to computer viruses, it might install virus scanning software across the entire organisation.

▶ Obfuscation

Obfuscation concerns itself with hiding or distributing assets so that any damage caused can be limited.

One means by which such a strategy can be implemented is by monitoring *all* of the organisation's activities, not just those related to the use of its information systems. This provides a more comprehensive approach to security than containment or deterrence, since it also provides a measure of protection against theft and other threats.

A second method involves carrying out regular **audits** of data, hardware, software and security measures. In this way, the organisation has a more complete overview of its information systems and can assess threats more accurately. A regular software audit, for example, might result in a reduction in the use of illegal software. In turn, this might reduce the number of virus infections suffered by the organisation, avoid potential litigation with software companies and detect illegal or unauthorised use of programs and data.

The dispersal of assets across several locations can be used to discourage potential intruders and can also limit the damage caused by a successful attack. The use of other techniques, such as backup procedures, can be used to reduce any threats further.

Audit

The process of monitoring an organisation's hardware and software resources. In general, audits are used as a deterrent against theft and the use of illegal software.

▶ TYPES OF CONTROLS

There are five main categories of controls that can be applied to information systems. These are: physical protection, biometric controls, telecommunications controls, failure controls and auditing. The types of controls are summarised in this section, and in the next the details of the techniques used to implement these controls are described. We also describe a different type of control – the external legal control introduced by government legislation.

▶ Physical protection

Physical protection involves the use of physical barriers intended to protect against theft and unauthorised access. The reasoning behind such an approach is extremely simple: if access to rooms and equipment is restricted, the risk of theft and vandalism is reduced. Furthermore, by preventing access to equipment, it is less likely that an unauthorised user can gain access to confidential information.

Techniques of physical protection: locks, barriers and security chains.

▶ Biometric controls

These controls make use of the unique characteristics of individuals in order to restrict access to sensitive information or equipment.

Techniques of biometric control: scanners that check fingerprints, voice prints or even retinal patterns.

Until relatively recently, the expense associated with biometric control systems placed them out of the reach of all but the largest organisations. In addition, many organisations held reservations concerning the accuracy of the recognition methods used to identify specific individuals. However, with the introduction of more sophisticated hardware and software, both of these problems have been largely resolved. Many organisations have now begun to look at ways in which biometric control systems could be used to reduce instances of fraud. Within five years, for example, banks are expected to introduce automated teller machines (ATM) that use fingerprints and retinal patterns to identify customers.

▶ Telecommunications controls

These controls help verify the identity of a particular user.

Techniques of communications controls: passwords and **user validation** routines.

User validation

Checks made to ensure the user is permitted access to a system. Also known as access control systems they often involve user names and passwords, but can also include biometric techniques.

As an example, when a new network account is created for a given user, they may be asked to supply several pieces of personal information, such as the name of a spouse or a date of birth. When the user attempts to connect to the network system via a modem, they will be asked to confirm their identity by providing some of the information given when the account was created.

▶ Failure controls

Failure controls attempt to limit or avoid damage caused by the failure of an information system.

Techniques of failure control: regular backups of data and **recovery** procedures.

Recovery

The process which is used to restore backup data.

▶ Auditing

Techniques of auditing: taking stock of hardware, software and data at regular intervals.

With regard to software and data, audits can be carried out automatically with an appropriate program. Auditing software works by scanning the hard disk drives of any computers, terminals and servers attached to a network system. As each hard disk drive is scanned, the names of any programs found are added to a log. This log can be compared to a list of the programs that are legitimately owned by the organisation. Since the log contains information concerning the whereabouts of each program found, it is relatively simple to determine the location of any unauthorised programs. In many organisations, auditing programs are also used to keep track of software licences and allow companies to ensure that they are operating within the terms of their licence agreements.

A software licence enables a company to make several copies of a program, allowing it to acquire important programs at reduced cost. Typically, a company will purchase a single copy of the program and install this on as many computers as required. Since only one copy of the program and any accompanying documentation is required, costs are reduced for both the company and the supplier. The terms of the software licence will determine how many copies of the program can be made. A 10-user licence, for example, allows a company to make up to 10 copies of a program for use by its employees.

▶ Legal controls

In addition to the physical and procedural controls mentioned above, control is also available from legislation. Governments can use this to their advantage in preventing security breaches. The relevant legislation in the UK is as follows.

Computer Misuse Act (1990)

This covers unauthorised access to information systems, popularly known as **hacking**. If a company finds that its security has been breached it can invoke this act and bring charges. Note that this is a retrospective action and the damage may already have been done.

Examples of prosecutions brought about under the Act and further details on its coverage are provided in Chapter 18.

Data Protection Act (1984)

The Data Protection Act 1984 is defined by the Data Protection Registrar as:

An Act to regulate the use of automatically processed information relating to individuals and the provision of services in respect of such information.

The Act is mainly intended to cover the individual's rights to view the information stored on them and ensure that it is accurate. Beyond this, it could also be used if an outside company had gained unauthorised access to a company's systems to find out information about an individual.

The Data Protection Act is considered in more detail in Chapter 18.

Companies Act and Financial Services Acts

These require that financial institutions use a disaster recovery service as described in the case study on disaster recovery. This specific legislation is to protect the customer, but of course is also in the interests of the company.

▶ SOME TECHNIQUES FOR CONTROLLING INFORMATION SYSTEMS

In this section the techniques referred to above that help in achieving control are described in more detail. Some of the most common techniques used to control computer-based information systems include:

- formal security policies;
- passwords;
- file encryption;
- organisational procedures governing the use of computer-based information systems;
- user validation techniques.

▶ Formal security policy

> Only 46 per cent of organisations have a formal security policy (*Information Security Breaches Survey*, 1996).

Perhaps the simplest and most effective control is the formulation of a comprehensive policy on security. Among a wide variety of items, such a policy will outline:

- what is considered to be an acceptable use of the information system;
- what is considered an unacceptable use of the information system;
- the sanctions available in the event that an employee does not comply with the security policy;
- details of the controls in place, including their form, function and plans for developing these further.

Once a policy has been formulated, it must be publicised in order for it to become effective. In addition, the support of management is essential in order to ensure that employees adhere to the guidelines contained within the policy.

▶ Passwords

The password represents one of the most common forms of protection for computer-based information systems. In addition to providing a simple, inexpensive means of restricting access to equipment and sensitive data, passwords also provide a number of other benefits. Among these are the following:

- Access to the system can be divided into levels by issuing different passwords to employees based on their positions and the work they carry out.
- The actions of an employee can be regulated and supervised by monitoring the use of his or her password.
- Passwords are changed frequently to reduce the risk of their becoming known.
- If a password is discovered or stolen by an external party, it should be possible to limit any damage arising as a result.

CASE STUDY: TOPIC AREA

FT

Passwords

Computer fraud: screen out divers and surfers

Contrary to popular belief, most computer fraud is not technically sophisticated, and is often due to a lack of basic controls.

'A company's head of IT needs to keep abreast with the latest developments and have regular security revisions,' says Mark Morris, senior manager of UK-based Computer Forensics Investigations.

Many fraudsters, he says, rely on human behaviour rather than technology. 'Social engineers', for example, are often temporary workers who will telephone the accounts department with a bogus tale about a computer crash that has deleted the password files. The fraudster will ask for the passwords, so that employees can gain access to their computers.

'Dumpster divers', meanwhile, search rubbish bins for notes with passwords scribbled on them.

'Shoulder surfers' look over the shoulder of someone entering a password on a computer. There are also password-cracking programs that can search through vast dictionary databases to find passwords. 'Passwords should be alphanumeric, and they should only mean something to you,' says Mr Morris.

Another UK company, Priority Data Group (PDG), whose clients include Citibank, computer services company EDS, the computer services company, and General Motors, has developed a system that automatically blanks a PC screen when the user is away from it. The screen is reactivated by using a password. 'People can leave sensitive data on a computer screen while they go to the coffee machine or leave the office,' says Alec Florence, PDG's chief executive.

US-based Finjan has developed SurfinShield Corporate, designed to protect computers against rogue programs attached to ActiveX or Java-created programs. SurfinShield monitors the behaviour of the downloaded program and if it attempts to breach the computer's security system, the program is eliminated.

Source: Financial Times, 8 April 1998

Questions

1 Why should an organisation use passwords to protect equipment and sensitive data from unauthorised users?

2 The case study describes several ways in which fraudulent users are able to obtain important passwords. What measures can an organisation take to protect against some of the methods described?

3 Describe the password protection features provided by a typical operating system, such as Windows NT or Novell Netware.

◆ The use of passwords can encourage employees to take some of the responsibility for the overall security of the system.

▶ Encryption

An additional layer of protection for sensitive data can be provided by making use of encryption techniques. Modern encryption methods rely on the use of one or more keys. Without the correct key, any encrypted data is meaningless – and therefore of no value to a potential thief.

▶ Procedures

Under normal circumstances, a set of procedures for the use of an information system will arise from the creation of a formal security policy. Such procedures should describe in detail the correct operation of the system and responsibilities of users. Additionally, the procedures should highlight issues related to security, should explain some of the reasoning behind them and should also describe the penalties for failing to comply with instructions.

▶ User validation

Of relevance to telecommunications is the use of user validation techniques. It is necessary to verify the identity of users attempting to access the system from outside the organisation. A password is insufficient to identify the user since it might have been stolen or accidentally revealed to others. However, by asking for a date of birth, National Insurance number or other personal information, the identity of the user can be confirmed. Alternatively, if the location of the user is known, the system can attempt to call the user back at their current location. If the user is genuine, the call will be connected correctly and the user can then access the system. Although such methods do not offer total security, the risk of unauthorised access can be reduced dramatically.

▶ Backup procedures

A sudden loss of data can affect a company's activities in a variety of ways. The disruption caused to normal activities can result in significant financial losses due to factors such as lost opportunities, additional trading expenses and customer dissatisfaction.

The cumulative effects of data loss can prove detrimental in areas as diverse as corporate image and staff morale. Perhaps the single most compelling reason for introducing effective backup procedures is simply the expense involved in reconstructing lost data.

Grandfather, father, son

A common procedure used for creating backup copies of important data files.

One of the most common methods of protecting valuable data is to use the 'grandfather, father, son' technique. Here, a rotating set of backup disks or tapes are used so that three different versions of the same data are held at any one time.

To illustrate this method, imagine a single user working with a personal computer and using three floppy disks to store their data. Each day, all of the data being worked on is copied on to the disk containing the oldest version ('grandfather') of that data. This creates a continuous cycle that ensures that the oldest backup copy is never more than three days' old.

Table 15.1 illustrates the operation of the 'grandfather, father, son' method.

Table 15.1 The 'grandfather, father, son' backup method

Day 1	Day 2	Day 3
Disk 1 Grandfather	Disk 2 Grandfather	Disk 3 Grandfather
Disk 2 Father	Disk 3 Father	Disk 1 Father
Disk 3 Son	Disk 1 Son	Disk 2 Son

As can be seen, each disk or tape moves through three generations. Since three copies of the data are maintained, the risk of data loss is reduced considerably. In the event of the original data becoming corrupted or damaged in some way, only the

changes made since the last backup copy was made would be lost. In most cases, this would amount to new or altered data produced during the previous day. In addition, since only three sets of reusable media are required in order to make backups, the costs involved can be considered low.

It is worth noting several general points concerning backups of data:

◆ The time, effort and expense involved in producing backup copies will be wasted unless they are made at regular intervals. How often backups are made depends largely on the amount of work processed over a given period. In general, backups will be made more frequently as the number of transactions carried out each day increases.

◆ Backup copies of data should be checked each time they are produced. Faulty storage devices and media may sometimes result in incomplete or garbled copies of data. In addition, precautions should be taken against computer viruses, in order to prevent damage to the data stored.

◆ The security of backup copies should be ensured by storing them in a safe location. Typically, an organisation will produce two sets of backup copies: one to be stored at the company premises, the other to be taken off the premises and stored at a separate location. In this way, a major accident, such as a fire at the company premises, will not result in the total destruction of the organisation's data.

◆ It is worth noting that not all data needs to be backed up at regular intervals. Software applications, for example, can normally be restored quickly and easily from the original media. In a similar way, if a backup has already been made of a given item of data, the production of additional copies may not be necessary.

◆ Backups are often only made of a company's file servers. While this will protect information stored on the network, information saved to individuals' hard disks will not be saved. Policies should be put in place to ensure that employees save all their work to the network, where it will be backed up.

In order to reduce the time taken to create backup copies, many organisations make use of software that allows the production of **incremental backups**. Initially, a backup copy of all data files is made and care is taken to ensure the accuracy of the copy. This initial, complete backup is normally referred to as a **full backup** (sometimes also known as an archival backup). From this point on, specialised backup software is used to detect and copy only those files that have changed in some way since the last backup was made. In the event of data loss, damaged files can be replaced by restoring the full backup first, followed by the incremental backups. One of the chief advantages of creating incremental backups is that it is possible to trace the changes made to data files over time. In this way, any version of a given file can be located and restored.

Incremental backup

Includes only those files that have changed in some way since the last backup was made.

Full backup

A method of producing copies of important data files by including all data files considered to be important.

▶ Controlling security risks of Internet and inter-organisational access to a company

Chapter 17 describes the benefits of using networks such as the Internet to improve communications with customers, suppliers and distributors. The benefits are attracting an ever increasing number of companies to use these public networks to reduce the cost of managing transactions with third parties. As well as representing an opportunity, the Internet also represents a major challenge for the IS manager of a

company in avoiding malicious damage to company information. This section describes some of the techniques to reduce the risks.

Particular measures for controlling access from outside a company are:

1 *Standard techniques*. The basic techniques mentioned throughout this chapter are still relevant here, namely backing up data to ensure that it can be restored if it is maliciously deleted and using passwords to prevent access.

2 *Firewalls*. A firewall is a software application mounted on a separate server at the point the company is connected to the Internet. Firewalls may have the following types of facilities to monitor access requests to a company and take preventive action.

◆ Firewall software can be configured only to accept links from trusted domains representing other offices in a company or trading partners. However, IP address spoofing (simulation of these other addresses) can be used to gain access. For this reason, security measures are continually evolving. New standards, such as the authentication of IP addresses in new IP standard version 6 for example, should reduce the problem of IP spoofing.

◆ They support encryption of data packets as they leave the site to other company offices, and decrypting on arrival will become standard to make things more difficult for eavesdroppers.

3 *Locate Web and mail servers beyond the firewall*. A company's corporate system inside the firewall will be more secure if Web servers (which will be accessed by people outside the company) are not on the same network as the company data. Many companies have outsourced their Web server hosting to third parties, partly because of this reason.

4 *Encryption*. This can be a built-in function of firewalls or it can be included as a function of Web browsers. Encryption involves the 'scrambling' or encoding of data before it is transferred so that it cannot be understood if it is intercepted when in transit. When data is received, it is decoded or decrypted and it can then be read by the recipient. This decryption can be made more secure if it is only available to third parties who have the authority to decode the data. This uses a technique known as digital certificates, described in the box.

5 *Virtual private networks (VPNs)*. VPNs were described in Chapter 5. They are secure networks which make use of the Internet infrastructure, but use techniques such as firewalls and encryption to secure transactions. It is predicted by many analysis that VPNs will become widely used once companies become aware of the promise of security and relatively low cost available with this option.

FOCUS ON

▶THE COMPUTER VIRUS

▶ What is a computer virus?

Computer virus

A computer program that is capable of self-replication, allowing it to spread from one 'infected' machine to another.

The origin of the term '**computer virus**' is credited to Fred Cohen, author of the 1984 book *Computer Viruses: Theories and Experiments*. However, 'natural' computer viruses were reported as early as 1974 and papers describing mathematical models of the theory of epidemics were published in the early 1950s.

The first deliberate attempt to create a computer virus is attributed to Basit and Amjad Farooq, believed to have written the Brain virus in 1985 as a means of keeping track of

Digital certificates

The use of digital certificates or public key cryptography fulfils all the criteria for secure transactions described above.

In this method, two keys are used: one key to encrypt the message and the other to decrypt the message. The two keys are mathematically related so that data encrypted with either key can only be decrypted using the other. Each party such as a customer has two keys: a public key and a private key. The public key is freely available from an 'authentification authority' which will hold keys for individuals and organisations. Because of the mathematical relationship between the two keys, the user and anyone receiving the public key can be assured that data encrypted with the public key and sent to the user (or vice versa) can only be decrypted when the user uses the private key. Of course, this is only true as long as the private key is kept by the user. Figure 15.2 shows the relationship between the public and private key.

| Original document | Public key | Encrypted document | | Encrypted document | Private key | Original document |

Fig 15.2 Public Key Cryptography

the pirated software they sold. Although the virus spread rapidly around the world, it received little attention since few people seemed to perceive it as a threat. The attention of the public first turned to the issue of computer viruses in 1987, when two relatively innocuous programs, now called the IBM Christmas Card and MacMag viruses, affected thousands of machines across the US. Fortunately, neither program was the result of a deliberate attempt to create and distribute a virus; both programs were released accidentally, both were harmless and no reports of loss or damage were recorded.

The release of the Internet Worm in 1988 caused widespread concern when it was learnt that estimated losses were between $10 million and $90 million. Similar reactions occurred in Britain when details of the Aids Virus Trojan emerged. It is estimated that 27 000 disks were sent out from London to addresses all over the world. Users were tricked into believing that the disks contained important information regarding the AIDS virus. When the disks were used, a virus was activated that encrypted the contents of the user's hard disk drive. In order to retrieve their data, users were instructed to send a payment to an address in Panama.

Both the Internet Worm and the Aids Virus Trojan led to new legislation dealing with computer crime. In the US and Canada, new federal laws were passed that imposed severe penalties for those causing deliberate damage to data. In Britain, the Computer Misuse Act of 1990 was introduced by Michael Colvin and new powers were granted to FAST (Federation Against Software Theft) in order to increase its effectiveness against virus writers.

▶ Types of computer virus

There are three main types of computer virus: boot sector, link and parasitic. The *boot-sector virus* is capable of infecting both floppy and hard disks. The boot sector of a disk contains a set of instructions that will be executed each time the computer is switched on or reset. If a virus infects the boot sector of a disk, it will be executed before any other program, including virus detection utilities. Overall, this type of virus accounts for approximately 50 per cent of all virus infections, although only around 10 per cent of viruses are of this kind.

> By dividing processor time among a number of tasks, it is possible to run several applications simultaneously. Users will normally be unaware that more than one program is running at a time, since the application that receives the largest share of the processor's time (known as the *foreground task*) disguises the operation of any other *background tasks.* A **terminate and stay resident** program is one that is stored in the computer's memory and functions as a background task.

A *link virus* attaches itself to the directory structure of a disk. In this way, the virus is able to manipulate file and directory information. Link viruses can be difficult to remove, since they become embedded within the affected data. Often, attempts to remove the virus can result in the loss of the data concerned.

Finally, *parasitic viruses* (sometimes known as *file infectors*) insert copies of themselves into legitimate programs, such as operating system files, often making little effort to disguise their presence. In this way, each time the program file is run, so too is the virus. Additionally, the majority of viruses are created as **terminate and stay resident (TSR)** programs. Once activated, the virus remains in the computer's memory, performing various operations in the background. Such operations might range from creating additional copies of itself to deleting files on a hard disk.

Terminate and stay resident (TSR)

A program that is stored in the computer's memory and functions as a background task, receiving only a small share of the processor's time.

With the possible exception of *anti-viruses* (described in more detail later), all viruses must be considered to be harmful. Even if a virus program does nothing more than reproduce itself, it may still cause system crashes and data loss. In many cases, the damage caused by a computer virus might be accidental, arising merely as the result of poor programming.

There is also evidence to suggest that viruses may be capable of causing physical damage to hardware components. It is possible, for example, to construct a virus that instructs a disk controller to attempt to read a non-existent track, causing immediate and irreparable damage to the hard disk drive.

> Until quite recently, it was thought that computer viruses could not be attached to data files, such as wordprocessing documents. However, the built-in programming languages featured within many modern applications mean that data files may now be used to transmit viruses. A typical example is the Word for Windows *macro viruses*, which attach themselves to a document template and duplicate themselves each time a new document is created. Using an infected document on another machine automatically infects the user's copy of Word for Windows.

Two other kinds of program are related to computer viruses: worms and Trojans. A **worm** is a small program that moves through a computer system randomly changing or overwriting pieces of data. A **Trojan** appears as a legitimate program in order to gain access to a computer system. Trojans are often used as delivery systems for computer viruses. A good example of this was McAfee Scan V84, originally released in 1991. This program appeared to be a genuine version of a popular virus detection utility, but was actually the delivery system for a particularly destructive computer virus. By assuming the identity of a new version of the world's most popular virus detection program, the Trojan was able to gain extremely wide distribution in a very short time.

▶ The transmission of computer viruses

A number of reports suggest that consultants, maintenance engineers and employees are responsible for approximately 40–60 per cent of all virus infections. Often, a virus infection occurs as a result of employees bringing disks into work from their machines at home. However, several other factors have also been identified and these may help explain how viruses are transmitted between home users.

The sheer volume of illegal software copying is almost certainly responsible for a large number of virus attacks. The severity of the piracy problem gives an indication of its importance as a factor in the transmission of viruses: it is estimated that software piracy in Europe exceeds more than $2.5 billion per year and that as much as 34 per cent of all software in the UK is illegal. Worldwide, estimates suggest that software piracy and counterfeiting cost the software industry more than $11 billion each year in lost sales.

The widespread use of illegal software may go some way to explaining how viruses are able to 'emigrate' to other countries within days or weeks of their release. For example, the Michelangelo virus originated in Australia in April 1992. By December, it had been discovered in Europe, the US and the Far East. Within this short time, it was estimated that five million machines worldwide had been infected.

Commercial software may also be responsible for a small number of virus infections each year. In one incident, for example, some 50 000 copies of an infected utility disk were circulated in Germany.

Bulletin board systems and shareware are also regarded as significant factors in the transmission of computer viruses.

Bulletin Board Systems (BBS) can be described as electronic noticeboards, where users can send or receive messages related to a wide variety of subjects. A typical BBS will provide users with e-mail facilities, discussed forums and access to software libraries containing Freeware and Shareware. In the US, estimates suggest that bulletin board systems are responsible for approximately 7 per cent of all infections.

A BBS may house a number of different discussion forums, each dedicated to a specific subject. Users may browse the message left by others, reply to messages or post new messages in order to initiate further discussion. Many users often make use of discussion forums in order to obtain information that can be used to solve technical problems. Companies often contribute to discussion forums in order to provider customers with additional support, announce new products and monitor customer attitudes towards products and services.

The popularity of bulletin board systems has declined steadily since the mid-1980s. Much of this decline can be attributed to the fact that the services offered by many bulletin board systems have become redundant as the Internet has grown in

Worm

A small program that moves through a computer system randomly changing or overwriting pieces of data as it moves.

Trojan

A Trojan presents itself as a legitimate program in order to gain access to a computer system. Trojans are often used as delivery systems for computer viruses.

popularity. As an example, the relatively small number of (generally local) discussion forums hosted by bulletin board systems are not often ignored in favour of Usenet services. Usenet is a collection of international discussion forums (known as newsgroups) that can be assessed via the Internet. As many as 20 000 individual newsgroups can be accessed by users.

ACTIVITY

List some of the advantages of using discussion forums or newsgroups as a means of providing technical support to customers.

Shareware is often described with the phrase 'try before you buy'. Shareware programs can be obtained free of charge or at very low cost from a wide variety of sources, including computer magazines, bulletin board systems, via the Internet and specialised Shareware libraries. Users are entitled to use Shareware programs free of charge for a specified period of time. Having been given the opportunity to evaluate the software, the user is then required to pay the author a registered fee or remove the software from their system. Shareware often provides a viable and economical alternative to commercial software packages.

The author of a Freeware program allows users to copy, distribute and use of the software free of all charge. However, although the author has waived copyright to the software, the user is often required to abide by conditions of use. Such conditions often include an agreement that the software may not be sold for profit and that the user will not attempt to reverse engineer the program.

Although often criticised for being of poor quality, there are some exceptionally well-known and popular Shareware and Freeware packages. A good example concerns the packages developed in association with the Free Softward Foundation, an organisation founded by Richard Stallman with the aim of creating software packages that are freely available to all users. The organisation's GNU project has resulted in the development of Linux – a free version of the Unix operating system – and thousands of additional support programs. Linux has achived such popularity that it is used by numerous organisations and educational institutions around the world. Similarly, the DJGPP C++ software compiler is also used worldwide.

Many writers and IT specialists take a combative stance and view viruses as a weapon used by unethical programmers. They argue that, just as missiles are used to deliver explosive warheads to the enemy, viruses are the *delivery systems* for destructive *payloads* to computer systems. Although some viruses are unique, the majority of payloads generally fall into a very small number of categories.

The action that a virus carries out when activated is normally referred to as the *payload*. An example of a payload might be issuing the command to delete all of the files from the user's hard disk drive when a certain condition is met, such as when a particular date or time is reached.

A major use of the payload is to display messages on the screen and play practical jokes on the user. The VirDem virus, for example, is harmless to data files but forces the user to play a simple 'guess my number' game before allowing them to use the machine. An increasing number of viruses are also being used to promote political messages. The Bloody! virus, for example, displays the message 'Bloody! Jun. 4, 1989' when activated – an obvious reference to the date of the 'Beijing massacre'.

Many viruses are designed to damage or destroy the data on a computer system. When activated, such viruses may simply alter certain parts of a data file or erase it altogether. Viruses may also be targeted against specific types of data. The DBF virus, for example, attacks only dBase files, leaving all others intact. Occasionally, a virus is programmed to activate at a certain time or in reaction to a specific event. This kind of virus is often called a **logic bomb** (sometimes also known as a *time bomb*). The number of such viruses in circulation is alarming; some sources suggest that logic bombs exist for each day of the year.

Good examples of logic bombs are the viruses based on the Jerusalem and Fu Manchu strains. These activate on any Friday the 13th, when they attempt to erase all of the data on the user's hard drive. The Michelangelo virus attacked an estimated 600 000 computers worldwide when it activated on 6 March 1992.

> The belief that an active computer virus can be transmitted to other users as part of an e-mail message is incorrect. However, any files or programs attached to e-mail messages *can* contain a virus. Simply transmitting a file will not activate a virus program – the file must be executed or manipulated in some way first.

A small number of viruses are created to assist with criminal activities such as fraud. It has been suggested that some programmers create viruses designed to give them unlimited access to an infected system (and therefore all of the data it contains). A variation on this theme is the *call-me virus*, which instructs the infected computer to call the programmer's system automatically, so that the owner of the infected system bears the brunt of any phone charges.

It could be argued that computer users themselves are often responsible for damage arising as a result of virus infections. Few users take adequate security measures, such as backing up data. It is estimated that fewer than 5 per cent of computer users are capable of carrying out backup procedures. Furthermore, inadequate training and incorrect responses to virus infections often exaggerate the problem, since anxious users may cause more damage than the virus itself.

There are few estimates of the financial loss caused by computer viruses each year. This is undoubtedly due to the reluctance of major companies to disclose the fact that their systems have been compromised. However, surveys suggest that approximately 65 per cent of major corporates come into contact with computer viruses each year. The real rate of infection may be substantially higher, since companies are unlikely to admit any major losses arising as a result of computer virus infections.

▶ Detecting and preventing virus infection

> Most viruses contain a message to be displayed on screen or a hidden piece of text. Additionally, a virus program may also contain a unique series of values in its program file. These unique features are known as the **signature** of the virus.

Signature
Unique features of a virus such as the unique series of values in its program file or message displayed on screen or hidden text.

The risk of virus infection can be reduced to a minimum by implementing a relatively simple set of security measures:

1 Unauthorised access to machines and software should be restricted as far as possible.

2 Machines and software should be checked regularly with a virus detection program.

3 All new disks and any software originating from an outside source should be checked with a virus detection program before use or floppy drives can be removed from networked machines entirely, with one central access point.

4 Floppy disks should be kept write-protected whenever possible, since it is physically impossible for a virus to copy itself to a write-protected disk.

5 Floppy disks should not be kept in the drive when the machine is switched off. Most virus infections come from so-called boot-sector viruses, which are enabled when a machine is switched on with an infected disk in the floppy drive.

6 Regular backups of data and program files must be made in order to minimise the damage caused if a virus infects the system.

> A *polymorphic* virus is capable of altering its form, so that the 'standard' signature of the virus is not present. This means that a virus scanner may not always identify the virus correctly.

Virus scanner

Intended to detect and safely remove virus programs from a computer system.

Virus scanners are intended to detect and then safely remove virus programs from a computer system. The most common method of detection used by these programs involves scanning for the **signatures** of particular viruses. It is often possible to locate a virus by simply searching every file on an infected disk for these identifying characteristics. However, since new viruses are discovered quite frequently, the list of signatures contained within a detection program quickly becomes dated. For this reason, most software developers insist that regular program updates are essential. However, the introduction of new kinds of viruses, such as polymorphic and stealth viruses, mean that signature checking alone can no longer be regarded as a completely secure method of detection. For this reason, most virus scanners use a combination of techniques to enhance their efficiency. Among the methods used are checksums, virus shields, anti-viruses and inoculation.

> A *stealth* virus is specifically designed to avoid detection. Such programs are normally written with the intention of defeating common or well-known virus scanning programs.

Virus shield

Virus shields are programs that constantly monitor and control access to a system's storage devices. Any unusual attempt to modify a file or write to a disk drive will activate a message asking the user to authorise the operation.

One of the most effective methods of detecting virus infections uses a process known as cyclic redundancy checking or CRC. This involves the creation of a list of unique identification numbers for every file on a hard or floppy disk. By comparing the current CRC number to the original, it is possible to detect if any changes have been made to a file. Thus, cyclic redundancy checking is able to detect the presence and activity of virus, Trojan and worm programs with almost perfect accuracy.

Virus shields are TSR programs that constantly monitor and control access to a system's storage devices. Any unusual attempt to modify a file or write to a disk drive will activate a message asking the user to authorise the operation. A similar task is performed by hardware virus detection devices. Modern hardware protection devices can be extremely sophisticated, featuring their own processors, disk controllers and other expensive components. However, despite the claims of the manufacturers of these devices, there is little evidence to suggest that they are any more effective than software solutions.

The use of **anti-virus** software is particularly popular with owners of home computers. Essentially, an anti-virus is a benevolent virus program that copies itself to the boot sectors of unprotected floppy disks. If another virus attempts to overwrite the anti-virus, it displays a message on the screen warning the user of infection. A similar technique is used to protect individual programs by adding a small amount of inoculation code to the end of them. Each time the program is run, the inoculation routine evaluates the program's checksum number and issues a warning if the file has been altered in any way. However, a drawback of this technique is that only a relatively small number of programs can be treated in this way.

> A distinction is made between *erasing* and *deleting* a file. Erasing a file merely removes its entry in the disk's directory structure: the file remains intact until another file overwrites it. For this reason, virus killers delete the virus completely by overwriting it with new data.

Once a virus has been detected there are three methods of removing it. The first, *disinfection*, attempts to restore damaged files and directory structures to their original condition. However, disinfection is not possible in all cases, particularly when dealing with parasitic viruses. The second technique involves *overwriting* the virus program so that it is permanently and irrevocably deleted from the disk. The third and final method of removing a virus is by restoring a backup of the disk before infection to the system. The process of writing files to the disk effectively overwrites the virus and restores the system to its original state.

Despite the sophistication of scanning programs, none is capable of offering complete protection against infection. Many tests have been carried out to determine the efficiency of specific virus scanning programs. In all of these tests, no program has yet achieved a perfect score. The detection rate of some programs was found to be as low as 50 per cent.

▶ Trends

In 1989, it was believed that there were fewer than 50 viruses in circulation. Recent reports estimate that between 1500 and 3000 viruses exist at present. Furthermore, other estimates suggest that new viruses are being discovered at a rate of more than 50 a month.

There is a distinction to be made between the number of viruses that actually exist and those found 'in the wild'. It should be recognised that a large number of computer viruses are created as experiments and are not intended to be distributed. In addition, the vast majority of computer viruses that are created are often incapable of surviving long enough to achieve widespread distribution. Poor programming, for example, may mean that a particular computer virus is unable to travel beyond the author's computer. Similarly, since many new computer viruses are created as variants on existing ones, they are often easy to detect and neutralise using virus detection software.

Thus, although some estimates suggest that there may be as many as 20 000 different computer viruses in existence, a much smaller number will actually be in circulation at any one time.

There is evidence to suggest that the competition between virus writers and anti-virus experts is responsible for a surge in new types of virus. Apart from the growth in the numbers of new viruses, this competition has almost certainly led to the appearance of new stealth and polymorphic viruses. Stealth viruses – named after US aircraft technology – use various techniques to hide their presence from virus scanners, while polymorphic viruses are capable of changing their basic file structure, making it almost impossible to detect a signature.

The situation has deteriorated further with the release of *virus mutation engines*, menu-driven programs that can be used by amateurs to produce sophisticated viruses in minutes. For example, it is known that the mutation engines produced by the Dark Avenger group and the Chaos Computer Club have already been used to produce a number of new stealth and polymorphic viruses.

Improved access to technology, an increase in the use of networks and new communications technology have increased the vulnerability of many users to virus infections. At most risk are universities and other large sites, such as public services.

It has been alleged that government agencies, terrorists, criminals and even corporates are beginning to take an active interest in developing viruses. Some of the allegations made in recent years include:

◆ US intelligence services have conducted research into the use of viruses as weapons of war.

◆ Major corporations have examined the possibility of using viruses for industrial espionage. Possible applications included the destruction of competitors' database files and new kinds of call-me viruses.

◆ The Jerusalem virus was created by the PLO for use against Israeli computer systems.

The Aids Virus Trojan demonstrates the ease with which viruses can be employed in criminal activities. Financial systems are particularly vulnerable to electronic theft and blackmail attempts. Although no evidence exists to suggest that viruses have yet been used in this way, the possibility remains.

CASE STUDY: TOPIC AREA

FT

Computer viruses

Computer viruses: concerns grow as figures double

New computer viruses which can damage companies' software and cause costly disruption to businesses have more than doubled in the past 18 months.

The number of new viruses discovered each month has risen from about 200 to 500 worldwide, raising serious concerns in the computer industry.

The problem is blamed on the rapid adoption of software using easily-corruptible instructions, and the growing use of the internet as a means of transmission.

Geoff Leahy, chief executive of Dr Solomon's, Europe's biggest anti-virus computer software company, said: 'It's not out of control yet, but this is a serious problem affecting thousands of computer users.'

Nick Fitzgerald, who edits the industry magazine *Virus Bulletin*, said: 'It is getting to the point where the anti-virus industry will have to start re-evaluating how it tackles the problem.'

The computer crime unit at the central police headquarters in London said it was aware of the problem and was watching developments carefully but it could only act on complaints and few businesses were prepared to admit they had a virus problem.

There are some 18 000 known viruses, with a further several hundred undiscovered strains in circulation among computer users. Once identified, most viruses – almost wholly written and sent by adolescent boys – are easily prevented from damaging a computer's hardware or software.

However, the emergence of so-called 'macro-viruses' has added a new dimension. A macro is a set of instructions which runs automatically when a file is opened. Macro is used in Word and Excel, two of the most popular programmes by Microsoft, whose software is used in about 80 per cent of the world's PCs.

Jan Hruska, technical director of Sophos, the UK anti-virus group, said: 'Macro is easy to write into, and so it is easy for virus writing. The internet has also made it easy to spread.'

The International Computer Security Association, an anti-virus industry group, estimates that more than a third of all viruses are carried through files attached to electronic mail via the internet. The association also estimates that the average cost to computer users of a virus incident has doubled in the past two years to almost £2000.

Graham Kluley, senior technical director at Dr Solomon's, said the number of incidents of infection being reported from the group's 50 000-strong customer base was rising in proportion to the increase in new strains.

From the company's figures, he estimated that a company with 1000 machines would have an average of 46 infected by a virus every month. 'One of our large clients gets 200 viruses a week,' he said, most sent via e-mail.

To the chagrin of the anti-virus industry, virus writers can operate openly because the act of writing is not a crime. 'We do spend a lot of time discouraging them and we have made a few converts,' said Mr Kluley. 'But they are basically young boys who have yet to discover girls.'

Source: *Financial Times*, 23 February 1998

Questions

1 Why are macro viruses of particular concern to business organisations?

2 What factors might explain why the average cost of a virus incident is £2000?

3 The case study suggests that a company with 1000 machines would have an average of 46 infected by a virus each month. How can such a high incidence of virus infection be explained?

▶ SUMMARY

1 Controls on computer-based information systems are needed to ensure the accuracy of data held by an organisation and to prevent against loss or damage. The use of passwords to prevent unauthorised access and regular backups are the most important controls that should be in place for all companies.

2 Computer-based information systems should be protected against deliberate or unintentional sabotage. The most common threats to computer-based information systems include accidents, natural disasters, sabotage, vandalism, theft, unauthorised use and computer viruses.

3 There are four basic control strategies that can be applied to the security of computer-based information systems:
   ◆ Containment using passwords attempts to control access to an information system and often involves making potential targets as unattractive as possible.
   ◆ Deterrence uses the threat of punishment to discourage potential intruders.
   ◆ Obfuscation involves hiding or distributing assets so that any damage caused can be limited.
   ◆ Recovery recognises that, no matter how well defended, a breach in the security of an information system will eventually occur, so information should be backed up to avoid loss even if it is deleted.

4 Types of control for computer-based information systems include:
   ◆ Physical protection involves the use of physical barriers intended to protect against theft and unauthorised access.

- ◆ Biometric controls make use of the unique characteristics of individuals, such as fingerprints, in order to restrict access to sensitive information or equipment.
- ◆ Telecommunications controls, such as passwords and user validation routines, help verify the identity of a particular user.
- ◆ Failure controls attempt to limit or avoid damage caused by the failure of an information system using backup and disaster recovery techniques.
- ◆ Auditing involves taking stock of procedures, hardware, software and data at regular intervals.

5 Backup procedures enable an organisation to protect sensitive files by making copies that can be stored at a safe location. The 'grandfather, father, son' technique is one of the most popular methods of making backups. An incremental backup provides a means of copying only those files that have changed in some way since the last backup was made.

6 Computer viruses, worms, Trojans and logic bombs represent a growing threat to information systems security. A computer virus is a computer program that is capable of self-replication, allowing it to spread from one 'infected' machine to another. All computer viruses are considered harmful and steps should be taken to protect valuable data from infection.

▶ EXERCISES

▶ Self-assessment exercises

1 What are the two basic reasons for the need to control computer-based information systems?

2 List some of the advantages and disadvantages of using passwords to protect equipment and sensitive data from unauthorised users.

3 What types of controls can be used to protect a computer-based information system against vandalism, theft and unauthorised access?

4 What are the advantages and disadvantages of an approach to controlling computer-based information systems that is based on containment?

5 Describe some of the ways in which accidental damage can occur to a computer-based information system.

6 Explain why virus scanning software and anti-virus programs are often only of limited value in detecting and removing computer viruses.

7 Explain what is meant by disaster recovery planning.

▶ Discussion questions

1 What motivates an individual or organisation to create a computer virus?

2 No computer-based information system can be considered completely secure – all organisations should base their control strategies on recovery. Make a case in favour of or against this argument.

▶ Essay questions

1 Conduct any research necessary and produce a formal security policy governing student access to the computer systems at the institution that you attend. In addition to providing details of any controls already in place, your work must also address the areas listed below. For each of these areas, you should also justify any decisions or choices made.
   (a) what activities are considered acceptable;
   (b) what activities are considered unacceptable;
   (c) the sanctions that may be used against those failing to comply with the policy.

2 Select an organisation with which you are familiar, such as a university or bank. Conduct any research necessary to address the following tasks:
   (a) Describe the potential impact of infection by computer viruses on the organisation's computer-based information systems.
   (b) Consider the effectiveness of tools, methods and procedures designed to protect computer-based information systems from computer viruses.
   (c) Evaluate the level of risk posed to the organisation by computer viruses and produce a set of recommendations that may assist the organisation in reducing this risk.

▶ Examination questions

1 Computer viruses represent a significant threat to the security of organisational computer-based information systems. It is estimated that as many as 500 new computer viruses appear each month. You are required to:
   (a) Provide a definition of the term 'computer virus'.
   (b) Using relevant examples, describe the ways in which computer viruses can be transmitted.
   (c) Discuss some of the ways in which organisations can protect against computer viruses. Highlight some of the advantages and disadvantages of each method described.

2 With regard to the control of computer-based information systems, you are required to:
   (a) Describe some of the common security threats facing organisational computer-based information systems.
   (b) Explain the four basic approaches to controlling computer-based information systems. Highlight the advantages and disadvantages of each approach.
   (c) More effective protection for a computer-based information system can be achieved by employing a combination of the four basic approaches to control. Using relevant examples, discuss this statement.

3 A formal security policy can provide an effective means of protecting an organisation's computer-based information systems against theft, damage and other hazards. You are required to:
   (a) Provide an overview of the areas that will be outlined by a typical formal security policy document.
   (b) Describe the ways in which a formal security policy can help protect an organisation's computer-based information systems.
   (c) A number of factors will determine whether or not a security policy works effectively. Using relevant examples, provide a brief discussion of some of these factors.

4 Safeguarding company information is an important responsibility of an IS manager or any departmental head. Describe the main threats to company information and define a strategy to ensure that information is not lost or corrupted. You should describe the full range of threats to information security.

▶ References

Price, C. (1998) 'Computer viruses: concerns grow as figures double', *Financial Times*, 23 February.

▶ Further reading

Baum, D. (1997) 'Planning and implementing a data warehouse', *BYTE*, June.

Burger, R. (1989) *Computer Viruses: a High-Tech Disease*, 3rd edition, Data Becker, New York.

Cohen, F. (1984) *Computer Viruses: Theory and Experiments*, IFIP TC-11 Conference, Toronto, F899, 240–255. This is the first paper to refer to viruses.

Fites, P., Johnston, P. and Kratz, M. (1992) *The Computer Virus Crisis*, 2nd edition, Van Nostrand Reinhold, New York.

Forester, T. and Morrison, P. (1990) *Computer Ethics*, Basil Blackwell, Oxford.

Laudon, K. and Laudon, J. (1995) *Management Information Systems: Organization and Technology*, 3rd edition, Macmillan.
Chapter 18 deals with issues related to the control of computer-based information systems.

Levy, S. (1994) *Hackers: Heroes of the Computer Revolution*, Penguin, Harmondsworth.
An investigation into the behaviour of computer hackers, including Steve Wozniak, who later formed Apple Computers.

▶ Web references

http://www.bsi.org.uk British Standards Institute. Provides details on the BS7799 standard on information security.

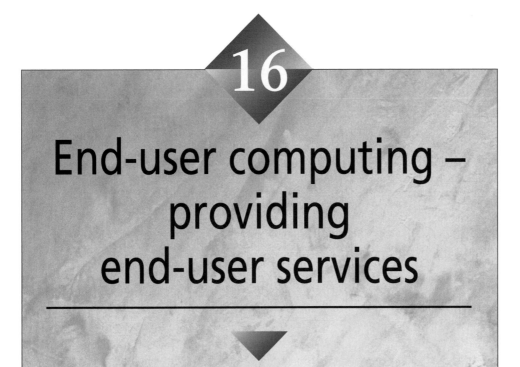

End-user computing – providing end-user services

INTRODUCTION

This chapter considers some of the many tasks to support end-users that need to be performed by an information systems manager in the modern organisation. At the top of the list of priorities is the management of user information within the organisation – ensuring that it is secure, that backups are made and that its quality is maintained. A further important aspect of managing the information quality is ensuring that it is delivered to the user in a reliable and timely way. The management of the network is key to achieving this, but ensuring reliable access to the applications needed to work with the data is also important. This is particularly true with mission-critical applications – the operational systems used to deal with customers for taking orders and reservations. When a new version of the EuropCar car reservation system failed, for example, it is estimated to have cost the company $300 000 in lost orders over three days.

The protection of information is one type of end-user service that has been covered in the previous chapter. As well as managing information, the network and applications, the IS manager has to manage other services provided to end-users to help them work with this application. These 'soft' services include advice, troubleshooting various problems and assisting users in developing their own applications. End-user development is an increasingly important activity with the move to PCs from a central mainframe and dumb terminal arrangement, giving more opportunities for tailoring of applications. This chapter will focus on the management of these 'soft' services and examine how they should be integrated into a company's overall IS strategy.

End-user service provision is often considered under the heading 'end-user computing'. This covers a wide range of activities. In this chapter, the distinction is

End-user computing (EUC)

All uses of computers by business people who are not Information Systems professionals.

End-user development (EUD)

Systems development and programming undertaken by non IS staff.

made between the *use* of applications created by others by the end-user (**end-user computing**) and the *creation* of applications by the end-user (**end-user development**). The chapter considers how to provide services to support both classes of activity. Supporting both activities is certainly important – Robson (1997) suggests that what she defines as user-controlled computing has increased from 25 per cent of IS budgets in the early 1980s to 75–90 per cent in the 1990s.

▶ Learning objectives

After reading this chapter, readers will be able to:

◆ appreciate the range of services that must be delivered to support end-users effectively;

◆ distinguish between the general term end-user computing and the more specific end-user development;

◆ analyse the risks associated with pursuing end-user development of information systems as part of a company's IS strategy;

◆ recommend policies for the effective management of end-user computing within an organisation;

◆ recommend new information systems applications that could reasonably be developed by end-user staff within an organisation.

▶ Links to other chapters

Protecting information, another key role of the IS manager, is covered in Chapter 15. Attributes of good-quality data were covered in Chapter 2.

End-user computing and the location of support services are elements of IS strategy that are described in Chapter 14.

End-user IS services

All services required to support end-users in running their PCs and developing and using applications.

▶ END-USER IS SERVICES

The main end-user services that the information systems manager has to provide are as follows:

1 *Provide a help-desk service.* This will solve problems that users are having in using their software. This will involve troubleshooting to work out the source of the problem, which could be caused by:
   ◆ the way the user is using the software;
   ◆ a problem with the way the software has been installed;
   ◆ a bug in the software;
   ◆ an underlying hardware or networking problem.

This service must be delivered as rapidly as possible, but this is often difficult to achieve since a help desk will have to juggle many requests, some of which may be quite time consuming to solve.

2 *Achieve standardisation of software.* Applications used across departments should be standardised to reduce the cost of purchase through volume discounts and to ensure easy transfer of information through the organisation (Chapter 3).

3 *Ensure network efficiency.* Users should not experience 'downtime' when the network is unavailable (Chapter 5).

4 *Provide training.* Users require training in the use of standard and company applications and where necessary in how to develop applications or manage information when end-user development is undertaken.

5 *Delivering services to end-users cost effectively.* This is referred to as minimising the 'total cost of ownership', which includes both the initial cost of purchase of hardware and software and the ongoing cost of maintenance.

At a more strategic level, the IS manager will be responsible for:

◆ setting the organisation's IS strategy covering issues such as integration with business strategy, investment levels and whether services are centralised or decentralised (Chapter 14);

◆ establishing IS infrastructure (networks, hardware and software services);

◆ implementation of corporate strategy through developing line-of-business systems;

◆ ensuring that the company follows ethical or legal codes for health and safety and data protection (Chapter 18).

▶ MANAGING NETWORK SERVICES

▶ Network management services

Network management services are part of the goal of integrated information management. This will include the following end-user services that are normally managed centrally:

◆ Maintaining servers, including file (document) servers, database servers and Web servers for intranets (Chapter 5 describes types of servers).

◆ Ensuring availability of end-user applications.

◆ Backup/restore of information.

◆ Network maintenance.

In many companies, the magnitude of the cost of managing user services is not recognised. To start with, the number of PCs and the different applications they run must be audited. The number of PCs that have been purchased and applications being used may be a surprise. For example, on completing its first audit, Nottinghamshire County Council discovered 6500 PCs across 830 sites. A recent survey in the UK of 500 IT and finance directors by market research company Banner discovered that 47 per cent had no tools to help in auditing the software applications used or for troubleshooting. This shows that network management and end-user services can be neglected in some organisations.

▶ Cost-effective delivery of IS services

A growing realisation among many IS and financial managers is that the total cost of ownership of each PC in a company is significant when summed across all PCs in an organisation. Traditionally, companies have costed PCs on the initial purchase price or the cost of leasing, without explicitly costing the other services required to support a PC and its users. These other costs are all the end-user services referred to above, such as running a help desk to solve end-user problems and managing user information. It also includes other costs such as:

◆ the loss of productive work time when users are unable to use their computer;

◆ the loss of productive work time when someone is trying to fix a colleague's problem (this type of unofficial support can be very costly);

◆ the cost of consumables such as paper and toner for printing.

Total cost of ownership (TCO)

TCO refers to the total cost for a company operating a computer. This includes not only the purchase or leasing cost, but also the cost of all the services needed to support the end-user.

This issue was highlighted in the US by studies by the Gartner Group which have shown that the annual cost of servicing a PC, known as the **total cost of ownership** (TCO), runs at $8000 per year.

Figure 16.1 shows the breakdown of the TCO. Costs in these categories can be attributed to 'desktop costs', related to the PC hardware and software, and 'network costs', related to managing communications and the network operating system. Desktop costs account for about two-thirds of the TCO. Note the relatively small proportion that is spent on capital and that all the other costs can be considered as aspects of supporting end-user computing. Further studies have shown that if companies carefully manage their PC resources, they can achieve cost savings of up to $3100 per PC per annum.

In 1996, US PC manufacturer Compaq launched a marketing initiative based on the cost of ownership that claims that Compaq 'costs you less than other computers' due to tools bundled with the computer to reduce TCO. Microsoft's initiative of Zero Administration Windows (ZAW) and tools such as Systems Management Server (SMS) are aimed at reducing the cost of distributing and maintaining software. SMS provides:

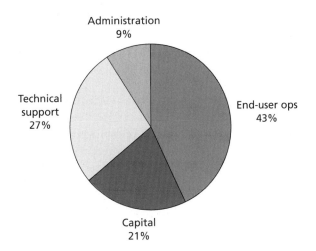

Fig 16.1 Breakdown of the total cost of ownership

Source: Gartner Group (1996)

- automated software distribution and upgrades;
- metering of which applications are being used;
- hardware and software inventory for each machine;
- troubleshooting diagnostics of each machine from a remote location (i.e. users' machines can be monitored from a help desk).

The TCO can also be reduced by using simpler, less expensive hardware, which is the idea behind the network computer and NetPC. The mini case study on using network computers shows how the savings can be achieved.

Using network computers to reduce the total cost of ownership

MINI CASE

A further response to reducing TCO is to treat the problem at its root cause – the complexity of the PC. By reducing the options to configure each PC and its software individually, there is less risk of its failing and the need for support. This has led to the idea of the network computer (introduced in Chapter 3). This is a simplified computer that runs the software on a network server. This reduces the purchase cost, since the computer needs less RAM memory, no hard disk, no floppy disk and a less powerful processor than a PC. It also reduces the cost of ownership, since there are fewer hardware items to fail and the software can be managed by central support staff rather than the end-user. Of course, simplifying the maintenance of the computer in this way also reduces the flexibility of options available for the end-user.

Since the NC concept was first discussed in 1995, a number of companies have purchased large numbers of NCs to help reduce the TCO. For example, in the UK retailer Safeway and insurer Eagle Star have each bought several hundred, and in the US Boeing has committed to buying several thousand. Despite large individual purchases, it should be noted that the market for NCs is still less than 1 per cent of the desktop computer market.

The network computer concept was chiefly promoted by Oracle and IBM. It represents a threat to rival companies Microsoft and Intel, since typically it would not use Windows for the operating system or Intel processors. To counter this, several counterinitiatives have been launched. These include a hardware initiative through the concept of a Net PC, which can be thought of as a hybrid between a PC and an NC, with the aim again being to reduce the TCO, but without removing all the flexibility of the PC. There are two main software initiatives to date. The first is Hydra, included in Windows NT 5.0 to allow Windows-based applications to be run on a server while the user only uses a relative low-cost Windows terminal from a manufacturer such as Wyse. The second is to build tools into the operating system to make central administration of PCs, NCs and Windows terminals more effective. This is known as ZAW or Zero Administration Windows.

▶ END-USER COMPUTING

▶ What is end-user computing?

The term **end-user computing** has different meanings according to the context in which it is used. The following statements could all refer to end-user computing:

◆ All tools by which non-data processing staff handle their own problems without professional programmers.

◆ Creative use of data processing by non-data processing experts.

◆ Complex computing by non-data processing professionals to answer organisational information needs.

◆ Non-technical end-users using user-friendly, fourth-generation languages (4GLs) and PCs to generate reports or build decision support systems.

◆ The use of computer hardware and software by people in organisations whose jobs are usually classified as net users of information systems rather than net developers of information systems.

The common theme is that staff whose main job function is not building information systems are doing some system development. The definitions vary in what is meant by 'system development'. For some staff this may mean just that: developing a complete information system. More frequently, it will mean users building their own spreadsheet model or using a report generator. The three main types of end-user computing can be defined as:

1 End-user developed computer-based information systems for personal, departmental or organisation-wide use, where the end-user is a non-IT professional.

2 End-user control of which hardware and package applications are purchased for use in their department.

3 End-user use of existing information systems.

Clearly, each type of end-user computing represents a different challenge for the information systems manager. In this chapter we will consider end-user computing and end-user development separately.

▶ What are the drivers for end-user computing?

The primary business driver for EUC from the *organisational perspective* is greater control in end-user departments over choosing which applications are developed. Where there is a backlog of applications that need to be developed, this also leads to a reduced time for a system to be implemented if it is developed by end-users. EUC can also lead to the empowerment of staff in functional areas of an organisation to follow through creative ideas for using information systems to improve the efficiency of their work. Innovative ideas may be fostered in this way when they would otherwise be stifled if there was no outlet or mechanism for their being implemented.

The reasons given above for the development of end-user computing have been supported by *technology* becoming more readily available to support end-user development. Such technical support has become possible through increased availability of:

◆ personal computers or workstations on users' desktops with graphical user interfaces that (unlike simple terminals) are appropriate for end-user development;

◆ 4GLs (Chapter 4) that enable systems to be developed with limited programming skills;

◆ visual development tools such as Visual Basic, PowerBuilder and Delphi, which make it easier to prototype application screen layouts and navigation between data views – these tools also enable screen elements such as tables to be readily integrated with information from a database;

◆ support for extending productivity applications. For example, Microsoft Word or Excel can be extended to an end-user application using the Visual Basic for Applications tools.

Finally, EUC has also been enabled by IS skills among the workforce increasing as the overall standard of IT familiarity grows through staff using IT throughout their education and into the workplace.

The specific reasons for and possible problems with end-user development are described in more detail on page 579.

▶ Which company staff are involved in end-user computing?

A common method of describing end-user computing is according to the skills of the end-user. This method was described in a paper from the early 1980s by Rockart and Flannery, summarised in Table 16.1. Some of the terms used have been superseded (updated equivalents shown in brackets), but the basic definition does remain valid. The classification does not represent a continuum from Class 1 to 6, but rather two different groupings: first business users of different skills levels in Classes 1 to 3, and then support personnel in Classes 4 to 6. Blili *et al.* (1996) present a more recent review of how end-user computing can be defined, grouping work into types of user, types of application and end-user behaviour.

Table 16.1 Different types of end-user personnel as categorised by Rockart and Flannery (1983)

Class	Term	Description
1	Non-programming end-users	These are users of software developed by others
2	Command-level end-users (power users)	These are users who use more sophisticated functions of a package, such as formulas and macros in a spreadsheet such as Excel
3	Programming-level end-users	Here users write their own functions using add-on application languages such as Visual Basic for Applications
4	Functional support personnel (business analysts and developers)	These are support staff who work in one area of the business to provide end-user development and support
5	End-user computing support personnel (help desk staff)	These are the support staff who exist to troubleshoot hardware and software problems that are encountered by users in Classes 1 to 3.
6	Data processing programmers (application developers)	This type of programming staff has traditionally worked on company operational or reporting systems

A further important method of describing end-user computing is according to the way in which it is controlled. This will typically vary in line with the maturity of end-user computing in an organisation. Initially there will be no control and an organic growth of EUC. As EUC becomes more prevalent, problems caused by the lack of control will occur and a need will be identified by business and IS managers to take measures to control it. Control measures are referred to below.

▶ THE INFORMATION CENTRE

Information centre (IC)

A central facility in an organisation which provides end-user help-desk services such as phone support for troubleshooting end-user software and hardware problems, training, guidance on end-user development and management of user information.

Information centre (IC) is an American term that has arisen from a concept developed by IBM in the 1980s. Typical information centres developed at this time are described by Christy and White (1987). In the UK and Europe, the equivalent is usually referred to by the less grand terms 'IT support' or 'help desk'. However, the IC or modern IT support centre offers much more than phone support to users – it provides all the services required for end-users to use and develop applications.

The range of services offered by a typical information centre are:

1 *Help desk support for user problems.* The case study on Pfizer's help desk illustrates the different levels of support that are offered.

2 *Advice on software purchase.* This ensures that the software is suitable for its purpose and is compatible with hardware, other software and company purchasing schemes.

3 *Advice on hardware purchase.* This will usually be a centralised standard, again to take advantage of discounts and limiting support contracts.

4 *Advice on how end-user development should be approached.* The support person will suggest the best approaches for developing software, such as following the main parts of the lifecycle. These can be defined through more detailed training.

5 *Application development.* For larger systems, the IC staff may be involved in performing the systems analysis and design or more difficult aspects of the programming.

6 *Training.* In particular, on packages or development techniques.

7 *Data management.* Management and supply of data to end-users or explanations of formats used.

The main difficulty with information centres is getting the balance right between providing a flexible service and exerting controls that are too restrictive. The information centre can be valuable in providing controls to prevent the type of problems that are described in the following section.

As part of the trend to outsourcing of IS described in Chapter 14, many help desks are now outsourced to other companies. For example, within Rolls-Royce UK, user support is now provided by EDS staff. Microsoft outsources its help desk for its applications and operating systems to companies such as Digital (now part of Compaq). The case study on Pfizer's help desk illustrates how a company has taken steps to avoid the problems that could occur through outsourcing. It highlights a common three-tier method of profiling user problems so that they can be dealt with efficiently. The case study also illustrates how a company is evolving the strategy for its help desk.

CASE STUDY: TOPIC AREA

Pfizer's help desk wins award

In recent years computer service departments have come under increasing pressure from business units to significantly raise the level of support they provide. As a result, service level agreements have become an accepted way of life. Yet at the same time, as many companies look to focus their internal expertise on core business rather than support services, these departments are under the constant threat of outsourcing as well as pressure to contain, if not reduce, ongoing costs.

Key to providing that service is an integrated and efficient help desk. Pfizer Central Research, part of pharmaceutical giant Pfizer, has recently been awarded Help Desk of the Year by the Help Desk User Group. Steve Ladyman, head of computer user support at Pfizer, attributes the award to the company's 'very professional approach to the help desk'. He says, 'We have an innovative approach to resolving help desk problems.' A key element of that innovative approach has been the adoption of a co-sourcing agreement for the staffing of the help desk. As Ladyman explains, most firms in this competitive market are concentrating on core business. 'Pfizer employees are focused on drug discovery and development rather than IT,' he says. Pfizer, like many rivals, initially took the contracting approach to help desk staff. 'We found they were not fully committed to us which created a morale problem,' Ladyman says. With average staff turnover hitting six months, the obvious lack of training programmes and a career development path was significantly affecting the ongoing level of service the help desk could provide Pfizer employees.

So Pfizer adopted a co-sourcing strategy. 'The help desk staff are not Pfizer employees, but are full time for DCS [the outsourcing firm which holds the contract],' he says. And, to overcome that morale problem, the contract between Pfizer and DCS stipulates a training plan and clear career development must be in place. They work to similar terms and conditions of both pay and holiday as Pfizer employees,' he says.

Since this strategy was implemented early in 1995, the help desk has lost only one staff member – a clear indication, says Ladyman, of the success of co-sourcing. But, to ensure the help desk is still under Pfizer's firm managerial control, each of the three tiers of the help desk is managed by a Pfizer employee. This three-tier help desk architecture

is, according to Ladyman, Pfizer's other innovative solution for creating a truly supportive help desk.

The first tier attempts to solve the user's problem there and then, usually over the phone. These are calls relating to recognised, standard problems that are documented and have a clear, predefined response. Pfizer's target is to solve 60% of calls this way and the company is already achieving a 50% resolution rate. The second tier is also for recognised problems, but those that require actual physical work on the system – and a visit to the user's site. The third tier deals with unrecognised problems. 'The third tier expert is given time not only to find and fix the problem, but to document it and train second tier staff to solve it themselves in a predefined manner should that problem occur again,' Ladyman says.

The target is to ensure a third tier problem should arise once only – once solved it has a standard fix and can be handled by one of the first two tiers. Pfizer has not yet attained this goal. 'We are trying to capitalise learning within a documented solution and contain support costs,' says Ladyman. Controlling staff turnover on the help desk is key to attaining these targets: previously without good documentation and follow-up training, rapid staff turnover meant problems were having to be regularly resolved. 'Rapid staff turnover means that, without adequate documentation of problems, when a problem recurs you have to go back to the beginning,' says Ladyman. 'We are trying to be much more careful in our documentation of solutions, which means we have a greater likelihood of the expertise being on site if a problem returns.'

Underpinning this new strategy has been the replacement of the firm's existing help desk software with Utopia from Utopia. As one of the new breed of client/server help desk products, Utopia enables Pfizer to build an extensive database of user problems, providing the opportunity to spot trends and track problem resolution to ensure a satisfactory response to user demands.

Ladyman says, 'Our target is to contain costs.' He says, 'Pfizer has a highly technical user population. They are very bright and tend to be pushing IT to the limits. We don't want users trying to solve problems that we can solve more quickly for them. The strategy is not about reducing calls to the help desk, but increasing the efficiency with which they are solved.' Ladyman cites two recent trends spotted by help desk staff where specific departments were logging a higher-than-average number of calls. One department had many calls about cc:mobile which, after analysis, the help desk team was able to link to the fact that members of that department are constantly on the road. 'The other department is clearly pushing technology to the limit,' he explains.

Using this information, Pfizer is starting to work out specific training programmes for cc:mobile users to help them with problem solving. In addition, Ladyman says the information will prove critical in negotiations with user departments about service level agreements. 'The previous help desk software gave us no information to help us to put agreements in place. It was a driving reason for replacing the help desk software,' says Ladyman.

Having achieved the first phase of the implementation, Pfizer will now look to setting up an improved asset register for asset management in the next phase which will, eventually, be followed by change management. 'Effective asset management is a big target,' he concedes. 'We have 2300 PCs to support and if we do an audit one day, you can guarantee the next day some of those PCs will have

moved. This has always been a headache.' Despite the early success of the help desk strategy, Ladyman remains pragmatic. 'I don't think anyone has help desks right yet. The demand for support services is always ahead of what you can economically provide and there is always someone who needs help quicker than you can provide it. But with our three tier model, co-sourcing and the tools set we have implemented, we have an advantage over other organisations running help desks in this environment.'

Source: 'IT help desk: questions and answers', *Computer Weekly*, 12 September 1996.

Questions

1 Explain the three-tier method used for targeting the type of enquiry being made.

2 How has Pfizer attempted to keep the help desk staff well integrated with business users, despite their being employed by another company?

3 Summarise the future strategy that Pfizer has developed for managing its help desk.

▶ Help desk technologies

In this section we briefly review the way in which information systems are used to support the use of other information systems within a company!

1 *Asset management software*. Help desk staff need to know the technical details of the systems being used in the company and the software loaded on them. This is achieved by asset management software such as Microsoft Systems Management server. This can also distribute new software automatically.

2 *Computer telephony integration (CTI)*. CTI gives automatic phone number identification and the system will then load up the details of the computer, its current user and configuration. This allows first-tier calls to be answered much faster.

3 *Case-based reasoning*. These systems use artificial intelligence techniques (Chapter 6) to guide the user or help desk staff through the process of solving the problem.

4 *Web-based intranet access*. Users can access frequently asked questions, send an e-mail or type in keywords describing their problems. Problems solved this way will save help desk staff the time spent dealing with straightforward queries.

5 *Workflow*. Workflow systems can be used to prioritise user queries and assign them to the staff best placed to deal with them. An example of a workflow queue used in a help desk is shown in Fig 16.2.

Further details on the type of facilities available in help desk software are provided by Utopia, one of the most frequently used products worldwide (*see* http://www.utosoft.com).

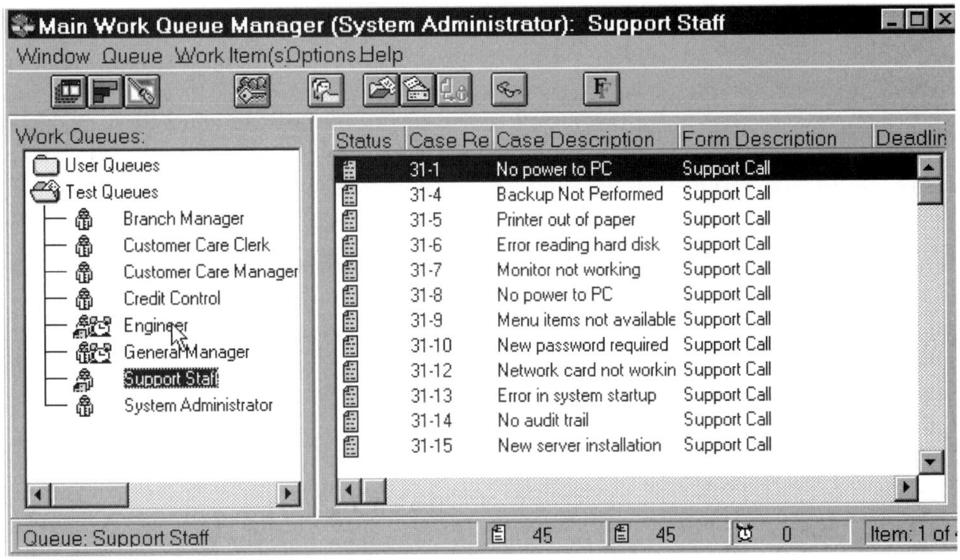

Fig 16.2 Workflow system from Staffware being used to prioritise support calls

▶ END-USER DEVELOPMENT

End-user development of applications represents a major trend in the use of information technology in organisations. An increasing number of users are writing their own software or spreadsheet models to help in decision making. This was not possible before there was a PC on every desktop. The user was then reliant on the IS department writing applications. Since the IS department focused on strategic applications, the users' requests for small-scale applications would often be ignored.

▶ Applications and tools for end-user development

There is a wide range of possible applications for end-user developed software that are listed below. Typically it is the smaller-scale, departmental applications that are most appropriate for end-user development. The development tools reflect these. These tools are usually high-level reporting and programming tools. It is rare for the end-user to program using a lower-level language such as C++ or Java, which would require extensive training. Possible types of applications include:

◆ Reports from a corporate database using standard enquiries defined by the IS/IT function.

◆ Simple *ad hoc* queries to databases defined by the user. For someone in an airline, for example, these might include access to a frequent flier database, customer reservation system or crew rostering system to monitor performance of each.

◆ What-if? analysis using tools such as spreadsheet models or more specialised tools such as risk or financial management packages or business intelligence software, used for monitoring sales and marketing performance of information stored in a data warehouse (Chapter 19).

◆ Writing company information for a company intranet (*see* mini case study on Delcam and details on intranets in Chapter 17).

◆ Development of applications such as a job costing tool or production scheduling system, using easy-to-use, high-level tools such as application generators, PC database management systems such as Microsoft Access or Borland, or visual programming environments such as Microsoft Visual Basic, Borland Delphi, Powerbuilder or Centura.

An example of a visual programming environment is shown in Fig 16.3. The user has easy-to-use tools to draw graphs and tables and to populate these with information from a database. Program code (shown in the window) may be required to achieve this.

▶ Reasons for the growth of end-user development

The reason for the increase in end-user developed applications is a combination of two main factors. The first is that it only became practical for end-users to develop software with the introduction of the PC and graphical systems development tools. With earlier mainframe and minicomputer systems, it was not practical for people who were not in the IS department to develop software; neither the tools nor the access were available.

The second reason is that users were not receiving the required response from the IS department in terms of building systems for them. This is often known as

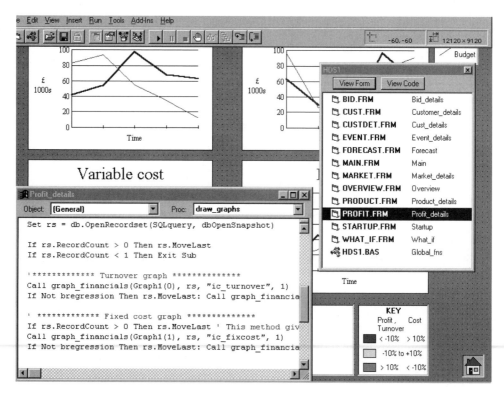

Fig 16.3 Visual Basic development tool showing onscreen forms and development code

CASE STUDY: TOPIC AREA

End-user development training at the Open University

In the fast-changing world of Windows, training staff can quickly rise from providing guidance on simple word processing to complex database development. Jason Hobby reports on how the Open University not only rose to the challenge, but found wider recognition in CW's coveted training awards. A team of just two systems analysts working on a shoestring budget have transformed more than 200 staff at the Open University (OU) from mere PC users to amateur systems developers. In the process they scooped for the university the End User Training Award, a category of the *Computer Weekly* IT Training Awards.

The hard graft on both the part of willing learners and the two experienced systems analysts falls under the mantle of the university's End User Development (EUD) Scheme, specifically geared to adapting IT to meet local needs directly. Essentially, it allows individuals or departments to develop the applications they choose without waiting for the IT department to do it for them.

The OU defines six levels of end-user computing, ranging from basic word processing to complex multi-user relational databases. It is at levels four and five that the EUD support team steps in, providing instruction in the development of simple, single-table databases to more complex office-modelling procedures. This is restricted to PC hardware, stopping short of university-wide systems.

The administrative staff at whom the scheme is aimed are expected to do much of the local data manipulation. Sandra Evans, one of the two systems analysts involved in the training project, explains. 'The basic word processing skills were already catered for, but there was this higher level where people started wanting to use tools such as Microsoft Access. They needed to write their own databases.'

In the beginning the trainers concentrated on teaching how to use only Microsoft Access but, 'Then we also realised they would need to do a small amount of systems analysis,' Evans says. 'Something slightly different from using Word and Excel – actually learning how to design a database properly.' So Evans set up a one-day Basic Systems Analysis course, classroom-based and with the intention of teaching the rudiments of systems development and providing guidance on key issues such as security, back-ups and data protection.

The trainees are taken step-by-step through the development process with a case study exercise. Next follows the two-day Microsoft Access course, which unlike the one-day Basic Systems Analysis course has a high hands-on content.

'A lot of people don't want to come and do the systems analysis course,' says Evans. 'They just want to get straight on and work with the PC. But once they've been through the course they realise it's very valuable, before they start using the PC, to be actually taught how to do it properly.'

The Microsoft Access course for the developers takes the system designed in the analysis course and leads the learner through the techniques required to develop it in Access. At the end of the course learners have built a five-table relational database with query, reporting and forms facilities. The course, says the OU, is designed for varying levels of ability with step-by-step instructions for the less confident and things to try for the more advanced who want to experiment. Afterwards, if the developers ask for something called 'mentor support', one of the support team is allocated to their particular project to assist in the development. 'People enjoyed the training,' says Evans, 'I think mainly because they actually wanted to do it. They know that back in the office they have to deal with a large amount of data and they can't teach themselves.'

In the beginning funding was hard to come by. 'We had to put a bid in ourselves to get funding for the course,' says Evans. 'We set up the training ourselves on a very, very limited budget to begin with.' So far, more than 200 staff have attended the courses and there are over 60 successful developments, with more currently under way. The major benefits, says the OU, have been found in regional offices where their particular requirements have never been met by central services. Applications include tutorial time tabling, exam deferrals, invigilator allocation and exam special needs. Several systems have been written in one department, and they have been so successful that the systems are adopted by others. Examples include an inventory database, holiday bookings, contacts database and tutor enquiries. There have also been examples of staff using the scheme to further their careers: one progressed to a project management job on the university's major student registration systems development.

'A lot of the paperwork has gone,' says Evans. 'People are more aware that they can get hold of data and do things with it instead of asking us. They are quite happy to have a go and do it themselves, a lot faster and a lot more effi-

▶

ciently, and not to have to wait several weeks for a program-mer from the IT department to come along and do it for them.' Plans for the future include offering more than just training on Access because the newly confident developers are thinking of using other tools. 'There are quite a lot of requirements other than just databases,' Evans says. 'We are also hoping to start encouraging departments to build up their own expertise in end-user development; to have their own local expert rather than keep coming to us for support.'

Source: (1996) OU Study, *Computer Weekly*

Questions

1 What different types of end-user computing does the Open University recognise?

2 What types of end-user developed systems have been produced?

3 What benefits has the scheme brought?

4 Why do you think staff didn't want to take the systems analysis course? Should it be compulsory, in your opinion?

Applications backlog

The demand for new applications by users exceeds the capacity of the IS department or IS outsourcing company to develop them.

the **applications backlog**. The IS department has rightly to focus on corporate, mis-sion-critical applications such as production, financial and customer services applications. It follows that they will not have the resources available to develop smaller-scale systems required in departments. As an example of this, one UK travel industry organisation has a backlog of nearly 100 systems required by users to add to over 120 existing systems. Any new system requested will almost certainly not be authorised by the IS department. For example, if the marketing department requires a new system to analyse sales performance and it requests this from the central IS, it will almost certainly be of a lower priority than items that were requested a year ago. As a result, the *only* option may be for it to be developed in the marketing depart-ment or to ask an outside consultant to develop it. Viewed in this way, end-user development could be considered as a failure of the IS department and IS strategy.

Less significant reasons for the growth of end-user development are:

◆ the desire by users to query and analyse data and generate reports from informa-tion stored on databases available across the corporate network;

◆ a trend to decentralisation of computing to user departments for systems to sup-port departmental activities;

◆ reduced expense of application development when conducted by end-users (from departmental rather than information systems budget);

◆ better fit between end-user developed software and their requirements (since no requirements translation is needed between the users and third-party developers). End-users are also less likely to 'overengineer' a solution to a basic problem than an IS professional who will want to treat every problem with rigour.

▶ Benefits of end-user development

There are many benefits claimed for end-user development. Some are those experi-enced by the end-users, such as more varied work and being able to use applications sooner. Additionally, IS personnel can concentrate on key, mission-critical applica-tions. Improvements in both these areas also accrue benefits to the organisation as a whole. The full range of benefits includes:

◆ Reduction in the number of professional analysts and programmers and IS employed by a company (and reduced cost of employing outside consultants).

◆ Reduction in communications overheads of users explaining requirements to IS professionals and also reduced risk of mistranslation of requirements.

◆ Help in reducing the applications development backlog associated with centralising applications development in an IS department.

◆ IS staff can focus on tasks requiring their expertise, such as the maintenance of corporate systems.

◆ Allows applications in departments to be developed more quickly, so the business can benefit from new facilities more quickly and gain competitive advantage.

◆ Can encourage innovation and creativity in the use of IS/IT, since bureaucratic barriers can be removed.

To balance these benefits, there are many potential problems. These include lack of standardisation, which leads to different software tools being selected by different users giving rise to incompatible software and data sources. Users may also take short cuts during development, such as missing out application design or testing, which will give rise to poor-quality software with bugs in it. These problems, and how to counter them, are described in more detail below.

MINI CASE

Delcam uses end-user developers to help internal communication using an intranet

Delcam is a Birmingham, UK-based software house with over 200 staff producing CAD software that is sold in more than 40 countries. It has developed an intranet which is used for corporate communication from directors to staff, and is also used extensively in the marketing department. Examples of the use of the intranet include:

◆ Company newsletter.
◆ Company phone directories.
◆ Reviews of client meetings and exhibitions attended.
◆ Price lists used by agents in different countries.
◆ Technical information on products for prospective customers.
◆ Support information for existing customers.

The intranet Web pages are produced by end-user developers mainly based in the marketing department, who write them in Microsoft Word before converting them to HTML pages that are read through a Web browser. The advantages of end-users developing these pages are:

◆ The pages can be updated immediately by end-users as soon as the need arises – there is no need to wait for the IS department to make the changes.
◆ The pages have a distinctive, informal 'look and feel' that is consistent with the mindset of the staff who use them.
◆ The cost of changes to Web pages can be borne by the marketing staff and does not have to be charged out.
◆ Confidential data is only seen by marketing staff with the access permissions to view it.

▶ The development of EUD in an organisation

The stage model of Huff *et al.* (1988) indicates how the use of end-user computing might develop in a typical organisation. This is loosely based on Nolan's stage model of computing use in organisations (Chapter 14). The stages of development are:

1 *Isolation*. A few scattered pioneers of EUD develop small-scale business tools within their area. Initially, little support from central IS.

2 *Standalone*. Larger-scale applications are developed that may be of importance to a department. Examples might include a staff rostering system or an application for anticipating demand for raw materials. At this stage, an information centre may be developed to support an increase in demand for user computing services.

3 *Manual integration*. Here, different EU applications need to exchange data. This happens through manual intervention, with files being transferred by floppy disk or across the network or even with rekeying of information. IC development has continued to support the needs of these larger-scale applications by providing training and skills and specifying standards for hardware, software and the development process.

4 *Automated integration*. Users start to link into corporate applications to gain seamless access to information. For example, end-users may download information from a central data warehouse, which is then used to profile customers for a new product launch or marketing campaign.

5 *Distributed integration*. At this stage of development, there is a good level of integration between different end-user applications and corporate systems. Good standards of metadata (or data describing data in a data dictionary) are required to help achieve this.

Since this model was proposed, experience indicates that although a natural progression can be seen in many organisations, the development beyond Stage 3 may not be practical or desirable. Once end-user developed applications become important or 'mission critical' to a department or an organisation, the question which must be asked is: 'Are end-users the right people to maintain an application of this importance?' The answer will usually be 'no', since end-users will not have the skills to develop such an application and if they are trained to levels necessary to do this, they will no longer be end-users fulfilling their original function, but specialist application developers!

▶ Problems of end-user development

The problems of end-user development are usually the result of a lack of sufficient training in software development or the inability of management to ensure that this training occurs. This can manifest itself in different ways. Perhaps the best way to consider these problems is to review where they may occur over the course of end-user development using the software lifecycle model as a framework (Table 16.2).

The problems referred to in Table 16.2 could have serious consequences if they occurred during the development of a large, new information system. However, for small-scale end-user developed software that will only be used by a limited number of staff and is not vital to the business, such errors are less important.

Note that Table 16.2 is based on assuming that end-user development follows a similar pattern to a large-scale systems development. However, some authors, such as Lally (1995), note that additional stages of promotion or dissemination of information about the product are required. The product may then need to evolve for it to be adopted more widely in a company.

Table 16.2 Review of problems associated with EUD and where they occur in the systems development lifecycle (SDLC)

Stage of SDLC	Typical problem
Initiation	*Absent or limited feasibility study.* If omitted, the user may be developing a system that is not required or solving a problem that has been solved before. *Insufficient review of cost–benefit and acquisition alternatives.* Other end-user software with the same function may be available elsewhere in the organisation. Off-the-shelf software may also be available.
Analysis	*Limited analysis.* Since the end-user may know their own requirements, they may not consult others in the company who may have a different perspective. This may alienate potential users and mean that the software is unsuitable for its application.
Design	*Omitted completely!* This stage is often omitted and programming will occur straightaway. This may occur since users may not have the design skills or understand the importance of design. This will adversely affect the usability, speed and security of the software.
Build	Programming will occur as normal, the problem is that ancillary activities may be omitted. *Documenting* the work and *testing* are areas that should not be omitted.
Implementation	Implementation becomes more difficult for large systems. For a standalone piece of end-user developed software, there should not be too many problems.
Maintenance	Problems at this stage are minor compared to those that may have happened before. Users may not keep an adequate list of problems that need to be fixed. There is also a tendency to release updates to the software without good version control.

Among the general risks or misuse of information associated with end-user developed information systems are:

◆ using information that is out of date;

◆ information requires export from other information systems before it can be analysed by the end-user application;

◆ corruption of centrally held data by uploading erroneous data;

◆ development of insecure systems without password control that are vulnerable to accidental and deliberate damage.

A final problem to be mentioned is the hazard of personal or private systems that are unreadable, undocumented and not transferable to any other users. This is a particular problem if the developer of the software leaves. This can be a common scenario with end-user developed software. The only solution to this problem is often to rewrite the software, since the source code and documentation may be impossible to follow or non-existent.

▶ MANAGING EUC AS PART OF IS STRATEGY

It could be argued that the IS manager has two basic choices when considering the relationship between IS strategy and end-user computing. These could be paraphrased as 'ignore it' or 'embrace it'. The 'ignore it' option may be appealing to the IS manager who sees EUC as a threat that is eroding their control. In reality, they will not ignore it completely, rather they will not take any steps to encourage it. Those IS managers who wish to embrace it will probably have realised that EUC is inevitable, given the reasons mentioned earlier in the chapter such as insufficient availability of staff to develop applications, increasing skills among staff and availability of tools to produce the applications. EUC should be encouraged to reduce the applications backlog and will help in ensuring that the requirements of end-users are well understood and are met by the software developed.

We have seen that quite serious problems can develop with EUC due to inexperience in systems development and management among the end-users and their managers. Given this, it is vital that there is a strategy to support *and* control EUC, whether the IS manager is ignoring it or embracing it. Many of these risks and problems arise through a lack of experience of system development, coupled with a lack of training for end-users. End-user development should be recognised as part of the IS strategy and guidelines should be developed that cover the techniques below. Techniques that could be used to improve control of end-user development include:

1 *Training.* Provision of relevant training courses both in how to program and in how to approach systems development in a structured way (the second of these is often omitted). This happened at the Open University, where many of the end-users wanted to omit the analysis course.

2 *Suitability review.* Authorisation of major end-user new developments by business and IS managers to check that they are necessary (this should not be necessary for smaller-scale developments since otherwise creativity may be stifled).

3 *Standards for development.* Such standards will recommend that documentation and structured testing of all user developed software occurs. Detailed standards might include clear data definitions, validation rules, backup and recovery routines and security measures.

4 *Guidance from end-user support personnel.* IC or help desk staff can provide training in techniques used to develop software.

5 *Software and data audits.* Regular audits should occur of software produced by end-users for data and application quality. There is an apocryphal story of a company that had an end-user developed spreadsheet for making investment decisions which had an error in a formula that lost the company millions of pounds each year!

6 *Ensuring corporate data security.* Ensure that users are not permitted to enter data directly into central databases except via applications especially written for the purpose by the IS department which have the necessary validation rules to ensure data quality. For analysis of corporate data, data should regularly be downloaded from the central database to the PC for analysis, where it can be analysed without causing performance problems to the corporate system.

It will be apparent from the list of potential measures that a careful balance has to be struck between being overrestrictive, which may cause a stifling of innovation, or too open, which will result in the type of problems referred to above.

As a summary to this chapter, the case study reviews how British Sugar has modified its help desk strategy, moving to what is now referred to as a service desk, which has agreed levels of service such as a guaranteed 30-minute response. It also discusses how the tools it use have changed to accommodate support for 1800 people at over 50 sites.

CASE STUDY: TOPIC AREA

FT

Sweetening the British Sugar help desk

British Sugar is one company that has reaped extensive rewards from the desktop revolution. The company based its IT strategy around a mainframe-based solution with dumb terminals until five years ago, when user demands led the IT department to introduce PCs on a phased basis. The company has a big task on its hands when it comes to maintaining an efficient IT infrastructure. In addition to its central office, it has nine factories and 50 depots which it uses for distribution. It has 1800 people on its books, any of whom may need to report an IT query at some stage. Until it installed its PCs, the company had been using a proprietary bespoke help desk solution which took calls on an *ad hoc* basis. With the introduction of the desktop equipment, change co-ordinator for the service team Barry Elmore explains that the company needed a more sophisticated solution. In 1992 the firm bought Quetzal, a DOS-based product which it used for roughly a year and a half. 'As Windows came in we were led towards looking for a Windows solution,' explains Elmore. 'We drew up a list of different products that we could pick up from magazines and Support Magic (from Magic Solutions) was one of those products.' This choice was driven by the fact that most of the applications in British Sugar's computing environment were Windows-based by this time.

Elmore explains that the more sophisticated features within Support Magic had enabled him to provide his users with a more pragmatic solution, in line with a corporate requirement to increase the efficiency of the individual departments on an internal market basis. The company could now get better value for money from the IT department as a whole, because it was able to use better reporting facilities to structure the support strategy more intelligently.

'What we have been doing with Support Magic over the last three years is trying with the reporting facility to implement service level agreements because that is the driving factor. We have to provide a service desk now as opposed to a help desk. Having introduced the reporting facility, we are able to respond within 30 minutes,' he says. Although the IT department cannot guarantee a 30-minute fix time, the fact that it can at least respond to calls in this period serves to increase customer satisfaction. Elmore emphasises the fact that he designed the reporting solution in reverse, making sure that he knew what it was that he wanted to report on and then constructing the solution around that requirement. This makes it much easier to extract the information, he explains, enabling the IT department to analyse support calls more effectively.

British Sugar has three people managing the help desk and producing the reports. The operators receive roughly 2500 support calls per month and, of that, just over a thousand problems are generated. The next phase of Elmore's service strategy involves using the help desk software database facility to construct a knowledge base of commonly perceived problems. He explains that this is difficult because what appears to be the same problem initially may be an entirely different problem upon closer investigation.

Source: Computing, 3 June 1998

Questions

1 Describe the evolution of software used to support the help desk at British Sugar.

2 Explain the move to a service desk rather than a help desk and the introduction of service-level agreements.

▶ SUMMARY

1 End-user computing (EUC) describes the use of information systems by non-IT staff.

2 Providing end-user services is an important function of the IS department, since many company staff rely on analysing data for decision making.

3 End-user development (EUD) is one type of EUC that is significant in many organisations, since it provides a low-cost method of reducing the applications backlog.

4 The key benefits of end-user development are:
   ◆ shorter wait for system before it can be used in the organisation;
   ◆ users understand their requirements better than IS specialists;
   ◆ lower cost than paying a third party.

5 The principal problem with end-user development is that users may omit some essential activities in software development, such as assessing the best solution, documenting their work, design or thorough testing.

6 An information centre or help desk is provided by many medium and large organisations to provide guidance, support and troubleshooting for end-users.

7 Given the potential problems of end-user developed applications, they are most appropriate for small-scale applications within departments.

8 The cost of providing end-user services can be high, which is partly responsible for the high total cost of ownership (TCO) of PCs in many organisations and a trend to using thin clients to reduce this (Chapter 19).

9 EUC and EUD have great potential, but enthusiasm can be misdirected due to inexperience. EUC must be an element of overall IS strategy to ensure that it is effectively controlled and supported.

▶ EXERCISES

▶ Self-assessment exercises

1 What are the principal end-user services that must be provided by the information systems manager?

2 What is the significance of the total cost of ownership?

3 What is the role of the network computer and other thin clients in reducing the total cost of ownership (see Chapter 12).

4 What is the difference between end-user computing and end-user development?

5 What are the different types of end-user development?

6 What are the main reasons for the growth in end-user development?

7 Which activities in the software development lifecycle are often omitted by end-users?

8 What facilities can be provided to support end-user development?

▶ Discussion questions

1 It has been argued that end-user computing has been driven by a failure of central information systems departments to develop applications quickly enough (the applications backlog). Is this statement true or is there an alternative explanation?

2 Examine the reasons for the growth of end-user computing in companies of all sizes. You should consider the balance between practical necessity and strategic planning.

3 What do you see as the future for end-user computing? Will the growth continue, or will there be a backlash against the problems experienced by some companies using this approach?

▶ Essay questions

1 End-user applications development poses a new set of management problems in companies that adopt this approach. Identify the nature of these problems and suggest measures to overcome them.

2 Intranets are now widely used by many companies. Examine the suitability of end-users for the control, development and maintenance of intranets.

3 End-user computing can only be successful if users have a knowledge of the software lifecycle and the activities required to produce good-quality information systems. Which activities do you consider essential to achieving this, and which are likely to be omitted?

4 Imagine that you are the IS manager of a medium to large company with 500 staff. Explain the strategy you would develop to encourage end-user computing, while seeking to control any problems that may arise.

▶ Examination questions

1 What are the main benefits provided by end-user computing?

2 Why are end-user developed applications unsuitable for cross-enterprise applications?

3 What factors contribute to the total cost of ownership. Why is it significantly higher than the purchase cost?

4 How does the network computer differ from the personal computer? Why might this appeal to:
   (a) the IS manager;
   (b) the finance manager;
   (c) the end-user.

5 Name and explain three services that can be provided by an information centre.

6 What is the applications backlog and how is end-user development significant in relation to this?

7 Give three reasons that it is important for end-user computing to be part of a company's overall IS strategy. Briefly justify each.

▶ References

Blili, S., Raymond, L. and Rivard, S. (1996) 'Definition and measurement of end user computing sophistication', *Journal of End User Computing*, Spring, 8, 2, 13–23.

Carr, H. (1988) *Managing End-User Computing*, Prentice Hall, London.

The Gartner Group (1996) *Total Cost of Ownership: Reducing PC/LAN Costs in the Enterprise*, February 9, The Gartner Group, Boston.

Huff, S., Munro, M. and Martin, B. (1988) 'Growth stages of End-User Computing', *Communications of the ACM*, 31, 5, 542–50.

Lally, L. (1995) 'Supporting appropriate user-developed applications: guidelines for managers', *Journal of End User Computing*, Summer, 7, 3, 3–11.

Robson, W. (1997) *Strategic Management and Information Systems: An Integrated Approach*, Financial Times Pitman Publishing, London.

Rockart, J. and Flannery, L. (1983) 'The management of End-User Computing', *Communications of the ACM*, 26, 10, 776–84.

White, C.E. and Christy, D.P. (1987) The Information Centre concept: A normative model and a study of six installations, *MIS Quarterly*, December, 450–58.

▶ Further reading

Alavi, M.R., Nelson, R. and Weiss, I.R. (1988) 'Strategies for end-user computing: an integrative framework', *Journal of Management Information Systems*, 4, 3.

Brancheau, J. and Brown, C. (1993) 'Management of end-user computing', *ACM Computer Surveys*, 437–82.

Computing special issue on help desks, 3 June 1998 – contains many case studies.

Nelson, R. (1989) *End-User Computing: Concepts, Issues and Applications*, James Wiley, Chichester.

Regan, E.A. and O'Connor, B.N. (1994) *End-User Information Systems: Perspectives for Managers and Information Systems Professionals*, Macmillan, New York.

Tourniaire, F. and Farrell, R. (1996) *The Art of Software Support: Design and Operation of Support Centres and Help Desks,* Prentice-Hall, London.

▶ Web references

http://www.helpdeskinst.com This site provides resources for practitioners to manage held desks. It includes articles on measuring help desk effectiveness and how to improve service levels.

Computing special issue on help desks has many case studies, 3 June 1998.

http://www.vnunet.co.uk

Managing Internet- and intranet-based information systems

INTRODUCTION

The rapid adoption of the Internet for business use is one of the most dramatic changes in the short history of computing. An Internet presence is now seen as a vital business tool, given the number of consumers and companies accessing the World Wide Web.

This chapter explores different opportunities for business use of the Internet. This is already extensively used for marketing purposes, ranging from promotion of a company and its products through to online sales or electronic commerce. How a company can use the Internet for the full range of marketing functions that occur as an essential part of running any business is discussed. The chapter describes what steps an IS manager working in conjunction with marketing staff must take to ensure that the Internet is used effectively and does not introduce additional problems, such as disruption to work or security risks. These measures are also relevant to when Internet management is outsourced to a third party such as an Internet service provider. Their role in providing Internet services is described.

The chapter also reviews the role of the increasingly popular intranet or 'internal Internet' for sharing business information. The chapter concentrates on the use of the World Wide Web for the Internet and intranets, since this has been the most important tool prompting business adoption of the Internet.

> ## Learning objectives
>
> After reading this chapter, readers will be able to:
>
> ◆ understand the difference between the Internet, World Wide Web, intranets and extranets;
>
> ◆ know the potential for using the Internet and intranets for different business purposes, in particular different marketing functions;
>
> ◆ put together a strategy for exploiting the Internet;
>
> ◆ understand the different options for connecting to the Internet and setting up a Web site;
>
> ◆ use the Internet to search for information.

> ## Links to other chapters
>
> This chapter is relatively self-contained and it is not necessary to read earlier chapters first.
>
> Chapter 4   provides a brief introduction to the features of software used to access the Internet, such as e-mail and Web browsers.
>
> Chapter 15   describes some of the methods of securing information transmitted over inter-organisational networks.

▶ INTRODUCTION TO THE INTERNET

▶ A brief history of the Internet

The Internet

A network that links computers across the globe. It consists of the infrastructure of servers and communication links between them.

The history and origin of the **Internet** are well known. It started life in 1969 as the ARPAnet research and defence network in the US, which linked servers used by key military and academic collaborators at the time of the Cold War. It was established as a network that would be reliable even if some of the links were broken. This was achieved since data and messages sent between users were broken up into smaller packets and could follow different routes. Although the Internet was used extensively by academic and defence communities, it has only recently been catapulted into mainstream business and consumer use.

Although the Internet has many tools to help users navigate between the information resources and transfer files between servers, it is really the increase in use of World Wide Web browsers in the 1990s that has caused this sea change in computing. Web browsers such as Netscape Navigator and Microsoft Internet Explorer provide an easy method of accessing and viewing Web documents stored on different servers.

▶ From Internet to intranet

Intranet

An intranet uses web servers, browsers and e-mail within a company to share company information and software applications. The intranet is only accessible to company employees.

The Internet is a well-established term, whereas **intranet** only came into existence in the mid-1990s. Intranets arose because companies which experimented with using Internet tools to share company information realised that intranets offered several benefits over traditional information systems. Early adopters found that intranets can be relatively:

- ◆ quick to set up;
- ◆ cheap to maintain;
- ◆ easy to use and popular with users.

Although, as we shall see, they are not without their problems, intranets use the tried and tested standards and tools of the Internet, but within an organisation rather than between companies. Of course, security becomes important to stop unauthorised access to company data.

Intranets are now used by over 90 per cent of large US corporations, but adoption in the UK is at a lower level. Many analysts believe that the UK figure is set to increase rapidly to US levels, however.

To derive full potential from an intranet, a company will want to share information with collaborators. The term **extranet** has been coined to describe an intranet that is extended beyond the boundaries of a company. The extranet can be accessed by authorised people outside the company, such as collaborators, suppliers or major customers, but information is not available to everyone with an Internet connection – only to those with password access. An example of two extranets that have been set up to link to customers and suppliers is described in the mini case study on Tesco supermarkets.

Extranet

An intranet with restricted access which is extended to suppliers, collaborators or customers.

MINI CASE

Tesco supermarkets use extranets to communicate with customers and suppliers

Customer extranet

Of the major supermarkets in the UK, Tesco has been quickest to respond to the possible threat from competitors eating into its market share. The Tesco Internet Superstore (www.tesco.co.uk) now offers over 22 000 products to anyone who lives within a five-mile radius of stores in Leeds, Hammersmith, Osterley, Romford and the Lea Valley. As with many current Internet retailers, Tesco is not looking to achieve an immediate return, rather it is preparing for the future by gaining experience in the technology and how its customers react to it. So far, Tesco has found that the majority of customers using the site are young professionals, with an even split between males and females. The main difficulties with the service are the difficulty of selecting from many products and the time taken to download the details.

The initial site was built in 13 weeks using products from Microsoft. Tesco is not only relying on the Internet; it also offers an Internet, CD-ROM or paper-based catalogue.

Supplier extranet

Tesco is also utilising the Internet to improve its links with suppliers through a project known as the Tesco Information Exchange (TIE).

The aim of this project is to enable suppliers to provide goods necessary to support an in-store sales promotion. The project sets out to solve the perennial problem of either oversupply, leading to wastage, or undersupply, giving rise to irritated customers and lost potential sales. This is achieved by using the Internet as a relatively low-cost method for the 600 Tesco branches to link to both large and small suppliers and exchange information on

▶

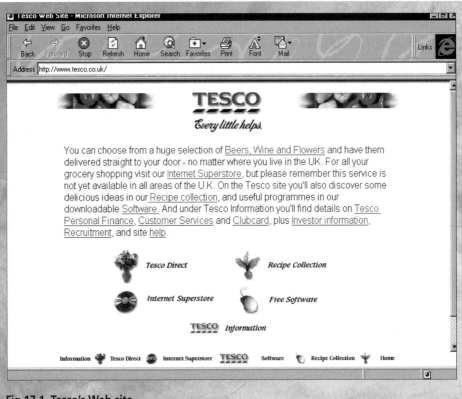

Fig 17.1 Tesco's Web site

availability and demand for products. Previously, such a link would only have been available to the largest suppliers which could afford a leased line, wide area link (Chapter 5).

TIE uses a secure Web site that can only be accessed by suppliers with password authorisation. It also uses firewalls to ensure that hackers cannot access the information.

TIE is part of a new product offered by General Electric – the GE-Trading Information Exchange. General Electric is the world's largest corporation with a turnover of around $90 billion, so it is likely that this type of system will be widely adopted. One of the benefits of using the Internet for the service provider is that central facilities can be provided to serve Europe. The database used for the Tesco system is based in Amsterdam, the Netherlands.

▶ Essential terms

The use of the Internet as a business tool has introduced a host of new terms. We will highlight the most significant ones in this introductory section.

Internet

The **Internet** refers to the physical network that links computers across the globe. It consists of the infrastructure of network servers and wide area communication links between them that are used to hold and transport the vast amount of information on the Internet.

Internet tools

The Internet has many tools, such as e-mail, FTP, Gopher and Telnet, that are used to navigate and transfer files between servers. The **World Wide Web (WWW)** is another of these tools that has become very popular and is responsible for the growth in the use of the Internet as a serious business tool. Of the other tools, Internet-based e-mail is most important to businesses as a means of facilitating communication between different businesses and their customers. Table 17.1 highlights some of the uses of Internet tools.

Table 17.1 Business uses of different Internet tools

Internet tool	Business use
Electronic mail or e-mail	The cost of communication within and between businesses has been greatly reduced through the use of e-mail. Through using file attachments, wordprocessed documents and spreadsheets can also be transmitted by e-mail.
Internet relay chat (IRC)	This is a synchronous communications tool which allows text-based 'chat' between different users who are logged on at the same time. It is not used for many business applications, since asynchronous discussions are more practical – not all team members need to be present at the same time.
Usenet newsgroups	Usenet is mainly used by special-interest groups, for example people discussing their favourite pastime such as fishing or archery. They are not used much by businesses, unless it is as a means of studying consumer behaviour. There are some newsgroups for announcing the introduction of new products or staff vacancies. To access newsgroups via the Web use http://www.dejanews.com.
FTP file transfer	The File Transfer Protocol is used as a standard for moving files across the Internet. The most common use is for releasing fixes to software applications. Documents can be transferred by this means. FTP is available as a feature of Web browsers for downloading files.
Gophers, Archie and WAIS	These tools were important before the advent of the Web for storing and searching documents on the Internet. They have largely been superseded by the Web, which provides better searching and more sophisticated document publishing.
Telnet	This allows remote access to computer systems. For example, a system administrator on one site could log in to a computer elsewhere to check that it is running successfully. Telnet is widely used in the retail industry. For example, a retailer could check to see whether an item was in stock in a warehouse using a Telnet application. Such Telnet applications will not usually be run over the public Internet, but rather over secure lines.
World Wide Web	The Web is widely used for publishing information and running business applications over the Internet. It is the main tool described in the remainder of this chapter.

The coverage of business use of the Internet in this chapter concentrates on the use of e-mail and the World Wide Web, since these tools are now most commonly used by businesses.

World Wide Web (WWW)

The **World Wide Web**, or 'Web' for short, is a medium for publishing information on the Internet in an easy-to-use form. If we take the analogy of television, then the Internet would be equivalent to the broadcasting equipment such as masts and transmitters, and the World Wide Web to the content of different TV programmes. The medium is based on a standard document format known as **HTML (Hypertext Markup Language)**, which can be thought of as similar to a wordprocessing format. It is significant since it offers hyperlinks that allow users to move readily from one document to another – the process known as 'surfing'. Examples of HTML are given later in the chapter.

Web browsers

Browsers such as Netscape Navigator or Microsoft Internet Explorer provide an easy method of accessing and viewing information stored as Web documents on different servers. Text and graphical information can be displayed in a browser. Business applications requiring input of data in fields can also be accessed through a Web browser. These use technology known as **Java**, **Active-X** and the **Common Gateway Interface (CGI)**. The Web pages, stored as HTML files on the servers, are accessed through a particular standard supported by the Web browsers: the hypertext transfer protocol (http), which you will always see preceding the Web address of a company. For example, http://www.derby.ac.uk defines the university home page at Derby.

Web addresses (uniform resource locators – URLs)

Web addresses refer to particular pages on a **Web server** which are hosted by a company or organisation. The technical name for these is uniform resource locators, so you often see them referred to as URLs. They are usually prefixed by http://www. to denote the Web protocol and then are broken down as follows:

http://www.domain-name.extension/filename.htm

The **domain name** refers to the name of the Web server and is usually selected to be the same as the name of the company. The extension indicates its type. The extension is also commonly known as the global top level domain (gTLD):

◆ **.com** represents an international or US company, such as http://www.travel agency.com;

◆ **.co.uk** represents a company based in the UK, such as http://www.thomas cook.co.uk/.

Intranet

An **intranet** is a network within a single company that enables access to company information using the familiar tools of the Internet, such as Web browsers. The relationship between an intranet and the Internet is shown in Fig 17.2. Only staff within the company can access the intranet, which will be password protected.

World Wide Web

The World Wide Web is a medium for publishing information on the Internet. It is accessed through Web browsers which display Web pages and can be used to run business applications. Company information is stored on Web servers which are usually referred to as Web sites.

HTML (Hypertext Markup Language)

HTML is the method used to create Web pages and documents. The HTML code used to construct pages has codes or tags such as <TITLE> to indicate to the browser what is displayed.

Java

A programming language standard supported by Sun Microsystems which permits complex and graphical customer applications to be written and then accessed from a Web browser. An example might be a form for calculating interest on a loan. A competitor to Active-X.

Active-X

A programming language standard developed by Microsoft which permits complex and graphical customer applications to be written and then accessed from a Web browser.

Common Gateway Interface (CGI)

CGI offers a way of providing interactivity through the Web. With a form type HTML document, a user type in information and structured information or queries sent using the Web.

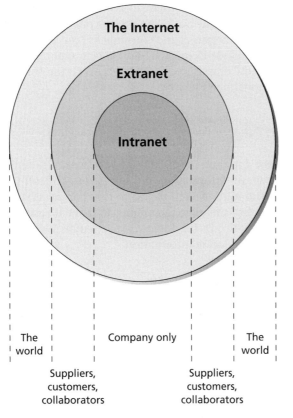

Fig 17.2 The relationship between intranets, extranets and the Internet

Extranet

An **extranet** can be formed by extending the intranet beyond a company to customers, suppliers, collaborators or even competitors. This is again password protected to prevent access by Internet users.

Protocols

The Internet functions through a series of standard **protocols** that allow different types of machines to communicate with each other. The passing of data packets around the Internet occurs via the TCP/IP protocol, which stands for Transfer Control Protocol/Internet Protocol. For a PC to be able to receive Web pages or for a server to host Web pages, it must be configured by a technician to support this protocol. The HTTP protocol is used to allow computers to transfer and process HTML files. Thus the letters http:// are used to prefix all Web addresses.

SMTP is a mail protocol to allow e-mail to be sent across the Internet, and FTP allows other types of files to be uploaded and downloaded.

Internet service provider (ISP)

These are telecommunications companies that provide access to the Internet for home and business users. ISPs have two main functions. First, they can provide a link to a

Web addresses

Web addresses refer to particular pages on a Web server which are hosted by a company or organisation. The technical name for these is uniform resource locators (URL).

Web servers

Used to store the Web pages accessed by the Web browsers. They may also contain databases of customer or product information which can be queried and retrieved from the browser.

Domain name

Refers to the name of the Web server. The extension is also commonly known as the Global Top Level Domain (gTLD). http://www.domain-name.extension.

Protocols

The Internet functions using a series of standard protocols which allow different computers to communicate with each other. Passing of data packets around the Internet occurs via the TCP/IP protocol which stands for Transfer Control Protocol/ Internet Protocol. The HTTP (hyper text transfer protocol) protocol is used to allow computers to transfer and process HTML files.

Internet service provider (ISP)

Companies which provide access to the Internet and Web page hosting for home and business users. Online service providers access to the Internet plus their own content.

company or individual that enables them to access the World Wide Web and send Internet e-mail. Second, they can host Web sites or provide a link from a company's Web servers to allow other companies and consumers access to a corporate Web site.

Examples of UK ISPs include Demon, BT and U-Net. Online service providers such as AOL, BT LineOne and Compuserve provide access to the Internet plus their own content, such as additional news services.

▶ FINDING INFORMATION ON THE INTERNET

Many new users of the Internet are discouraged because, although there appears to be good potential for useful information, it often proves difficult to find what is relevant. There are over 100 million Web pages, so it is natural that useful information will be difficult to find, but there are techniques to make it easier. In this section, we review a number of methods for locating particular Web pages and describe approaches using criteria to locate information.

▶ Web-based information resources

Content

Content is the design, text and graphical information which forms a Web page.

Search engines

Search engines provide an index of all words stored on the World Wide Web. Keywords typed in by the end-user are matched against the index and the user is given a list of all corresponding Web pages.

Web directories or catalogues

A structured listing of Web sites grouped according to categories such as business, entertainment or sport. Each category is then subdivided further.

Figure 17.3 shows the range of methods used to find the information or **content** of a Web site. From the perspective of the company or organisation that has created the Web site, all of these methods should be targeted when promoting a Web site to ensure that as many customers visit as possible. Staff monitoring Web sites find that the most common method for visiting is **search engines** or **directories**. Such sites are collectively referred to as portals since they provide a gateway to accessing information on the WWW. These will often account for 80 per cent of all Web referrals to a site. These methods are described in mini case on methods of finding information on page 602. The two other main methods are links from other sites where the company is listed, or through Web-based banner adverts that occur at the top of a Web page and invite the user to 'click-through' to another page. Banner adverts are described later in the chapter.

Search engines provide an index of all words stored on the World Wide Web. Keywords typed in by the end-user are matched against the index and the user is

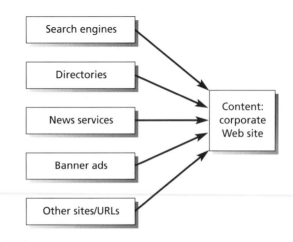

Fig 17.3 Web-based information systems

given a list of all corresponding Web pages containing the keywords. By clicking on a hyperlink, the user is taken to the relevant Web page.

Web directories or catalogues provide a structured listing of Web sites. They are grouped according to categories such as business, entertainment or sport. Each category is then subdivided further, for example into football, rugby, swimming etc.

How do you ensure that your company site appears on Web search engines and directories?

Search engines

Search engines use special automatic tools to index Web pages. These are known as spiders or robots, since they crawl or rove around all the hundred million-plus Web pages located on Web servers around the world and build up an index of each word on every page. To help identify key information on a particular page, special keywords can be used to highlight information. These are known as metatags – an example of metatags used by the Internet Bookshop (http://www.bookshop.co.uk) is given below:

◆ The 'keywords' metatag highlights the key topics covered on a Web page. For example, <meta name="keywords" content="book, books, shop, store, book shop, bookstore, publisher, bookshop, general, interest, departments,">

◆ The 'description' metatag denotes the information that will be displayed in the Web browser when a Web page is found. For example, <meta name="description" content="The largest online book store in the world.">

Directories

Directories such as Yahoo (http://www.yahoo.co.uk) and the UK online yellow pages (http://www.yell.co.uk) are used regularly by Internet visitors, so it is important that a company is registered with them. Yahoo and its specific sites in each country are the most popular sites in the world, attracting over 30 million hits a day. Fortunately, it is easy to ensure that a company is listed with these directories, since an e-mail notification of the Web address and category in which to place the site is all that is required.

▶ Finding information on the World Wide Web

Information can be found on the World Wide Web in four main ways:

◆ typing in the Web address of a known page (URL);
◆ search engines;
◆ directories (or Web catalogues/indexes);
◆ 'surfing'.

Web addresses or URLs (universal resource locators)

The preferred (fastest) method of reaching a Web site is through typing in the **Web address** (if you know it) or URL directly into the Web browser's address box. While it may be obvious for a company such as IBM (http://www.ibm.com), it is less obvious for a company with a longer name, such as the Alliance and Leicester Building Society (http://www.allianceandleicester.co.uk).

Web addresses must start with 'http://' as given below and have any full stops and forward slashes in the correct location. In the latest browsers it is not necessary to type in the http://prefix.

Search engines

Search engines provide an index of all words stored on the World Wide Web. Keywords typed in by the end-user are matched against the index and the user is given a list of all corresponding Web pages containing the keywords. By clicking on a hyperlink the user is taken to the relevant Web page.

Search engines to try are:

http://www.altavista.digital.com

http://www.excite.com/

http://www.hotbot.com/

http://www.infoseek.com/

http://www.lycos.com/

as well as meta search engines such as http://www.metacrawler.com/ (combines several search engines).

Tips for using a search engine such as AltaVista

- ◆ Use several words (or synonyms) to narrow down the search – London fire.
- ◆ Use inverted commas to define a phrase – 'Fire of London'.
- ◆ Use + and – to include or exclude words – +'Fire of London' +1666 –Wren.
- ◆ Use a European site if you know it, e.g. www.altavista.telia.com., or www.yahoo.co.uk or restrict your search to UK or European sites where this option is available.

ACTIVITY

Search engines

Type the following into the AltaVista search box (and hit return or enter), noting the number of Web pages returned each time:

1 channel tunnel

2 'channel tunnel'

3 'channel tunnel' fire

4 +'channel tunnel' +fire

5 +'channel tunnel' +fire –news

Web catalogues or directories

Web directories provide a structured listing of Web sites. They are grouped according to categories, such as business, entertainment or sport. Each category is then subdivided further, for example into football, rugby, swimming etc.

Web catalogues such as http://www.yahoo.co.uk work differently, in that they have a hierarchy of information stored under different categories. For example, to find a UK travel agent specialising in cheap flights, you would move down the hierarchy to select:

Regional:Countries:United Kingdom:
Business:Companies:Travel:Agents:Direct

This would then lead you to the site of http://www.cheapflights.co.uk, which claims that it is 'The best source for bargain air tickets from the United Kingdom'. Categories can be quicker to use than broader search facilities.

Web catalogues

1 Type the name of a sports team or pop group into the yahoo search engine, move to this location and note its position in the hierarchy.

2 Find this position in the hierarchy:
　　:Regional:Countries:United_Kingdom:Business_and_Economy

3 and this one:
　　:Regional:Countries:United_Kingdom:News_and_Media:Newspapers

ACTIVITY

Navigating or 'surfing'

Surfing is a relatively inefficient method of finding information by following hyperlinks between related Web pages. It is probably most useful for finding information you didn't know you were looking for!

Try any of these methods:

1 Click on underlined *hyperlinks* (usually coloured blue by default) to move from one page to the next.

2 Use *Back* or *Forward* buttons to move between pages visited already (a right mouse click also gives this option).

3 Use *Go* menu in Internet Explorer to move to previous choices.

4 Use *Go*, Open *History* Folder to move to previous choices.

5 Use *Favorites*, *Add* To Favorites to retain a page for revisiting later. These are personal bookmarks retained on the hard disk.

6 Use *Edit*, *Find* to search for a word in the page that is currently loaded.

▶ Search strategies for market research

When researching projects or undertaking market research, your search strategy should vary according to the type of information you are looking for. We would recommend the following.

MINI CASE

Methods of finding information

Search engines

This example uses AltaVista, one of the most common search engines. Imagine you wanted to find out information on holidays available in Spain. You could start by typing in a general word such as 'holiday'. The problem with a non-specific search is that there is such a large volume of information on the Web. This search would return some 600 000 references to Web pages. To use the Web efficiently it is necessary to know the syntax provided by search engines to narrow down the search. For example, + 'holiday inn' + 'Costa del Sol' returns a handful of pages, since we have indicated through the + symbol that both phrases must be present and through enclosing it in inverted commas that the words must appear in the order shown.

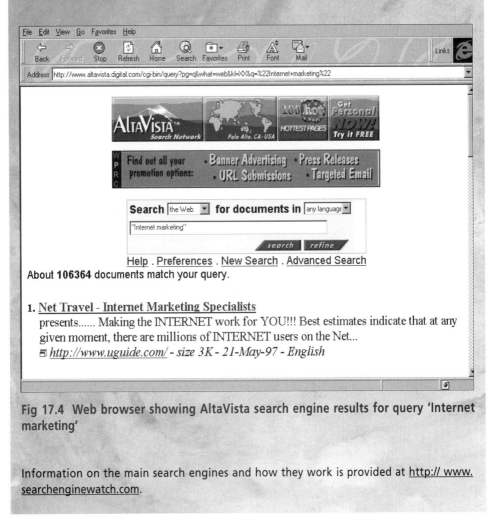

Fig 17.4 Web browser showing AltaVista search engine results for query 'Internet marketing'

Information on the main search engines and how they work is provided at http:// www. searchenginewatch.com.

For information about *companies and different business markets*, directories such as Yahoo or Yell represent the best method:

http://www.yahoo.co.uk

http://www.yell.co.uk

For information about *products and services*, use the search engines, as discussed above.

For *local companies*, use the Yellow Pages or Thomson databases, which allow you to search locally. Electronic Yellow Pages offers a search by postcode or county. Thomson is better for nationwide information:

http://www.thomson-directories.co.uk

http://www.eyp.co.uk (Electronic Yellow Pages)

Try searching *newsgroups* for industry information. Search them using the Web site http:// www.dejanews.com.

For example:

clari.biz.industry.textiles

clari.biz.industry.transportation

clari.biz.marketreport.europe

misc.industry.pulp-and-paper

uk.rec.fishing.sea

An example of specialist information on pharmaceuticals is shown in Fig 17.5.

To avoid a recurring need to use search engines or directories, it is useful to identify *reference sites* which fit your interest. For example, www.cyberatlas.com is a site

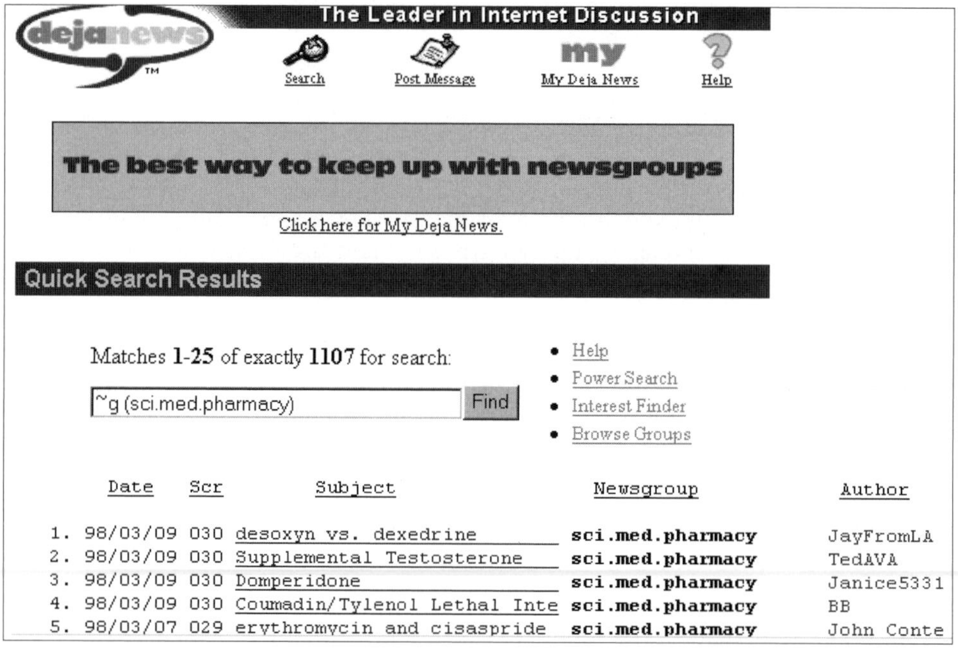

Fig 17.5 Screenshot frrom DejaNews showing information on pharmaceuticals

that is updated monthly on the latest business developments on the Internet. It is more efficient to visit this site regularly than to try to find the information yourself – the compilers of the site have done the searching for you. A further useful reference site for business students and practitioners is Business Researchers' Interests (BRINT) (www.brint.com). This site has research compiled on many topics, such as business process reengineering, organisational learning and electronic commerce.

▶ USAGE PATTERNS OF THE INTERNET

The Internet offers great opportunities for businesses to market and sell their products to customers. It delivers a new route by which customers worldwide can find out about the availability of products, and purchase them. These customers include 44 million consumers in the US, 4 million in the UK and 112 million worldwide who used the World Wide Web in 1998. The number of people accessing the Web is growing rapidly. UK opinion pollsters NOP found in a 1997 survey that the number of people accessing the Internet, most commonly from home, had increased by 150 per cent over a 12-month period. These users are not only searching the Internet to find information, but are using it as a new method of purchasing. Buying transactions arising from Internet use were estimated to exceed £1 billion in 1997.

Households worldwide with access to the Internet

Jupiter Communications estimates a total of 23.4 million households had access to the Internet in 1996, with 66% of the total in North America, 16% in Europe and 14% in Asia/Pacific. By 2000 their estimate is for a total of 66 million households connected with 58% in the US, 25% in Europe and 15% in Asia/Pacific.

Source: The Economist, 10/16 May 1997

Despite these growth rates, cynics point out the relatively small number of people who can be reached compared to the mass media. They ask searching questions such as: 'how does the Internet affect the bottom line?' and 'are these companies turning a profit on their Web operations?' These are certainly valid questions and the intention here is not to be swept up by the 'cyberspace hype', but to take a balanced view.

Cyberspace and cybermarketing

The prefix cyber indicate a blurring in distinction between humans, machines and communications. Cyberspace is a synonym for Internet.

Cyberspace and cybermarketing are terms often preferred by science fiction writers and tabloid writers to indicate the futuristic nature of using the Internet. The prefix cyber indicated a blurring between humans, machines and communications. The terms are less frequently used today, since Internet, intranet and World Wide Web are more specific and widely used.

▶ Why is the Internet proving popular?

The recent dramatic growth in the use of the Internet has occurred because the World Wide Web changed the Internet from a difficult-to-use tool for academics and technicians for accessing technical information to an easy-to-use tool for obtaining

UK Internet usage

More than 7 million people used the Internet in 1997, according to a recent study; in the four weeks prior to being interviewed the number was 4.3 million. Home use rose dramatically by a factor of two, from 420 000 users to over a million surfers between end 1995 and end 1996.

Female Internet surfers now account for 35 per cent of all surfers – which reflects the approximate proportion of PC owners in the UK (one-third female to two-thirds male). In the workplace, two-thirds of users are from firms with 200 or more employees (classified as large businesses).

Source: NOP Research Group, March 1998

useful business and consumer information. The Internet offers a vast amount of information (more than 100 million pages at a recent count) which is readily accessible and has a low cost.

The use of straightforward Web browsers to access the Web provides a range of benefits. Many of these benefits can be turned to advantage by the marketing executive. They include the following:

◆ It is easy to use, since navigation between documents is enabled by clicking on hyperlinks or images. This soon becomes a very intuitive way of navigation that is similar across all Web sites and applications.

◆ It can provide a graphical environment supporting multimedia that is popular with users. This also provides a visual medium for advertising and is also popular with marketers.

◆ There is a large and growing target market. The number of users connected to the Web is estimated to be about 150 million by the year 2000 (Table 17.2). The demographics of this market are slanted towards high-income professionals with a high disposable income.

The business benefits that the Web confers are advantageous both to the large corporation and the small to medium enterprise. Together with the large number of potential customers on the Internet, there are compelling reasons for establishing a presence. These include:

Table 17.2 IT users worldwide

Millions	1995	1996	1997	1998	1999	2000
PC users	144	167	184	203	217	225
E-mail	35	60	80	130	180	200
Web	9	23	46	81	122	152
Online	8	13	18	23	27	30

Source: IDC, October 1996; Morgan Stanley, February 1996

◆ a new medium for advertising and PR;

◆ a new channel for distributing products;

◆ opportunities for expansion into new markets;

◆ new ways of enhancing customer service;

◆ new ways of reducing costs by reducing the number of staff in order fulfilment.

For customers, the potential benefits are convenience through shorter times for selecting a product or service, improved customer service with better access to information and lower product costs, as the companies do not have to have such a significant high street presence.

ACTIVITY

Explain the pattern of growth of different types of IT users in Table 17.2. In particular, explain the following:

◆ the declining rate of increase of PC users;

◆ the narrowing gap between the number of e-mail and Web users;

◆ the meaning of 'online' users as opposed to those described as 'Web' users.

Using the Internet for marketing also offers benefits leading to lower costs for promotion and the ability to provide a wealth of customer service information. At the same time, there is the traditional problem of competing for attention on the 100 million Web pages that are indexed by search engines. The box on the Internet as a new marketing medium explores some of these issues in more detail.

The Internet – a new marketing medium

Internet marketing differs from conventional marketing in several ways. With the new medium comes a different type of customer behaviour and a different set of values. This means that some approaches, such as direct mail, that traditionally work well may fail when applied to the Internet community or 'netizens'. Rather than using conventional 'push' methods of promoting the product, marketers need to think in terms of which information is valuable to the customer. This more subtle approach is more likely to result in a sale if a company supplies the information that customers need to make their buying decisions.

Another key difference is that marketing can be more interactive. Customers can ask questions and the company can reply, and vice versa. This gives the chance for new methods of direct and relationship marketing.

Daniel Janal (1997) looks at how Internet marketing differs from traditional marketing in a number of key areas. These are summarised in Table 17.3. The main differences that should be noted are:

◆ The cost of advertising is reduced in the new media as more space becomes available.

◆ It is the customer who initiates the dialogue and who will expect their specific needs to be addressed.

◆ The user's time is valuable and the time interacting with them will be limited, so this time must be maximised.

> ◆ Information is the main currency. Supplying information is as important as appealing to emotions. If your company doesn't supply it, a competitor will.
>
> The key ways of ensuring success on the Internet are often summarised as content, community and commerce content to capture and retain people's attention, community to enable specialists to work together and commerce to support sales.

Table 17.3 Key concepts of marketing in the new and old media

	Old media	New media
Space	Expensive commodity	Cheap, unlimited
Time	Expensive commodity for marketers	Expensive commodity for users
Image creation	Image is everything	Information is everything
	Information is secondary	Image is secondary
Communication	Push, one-way	Pull, interactive
Call to action	Incentives	Information (incentives)

▶ What are the characteristics of potential users?

Table 17.2 shows that, despite the hype and rapid growth in the number of users, the size of the Internet market is still small compared with global market potential. However, it is the nature of the market that is attractive to marketers. While early users tended to be students or technophiles, the growth in use has occurred as young professionals with high disposable incomes become connected at work or at home. There are many surveys that define the demographics of the users. The following figures are taken from the Graphic, Visualization, & Usability Center's (GVU) 6th International WWW User Survey in 1997:

◆ average age of user is 34.9 years old;

◆ 31.4 per cent female and 68.6 per cent male;

◆ 63.6 per cent access the Web from home;

◆ average household income $60 000.

And these from the eighth survey in 1998:

◆ average age of user is 35.7 years old;

◆ 38.5 per cent female and 61.5 per cent male (22 and 72 per cent in Europe);

◆ 65 per cent access the Web from home (29 per cent in Europe);

◆ average household income $53 000.

It can be seen that the pattern of usage is changing to become more in line with the 'average' population.

The best location for statistics on Web usage, including the regular GVU surveys, is http://www.cyberatlas.com/.

In terms of the geographic spread of the market, the current location of Web users is not representative, with the US market overrepresented. In 1996 about 73 per cent of Web users were from the US, 11 per cent from Europe and 8 per cent from Canada and Mexico (*source*: NUA, Internet Surveys (http://www.nua.ie). In September 1998 there were 148 million Web users in total, 59 per cent of which were from the US and Canada, 22 per cent from Europe and 15 per cent from Asia/Pacific (compiled from various sources).

▶ What are Web sites being used for?

The Durlacher quarterly Internet report of Quarter 3, 1997 reported that 39 per cent of UK small and medium enterprises were using the Internet, with over three-quarters of larger companies accessing it. Table 17.4 shows that company Web sites in the UK are being used for a variety of purposes. Each use has a clear marketing application. Significantly, most UK companies are not fully tapping the potential for marketing, with the display of basic marketing information the most common application.

Table 17.4 Survey of Web site use in British companies

Use		Percentage adoption
1	Putting up PR and marketing information	70%
2	Displaying product information and catalogues	40%
3	Displaying customer contacts	27%
4	Facilitating customer feedback	20%
5	Displaying detailed product information (data sheets and white papers)	18%
6	Distributing paid-for information (software and reports)	10%
7	Taking orders online	8%
8	Carrying paid-for advertisements	5%

Source: *Business Computer World*/Spikes Cavell, February 1997

Table 17.4 is a snapshot of what companies are using the Internet for. As companies become established on the Internet, the importance of the items further down the list will increase.

▶ BUSINESS APPLICATIONS OF THE INTERNET

In this section we look systematically at how the Internet can be used within a company for the different functions comprising the value chain, from service supply through to logistics and support. When thinking about how to integrate the Internet with business functions, it is useful to put this in the context of Michael Porter's value chain, discussed in Chapter 14. If the Internet is only used within the marketing function, or different Internet solutions are implemented in different parts of the organisation, this stores up problems for the long term, since when information needs to be transferred from one part of the organisation to the next it will be difficult. Furthermore, the use of the value chain helps an organisation think about how it can maximise value at each stage. Table 17.5 shows how the Internet can be applied in different parts of an organisation that are defined as elements in the value chain.

Table 17.5 Applications of the Internet for different elements of the value chain

Component of value chain	Internet application
Support activities	
Administration and infrastructure	Use of groupware and administrative workflow between different offices across the Internet to assist in information management
Human resources management	Sharing of HR information in remote offices
Product research and development	Design teams in different offices using Internet as low-cost medium
Procurement	Links to suppliers (extranet) for exchanging ordering and availability information
Primary activities	
Inbound logistics	See procurement
Operations	Limited application unless production is distributed in different sites
Outbound logistics	Links to distributors of product
Sales and marketing	Use of Web site for promotion and electronic commerce
Services	Internet-based customer services such as online help desks

It can be seen from Table 17.5 that true, unrestricted Internet access is most commonly used in the marketing function. Other business applications commonly involve an intranet (which is restricted to company staff sharing information between offices) or an extranet (with restricted access to third-party suppliers or distributors). An extranet can also involve customers. For example, where the product is sent directly to the customer, then the customer can use the Internet to query the delivery of the product. An example of this is querying the delivery status of parcels sent by couriers such as DHL and Federal Express.

Chapter 14 showed how the value chain concept can be extended to suppliers. Long-term consideration should be given to how the Internet can be used in relation to different players in your market.

In this section we consider some of the applications of the Internet in sales and marketing. In the following section we look at applications of extranets in other departments.

▶ Advertising and brand management

The volume of advertising on the Web and other new media is currently dwarfed by traditional media such as newspapers and television.

In the UK in 1996, Web advertising accounted for only £4 million of a total advertising spend of several billion, with radio accounting for £300 million, direct mail £1.2 billion and television £2.2 billion. A similar picture exists throughout the world.

One of the reasons for the slow growth in advertising is the relatively low target audience, estimated at about 4 million in the UK and about 10 times that in the US.

These figures could be taken to show that the Web is a failed medium as far as advertising is concerned. However, advertising spend is growing rapidly from a base of zero only a few years ago. An increase of over 250 per cent was reported in the first six months of 1997 in the US on a baseline figure of $343 million for 1996. Also, it is likely that 'paid-for' advertising is not common on the Web, because the medium is not really suited to it. The Web is a 'pull'-based medium, where users search for the information they want. Adverts do not fit in well with this model, unlike television where the 'push' model is predominant. This does not mean that marketing communications cannot occur, rather they are taking different forms with promotion and public relations occurring at low cost via company Web sites.

Which advertising methods are used?

Figure 17.6 shows a useful method for classifying Internet advertisements. This model divides adverts into paid-for media buys and content on Web sites, which is cost only.

Banner advertising is the most commonly used method, normally employing animated graphics to attract attention at the top of a page, which can be clicked on for further information by a 'click-through'. Incentives are used to encourage users to click

Banner

A rectangular graphic displayed on a Web page for the purposes of advertising. It is normally possible to perform a click-through to access further information. Banners may be static or animated.

Ad clicks

An IFABC standard indicating the number of audited occasions a Web banner or interstitial has been clicked on by a user to view an advert.

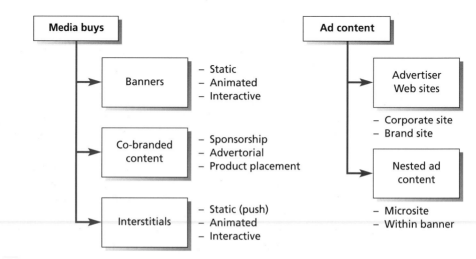

Fig 17.6 An Internet advertising model

through; these include product discounts, a prize or a competition. **Interstitials** are a related form of advertising with a small, animated advert within the body of the Web page. Early adverts were static, but now most are animated to attract more attention. Co-branded content such as sponsorship is similar to that used for television drama.

What does it cost?

The cost of advertising is usually measured in **CPM** or **cost per thousand impressions**. This currently varies between $25 and $35 in the US. The *Daily Telegraph*, one of the most popular sites in the UK, charges £35 per 1000 impressions and the home page of the *Guardian* £4000 per month. A two-week slot on a search engine or Web directory such as Yahoo, which would receive millions of visits, costs $50 000. In the future, it is envisaged that when micropayments (low cost transactions of a few pence or fractions of a penny) become popular, advertisers may pay viewers a small incentive. This would reverse the 'pay-per-view' model.

Where can companies advertise?

A range of choices exist for placing banner advertising. Those most commonly used at the moment are high-volume, general-interest sites such as:

◆ search engines and directories;

◆ news sites such as CNN and PA;

◆ specialised niche sites, e.g. on sporting events;

◆ **cybermalls**.

In the future, the opportunities for targeting special-interest groups for advertising are likely to increase.

▶ Is auditing possible?

As with all forms of advertising, advertisers need to know the size and makeup of the audience. The Web offers a number of advantages over traditional media, since automatic collection of data is possible. Page impressions and ad impressions or number of visitors are the preferred method for establishing audience levels. **Hits** are less accurate, since these refer to the number of graphical images or blocks of text downloaded. One person viewing a single page could record 10 hits.

Formal auditing and registration of sites is now offered by the ABC and BPA, which also fulfil this role for the printed media. Details of these services are available at their sites: http://www.abc.org.uk and http://www.bpai.com. Both are auditing bodies who independently assess the number of visits to Web sites for media buying purposes.

Push technology for Web broadcasting

The 'push' paradigm is changing the way content is provided and accessed on the Web. Rather than users having to search the Web to find what they want, they can now subscribe to the services providing the content in which they are interested and this information is broadcast to them. This happens in a manner similar to a conventional TV broadcast with a subscriber choosing from a number of channels. The content is hosted on a server acting as a transmitter, which broadcasts information at intervals. This is also known as Web or 'netcasting'.

Interstitial

A small, rectangular area within a Web page used for advertising. May be animated or static.

CPM

Cost for advertising is specified as CPM or cost per thousand impressions (Varies in 1997 between $25–35 CPM in United States).

Page impressions

Number of occasions a single page has been delivered to a user. Several hits may be recorded during one page impression according to the number of separate graphics and text blocks that need to be downloaded.

Cybermall

A single Web site which gives online access to goods from a range of shops in a similar way to physical shopping malls enable shoppers to make purchases in one location.

Hits

A measure of individual files delivered to the browser when requesting a URL. Hits usually overstate access to a Web page. Page-impressions and ad-impressions are more accurate.

Push technology

Push is used to deliver Web pages to the users desktop PC without them specifically requesting each page. It is the Internet equivalent of a TV channel hence it is sometimes also known as NetCasting.

Repeaters can be set up to repeat signals from the server and reduce bandwidth constraints. The information can enter a company through a specialised transmitter on a proxy server outside the company firewall. Meanwhile, a tuner residing on the client machine will poll for updated information at set intervals and then download when appropriate, such as when a screensaver starts up if the PC has not been used for a period. Options are also available to personalise information to the individual. Lotus Domino.Broadcast server was released in 1996 to provide this technology. Other major players are Marimba, with its Castanet product, and PointCast, which has teamed up with CNN to broadcast news. Relevant URLs include:

http://www.pointcast.com

http://www.marimba.com

http://www.my.yahoo.com

▶ Direct marketing

It could be argued that all Internet marketing methods are direct, but in this section we look at equivalents to traditional direct marketing. The best-known parallel to traditional methods is direct e-mail, or 'spam' as it is known. The origin of the term spam is obscure, but it quite possibly dates back to the 1960s *Monty Python* television series. US companies have pioneered this direct e-mail approach, sometimes also known as guerilla Internet marketing. Unsolicited e-mail does not fit in with the culture of the Internet and is not well received. Hostility from 'netizens' who reply to a 'spammer' can result in the company from which the message is sent being overloaded by the number of messages received, and it or the ISP responsible may have to shut down its operations. Owing to this, the way forward is probably the use of opt-in systems such as that proposed by www.postmasterdirect.com. With this arrangement, e-mails are only sent to customers who have expressed an interest in a specific area.

A different method of successful direct marketing is needed for the Web. This is incentive based and involves the user providing their details in exchange for information such as a catalogue or information about a new product. Users seem happy to fill in their details when requesting information from companies. In this way, they are self-selecting and companies can build a one-to-one relationship with the customer and interactive marketing can occur.

The catalogue sector has an obvious Internet equivalent and this method is being used by existing catalogue vendors. Direct-response press and television campaigns can also be augmented by providing a Web address offering further information about the product or service.

The Open Profiling Standard

Open Profiling Standard

A standard method of collecting personal details about customers. An initiative, begun by Netscape and Firefly, now supported by many players including Microsoft. http://www.firefly.net/ OPS/OPS.html.

This initiative, begun by Netscape and Firefly (http://www.firefly.net/OPS/OPS.html), is now supported by many players, including Microsoft. Its purpose is to reduce the barrier to customer involvement that requires users to fill in details such as name and address at each site where a dialogue with the company is required. When this standard becomes widely supported, users will only have to fill in their details once and they will be accessible to all companies supplied with your identification number.

▶ Electronic commerce in the consumer market

Electronic commerce divides into the consumer market and the business-to-business market. A great deal of media-generated hype has occurred about online supermarket shopping and cybermalls. To date, the turnover of some of these sites has been less than spectacular.

Barclaysquare, one of the first UK-based cybermalls, is rumoured to have taken only £10 000 in sales in its first 18 months of operation and has recently been relaunched. This amount is small in comparison with the average out-of-town supermarket, which turns over more than £30 million a year. However, some examples show that it is possible to make consumer sites work.

The most successful consumer sites are those of US computer manufacturer Dell and software company Microsoft. These two sites show the potential of online consumer commerce where the product is right. Dell now estimates that it receives over $5 million worth of orders each day which are supported by the Web site. It should be noted that this estimate includes different types of behaviour:

1 Customers researching product information and prices online ('shopping') whose buying decision is supported by the Web site, but who purchase through a conventional channel such as mail-order or through a shop.

2 Customers who place an order online, but who pay by another method such as phone or through the post.

3 Customers who place the order online and whose payment transaction by credit card is also made online.

The actual number of customers who purchase online is relatively small compared to the customers in the other categories. However, the Web site is performing a valuable function to Dell by supporting the buying decision and then providing after sales customer service.

The two biggest obstacles to the spread of electronic commerce are:

◆ the relatively small numbers of consumers and businesses connected to the Internet;

◆ fears about the safety of confidential or personal information transmitted across the Internet (particularly credit card numbers).

Electronic commerce
Transactions of goods or services for which payment occurs over the Internet or other wide-area networks.

The Internet Bookshop

This UK-based startup has achieved sales of £2 million a year, increasing by 20 per cent a month. It is successfully tapping overseas markets, with 80 per cent of sales occurring outside the UK. In the US Amazon, an equivalent operation, saw sales in 1997 rise by $16 million.

Despite flotation on the London alternative investment market and this level of sales, Internet Bookshop is still not turning a profit due to the high infrastructure cost. Competitors such as traditional booksellers Blackwells and Waterstones are now fighting back strongly. The traditional booksellers have increased buying power, hold higher levels of stock and have better established distribution methods.

In 1998, the Internet Bookshop was purchased by traditional UK bookseller, W H Smith for £9 million.

MINI CASE

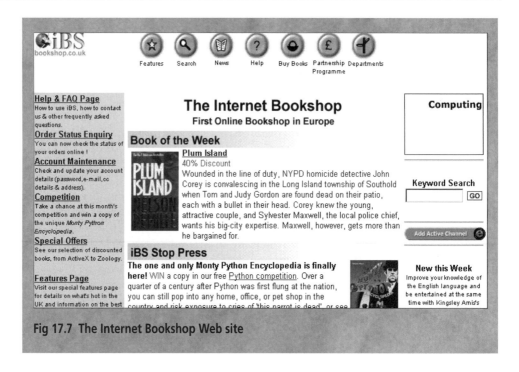

Fig 17.7 The Internet Bookshop Web site

As we have seen, the number of users will continue to increase, but will their attitudes change? Our personal view is that as new secure payment methods become available and are promoted, the security issue will disappear, but not for several years. After all, offering a credit card for payment in a restaurant or a shop probably has much greater potential for the card number to be copied than an encrypted transaction over the Internet.

The feasibility of direct sales

Whether a company can use the Internet for direct sales will, of course, depend on the nature of its products and services. High-volume, low-cost items such as groceries will not be sold direct from the manufacturer, but via wholesalers and retailers as currently. The mini case study earlier in the chapter shows how food retailer Tesco is exploiting the Web.

High-volume, moderate-cost consumer products and information products such as books, records and videos are most suitable and, as we have seen, are already showing significant success.

Payment methods

A large range of payment methods have been developed by a number of different parties, and the number and complexity of methods itself represents a further barrier to the growth of online transactions. Note that with all these methods, links need to exist through to fulfilment of order to the customer. To deliver good-quality customer service, the payment system must be integrated with sales order processing, stock control and distributing systems. After a customer makes a payment for a book they will rightly expect it to be delivered promptly.

ACTIVITY

> How will electronic commerce affect distribution channels for products? Consider the examples of:
>
> ◆ coffee filter paper – a low-interest item;
> ◆ fresh fruit and vegetables;
> ◆ compact discs;
> ◆ financial services such as life insurance.
>
> Consider the following factors when assessing feasibility:
>
> 1 Is the product right – is unseen purchase possible, can it be dispatched?
> 2 Is use of the phone sufficient to give other information, such as location of branch or distributor?
> 3 Will sufficient revenue be generated to cover setup? If not, does this matter!?
> 4 Does the company already have a mail-order infrastructure?
> 5 Can sales be achieved by a third party? A wholesaler or in a catalogue?
> 6 Payment method – is this possible by phone or online?

Before looking at the main payment methods, we will look at the different requirements that any secure payment system should fulfil:

1 *Authentication*. Are parties to the transaction who they claim to be? This is achieved through the use of digital certificates.
2 *Privacy*. Is transaction data protected? The consumer may want to make an anonymous purchase, which is not possible with credit cards currently.
3 *Integrity*. Check that message sent is complete, i.e. that it isn't corrupted.
4 *Non-repudiability*. Sender cannot deny sending message.

Notice that low cost is not one of these requirements. The cost of securing each transaction is governed by the purchase price of an item. A low-cost item does not need such a high degree of security as a high-cost item.

A new proposed standard that is touted as a method to accelerate the uptake of Internet commerce is the SET or Secure Electronic Transactions standard proposed by Barclaycard and Mastercard. This method is based on the exchange of digital certificates between the consumer, merchant and an authentification authority or bank. *See* http://www.mastercard.com/set.

Figure 17.8 indicates the sequence of events that occur when a **secure electronic transaction (SET)** occurs. First, the customer identifies the item they want from the retailer's Web site, puts it in their 'virtual shopping basket' and clicks 'OK' to purchase. The price of the item is transferred to the customer's PC (1). The e-cash software on the PC, which is integrated with the Web browser, then automatically sends a request for some e-cash to the value of the product to the customer's bank (2). This is authorised and the e-cash is returned to the customer (3) and on to the supplier (4). The customer's bank and supplier's bank then negotiate (6) and the payment is made. Further information on keys and **digital certificates** is given on page 557.

There are five main methods of making digital payments over the Internet. These are outlined below:

Secure electronic transactions (SET)

A method developed by Visa and Mastercard proposed for enabling credit-card based electronic commerce based on digital certificates.

Digital certificates

A method of ensuring privacy on the Internet. Certificates consist of a private key for encrypting data or documents and a corresponding public key for reading the data. An independent certification authority issues public and private keys. Basis for SET.

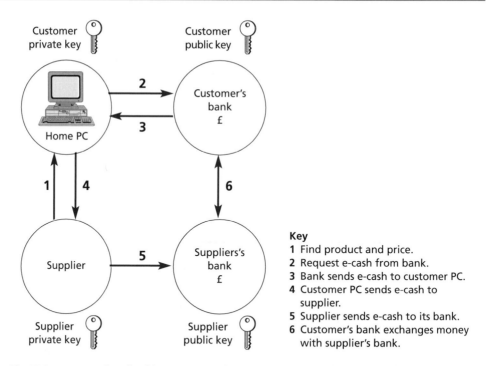

Customer private key

Customer public key

Home PC

Customer's bank £

2

3

1 4

6

5

Supplier

Suppliers's bank £

Supplier private key

Supplier public key

Key
1 Find product and price.
2 Request e-cash from bank.
3 Bank sends e-cash to customer PC.
4 Customer PC sends e-cash to supplier.
5 Supplier sends e-cash to its bank.
6 Customer's bank exchanges money with supplier's bank.

Fig 17.8 Processes involved in an secure electronic transaction between a customer and a supplier using electronic cash

1 *Credit cards*. This is the most commonly used method of consumer purchase over the Internet. Companies usually give the option of encrypting the number when transmitted. If a user has an earlier version of a browser and is not comfortable with transmitting their credit card number, an option must be available for the payment to be made by phone. Much consumer commerce is still performed in this way. Encryption currently occurs using the **Secure sockets layer (SSL)** method pioneered by Netscape. Note that the cost of conducting credit card purchases will preclude them from being used for small-value items or 'micropayments'. This leaves a number of other contenders such as Millicent to tackle this area (*see* method 5).

Secure sockets layer (SSL)

A standard used within Web browsers to encrypt data such as credit card details sent over the Internet.

2 *Smart cards*. These are similar to the Mondex cards that are being trialled in Swindon, UK. The cards contain a chip that is used to store money. They can be recharged from auto-teller machines. Low-cost items such as milk or newspapers can be purchased by this means since the cost of the transactions are low. They are effectively electronic wallets which require a physical device to read them. For making payments from home on the Internet, PCs or set-top boxes would need to have a smart-card reader.

3 *Digital cash and e-checks*. Cybercash and Digicash have both promoted methods for payment from 'software wallets' that do not require a physical card. Cybercash has set up a package that enables funds transfer from a bank account to a merchant or retailer using a range of payment methods such as electronic cash or credit cards (using SET).

4 *Third-party schemes*. A user sets up an account with First Virtual, for example, paying by credit card. FV then acts as a broker when payments are made. When a

sale is made, credit card details are not passed across the Internet, just the reference to the First Virtual account. *See* http://www.fv.com.

5 *Micropayments*. These have been developed by Digital for very small amounts down to a fraction of a cent and are known as the Millicent method. Small amounts would be used for buying information products such as newspapers, stocks or company reports. The method of security is less secure since lower-value items are involved.

▶ Electronic commerce in the business-to-business market

Despite the hype about the consumer market, it is probable that the business-to-business area will see the largest volume of transactions. By the year 2000 the Yankee Group estimates that worldwide:

◆ consumer electronic commerce will reach $10 billion;

◆ business-to-business electronic commerce will exceed $130 billion.

Electronic transactions between businesses are not a recent phenomenon like consumer Internet commerce. They are merely a different method of EDI (electronic data interchange), which has been used for many years by large companies linked by leased lines. It is commonly used for supply of products in a 'just-in-time' environment to minimise holding costs, as described in Chapter 6. Using the Internet as the medium for EDI will reduce the costs involved, and open it up to more small to medium companies.

MINI CASE

Business-to-business commerce

Boeing PART

A good indication of the importance that the Internet will have for future business-to-business commerce is provided by Boeing. The PART system became operational in November 1996 and by the end of 1997 over 500 000 transactions, equivalent to over $1 billion in sales, were achieved. Across the different models of plane there are 410 000 different parts that need to be supplied to the operators. The PART system is used to manage this process.

Cisco Systems (http://www.cisco.com)

This business-to-business Web site was set up to enable customers to purchase gateway electronic products such as hubs and routers. Cisco is now achieving $2 billion in annual sales from the Web site, about 30 per cent of its total revenue.

Marshall Industries (http://www.marshall.com)

This company is another distributor of electronic equipment. A large proportion of its $1.2 billion in annual sales are online using the CyberCash system. The site also features order status tracking, so customers know the anticipated delivery date of the item they have ordered.

IndustryNet (www.industry.net) is an online business-to-business directory that has links from companies' catalogues to back-end order entry, fulfilment and payment systems. It has more than 300 000 buying members and 4500 manufacturers and distributors that have paid for a presence on the site. In the US, CommerceNet has also been active in promoting business commerce between companies. The equivalent organisation in the UK is the Electronic Commerce Organisation at http://www.eca.org.uk.

Most business-to-business sales are currently conducted directly between the customer and the supplier. In the future, an alternative model will also operate. In the UK, a similar scheme to IndustryNet, known as Trading Places (http://www.trading-places.co.uk), is being trialled by BT. In the example shown in Fig. 17.9, the user has selected a PC and is given prices and availability from three different suppliers. They can select one of these or negotiate online to drive the price down further.

Features of a typical business-to-business site

A range of corporate information can be presented on a business Web site. The box shows a typical arrangement. Many businesses don't exploit their site's full potential by simply omitting key pieces of information, such as:

◆ Who are we?

◆ What products do we sell and where can they be bought?

◆ How can we be contacted?

◆ Where can you find out more?

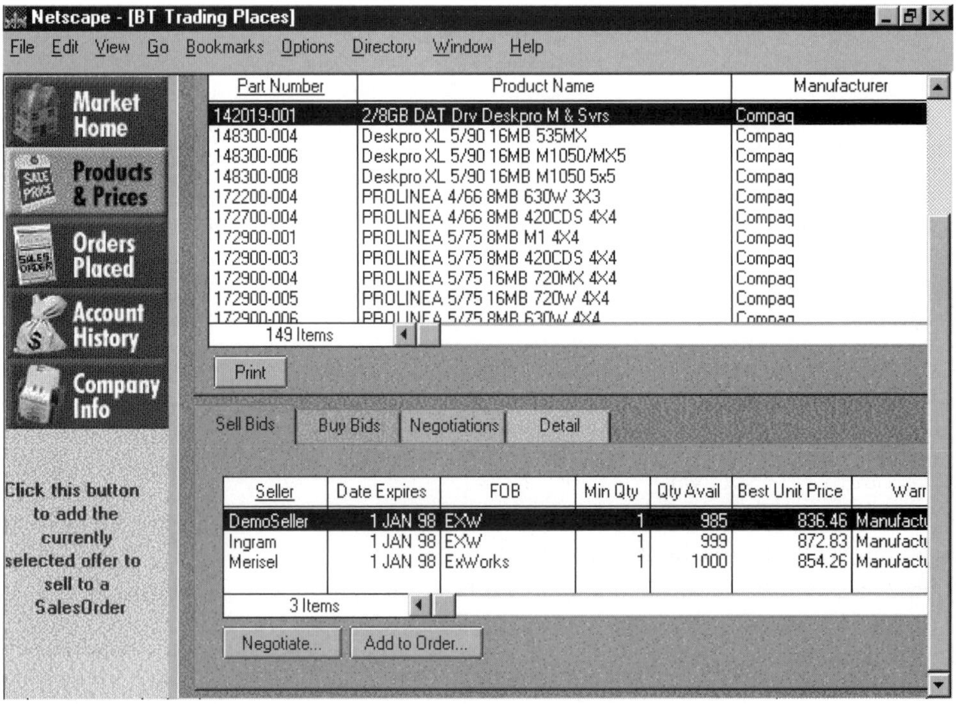

Fig 17.9 Electronic commerce using BT's Trading Places system

---

A comprehensive Web site checklist

About the company
- History
- Contacts
- Office locations – addresses and maps
- Company annual reports
- Financial performance

Products and services
- Catalogue of products, prices
- Online sales from product
- Current stock levels and delivery times
- Detailed technical specifications
- Customer testimonials and client list
- White papers
- Press releases
- Special offers
- Demonstrations
- Where to obtain them

Customer services
- Product returns
- Electronic help desk
- Frequently asked questions

Events
- Seminars
- Exhibitions
- Training

General information
- Contact us
- What's new or media centre (for PR)
- Job vacancies
- Index or site map
- Search
- Links to related sites

▶ Customer service and support

A wide range of information useful to customers can be stored on a company Web site. Useful information will encourage repeat visits and reduce the volume of queries through normal support channels, which need to be staffed. The greater the range of information, the more likely you are to attract new visitors and repeat visits. Customer service information could include:

- product availability;
- discounts and bargains;
- electronic help desk where customers ask questions by e-mail or the Web – all questions are then available to other customers;
- frequently asked questions (FAQ) from customers, e.g. for a travel agent, how soon will my tickets arrive before departure?
- customer feedback forms can be set up for customers to tell you what they think of the Web site or company;
- links to other information, for a travel company, this will be to guides such as http://www.lonelyplanet.com, currency converters, foreign exchange, health precautions.

These types of information will usually be password protected, and only customers who hold accounts or who have registered at the site will be provided with information. In this way, customer service can be linked in with direct marketing and new prospects as well as existing customers can be identified.

E-mail is also a powerful way of providing support. Companies can:

◆ use standard mail addresses such as support@company-name.co.uk or returns@ company-name.co.uk to target support more closely;

◆ use auto-reply services known as mail-bots or auto-responders to reply automatically to customers. For example, on receipt of an e-mail with a subject 'FAQ' or 'New products' in the header, the corresponding information will automatically be sent back to the customer;

◆ e-mail all customers if a product problem occurs.

▶ PR

The Internet can be used to facilitate traditional methods of public relations. It can also be used to expand the depth and breadth of PR.

Most press agencies now use the Internet as a primary source of information. Press releases can be sent by e-mail to agencies with which you are registered and also made available on your Web site.

With this new method of PR, a key difference is that a company can talk directly to the market via the corporate Web site. Third-party agencies and physical media still have a role, because of their credibility as independent sources of information and their wider circulation. Agency information can be supplemented by more detailed and timely information directly from the corporate Web site. Another difference with the new PR is that traditional weekly and monthly publishing deadlines disappear as new stories appear by the minute. This has the obvious benefit that you can make an immediate impact and be better aware of the changing marketing environment. The obvious problem of the new PR is that your competitors have these advantages too. So it is likely that there will be an increased need for defensive PR.

▶ Marketing research and planning

The Web can be used to find out more information about the marketing environment in which a company operates. For each of the main categories that make up the environment, the following techniques can be used:

1 *Competition.* Visit rival companies' Web sites; use tools to monitor when they change (such as smart bookmarks); look at financial status if relevant; monitor online newspapers and industry/trade papers. To find competition use search engines and lists or catalogues. To find information on competitors and the state of the market, reference sites such as Infoseek Industrywatch (www.infoseek.com) are valuable (Fig 17.10).

2 *Market demand* (economic and lifestyle data). Use the traditional research organisations, which are all online (e.g. Experian, Nielsen and NOP) plus summaries of new media behaviour (http://www.cyberatlas.com).

3 *Political and legal forces* (legal, social and political situation). Look at the trade associations for the relevant market.

4 *Technology.* Access the sites of IT suppliers and use new media and IT magazines.

Techniques for using the Internet to find information about products and customers have been examined in an earlier section.

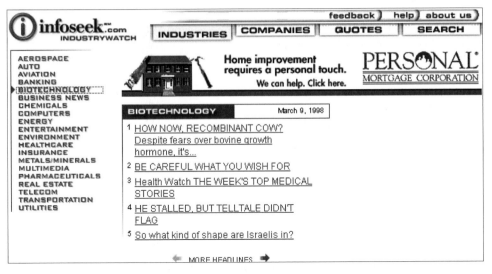

Fig 17.10 Infoseek Industrywatch – a reference site giving specific industry news

▶ BUSINESS USE OF INTRANETS

▶ Intranet benefits

Intranets are private networks for staff within a company that use the standards, protocols and tools of the Internet, such as Web browsers. They provide a cheap and easy way for connecting key people in organisations with the information they need.

When intranets are extended to allow restricted access to third parties such as customers, suppliers or distributors, they are known as **extranets**.

Intranets for the enterprise

According to a recent study by Computer Intelligence, nearly 50 per cent of 150 large companies surveyed said that they are reconsidering their entire network infrastructures to take into account intranets. More than 66 per cent are increasing their intranet budgets and over 17 per cent will spend at least $1 million on an intranet this year.

Source: Computerworld, 25 March 1997

The Durlacher quarterly Internet report of Q3, 1997 reported that only 11 per cent of UK small to medium companies were using intranets, but 60 per cent of large corporates had established them. Durlacher expected penetration in the small to medium sector to grow by 35 per cent over 1998.

Intranets can include the following types of information:

◆ Staff phone directories.

◆ Staff procedures or quality manuals.

◆ Information for agents such as product specifications; current list and discounted prices; competitor information; factory schedules; and stocking levels – this normally has to be updated frequently and can be costly.

◆ Staff bulletin or newsletter.

◆ Training courses.

Intranets are popular since they can produce major cost savings, as is shown in the mini case study on BT. The intranet also offers advantages to network managers looking for more efficient and flexible means of running business applications. Intranets give the following opportunities:

◆ A cross-platform medium for delivering applications, which is important for large corporations with a range of client computers such as Windows PCs, Apple Macintoshes and Unix workstations. By this means a range of computer users are reached.

◆ Lower support costs and costs of ownership to the IS providers in a company, since Web browsers are relatively easy to configure and administer compared to other applications.

MINI CASE

BT's intranet

As a large multinational with over 125 000 staff, information management is a major challenge for British Telecom. In 1994, it decided to experiment with using Internet technology to help its internal information management. To date, it has developed an intranet with over 2 million pages which is accessed by over 65 000 users and is now described as the company's 'central nervous system'.

Information available includes:

◆ product price lists;

◆ operations manuals and policies;

◆ HR support and staff directories;

◆ training information;

◆ company news.

Much of this information used to be modified weekly and sent out as costly updates to staff around the world. The cost savings are substantial because there is now no need to run through the paper cycle of reprinting and distribution. To take an example, the worldwide product pricing manual was regularly updated and distributed around the globe. The annual direct costs of production and distribution were £800 000 before the introduction of the intranet. Indirect costs were estimated as much higher, at between £15–20 million. This amount was so high due to the cost of individuals having to update their own manual and time spent searching through it. Overall savings through reducing these costs have been calculated at £305 million for 1995/96 and £747 million for 1996/97. As well as these changes, there has been a change in the culture, with a move from information being pushed out from the centre of the organisation to people searching for or 'pulling' the information to their desktop, as they need it.

▶ What can a marketing intranet achieve?

Intranets can be set up in different parts of a company, but are particularly beneficial in the marketing department. A marketing intranet has the following advantages:

◆ Reduced product lifecycles – as information on product development and marketing campaigns is rationalised, products reach markets faster. Figure 17.11 shows an intranet homepage for a team collaborating on designing a new watch.

◆ Reduced costs through higher productivity, cheaper tools and saving on hard copy.

◆ Better customer service – responsive and personalised support with customers accessing over the Web.

◆ Globalisation.

Saatchi and Saatchi have adopted Groupwise for 5000 users on an intranet. This gives them a single global address book or staff directory and the ability to share information on draft campaigns and work on a global basis.

▶ Setting up an intranet

An intranet is straightforward to set up if staff already have access to the Internet, since the same protocols such as TCP/IP and tools such as Web browsers are used. Authoring of information to put on the intranet uses the same methods as for the Internet.

Fig 17.11 Livelink intranet being used for coordinating product design

The two main problems that companies report with using intranets are security and the cost of maintenance. Security is an obvious concern, since if staff are accessing the Internet, it may be possible for people outside the company to access information on the intranet. To counter this, a simple solution is to restrict access to the intranet to staff who have usernames and passwords. Commonly, a device known as a firewall is installed. This is described in Chapter 15.

▶ DEVELOPING AN INTERNET STRATEGY

Errors in developing an Internet strategy are common since it is such a new medium, so it is difficult to know how to approach it. As a result, many companies don't have a strategy, rather they have a site or are thinking of having a site, perhaps as a short-term tactical response to the competition. Common errors are:

◆ Not committing and unleashing the power of the Internet because of fears of security, staff time misuse or immature technology.

◆ Setting the scope too narrow – just limiting it to establishing a presence.

◆ Site meets the developers' needs rather than those of customers. For example, developers use large graphics that are slow to download.

◆ Allowing all departments to produce their own sites, leading to fragmentation.

◆ Insufficient investment – without money for maintenance the site will fade away.

The cost of implementing the Internet strategy is not solely concerned with the cost of the information systems. A Web server and a connection to the Internet via an ISP to provide a good service to clients can be purchased relatively cheaply. Rather, it is the cost of staff to author the Web pages and then maintain them that is important. Promotion of the Web site in other media or via Web-based advertising can also be costly.

▶ Alternative Internet strategies

In creating a marketing vehicle for the new medium many companies have found the following to be a natural progression. The IS manager of a company will be asked to provide an increasingly sophisticated Web site, as implied by the evolutionary strategy below:

1 Use a directory insert such as www.yell.co.uk or www.yahoo.co.uk to make people searching the Web aware of the existence of your company or products. You do not need a Web site at this stage.

2 Simple static Web site with basic company and product information.

3 Simple interactive site where users are able to search the site and make queries to retrieve information, such as product availability and pricing.

4 Fully interactive commerce site for direct sales if this is feasible for the type of product you sell.

Such an evolutionary model of Internet application has been developed by Quelch and Klein (1996). They identify two alternative models according to the type of products a company sells. Products that lend themselves to sales on the Internet will follow the stages of the transaction–information model:

1 Transactions.

2 Customer support/service.

3 Image/product information.

4 Information collection/market research.

The majority of companies which do not have the right type of product for electronic commerce, or if there is little market demand, will follow the information–transaction model:

1 Image/product information.

2 Information collection/market research.

3 Customer support/service.

4 Internal support/service.

5 Transactions.

A centre for research on how companies are using the Internet as part of their business strategy was established in 1994 at Owen Graduate School of Management, Vanderbilt University. Project 2000 is directed by professors Donna Hoffman and Tom Novak, and its aim is to study the marketing implications of commercialising the World Wide Web. *See* http://www2000.ogsm.vanderbilt.edu/.

Hoffman and Novak (1996) provide an overview that distinguishes between the application of electronic commerce and other forms of traditional commerce.

The Dell case study provides an excellent example of a company that has successfully made use of the Internet to retail goods directly to its customers. Its strategy has resulted in sales attributed to the Internet site of $4 million each day, with the company forecasting that over half its sales will be achieved this way by the year 2000.

▶ IMPLEMENTING THE INTERNET STRATEGY

▶ How to set up Internet access

The following stages are involved in setting up Internet access for a company to allow employees to browse the Internet, send e-mail and read newsgroups:

1 Select an ISP and connection method.

2 PCs need to be configured with TCP/IP and Windows sockets.

3 PCs must have a Web browser such as Microsoft Internet Explorer or Netscape Navigator.

4 Gateway server needs a firewall for security.

A standard client PC will need to be configured with drivers to access the Internet using the TCP/IP protocol. For PCs accessing the Internet using the TCP/IP protocol, connectivity must be set up; one of the most popular Windows sockets options is Trumpet Winsock. A Web browser program is used to access the Web by selecting which pages to download from the Web servers, display the images and navigate between different sites. These also give e-mail and newsreading facilities. Netscape Navigator and Microsoft Explorer are the two main browsers in use today.

Firewalls

A specialised software application mounted on a server at the point the company is connected to the Internet to prevent unauthorised access into the company from outsiders.

625

CASE STUDY: TOPIC AREA

FT

Dell Computer Corporation

Scalability: Dell is with the Woolwich

by Ray Attwood and Andrew Parker

Fig 17.12 Dell European Web site home page

Scalability is a term regularly used in the IT world to describe the ability of a piece of software and the hardware platforms across which it is being used to meet the increasing demands placed upon it. The term might equally describe the sales and profits figures of the Dell Computer Corporation as it goes on posting ever more impressive results in its drive to adopt the Internet as a prime sales channel for its products. The company seems to have learned quickly how to position itself with consummate success in the fast growing area of Electronic Commerce.

Like many other American corporations Dell is rapidly expanding its global influence and using the Internet as a central plank in its strategy. Unlike many of its contemporaries, however, it is also making healthy profits in the process. The new European operations of Dell are showing that even in a more culturally diverse marketplace the direct selling method, combined with Internet based commercial operations, can rapidly expand and develop across national boundaries.

Sales have been particularly strong in the corporate sector where according to IDC, Dell's revenues grew by 50% in Western Europe. Significantly the proportion of Dell's worldwide sales revenues generated online, which frequently hit the headlines, reached over $4m per day by the end of 1997. Less than a year on from the launch of the first European Internet site, European revenues from the Internet have now risen to $5m a week, indicating the growing acceptance of electronic commerce in Europe. Reflecting the growing importance of this market there are now 16 European online stores in seven European languages where customers can electronically configure, price and purchase systems simply by clicking on the 'Buy a Dell Icon' on Dell's Web page.

In addition to its online stores Dell has also developed a Premier Page programme for its European corporate customers. These are based on the model successfully used in the USA and have grown rapidly from around 60 corporate users in the autumn of 1997 to almost 300 in the Spring of 1998. The Premier Pages have been specifically developed to make it easier for large corporations to do business with Dell. Customers have access to their own secure and customised Web pages where they have information on all aspects of

their account, from corporate pricing strategy and product specifications to order status and service and support.

As Dell continues its drive into the enterprise, the support functions offered by these Premier Pages are beginning to demonstrate their fundamental importance to the continued success of Dell's global strategy. They also show how the Internet is claiming a central role in this development and becoming an indispensable feature in the business process.

Dell's Premium Pages have been providing one of the UK's largest financial companies – Woolwich PLC – with a customised Web based support service, and offering the potential for recording cost savings from standardized ordering across its organization. They have also provided some useful insights into the need for re-engineering some existing business processes in the Woolwich's drive towards de-centralisation.

When it awarded Dell Computer Corporation its branch roll-out contract in 1997, Woolwich became one of the first European based companies to take advantage of the unique Premier Page Programme operated by Dell. Now, several months into the roll out programme, Andy Chavez, responsible for Information Technology at the Woolwich, reviews the major gains for his company from this online support service and notes some unexpected side-benefits.

Dell Premier Pages offer secure and customised Web based support for many of Dell's major corporate clients and since their introduction into Europe nine months ago have already claimed more than 300 corporate users. As Chavez states: 'The old system of communicating with our IT suppliers used a combination of face to face meetings/faxes/phone calls and post. This led to mistakes being made in order specifications with outdated information being used and incorrect prices being charged. These problems created operational delays and confusion in the whole process.'

The opportunity to make use of the Internet to improve this situation was suggested by Dell based on its successful experience in implementing the Premier Page support service to hundreds of corporate clients in the USA. With a major IT client/server roll-out operation now planned for its 400 branches, and the close scrutiny of its new shareholders to take into account, the Woolwich readily grasped this opportunity. A system that could improve its IT procurement procedures, provide costs savings and transfer some of the workload from the service desk to the Web seemed an attractive option to Chavez and his colleagues.

Before the system could become fully operational the Web pages had to be customised to suit the specific requirements of Woolwich PLC. With numerous variations in IT equipment and software specifications constantly being received from all its branches, this task was not straightforward.

The Central IT unit at the Woolwich HQ in Bexleyheath had to consider both the technical aspects of the operation and the commercial imperatives involved. This meant close and often prolonged internal discussion and negotiation between departments to ensure the correct specifications

were given to Dell. As Chavez points out: 'We had to marry the process Dell had engineered to the process that the Woolwich required.' Doing business over the Web on an ongoing basis and replacing paper based systems with electronic communications also involved legal implications.

Previous written terms and conditions of sale required additional legal scrutiny and re-negotiation before progress could be made. This was eventually achieved and standard IT specifications for the Premier Pages were finalised with centrally negotiated price agreements attached.

The new Premier Page system is flexible and allows for additional variations to the standard product specifications to be added with updates advised from either side. Prices are re-negotiated centrally on a quarterly basis, and for Chavez and his colleagues the importance of processing orders through a single point is paramount.

Currently around 20 employees from the Woolwich have access to the Premier Pages and deal with five staff from Dell who are employed in a mixture of sales and technical support roles. Access to information can be slow at times primarily due to the combination of server capacity and network infrastructure used by the Woolwich. At present access is made via standalone PC's generally using 28.8kbps modems but plans are underway to install and develop a 2mb leased line connection with a networked system behind a corporate firewall.

Such improvements to the system should enable the fast and effective use of the Premium Page support service and fits neatly with the plans by Woolwich PLC to de-centralise its operations. For Chavez it is precisely in this de-centralising process that the Dell Premium Pages can prove their effectiveness. Moves to allow some of the larger departments in the Woolwich to become autonomous and accountable profit centres also require they have the ability to control their own purchasing budgets and deployment of IT equipment. For Chavez this may be a double-edged sword if not carefully implemented. 'It is no good speeding the ordering process if you don't link this in with the installation and delivery to the desktop,' he says.

Dell's Premium Page support can be used autonomously by departments or remote branches, promising operational efficiencies with associated cost savings. This does, however, involve the careful re-thinking of some previously accepted business processes, control issues and working practices by the departments involved. Co-ordinated planning within the Woolwich management system is vital to ensure the process works smoothly.

As each business unit in the Woolwich becomes responsible for its own budget Chavez sees the Central IT department taking on more of a brokering role. For Chavez this new way of operating '. . .challenges the way IT departments organise themselves by identifying previous failings and forcing fundamental re-thinking on service and control issues'.

In the past, mistakes in pricing, specification or delivery could have been difficult to attribute and easy to blame on third parties, but with the Premium Pages in place and their accurate notification and recording of all details in the sales and support process, this is no longer a possibility. Orders need to be placed against agreed criteria by approved personnel and they can be tracked constantly. Getting it right first time needs careful pre-planning but by using the Internet and the expertise of both in-house and support staff from Dell, the ultimate cost savings for the Woolwich could be significant.

Source: Financial Times, 2 April 1998

Questions

1 What factors have contributed to Dell's successful use of the Internet as a marketing tool?

2 Identify and explain some of the advantages and disadvantages of Dell's approach to carrying out business over the Internet.

3 What are the benefits of Dell's Internet services to customers?

A connection to the Internet for the mobile or teleworker can be established using a modem and registering them as a user with an ISP (Internet service provider) such as AOL. This arrangement can also be used for the small business. For a larger company a secure server will be used as the gateway to the company.

▶ How to set up a Web site

The IS manager has to be aware of the following stages involved in hosting a Web site:

1 Register the domain name or Web address. It is a good idea for a business to register its company name as the domain name as soon as possible, to avoid possible conflicts with other companies with a similar name. Examples of this problem are illustrated below.

2 Select a PC or UNIX machine to act as a Web server to host:
   ◆ Web pages using the http protocol;
   ◆ remote file access for clients who may wish to download software or documents about the company using the ftp protocol;
   ◆ SMTP Internet e-mail. Note that a company may already have an existing mail server that will need to be connected via a gateway, which converts the internal e-mail from groupware systems such as Lotus Notes or Microsoft Exchange to the Internet.

3 Identify an ISP as a method of attaching the Web site to the Internet.

Domain name registration

A company wanting to establish a Web presence has to register a domain name that is unique. The resulting URL becomes a marketing tool that should be used on all company publications and adverts. Internet domain names have become a commodity, with some individuals registering a name such as 'www.mcdonalds.com' and then attempting to sell it to that company. There have also been legal battles between companies using the same name. For example, the UK training company Prince set up a site www.prince.com. This was contested by the US sports manufacturer Prince, which also wanted to use the name. In this case, the UK courts found in favour of the UK company, since it had established the site first.

A domain name is unique to each site. It has the form:

www.company-name.co.uk for a UK company, such as boots.co.uk

or:

> www.company-name.com for an international or US company, such as www.ibm.com.

Domain names can be registered via an Internet service provider or at more favourable rates direct from the domain name services:

1 InterNIC – www.internic.net. Registration and information about sites in the .com, .org and .net domains.
2 Nomination – www.nomination.uk.com. An alternative registration service for the UK, allowing you to register in the uk.com pseudo-domain. (Also provided by AlterNIC.)
3 Nominet – www.nominet.org.uk. Main co.uk site.

Choices in hosting a Web site

A company must decide between an internal and external site. If a company does not have the technical expertise to host its own Web site, it can publish information via an ISP by renting space on that Web server. Alternatively, it can house a separate Web server inside the company. The second option poses a security risk to the company, since access to the Web site is open, but access to internal systems must be restricted. The use of a firewall reduces the risk of access to the company's systems.

What specification of hardware is required?

Early Web servers were frequently UNIX based and these are still very common, often using the Apache freeware Web server software. PC-based Web servers are also increasingly being used. A Pentium processor-based PC with 64 to 128Mb of RAM is a typical entry-level configuration for a site with a moderate number of visitors or hits. The preferred software for running an in-house PC Web server is Windows NT running Microsoft IIS (Internet Information Server).

What software is required?

To publish information on the Web server you will need additional tools to create content in HTML standard format. If you are simply publishing documents, there are many HTML editors to achieve this or there are converters such as the Microsoft Internet Assistant or the rtftohtml tool that convert wordprocessed documents to HTML with little knowledge of the tags required. Although these may be useful for publishing company information to create the interactive applications required for Web-based groupware and workflow, more powerful tools are usually required. Tools include Webedit Pro, HotMetal Pro, Adobe PageMill and Microsoft FrontPage. Server software such as Microsoft Internet Information Server are also required to deliver the pages from the Web server.

How easy is it?

HTML (Hypertext Markup Language) is the method used to create Web pages and documents. An example is given in the box. The HTML code used to construct pages has codes or tags such as <TITLE> to indicate to the browser what should be displayed.

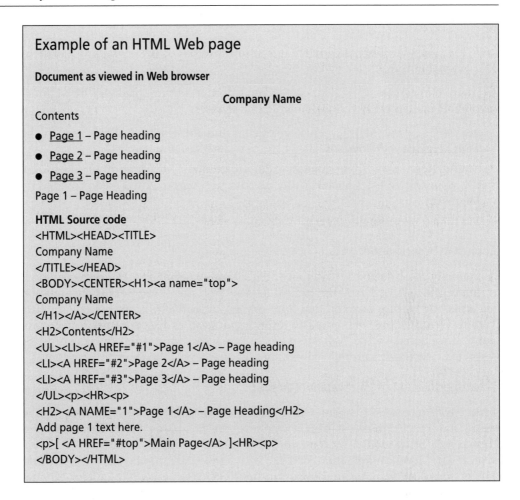

The simplicity of HTML compared to traditional programming languages makes it possible for a simple Web site to be developed by non-specialists such as marketing assistants. However, this is not practical for online catalogues or commerce-enabled sites, which require database expertise.

▶ How much does it cost?

The national median in the US for developing a Web site is shown on www.netb2b.com as $13 500 (small), $33 500 (medium) and $66 250 (large).

Durlacher reports that quotes from an ISP or designer in the UK range from £120 to more than £10 000. Larger sites can cost hundreds of thousands of pounds. For small to medium companies the average spend was just £3000.

▶ Is it working? Indicators of success

Ellsworth and Ellsworth (1997) identify the following options for assessing whether a site is successful. These break down into monitoring the use of the site and the effect on the bottom line. This is difficult to assess unless customers are questioned to see whether they purchased as a result of information on the Web or use the Web to receive orders directly. Indicators include:

- Access levels – who is visiting from where, what is their behaviour?
- Activity – guest book signings.
- Number of references to site from others.
- Sales/transactions resulting directly onsite or product awareness originating from site.
- Advertising volume and revenue.
- Media attention.
- Awards and inclusion in lists of 'hot sites'.

The Web provides a powerful means of profiling customers. It is possible, with the right tools, to establish which country the customers originate from, when they are accessing the site, how long they spend on particular pages and whether a purchase results. Through analysing this information the design of the site can be improved further.

Measuring Web site access

The number of visitors to Web sites can be readily analysed using tools that query the Web log file. Such tools include WUsage, Web Analyser and SurfTool.

▶ SUMMARY

1 The Internet is an international network which is increasingly being used by businesses to:
   - market their company, brands and products;
   - sell their products;
   - set up relatively low-cost links with customers, suppliers and distributors.

2 The World Wide Web is accessed by Web browsers and provides an easy-to-author and easy-to-use publishing and information retrieval system that is largely responsible for the growth of business use of the Internet.

3 When Internet technologies such as Web browsers and servers are used to connect to third-party companies, this is known as an extranet.

4 When these technologies and e-mail are used within a company to share information and to aid collaboration, these are referred to as intranets.

5 Internets, intranets and extranets can be set up by using an Internet Service Provider (ISP) to link to the Internet. ISPs are also used by consumers to access the Internet.

6 Information can be located on the World Wide Web using a variety of techniques:
   - typing in the Web address or uniform resource locator (URL) into a Web browser to go straight to the Web site;
   - using a search engine such as AltaVista to type in keywords, which are then searched for in an index of all Web pages. Relevant pages can be viewed using hyperlinks that move the user to the Web site;
   - using a directory such as Yahoo to find information according to the category in which it is placed, such as Media:Newspapers:Financial Times.

7 Internet marketing strategies involve a combination of publishing interesting content that customers will want to read and return to when it is updated, and promoting the Web site to capture customers through both conventional media and the new media to ensure that it is easy to find via search engines and directories. Community or shared interests can also be used to encourage awareness and commerce can occur if appropriate. Together these can be referred to as the '4 Cs' of Internet marketing strategy:

◆ capture;
◆ content;
◆ community;
◆ commerce.

▶ EXERCISES

▶ Self-assessment exercises

1 Distinguish between the Internet and World Wide Web.

2 What are the business benefits that a company gains by being connected to the Internet? Distinguish between access for staff and setting up a Web site.

3 What are the key stages involved in setting up a Web site that a company plans to manage in-house?

4 What are the main issues in managing staff Internet and intranet access?

5 Explain the different methods of advertising on the World Wide Web.

6 What is the purpose of a Web address or universal resource locator (URL)? How does the standard format of these help indicate different companies, organisations and countries?

7 What is the difference between an intranet and an extranet?

8 How can a company achieve cost savings through conducting business-to-business commerce over the Internet?

▶ Discussion questions

1 The revenue that is generated through Internet advertising is small compared with traditional media such as television and newspapers. Does this imply that the Internet is not an effective medium for advertising?

2 The Internet is not appropriate for undertaking direct marketing campaigns due to the hostility this could generate from customers. Discuss.

3 The marketing department of a company should always be responsible for the creation and maintenance of the company Web site and intranet. This is too important a task to be left to the IT department. Discuss.

4 What do you see as the main barriers to electronic commerce? Do you think these barriers will ever be overcome?

5 Business-to-business commerce on the Internet is predicted to exceed consumer commerce. What do you think the reasons are for this?

6 What are the alternative methods for direct marketing over the Internet? Which do you think is most effective?

▶ Essay questions

1 The Internet is a major new medium for achieving sales. What benefits does it offer over other media? Are these advantages sufficient for it to become the main method of commerce in the future?

2 The adoption of intranets in the UK is significantly less than in the US. Examine the reasons for this.

3 Examine the reasons for the relatively slow growth of consumer electronic commerce in the UK.

4 Until recently, the World Wide Web has followed a 'pull' model of information access. With the advent of 'push' technology such as Pointcast, Marimba Castanet and the inclusion of 'net' or 'Webcasting' in the browser products from Microsoft and Netscape, this looks set to change. Discuss whether the new 'push' methods will change the Internet to being like any other advertising medium.

▶ Examination questions

1 Briefly explain how a business would exploit the different forms of Internet access for business advantage. Give examples of the application of each.
   (a) Internet;
   (b) intranet;
   (c) extranet.

2 Describe what will occur at each of these stages of setting up a company Web site:
   (a) domain name registration;
   (b) connecting to an ISP;
   (c) content authoring.

3 How do the following aspects of marketing differ in the Internet environment:
   (a) advertising;
   (b) PR;
   (c) customer service.

4 Explain how an intranet or extranet can save a company money in the following areas of business:
   (a) sales;
   (b) human resources management;
   (c) product development.

5 There are a number of terms defining the standards and protocols used to enable Web access over the Internet. Explain the following:
   (a) TCP/IP;
   (b) hypertext transfer protocol (http://);
   (c) Hypertext Markup Language.

6 For Internet commerce to be successful, there are a number of criteria that it must meet. Explain the following, in plain language:

(a) authentication;

(b) privacy;

(c) integrity;

(d) non-repudiability.

7 There are a number of different methods for finding information on the World Wide Web. Distinguish between these types:

(a) search engines such as AltaVista or Lycos;

(b) directories or catalogues such as Yell and Yahoo;

(c) 'surfing' by following hyperlinks.

8 Explain how the four main factors of the 'marketing mix' are supported by the Internet:

(a) price;

(b) product;

(c) place;

(d) promotion.

▶ References

Cronin, M. (1996a) *Internet Strategy Handbook*, Harvard Business School Press, Boston, MA.

Cronin, M. (1996b) *Doing Business on the Internet*, Harvard Business School Press, Boston, MA.

Ellsworth, J.H. and Ellsworth, M.V. (1997) *Marketing on the Internet*. John Wiley, New York.
Good for practical design tips and information resources. Limited on strategy development.

Hoffman, D.L. and Novak, T.P. (1996) 'Marketing in hypermedia computer-mediated environments: conceptual foundations', *Journal of Marketing*, July, 50–69.

Quelch, J.A. and Klein, L.R. (1996) 'The Internet and international marketing', *Sloan Management Review*, Spring, 60–76.

▶ Further reading

Allen, C., Kania, D. and Yaeckel, B. (1998) *Guide to One-To-One Web Marketing*, Wiley Computer Publishing, New York.

Bayne, K. (1997) *The Internet Marketing Plan: A Practical Handbook for Creating, Implementing and Assessing Your Online Presence*, John Wiley, New York.

Bickerton, P. and Pardesi, U. (1996) *Cybermarketing*, Butterworth-Heinemann, Oxford. Chartered Institute of Marketing series. Available online for partial preview at: http://www.marketingnet.co.uk.

Butler Group (1997) *Business on the Web*, the Butler Group, Hessle.

Campbell, D. and Campbell, M. (1995) *The Student Guide to Doing Research on the Internet*, Addison Wesley, Reading, MA.

Chase, L. (1998) *Essential Business Tactics for the Internet*, Wiley Computer Publishing, New York.

Ghosh, S. (1998) Making Business Sense of the Internet, *Harvard Business Review*, March–April, 126–35.

Hills, M. (1997) *Intranet as Groupware*, John Wiley, New York.

Janal, D. (1997) *Online Marketing Handbook: How to Promote, Advertise and Sell Your Products and Services on the Internet*, Van Nostrand Reinhold, New York.

Kalakota, R. and Whinston, A. (1997) *Electronic Commerce: A manager's Guide*, Addison Wesley, Reading, MA.

Magretta, J. (1998) The power of virtual integration: an interview with Dell computer's Michael Dell, *Harvard Business Review*, March–April, 73–84.

Sterne, J. (1995) *World Wide Web Marketing: Integrating the Internet into York Marketing Strategy*, Wiley, New York.

Winship, I. and MacNab, I. (1996) *The Student's Guide to the Internet*, Library Association Publishing, London.

Business Computer World (monthly) and *Computing* (weekly) both provide good case studies and give updates on changes to the technology.

▶ Web references

http://butlergroup.co.uk Reports on different aspects of applying the Internet to business (in publications section).

http://www.computerweekly.co.uk *Computer Weekly*. Weekly technology paper. Weekly feature 'Getting Wired' covers all Internet and intranet developments.

http://www.ibmag.co.uk *Internet Business*. Independent monthly. Good for practical advice.

http://www.mag.net *Internet World*. Good monthly, but tends to be technology rather than business oriented. Full text available online.

http://www.marketing-haynet.com

http://www.marketing.online.co.uk An extensive collection of web references relating to all aspects of Internet marketing including site infrastructure, development and promotion, produced by Dave Chaffey.

http://www.marketing-week.co.uk

http://www.nma.co.uk *New Media Age*. Available by subscription only.

http://www.revolution.haynet.co.uk *Revolution*. New monthly magazine devoted to new media.

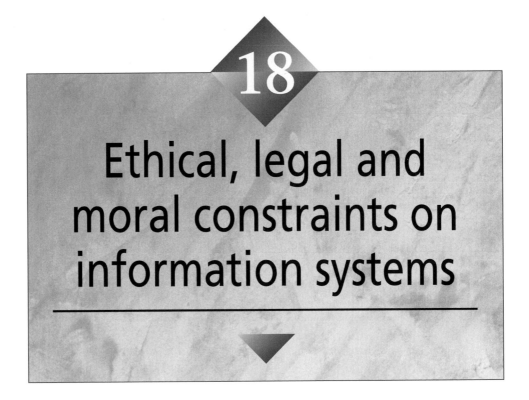

18

Ethical, legal and moral constraints on information systems

INTRODUCTION

This chapter considers the moral, legal and ethical responsibilities of those involved in designing, developing and managing computer-based information systems.

The chapter will cover:

◆ legislation relevant to the management and use of computer-based information systems;

◆ the social and professional responsibilities of those involved in the management, development and use of computer-based information systems;

◆ major and contemporary social issues related to computer-based information systems, such as the impact of technology on employment and personal privacy.

> ▶ **Learning objectives**
>
> After reading this chapter, readers will be able to:
>
> ◆ analyse decisions and courses of action from professional, ethical and moral perspectives;
>
> ◆ select appropriate and legal courses of action in keeping with professional codes of conduct;
>
> ◆ understand and respond to issues of concern, such as personal privacy.

▶ **Links to other chapters**

Chapter 13   deals with a number of issues relevant to this material, such as managing organisational change.

Chapter 15   considers common threats to the security of computer-based information systems, such as unauthorised access.

▶ PROFESSIONALISM, ETHICS AND MORALITY

We expect the developers, managers and users of computer-based information systems to behave in a professional manner at all times. They have to balance the needs of their employer and the requirements of their profession with other demands such as a responsibility to society. The terms ethics, morality and professionalism are often used to describe our expectations of managers and employees:

◆ **Professionalism** can be described as acting to meet the standards set by a profession in terms of individual conduct, competence and integrity.

◆ **Ethics** describe beliefs concerning right and wrong that can be used by individuals to guide their behaviour.

◆ **Morality** is concerned with an individual's personal beliefs about what is right and wrong.

IS professionals are in a difficult position when undertaking their work since there are a number of constraints affecting their behaviour. These constraints are indicated on Fig 18.1. They may not necessarily conflict, but the employer may place demands on the manager which go against any of these constraints. What should a project manager do, for instance, if the company asks her to reduce the time taken for testing on a project (in order to meet a deadline) which may affect public safety? The following sections examine some of the responsibilities of the IS manager in each of these areas.

Professionalism

Acting to meet the standards set by a profession in terms of individual conduct, competence and integrity.

Morality

Individual character or personality and beliefs governing right and wrong.

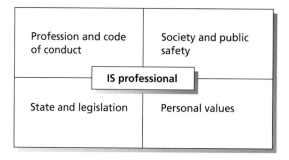

Profession and code of conduct	Society and public safety
IS professional	
State and legislation	Personal values

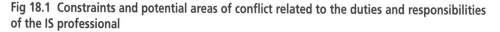

Fig 18.1 Constraints and potential areas of conflict related to the duties and responsibilities of the IS professional

▶ Codes of conduct

In addition to personal beliefs concerning right and wrong, professionals must also ensure that they obey the law and meet the standards set by their professional association.

A professional association is entitled to set entrance requirements that govern minimum levels of experience and qualifications for new members. Gaining membership affords status to members and implies that they have achieved a high level of competence in their field. Membership also provides a variety of other benefits, such as training and official representation. However, in return for membership, the individual accepts a duty to meet certain standards of conduct and behaviour. All professional associations expect members to adhere to a **code of conduct** that sets out the association's principles.

In the UK, the **British Computer Society (BCS)** is regarded as the leading professional association for those involved in the design, use and management of computer-based information systems. The BCS code of conduct provides clear and firm guidance concerning a member's duties and responsibilities.

Code of conduct

Members of professional associations are expected to abide by a set of principles that sets out minimum standards of competence, conduct and behaviour.

British computer society (BCS)

Widely regarded as the UK's leading professional association for those involved in the management and development of computer-based information systems.

British Computer Society – Code of Conduct

The Public Interest

1 Members shall in their professional practice safeguard public health and safety and have regard to protection of the environment.

2 Members shall have due regard to the legitimate rights of third parties.

3 Members shall ensure that within their chosen fields they have knowledge and understanding of relevant legislation, regulations and standards and that they comply with such requirements.

4 Members shall in their professional practice have regard to basic human rights and shall avoid any actions that adversely affect such rights.

Duty to Employers and Clients

1 Members shall carry out work with due care and diligence in accordance with the requirements of the employer or client and shall, if their professional judgment is overruled, indicate the likely consequences.

2 Members shall endeavour to complete work undertaken on time and to budget and shall advise their employer or client as soon as practicable if any overrun is foreseen.

3 Members shall not offer or provide, or receive in return, inducement for the introduction of business from a client unless there is full prior disclosure of the facts to the client.

4 Members shall not disclose, or authorise to be disclosed, or use for personal gain or to benefit a third party, confidential information acquired in the course of professional practice, except with prior written permission of the employer or client, or at the direction of a court of law.

5 Members should seek to avoid being put in a position where they may become privy to or party to activities or information concerning activities which would conflict with their responsibilities in 1–4 above.

6 Members shall not misrepresent or withhold information on the capabilities of products, systems or services with which they are concerned or take advantage of the lack of knowledge or inexperience of others.

7 Members shall not, except where specifically so instructed, handle clients' monies or place contracts or orders in connection with work on which they are engaged where acting as an independent consultant.

8 Members shall not purport to exercise independent judgment on behalf of a client on any product or service in which they knowingly have any interest, financial or otherwise.

Duty to the Profession

1 Members shall uphold the reputation of the Profession and shall seek to improve professional standard through participation in their development, use and enforcement, and shall avoid any action which will adversely affect the good standing of the Profession.

2 Members shall in their professional practice seek to advance public knowledge and understanding of computing and information systems and technology and to counter false or misleading statements which are detrimental to the Profession.

3 Members shall encourage and support fellow members in their professional development and, where possible, provide opportunities for the professional development of new entrants to the Profession.

4 Members shall act with integrity towards fellow members and to members of other professions with whom they are concerned in a professional capacity and shall avoid engaging in any activity which is incompatible with professional status.

5 Members shall not make any public statements in their professional capacity unless properly qualified and, where appropriate, authorised to do so, and shall have due regard to the likely consequences of any statement on others.

Professional Competence and Integrity

1 Members shall seek to upgrade their professional knowledge and skill and shall maintain awareness of technological developments, procedures and standards which are relevant to their field, and shall encourage their subordinates to do likewise.

2 Members shall seek to conform to recognised good practice including quality standards which are in their judgment relevant, and shall encourage their subordinates to do likewise.

3 Members shall only offer to do work or provide a service which is within their professional competence and shall not claim to any level of competence which they do not possess, and any professional opinion which they are asked to give shall be objective and reliable.

4 Members shall accept professional responsibility for their work and for the work of their subordinates and associates under their direction, and shall not terminate any assignment except for good reason and on reasonable notice.

5 Members shall avoid any situation that may give rise to a conflict of interest between themselves and their client and shall make full and immediate disclosure to the client if any conflict should occur.

▶ Professional responsibilities

Another way in which the responsibilities of managers, developers and users can be described is by considering some of their obligations to their employers, the public and the state. In this way, we can illustrate some of the areas in which conflicts of interest might occur.

Employers and employees

Both managers and employees are expected to balance a number of duties and responsibilities in the course of their activities. These can be divided into two broad areas: the responsibilities of all staff to the employer and the responsibilities of managers to the staff they supervise.

Some of the responsibilities that employers expect their staff to assume include:

◆ All employees should look for ways in which they can help the company to achieve its aims. In many cases, this will involve finding new or more efficient ways to complete their work.

◆ All staff should take responsibility for their actions and the quality of their work.

◆ Managers should assess projects carefully, considering areas such as cost and risk in relation to the aims of their employer.

◆ Staff should work to ensure the security of equipment, software and data.

◆ All employees should attempt to protect and maintain the accuracy of the data held by the company.

◆ All employees should only attempt work that they feel competent to perform. In the event that they feel unable to manage a task correctly, they should seek appropriate help and advice.

◆ All employees should maintain up-to-date knowledge of their area of expertise and seek training when required.

In addition to their responsibilities to their employer, managers must also assume additional responsibilities for the staff under their supervision. Some of these responsibilities include:

◆ Managers should assign tasks to employees based on skills and experience. Staff should not feel that their skills are being underemployed, nor should they feel pressured into attempting work that they are not capable of carrying out competently.

◆ Managers should ensure that their staff are adequately trained and should assign responsibilities carefully and fairly.

◆ Resources should be applied in the most efficient ways possible. Managers should be accountable for how the resources they control are used.

These points should help illustrate some of the difficulties that can arise in the workplace. As an example, consider a manager charged with completing a complex technical project with only a limited budget. Some of the possible approaches to the task might be as follows:

◆ The manager might approach a superior and ask for additional resources, or could continue with the work knowing that the assigned budget would be exceeded.

◆ The manager could attempt to distribute the work among staff members, potentially placing them under extreme stress by asking them to complete work that might be beyond their capabilities.

◆ The manager could use part of the budget to provide additional training for staff. This would enable the work to be completed, but might affect the timescale allowed for the project and cause difficulties for the company later on.

In each of these cases, there is a clear conflict between the manager's responsibilities to the employer and their responsibilities towards staff. In attempting to seek a solution to such a problem, the manager must deal with a number of professional and ethical issues, often relying on personal judgement and experience.

The public

The responsibilities of managers, developers and users to the public can also raise a number of ethical and professional issues. Two of the most important obligations placed on professionals concern the duty to protect confidential information and a duty towards public safety.

The duty to protect sensitive or confidential information is normally described in terms of developing security measures to prevent hackers and other unauthorised users from gaining access to company data. However, in terms of a duty to the public, this responsibility can be extended to encompass areas relevant to civil liberties, such as censorship, the right of individuals to view personal data held on them and the privacy of e-mail messages and other communications.

In a similar way, the duty to maintain public safety is not to be restricted simply to ensuring that safety critical systems function correctly. Managers and developers must also take responsibility for the quality of the systems with which they work.

Many computer-based information systems can have an indirect impact on public safety by producing inaccurate or incomplete information that is relied on by users. As an example, many companies publish medical software programs designed to help home users find information related to illnesses and their treatment. Despite the prominent warnings displayed by these programs, there is clearly a danger that users may accept a suggested diagnosis or treatment and act on the information.

If some people can place too much reliance on computer-based information systems, then the opposite is also true. An unreliable or ineffective system could also have consequences for public safety. In 1990, the pilot of a British Airways aircraft, Captain Tim Lancaster, was nearly sucked out of his cockpit window after the bolts securing the windscreen gave way. It was later found that an engineer had used the wrong bolts when fitting the windscreen. Although the engineer had access to a computer-based information system that could have been used to identify and select the correct bolts, he had chosen not to use it since it was considered unreliable and inaccurate (*Independent on Sunday*, 15 November 1992).

A controversial aspect of public safety concerns issues related to child pornography and information that could be used to support criminal and terrorist activities. While some argue that all information should be freely available, others are concerned that steps should be taken to control potentially dangerous information and protect the vulnerable, such as children.

The state

The state attempts to maintain standards and behaviour by enacting legislation to regulate the behaviour of companies and employees. Although specific pieces of legislation, such as the Computer Misuse Act (1990), are aimed directly at those working in the field of computer-based information systems, companies and employees must also observe more general laws. As an example, the Health and Safety at Work Act (1974) means that all employees are responsible for safety in the workplace. Staff are required to take immediate action in response to any hazard or danger to health. Furthermore, employers are expected to ensure that the workplace is safe through actions such as providing safety equipment.

Other aspects of legislation relevant to those working in the field of computer-based information systems are described in more detail later on.

CASE STUDY: TOPIC AREA

FT

Internet self-regulation

A global consensus is emerging that pornography and other undesirables on the Internet should be controlled mainly by self-regulation rather than by law.

The issue is extremely hard to resolve because although the Net is a global medium – and different cultures take very different attitudes to what material is permissible, how it should be controlled, who is responsible and what penalties are appropriate for abuse.

Unregulated, the Internet could become a medium not only for hard-core pornography but also recipes for bomb-makers, incitements to racial hatred, credit-card copying instructions and the nefarious activities of hacking, piracy and libel.

That the Internet looks likely to avoid strict legislation is partly because the libertarians have won the argument in the US (from where the Internet is run) and partly because it has so far proved impossible to impose effective global controls.

A landmark in the history of the Internet came in June last year when the US Supreme Court threw out the proposed Communications Decency Act. That act was introduced by Congress to impose a criminal liability on service providers and network users who transmitted obscene material.

It aroused much hostility in the US. Objectors said it was so broad that it could even incriminate phone companies for allowing lovers to talk intimately across their networks.

In an appeal case brought by the American Civil Liberties Union and others against the Attorney-General Janet Reno, the court ruled that the act was unconstitutional because it abridged the freedom of speech protected by the first amendment of the constitution.

After that, it was back to the drawing board. President Clinton quickly threw his authority behind a self-regulatory approach, urging the computer industry to make the Net 'family-friendly'. Parents and teachers should be given the tools to prevent children from getting access to undesirable material, he said.

In December, a conference in Washington brought together the US government, the industry, parents and teachers to discuss controls, particularly how enforceable codes of conduct could be formulated to make the Internet 'family friendly'. Vice-President Al Gore pressed the industry to come up with solutions within six months.

The EU and other European countries are heading in the same direction. Last July, 29 European ministers meeting at a conference in Bonn came out in favour of an Internet as lightly governed as possible, with the emphasis on self-regulation and private initiative. They also stressed the need for the computer industry to produce content rating systems.

However, they diverged from the US policy on encryption. The US still prevents the general export of strong encryption software products without first depositing the key with the authorities because it sees encryption as opening a channel for organised crime.

European ministers, however, backed the adoption of encryption following the line of the Organisation for Economic Co-operation and Development. Germany's economics minister Gunter Rexrodt said he favoured encryption as essential to preserving data integrity and personal privacy.

In October, the European Commission took the view that since encryption was already becoming widespread the EU should work towards adopting it by the year 2000 as the only way of effectively protecting confidentiality.

The Commission is following the same line as the US in backing an action plan to make the Internet 'safe', which hinges on a campaign of self-regulation. The campaign comprises an effort at spreading awareness of the problem, speeding up development of filtering systems and establishing hotlines for users' complaints and a content rating system.

The Commission argues that although service providers cannot be held responsible for all content on their networks, they have a duty to respond to complaints about content by investigating and taking appropriate steps to remove illegal material and to help block offensive material.

However, there is still a lot of detail to be worked out. A content rating system could be established whereby any material which is not labelled is treated as undesirable and blocked; alternatively, all material could be allowed unless it is labelled for restricted access.

As yet, the industry has not formulated a policy on this. The Commission stresses that whatever is decided rating systems must be compatible with each other so that a global standard emerges.

In the meantime, service providers have been trying to promote self-regulation, providing software with which users can impose censorship on themselves and on their families.

Jonathan Bulkeley, UK managing director of service provider America Online (AOL), says the biggest part of the problem is protecting children.

'The responsibility must lie with parents to supervise their children's use of the Internet, as they should supervise their use of television,' he says. But there are things service providers can do to help, he adds.

AOL is introducing into the UK a 'Kids' Only' account which guarantees that all the sites accessible are decent and suitable for children.

The account has already proved popular in the US, says Mr Bulkeley. It may be harder for service providers which do not have proprietary networks but only give access to the Internet to offer such facilities.

Mr Bulkeley says that AOL's policy is to protect the customer's right to privacy unless there is strong evidence that a crime has been or could be committed. He says there is a growing number of complaints being made on which the service provider has to make a difficult judgement.

For example, if someone complains of harassment by e-mail, it is very hard for a service provider to distinguish between a message which is a legitimate though offensive complaint and one which a court might rule was harassment.

Source: Financial Times, 1 April 1998

Questions

1 What social and ethical issues are involved in the debate over legislation versus self-regulation?

2 Who is responsible for the protection of Internet users from hazards such as pornography, harassment and racial hatred? Consider whether separate rules or arrangements are needed to protect children and young people.

3 Assuming that new legislation is introduced to regulate the Internet, what problems might be faced in enforcing it?

▶ SOCIAL ISSUES

The **information society** is a term that has been coined to describe a modern population that is conversant with – and reliant on – information and communications technology. In this section, we consider a selected range of social issues that concern both individuals and organisations.

Information society

Describes a modern population that is conversant with – and reliant upon – information and communications technology.

▶ Employment

There can be no doubt that technology has made a significant impact on patterns of employment. In the office environment, the positions and tasks of many employees have been taken over by computer-based information systems. Where a number of clerks may have been needed to maintain records or handle everyday transactions, many tasks are now carried out automatically through technologies such as EDI and computer telephony. In manufacturing organisations, industrial robots and automated manufacturing processes have replaced many thousands of skilled workers.

However, while it is certainly true that technology has been responsible for the loss of many jobs in manufacturing and service industries, it is also apparent that a wealth of new employment opportunities have been created in their place:

◆ In order to make use of technology within industry, highly skilled workers are needed to design, produce, market and maintain the required hardware and software. In addition, other areas of employment, such as education and training, have expanded in order to service the needs of those adopting new technology.

◆ The use of technology has also allowed organisations to develop more sophisticated goods and services, creating whole new industries in a matter of just a few years. The Internet, for example, has grown rapidly over the past five years and provided many thousands of employment opportunities in areas such as Web page design and e-commerce.

▶ Personal privacy

It has long been recognised that technology enables companies, government departments and other organisations to collect large amounts of personal information. Although the use of such information is controlled by various mechanisms, such as legislation, many people are concerned by the potential threat to personal privacy.

This threat is perceived to arise from the basic functions of computer-based information systems, namely their ability to store, process and retrieve data quickly and efficiently. Two examples can be used to illustrate common concerns related to privacy:

◆ The use of computer-based information systems enables an organisation to combine or analyse data in ways not previously possible with manual systems. As an example, a bank might build up profiles of its customers by analysing their spending, borrowing and saving habits. This information could be supplied to other organisations involved in marketing relevant goods or services.

◆ Communications technology allows organisations to share data, enabling them to develop a comprehensive pool of information regarding individuals. An insurance company, for example, might gather medical information before deciding whether or not to offer a policy to an individual.

A further issue related to privacy concerns the quantity and accuracy of the personal data held on individuals. It is estimated that an average adult may be listed on as many as 200 computer files. Furthermore, there may be a 2 per cent error rate in the information held (*Guardian*, 12 May 1997). Other estimates suggest that up to 43 per cent of consumer credit files may contain errors. Holding inaccurate personal data on an individual can result in a number of problems, for example an incorrect health service number might result in an error in a person's treatment.

Another area of concern is the use of computer monitoring to gather information concerning the behaviour of people in the workplace. Although such monitoring has legitimate uses, for example measuring workflow and productivity, it can also be used to violate an employee's privacy. In fact, in Germany this is not a legitimate use since the law protects workers from this type of electronic monitoring.

Computer monitoring

The use of computer and communications technology to monitor the activities of individuals.

Computer monitoring is also used in a number of other areas, for example a security firm may use a combination of computers, video cameras, sensors and other devices to maintain the security of a large building.

The monitoring of communications, such as telephone calls and e-mail messages, is also a major area of concern for many users. Although there seems little evidence to suggest that all communications are monitored at all times, many companies and individuals have turned towards methods such as encryption to protect sensitive business or personal information.

ACTIVITY

> It is estimated that a typical adult may be listed in as many as 200 computer files.
>
> 1 How many organisations hold data on you? List as many organisations as you can think of and describe the data held.
>
> 2 Imagine that you have access to all of this data and wish to build a profile of a person's characteristics. Describe what such a profile would contain and what other assumptions could be made.
>
> 3 If a government department or commercial organisation were given access to all of this information, to what uses could they put it?

▶ Crime

As the use of technology has become more widespread, so too have incidences of computer crime. Acts such as theft, fraud, unauthorised access and vandalism have become almost commonplace and the losses or damage caused by such acts have increased dramatically.

> The Association for Payment Clearing Services suggests that card fraud cost the banks more than £97 million in 1996, with more than £13 million from false magnetic stripe cards, twice the amount recorded in 1995.
> *Source: Guardian, 24 September 1997*

Computer criminals

Those who commit computer-related crimes can be divided into three basic categories:

1 **Computer criminals** as well-educated, white-collar workers who feel undervalued or bear some resentment to an employer or former employer (Parker, 1976). Such individuals resort to sabotage, vandalism or theft as a means of revenge against the employer. Other computer criminals may stumble on ways of compromising system security and take advantage of these in order to steal money, goods or services.

2 Schwartau (1994) describes **information warriors** as those who seek to obtain data by any means necessary. These people may resort to illegal methods, such as hacking, in order to obtain the information they require. It is worth noting that the information obtained may not necessarily be used in pursuit of criminal activities, for example a police officer might feel the need to resort to such methods in order to gather evidence against a suspect.

3 **Hackers** are often described as individuals who seek to break into systems as a test of their abilities. Few hackers attempt to cause damage to the systems they access

Computer criminals

Make use of technology to perform a variety of criminal acts, ranging from vandalism and sabotage to hacking and fraud.

Information warrior

Seeks to obtain data by any means necessary. Such people may resort to illegal methods, such as hacking, in order to obtain the information they require.

Hacker

Individuals who seek to break into systems as a test of their abilities. Few hackers attempt to cause damage to the systems they access and few are interested in gaining some sort of financial profit.

and few are interested in gaining some sort of financial profit. It can be argued that there are four basic motives behind the actions of hackers (Johnson, 1994):

(a) Some hackers hold the belief that all information should be free. They feel a duty to ensure free access to information held by government departments and private companies.

(b) Many hackers believe that they provide an important service to companies by exposing flaws in security.

(c) Some people believe that hacking serves an educational purpose by helping them to improve their knowledge and skills. Since no harm is caused to any systems accessed, their actions are acceptable and should not be considered threatening.

(d) A final motive for hacking is simply for enjoyment or excitement. Many hackers find stimulation in the challenge of defeating the designers of the security measures used by a given system.

Types of computer crime

Computer crime can be divided into a number of different categories:

Theft

In terms of computing, theft normally, but not always, involves altering computer records to disguise the theft of money. The theft of services can include a variety of acts, such as the unauthorised use of a company's information systems.

Software theft

Software theft, also known as software piracy, involves making unauthorised copies of software applications.

Data theft

Data theft can involve stealing sensitive information or making unauthorised changes to computer records.

◆ **Theft** normally, but not always, involves altering computer records to disguise the theft of money. An employee of an insurance company, for example, might create a number of fictitious clients and then make claims on their behalf.

◆ The *theft of services* can include a variety of acts, such as the unauthorised use of a company's information systems. Although many of these acts may appear innocuous, it should be noted that their effect can lead to significant losses. Making intensive use of a company's computer systems, for example, can temporarily deprive the organisation of its resources, leading to financial losses through decreased productivity.

◆ **Software theft** involves making unauthorised copies of software applications. This topic is described in more detail later on.

> In 1996, entertainment software piracy cost the global industry $3 billion in lost revenues.
> *Source: Guardian, 23 April 1997*

◆ **Data theft** can involve stealing sensitive information or making unauthorised changes to computer records.

◆ The *destruction of data and software*, for example by creating and disseminating computer viruses, can lead to significant losses. The International Computer Security Association, for example, estimates that a virus infection costs a company an average of £2000 (*Financial Times*, 23 April 1998). The impact of computer viruses is described in more depth in Chapter 15.

◆ A number of well-known cases have highlighted the risks posed by *hackers*. Two well-known examples are the following:

(a) In 1988, Robert Morris, a student at Cornell University, released a computer program onto the Internet that later became known as the Internet Worm.

The program, it was later argued, was intended to demonstrate weaknesses in the security of networked computer systems. The program infected academic, corporate and military computer systems throughout the US and beyond, causing damage estimated at between $10 million and $90 million. The cost of removing the program from each affected site was estimated to be from $200 to more than $53 000. The Morris case is widely regarded as the first international incident to involve hacking and computer viruses.

(b) In 1996, 24-year-old Russian hacker Vladimir Levin used a laptop computer in an attempt to steal $400 000 from Citibank. Following his arrest, the US began extradition proceedings and it emerged that Levin had actually attempted to steal more than $10 million. This case generated international publicity, since Levin had allegedly worked alone and yet had been able to breach the defences of one of the world's largest corporations (Flohr, 1995).

CASE STUDY: TOPIC AREA

FT

Computer fraud

Hi-tech sleuths aim to crack computer fraud

by George Cole

Internet technology has made corporate theft easier than ever. George Cole reports on a new breed of 'detectives' dedicated to stopping it.

Financial fraud investigations are often called paper-chasing exercises, but these days a fraud investigator is more likely to use a computer than piles of paper to investigate a possible crime.

Today's global financial system uses computer networks to transfer funds worldwide, and most companies store financial records on computer. So information technology has become a powerful tool for cracking fraud cases.

'Computers are used by fraudsters for recording information rather than pen and paper,' says Andrew Durant, senior manager of the fraud services unit at Arthur Andersen, the accountancy group. 'They often hold a lot of information that is extremely helpful to the fraud investigator, such as banking transactions, contacts, and names and addresses.'

Forensic computing is the name given to a relatively new science that recovers and analyses data stored on computers, which could form part of a criminal investigation. Many of the tools used by forensic computing investigators are designed for notebook PCs, allowing them to be used outside a forensic laboratory.

Computer fraud costs companies hundreds of millions of pounds annually. A survey of 800 international compa-nies by Ernst & Young, another accounting firm, found that in 1995, IT fraud had cost them $640m. In February, the UK Audit Commission, which monitors public sector organisations, released a report on IT fraud and abuse. Of the 900 public and private sector organisations that took part, 45 per cent reported incidents of IT fraud and abuse compared with 36 per cent in 1994.

There are many types of computer fraudsters, from the finance controller who creates bogus employee records and directs company money into false accounts, to the hacker who gains access to a company's financial records. The growing use of the internet exposes many more organisations to computer fraud, either by employees using the internet to transfer funds, or by external agents gaining unauthorised access.

Most companies use passwords and firewalls – electronic filters placed between the company's computer network and the outside world – to reduce the risk, but fraudsters are becoming increasingly sophisticated.

Many web sites use miniature programs created with ActiveX, a system developed by Microsoft, or Java, the programming language developed by Sun Microsystems. ActiveX and Java-created programs are downloaded on to a PC hard disk and used for playing video, animation and other multimedia programs from the web.

▶

But hidden programs can also be downloaded at the same time, which can copy files held on hard disk and e-mail them to another address. However, most IT fraud is low-tech and carried out by a company's own employees.

'When people use computers for committing fraud, they leave a lot of trails,' says Tim Allen, director of UK-based Computer Forensics Investigations.

Howard Schmidt, director of information security at Microsoft, adds: 'A lot of people believe that when they press the delete button on their PC or re-format the hard disk they are destroying all the data. Not so.'

A number of programs can be used to recover deleted data and even files that have not been saved on the PC. 'One fraudster created a set of false invoices on a PC and printed them without saving the files. What he didn't realise was that the computer had created a temporary file which we were able to recover,' says Peter Verreck, director of Computer Forensics, which has developed technologies used by forensic computing investigators around the world.

One of the first steps in a forensic computing investigation is to copy the data from the suspect's PC on to another computer. But the data must be copied in a manner that makes any evidence acceptable in court. This is not as straightforward as it seems. 'You must not alter the original hard disk contents in any way, and by simply copying the data you can write new files to the original hard disk,' says Mr Verreck.

Computer Forensics has developed a disk image system that creates a perfect copy of the data on an optical cartridge without affecting the original data. Known as Dibs, the software can be used to find data that has been hidden, deleted, password-protected or encrypted.

The resulting amount of data can be vast. For example, if all the information on a 500MB hard disk, which is quite small by today's standards, was printed, the reams of paper would fill a small room.

A new system, visual intelligence analysis, has transformed IT fraud investigations. 'The traditional way of analysing data was to use a working chart, but in some cases this could be over 20ft in length,' says Mike Hunter, managing director of UK company i2.

But i2 has developed the Analyst's Notebook, a sophisticated database used by many agencies worldwide, including all UK police forces, Interpol, Europol, and the FBI. This makes it easier for investigators to analyse and display complex information including spreadsheets, photographs and documents, by creating links and graphical displays.

Emerging technologies could also make life easier for IT fraud investigators. Mr Durant is enthusiastic about the potential of imaging technology. 'When optical character recognition software improves, we'll be able to scan documents directly into a PC and eliminate the need for manually entering them. This will save a lot of time,' he says.

Voice-recognition technology will also be useful, he says, although the existing technology is not quite good enough.

Another promising area is neural computing, which uses computer programs that work more like the human brain, and can 'learn' from experience. This is useful for analysing patterns of behaviour, says Peter Baxendale, commercial director of UK-based Neural Technologies.

The company is working on a long-term project with a merchant bank that could result in a highly sophisticated anti-fraud computer system.

The system would monitor an employee's normal pattern of behaviour, such as the files he or she normally accesses, or the destinations data are usually sent to.

If the employee's behaviour deviates from normal, the system would put out an alert.

But technology alone will never eradicate IT fraud. 'What we now need is a new generation of police officers and investigators with computer science degrees rather than law degrees. It's the only way we are going to keep up with the IT fraudster,' says Mr Schmidt at Microsoft.

Source: Financial Times, 8 April 1998

Questions

1 From the material contained in the case study, identify and describe some common methods used to commit fraud.

2 From the material contained in the case study, identify and describe some common methods that can be used to counter fraud.

3 What are some of the problems faced by those attempting to prevent acts of fraud?

4 What methods can an organisation use to reduce the risk of fraud?

5 Describe how legislation, such as the Computer Misuse Act, can be used to deal with acts of computer fraud.

▶ LEGAL ISSUES

In this section, we consider some of the legislation relevant to managers, users and developers of computer-based information systems.

It is worth noting that, while this section is primarily concerned with UK legislation, many other countries have similar laws and guidelines that deal with the same issues. In general, the majority of the material in this section will be relevant to all European Union members, the US and other nations such as South Africa, Australia and New Zealand.

▶ Computer Misuse Act (1990)

The origin of the Computer Misuse Act is often attributed to the events surrounding a court case involving unauthorised access to private customer identification information of members belonging to the Prestel service. In 1984, Stephen Gold and Robert Schifreen were arrested and charged with hacking into the Prestel system and leaving a number of messages in the Duke of Edinburgh's private e-mail account. Although both defendants claimed that they had no intention of profiting from their actions and merely wanted to demonstrate their skills, they were convicted under forgery legislation and sentenced accordingly. However, a High Court appeal in 1986 was upheld on the basis that forgery legislation was inappropriate to offences involving computer misuse. The need for new legislation governing computer misuse resulted in a Royal Commission that eventually led to the enactment of the Computer Misuse Act (1990).

> **Computer Misuse Act (1990)**
> Legislation intended to protect sensitive equipment and data from unauthorised access, alteration and damage.

The full title of the Computer Misuse Act (1990) can be used to clarify its intent:

> An Act to make provision for securing computer material against unauthorised access or modification; and for connected purposes.

A number of offences are covered by the Act. Among these are the following:

(a) Unauthorised access to computer material.

(b) Unauthorised access with the intention of carrying out or assisting others with the commission of further offences.

(c) Unauthorised modification of computer material.

(d) Impairing the operation of a program or the reliability of data.

(e) Preventing or hindering access to any program or data.

It is worth noting several general points in relation to the offences outlined here. First, the Act makes it clear that offences need not be directed at any particular program, data or computer system. This provides the Act with far-reaching authority, allowing action to be taken in a wide variety of circumstances.

Second, the Act states that an individual is guilty of an offence if they have the 'requisite knowledge and intention', meaning that individuals must be aware that their actions are unauthorised and they must have the intention to cause some form of damage or harm. This offers a measure of protection to those users who unintentionally gain unauthorised access to a computer system or cause accidental damage.

Third, the Act makes no distinction between acts that cause permanent or temporary changes to programs or data. In this way, even a practical joke, such as changing a user's password without their permission, could be considered a criminal act.

The Act deliberately makes no attempt to define what is meant by a computer. It was recognised very early on that it would be impossible to create a definition that could encompass the technological changes likely to occur over the next few decades. Instead, it was decided that the courts should use the common, everyday meaning of the term. This enables the Act to remain relevant for longer by allowing it to keep pace with technology.

The focus of the Computer Misuse Act is on the protection of computer systems, not on the data they hold. It can be argued that only by protecting computer systems can the data held be safeguarded.

Oddly, the Act does not extend to damage caused to data held on offline storage media, such as compact discs and magnetic tapes. However, other legislation can be used to provide additional protection. It is an offence under the Criminal Damage Act (1971), for example, to destroy or damage any property. This legislation has been extended to cover storage media by suggesting that certain actions, such as deleting data from a floppy disk, can be said to cause damage by reducing the value or usefulness of the media.

Other notable omissions from the Act include electronic eavesdropping, software piracy and the writing of viruses. Although relatively uncommon at the time the Act was passed, incidences of electronic eavesdropping have grown rapidly over the past five years. Much of this growth can be attributed to increased sales of mobile telephones and the rapid development of e-commerce. Software piracy is considered to be covered adequately by existing counterfeiting and copyright legislation. Although the dissemination of computer viruses has become illegal, the act of creating a computer virus is not covered by the Act.

Electronic eavesdropping	**Electronic eavesdropping** describes the act of gaining access to confidential information by intercepting or monitoring communications traffic. Some examples include:
Describes the act of gaining access to confidential information by intercepting or monitoring communications traffic.	◆ Calls made using cellular telephones can be monitored using relatively inexpensive radio receivers. ◆ Police, emergency services and air traffic control radio transmissions can be monitored using a domestic radio receiver. ◆ Material sent via the Internet, such as e-mail messages, can be intercepted at a number of different points. This allows individuals to gain access to any sensitive information transmitted in this way, such as credit card numbers. ◆ Comparatively inexpensive receivers can be used to view the display shown on a computer monitor being used in another location. Although monitors can be shielded to prevent this, relatively few organisations seem aware of the risk.

The penalties for offences covered by the Act can include a fine of up to £2000 and up to six months' imprisonment. More serious offences can result in an unlimited fine and up to a maximum of five years' imprisonment.

Some of the early convictions achieved under the Act demonstrate the wide scope of the offences covered and also highlight some of its deficiencies:

◆ The first conviction achieved under the Act involved Ross Pearlstone, who was convicted in April 1991. It was alleged that Pearlstone used his ex-employer's Mercury telephone account to place a number of calls to the US. Although he later repaid the amount, he was still prosecuted under the Act and received a £450 fine.

◆ The first true hacking case to be tried under the Act involved a two-year investigation and resulted in a trial lasting several weeks. The defendant, Bedworth, was acquitted in 1991 after claiming he was a computer addict and that there was no criminal intent behind his actions.

◆ Strickland and Wood were jointly accused with Bedford of various offences and became the first people to be imprisoned under the Act. The offences included causing damage of more than £25 000 to a share index database belonging to the *Financial Times* and causing the European Organisation for the Research and Treatment of Cancer (EORTC) in Belgium to suffer telephone charges of more than £10 000. With the acquittal of Bedford, the Crown Prosecution Service decided to charge Strickland and Wood with more serious offences under the Act, hence the prison sentences on conviction.

▶ Data Protection Act (1998)

The **Data Protection Act (1998)** is defined as:

> An Act to regulate the use of automatically processed information relating to individuals and the provision of services in respect of such information. (Office of the Data Protection Registrar)

The Act sets out to define the rights of organisations and individuals in terms of how personal information is gathered, stored, processed and disclosed. One of the most important aspects of the Act is a focus on the individual's rights to view the information stored on them and ensure that it is accurate.

In order to understand the Act fully, it is important to define three important terms:

◆ *Personal data* describes data related to an identifiable, living person. It is important to note that the Act protects individuals; companies and organisations are not covered. In addition, the term refers only to data processed automatically, that is, by a computer-based information system.

◆ *Data users* are those who collect, control and process personal information, usually a company or government organisation. In general, a company that records personal data is known as a *computer bureau* or *data bureau*, reflecting the emphasis placed on the fact that the Act deals only with data processed automatically.

◆ *Data subjects* are those people whose personal data has been recorded.

Data Protection Act (1998)
Legislation setting out the rights of organisations and individuals in terms of how personal information is gathered, stored, processed and disclosed.

Principles

The Data Protection Act is based on eight general principles (Office of the Data Protection Registrar):

1 The information to be contained in personal data shall be obtained, and personal data shall be processed, fairly and lawfully.

2 Personal data shall be held only for one or more specified and lawful purposes.

3 Personal data held for any purpose or purposes shall not be used or disclosed in any manner incompatible with that purpose or those purposes.

4 Personal data held for any purpose or purposes shall be adequate, relevant and not excessive in relation to that purpose or those purposes.

5 Personal data shall be accurate and, where necessary, kept up to date.

6 Personal data held for any purpose or purposes shall not be kept for longer than is necessary for that purpose or those purposes.

7 An individual shall be entitled:
   (a) at reasonable intervals and without undue delay or expense –
       (i) to be informed by any data user whether he holds personal data of which that individual is the subject; and
       (ii) to access to any such data held by a data user; and
   (b) where appropriate, to have such data corrected or erased.

8 Appropriate security measures shall be taken against unauthorised access to, or alteration, disclosure or destruction of, personal data and against accidental loss or destruction of personal data.

Enforcement

The Act describes a number of offences. Under certain conditions, these can include:

(a) the unregistered holding of personal data;

(b) incorrectly registering a data user or computer bureau;

(c) failing to comply with the data protection principles;

(d) transferring personal data to another country;

(e) disclosing personal data.

The penalty for failing to comply with the Act is a fine of up to £2000. However, to date, there have been relatively few prosecutions brought under the Act and the majority of these have been for failure to register as a data user.

The Data Protection Registrar may act against a data user who fails to comply with the eight principles outlined earlier. In many cases, the Registrar will issue an enforcement notice that requires the data user to conform to the principles of the Act. However, this can be a lengthy process and is not always successful. Data users registering under the Act are exempt from action taken by the Registrar for a two-year period. Even after that period has elapsed, the Registrar may only act if there is sufficient evidence to show that the data user has acted against the principles of the Act. This condition reveals a paradox commonly used as a criticism of the Data Protection Act: on some occasions the Registrar may be constrained by a need to demonstrate that there is sufficient evidence to warrant the gathering of further evidence.

However, even if an enforcement notice is served against a data user, the user may appeal to a tribunal selected by the Home Secretary. Although the tribunal's decision is final, it may take several years for the matter to be resolved. This leaves the possibility that the data user may continue to act against the principles of the Act until a ruling is made.

Registration

Organisations that make use of personal data are required to register by applying to the Data Protection Registrar. If the application is accepted, the data user is added to the Data Protection Register and the details of the application are made available for public inspection. Although comparatively few applications are rejected, if an application is refused, the data user must cease processing personal data immediately, since this constitutes a criminal offence.

Exemptions

As mentioned earlier, the Data Protection Act applies only to personal data processed automatically. Manual records, such as paper files, are exempt from the Act and data users have no rights concerning access to personal data held in this way. Many organisations use their computer-based information systems merely to record the physical location of information held on paper or microfilm.

A number of other exemptions to the Data Protection Act also exist. Under certain circumstances, *subject access exemption* allows the data user to deny a data subject access to personal information. *Disclosure exemption* enables an organisation to pass data to another organisation not specifically listed in the original application to the Data Protection Registrar. *Total exemption* can be applied to information considered of little or no relevance to personal privacy, such as payroll details. Other applications given exemption are those related to national security, the detection of crime and the collection of taxes. The security services, for example, have no obligation to inform the Data Protection Registrar of any personal data held or the purposes to which it is put. In addition, there is no obligation to inform the data subject that personal data is held nor to provide access to the data.

One of the most common criticisms of the Act concerns the ability of data users to deny a data subject access to personal data if the data might identify another individual. In such cases, the data user is obliged to provide access to the data only if they have received the consent of any other individuals concerned. This exemption, critics argue, illustrates a fundamental paradox: how can a data subject gain the consent of any other individuals without knowing their identities? Fortunately, the Act goes some way towards dealing with this issue by requiring data users to supply as much data as possible without revealing information that might be used to identify another individual. For example, in many cases this could be achieved by simply removing names, addresses and other personal details from the information supplied to the data subject.

> Data subjects have the right to have access to any personal data held on them. The data user is allowed to impose a small charge to cover the costs associated with supplying the information requested. Although data users can charge up to £10 for each set of information supplied, many provide the information free of charge or request only a nominal fee of £1.

Corrections to personal data

Although data subjects have the right to have corrections made to personal data held by data users, the exercise of this right is often problematic. Before attempting to correct inaccurate personal data, one must become aware that a given organisation holds such data and must then be able to obtain a copy of it. If it is determined that the data contains errors, the data subject may then request that corrections are made by the data user. If the data user refuses to comply, the data subject may need to take legal action in order to force the data user to make the required changes.

The expense involved in taking court action against a data user is likely to discourage many data subjects from attempting this course of action. Although the data subject may receive compensation, the level of damages received is likely to be relatively low. In addition, in some cases, the court may decide that the data user is not required to alter or delete the information, ruling in favour of the data user. Furthermore, a loophole in the Data Protection Act can be used to provide a simple but effective defence against a data subject's claims. This loophole entitles a data user to consider information provided by a third party as being accurate. Effectively, the data user's responsibility is limited to ensuring that the information has been recorded correctly, even if the information itself is entirely wrong.

CASE STUDY: TOPIC AREA

Personal privacy

Personal privacy: a cause for concern

The vast amount of data on the information superhighway is causing concern about the 'Big Brother' age in which we live, reports Paul Taylor.

Fifty years ago, Justice Louis Brandeis, a US Supreme Court judge, described privacy as, 'the right to be left alone – the most comprehensive of rights, and the right most valued by a free people.'

But in recent years, the rapid commercialisation of the internet and the exploitation of other technologies such as 'data mining' have focused new attention on personal privacy and sparked an active debate on both sides of the Atlantic about the 'big brother' age we are living in.

Among the participants, Alan Greenspan, Federal Reserve Board chairman, expressed his concerns during a speech on privacy and electronic payment systems last year. Mr Greenspan noted the need for policies that 'avoid the risk of a gradual, long-term erosion of privacy.'

High profile cases such as the recent dismissal of a US Navy sailor after America Online turned over confidential information to a Navy investigator – a move which forced AOL to admit that it violated its own internal privacy policy and led to a ruling from the courts last week that the Navy must reinstate the man – have catapulted the issue into the headlines.

The debate on privacy could have far-reaching consequences for both individuals and companies, involves the tangled moral and economic issues surrounding the collection and transfer of information gleaned from consumers by commercial organisations, governments and others.

This information can be collected from online sources, at a supermarket checkout counters, through loyalty card programmes and other sources. However, it is the implications of the internet for privacy which has ignited most passion.

Indeed, some campaigners have grown so concerned about the sheer volume of data that is now collected about individuals over the internet – much of it available at a price to others – that they are now calling for new, tougher legislation to control the activities of modern-day marketers.

One bill now before the US congress – the Consumer Internet Privacy Protection Act of 1997 – would require written consent before a computer service disclosed a subscriber's personal information to a third party and would allow consumers to access and correct information.

Meanwhile, the Federal Trade Commission's decision to sidestep legislation and endorse, instead, US industry guidelines governing the operations of so-called 'look-up' computerised databases which disseminate personal information for a fee, has caused a storm of protest from organisations such as the Electronic Privacy Information Center (Epic), a Washington-based public pressure group.

Announcing the decision in December, Robert Pitofsky, FTC chairman, said 'consumers have been justifiably concerned about the extent to which their personal information has become publicly available.'

But he added: 'The information industry's innovative and far-reaching, self-regulatory programme will go a long way to address these concerns and lessen the risk that these services will be misused.'

Epic, however, protests that the industry guidelines – which will restrict for example the disclosure of information such as Social Security numbers, mother's maiden name, birth date, credit history, financial history, medical records or similar information – 'lacks enforcement and provides no legal rights for aggrieved parties.'

Meanwhile, in Europe, member-states must implement the EU Data Protection directive by October 24 and several Asian countries, including Japan, are set to adopt the EU Directive's tough but cumbersome privacy standards.

The directive which seeks to harmonise privacy legislation in Europe lays down rules on issues such as database registration and rights of access. 'We have been strong supporters of the directive,' says Tom Robb, group director of Equifax, one of the industry leaders in the provision of customer credit checks. Equifax holds 300m consumer credit profiles worldwide and processes 2000 consumer names for lenders every second.

Once implemented, the EU directive will strengthen existing legislation in many European countries, including Britain. Among its provisions, companies with an international presence must ensure that personal information on the internet is processed fairly and lawfully, collected and processed for specified, explicit, legitimate purposes, is accurate and current and is not kept any longer than necessary to fulfil the stated purpose.

User's information privacy rights include a right to access, right of correction, erasure or blocking of information, the right to object to usage, right to oppose automated individual decisions and rights to judicial remedy and compensation.

But even ahead of implementation, Mr Robb acknowledges that many individuals are probably unaware of what data is currently held on them, or how to gain access to it.

There is, however, no doubt that concern about online privacy is growing. For example, a recent survey of the world wide web conducted by the Graphic, Visualisation & Usability Center revealed that privacy has now become the most important issue facing the internet ahead of censorship and navigation.

The same study reveals that 72 per cent of 'Net users believe there should be new laws to protect privacy on the internet and that an overwhelming 82 per cent of users object to the sale of personal information.

It is the ability of web site operators to track users' activities and match their findings with personal information gathered from registration forms that is of particular concern to many internet users. Last summer, Epic, which advocates government regulation of privacy standards, released a survey of 100 popular web sites which found nearly half collected personal information from users.

Only eight gave users any control over how that information could be disseminated, and 23 use automated 'cookies' – small software programs that plant information on a personal computer hard disk – to tag users so that they can be identified if they returned to the sites.

But while many users favour tougher legislation to protect online privacy, software developers and web site operators are generally opposed to laws or regulations that might put a crimp in their activities. Instead, they favour self-regulation.

Microsoft and Netscape Communications, the leading providers of internet browser software, have both proposed technology solutions that would give web users greater control over the personal information they share – the latest versions of both company's software include a number of options for handling cookies.

Another layer of consumer protection may come from TRUSTe, a new industry group that aims to foster user-trust and confidence in the internet and create a recognised seal of approval for web sites. Only sites committed to strict privacy guidelines would be entitled to use the seal.

Among its services, TRUSTe also publishes 'tips for protecting your privacy online.'
These include:

◆ Look for the TRUSTE logo. Clicking on it will display the site's privacy policy.
◆ Be aware that when you provide your name and/or messages to others online, they will probably be able to find out how to communicate with you.
◆ Check whether the site has an 'opt-out' policy which allows you to prevent further solicitation or sharing of information with third parties.
◆ If they don't already have one, ask your favourite sites to post easy-to-find statements of their privacy policy.
◆ Guard your password, change it often and never give it to anyone who asks for it online.
◆ Tell children never to give out their name or other personal information without your permission.
◆ Investigate software tools such as 'anonymisers' and 'cookie-cutters' that provide an additional layer of privacy protection. Consider encrypting e-mail.
◆ Report privacy violations and misuse of trust-marks to TRUSTe or the appropriate authorities. Proponents of self-policing approaches towards privacy argue that they are good for business and for the internet. TRUSTe points to a study by the Boston Consulting Group which found that electronic commerce would grow twice as fast if consumers' fears about internet privacy were erased.

One problem is that the bulk of revenues being generated by most web sites come from advertising, rather than selling. While businesses offering goods and services to consumers over the internet may want to adhere to privacy guidelines, their advertisers are equally determined to gather as much information as possible about individual users.

Organisations such as Forrester Research, the US-based technology consultancy, argue that 'a privacy time-bomb is ticking', and that leading companies 'will need to adopt consensual marketing to survive.'

In a survey of consumers about their privacy, Forrester notes that 'a string of high-profile marketing debacles has thrust personal privacy into the spotlight.'

The report adds: 'The internet gives marketers a unique and somewhat frightening power – the ability to collect data surreptitiously and impersonally, distribute previously inaccessible data worldwide, and link new data with old data.'

The Forrester report reaches three main conclusions:

First, it notes that people dislike telemarketers and fear losing control of privacy. On-line, users hate junk e-mail, and steer away from data-gathering sites. They also worry about child exploitation.

Second, new technologies will not solve the problem. By the end of the decade, tools such as filters, agents, profilers and anonymisers will be used by only 7m people, only 10 per cent of internet users. 'The masses will suffer repeated invasions of privacy until an acute event triggers an explosion,' warn the analysts.

Third, leaders will adopt consensual marketing to survive. 'Intrusive "in-your-face" methods will give way to quid pro quo deals that provide value to consumers who share information with respectful marketers.'

In much the same way most loyalty schemes reward users with points or discounts in return for both their custom and – most importantly – the information which users knowingly supply when they apply and implicitly provide each time they use a loyalty card.

Predictably, however, not everyone agrees. For example, Ms Solveig Singleton, director of information studies at the Washington-based Cato Institute, argues strongly that 'mandatory opt-in' schemes in particular would 'conflict with our tradition of free speech and do real economic harm.'

Ms Singleton also warns that 'privacy concerns should focus on government, not on private data . . . we have little to fear from private collection and transfer of consumer information,' she says. 'Our attention should shift to threats from government databases.' And she argues passionately that regulating the collection of consumer information 'would hurt small and new businesses.'

Source: Financial Times, 4 February 1998

Questions

1 What issues related to personal privacy are highlighted by the case study?

2 How can users safeguard personal information and prevent invasions of privacy?

3 What are the arguments for and against allowing organisations to gather personal data?

▶ Copyright, Designs and Patents Act (1988)

Copyright, Designs and Patents Act (1988)

Legislation that can be used to provide organisations and software developers with protection against unauthorised copying of designs, software, printed materials and other works.

Intellectual property

A generic term used to describe designs, ideas and inventions. In general, intellectual property covers the following areas: patents, trade marks, designs and copyright.

The **Copyright, Designs and Patents Act** provides organisations and software developers with protection against unauthorised copying of designs, software, printed materials and other works.

Copyright legislation allows a company to safeguard its **intellectual property rights (IPR)** against competitors and others who might wish to profit from the company's research and investment.

Copyright

Copyright exists automatically as soon as a given work is completed and no action is necessary to gain copyright. The copyright to a given work can exist for up to 50 years following the author's death. Authors of copyrighted works can transfer their rights to others, selling or leasing them if they wish.

For managers involved with computer-based information systems, copyright legislation raises a number of important issues. The two most significant are:

1 *Ownership of bespoke software developed for the company by a consultant.* The possibility of disputes means that organisations should introduce procedures that can be used to establish ownership of copyright. Quite a common problem is when a bespoke system is developed for a company by a consultant. Unless specified in the contract, the copyright or IPR will reside with the consultant. The consultant can then sell the same software (which was of course paid for) to a competitor of the first company. This is obviously undesirable and needs to be included in the contract for development of the system.

Consider a dispute concerning two writers claiming ownership over the contents of a book or article. Unless one of the authors can prove that they were the original creator of the material, it may not be possible to resolve the argument. For a company, such copyright disputes might result in lengthy and expensive legal battles, leading to lost revenues and adverse publicity. A common solution to this problem is to register all copyright materials with an agency, government department or legal firm. However, this requires organisations to put procedures in place in order to ensure that all important materials are protected in this way.

In the UK it is worthwhile including a **source escrow** clause in a contract for bespoke software. Under this arrangement software (both media and source code instructions) is stored at the National Computing Centre in Manchester and if the company developing the software becomes insolvent, the company which originally contracted it can still attempt to use the source code to fix maintenance problems.

Source escrow

An arrangement where a third party stores software that can be used for maintenance purposes if the original developer of the software becomes insolvent.

> Many countries allow companies to lodge materials with a government department in order to register copyright. In the US, for example, materials can be lodged with the US Copyright Office for a small fee.

2 *Employee 'takes' software to another company.* Another problem concerning ownership of copyright involves materials produced by the employees of an organisation. Although many organisations assume automatic ownership to the copyright of any materials produced by their employees, this may not necessarily be the case. Unless specifically stated by the employee's contract, or implied on the basis of the employee's usual work for the organisation, the company may have no rights to any materials created.

> You are employed as a clerk in a large sales organisation. In your spare time, for example during lunch breaks, you develop a computer program that could be of significant value to your employer. Your employer claims ownership of the program on two grounds: that the program is related to your normal activities as an employee and that you used their equipment when creating the program. You dispute this on the grounds that the work was carried out during your own time and that the majority of the work was completed at home, using your own personal computer.
>
> **Questions**
>
> 1 What legal, moral and ethical issues are involved in this case?
>
> 2 Who owns the program?

ACTIVITY

An example may help to make this point clearer. A computer programmer moves to another company, taking with them a program that was under development. The programmer argues that they are entitled to take the program since the contract they worked under made no reference to ownership of copyright. However, since the programmer was formerly employed to produce computer programs, the original employer has implied rights concerning the uncompleted program. In such a case, it is likely that the original employer would be successful if they took legal action against the employee.

This example should help illustrate the importance of ensuring that employees' contracts take account of copyright issues. Many organisations routinely issue employment contracts containing clauses that concern copyright to all employees, regardless of their position or function.

Note that copyright protection applies only to materials that have been recorded in some way and cannot be used to protect ideas or concepts. The operation of a computer program, for example, is not normally protected by copyright legislation; although the actual source code may be subject to copyright, there may be little to stop a competitor creating a similar program to fulfil the same purpose.

In general, breach of copyright involves making a direct copy of part or the whole of a given work, such as an article. However, copyright can sometimes be extended to include the expression of a work and derivative works. As an example consider the following.

A programmer develops a program that produces precisely the same screen displays, in terms of content and presentation, as an existing commercial product. Copyright infringement could be argued on the basis that the new program is merely an expression of the original commercial product. However, if the displays produced by the program were sufficiently different to the original, it might not be possible to prove infringement.

For business organisations, these aspects of copyright legislation can present a major dilemma. Although copyright legislation can be used to gain a measure of protection for certain works, for example computer programs, such protection is often limited and may not be sufficient in the case of particularly valuable or important works. As a result, large amounts of expense and time can be involved in pursuing copyright infringement via legal action.

3 *Software piracy*. Copyright is also infringed when software is copied by employees in the organisation so that it can be installed on more machines than licences have been paid for.

Patents

Patent

Provides its owner with a monopoly allowing them to exploit their invention without competition. The protection offered by a patent lasts for a number of years but does not begin until the patent has been granted.

A **patent** provides its owner with a monopoly allowing them to exploit their invention without competition. The protection offered by a patent lasts for a number of years but does not begin until the patent has been granted. The application process for a patent can take as long as five years. During this time, the applicant must not disclose the details of the invention or the application will be rejected.

A patent can only be granted for original inventions that are considered to be 'non-obvious'. A simple modification to an existing item, for example, would be considered obvious and unoriginal.

Since the patent application will describe the method used to create the item and the way in which it functions, the owner's work is protected in its entirety. Once the patent has been granted, competitors are prohibited from duplicating the item.

Unlike copyright, where international agreements provide automatic protection for an author's work in other countries, separate applications may need to be made to patent offices in other countries. It is common, for example, for companies to register patents in the UK, Europe and the US in order to protect these potential markets from competitors.

The rights assigned by a patent can be sold or licensed to others. This enables smaller companies to form partnerships with others in order to exploit foreign markets. Cross-licensing agreements allow companies to share patents so that each can produce and market a wider range of products.

In many countries, patents can be used to protect computer programs by registering the methods and techniques used in their creation. As an example, PKZIP is a leading data compression utility that uses a number of specialised techniques to compress data quickly and efficiently. It is these techniques that distinguish the program from others, allowing it to provide an original and non-obvious approach to data compression. In the UK, patents are not granted for computer programs, although this is likely to change in the near future.

Reverse engineering represents one of the ways in which companies attempt to circumvent the restrictions imposed by copyright and patent legislation. Reverse engineering attempts to recreate the design of an item by analysing the final product. This can be compared to the 'black box' approach to systems analysis, where the outputs from the system are analysed in order to determine the inputs and processes involved.

Microprocessors compatible with Intel's range of Pentium processors are often created using reverse engineering methods. Typically, a team of developers is assembled and made to work in a 'clean room', that is, an environment where there is no access to information concerning the item to be reproduced. The development team is then given information concerning the functions performed by the processor to be duplicated and works to reproduce all of these functions. Since the developers have no access to the original processor and information concerning its operation, the new processor design cannot be claimed to be an identical copy. However, this does not necessarily mean that reverse engineering is considered an acceptable activity; this area continues to be a subject of legal controversy.

Cross-licensing agreement

Agreements allow companies to share patents so that each can produce and market a wider range of products.

Reverse engineering

Attempts to recreate the design of software or hardware by analysing the final product.

Registered designs

The aesthetic aspects of items such as clothing, furniture, electrical goods and jewellery can be protected by registering their designs. Registered designs can be thought of as similar to patents, except that they deal only with the appearance of a given item.

Trademarks

A trademark distinguishes a company's goods or services from those of its competitors. The 'Intel Inside' campaign is an excellent example of how a trademark can help establish a strong product or brand identity. As with patents and designs, trademarks can be protected by formally registering them.

▶ SOFTWARE PIRACY

FOCUS ON

Copyright theft, in the form of software piracy, continues to be one of the most common crimes associated with computer systems. This section considers software piracy from several perspectives with a view to improving understanding of this complex area.

▶ Background

The recognition of software theft as a major problem for software companies and distributors can be traced back to the early 1980s. During this period, the personal computer 'boom' began with the launch of the original IBM personal computer in the US and the launch of a series of inexpensive home computers by Sir Clive Sinclair in the UK. The sudden popularity of personal computers created a huge demand for software applications and resulted in the creation of thousands of small software companies around the world.

However, as the number of applications increased, so too did incidences of illegal copying. Comparatively few business applications existed and the majority of commercial software packages consisted of leisure programs, such as computer games. Many users considered computer games to be luxury items and were unwilling to purchase legitimate copies of the programs they desired. Within this environment, a small industry soon developed that was dedicated to helping users create and distribute illegal copies of popular software titles.

Prior to the widespread adoption of CD-ROM, most software applications were distributed via floppy disk and magnetic tape. Programs distributed via magnetic media, such as the floppy disk, were relatively simple to copy, since few software companies made use of **copy protection** methods. However, even the use of copy protection techniques did little to deter users. A number of companies existed which supplied various hardware and software items that could be used to circumvent common copy protection techniques. Such items were often sold as legitimate products, for example special utility programs designed to help users duplicate copy protected software were often sold as legitimate backup utilities.

Copy protection

Methods that can be used to prevent unauthorised copies being made of a software package.

> **Copy protection** describes a number of methods that can be used to prevent unauthorised copies being made of a software package. The most common form of copy protection is the use of passwords and registration codes; unless the user possesses the correct registration information, the software will not function. It is worth noting that some software companies make use of hardware copy protection devices. Specialised programs are sometimes supplied with a hardware key, often called a **dongle**. The hardware key must be connected to the computer in order for the software to function. This provides a highly effective, if inconvenient, means of preventing illegal copies of the program from being made.

Dongle

A hardware device used to prevent unauthorised copies of a program being made. The hardware 'key' must be connected to the computer in order for the software to function.

As more sophisticated personal computers became available, the cost of software began to increase and the problem of software theft grew even greater. Many individuals saw an opportunity to profit by distributing counterfeit versions of popular programs. Organised groups began to sell counterfeit software through a number of different channels, for example via mail order. New programs were obtained through a variety of different methods. As an example, *cracking groups* were made up of users who gained satisfaction by defeating the copy protection methods used by software companies. Collections of programs where all copy protection had been disabled were created and sold on to others. In some cases, individuals imported software from countries without effective copyright legislation or where software theft was regarded as unimportant.

The advent of CD-ROM as a distribution medium in the early 1990s briefly obstructed the making of illegal copies. The sheer quantity of data held on a compact disc made it impractical for individuals to transfer data on to magnetic tape or floppy disk. In addition, the costs involved in duplicating large numbers of disks or tapes also served to hinder the activities of the organised groups. However, the introduction of inexpensive CD-recordable (CDR) units reversed the situation by making it possible to store and distribute numerous applications on a single compact disc.

As DVD (digital versatile disk) units become widespread, the problem of software theft is likely to decline. The DVD format offers a number of features designed to prevent illegal copying of software and data. However, the planned introduction of recordable DVD units may present the same problems as associated with CD-R.

▶ The growth of software piracy

Produced on behalf of the **Business Software Alliance (BSA)** and the **Software Publishers' Association (SPA)**, the annual *Global Software Piracy Report* charts changes and trends in software piracy across the world.

The report gives a number of statistics that illustrate the severity of the problem of software piracy:

Business Software Alliance (BSA)

An organisation formed to act against software piracy.

Software Publishers' Association (SPA)

An organisation formed to act against software piracy.

◆ In 1996 it was estimated that 523 million business applications, both legal and illegal, were in use.

◆ In 1996 more than 225 million business applications were pirated, representing a 20 per cent increase on 1995.

◆ Worldwide losses from software piracy were estimated at $11.2 billion in 1996, $13.3 billion in 1995 and $12.3 billion in 1994.

◆ Although values varied from region to region, the average worldwide piracy rate was 43 per cent in 1996, 46 per cent in 1995 and 49 per cent in 1994.

◆ In the UK, the piracy rate for 1996 was estimated at 34 per cent.

Figures 18.2 and 18.3 illustrate selected software piracy rates by region and country.

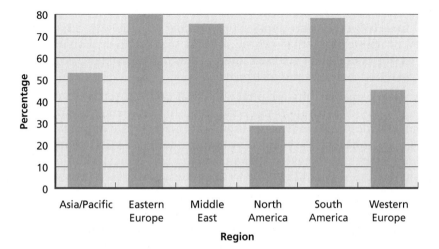

Fig 18.2 1996 software piracy rates by region

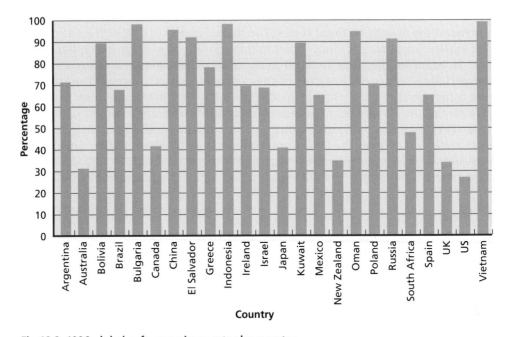

Fig 18.3 1996 global software piracy rates by country

In this section, we consider software piracy from three perspectives: a typical end-user, software development companies and business organisations.

End-users

On an individual basis, making illegal copies of computer programs holds a number of attractions:

◆ Software packages can be acquired at a very low cost. After an initial outlay for any specialised software or hardware needed, users face only the ongoing costs of blank media.

◆ Many users collect software applications in order to trade with others or create a library of applications that can be used to support their activities. It is not unusual, for example, for a person interested in programming to acquire a collection of editors, compilers and interpreters.

◆ Many users consider software piracy a trivial offence; some even believe that making copies of software is perfectly legal. In truth, since software piracy is extremely widespread, individual users who make copies of programs for their own use are unlikely to be pursued by agencies such as FAST (**Federation Against Software Theft**). In the event that a user is caught in possession of illegal software, prosecution is unlikely due to the time and expense involved in taking legal action.

◆ A significant minority of users produce and distribute illegal copies of software in order to generate an income that can be used to support their hobby. In many cases, the distribution of software is seen as a business venture and used as a source of revenue.

Federation Against Software Theft (FAST)

An organisation formed to act against software piracy.

There are several common arguments put forward by individuals who advocate the copying of software and associated materials, such as manuals.

One argument suggests that software houses provide too little information concerning their products. Software houses and retailers are also seen as being reluctant to provide demonstrations or allow users to purchase products on a trial basis. These factors can sometimes mean that the software chosen for a particular task proves to be unsuitable. In some cases, the user may not be able to reclaim the cost of the software, since retailers and manufacturers are sometimes reluctant to offer refunds. In view of these factors, many users feel that it is unfair to ask them to bear the full cost of a decision made on the incomplete or inaccurate information provided by the retailer or software house. Copying a given package, some argue, allows a full and careful evaluation to be made of the software. If it is felt that the package is appropriate to their needs, users are likely to purchase a genuine copy of the program in order to receive manuals, technical support and other benefits. On the other hand, if the software is considered unsuitable, the user will delete any copies made since they are of little or no value.

A second argument in favour of copying software involves the sometimes restrictive licence conditions adopted by software houses. When a user purchases a software package, they are merely buying the right to make use of the package for an unspecified period. In general, the software house retains ownership of the software, all accompanying documentation and the distribution media itself. A licence agreement may also forbid users from making a backup copy of a package and the software may incorporate copy protection in order to prevent users from making copies. In addition, licence agreements often include statements that disclaim responsibility if the software does not function correctly or if the distribution medium becomes damaged or corrupt. If the terms set out in the software licence agreement are broken, the user may be required to return all of the materials supplied at their own expense. Many users believe that they should have the right to safeguard their investment in a software package by making one or more backup copies. Such users will see the terms of the licence agreement as being unreasonable and will often disregard any clauses regarding backup copies.

A third argument concerns the pricing policies adopted by software companies. Some users argue that software companies have deliberately inflated their prices, placing some packages out of the reach of individuals and small companies. Copying software, it is argued, causes no harm to the software companies involved, since the software would never have been purchased in the first place.

Software developers

Software companies make a number of powerful arguments against the copying of software.

Perhaps the simplest and most compelling argument made by software companies is that software is protected under international copyright laws. In most countries, the copying of software is regarded as theft and exposes the individual to both criminal and civil liability.

A second argument involves a defence of the pricing policies adopted by many software companies. The costs involved in the development of a sophisticated, comprehensive application program can be extremely high. The effort involved in developing an application is normally measured in terms of labour hours. A wordpro-

cessing program, for example, may take several years to develop and can involve the efforts of hundreds of staff. Such a program might require many millions of labour hours before it is released to the public. Since the cost of development must be recovered, it is reflected within the price of the application. In addition, the cost of the software also includes sums that support the continued development of the application and research into new products. Copying software, it is argued, reduces the revenues generated from the sale of the software and jeopardises new developments.

This leads to a related argument concerning the pricing of software. As incidences of illegal copying increase, software companies face a need to safeguard profit margins and recover development costs as quickly as possible. In order to do this, prices must be increased so that the losses made due to illegal copying can be recovered. In this way, it is argued, those that make illegal copies of software are directly responsible for the higher prices faced by legitimate customers.

Business organisations

The preceding sections should make clear some of the problems that face modern business organisations.

Smaller organisations, with limited budgets, are sometimes tempted to make additional copies of a given software package. As mentioned earlier, although the risk of detection is relatively low, the use of illegal software can lead to a number of repercussions. Some examples include:

◆ Organisations found in breach of copyright can suffer severe financial penalties. It is not uncommon for an organisation to be required to purchase licences for all illegal programs found on the company's premises. In addition, the company may face criminal or civil proceedings that result in significant fines.

◆ By encouraging employees to make use of illegal software, the company exposes itself to action from unions, employees and other parties. As an example, an employee accused of using illegal software in the course of their duties might take legal action against the employer. In addition, staff morale might be reduced, leading to productivity losses and labour disputes.

◆ Action taken by organisations such as the Business Software Alliance often result in negative publicity for an organisation. This could have a major impact on relationships with customers and suppliers.

◆ The organisation's profitability can be damaged if it is deprived of the applications software needed to support day-to-day activities. In some companies, even a temporary disruption might lead to long-term effects. As an example, relationships with clients could be harmed if a sales organisation was unable to offer high levels of customer service.

It is worth noting that, as the size of the organisation increases, so too does the risk of detection and the severity of the possible consequences. Organisations such as the Federation Against Software Theft (FAST) and the Business Software Alliance (BSA), for example, encourage employees to report software piracy by their employers, sometimes offering a substantial reward for information leading to a successful prosecution.

Large organisations must also recognise a number of issues and responsibilities that influence the way in which they operate. A key issue facing many organisations is the need to reduce or eliminate the use of illegal software within their computer-

based information systems. Only by taking an active stand against software piracy can a company gain a measure of protection against prosecution and the other losses outlined in this section. In addition, only such a stance can protect the company's reputation and industry status.

At the simplest level, an organisation seen to be making an effort to control how software is used in its computer systems is likely to be dealt with less severely than one that takes no action at all. However, such an approach can also lead to a number of other, somewhat more tangible benefits. Consider some of the benefits to be gained by using methods such as regular software audits in order to control which software applications are used by a company's computer-based information systems:

◆ In the UK and many other countries, an employer, ultimately the managing director, is held responsible for the actions taken by employees during the course of their work. In this way, the employer could be held jointly responsible if an employee uses illegal software with the company's computer-based information systems. The use of methods such as software audits can help reduce instances where employees install or use illegal programs on the company's systems. In turn, this acts to reduce the risk of the company facing prosecution due to the employee's actions.

◆ By reducing the number of illegal or unauthorised programs used with the company's systems, employees can be encouraged to focus on their work more closely. Games and Internet browsers, for example, are well-known distractions that cost organisations many millions of labour hours each year.

◆ With a reduction in the use of unauthorised or illegal software also comes a reduction in the risk of infection by computer viruses. In turn, this decreases the costs and damage associated with virus infection.

◆ By preventing the use of unauthorised or illegal software, employees can be encouraged to adhere to organisational standards for the use of the company's computer-based information systems. This can provide a number of benefits related to the way in which the organisation produces, manages and makes use of its data. As an example, if only programs that have been approved by the organisation are used, then the accuracy of data can be maintained or improved.

ACTIVITY

An employee makes use of an unauthorised program in order to generate financial information for a senior manager. Although the program is legitimately owned by the employee, the information is stored in a form that is incompatible with the program that will be used by the manager.

Questions

1 Should the employee have been made to use the company's standard financial software package?

2 What problems and costs might be associated with converting the information so that the manager can use it directly?

3 Assuming that the employee should have been made to use the company's standard financial software package, what steps could be taken to ensure that this happened in future?

▶ SUMMARY

1 Managers, developers and users of computer-based information systems are required to balance the needs of their employer and the requirements of their profession with other demands, such as a responsibility to society.

2 Membership of a professional association brings with it the requirement to abide by a professional code of conduct. The code of conduct provides guidance related to the individual's legal, social and professional responsibilities.

3 An alternative view of the responsibilities of managers, developers and users involves considering some of their obligations to their employers, the public and the state. Conflicts of interest can arise from the need to serve the duties and responsibilities imposed on the individual.

4 The impact of technology on personal privacy has manifested itself in many different ways. A contemporary issue related to personal privacy is the increase in the use of computer monitoring techniques. Computer monitoring can involve a wide variety of activities, from observing the behaviour of employees in the workplace to intercepting private e-mail messages.

5 Acts of computer crime can include theft of goods or services, software theft, data theft, damage to data or software and hacking.

6 Some of the legislation relevant to those involved in managing or developing computer-based information systems include:
   ◆ The Copyright, Designs and Patents Act (1988) provides limited protection for an organisation's intellectual properties. Such legislation also places a responsibility on companies to ensure that they do not infringe the copyright of others, for example by making or using unauthorised copies of computer programs.
   ◆ The Computer Misuse Act (1990) attempts to prevent unauthorised access to computer-based information systems. In addition, such legislation also makes it an offence to cause damage to hardware, software or data.
   ◆ The Data Protection Act (1984) defines the way in which companies may gather, store, process and disclose personal data. In addition, the Act provides individuals with a number of rights allowing them to view or modify the personal data held on them.

7 Software developers see software piracy as a major threat to their business activities and the continued growth of the software industry. Business organisations face severe penalties unless they take an active stand against software piracy.

▶ EXERCISES

▶ Self-assessment exercises

1 Describe the offences covered by the Computer Misuse Act (1990).

2 What is meant by computer monitoring?

3 What are eight guiding principles of the Data Protection Act (1984)?

4 What are the most common types of computer crime?

5 Identify the legislation that covers the following actions:
   (a) distributing a computer virus;
   (b) making an unauthorised copy of a computer program;
   (c) gaining unauthorised access to a computer-based information system;
   (d) vandalising computer hardware;
   (e) creating a computer virus;
   (f) placing an unauthorised computer program on a network system;
   (g) stealing a backup copy of a data file;
   (h) photocopying a software manual.

6 For each of the following acts, state whether or not they are permissible under the Computer Misuse Act (1990) or Data Protection Act (1994):
   (a) storing inaccurate or misleading personal data;
   (b) damaging data held on offline storage media;
   (c) electronic eavesdropping;
   (d) preventing access to personal data held in manual files, such as microfilm;
   (e) software piracy;
   (f) accidental damage to hardware, software or data;
   (g) disclosing personal data without the permission of the individual;
   (h) preventing access to personal data.

7 What is reverse engineering?

8 What is a professional code of conduct?

▶ Discussion questions

1 You are given the responsibility of managing a technical project that may result in hundreds of job losses. Decide whether or not you should continue with the project and justify your decision on professional, moral and ethical grounds.

2 Do the security services and government departments have the right to monitor personal communications, such as e-mail messages? Justify your answer.

3 The cost of software applications leaves some users no choice but to make illegal copies. Make a case in favour of or against this argument.

▶ Essay questions

1 Discuss changes in employment patterns brought about by increased levels of automation and the introduction of computer-based information systems.

2 What are some of the moral, ethical and professional issues faced by the managers of information systems? Illustrate your answer with relevant examples.

3 Using relevant examples, critically review the major pieces of legislation relevant to the ways in which organisations use computer-based information systems. Your discussion should refer to areas such as copyright, unauthorised access, the use of personal data and any other relevant issues.

▶ Examination questions

1 The Data Protection Act (1984) regulates the ways in which organisations may gather, store, process and disclose personal information. You are required to:
   (a) Describe the principles on which the Act is based.
   (b) Discuss some of the responsibilities placed on organisations by the Act.
   (c) Critically evaluate the strengths and weaknesses of the Act in terms of the right given to individuals to view and amend any personal data held on them.

2 The ability of computer-based information systems to store, process and retrieve data quickly and efficiently raises concerns related to the privacy of individuals. You are required to:
   (a) Explain the meaning of 'personal privacy'.
   (b) Describe some of the ways in which technology can allow an individual's personal privacy to be invaded.
   (c) Using relevant examples, discuss the moral and ethical issues involved in gathering, storing and making use of personal data.

3 Members of associations such as the British Computer Society are required to abide by a professional code of conduct.
   (a) Describe the areas that a professional code of conduct is likely to include.
   (b) Using relevant examples, discuss some of the ways in which a manager's ethical and professional responsibilities can conflict.
   (c) An individual's professional and legal obligations always take precedence over moral and ethical concerns. Adopt a position in favour of or against this argument and justify your response.

▶ References

Black, G. (1998) 'Internet: self-regulation', *Financial Times*, 1 April 1998.

Cole, G. (1998) 'Hi-tech sleuths aim to crack computer fraud', *Financial Times*, 8 April 1998.

Dworkin, G. and Taylor, R. (1992) *Blackstone's Guide to the Copyright, Designs & Patents Act 1988*, Blackstone Press, London.

Flohr, U. (1995) 'Bank robbers go electronic', *BYTE*, November.

Global Software Piracy Report: Facts and Figures, 1994–1996, Software Publishers Association Europe.

Price, C. (1998) 'Computer viruses: concerns grow as figures double', *Financial Times*, 23 February 1998.

Taylor, P. (1988) 'Personal privacy: a cause for concern', *Financial Times*, 4 February 1998.

▶ Further reading

Bainbridge, D. (1995) *Introduction to Computer Law*, Financial Times Pitman Publishing, London. Coverage of legal issues related to computer-based information systems. Includes the Computer Misuse Act and discusses areas such as reverse engineering.

Edwards, C. and Savage, N. (1986) *Information Technology and the Law*, Macmillan, London.

Fuori, W. and Gioia, L. (1995) *Computers and Information Systems*, Prentice-Hall, Englewood Cliffs, NJ. Chapter 1 provides an introduction to computer crime and the social impact of computer technology.

Hussain, K. and Hussain, D. (1995) *Information Systems for Business*, Prentice Hall, Hemel Hempstead.
   Chapter 16 describes issues related to privacy and security.

Johnson, D.G. (1994) *Computer Ethics*, 2nd edition, Prentice-Hall, Englewood Cliffs, NJ.

Laudon, K. and Laudon, J. (1995) *Management Information Systems: Organization and Technology*, 3rd edition, Macmillan.
   Chapter 20 deals with professional, ethical and social issues.

O'Brien, J. (1993) *Management Information Systems: a Managerial End User Perspective*, 2nd edition, Richard D. Irwin.
   Chapter 15 deals with ethical issues.

Parker, D.B. (1976) *Crime by Computer*, Charles Scribner's Sons, New York.

Schwartau, W. (1994) *Information Warfare*, Thunder's Mouth Press, New York.

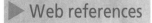

▶ Web references

Comprehensive details of the Data Protection Act can be located at http://www.hmso.gov.uk (Acts) and http://www.open.gov.uk.

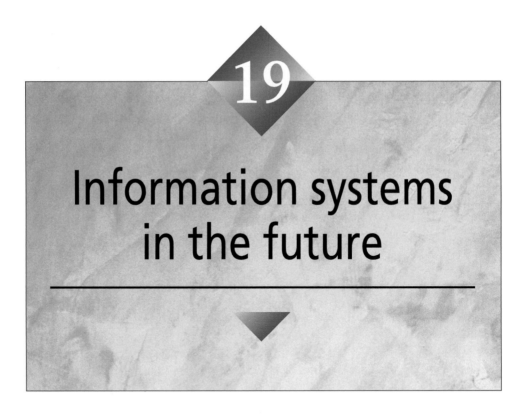

19

Information systems in the future

INTRODUCTION

This chapter explores the ways in which information systems may be used in the future. We also review major trends in technologies and the application of information technology that are likely to continue into the future. This is achieved through examining some examples of companies which are currently making use of new technology. The chapter also considers some of the difficulties for businesses caused by rapid changes in technology and how companies can respond to the constantly changing technological environment.

> ▶ Learning objectives
>
> After reading this chapter, readers will be able to:
>
> ◆ assess how a company should deal with technological change;
>
> ◆ identify significant trends in technology and how they may affect businesses;
>
> ◆ understand the purpose of technologies such as groupware and workflow software, expert systems, data warehouse and business intelligence and object-oriented technology;
>
> ◆ plan how future technology developments may affect a company.

> **Links to other chapters**

This chapter draws on material from several chapters, but is not directly linked to any particular one.

Chapter 17   provides additional details on the application of the Internet to marketing.

Chapter 6   provides more detail on data warehouses.

▶ FUTURE WAYS OF DOING BUSINESS

▷ The global business

Many multinational companies are now using information technology to enable them to do business in different countries. While companies have always been able to operate in different countries, new technology has made this more efficient. It is now possible to use fewer staff or base more of them in the country of the parent company and give better control with faster response to the conditions in the local market. It is the availability of wide area networks, the Internet and distributed client/server technology that have made this possible.

An example of how these technologies are harnessed by the **global business** is provided by Hamamatsu electronics, a Japanese-based company that sells in Europe and the US. This case study also shows how distributed client/server technology and groupware enable the server computers in different countries to communicate, thus allowing end-users in different locations to share information.

A further example of how IT is used by the global business is provided by the way British Telecommunications manages its human resources. Until recently, BT used six separate systems for functions such as payroll, appraisal and training, which had to be operated individually in each country. Now it has a single package based on the Oracle HR database management module. This system can be used to provide HR services to its 120 000 employees across the globe. The use of a single off-the-shelf package to replace separate bespoke packages is also another significant trend in the use of software, which is referred to later in this chapter.

Global business

A company which operates in several countries which uses information technology to assist in the control of operations and performance in each country.

▷ The growth of virtual teams and virtual corporations

A logical extension of the new way in which the global business is operating is that international boundaries will dissolve. The **virtual organisation** is now suggested as the shape of the future business by many authors, such as James Martin in his book *Cybercorp*. A virtual organisation makes use of networking to set up communication between its employees, suppliers and customers in such a way that there are no physical boundaries or constraints on the company. Employees may work in any time zone and customers are able to purchase tailored products from any location. The absence of any rigid boundary or hierarchy within the organisation should lead to a more responsive and flexible company. This also extends to 'virtual products', where mass production is replaced by the ability to tailor the product to the customer's

Virtual organisation

An organisation which uses technologies to allow it to operate without clearly defined physical boundaries between different functions.

MINI CASE

Hamamatsu Electronics uses client/server technology to improve customer service

Hamamatsu makes use of distributed client/server technology and groupware to provide customer service and product fulfilment through its agents and satellite offices. It uses the groupware product Lotus Notes to respond to requests from customers for product information and customer support in the countries in which it operates. The information is collected in each country and then processed by the product specialists at the home base. To assist the information flow between countries, a process known as replication is used to synchronise the information in the databases in each country.

This information includes product prices, specifications and answers to customer support problems. Such information would previously have been transferred by air-mail or fax and is now all transmitted electronically. The mechanism for replication is shown in Fig 19.1. At regular times, twice daily, information is transmitted from the server computer in Japan to European head office in Germany and other offices in Europe such as that in London. At the same time, any updates and queries to the database are also transmitted back to Japan.

Replication (server)

A process in which information on server computers at different locations is transferred and synchronised so users in different locations can view the same data.

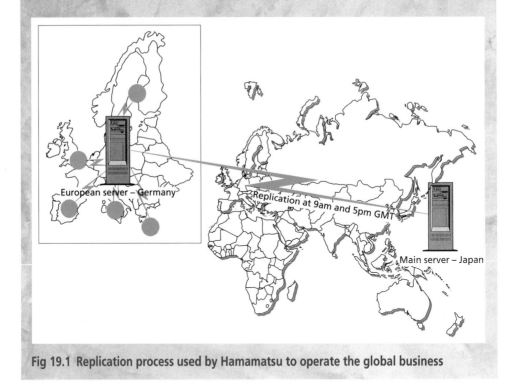

Fig 19.1 Replication process used by Hamamatsu to operate the global business

need. The Internet and wide area networks are used to set up the links between the players in the virtual organisation. Software such as e-mail, groupware and workflow will all be used to aid collaboration between people in the organisation.

Davidow and Malone (1992) describe the virtual corporation as follows:

To the outside observer, it will appear almost edgeless, with permeable and continuously changing interfaces between company, supplier and customer. From inside the firm, the view will be no less amorphous, with traditional offices, departments, and operating divisions constantly reforming according to need. Job responsibilities will regularly shift.

Virtual jeans from Levi's

An example of a 'virtual product' facility is provided by the jeans manufacturer Levi's. From its Internet site it is possible to specify your individual measurements for a pair of jeans. Details of your bespoke measurements are then sent to a factory in Belgium, which manufactures a product for your size that is then dispatched by post. All this occurs without the customer meeting the retailer directly, another feature of the virtual organisation.

Information systems software is increasingly being developed using a virtual teaming arrangement. For example, in his book *The Decline and Fall of the American Programmer*, Edward Yourdon describes how much software development is now subcontracted to teams of professional programmers in India and Asia, who achieve quality work at a much lower rate than their US equivalents.

James Martin (1997) uses a similar term to refer to such organisations. This is the 'cybercorp':

A corporation optimized for the age of cyberspace. A cybernetic corporation has senses constantly alert, capable of reacting in real time to changes in its environment and customer needs, with virtual operations or agile linkages of competencies in different organisations when necessary. A corporation designed for fast change, which can learn, evolve and transform itself rapidly.

▶ Call centres

Call centre is a office devoted to answering telephone enquiries from customers, commonly used for financial services and retail customer support.

The number of call centres is increasing rapidly. It is estimated by research group Datamonitor that there are nearly 200 000 employees at call centres in the UK and approximately double this number in Europe. Growth is such that it is estimated that by 2001 approaching half a million UK staff will be employed in call centres, which represents 2 per cent of the workforce. Current employers using call centres include:

Call centre
An office which is devoted to answering telephone enquiries from customers, call centres are commonly used for financial services and retail customer support.

◆ Direct Line insurers which has eight call centres (3400 staff);

◆ BT's customer centre in Warrington with 2000 staff;

◆ Sitel UK Ltd (a subsidiary of US-based Sitel Corporation), which operates six call centres in the UK with about 600 staff at each. Clients include Nissan, Cable and Wireless, British Gas and Disneyland Paris.

The principal reason for the growth of call centres is the ability to reduce the cost of customer service. Other factors include:

◆ The availability of LAN technology with computer telephony integration and workflow systems to retrieve customer details when a customer rings or to dial out automatically when a customer needs a reminder (the system only passes a call to the operator if the customer answers).

◆ Economies of scale of operating a single national call centre rather than several regional ones.

◆ The wish for 24-hour customer service can best be met by concentrating employees at one location.

◆ Standardisation and improved quality of customer service through operating from one location where staff can be trained and monitored.

From the growth rates it appears that these arguments are strong ones and the growth looks set to continue. However, some commentators have noted that for the workers, call centres represent a backward step and are the modern equivalents of Victorian workhouses. A *Guardian* article on call centres (2 June 1998) noted that, writing in 1977, French philosopher Michel Foucault anticipated a dark future in which:

> All that is needed, then, is to place a supervisor in a central tower and to shut up in each cell . . . a worker. They are like so many cages, so many small theatres, in which each actor is alone, perfectly individualised and constantly visible . . . there are no disorders, no theft, no coalitions, none of those distractions that slow down the rate of work, make it less perfect.

Whether employers will be concerned about the working environment remains to be seen, but the need to retain quality staff who will move to a better call centre environment if not satisfied could be one factor that will prevent this situation arising. It has already led to a rise in salaries to counter staff mobility.

▶ Teleworking

Teleworking

The process where company staff work remotely from their company office. Most commonly it is applied to 'home-workers' who spend at least 3 days a week working in this way.

Teleworking is the term used when workers fulfil their job functions remotely from the office where they are based. Most commonly it applies to employees 'working from home', but it can also refer to employees working at other company sites. The definition of teleworking varies. It is usually taken to indicate that an individual spends more than three days a week working at home. In the US it is estimated that there are more than ten million teleworkers. In the UK, proponents of teleworking such as British Telecom suggest that there may be more than a million teleworkers who work from home one day or more each week. If a stricter definition involving working at home for more than three days a week is used, then the figure is probably nearer to 200 000. (Refer to the case study for a discussion of estimates of the number of teleworkers.)

The costs of setting up an employee for teleworking are relatively modest. A leased personal computer, modem, software including groupware such as e-mail and tasks lists plus phone charges can cost as little as several hundred pounds per year. Companies such as British Gas have reduced their office space requirements by over 25 per cent through teleworking. This amounts to a substantial cost reduction.

Although it might be thought that teleworking would lead to staff not undertaking sufficient work due to domestic distractions, surveys indicate that this is not the case. If the right staff are chosen, then staff motivation and productivity can

Table 19.1 Benefits and disadvantages of teleworking

To the company		To the employee	
Benefits	**Disadvantages**	**Benefits**	**Disadvantages**
Reduced office and parking space requirements	Shortages of resources when staff are in the office ('hot-desking')	Less commuting, more time available and reduced travel costs	May miss social stimulus of working in office
Improved staff to motivation and retention	Difficulties for managers in monitoring and controlling staff	More flexibility in work hours	Not being able 'escape' work
Improved staff productivity	Additional cost of providing employee with home computer, software, modem and communications		Distractions from family
	Possible security threat to sensitive company data		Difficulties in understanding work required

increase. At the same time, costs can be reduced due to lower requirements for office space. The benefits and disadvantages of teleworking are summarised in Table 19.1.

The table indicates that the decision to adopt teleworking is not a clear one, either for the company or the employee. Although advantages have been demonstrated in terms of staff motivation and productivity, these are likely to depend on the individual. As a result, teleworkers must be carefully screened for individual suitability and the type of job function must be appropriate. The most common type of teleworkers are either managers, technical design staff or staff in a 'virtual call centre' answering phone queries that are then logged to a workflow system for staff elsewhere to deal with.

The case study on teleworking gives an insight into the adoption of teleworking in the US and Europe and summarises its benefits.

▶ Knowledge management and organisational learning

Knowledge management is intended to make the information assets of a company an integral part of its success. David Taylor (the founder of the Association of IT Directors in the UK) describes it as:

> a discipline that manages and improves organisational learning process and promotes an integrated method of identifying, controlling and sharing all of an enterprise's information assets.

Knowledge management has a particular focus on assisting decision making at a strategic level, as described in Chapter 6. As such, it is closely allied to technologies described in Chapter 6 such as business intelligence software (data warehouses and

CASE STUDY: TOPIC AREA

Teleworking

Teleworking: US leads the way

by Lindsay Nicolle

Europe is still way behind the US in adopting teleworking – or telecommuting, as it is often known.

Where the US has been encouraged to set up more flexible working methods by its architectural and industrial youth, sheer size, and its freethinking entrepreneurial spirit, many Europeans are typically huddled together in prewar buildings not designed for the modern working world, paying higher telecommunications costs, and hidebound by corporate management cultures which historically 'feed' on office-based workers.

The buildings and telecom costs are issues that Europeans can do something about – and they are making progress – with properties being built with distributed IT in mind and competition being encouraged to cut communications costs. But it is going to take longer to overcome the greatest inhibitor to teleworking in Europe today: corporate culture.

'Cultural change takes longer than changes in technology,' says Frank Shepherd, who is employed in workstyle consultancy for British Telecom. 'It's a historical thing. The mindset of senior managers needs to change.'

The UK has a corporate culture that still values 'face time' at the desk. Out-of-sight means 'out-of-control' to many managers who simply do not trust their staff to work unsupervised. Worse, middle managers fear losing their power base – or even their jobs – if staff are allowed effectively to manage themselves.

Clearly, teleworking needs to be driven from the top of the company with every director championing the concept. In Europe, it is still seen as an option for managers to pursue if they choose, all too often creating a situation where the teleworking project collapses when the champion leaves.

In the US, apart from a more liberated management attitude towards teleworking in the first place, a significant difference to the European experience is that American workers are far more vocal about wanting to take on telework.

A growing number of North Americans are taking control of their lives through flexible working. They claim it has helped their careers and enhanced their home relationships, while causing minimal isolation.

'Baby boomers' are leading teleworking in the US, according to a study by AT&T. One in six is aged between 33 and 51 and the favoured occupations include salespeople,

executives and managers, business professionals, technician/computer programmers, and teachers. They sit in log cabins, New York lofts and Californian condos, working away on PCs with Internet/intranet and e-mail capabilities, fax and phone, for employers based across state lines.

Meanwhile, in the UK, when the lobbying organisation, the Telework Platform, launched a manifesto for flexible working recently, 15 members of Parliament turned up, including a government minister and a select committee chairman – and another 65 MPs expressed their interest.

Could government ministers become teleworkers in the future? Someone with a high profile needs to lead the way soon since the notion of teleworking is already being regarded as a mythical proposition touted by idealists whose mantra over the past decade is beginning to wear thin.

Teleworking is trotted out as a solution every time the UK worries about the performance of the economy in a shrinking world of global competition, or the skills shortages, or the medical expense of treating office stress-related illnesses, or the irreparable harm commuting does to the ozone layer.

It is true that the benefits of teleworking via telecommuting, a virtual office, a telework centre, or so-called 'hot-desking', are many: a more flexible workforce drawn from a wider pool of people, not just able-bodied white males, based virtually anywhere in the country; happier, more personally fulfilled staff who, in turn, are more productive; flatter management structures which do away with divisive hierarchies and office politics; reduced office overheads; fewer cars on the road, making less pollution, and so on.

So why are so many in Europe still wending our weary way to the office every Monday morning? Why aren't they all telecommuting to work from rural idylls, or even palm beaches, away from traffic jams, late trains, and fatty, staff canteens?

Despite earlier forecasts from respected research companies that Britain would have 3.5m teleworkers by 1996, there are still only around 1.5m using computers and communications to work remotely. Yet there is no doubt that today, the spread of PCs and improved telecoms not only makes it possible for Britons to work from home but has the potential to change many jobs so that they can be done anywhere without physical contact with other people.

Boundaries

Technology has blurred the old home/work boundaries. So why isn't everybody teleworking? Is it just a myth too good to come true?

'It's not a myth, it's just that we're still at the experimental stage. But there is some evidence to suggest it is taking off,' says Alan Denbigh, executive director of the UK Telework, Telecottage and Telecentre Association (TCA).

'The trouble is, teleworking was oversold, early on,' he says. 'Initial forecasts were misleading since they tended to count the kind of jobs suited to teleworking without taking into account the necessary changes required in the economy, corporate cultures and social pressures.

'But the UK is leading Europe in this sector, apart from Scandinavia, and we've seen a doubling of the number of teleworkers in the last five years.'

Already, companies such as British Gas, Barclays and Xerox are saving up to £1000 a head every year in office costs by equipping staff with PCs and links to central systems and switchboards so they can work from home or while out on the road.

IT and management companies, including IBM, Andersen Consulting and Digital Equipment, have hot-desking schemes, in which home-based staff book office facilities for the day or two a week that they go in to the main offices.

Across most of Europe, people commute like automatons to the office, their second home, dreaming of taking control of their lives and working to live.

But there's hope. The Telework Platform claims that in 10 years' time teleworking will be the norm in the UK, just as computers have come to be taken for granted.

Whether this will happen because of political will, employer enlightenment or staff pressure is a moot point. More likely the drop in the birth rate, the escalating skills shortages to feed a service-based economy, and crippling city centre property prices will force teleworking on to the agenda and then gather staff support.

'By 2005, 25 per cent of companies expect that more than half their office space will support team activity, rather than individuals,' says John Lane, director of IT at Pagoda Associates, the business change consultancy. 'Offices will exist primarily to provide corporate identity and occasional social interaction.'

Roll on the day. . . .

Source: Financial Times, 1 April 1998

Questions

1 What benefits can an organisation gain by moving towards teleworking?

2 What software applications is a teleworker likely to make use of?

3 Identify any potential problems that might arise as organisations make extensive use of teleworking.

4 What is the impact of teleworking on employees?

data mining) and artificial intelligence techniques. Although IS can assist in the capture and distribution or sharing of knowledge, it currently only plays a minor role in applying this knowledge to take the decisions. It is reassuring that managers are unlikely to be made redundant by technology in the foreseeable future!

Organisational learning is a related development of the concept of total quality management. According to Huber (1991) four supporting factors for organisational learning are:

◆ knowledge acquisition;
◆ information distribution;
◆ information interpretation;
◆ organisational memory.

The learning can be thought of as a natural part of the evolution of an organisation. As a company develops it will learn from its mistakes and its successes. The link with knowledge management is to provide information on past behaviour to assist with learning from mistakes. Sveiby (1997) notes that the focus on knowledge rather than information is crucial to organisations, since this emphasises the knowledge that is held by people and that is a result of social interaction.

Given the increased recognition of knowledge management as a business improvement tool, it is likely that some of the techniques discussed in this chapter, such as business intelligence software and artificial intelligence, will increasingly be used to support organisational learning.

▶ TRENDS IN MANAGING INFORMATION SYSTEMS

▶ ERP deployed across organisations

One main trend in the way that applications are bought is that of 'single sourcing'. Rather than obtaining best-of-breed software from a range of companies, companies are now tending to purchase a single application or suite from a single vendor. The different modules will work across a range of business functions. This type of software is known as **enterprise resource planning (ERP) software**, since it can be used across a company for management of all resources such as material requirements planning, financial and human resources management. A 1997 survey by consultants Ovum showed that ERP expenditure worldwide was $12 billion, with a growth rate of 23 per cent.

Figure 19.2 compares an ERP application with the previous company arrangement of having separate data silos and applications (sometimes known as 'information islands') in different parts of the company. ERP software is produced by the German company SAP, the Dutch company Baan and US companies such as JD Edwards and Peoplesoft. The database manufacturer Oracle also operates in this area, with separate modules Oracle Financials and Oracle Human Resources.

The benefits of 'single sourcing' software are principally that the modules are easier to integrate when they are from the same manufacturer. This enables data to be transferred between different functional areas more easily, which is important for operational purposes, but also gives tactical benefits, in that an overview of company

Enterprise resource planning (ERP) software

A software system with integrated functions for all major business functions across an organisation such as production, distribution, sales, finance and human resources management.

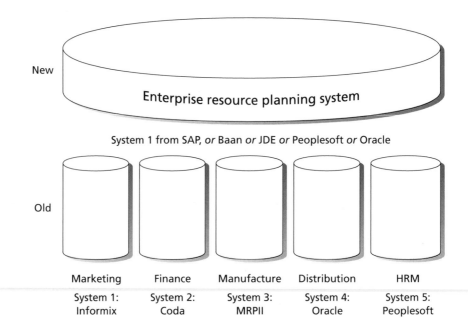

Fig 19.2 ERP application in comparison to separate functional applications

performance is available to senior managers. Reduced cost and a single source for support are further reasons for following this route. Reduced cost (at least in the short term) is not a strong argument for these products, however, since they are in such high demand that the companies and consultants implementing them can charge a premium for the functionality they offer. These systems have been adopted by many companies looking for a solution to the millennium bug in their legacy systems, for example. Rather than fixing millions of lines of legacy code, it is often a more practical proposition to buy an ERP system that is year 2000 compliant.

A significant feature of adopting ERP systems is that they tend to impose a particular business model on a company. In introducing such a system, companies will probably have to change their business practices. This will often bring improvements in efficiency, but only at the cost of the disruption that new systems can bring. Although there is a general business process model that is followed in introducing these systems, the products are designed to be configurable at the detailed level and much of the implementation cost is concerned with the detailed implementation and tailoring. For example, SAP has over 800 detailed business activities defined in its model, such as 'post an accounting entry'.

The increased use of ERP packages has arisen as a consequence of lessons learnt following the introduction of personal computers and the first wave of client/server systems in the early 1990s. During this period, IT selection became devolved, with the end-users in individual departments making their own purchasing decisions. This often led to separate applications from different vendors in different departments, often without good data transfer between applications. At the same time, client/server technologies have become more mature and can cope more effectively with the transactions required by large systems. In the future, the trend towards using ERP applications is likely to continue in large and medium companies. While small companies cannot usually afford packages such as SAP or Baan, an equivalent approach is becoming possible as cheaper, PC-based accounting packages are extended to functions beyond the key accounting functions. For example, Sage Sovereign has modules for sales order processing, payroll and stock control.

▶ Software obtained off the shelf rather than bespoke

The choice between off-the-shelf and bespoke acquisition of information systems was described in Chapter 7. A significant trend is that companies are now more likely to purchase off-the-shelf software than develop their own. This is also an additional reason for the popularity of ERP software, which is usually purchased as a tailored off-the-shelf solution.

This trend appears to be the result of a growing realisation that developing bespoke software is a lengthy and costly process. Although bespoke software is likely to fit the business requirements more closely, it may also have more errors than off-the-shelf software.

The benefits of off-the-shelf software, namely lower costs and fewer errors, are due to the fact that the software is purchased and used by many companies. The cost of purchase is shared between companies and with a standard product more effort can and needs to be applied to finding and fixing errors. A further trend that has accompanied the growth in popularity of off-the-shelf solutions is that modules are now more easy to tailor, if necessary, to an individual company's requirements.

▶ IMPORTANT FUTURE TECHNOLOGIES

▶ The Internet and World Wide Web applications

The growth of the Internet will be a major trend in the future use of information systems by businesses. This was described in Chapter 17, so is not reconsidered here in detail. In the near future, the Internet is expected to be most commonly used for business-to-business commerce. This was estimated in *The Economist* of 10 May 1997 to be between 60 and 160 billion by the Year 2001. The success of some companies in business-to-business commerce is indicated in the mini case study. Both of these companies expect to have more than half their turnover from the Internet before the millennium.

MINI CASE

Cisco aims for 50 per cent of sales to be made via Internet

By the end of 1997, Cisco, a supplier of network infrastructure, had achieved daily Internet-based sales of $7 million, which represented 39 per cent of sales. By early 1998, the computer manufacturer Dell was selling $4 million of personal computers via its Web site each day. Note that not all of these sales were achieved directly over the Web – some were still placed by phone or fax following the buying decision taken using the Internet.

Source: San Francisco Chronicle, 11 November 1997

Meanwhile, consumers will tend to continue to use existing retail channels, and consumer electronic commerce will remain at approximately 10 per cent of the level of business-to-business trade. Consumer commerce is likely to remain the poor relation, since the preferred medium for consumer purchases seems to be through normal retail channels. Other new consumer distribution channels, such as TV-based home shopping have only occupied a niche market compared to total retailing, even in the US where they are well established. Further barriers to the growth of Internet retail commerce are fears about the security of credit card transactions and also the number of consumers who have limited access to a Web-enabled computer at work or at home. The number of consumers with PC access will only grow relatively slowly. If and when the Internet becomes a standard service supplied with televisions, then consumer use of the Internet will increase dramatically.

Information 'haves' and 'have nots'

Another aspect to be considered in the future application of Internet technology is the concern about information 'haves' and 'have nots'. Fears have been expressed throughout the western world that there will be a polarisation of the better off and the poor in countries as IT skills and access to the Internet become vital for prosperity. This fear has resulted in initiatives to make IT skills and hardware available to the less privileged through schools and local government.

On a global scale, there is a worry that there will also be further polarisation between the less developed and developed nations. This will be more difficult to manage than variations within an individual country. Some countries are taking the initiative to ensure that they do not fall behind in communications technology, since they believe that this would adversely affect their development.

▶ Data warehouses and business intelligence software

Industry analysts such as Gartner, IDC and the Meta Group now estimate that data analysis tools, known collectively as **BI (business intelligence) software**, may be worth up to $30 billion by the year 2000 with hundreds of thousands of users. Such products have previously been referred to as online analytical processing (OLAP) tools. Products from companies such as Business Objects, Cognos and Gentia each have tens of thousands of users among business analysts, marketers and senior managers. These tools are intended to assist managers in analysing the performance of a business, in particular the success of the marketing and sales teams in promoting particular products to customers. In a 1998 report by IT analysts DataQuest of 177 early adopters in Europe, the most important reason for implementing **data warehouses** was to provide better information for decision support, together with using the technology to gain or keep a competitive edge.

The technical and business benefits of this technique are also covered in Chapter 6.

As with many new technologies, data warehousing has experienced some initial difficulties in implementation. Most of these problems have arisen from the scale of the implementations. For a large company to take information from all its operational systems involves managing the conversion of many gigabytes of data. In fact, a data warehouse is sometimes defined as starting at 80 gigabytes. For a large organisation a data warehouse may occupy terabytes of information – in the US, Walmart is building a data warehouse that holds 24 terabytes of data, equivalent to approximately 2400 one-gigabyte hard disks. All this information has to be converted from different systems so that it is in a consistent form suitable for analysis in the data warehouse. This data transformation and cleaning process can be difficult, since products, customers and date formats will be stored under different codes in different systems and these have to be unified.

Data warehouse projects also face all the other problems of large systems developments, such as initial estimation of a project that will be a new initiative for most companies and then keeping it on target as the business requirements and the tools available change. As a response to these difficulties, many companies have decided to embark on a smaller-scale initial project to analyse the data in one part of the company, such as marketing, finance or production. These smaller-scale projects use software known as **data marts**, which uses a similar approach to data warehouses, but has a smaller capacity and uses less expensive tools.

▶ Collaborative and workflow systems

Groupware and workflow systems are relatively new software technologies. Given this, and their ever increasing usage in business, there are many ways in which they will develop further. A key influence is likely to be the growth in use of the Internet and intranet. Groupworking applications such as Lotus Notes, Microsoft Exchange and Novell Groupwise will be accessed directly via a familiar Web browser such as Netscape Navigator rather than a proprietary client. There will also be more incorporation of groupware features into all types of software applications whose primary function is not groupworking. For example, accounting software was traditionally

Business intelligence (BI) software

A general term used to describe analysis software which makes use of functions available in data warehouses, data marts and data mining.

Data warehouses

Large database systems (often measured in gigabytes or terabytes) containing detailed company data on sales transactions which are analysed to assist in improving the marketing and financial performance of companies.

Data marts

Small-scale data warehouses which do not hold information across an entire company, rather they focus on one department.

British Midland uses multidimensional analysis of a data warehouse to assess sales performance on different routes

During 1996, British Midland introduced an Essbase multidimensional database as part of a sales and market decision support system. Prior to this, the sales and marketing database had only been available on hard-copy printouts, which made it difficult to analyse the data and arrive at early conclusions on how to react to current market conditions. The old system was based on an eight-year-old database. During this time the number of reports had been increased to 35, which consisted of 40 000 pages of data each month. Each report would take three days to create and print and a further two days to copy and distribute to UK users, still longer for users overseas.

The new system, known as SMART (Sales and Marketing Analytical Reporting Tool), was intended to provide a fast, easy-to-use delivery system for analysing sales information on flights by route, region, fare type and source (primarily agents). Sales information can be displayed as passengers, revenue or yield, giving a history across 36 months. The capabilities of SMART enable users to drill down to agent level in some countries, but not others where the number of agents precludes the reports being generated due to system limitations. The current system is approximately 50 Gb in size. To analyse the other 15 000 agents would require an increase in capacity of the system to 355 Gb. Given the cost and possible performance problems this could give, it is not thought to be a viable solution. Other solutions involve a trade-off between the detail required for analysis and the size of the data warehouse. One approach would involve breaking up the data warehouse into smaller data marts to cover each individual market, such as Asia, North America, Europe and so on. Another involves reducing the number of fare types from 500 to 27.

A further problem is logistical in nature. Where the reports need to be viewed by overseas users, this is not possible since the current system only functions over a local area network. The company is hoping to set up an extranet facility that would allow analysis of data by overseas users. A potential problem with this approach is that overseas users are often agents who represent other carriers.

Questions

1 Why do you think British Midland decided to introduce this system? Will it provide it with a competitive advantage?

2 Describe some of the problems that British Midland has faced as an adopter of this software. Are solutions possible? What are the compromises?

3 Do you think the company should have waited until the data warehouse market was more mature?

software for individuals. Today it has functions to enable teams of accountants to work together. Figure 19.3 summarises the typical trends of groupware software.

The main trends evident from the figure are:

◆ All applications will include groupworking functions.
◆ Web browsers accessing data across TCP/IP-based networks will become the primary means of deploying group applications.

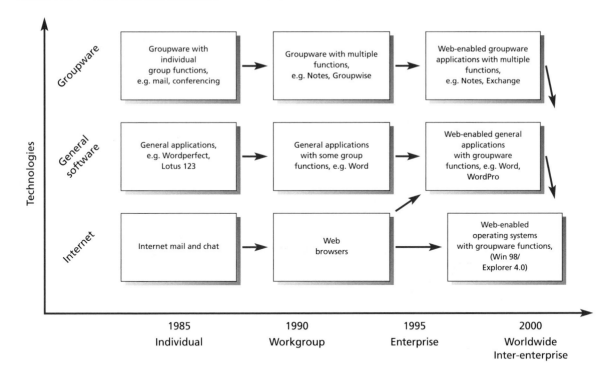

Fig 19.3 Future evolution of group-enabled systems

◆ Applications accessed from Web browsers will be incorporated as plug-in functions and Java or Active-X applets (which are computer software having a limited number of functions, but which are small in size).

◆ Operating systems will incorporate groupworking functions such as e-mail, news and conferencing.

▶ Object-oriented technology

Using object-oriented techniques for building software will become increasingly common in the future. More than half of major UK firms are already using object technology for some projects, according to a 1997 survey by services supplier Admiral of 150 medium to large UK-based organisations.

Objects can be thought of as building blocks that are brought together to build an information system. They are described in more detail in Chapter 12. The key concept here is reusability – a generic software object such as a payroll object or a sales analysis object can be used by different companies. The use of object-oriented techniques has been embraced by ERP vendors such as SAP, which offers over 170 different business objects describing a wide range of business processes and entities such as 'employee', 'customer' and 'product'. Each of these objects has a set of standard functions that can be used for every instance of an object in a business. For example, the standard functions (or methods) for an invoice object are:

◆ Create (a constructor function for when the invoice is created);

◆ Revise (modifications to the invoice);

◆ Post (when the invoice is paid and posted into accounts payable);

◆ Delete (a destructor for removing this object from the system).

The use of the Java language for developing applications to run in Web browsers and its promise of cross-platform portability (the ability to run on different types of machines) offer further reasons for the increase in the use of object-oriented techniques. Object-oriented techniques are being incorporated into other development tools such as Visual Basic and PowerBuilder. Object-oriented database management systems (OODMS) are also being used more widely. The Rover Group in the case study uses this technology. OODMS have yet to enter the mainstream and are unlikely to replace relational databases such as Microsoft Access for the foreseeable future.

A further key benefit of the use of objects is that each object can be tailored to a degree to fit the needs of an individual business. Making use of the existing functions of an object leads to more rapid development and lower costs. Reuse in object-oriented systems is a consequence of the ease with which generic objects can be incorporated into programming code. This is a result of inheritance, where a new object can be derived from an existing object and its behaviour modified.

MINI CASE

Rover and object-oriented technology

Rover Cars (now part of BMW) has used object-oriented technology to improve customer service when customers are selecting cars. It has developed a system that allows customers to specify, in detail, the features of cars (which are specified as different types of objects). The features specified are then electronically passed through to the production facility and the aim is to produce the car within a period of two weeks.

▶ Artificial intelligence and expert systems

Expert systems are not a new technology. The idea of using software that has intelligence programmed into it and making it capable of human decisions dates back to when computers were first introduced. However, real business applications making use of artificial intelligence techniques only became feasible in the 1970s and 1980s, when research in this field had been undertaken and computers became powerful enough to perform the processing. At this stage there was a great fanfare about how expert systems would replace much of human decision making. This did not happen and to date expert system applications in business have been limited to particular niche areas such as medical diagnosis and financial risk assessment. These applications and some technical background are described in Chapter 6.

In the future, it is probable that expert systems will remain a niche product that is not widely used in business. One exception to this may be the use of expert systems techniques to help in data mining for business intelligence applications, which will be used by many medium and large businesses. Here, expert systems will identify patterns and relationships in sales data that can be used to suggest changes to the method of promoting products.

Software agents will also be used on individual machines to take the drudgery out of using computers. A software agent can be set up to perform a routine task that would otherwise have to be performed by the user. An agent for an operating system might constantly monitor disk performance and then suggest defragmentation of the disk when operation becomes slow. An agent for the Internet might automatically scan the World Wide Web for the type of information you were interested in after monitoring your preferences, for example.

► MANAGING TECHNOLOGICAL CHANGE

A major difficulty for companies looking to apply information systems to help their businesses is how often technology changes. The speed of this change occurs through the competitiveness of the IT industry. If the leading vendors do not introduce new products, they can quickly be overtaken by smaller companies, or even startups. Witness the speed at which Microsoft moved from a small player to one of the world's leading software companies.

The speed of change is governed by the rate at which processing power increases and by new software developments. Improvements in processing power are indicated by Moore's law. Gordon Moore, the co-founder of Intel, predicted in 1965 that the transistor density of semiconductor chips would double roughly every 18 months. This prediction has actually happened as we have moved from different generations of processors, such as from 8086 to 80286 and through to the Pentium II. Alongside this increase in the capacity and speed of processors, the capacity and speed of primary RAM storage and secondary magnetic disk storage have also increased dramatically, allowing larger, more complex software to be run. The hardware improvements have permitted more complex software to be built and this in turn requires newer hardware, since software designers tend to design new systems for the fastest machines available.

How do these technical changes affect a business? Many managers would answer that they result in unnecessary expense and disruption. While this may be true, managers do not have to adopt the latest technologies if they do not believe that they are delivering benefits. So why are new technologies adopted? The reason is often that if your competitor has upgraded to the latest version of an ERP system or has just introduced a new data warehouse, then it is likely to have a competitive advantage. If you perceive that your competitor has, or may develop, a competitive advantage, then this is a powerful incentive to invest in new systems. Note that your competitor may only have a *perceived* competitive advantage.

Much of this investment cycle may be driven by uncertainty and the fear of falling behind. Industry figures seem to suggest that companies overestimate the benefits that new systems can give them and underestimate the risk of project failure. The failure rate of reengineering projects, which usually involve a high IS content, has been put at 70 per cent or higher. Furthermore, studies in the 1980s and 1990s summarised by Strassman (1997) seemed to suggest that there is little or no correlation between a company's investment in information systems and its business performance measured in terms of profitability or stock returns. This is often known as the **productivity paradox**. Brynjolfsson and Hitt (1996) argue that this paradox may exist for a number of reasons, including:

Productivity paradox
Studies show that large investments by a company in Information Systems do not necessarily result in greater business benefits. In fact there is a poor correlation between these variables.

- mismanagement of projects;
- mismeasurement;
- lags occurring between the initial investment and payback.

They take these factors into account and conclude that expenditure on computer capital and IS staff does contribute significantly to total company output. However, their view is probably a minority one and there is much anecdotal evidence of new systems failing to deliver, hence a detailed feasibility study should always be conducted for major investments.

▶ Techniques for dealing with change

Early adopter

Companies or departments who invest in new technologies when they first become available in an attempt to gain a competitive advantage despite the risk with deploying new systems.

There are two main strategic alternatives for a company adopting new technology. The first is to be an **early adopter**, who always tries to be the first to make use of new technologies to gain a competitive advantage. The second is to use a more conservative, 'wait-and-see' approach and not use new software until its benefits have been successfully demonstrated by other companies in your sector. Of course, there is a continuum here and most companies would seek to position themselves somewhere between the two extremes.

The problem with being an early adopter is that the leading edge of development is often also referred to as the 'bleeding edge' of technology due to the risk of failure. New systems may have many bugs, may integrate poorly with the existing system or may simply not live up to their promise. The counterargument to this is that, although the risks of adoption are high, so are the rewards, since you may gain an edge on your rivals. American Airlines gained a considerable advantage over its rivals

---

Keeping pace with PC software and hardware

There is a tendency for hardware vendors to retain their entry-level price as technology improves. For $1000 or £1000 the specification that is available has increased dramatically over the past five years. Yet this price bracket seems to be that most commonly used in adverts. The result of this is that a business manager may be forced to overspecify the equipment needed for end-users. Does an administration assistant really need the latest-generation PC with a very fast processor and full memory complement for simple wordprocessing?

A further problem is upgrading to new versions of operating systems and applications software. For example, a company such as Microsoft needs to produce new versions of software every few years to maintain its revenue stream. The question for the business user is, do we really need these latest versions? Companies will often find that the benefits of the new software are marginal and the costs and disruption of upgrading may be significant. Remember that costs will not only include upgrading to the software, but upgrades to hardware such as RAM and processors to run the new software and also training for staff. For these reasons, in August 1995 when Microsoft introduced Windows 95, many companies decided to continue using Windows 3.1 and DOS for their operating system since it fulfils the main functions required. Similarly, in 1997 when Microsoft, Lotus and Corel upgraded their Office suites for wordprocessing and spreadsheets, many companies decided to keep using their existing software because they perceived that the benefits were marginal and would probably be exceeded by the costs..

when it first introduced the SABRE customer reservation system; similarly, the banks which first introduced new techniques such as auto-teller machines and phone banking facilities also managed to increase market share.

In Chapter 14 McFarlan's strategic grid model was considered, which classifies companies' ambitions with respect to deploying technology. When using this model to decide which strategy to adopt, it is important to remember that the appropriate type of strategy may vary between industries. For example, in the financial services industry where the emphasis is on customer service, technology can be vital to achieve this. The early adopter of, for example, PC banking could gain a significant competitive advantage. To illustrate this, Capital One, a $14 billion company with over 12 million customers, considers information so crucial to its business that it states that its success is founded on its information-based strategy. It claims that this strategy allows it to:

> identify, manage and rapidly exploit business opportunities across a wide spectrum of applications. This has enabled us to become one of the world's largest issuers of credit cards in just three years.

Capital One uses data warehousing and data mining to assist in its objectives. Quoted in *PCWeek* (10 March 1998), Dave Buch, IT director at Capital One, said: 'Back in 1987 we figured that our business is nothing to do about credit cards, its about information.'

In the construction or chemical industry, in contrast, information technology may be less important and there will be lower gains available to the early adopter.

A further problem with dealing with change is identifying what are genuinely new significant technologies that should be adopted and what are relabelled ideas or new ideas that won't actually deliver much benefit. Spotting which is which is difficult, since technology supply companies are continually innovating and producing new products. For each major new development there will be a great deal of marketing hype and support from PR companies, industries and analysts, since it is in the interest of all these parties to support the latest trend. Objective studies will not be available until many companies have already taken the plunge and have learnt the hard way whether the technology is worth adopting.

The short history of the IT industry is full of examples of new techniques which were hyped, but have failed to deliver all that was promised. Some or even all of the new technologies mentioned in this chapter may fit into this category, since the hype can often exceed the benefits delivered. For example, expert systems were originally claimed to lead to massive cost reductions through deskilling as experts were replaced by software. This hasn't happened, and in fact expert systems are only used in particular specialised applications. Today, many are suggesting that the Internet will revolutionise the way business occurs and companies have felt a need to be part of this and establish a Web site. Those that have are often disappointed by the results. Many other technologies have failed to live up to the hype, including computer-aided software engineering, software tools that would automatically produce program code for users, object-oriented technology and the latest Java programming technique. The same could also be said for methodologies such as SSADM, soft systems methodologies, business process reengineering and total quality management.

For each of these techniques a simple lifecycle can be identified:

1 *Creation*. Creation of new technology or technique. Very few users (who are probably involved in testing early versions of the product).

2 *Adoption*. Initially by limited number of users with limited media exposure. With successful early deployments, media hype grows, as does number of users planning to deploy technology.

3 *Disappointment*. Reports of failures or poor results start to become more common in media. Number of users then starts to fall as they revert back to previous ways of working.

4 *Decline*. The media latches on to the next major trend and the technology falls out of the news.

CASE STUDY: TOPIC AREA

Data warehouse – problems in store

It's all too easy when building a data warehouse to get carried away by the technical issues. But agonising between choosing a massively parallel computer or the intricacies of online analytical processing (Olap) can detract from facing up to larger concerns.

The primary management concern associated with data warehousing is that of cost-justification. Despite the fact that the average spend on a data warehouse is something like £3m, a frightening number of organisations do not have any rigorous estimate of the commercial benefits that that spend will bring about. According to a survey published earlier this year by analysts Data Warehouse Network and Sun, about 70% of organisations investing in data warehousing do so simply as an act of faith. This may be for several reasons.

It could be that since rigorous cost-justification for any kind of IT investment is extremely difficult to calculate, users simply cannot face doing it for their investment into data warehousing. It could also be that there is a growing perception that the cult of the data warehouse is being driven by business managers – especially marketing managers – carried away by the prospect of drilling down into their sales performance in ever greater detail. This 'management by magazine' whereby a business manager is persuaded of the huge business advantage to be gained by a particular line of IT by having read a glowing, supplier-sourced article in the business press, has already been seen in client/server migration. It is not surprising to find it cropping up again in data warehousing. Given a bevy of gung-ho marketing managers all crying out for a data warehouse, why should the IT manager turn down the opportunity to keep his department happy and busy for the next three years working on exciting new technology? If business is happy not knowing its return on investment, why should the IT department worry?

This, ironically, is a reprise of what happened in the 1980s with the first, Teradata-led generation of data warehouses, which were bought by business managers frustrated by the mainframe's inability to give them the level of detail and fast response to business queries they craved. At least this time around neither MPP nor, to a lesser extent, Olap is seen by the IT department as a threat to their dominance – rather the converse. The data warehouse is not a replacement but an extension of existing systems.

Nevertheless, like any major IT project, it is essential that a data warehouse has a business sponsor and a business project manager, otherwise there is a danger of rejection or complaint by business users, and ultimate relegation to an unvisited 'data basement'. Moreover, whether or not the cost of building – and running – a corporate data warehouse is formally justified (whether it is charged to a business department or is signed off as an infrastructure project), it is essential that both business and IT are in agreement. If IT thinks a return on investment is not required, it had better ensure that business thinks so too, or there will be unpleasant acrimony at budget time.

Where will the data warehouse budget be spent? If the decision has been to opt for a top-end big data warehouse, rather than the departmental data mart approach, then it is easy to assume that the major costs will be associated with the very large computer it needs to run on. However, such is the hunger of hardware vendors at the moment, all of whom are extremely keen to accrue market share and accumulate invaluable reference sites, that there are excellent opportunities to strike some very sweet deals indeed. Putting it bluntly, some suppliers are coming close to giving the boxes away. Certainly, as Will Gee, information delivery manager at Woolworth's discovered, it is pretty easy to get the hardware vendors to run free customer benchmarks. Gee put several hot-box vendors through the benchmarking hoop before opting for Tandem's Himalaya MPP machine – he has also stipulated that the contract with Tandem is for a given level of performance, irrespective of how many nodes it takes to achieve that. What it will cost, however, is anyone who knows how to build and run a data warehouse.

Data warehousing skills are still in very short supply, and most have been snapped up by consultants and suppliers. Even these are not always what the service providers might want to persuade you they are – Gee was frankly depressed by the relatively low level of expertise he found when researching data warehousing a year ago. 'Some of the consultants had simply gone round the suppliers and talked to each of them for an hour,' he says. Although, like any skills shortage, the problem is easing with time as more specialists come on stream, one difficulty with data warehousing is that, unlike Notes, mainframe Cobol or C++, which are also in a jobs boom at the moment, data warehousing is fundamentally difficult, and will therefore remain a premium-priced skill. It is technically difficult for several reasons. First, it requires a level of understanding of database design and database management that has to encompass both a huge amount of data and a very wide variety. A data warehouse needs to be fed by data from many, if not all, an organisation's production systems, as well as external data, such as market research data, and, warns Andy Bailey of Oracle, before long it will also need to take in non-standard data such as free text and images, for example geographical demographic information. Second, both Olap and MPP are still arcane and tricky technologies. How do you set up the most useful and speedily accessed summary tables for a multidimensional database? How do you provide the most effective hints to the Oracle SQL parallel optimiser so that it executes the query as efficiently as possible? How do you split up the data warehouse database across the multitude of nodes in a parallel computer so that you minimise the number of joins and maximise speed of response and throughput? Finally, although different people can be found to provide different skill sets – from Business Objects to parallel SQL – there will be a need for

someone with the top-level architecture skills needed to pull the whole thing together. People who can master the plethora of tools in this area to the extent of knowing what works with what and what the pros and cons of each are, are going to be pretty scarce.

Whether or not the user hires a database architect directly, or simply pays for his skills via a service provider, it will not be cheap. Salaries for data warehouse architects can easily mop up £50 000 a year, and the TSB, for example, is currently paying £1000 a day for Oracle's data warehousing consultants. At the very top, parallel processing specialists can charge nearly £200 an hour for their expertise. Even if unpleasant scenes during budget discussions are avoided, it will be a rare IT director who escapes being caught in the cross-fire as user communities discover that their jealously guarded data is to be sucked up into the maw of the corporate data warehouse to become accessible to other departments.

The perceived threat is twofold, believes Andy Wright, vice-president of data warehouse repository vendor, Platinum Technology. It is not just fear that departmental data owners will lose their privileged position as the only people in the company who know that particular information. 'What they really fear is that the integrity of their data will be compromised in a data warehouse,' he says. Inevitably, user departments will react to the arrival of the data warehouse by duplicating all their data before letting it go, just to protect it.

Source: Computer Weekly, 30 May 1996

Questions

1 On which criteria does the article suggest that the investment decision on data warehouses is made?

2 Would you say that the difficulties in implementing data warehouses are mainly technical or are other factors such as skills availability more important?

3 Summarise the history of data warehouse applications and predict the future for the technology.

This lifecycle is summarised in Fig 19.4. It is similar to Nolan's stage model referred to in Chapter 14, except that the Nolan model refers to use of an information system within a single company. Figure 19.4 refers to adoption of a particular type of system across industry. An industry model has also been proposed by Higgins (1985) which identifies stages of emergence, growth, mature and declining for all industries. In the IT industry, however, this situation is more polarised and the lifecycle tends to be shorter.

So what can companies do to avoid jumping on the wrong technology bandwagon or, equally bad, failing to jump on the right bandwagon? First of all, experienced managers will be aware of this problem and will be able to identify the

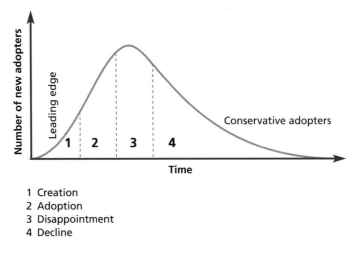

1 Creation
2 Adoption
3 Disappointment
4 Decline

Fig 19.4 Graph of proportion of adopters of technology through time

latest fad that is being proposed by suppliers. Second, they need to scan the market-place and evaluate the success of new technologies by benchmarking against the results of companies who are early adopters. If good results are being obtained, then this may be a good time to investigate using the technology. Care needs to be taken, since the growth of these technologies is fired by a limited number of success stories – these may not be realistic or representative. So a conservative, cynical approach is probably the best one. As well as these measures, the traditional tools of controlling investment decisions centrally, not overspecifying for function and careful cost–benefit and feasibility analysis should be used on all major new decisions.

▶ SUMMARY

The main trends identified in this chapter are as follows:

1 Web browsers will become established as the main end-user and administrative clients for all types of applications, from wordprocessors and spreadsheets to work-flow applications, which will all run within the Web browser, and this will effectively become part of the operating system.

2 Such applications will be used within companies over an intranet or between busi-nesses and or customers across the Internet as part of electronic commerce transactions.

3 Features to help groups of workers collaborate will become increasingly common in all classes of software, from operating systems to applications.

4 New systems will be purchased as off-the-shelf systems wherever practical and these will often be tailored to different companies' needs by purchasing packages made up of objects or components that can be assembled and tailored as required.

5 Enterprise resource planning systems such as SAP and Baan sourced from a single supplier will replace the many different bespoke and packaged solutions already used in a company.

6 Development and support of information systems will commonly be outsourced, not only for large companies, but also for small and medium enterprises.

7 Deciding which new technologies to adopt for a business will not become any easier and, given this, it is best to avoid being an early adopter who is exposed to the highest risk.

▶ EXERCISES

▶ Self-assessment exercises

1 What does the term virtual organisation mean?

2 Why is enterprise resource planning software being deployed by many companies?

3 What is the purpose of data warehousing software and how does this differ from data mining software?

4 What is teleworking?

5 Why is off-the-shelf or packaged software becoming more popular in comparison to bespoke software?

6 What are limiting factors on the growth of the Internet for electronic commerce?

7 What is the significance of object-oriented software?

8 Give examples of some business applications of expert systems.

▶ Discussion questions

1 What is the best approach for a company to deal with technological change?

2 There are less than one million teleworkers in the UK currently. Is the trend likely ever to become more significant than this?

▶ Essay questions

1 Using examples of evolving technologies, discuss the factors that govern why a new technology may become established in industry.

2 Investigate one of the following technologies in more detail to analyse its future adoption by industry and explain your reasoning:
   (a) object-oriented technology;
   (b) expert systems;
   (c) data warehouses and business intelligence software.

3 Describe the trend in the use of call centres to provide customer service. What factors are responsible for the number of staff now using these facilities? What are the disadvantages to staff? Are these likely to reduce the growth rate?

▶ Examination questions

1 What is the purpose of deploying a groupware system?

2 What are the main methods of dealing with technological change?

3 What do you understand by the term virtual corporation? Which are the main technologies that help such an organisation to function?

4 Explain why a company might prefer to use off-the-shelf or packaged software rather than bespoke software. Explain the meaning of each type of software in your answer.

5 Define a call centre. How has technology assisted in the growth of this phenomenon?

▶ References

Brynjolfsson, E. and Hitt, L. (1996) 'Paradox lost? Firm-level evidence on the returns to information systems spending', *Management Science*, 42, 4, 541–59.

Davidow, W.H. and Malone, M.S. (1992) *The Virtual Corporation: Structuring and Revitalizing the Corporation for the 21st Century*, HarperCollins, New York.

Davis, S. and Borkin, J. (1994) 'The coming of knowledge-based business', *Harvard Business Review*, Sep–Oct, 72, 5, 165–71.

Higgins, J. (1985) *Strategy: Formulation, Implementation and Control*, Dryden Press, Chicago.

Huber, G. (1990) *A Theory of the Effects of Advanced Information Technologies on Organizational Design, Intelligence, and Decision Making*, Academy of Management Review, 15, 47–71.

Martin, J. (1996) *Cybercorp: the New Business Revolution*, AMACOM (American Management Association), New York.

Strassman, P. (1997) *The Squandered Computer*, Information Economics Press, Connecticut.

Sveiby, K.E. (1997) *The New Organizational Wealth: Managing and Measuring Knowledge-Based Assets*, Berrett-Koehler, San Francisco.

Yourdon, E. (1992) *The Decline and Fall of the American Programmer*, Prentice-Hall, New York.

▶ Further reading

Davenport, T. and Prusak, L. (1998) *Working Knowledge: How Organizations Manage What They Know*, Harvard Business School Press, Boston, MA.

Inmon, W.H. (1996) *Building the Data Warehouse*, John Wiley, New York.

Metcalf, D. and Fernie, S. (1997) 'Hanging on the telephone', *Centrepiece*, 3, 1.

Senge, P. (1990) *The Fifth Discipline: The Art and Practice of the Learning Organization*, Currency/Doubleday, New York.

Strassman, P. (1990) *The business value of the customer*, Information Economics Press, Connecticut.

▶ Web references

http://www.brint.com The Business Researchers? Interests site has extensive references to knowledge management and organisational learning.

http://pwp.starnetinc.com/larryg Lany Greenfield's Data Warehousing Information Center.

Glossary

3DFx graphics card. A type of graphics card that features a sophisticated coprocessor used to manipulate an image so that it appears more realistic. Complicated calculations are required in order to perform actions such as smoothing jagged shapes or showing the shadows that an object might cast.

▶ A

Access control. *See* user validation.

Access time. In terms of storage devices, the access time refers to the average time taken to locate a specific item of data. Access times are normally given in milliseconds, for example a typical hard disk drive might have an access time of 11 ms.

Active-X. A programming language standard developed by Microsoft which permits complex and graphical customer applications to be written and then accessed from a Web browser. An example might be a form for calculating interest on a loan. A competitor to Java.

Ad clicks. An IFABC standard indicating the number of audited occasions a Web banner or interstitial has been clicked on by a user to view an advert.

Adaptive system. In general, an adaptive system has the ability to monitor and regulate its own performance. In many cases, an adaptive system will be able to respond fully to changes in its environment by modifying its behaviour.

Address Book. A folder that contains frequently used e-mail addresses. Rather than identifying other users by their e-mail addresses, individuals or groups can be given aliases or nicknames. E-mail addressed to an alias is automatically sent to the user(s) associated with that name.

Alias. The process of sending e-mail messages to specific individuals or groups of users can be simplified by making use of aliases. An alias – sometimes known as a nickname – usually consists of a description and the e-mail addresses of those grouped under the alias.

Alpha release and alpha testing. Alpha releases are preliminary versions of the software released early in the build process. They usually have the majority of the functionality of the system in place, but may suffer from extensive bugs. The purpose of 'alpha testing' is to identify these bugs and any major problems with the functionality and usability of the software. Alpha testing is usually conducted by staff inside the organisation developing the software or by favoured customers.

Analogue. Analogue data is continuous in that an infinite number of values between two given points can be represented. As an example, the hands of a clock are able to represent every single possible time of the day.

Annotation. A note or message that can be attached to a document. Voice annotations are spoken messages that can be embedded within a document.

Apple Macintosh. A family of personal computers produced by Apple Computers. Although less popular than IBM-compatible personal computers, the Apple Macintosh is widely used for professional desktop publishing applications, graphics and animation.

Applets. Small programs with limited functions typically running from within a Web browser.

Applications backlog. An applications backlog occurs when the demand for new applications by users exceeds the capacity of the IS department or IS outsourcing company to develop them. Over a period of a year a large number of applications are in the queue of required new work.

Applications generator. An application generator performs an action or creates a computer program based on a set of requirements given by the user. Many applications generators allow users to define a series of actions or requirements by arranging icons on a special design screen. The resulting design is then converted into a series of instructions or an executable program.

Artificial intelligence (AI). Artificial intelligence (AI) methods attempt to make a computer system behave in the same way as a human being. One application for AI is in natural language processing, where users can communicate with a computer system using English-like statements.

Assembly language. Assembly language represented an attempt to simplify the process of creating computer programs. Symbols and abbreviations were used to create sequences of instructions. An assembler was used to translate a completed assembly language program into the machine code required by the computer.

Asynchronous. When collaborators send messages that can be accessed at a later time these are known as asynchronous. Asynchronous exchange occurs with e-mail or discussion groups.

Attributes Of Information Quality. A group of characteristics by which the quality of information can be assessed. These attributes are normally grouped into three categories: time, content and form. Examples of attributes of information quality include accuracy, reliability and timeliness.

Audits. This describes the process of monitoring an organisation's hardware and software resources. In general, audits are used as a deterrent against theft and the use of illegal software.

▶ **B**

Back door. The back door is a section of program code that allows a user to circumvent security procedures in order to gain full access to an information system.

Back up. To create a duplicate copy of information to reduce the risk fo losing information.

Backup site. A backup site houses a copy of the organisation's main data processing facilities, including hardware, software and up-to-date data files. In the event of an emergency, processing can be switched to the backup site almost immediately so that the organisation's work can continue.

Banner. A rectangular graphic displayed on a web page for the purposes of advertising. It is normally possible to perform a click-through to access further information. Banners may be static or animated.

Bar code. A bar code is a means of displaying a unique identification number as a series of thick and thin lines. The sequence and width of the lines in the bar code can be translated into a sequence of digits. Bar-code numbers are normally produced according to specific method. The Universal Product Code, for example, is a standard method for creating and using bar codes.

Bar code reader. A bar-code reader measures the intensity of a light beam reflected from a printed bar code

to identify the digits making up a unique identification number. The digits making up the identification number are also printed at the foot of the bar code. If a label containing a bar code becomes damaged or cannot be read for some other reason, it may still be possible to enter the identification number manually.

Batch processing. Data is 'post-processed' following collection, often at times when the workload on the system is lower. Batch processing usually occurs without user interaction as a 'background job'.

Baud. A simple means of measuring the performance of a modem or other device. Early modems operated at speeds of 1200 baud, the equivalent of approximately 100 characters per second. Data transmission rates can also be expressed in bits per second (bps). In general, the higher the baud rate or bps value, the faster and more efficient the device.

Bench marks. This describes the process of testing the performance of computer equipment. Having carried out a series of bench mark tests, the results can be compared against similar items in order to make the best selection.

Bespoke development. An IS is developed 'from scratch' by an IS professional to suit the business requirements of the application.

Beta release and beta testing. Beta releases occur after alpha testing and have almost complete functionality and relatively few bugs. Beta testing will be conducted by a range of customers who are interested in evaluating the new software. The aim of beta testing is to identify bugs in the software before it is shipped to a range of customers.

Big-bang changeover. Immediate cutover is when a new system becomes operational and operations transfer immediately from the previous system.

BIOS (Basic Input/Output System). Housed in a memory chip on the computer's motherboard, the BIOS contains software that controls all of the computer's most basic activities. It is the BIOS that allows the keyboard, display, hard disk drives, serial ports and other devices to function. The BIOS is stored in ROM so that it is always available and cannot be accidentally damaged or erased.

Bit. A single binary digit representing a zero (0) or a 1.

Bit map image. A bit map image is made up of small dots (pixels) arranged in a grid. The finer the grid, the higher the resolution of the image.

Bookmarks. All Web browsers allow users to maintain a directory of WWW sites. The directory will enable users to add, edit, delete and organise addresses in the form of bookmarks.

Bottom-up design. The bottom-up approach to design starts with the design of individual modules, establishing their inputs and outputs and then builds an overall design from these modules.

Boundary. This describes the interface between a system and its environment. Everything within the boundary forms part of the system, everything outside the boundary forms part of the external environment.

Brainstorming. Uses the interaction between a group of staff to generate new ideas and discuss existing problems. It is the least structured of the fact-finding techniques.

British Computer Society (BCS). The British Computer Society is widely regarded as the UK's leading professional association for those involved in the management and development of computer-based information systems.

Bubble jet printer. A bubble jet printer works in similar manner to an inkjet printer, but transfers the character by melting the ink droplets onto the paper.

Bug. Software bugs are defects in a program which are caused by human error during programming or earlier in the lifecycle. They may result in major faults or may remain unidentified.

Bulletin Board System (BBS). Bulletin Board Systems can be described as electronic noticeboards, where users can send or receive messages related to a wide variety of subjects. A typical BBS will provide users with e-mail facilities, discussion forums and access to software libraries containing Freeware and Shareware.

Bus-width. Describe how many pieces of data can be transmitted or received at one time by the bus connecting the processor to other components of the PC.

Business aligning IS strategy. The IS strategy is used to support the business strategy.

Business impacting IS strategy. The IS strategy is used to favourably impact the business strategy, perhaps by introducing new technologies.

Business Information Systems. This describes information systems used to support the functional areas of business. For example, an organisation might use specialised information systems to support sales, marketing and human resource management activities.

Business intelligence (BI) software. BI software is a general term used to describe analysis software which makes use of functions available in data warehouses, data marts and data mining.

Business process reengineering (BPR). Identifying and implementing radical new ways of carrying out work, often enabled by new IT capabilities.

Business process automation (BPA). Automating existing ways of working manually through Information Technology.

Business resource base. The resources that a company has available to it are known collectively as the business resource base. The business resource base is made up of physical and conceptual resources (also known as tangible and intangible assets).

Business rule. A rule defines the actions that need to occur in a business when a particular situation arises. For example a business rule may state that if a customer requests credit and they have a history of defaulting on payments, then credit will not be issued. A business rule is broken down into an event which triggers a rule with test conditions which result in defined actions.

Business Software Alliance (BSA). An organisation formed to act against software piracy. *See* Software theft.

Byte. Made up of eight bits and represents the amount of space required to hold a single character.

▶ C

Cache memory. In a computer system, cache memory is used to improve performance by anticipating the data and instructions that will be needed by the processor. The required data is retrieved and held in the cache, ready to be transferred directly to the processor when required.

Call Centre. An office which is devoted to answering telephone enquiries from customers, call centres are commonly used for financial services and retail customer support.

Capacity loading graphs. Capacity loading graphs show the resources required to undertake activities in a project.

CD-R (CD-Recordable). This describes a variation on the traditional CD-ROM. CDR drives cannot only read conventional compact discs but can also write data to special 'gold' discs. Compact discs produced in this way are known as write-once discs, that is, once data has been stored on the disc it cannot be altered or erased. *See* CD-ROM.

CD-ROM. A computer storage device offering a relatively high capacity. The acronym CD-ROM stands for Compact Disc – Read Only Memory, denoting the fact that CD-ROM discs are read only devices; data can-not be written to a CD-ROM by a conventional player.

CDRW. A more recent development in terms of compact disc storage are CD Re-Writable drives. In addition to providing the functionality of the CDR drive, the CDRW drive also allows the use of special compact disc media that can be written and erased many times. However, discs produced in this way are not compatible with standard CD-ROM drives and can only be used with a CDRW unit. *See* CDR and CD-ROM.

Central Processing Unit (CPU). This describes the microprocessor found in a computer system. The CPU controls all of the computer's main functions and enables users to execute programs or process data.

Centralised IS management. Centralised IS management will involve the control of all IS services from a central location, typically in a company head-office or data-centre.

CGI (Common Gateway Interface). CGI offers a way of providing interactivity through the Web. With a form type HTML document, a user type in information and structured information or queries sent using the Web.

Change (modification) requests. A modification to the software thought to be necessary by the business users or developers.

Changeover. The term used to describe moving from the old information system to the new information system.

Channels. Channels (sometimes described as netcasting) enable users to subscribe to particular sites on the Internet, in much the same way that one might subscribe to a newspaper or magazine. The use of channels allows both the user and the information provider to select the information to be sent and schedule its transmission.

Checksum digits. A checksum involves the use of an extra digit for ensuring the validity of long code numbers. The checksum digit is calculated from an algorithm involving the numbers in the code and their modulus (by convention modulus 11).

Chip theft. Chip theft describes a relatively new phenomenon involving the removal of small but valuable components from computers, such as memory modules and processors.

CISC (complex instruction set computer). A specific type of microprocessor which has a wide range of instructions to enable easy programming and efficient use of memory. CISC processors are best known as the Intel processors from 8086 to 80486 and the Motorola 68000 used in early Apple Macintoshes.

Client/server. The client/server architecture consists of client computers such as PCs sharing resources such as a database stored on a more powerful server computers. Processing can be shared between the clients and the servers.

Clock speed. This is measured in MHz (megahertz, or millions of pulses per second). The clock speed is governed by a quartz-crystal circuit. Computer clock speed tends to double every year. It is worth remembering that clock speed is only one measure of a computer's 'power' and it is not usually directly proportional to the performance level. For example, a 266MHz Pentium will not be twice as fast as a 133MHz Pentium. Other factors such as the architecture of the processor, the graphics card, the amount and speed of RAM and the access speed of the hard-disk storage will all affect the overall performance of the system.

Closed system. No or limited interaction occurs with the environment.

Closed questions. Closed questions have a restricted choice of answers such as Yes/No or a range of opinion on a scale of strongly agree to strongly disagree (Likert scale). Approach is useful for quantitative analysis of results.

Constructive Cost Model (COCOMO). A model used to estimate the amount of effort required to complete a project on the basis of the estimated number of lines of program code.

Code of conduct. Members of professional associations, such as the British Computer Society, are expected to abide by a set of principles that sets out minimum standards of competence, conduct and behaviour.

Cognitive Style. This describes the way in which a manager absorbs information and reaches decisions. A manager's cognitive style will fall between analytical and intuitive styles.

Comma separated values (CSV). A CSV file is a simple text file made up of items enclosed within quotation marks and separated by commas. The use of commas and quotation marks enables a program reading the file to identify individual items.

Command Line Interpreter (CLI). A CLI is used to pass instructions from a user to a computer program. The CLI accepts instructions from a user in the form of brief statements entered via the keyboard.

Commercial languages. This category of programming languages is intended to create applications that meet the basic information processing requirements of business organisations.

Compact disc (CD). This describes the media used by CD-ROM players. The data on a compact disc is encoded as a series of dips and raised areas. These two states represent binary data – the same number system used by microprocessors. The CD-ROM player shines a laser beam onto the surface of the disc and measures the light that is reflected back. The intensity of the light that is reflected back enables the player to distinguish individual binary digits. *See* CD-ROM.

Competitive Advantage. In order to survive or expand, organisations must seek to gain dominance over their competitors in the marketplace. This can be achieved by using variety of strategies to gain control of a market or prevent others from gaining control.

Compiler. The instructions that make up a computer program are often stored as a simple text file, usually called a source code file. A compiler produces an executable program by converting instructions held as source code into machine language.

Compound key. In a relational database, it is possible to retrieve data from several tables at once by using record keys in combination, often known as a compound key. *See* Record key and Primary key.

Computer Aided Design (CAD). Provides interactive graphics that assist in the development of product and service designs. Connects to a database allowing designs to be recalled and developed easily.

Computer Aided Manufacture (CAM). CAM involves the use of computers directly to control production equipment and indirectly to support manufacturing operations.

Computer Aided Software engineering (CASE) tools. CASE tools are software which helps the systems analyst and designer in the analysis, design and build phases of a software project. They provide tools for drawing diagrams such as ERDs and storing information about processes, entities and attributes tools.

Computer criminals. In general, computer criminals are well-educated, white-collar workers that feel undervalued or bear some resentment to an employer or former employer. Computer criminals make use of technology to perform a variety of criminal acts, ranging from vandalism and sabotage to hacking and fraud.

Computer-based Information System. This describes an information system that makes use of Information Technology in order to create management information.

Computer Misuse Act (1990). This legislation is intended to protect sensitive equipment and data from unauthorised access, alteration and damage.

Computer monitoring. The use of computer and communications technology to monitor the activities of individuals.

Computer network. A computer network can be defined as: 'a communications system that links two or more computers and peripheral devices and enables transfer of data between the components'.

Computer Output to Microfilm (COM). COM, also known as Computer Output Microfilm, is often used to archive large quantities of information for future reference. Information is processed via a personal computer and sent directly to a device that produces microfilm negatives.

Computer system. A computer system consists of a number of interrelated components that work together with the aim of converting data into information. In a computer system, processing is carried out electronically, usually with little or no intervention from a human user. The components of a computer system include hardware and software.

Computer virus. A computer virus is a computer program that is capable of self-replication, allowing it to spread from one 'infected' machine to another.

Conceptual Resources. Conceptual resources describe the non-physical resources owned by a company. Conceptual resources are also known as intangible assets. Examples include knowledge, experience and judgement.

Configuration management. Procedures which define the process of building a version of the software from its constituent program files and data files.

Contact manager. This describes a software application that can be used to maintain lists of information relating to customers, suppliers and other important individuals or organisations.

Content. Content is the design, text and graphical information which forms a Web page.

Content dimension. This describes several characteristics of information quality related to the scope and contents of the information. Among these characteristics are the accuracy, relevance and conciseness of information. As an example, information may be considered to be of high quality if it is accurate. Other dimensions of information characteristics include time and form. *See* Time dimension, Form dimension.

Context diagrams. A simplified diagram which is useful for specifying the boundaries and scope of the system. They can be readily produced after the information flow diagram since they are a simplified version of the IFD showing the external entities.

Control. If alterations are needed to the system, adjustments are made by some form of control mechanism. The function of a control mechanism is to ensure that the system is working to fulfil its objective.

Copyright, Designs and Patents Act (1988). Legislation that can be used to provide organisations and software developers with protection against unauthorised copying of designs, software, printed materials and other works.

Copy protection. This describes a number of methods that can be used to prevent unauthorised copies being made of a software package.

Cost of ownership. The cost of ownership describes a range of different expenses incurred by purchasing and maintaining a computer system. Such costs include the original cost of the hardware and software, upgrades, maintenance, technical support and training.

Cost per megabyte. The cost per megabyte presents a simple means of gauging the costs associated with a given storage device.

Cost per page. The cost per page provides a simple means of determining the overall running costs of a given printer. The figures given usually refer to the costs of consumables such as ink and replacement components (toner cartridges, drums and so on).

Coupling. Defines how closely linked different sub-systems are. Loose coupling means that the modules pass only the minimum of information between them and do not share data and program code. Close-coupled systems are highly dependent on each other.

CPM. Cost for Internet banner advertising is specified as CPM or cost per thousand page impressions.

Critical path. Activities on the critical path are termed critical activities. Any delay in these activities will cause a delay in the project completion time.

Critical Path Method (CPM). Critical Path diagrams show the relationship between activities in a project.

Critical Success Factors (CSFs). CSFs are measures which indicate the performance or efficiency of different parts of an organisation.

Cross-licensing agreement. Cross-licensing agreements allow companies to share patents so that each can produce and market a wider range of products. *See* Patent.

Cybermall. A single Web site which gives online access to goods from a range of shops in a similar way to physical shopping malls enable shoppers to make purchases in one location.

Cyberspace. The prefix cyber indicate a blurring in distinction between humans, machines and communications. Cyberspace is a synonym for Internet.

▶ **D**

Daisy chaining. This describes a method of connecting devices together in series. A new device is added by connecting it directly to the preceding device. The use of a SCSI interface, for example, allows a computer system to be expanded by adding up to seven additional devices. Other methods, such as the Universal Serial Bus connector, can allow up to 127 expansion devices to be connected to a computer system.

Daisywheel printer. The daisywheel printer functions in much the same way as a conventional typewriter. Characters are mounted on hammers arranged in the shape of a wheel. The wheel is rotated until the correct character is in the correct position for printing. As one of the earliest forms of printing technology, daisywheel printers are considered slow and noisy. However, they are also considered inexpensive and reliable. It should be noted that daisywheel printers are unable to print graphics.

Data. Data can be described as a series of facts that have been obtained by observation or research and recorded.

Data dictionary. A repository which is used to store the details of the entities of the database. It will define tables, relations and field details which are sometimes referred to as metadata or 'data about data'.

Data entry form. In an electronic database, a data entry form provides a convenient means of viewing, entering, editing and deleting records.

Data marts. These are small-scale data warehouses which do not hold information across an entire company, rather they focus on one department.

Data migration. Is the transfer of data from the old system to the new system. When data is added to a database, this is known as populating the database.

Data mining. This involves searching organisational databases in order to uncover hidden patterns or relationships in groups of data. Data mining software attempts to represent information in new ways so that previously unseen patterns or trends can be identified.

Data modelling. Data modelling involves considering how to represent data objects within a system, both logically and physically. The entity relationship diagram is used to model the data.

Data Process. A process used to convert data into information. Examples include summarising, classifying and sorting.

Data Processing. This describes the process of handling the large volumes of data that arise from an organisation's daily activities. Although data processing describes a wide range of activities, the most common are transaction processing and process control.

Data Processing (DP) Department. A term commonly used in the 1970s and 1980s to describe the functional area responsible for management of what is now referred to as information systems and applications development. It is interesting to note that the term focuses on the processing of data rather than the application of information. The head of this department was referred to as DP manager rather than Chief Information Officer or IS manager.

Data Protection Act (1998). This legislation sets out to define the rights of organisations and individuals in terms of how personal information is gathered, stored, processed and disclosed. One of the most important aspects of the Act is a focus on the individual's rights to view the information stored on them and ensure that it is accurate.

Data theft. Data theft can involve stealing sensitive information or making unauthorised changes to computer records. *See also* Software theft and Theft.

Data transfer rate. In terms of storage devices, the data transfer rate describes how quickly a device is able to read continuous blocks of data. This figure is normally expressed in terms of kilobytes or megabytes.

Data validation. Data validation is a process to ensure the quality of data by checking it has been entered correctly.

Data views. Different screens of an application which review information in a different form such as table, graph, report or map.

Data warehouses. Data warehouses are large database systems (often measured in gigabytes or terabytes) containing detailed company data on sales transactions which are analysed to assist in improving the marketing and financial performance of companies.

Database. A database can be defined as a collection of related information. The information held in the database is stored in an organised way so that specific items can be selected and retrieved quickly. *See* Database Management System.

Database Management System (DBMS). The information held in an electronic database is accessed via a database management system. A DBMS can be defined as one or more computer programs that allow users to enter, store, organise, manipulate and retrieve data from a database. For many users, the terms database and database management system are interchangeable. A Relational Database Management

System (RDBMS) is an extension of a DBMS and allows data to be combined from a variety of sources.

Dataflow diagrams (DFD). Define the different processes in a system and the information which forms the input and output datastores to the processes. They may be drawn at different levels. Level 0 provides an overview of the system with levels 1 and 2 providing progressively more detail.

Decentralised IS management. Decentralised IS management involves management of some services in individual operating companies or at regional offices.

Decision behaviour. Describes the way in which people make decisions.

Decision Support Systems. Decision support systems provide managers with information needed to support semi-structured or unstructured decisions.

Decision table. A matrix showing all the alternative outcomes of different decisions which occur when certain input conditions occur.

Decision tree. A diagram showing the sequence of events, decisions and consequent actions that occur in a decision-making process.

Deletion anomaly. It is not possible to delete a record from a relation without also losing some other information which might still be required.

Deployment plan. A deployment plan is a schedule which defines all the tasks that need to occur in order for changeover to occur successfully. This includes putting all the infrastructure in place such as cabling and hardware.

Desktop computer. The desktop computer is intended for office use and supports the day-to-day activities of an organisation's employees. These machines tend to be placed in a fixed location and connected permanently to items such as printers, scanners and other devices. The desktop computer is the most common type of microcomputer and is found in the majority of organisations.

Detailed design. Detailed design involves the specification of how an individual component of a system will function in terms of its data input and output, user interface and security.

Development programs. Development programs allow users to develop their own software in order to carry out processing tasks.

Dial-up networking (DUN). Dial-up networking software allows users to access a network at a remote location via a modem. Most home computer users, for example, access the Internet via dial-up networking.

Dialog. An onscreen window (box) which is used by a user to input data or select options.

Digital. Digital data can only represent a finite number of discrete values. For example, at the most basic level, a computer recognises only the values 0 (zero) and 1. Any values *between* 0 and 1, for example 0.15, cannot be represented.

Digital Audio Tape (DAT). A storage medium that combines some of the characteristics of magnetic tape and compact disc. Digital audio tape couples high storage capacities with improved speed and reliability.

Digital camera. A digital camera captures and stores still images in much the same way as a traditional camera. Images are held in the camera's memory or stored on disk until they can be transferred to a personal computer. The image is recorded using a charge-coupled device which recognises the different colours and intensity of light in the image.

Digital certificates. A method of ensuring privacy on the Internet. Certificates consist of a private key for encrypting data or documents and a corresponding public key for reading the data. An independent certification authority issues public and private keys. Basis for SET.

Digital ID. A Digital ID provides a means of confirming the identity of a specific user through the use of a small data file called a personal certificate. The certificate contains encrypted information relating to the user's identity.

Digital Versatile Disc (previously refered to as **Digital Video Disk) (DVD).** Although superficially similar to CD-ROM, DVD devices offer two important benefits to users. First, the discs used by a DVD player offer extremely high storage capacities, typically between 4Gb and 7Gb. Second, data held on DVD can be accessed at very high speeds. One of the most common applications for DVD as a distribution medium for full-length feature films. *See* CD-ROM.

Disaster recovery company. These maintain copies of important data on behalf of an organisation. They may also provide a service which can immediately supply replacement systems.

Direct capture. This describes a method of acquiring and storing data automatically with little or no human intervention. As an example, the sensors on an automated production line can be described as direct capture devices.

Direct file access. Random or Direct file access allows any record to be read or written.

Document Image Processing (DIP). DIP systems are used in industry to convert printed documents into an electronic format so that they can be stored, organised and retrieved more easily.

Documentation. Software documentation refers to end-user guidance such as the user guide and technical maintenance documentation such as design and test specifications.

Documentation review. Use information on existing systems such as user guides, or requirements specifications together with paper or onscreen forms used to collect information such as sales order forms.

Domain name. Refers to the name of the web server and is usually selected to be the same as the name of the company and the extension will indicate its type. The extension is also commonly known as the Global Top Level Domain (gTLD).

http://www.domain-name.extension/filename.htm

Dongle. This describes a hardware device used to prevent unauthorised copies of a program being made. The hardware 'key' must be connected to the computer in order for the software to function.

Document image processing (DIP). DIP applications are used to convert documents into pictures or images so that they can be stored directly to compact disc or tape.

Dot-matrix printer. The dot-matrix printer arranges a series of pins to form the shape of a required character. The character is transferred to the paper by striking the pins against an ink ribbon. The greater the number of pins used, the more detailed the character can be produced. As one of the earliest forms of printing technology, dot-matrix printers are considered slow and noisy. However, they are also considered inexpensive and reliable.

Dots per inch (DPI). The quality of a printer's output is normally measured in dots per inch. This describes the number of individual dots that can be printed within a space of one square inch. Quality is normally compared against professional typesetting, such as the equipment used to produce a book or magazine.

Dot pitch. This describes a common method of gauging the quality of a monitor's display and involves measuring the distance – known as the dot pitch – between the pixels on the screen. The smaller the distance between pixels, the finer the image will appear.

Dynamic systems development methodology (DSDM). A methodology which describes how RAD can be approached.

▶ **E**

Early adopter. Early adopters are companies or departments who invest in new technologies when they first become available in an attempt to gain a competitive advantage despite the risk with deploying new systems.

Economic feasibility. An assessment of the costs and benefits of different solutions to select that which gives the best value. (Will the new system cost more than the expected benefits?)

Editing. The process of entering or correcting text is known as editing.

Effort time. Effort time is the total amount of work that needs to occur to complete a task.

Elapsed time. Elapsed time indicates how long in time (such as calendar days) the task will take (duration).

Electronic commerce. Transactions of goods or services for which payment occurs over the Internet or other wide-area networks.

Electronic data interchange (EDI). The electronic exchange of information between businesses using wide area network. EDI transactions transfer structured data such as an electronic payment and also documents.

Electronic document management software (EDMS). Systems that convert documents into a digital format which allows storage, retrieval and manipulation of the document on computer.

Electronic eavesdropping. This describes the act of gaining access to confidential information by intercepting or monitoring communications traffic. *See also* Computer monitoring.

Electronic mail (e-mail). E-mail can be defined as the transmission of a message over a communications network.

Electronic meeting systems. This describes a category of Office Automation Systems that seeks to improve communications between individuals and groups. Examples of these systems include those that support teleconferencing, teleworking and group work. *See* Office Automation Systems.

Electronic publishing systems. This describes a category of Office Automation Systems that supports the production of documents, such as letters, reports and catalogues. Some of the typical programs used include wordprocessors and desktop publishing packages. *See* Office Automation Systems.

End-user computing (EUC). End-user computing includes all uses of computers by business people who are not Information Systems professionals. This may range from use of business applications through spreadsheet modelling through to developing programs to solve specific problems.

End-user development (EUD). End-user development is programming undertaken by non IS staff. It typically involves development of small applications for solving departmental problems rather than cross-departmental applications.

End-user IT services. These include all services required to support end-users in running their PCs and applications.

Enterprise resource planning (ERP) software. A software system with integrated functions for all major business functions across an organisation such as production, distribution, sales, finance and human resources management. It is normally purchased as an off-the-shelf package which is tailored by a consultant. A single package typically replaces many different previous packages.

Environment. This describes the surroundings of system. The environment of system can contain other systems and external agencies.

Eraseable programmable read only memory (EPROM). This is a form of ROM memory that retains its contents until changed using a special device known as a 'burner'. *See* Read-Only Memory.

Error rate. In many cases, it may be acceptable if an input device generates a certain number of errors. This is often referred to as the error rate and the acceptable level will vary according to the input device being used and the business application. Optical character recognition, for example, is generally considered a comparatively unreliable means of entering data. At present, a typical OCR software package will have an error rate of between 5 and 10 per cent.

Errors per KLOC. Errors per KLOC (thousands of line of code) is the basic defect measure used in systems development.

Estimation. Estimation allows the project manager to plan for the resources required for project execution through establishing the number and size of tasks that need to be completed in the project.

Ethics. In general terms, ethics describes beliefs concerning right and wrong that can be used by individuals to guide their behaviour. *See* Morality and Professionalism.

Executive information systems (EIS). These systems are used by senior management to select, retrieve and manage information that can be used to support the achievement of an organisation's business objectives. They need not be directly concerned with decision-making activities, but can help senior managers to become more efficient and productive in a number of other ways, for example by helping them to manage their time more efficiently.

Expansion card. Expansion cards can be used to extend a computer's capabilities by adding new devices to the system. An expansion card usually takes the form of a small circuit board that can be inserted into an expansion slot on the computer's motherboard. Some examples of expansion cards include modems, graphics cards and sound cards.

Expert systems. Expert systems are used to represent the knowledge, decision-making skills of specialists so that non-specialists can take decisions. They encapsulate the knowledge of experts by providing tools for the acquisition of knowledge, representation of rules and their enactment as decisions.

Export. The process of saving a file in a format compatible with another software package is known as exporting.

Extended Industry Standard Architecture (EISA). Standard superseding the 16 bit interface of ISA with 32 bit data transfer between CPU and motherboard. *See* Expansion card and Motherboard.

Extranet. An intranet with restricted access which is extended to suppliers, collaborators or customers.

▶ **F**

Fax-modem. A fax-modem combines the capabilities of a modem with the ability to send and receive fax transmissions.

Fax-on-demand. A service that allows users to select from a range of documents by using the keys on the telephone handset. Once a document has been selected, the system automatically telephones the user's fax machine and transmits the document.

Feasibility assessment. The feasibility study is the activity that occurs at the start of the project to ensure that the project is a viable business proposition. The feasibility report analyses the need for and impact of the system and considers different alternatives for acquiring software.

Feasibility assessment context. Input: Idea for initiation of a new information system.
Output: Feasibility report and recommendation to proceed.

Federation Against Software Theft (FAST). An organisation formed to act against software piracy. *See* Software theft.

Feedback. A feedback mechanism provides information on the performance of a system. An example of feedback might include quality control measurements taken on a production line.

Feedback control. In feedback closed-loop control systems the control loop compares the output of the process to the desired output and if a difference is found, adjusts the input or process accordingly.

Feedforward control. Feedforward incorporate a prediction element in the control feedback loop.

Field. The data in an electronic database is organised by fields and records. A field is a single item of information, such as a name or a quantity.

File attachment. E-mail messages can be used to transmit data files to other users. Files can be attached to messages and transmitted in the usual way. All types of data can be sent in this way including wordprocessor files, spreadsheet data, graphics and database files.

Filter. In a spreadsheet or database, a filter can be used to remove data from the screen temporarily. This allows users to work with a specific group of records. Filters do not alter or delete data but simply hide any unwanted items.

Firewalls. This is a specialised software application mounted on a server at the point the company is connected to the Internet. Its purpose is to prevent unauthorised access into the company from outsiders. Firewalls are essential for all companies hosting their own Web server.

First Normal Form (1NF). Transforming unnormalised data into its first normal form state involves the removal of repeating groups of data.

Flat file database. A flat file database can be described as being self-contained since it contains only one type of record – or table – and cannot access data held in other database files.

Flexible Manufacturing Systems (FMS). A group of machines with programmable controllers linked by an automated materials handling system and integrated by an IS that enables a variety of parts with similar processing requirements to be manufactured.

Floppy disk. Consists of a plastic disk, coated with a magnetic covering and enclosed within a rigid plastic case.

Font. The type face used in a document is referred to as the font. The size of the characters used is referred to as the point size.

Foreign (secondary) key fields. These fields are used to link tables together by referring to the primary key in another database table.

Form. An onscreen equivalent of a paper form which is used for entering data and will have validation routines to help improve the accuracy of the entered data.

Formal communication. Formal communication involves presenting information in a structured and consistent manner. Such information is normally created for a specific purpose, making it likely to be more comprehensive, accurate and relevant than information transmitted using information communication. An example of formal communication is an accounting statement. *See* Informal communication.

Form dimension. This describes several characteristics of information quality related to how the information is presented to the recipient. Among these characteristics are clarity, level of detail and the order of information. As an example, information may be considered to be of high quality if it is presented in a clear and consistent fashion (clarity). Other dimensions of information characteristics include time and content. *See* Time dimension, Content dimension.

Formula. In a spreadsheet, a formula is a calculation that is entered by the user and performed automatically by the spreadsheet program.

Free-form database. A free form database allows users to store information in the form of brief notes or passages of text. Each item held can be placed within a category or assigned one or more key words. Information is organised and retrieved by using categories or key words.

Freeware. The author of a Freeware program allows users to copy, distribute and use the software free of charge. However, although the author has waived copyright to the software, the user is often required to abide by conditions of use. *See also* Shareware.

FTP file transfer. The File Transfer Protocol is used as a standard for moving files across the Internet. The most common use is for releasing fixes to software applications. Documents can be transferred by this means. FTP is available as a feature of Web browsers for downloading files.

Full backup. A method of producing backup copies of important data files. A full backup includes all data files considered to be important. *See also* Incremental backup.

Function. In a spreadsheet, a function is a built-in command that carries out a calculation or action automatically.

Functional testing. Testing of particular functions or modules either following a test script or working through the module systematically.

Functionality. A term used to describe whether software has the features necessary to support the business requirements.

Function point analysis. A method of estimating the time it will take to build a system by counting up the number of functions and data inputs and outputs and then comparing to completed projects.

▶ G

Gantt charts. Show the duration of parallel and sequential activities in a project as horizontal bars on a chart.

Geographical information system (GIS). Uses maps to display information about different geographic locations such as catchments or branches. They are commonly used for performance analysis by marketing staff.

Gigabyte (Gb). A measure of storage capacity. Approximately 1000Mb, or the equivalent of one billion characters.

Global business. The Global business is a company which operates in several countries which uses information technology to assist in the control of operation and performance in each country.

Goal seeking. In a spreadsheet, goal seeking describes a way of automatically changing the values in a formula until a desired result is achieved.

Grandfather, father, son. A common procedure used for creating backup copies of important data files.

Graphics accelerator card. A type of graphics card containing its own memory and featuring a coprocessor. The coprocessor reduces the burden placed on the CPU by taking over the intensive calculations needed to produce complex graphical displays.

Graphics tablet. A graphics tablet is used in the same way as a writing pad. A stylus is used to draw images on a rigid pad located near to the computer. As the user draws with the stylus, the image is duplicated on the computer's display.

Graphical user interface (GUI). A graphical user interface allows the user to control the operation of a computer program or item of computer hardware using a pointing device, such as a mouse. In general, commands are issued by selecting items from menus, buttons and icons. *See* Icon, WIMP.

Groupware. Software which enables information and decision making to be shared by people collaborating within and between businesses.

▶ H

Hacker. Hackers are often described as individuals who seek to break into systems as a test of their abilities. Few hackers attempt to cause damage to the systems they access and few are interested in gaining some sort of financial profit.

Hardware. Describes the physical components of a computer system. The hardware of a computer system can be said to consist of: input devices, memory, central processing unit, output devices and storage devices.

Hard data. *See* Quantitative data.

Hard disk. A magnetic media that stores data upon a number of rigid platters that are rotated at very high speeds.

Hierarchical systems. Systems are hierarchical in nature, being made up of subsystems that may themselves be made up of other subsystems.

Hits. A measure of individual files delivered to the browser when requesting a URL. Hits usually overstate access to a Web page. Page-impressions and ad-impressions are more accurate.

Human activity system. A human activity system can be defined as a 'notional system (i.e. not existing in any tangible form) where human beings are undertaking some activities that achieve some purpose' (Patching, 1990).

Human computer interaction (HCI) design. HCI involves the study of methods for designing the input and output of information systems to ensure they are 'user-friendly'.

Hypertext. Hypertext is highlighted words or phrases that represent links to other documents activated by clicking the mouse.

Hypertext database. In a hypertext database, information is stored as series of objects and can consist of text, graphics, numerical data and multimedia data. Any object can be linked to any other, allowing users to store disparate information in an organised manner.

Hypertext Markup Language (HTML). HTML is the method used to create Web pages and documents. The HTML code used to construct pages has codes or tags such as <TITLE> to indicate to the browser what is displayed.

▶ I

IBM-compatible. The modern personal computer found in most business organisations developed from a family of personal computers launched by IBM in the early 1980s. The IBM-compatible computer is considered the standard for general business use.

Icon. An icon is a graphical representation of an object such as a disk drive or document. Within a graphical user interface, users are able to manipulate icons in order to issue instructions. As an example, in order to copy a file from a floppy disk to a hard disk drive, the user might place an icon representing the file above an icon that represents the hard disk drive. The graphical user interface would interpret and carry out the instruction without further interaction with the user. *See* Graphical User Interface.

If Then Else statement. These are common within programs since they govern the different actions taken by the program according to a condition. They are usually in the form:

IF Condition Then

   Action if condition is TRUE

Else

   Action if condition is FALSE

End If

Image processing systems. This describes a category of Office Automation Systems that allows users to create, edit, store and retrieve documents in electronic format. Document Image Processing (DIP) is an example of an image processing systems. *See* Office Automation Systems.

Immediate cutover (big bang) changeover. Immediate cutover is when a new system becomes operational and operations transfer immediately from the previous system.

Import. The process of loading a file created with another package is known as importing.

Incremental backup. A method of producing backup copies of important data files. An incremental backup includes only those files that have changed in some way since the last backup was made. *See* Full backup.

Index. In an electronic database, an index stores information concerning the order of the records in the database. The index lists the locations of records but does not alter the actual order of the database.

Industry Standard Architecture (ISA). This describes a common standard governing the way in which an expansion card interacts with a computer's motherboard and CPU. *See* Expansion card and Motherboard.

Informal communication. This describes information that is transmitted by informal means, such as casual conversations between members of staff. The information transmitted in this way is often less structured and less detailed than information transmitted by formal communication. In addition, the information may be inconsistent or may contain inaccuracies. Furthermore, the information may also include a subjective element, such as personal opinions. *See* Formal communication.

Information. Data that has been processed so that they are meaningful.

Information centre (IC). An IC is a central facility in an organisation which provides end user services such as phone support for troubleshooting end user software and hardware problems, training, guidance on end user development and management of user information.

Information flow diagram (IFD). A simple diagram showing how information is routed between different parts of an organisation. It has an information focus rather than a process focus.

Information kiosk. A multimedia system usually integrated with a touch screen to provide information for retail or community applications such as libraries or local government is known as information kiosk.

Information leadership. Information leadership involves enhancing a product or service with an organisation's specialised information or expertise. In many cases, organisations achieve information leadership by selling information or expertise in the form of a separate product. A good example might be selling a mailing list created from an organisation's customer database.

Information need. The object of producing information is to meet a specific purpose or requirement.

Information quality. Information considered to be of high quality will display a number of characteristics. These characteristics can be grouped into time, content and form dimensions. *See* Time dimension, Content dimension, Form dimension.

Information reporting systems (IRS). These systems are used to generate reports containing information that can be used to support managerial decision making.

Information society. The information society is a term that has been coined to describe a modern population that is conversant with – and reliant upon – information and communications technology.

Information system. This describes a system designed to produce information that can be used to support the activities of managers and other workers.

Information systems acquisition. Acquisition describes the method of obtaining an information system for a business. The main choices are off the shelf (packaged), bespoke applications developed by an in-house IT department or a software house or end-user developed systems.

Information warrior. Information warriors seek to obtain data by any means necessary. Such people may resort to illegal methods, such as hacking, in order to obtain the information they require. However, the information obtained may not necessarily be used in pursuit of criminal activities.

Initiation phase. The startup phase in an IS development project. Its aims are to establish whether the project is feasible and then prepare to ensure the project is successful. Input: Creative thought and/or systematic evaluation of IS needs. Output: Idea for initiation of a new information system.

Inkjet printer. An inkjet printer uses a print-head containing 50 or more small nozzles. Each nozzle can be controlled individually by electrostatic charges produced by the printer. Characters are formed by squirting small droplets of ink directly onto the paper. Inkjets are considered relatively inexpensive, near silent in operation and capable of producing good-quality results. It should be noted that inkjet printers also represent an economical means of printing in colour.

Input. The input to a system can be thought of as the raw materials for a process that will produce a particular output. Examples of inputs might include data, knowledge, raw materials, machinery and premises.

Input design. Input design includes the design of user input through onscreen forms, but also other methods of data entry such as import by file, transfer from another system or specialised data capture methods such as bar-code scanning, optical or voice recognition techniques.

Input device. Input devices are used to enter data, information or instructions into a computer-based information system.

Insertion anomaly. It is not possible to insert a new occurrence record into a relation (table) without having to also insert one into another relation first.

Intangible assets. Intangible assets describe the non-physical resources owned by a company. Intangible assets are also known as conceptual resources. Examples include knowledge, experience and judgement.

Intangible value. A value or benefit that is difficult or impossible to quantify.

Integrated Services Digital Network (ISDN). ISDN represents a standard for communications that allows data transfer rates that are up to five times faster than a 56600 bps modem. An ISDN telephone line provides two separate 'channels' allowing simultaneous voice and data transmissions. Since ISDN lines transmit digital data, a modem is not required to make use of the service. Instead, a special terminal adapter (often called an ISDN modem) is used to pass data between the computer and the ISDN line. *See* Modem and Baud rate.

Intellectual property. Intellectual property is a generic term used to describe designs, ideas and inventions. In general, intellectual property covers the following areas: patents, trade marks, designs and copyright.

Interactive kiosk. A typical application for touch screen systems, an interactive kiosk allows a user to purchase items or browse through a list of products by pressing buttons or other controls shown on the screen. Such kiosks are often found in banks, music stores and large catalogue stores. Many bookings systems, such as those used by airlines, theatres and travel agents, also make use of touch screens. *See* Touch screen.

Interdependence. Interdependence means that a change to one part of a system leads to or results from changes to one or more other parts.

Interface. In terms of systems, the interface describes the exchanges between a system and its environment or the system and other systems. In the field of Information Technology, the interface describes ways in which information is exchanged between users and computer software or hardware.

Interlaced. An interlaced display is one where each complete image shown on a monitor's display is drawn in two steps. A non-interlaced monitor refreshes the display in a single pass. A good-quality monitor is normally capable of supporting a non-interlaced display at a refresh rate of 70Hz or more.

Interoperability. A general term used to describe how easily different components of a system can be integrated.

Internal rate of return (IRR). A discounted cashflow technique used to assess the return of a project by considering the interest rate which would produce an NPV of zero.

Internet. The Internet refers to the physical network that links computers across the globe. It consists of the infrastructure of servers and communication links between them which is used to hold and transport the vast amount of information on the Internet.

Internet relay chat (IRC). This is a synchronous communications tool which allows a text based 'chat' between different users who are logged on at the same time. It is not used for many business applications since asynchronous discussions are more practical – not all team members need to be present at the same time.

Internet service provider (ISP). Companies which provide access to the Internet and Web page hosting for home and business users. Online service providers access to the Internet plus their own content.

Interpreted. An interpreted computer program can be run directly, without the need for compilation. As the program runs, each instruction is taken in turn and converted into machine language by a command interpreter.

Interstitial. A small, rectangular area within a Web page used for advertising. May be animated or static.

Interviewing. Recommended practice: a range of staff are interviewed using structured techniques to identify features and problems of the current system and required features of the future system.

Intranet. An intranet uses Web servers, browsers and e-mail within a company to share company information and software applications. The intranet is only accessible to company employees.

▶ **J**

Java. An object-oriented programming language standard supported by Sun Microsystems which permits complex and graphical customer applications to be written and then accessed from a Web browser. An example might be a form for calculating interest on a loan. A competitor to Active-X.

Javascript. A simple scripting programming language, which offers a subset of the features of the Java programming language.

Joypad. The joypad is similar to the joystick but uses a flat pad that is pressed with the fingertips. The pad tilts in the direction it is pressed and gives a wide range of movement.

Justification. In a wordprocessor, the alignment of text with the left and right margins can be controlled by specifying the justification. Text can be left justified, right justified or fully justified.

▶ **K**

Kilobyte (Kb). A measure of storage capacity. Approximately 1000 bytes, or the equivalent of 1000 characters.

▶ **L**

Label printer. This describes a type of printer that is designed specifically for producing printed labels. Such printers normally require special media, such as sheets containing rows of adhesive labels. One of the most common uses for label printers is in producing labels containing bar codes. *See* SCSI and USB.

Laser printer. The laser printer is commonly used for business applications requiring a combination of speed with high print quality.

Legacy system. When a new computer-based information system is developed, it may be necessary to retain hardware – but more often software – from the earlier system. In these cases, the software that has been retained is referred to as a legacy system.

Lightpen. A lightpen is a pointing device that can be used to control applications by pointing to items on the screen. Lightpens are also used for applications involving graphics, such as drawing packages, since images can be drawn directly onto the screen. *See* Pointing device.

Line printer. A line printer processes a document one line at a time. In contrast, a page printer processes a document one entire page at a time.

Live (production) environment. The term used to described the setup of the system (hardware, software and office environment) where the software will be used in the business.

Local-area network (LAN). A LAN is a computer network that spans a limited geographic area, typically a single office or building. A LAN consists of a single network segment or several connected segments which are limited in extent.

Logic bomb. Sometimes also known as a time bomb, a logic bomb is a destructive computer program that activates at a certain time or in reaction to a specific event.

Low level language. A low level programming language requires the programmer to work directly with the hardware of the computer system. Instructions are normally entered in machine code or assembly language.

▶ **M**

Machine language. This describes the natural language of a computer. Machine language instructions are made up of binary digits and use only the values of 0 (zero) and 1.

Machine oriented. A machine oriented programming language focuses on the requirements of the computer hardware being used, where programs are produced in a form that suits the way in which the microprocessor functions.

Macro. A macro is a sequence of instructions that can be used to automate complex or repetitive tasks. Macros can be used to emulate a sequence of keys pressed on the keyboard or can be programmed so that they can carry out more complicated processes.

Magnetic ink character recognition (MICR). This involves capturing data that has been printed using a special magnetic ink. This technology is normally associated with the banking industry, especially cheque processing. Some of the details on a cheque, such as

the cheque number, are printed in a special typeface using magnetic ink. The shape of each character means that it can be recognised by its magnetic field.

Mainframe. A traditional view of computing saw three main categories of computers: mainframes, minicomputers and microcomputers. Mainframes were considered the most powerful computers and were used for large-scale data processing.

Management Information Systems. These systems provide feedback on organisational activities and help to support managerial decision making.

Materials Requirements Planning (MRP) Software. MRP software is used to plan the production of goods in a manufacturing organisation by obtaining components, scheduling operations and controlling production. MRP II integrates the information system with other functional areas in the business such as finance and marketing.

McFarlan's Strategic Grid. This model is used to indicate the strategic importance of information systems to a company now and in the future.

Megabyte (Mb). A measure of storage capacity. Approximately 1000Kb, or the equivalent of one million characters.

Memory. Computer memory is used as a temporary means of storing data and instructions. Memory is used to store data awaiting processing, instructions used to process data or control the computer system, and data or information that has been processed.

Metadata. Reference data describing the structure and content of data in a data warehouse is known as metadata.

Microcomputer. A traditional view of computing saw three main categories of computers: mainframes, minicomputers and microcomputers. Microcomputers were considered less powerful than other types of computer but were more flexible and relatively inexpensive to purchase.

Middleware. A type of software that acts as a layer between other software to assist in data transfer between incompatible systems.

Milestone. This denotes a significant event in the project such as completion of a prototype.

Minicomputer. A traditional view of computing saw three main categories of computers: mainframes, minicomputers and microcomputers. Minicomputers offered an intermediate stage between the power of mainframe systems and the relatively low cost of microcomputer systems.

Modelling. Modelling involves creating a numerical representation of an *existing* situation or set of circumstances, while simulation involves *predicting* new situations or circumstances. In both cases, a model is produced that provides a numerical representation of the situation or circumstances being studied. Modelling and simulation are common activities carried out with the use of spreadsheet software. *See* Spreadsheet.

Modem (Modulator-Demodulator). A modem is a communications device that allows users to send and receive data via an ordinary telephone line. *See also* Fax-modem.

Module design. Detailed design involves the specification of how an individual component of a system will function in terms of its data input and output, user interface and security.

Module or Unit testing. Individual modules are tested to ensure they function correctly for given inputs.

Monitoring and control. Monitoring involves ensuring the project is working to plan once it is started. Control is taking corrective action if the project deviates from the plan.

Morality. In general terms, morality is concerned with individual character or personality and beliefs governing right and wrong. *See* Ethics and Professionalism.

Motherboard. The motherboard is the main circuit board within a computer and houses the processor, memory, expansion slots and a number of connectors used for attaching additional devices, such as a hard disk drive.

Mouse. A pointing device found on most modern personal computers. Moving the mouse over a flat surface causes a corresponding movement to a small pointer on the screen. Selections, such as menu items, are made by clicking one of the buttons on the mouse. *See* Pointing device.

Multidimensional data. Data broken down in analysis for a data warehouse into dimensions such as time period, product segment and the geographical location. Dimensions are broken down into categories. For time these could be months, quarters or years.

Multimedia. Multimedia can be defined as the combination of several media under the control of an interactive computer program. Such media can include text, graphics, sound, video and animation. In terms of computer hardware, a multimedia computer will incorporate a CD-ROM drive and sound card. In addition, current standards for multimedia computers specify minimum graphics capabilities and processor speed.

Multi-user testing. The effect of different users accessing the same customer or stock record is tested. Software should not permit two users to modify the same data at the same time.

▶ N

Natural keyboard. A variation on the conventional computer keyboard, a natural keyboard has the keys arranged so that users can locate them more quickly and easily. The keyboard itself is often shaped in a way that makes prolonged use more comfortable.

Navigating. The act of moving from one section of the Internet to another.

Net PC. A hybrid between a traditional PC and an NC, it will usually feature no floppy or hard-drive and limited memory and processor since it will use the power of the server to provide applications.

Net present value (NPV). A measure of the return from a system which takes into account the variation in monetary value through time.

Network computer (NC). The purpose of the network computer is to provide access to a network system, such as the Internet, at minimal cost. A typical network computer will feature limited disk storage, memory and expansion potential. In addition, the computer may also feature an older, less powerful processor than its desktop counterpart. Network computers are often associated with the thin client architecture and the concept of zero administration. *See* Thin client and Zero administration.

Network interface card. A network interface card is an expansion card that allows a personal computer to be connected to a network. The network card deals with all communications between the network and the computer.

Network operating system (NOS). This describes the software needed to operate and manage a network system.

Network topology. The physical layout of a LAN is known as a network topology. Bus, star, ring and combinations are most common.

Neural networks. These systems use a similar process to biological intelligence to learn problem solving skills by 'training' or exposure to a wide range of problems. The learning occurs through interactions between nodes which are similar to the neurons of the brain.

Nolan's stage model. This model is a six-stage maturity model for the application of information systems to a business.

Non-interlaced. An interlaced display is one where each complete image shown on a monitor's display is drawn in two steps. A non-interlaced monitor refreshes the display in a single pass. A good-quality monitor is normally capable of supporting a non-interlaced display at a refresh rate of 70Hz or more.

Non-volatile memory. The memory found in a personal computer is considered volatile, that is, anything held in memory is lost once the power to the computer system is switched off. However, non-volatile memory retains its contents until altered or erased.

Normalisation. This design activity is a procedure which is used to optimise the physical storage of data within a database. It involves simplification of entities and minimisation of duplication of data.

Notebook. A small portable computer, which is approximately the size of a sheet of A4 paper.

▶ **O**

Object-oriented database. An object-oriented approach to database design employs the concept of reusable objects in order to develop sophisticated or complex applications. An object combines data structures with any functions needed to manipulate the object or the data it holds.

Object-oriented design. This is a design technique which involves basing the design of software on real-world objects which consist of both data and the procedures that process it rather than traditional design where procedures operate on separate data.

Observation. This analysis technique is useful for identifying inefficiencies in an existing way of working either with a computer-based or manual information system. It involves timing how long particular operations take and observing the method used to perform them. It can be time consuming and the staff who are observed may behave differently to normal.

Off-the-shelf purchase or packaged software. An acquisition method which involves direct purchase of a pre-written application used by more than one company.

Offline. When a user is not connected to their Internet account, they are said to be offline.

Office automation systems. In business organisations, productivity software is often used to reduce the time needed to complete routine administrative tasks, such as producing documents or organising meetings. By attempting to automate many of the activities carried out within a typical office, organisations seek to improve efficiency, reduce costs and enhance internal communications. Computer-based information systems used in this way are generally referred to as office automation systems.

Office management systems. This describes a category of Office Automation Systems that assists users in scheduling projects and tasks. Examples of office management systems include Personal Information Managers (PIM) and project management software. *See* Office Automation Systems.

Online. When a user is connected to their Internet account, usually by a modem link, they are said to be online.

Online analytical processing (OLAP). OLAP can be considered to be a synonym for a data warehouse. It refers to the ability to analyse in real time the type of multidimensional information stored in data warehouses. The term online indicates the users can formulate their own queries compared to standard paper reports. The originator of OLAP, Dr E.Codd, defines it as the dynamic synthesis, analysis, and consolidation of large volumes of multidimensional data.

Open loop control system. An open loop control system is one in which there is an attempt to reach the system objective, but no control action to modify the inputs or process is taken once the process has begun.

Open Profiling Standard. A standard method of collecting personal details about customers. An initiative, begun by Netscape and Firefly, now supported by many players including Microsoft. The Web reference is http://www.firefly.net/OPS/OPS.html. This includes a demographics section.

Open system. Interaction occurs with elements beyond the system boundary.

Open systems interconnection (OSI) model. An international standard defining connectivity of links between computers at different levels.

Open questions. Not restricted to a limited range of answers such as Yes/No (closed questions). Asked to elicit opinions or ideas for the new system or identify commonly held views among staff. Open questions are not typically used for quantitative analysis, but can be used to identify a common problem.

Operating environment. This describes a number of programs intended to simplify the way in which users work with the operating system. Early versions of *Windows*, for example, provided a graphical user interface that removed the need for users to work with the more complex aspects of MS-DOS.

Operating system (OS). The operating system interacts with the hardware of the computer at a very low level in order to manage and direct the computer's resources. The basic functions of the operating system include: allocating and managing system resources, scheduling the use of resources and monitoring the activities of the computer system.

Operational feasibility. An assessment of how the new system will affect the daily working practices within the organisation. (Is the system workable on a day-to-day basis?)

Operations information systems. These systems are generally concerned with process control, transaction processing, communications (internal and external) and productivity.

Optical character recognition (OCR). Optical character recognition involves using software that attempts to recognise individual characters. An optical scanner is normally used to capture an image of a document. As the image is processed, the OCR program creates a text file containing all of the characters recognised. This file can then be edited further using a wordprocessor, text editor or other suitable program. *See* Optical scanner.

Optical mark recognition (OMR). A variation on optical character recognition is optical mark recognition, which involves detecting and recognising simple marks made on a document. *See* Optical Character Recognition.

Optical scanner. The optical scanner can be used to capture graphics and text from printed documents. A photograph, for example, can be captured and converted into a form suitable for use with a number of different applications. Images captured in this way are normally incorporated into wordprocessing or desktop publishing documents.

Organisational culture. This concept includes shared values, unwritten rules and assumptions within the organisation as well as the practices that all groups share. Corporate cultures are created when a group of employees interact over time and are relatively successful in what they undertake.

Organisational feasibility. Reviews how well the solution meets the needs of the business and anticipates problems such as hostility to the system if insufficient training occurs. (Considers the effect of change given a companies culture and politics.)

Outline design. A high-level definition of the different components that make up the architecture of a system and how they interact.

Output. An output is a finished product that is created by a system. Examples include information, products and services.

Output design. Output design involves specifying how production of onscreen reports and paper-based reports will occur. Output may occur to database or file for storing information entered or also for use by other systems.

Output devices. Output devices translate the results of processing – output – into a human readable form.

Outsourcing. Outsourcing occurs when all or part of the information systems services of a company are sub-contracted to a third party.

▶ **P**

Packaged software. An acqusition method that involves direct purchase of a pre-written application used by more than one company.

Packets. Units of data that are exchanged between different devices over communications media. The entire message to be sent is broken down into smaller packets since if an error occurs in transmission, only the packet with the error needs to be re-transmitted.

Page impressions. Number of occasions a single page has been delivered to a user. Several hits may be recorded during one page impression according to the number of separate graphics and text blocks that need to be downloaded.

Page printer. A page printer processes a document one entire page at a time. In general, page printers are capable of printing documents quickly and at high quality. In contrast, line printers process a document one line at a time.

Page requests. *See* Page impressions.

Pages per minute (ppm). This describes a simple means of measuring the speed of a printer. The speed of a page printer, such as a laser printer or modern inkjet model, is measured in terms of pages per minute.

Pages per month. Manufacturers often provide ratings for their printers that describe the typical workload appropriate for a given model. This value is often described in terms of pages per month.

Paint programs. Paint programs serve the same purpose as a sketch pad or easel and enable users to produce drawings using a variety of different techniques.

Parallel port. A type of connector that allows various devices to be attached to a computer system. Examples of common parallel devices include printers and external storage devices.

Parallel running. This changeover method involves the old and new system operating together at the same time until the company is certain the new system works.

Patent. A patent provides its owner with a monopoly allowing them to exploit their invention without competition. The protection offered by a patent lasts for a number of years but does not begin until the patent has been granted.

Payback period. The period after the initial investment, before the company achieves a net benefit.

Peer to peer network. A simple type of Local Area network which provides sharing of files and peripherals between PCs.

Peripheral component interconnect (PCI). This describes a common standard governing the way in which an expansion card interacts with a computer's motherboard and CPU. PCI devices often support the Plug and Play installation of devices. *See* Expansion card, Plug and Play and Motherboard.

Personal certificate. A data file containing encrypted information relating to the user's identity.

Personal digital assistant (PDA). A PDA can be thought of as a sophisticated personal organiser. It is normally a handheld device, often no larger than a pocket calculator. The purpose of the PDA is to help users manage their time more efficiently and effectively. The typical functions of a PDA can include: address book, appointment scheduler, calculator, expenses tracking, currency conversion, alarm clock, world time display and a variety of other features that allow users to store notes, such as to-do lists.

Personal information manager (PIM). A PIM can be thought as an electronic personal organiser. The program allows users to store, organise and retrieve personal information such as appointments, personal expenses, telephone numbers and addresses, reminders and to-do lists.

Phased implementation. This changeover method involves introducing different modules of the new system sequentially.

Photo-editing packages. Photo-editing packages enable users to capture, view and edit scanned images.

Physical resources. Physical resources are the tangible resources owned by a company. Examples include land, buildings and plant. Physical resources are also known as tangible assets.

Pilot system. The system is trialled in a more limited area before it is deployed more extensively across the business.

Plotter. A plotter uses a number of different coloured pens to draw lines upon the paper as it moves through the machine. Although capable of producing

characters, the quality of the text created is often very poor. Plotters are primarily used to create technical drawings, such as engineering diagrams but can also be used to record the results of the continuous monitoring of various events by creating charts. Some cardiac monitors, for example, use a simple plotter device to produce charts showing a patient's heart activity over time.

Plug and play (PnP). This describes a means by which expansion cards can be added to a computer system and configured automatically without the user needing to enter settings or make other changes. *See* Expansion card.

Plug-in. A plug-in is a small program or accessory that can be used to extend a Web browser's capabilities. For example, a number of different plug-ins exist that allow a Web browser to display video or animation sequences.

Pointing device. An input device that allows the user to control the movement of a small pointer displayed on the screen. The pointer can be used to carry out actions by selecting items from a menu or manipulating icons.

Portable computer. The portable computer is largely self-contained, featuring its own power supply, keyboard, pointing device and visual display unit. Variations on the portable computer include the notebook and sub-notebook.

Portal. Sites which provide the main method of access to other Web sites through providing services to locate information on the WWW are now commonly referred to as portals. Such portals are often set to the default or home page of the user's Web browser. Examples of portals include Yahoo (www.yahoo.com), Microsoft's MSN (www.msn.com) and the Netscape Netcenter (home.netscape.com).

Porter and Millar's Five forces model. Porter and Millar's Five forces model is for analysing the different competitive forces which impact on an organisation. The five forces are: rivalry between existing competitors, threat of new entrants, threat of substitutes, the power of buyers and the power of suppliers.

Positive and negative feedback. Negative feedback is used to describe the act of reversing any discrepancy between desired and actual output. Positive feedback responds to a variance between desired and actual output by increasing that variance.

Post implementation review. A meeting that occurs after a system is operational to review the success of the project and learn lessons for the future.

Power supply unit (PSU). All modern personal computers feature a power supply unit used to convert

AC current into DC current. The PSU regulates the amount of power supplied to the motherboard and any other devices installed within the case.

Presentation software. Presentation software enables users to create, edit and deliver presentations via a computer system.

Primary key field. These fields are used to uniquely identify each record in a table and link to similar secondary key fields (usually of the same name) in other tables.

Primary storage. Data and instructions are loaded into memory such as Random Access Memory. Such storage is temporary.

PRINCE. A project management methodology that has been developed to be compatible with the system development methodologies such as SSADM.

PRINCE structure. PRINCE defines an organisational structure and standard set of job descriptors.

Print preview. The print preview feature displays a document exactly as it will be printed, enabling users to check and correct the document without making unnecessary printouts.

Printer sharer. A printer sharer allows several computers to be attached to a single printer.

Private branch exchange (PBX). Enables switching between phones or voice and data using existing telephone lines.

Problem-oriented. A problem-oriented language focuses on the expression of a problem or set of information processing requirements. The language will provide a variety of features that allow programmers to express their requirements in a natural form.

Process. Inputs are turned into outputs by using a transformation process.

Process control systems. Used to manage manufacturing type processes. These systems deal with the large volume of data generated by production processes.

Process modelling. Involves the design of the different modules of the system, each of which is a process with clearly defined inputs, outputs and a transformation process. Dataflow diagrams are often used to define processes in the system.

Processor. Uses instructions from software to control the different components of a PC.

Production (live) environment. The term used to described the setup of the system (hardware, software and office environment) where the software will be used in the business.

Productivity paradox. The productivity paradox is that large investments by a company in Information Systems do not necessarily result in greater business benefits. In fact it is very difficult to demonstrate a correlation between these variables.

Productivity software. This describes a category of computer software that aims to support users in performing a variety of common tasks.

Professionalism. In general terms, professionalism can be described as acting to meet the standards set by a profession in terms of individual conduct, competence and integrity. *See* Ethics and Morality.

Programming language. Programming languages enable users to develop software applications in order to carry out specific information processing tasks.

Project constraints. Projects can be resource-constrained (limited by the type of people, monetary or hardware resources available) or time-constrained (limited by the deadline).

Project costs graphs. Show the financial cost of undertaking the project.

Project crashing. Refers to reducing the project duration by increasing spending on critical activities.

Project documentation. Documentation is essential to disseminate information during project execution and for reference during software maintenance.

Project evaluation and review technique (PERT). Sometimes used to refer to a critical path network diagram (PERT charts), but more accurately PERT replaces the fixed activity duration used in the CPM method with a statistical distribution which uses optimistic, pessimistic and most likely duration estimates.

Project plan. This shows the main activities within the project, providing an overall schedule and identifying resources needed for project implementation.

Projects. Projects are unique, one-time operations designed to accomplish a specific set of objectives in a limited timeframe.

Protocols. The Internet functions using a series of standard protocols which allow different computers to communicate with each other. Passing of data packets around the Internet occurs via the TCP/IP protocol which stands for Transfer Control Protocol/Internet Protocol. The HTTP (hyper text transfer protocol) protocol is used to allow computers to transfer and process HTML files.

Prototyping. A prototype is a preliminary version of part or a framework of all of an information system which can be reviewed by end-users. Prototyping is an iterative process where users suggest modifications before further prototypes and the final information system is built.

Pull technology. Information sent out as a result of receiving a specific request, for example a page is delivered to a Web browser in response to a specific request from the user.

Push technology. Push is used to deliver Web pages to the users desktop PC without them specifically requesting each page. It is the Internet equivalent of a TV channel, hence it is sometimes also known as NetCasting. Important players are Marimba, Pointcast, Microsoft (Internet Explorer 4.0) and Netscape (Netcaster).

▶ **Q**

Qualitative data. Also known as *soft data*, qualitative data describes the qualities or characteristics of an object or situation. Such data is often collected in order to help achieve a better understanding of a given situation. An interview, for example, might help the interviewer to understand an individual's personal beliefs and opinions.

Quantitative data. Also known as *hard data*, quantitative data tends to make use of figures, such as statistics. This data is often collected in order to measure or quantify an object or situation.

Query. In a spreadsheet or database, a query can be used to extract data according to a set of conditions specified by the user. The results of a query can be stored in another part of the worksheet or database so that the original data remains intact.

Questionnaires. Used to obtain a range of opinion on requirements by targeting a range of staff. They are open to misinterpretation unless carefully designed. They should consist of open and closed questions.

▶ **R**

RAID. RAID stands for Redundant Array of Inexpensive Disks. Essentially, identical copies of important data files are kept upon a number of different storage devices. If one or more of the storage devices fail, additional devices are activated automatically, allowing uninterrupted access to the data and reducing the possibility of losing transactions or updates.

Random access memory (RAM). RAM is used as working storage by a computer, holding instructions and data that are waiting to be processed. The contents of RAM are volatile, that is, any data held is lost when the power to the computer system is switched off. *See* Volatile.

Random file access. Random or Direct file access allows any record to be read or written.

Rapid applications development (RAD). A method of developing information systems which uses prototyping to achieve user involvement and faster development compared to traditional methodologies such as SSADM.

Ratings. Many Web browsers support the use of ratings in order to restrict access to inappropriate content, for example pornography. When a Web browser is used to access a site belonging to a given ratings scheme, the site's ratings are checked against the list of criteria set within the browser. If a site does not meet the criteria specified within the browser, access to the site is denied.

Read-only. In terms of storage devices, a read-only device can only be used to access data that is already present on the media. A CD-ROM player, for example, is unable to write data to a compact disc and can only read from it. *See also* Read Only Memory.

Read-only memory (ROM). The contents of ROM are fixed and cannot be altered. ROM is also non-volatile, making it ideal as a means of storing the information needed for a device to function properly. In a computer system, for example, the basic information needed so that the computer can access disk drives and control peripherals is stored in ROM. *See* Non-volatile.

Real-time processing. Data is processed immediately on collection. Such systems often involve user interaction.

Record. In an electronic database, a record is a collection of *related* fields. *See* Field.

Record key. In order to identify a specific item of information within a database, all records must contain an identifier, normally called the record key. The record key usually takes the form of a number or code and will be different for each record in the database.

Recovery. The process which is used to restore backup data.

Reduced instruction set computer (RISC) processor.

Designed so that it has to perform fewer instructions than a CISC processor and it can then operate at a higher speed. The IBM RS/6000 workstation is a well-known example of a computer that uses the PowerPC RISC processor. As new designs of Pentium processor are produced these are incorporating RISC features and are also making use of parallel processing.

Refresh rate. This describes a common method of gauging the quality of a monitor's display and involves measuring the number of times the image is drawn upon the screen each second. The refresh rate is normally measured in Hz, for example a refresh rate of 60Hz means that the image will be drawn upon the screen 60 times each second.

Regression testing. Testing performed before a release to ensure that the software performance is consistent with previous test results, i.e. that the outputs produced are consistent with previous releases of the software.

Relational databases. Data is stored within a number of different tables with each dealing with different subjects that are related (linked) using key fields.

Relational Database Management System (RDBMS). RDBMS is an extension of a DBMS and allows data to be combined from a variety of sources.

Relationship. In a relational database, data can be combined from several different sources by defining relationships between tables.

Remote access. Remote access describes a means of accessing a network from a distant location. A modem and specialised software allows users to send and receive information from home or an office when travelling.

Replication (server). A process in which information on server computers at different locations is transferred and synchronized so users in different locations can view the same data.

Replication (virus). The process by which a virus copies itself.

Request for proposals (RFP). A specification drawn up to assist in selecting the supplier and software.

Requirements specification. The main output from the systems analysis stage. Its main focus is a description of what all the functions of the software will be.

Resolution. The resolution of the monitor describes the fineness of the image that can be displayed. Resolution is often expressed in terms of pixels (picture elements) – the individual dots that make up an image on the screen.

Resource allocation. This activity involves assigning a resource to each task.

Response time. Many organisations make use of external companies to provide maintenance and technical support for their computer-based information systems. In such cases, the organisation may require the maintenance provider to guarantee a minimum response time for important repairs.

Return on investment (RoI). An indication of the returns provided by an IS. Calculated by dividing the benefit by the amount of investment. Expressed as a percentage.

Reverse engineering. Reverse engineering attempts to recreate the design of an item by analysing the final product. This can be compared to the 'black box' approach to systems analysis, where the outputs from the system are analysed in order to determine the inputs and processes involved. Reverse engineering can be used to duplicate both hardware and software.

Risk management. Risk management aims to anticipate the future risks of an information systems project and to put in place measures to counter or eliminate these risks.

▶ S

Safety critical system. Where human lives rely on the correct operation of a computer-based information system, this is normally referred to as a critical system.

Scalability. The potential of an information system, piece of software or hardware to move from supporting a small number of users to a large number of users without a marked decrease in reliability or performance.

Scientific languages. Scientific programming languages are designed to serve scientific and mathematical applications.

Scoring system. A means of selecting hardware, software and suppliers using a point-scoring system. Each item or supplier is assigned scores against a number of selection criteria. Final selection is based upon the total score achieved by each item or supplier. The relative importance of the selection criteria can be recognised through the use of weighting factors, resulting in the creation of a weighted ranking table.

Script. All modern Web browsers are capable of executing special commands that have been embedded within the body of a WWW page. These scripts can be used to control the appearance of the page or can provide additional facilities, such as onscreen clocks and timers.

Search engines. Search engines provide an index of all words stored on the World Wide Web. Keywords typed in by the end-user are matched against the index and the user is given a list of all corresponding Web pages containing the keywords. By clicking on a hyperlink the user is taken to the relevant Web page.

Second Normal Form (2NF). Second normal form states that 'Each attribute in a record (relation) must be functionally dependent on the whole key of that record.'

Secondary key fields. These fields are used to link tables together by referring to the primary key in another database table.

Secondary storage. Floppy disks and hard disks are secondary storage which provides permanent storage.

Security breach. A security breach is a deliberate or unintentional act that leads to unauthorised access to or loss/damage to information or an information system.

Secure electronic transactions (SET). A method developed by Visa and Mastercard proposed for enabling credit-card based electronic commerce based on digital certificates.

Secure sockets layer (SSL). A standard used within Web browsers to encrypt data such as credit card details sent over the Internet.

Serial port. A type of connector that allows various devices to be attached to a computer system. Examples of common serial devices might include a mouse, modem or printer.

Sensing device. Modern personal computers are capable of communicating with external devices via a number of different means. This allows them to be connected to a variety of sensing devices. Among these are motion detectors, light sensors, infra-red sensors (that can detect heat), microphones and many others.

Sequential access method. Sequential file access involves reading or writing each record in a file in a set order.

Server. A Server is a powerful computer used to control the management of a network. It may have a specific function such as storing user files or a database or managing a printer.

Shareware. Shareware is often described with the phrase 'try before you buy'. Users are entitled to use Shareware programs free of charge for a specified period of time. Having been given the opportunity to evaluate the software, the user is then required to pay the author a registration fee or remove the software from their system. *See also* Freeware.

Signature. Most computer viruses contain a message to be displayed on screen or a hidden piece of text. Additionally, a virus program may also contain a unique series of values in its program file. These unique features are known as the signature of the virus.

Signature file. A signature file contains information such as an address and phone number that can be automatically added to the end of an e-mail message.

Site certificate. A site certificate contains information regarding the identity of a particular site on the Internet. The site certificate is encrypted to protect the information it contains. When a user's Web browser accesses a given site on the Internet, the corresponding certificate is checked to ensure the authenticity of the site.

Small computer system interface (SCSI). This describes a common standard governing the way in which an expansion card interacts with a computer's motherboard and CPU. Up to seven separate devices can be attached to a single SCSI interface simultaneously. Connecting several devices in sequence is known as daisy chaining. *See* Expansion card, Plug and Play and Motherboard.

Soft data. *See* Qualitative data.

Soft systems methodology. A methodology which emphasises the human involvement in systems and models their behaviour as part of systems analysis in a way which is understandable by non-technical experts.

Software. A series of detailed instructions that control the operation of a computer system. Software exists as programs that are developed by computer programmers.

Software bug. Software bugs are defects in a program which are caused by human error during programming or earlier in the lifecycle. They may result in major faults or may remain unidentified.

Software metrics. Measures which indicate the quality of software.

Software Publishers Association (SPA). An organisation formed to act against software piracy. *See* Software theft.

Software quality. Measured according to its suitability for the job intended. This is governed by whether it can do the job required (does it meet the business requirements?) and the number of bugs it contains (does it work reliably?).

Software theft. Software theft, also known as software piracy, involves making unauthorised copies of software applications. Software theft represents a serious and growing problem for the software industry. Global losses due to software piracy were estimated at more than $11 billion in 1996.

Sound card. A sound card allows a personal computer to play speech, music and other sounds. A sound card can also be used to capture sound, music and speech from a variety of sources.

Source escrow. An arrangement where a third party stores software that can be used for maintenance purposes if the original developer of the software becomes insolvent.

Spam. Unwanted messages, such as advertisements, are received by most e-mail users. The act of sending out these messages is usually called spamming.

Speech synthesis. Speech synthesis software allows text to be converted into speech. The contents of spreadsheet files, e-mail messages, wordprocessing documents and other files can be converted into speech and played back via a sound card or other device.

Spiral model. An iterative systems development model developed by Boehm (1988) in which the stages of analysis, design, code and review repeat as new features for the system are identified.

Spreadsheet. A spreadsheet can be described as a program designed to store and manipulate values, numbers and text in an efficient and *useful* way. The work area in a spreadsheet program is called the worksheet. A worksheet is a grid made up of cells. Each cell is uniquely identifiable by its horizontal (row) and vertical (column) co-ordinates. A cell can contain text, numbers or a formula that relates to information held in another cell.

Stakeholders. All staff who have a direct interest in the system.

Storage devices. Storage devices provide a means of storing data and programs until they are required.

Structured decisions. Structured decisions tend to involve situations where the rules and constraints governing the decision are known. They tend to involve routine or repetitive situations where the number of possible courses of action is relatively small.

Structured English. A technique for producing a design specification for programmers which indicates the way individual modules or groups of modules should be implemented.

Structured query language (SQL). This describes a form of programming language that provides a standardised method for retrieving information from databases.

Sub-notebook. A small portable computer which is usually significantly smaller than a notebook due to a small screen and keyboard.

Subsystem. Large systems can be composed of one or more smaller systems. These smaller systems are known as subsystems.

Suprasystem. This describes a larger system that is made of one or more smaller systems (subsystems).

Synchronous. When people exchange information simultaneously as is the case with real-time chat or a telephone conversation this is known as synchronous.

Synergy. Synergy means that the whole is greater than the sum of the parts.

System. A system can be defined as a collection of interrelated components that work together towards a collective goal.

System build. System build is the term used to describe the creation of software by programmers. It involves writing the software code (programming), building release versions of the software, constructing and populating the database and testing by programmers and end-users. Writing of documentation and training may also occur at this stage.
Inputs: Requirements and design specification.
Outputs: Working software, user guides and system documentation.

System implementation. Implementation covers practical issues such as making sure the hardware and network infrastructure for a new system are in place; testing of the system and also human issues of how best to educate and train staff who will be using or affected by the new system. Implementation also involves the transition or changeover from the old system to the new.
Input: Working system, not tested by users.
Output: Signed off, operational information system installed in all locations.

System maintenance. Maintenance occurs after the system has been signed off as suitable for users. It involves reviewing the project and recording and acting on problems with the system.

System or outline design. A high-level definition of the different components that make up the architecture of a system and how they interact.

System objective. All systems are created to meet a specific objective or purpose. All of the components of system are related to one another by a common objective. When the components of a system no longer share the same objective, a condition of sub-optimality is said to exist.

System owners. These are managers who are directly responsible for the operational use of a system.

System sponsors. System sponsors are senior managers or board members who are responsible for a system at a senior level in a company.

System testing. When all modules have been completed and their interactions assessed for validity, links between all modules are assessed in the system test. In system testing interactions between all relevant modules are tested systematically.

Systems analysis. Systems analysis refers to the capture of the business requirements of a system from talking to or observing end-users and using other information sources such as existing system documentation.
Input: Terms of reference in feasibility report describing outline requirements.
Output: Detailed requirements specification summarising

system functions. Supported by diagrams showing the information flow and processes that are required.

Systems analysis and design method (SSADM). A methodology that defines the methods of analysis and design that should occur in a large-scale software development project. It is used extensively in the UK, particularly in government and public organisations.

Systems design. The systems design phase defines how the system will work in key areas of user interface, program modules, security and database transactions. Input: Requirements specification. Output: Detailed design specification.

Systems dynamics. Based on the view that the world can be regarded as a set of interdependent systems, it usually uses simulation models to try to understand why systems behave as they do.

Systems software. This form of software manages and controls the operation of the computer system as it performs tasks on behalf of the user.

Systems theory. The study of the behaviour and interactions within and between systems.

▶ T

Table. In an electronic database, data is organised within structures known as tables. A table defines the structure of a specific record.

Tangible assets. Tangible assets are the physical resources owned by a company. Examples include land, buildings and plant.

Tangible value. A value or benefit that can be measured directly, usually in monetary terms. With regard to information, tangible value is usually calculated as: value of information – cost of gathering information.

Tape streamer. A common form of storage device that uses magnetic tape as a storage medium.

Technical feasibility. Evaluates to what degree the proposed solutions will work as required and whether the right people and tools are available to implement the solution. (Will it work?)

Telecommunications. Telecommunications is the method by which data and information are transmitted between different locations.

Telecommunications channels. The media by which data is transmitted. Cables and wires are known as guided media and microwave and satellite links are known as unguided media.

Teleworking. The process where company staff work remotely from their company office. Most commonly it is applied to 'home-workers' who spend at least 3 days a week working in this way.

Telnet. This allows remote access to computer systems. For example, a system administrator on one site could log-in to a computer elsewhere to check it is running successfully. Telnet is widely used in the retail industry. For example a retailer could check to see whether an item was in stock in a warehouse using a telnet application. Such telnet applications will not usually be run over the public Internet, but rather over secure lines.

Tender document. A document used as an invitation to suppliers, asking them to bid for right to supply an organisation's hardware, software and other requirements.

Terabyte. Approximately 1000 Gb, or the equivalent of one thousand billion characters.

Terminate and Star Resident (TSR). A Terminate and Stay Resident program is one that is stored in the computer's memory and functions as a background task, receiving only a small share of the processor's time.

Test environment. A specially configured environment (hardware, software and office environment) used to test the software before its release.

Test plan. Plan describing the type and sequence of testing and who will conduct it.

Test specification. A detailed description of the tests that will be performed to check the software works correctly.

Theft. In terms of computing, theft normally, but not always, involves altering computer records to disguise the theft of money. The theft of services can include a variety of acts, such as the unauthorised use of a company's information systems. *See also* Software theft and Data theft.

Thermal printer. Thermal printers operate by using a matrix of heated pins to melt ink from a ribbon directly onto the paper.

Thin client. In a network system, this describes an architecture where the bulk of the processing is carried out by a central server. The results of the processing are then relayed back to a terminal or network computer. *See* Network Computer.

Third Normal Form (3NF). A record is in third normal form if each non-key attribute 'depends on the key, the whole key and nothing but the key.'

Three-tier client/server. The client is mainly used for display with application logic and the business rules partitioned on a second-tier server and a third-tier database server. Here the client is sometimes referred to as a 'thin client', because the size of the executable program is smaller.

Time dimension. This describes several characteristics of information quality related to the time period that the information deals with and the frequency at which the information is received. Among these characteristics are the timeliness, currency and frequency of information. As an example, information may be considered to be of high quality if it is received in good time (timeliness). Other dimensions of information characteristics include content and form. *See* Content dimension, Form dimension.

Top-down design. The top-down approach to design involves specifying the overall control architecture of the application before designing the individual modules.

Total cost of ownership (TCO). TCO refers to the total cost for a company operating a computer. This includes not only the purchase or leasing cost, but also the cost of all the services needed to support the end-user.

Touch screen. The touch screen is a transparent, pressure-sensitive covering that is attached to the screen of the monitor. Users make selections and control programs by pressing onto the screen. Although touch screens are simple to use, they are comparatively expensive and require special software to operate.

Trackball. A trackball is a pointing device that is controlled by rotating a small ball with the fingertips or palm of the hand. Moving the ball causes corresponding movement to a small pointer on the screen. Buttons are used to select items in the same way as the mouse. *See* Pointing device.

Transaction processing. This involves dealing with the sales and purchase transactions that an organisation carries out in the course of its normal activities. Banks, for example, handle millions of deposits and withdrawals each day.

Transaction processing systems (TPS). Transaction Processing Systems (TPS) manage the frequent external and internal transactions such as orders for goods and services which serve the operational level of the organisation.

Transformation process. A transformation process is used to convert inputs into outputs. A power station, for example, converts fuel into electricity.

Trojan. A Trojan presents itself as a legitimate program in order to gain access to a computer system. Trojans are often used as delivery systems for computer viruses.

Two-tier client/server. Sometimes referred to as 'fat client', the application running on the PC is a large program containing all the application logic and display code. It retrieves data from a separate database server.

▶ U

Unit testing. Individual modules are tested to ensure they function correctly for given inputs.

Universal product code (UPC). A standard for defining bar-codes used frequently in retailing.

Universal serial bus (USB). This describes a relatively new standard that governs the way in which an expansion card interacts with a computer's motherboard and CPU. In addition to offering very high data transmission speeds, USB also supports Plug and Play, the connection of up to 127 devices and hot plugging. *See* Expansion card, Plug and Play, Hot plugging and Motherboard.

Unstructured decisions. Unstructured decisions tend to involve complex situations, where the rules governing the decision are complicated or unknown. Such decisions tend to be made infrequently and rely heavily on the experience, judgement and knowledge of the decision maker.

Update anomaly. It is not possible to change a single occurrence of a data item (a field) in a relation (table) without having to change others in order to maintain the correctness of data.

Update query. An update query can be used to change records, tables and reports held in a Database Management System.

Usenet newsgroups. Usenet is mainly used by special interest groups such as people discussing their favourite pastimes. They are not used much by businesses, unless it is as a means of studying consumer behaviour.

User acceptance testing. This is the final stage of testing which occurs before the software is signed off as fit for purpose and the system can go live.

User validation. Checks made to ensure the user is permitted access to a system. Also known as access control systems they often involve user names and passwords, but can also include biometric techniques.

Utility programs. Utility programs provide a range of tools that support the operation and management of a computer system.

▶ V

Validation. This is a test of the design where we check that the design fulfils the requirements of the business users which are defined in the requirements specification.

Value added networks (VANS). Value added networks (VANS) give a subscription service enabling companies to transmit data securely across a shared network.

Value chain. Michael Porter's Value Chain is a framework for considering key activities within an organisation and how well they add value as products and services move from conception to delivery to the customer.

Vector image. Vector graphics are made up of shapes, rather than individual dots. Mathematical formulae determine the size, position and colour of the shapes that make up a given image.

Verification. This is a test of the design to ensure that the design chosen is the best available and that it is error free.

Video capture card. The video capture card records and stores video sequences (motion video). A playback device, for example a video cassette recorder, is connected to the video capture card and special software is used to capture, edit and manipulate video sequences. Once a motion video sequence has been processed, it can then be output to a television, video cassette recorder or other device.

Video Graphics Array (VGA). A common standard for graphics cards. All graphics cards support the VGA (video graphics array) standard which specifies a maximum image size of 640 by 320 pixels, displayed in 16 colours.

Video projector. A computer system can be connected directly to a projector so that output is directed to a projection screen. Some projectors convert the computer's output into a television picture before displaying it.

Virtual organisation. An organisation which uses technologies to allow it to operate without clearly defined physical boundaries between different functions. It provides customised services for customers by linking different human resources and suppliers at different locations.

Virtual private network (VPN). A data network that makes use of the public telecommunication infrastructure and Internet, but information remains secure by the use of a tunneling protocol and security procedures such as firewalls.

Virtual reality (VR). An interactive, artificial reality created by the computer. Users perceive the environment in three dimensions and are able to interact with objects and people. Using virtual reality goggles, for example, a user might interact with a body of data that appears as a three-dimensional model.

Virus. *See* Computer virus.

Virus scanner. Virus scanners are intended to detect and then safely remove virus programs from a computer system. The most common method of detection used by these programs involves scanning for the signatures of particular viruses. *See also* Signature.

Virus shield. Virus shields are TSR programs that constantly monitor and control access to a system's storage devices. Any unusual attempt to modify a file or write to a disk drive will activate a message asking the user to authorise the operation. *See also* Terminate and Stay Resident.

Visual display unit (VDU). This is normally used to describe the monitor connected to a computer system. but can also refer to any other form of display device.

Visualisation. This describes a variety of methods used to produce graphical representations of data so that it can be examined from a number of different perspectives.

Voice annotations. These can be described as spoken notes or reminders that can be inserted into data files, such as wordprocessing documents. Annotations are created and played back via a sound card. *See* Sound card.

Voice modem. Voice modems offer greater flexibility than conventional modems by combining voice, fax and data facilities. At a simple level, a voice modem can be used as a speaker phone or answering machine.

Voice recognition. This describes the facility to control a computer program or carry out data entry through spoken commands. The user issues instructions via a microphone connected to a sound card. Specialised software then attempts to interpret and execute the instruction given.

Voice-data integration. Sometimes known as computer telephony. A combination of different communications technologies that provide a range of sophisticated facilities, for example automated call-switching, telephone answering services and fax-on-demand. *See* Fax-on-demand.

Volatile memory. The memory found in a personal computer is considered volatile, that is, anything held in memory is lost once the power to the computer system is switched off. However, non-volatile memory retains its contents until altered or erased.

Volume testing. Testing assesses how system performance will change at different levels of usage.

▶ W

Waterfall model. Outlines the series of steps that should occur when building an information system. The steps usually occur in a predefined order with a review at the end of each stage before the next can be started.

Wax printers. Printers which employ a ribbon with a coloured wax coating to form images by heating sections of the ribbon and pressing it against the paper (dye-sublimation).

Web addresses. Web addresses refer to particular pages on a Web server which are hosted by a company or organisation. The technical name for these is uniform resource locators, so you often see these referred to as URLs.

Web browsers. Browsers such as Netscape Navigator or Microsoft Explorer provide an easy method of accessing and viewing information stored as Web documents on different servers. The Web pages stored as HTML files on the servers are accessed through a particular standard supported by the Web browsers (this is the hypertext transfer protocol (http), which you will always see preceding the Web address of a company). For example http://www.derby.ac.uk defines the university home page at Derby.

Web directories or catalogues. Web directories provide a structured listing of Web sites. They are grouped according to categories such as business, entertainment or sport. Each category is then sub-divided further, for example into football, rugby, swimming etc.

Web servers. Web servers such as Microsoft Internet Information Server are used to store the Web pages accessed by Web browsers. They may also contain databases of customer or product information which can be queried and retrieved from the browser.

What if? analysis. This describes the ability see the predicted effect of a change made to a numerical model. *See* Modelling and Spreadsheet.

Wide-area network (WAN). These networks cover a large area which connect businesses in different parts of the same city, different parts of a country or different countries.

Windows, icons, mouse and pull-down menus (WIMP). Often used to describe a GUI environment

Wordprocessor. A wordprocessor provides the ability to enter, edit, store and print text. In addition, wordprocessing packages allow users to alter the layout of documents and often provide a variety of formatting tools.

Word wrap. In a wordprocessor, as users type text and move towards the end of a line, the program automatically moves to the beginning of a new line.

Workbook. In a spreadsheet program, this describes a collection of worksheets. *See* Worksheet.

Work breakdown structure (WBS). This is a breakdown of the project or a piece of work into its component parts (tasks).

Workflow management (WFM). Systems for the automation of the movement and processing of information in a business according to a set of procedural rules.

Workgroup. A workgroup can be defined as a group of individuals working together on a given task. Each member of the workgroup will be attached to the organisation's network system so that tasks can be organised and information can be shared with other members.

Worksheet. An individual area or sheet for entering data in a spreadsheet program.

Workstation. This describes a powerful terminal or personal computer system, usually applied to specialised applications, such as computer-aided design (CAD) and animation.

World Wide Web. The World Wide Web is a medium for publishing information on the Internet. It is accessed through Web browsers which display Web pages and can be used to run business applications. Company information is stored on Web servers which are usually referred to as Web sites.

Worm (virus). A worm is a small program that moves through a computer system randomly changing or overwriting pieces of data as it moves.

Write Once – Read Many (WORM). A WORM storage device allows data to be written only once. Once the data has been written, it cannot be changed or erased.

▶ Z

Zero administration. In a network system, zero administration describes a point where the centralised management and control of the computers attached to a network server makes administration costs almost negligible. Zero administration is often associated with Network Computers. *See* Network Computer.

Index

Pages where the term is defined are in **bold**. Where a term is best known by its acronym, the acronym is given first, e.g. EDI (Electronic Data Interchange).